MARVEL MASTERWORKS

PRESENTS

THE Fantastic Four

VOLUME 7

COLLECTING

THE FANTASTIC FOUR NOS. 61 - 71
& ANNUAL NO. 5

STAN LEE · JACK KIRBY

Collection Editor
Cory Sedlmeier

Book Designer
Patrick McGrath

Special Projects Manager
Jeff Youngquist

Editor in Chief
Joe Quesada

Publisher
Dan Buckley

MARVEL MASTERWORKS: THE FANTASTIC FOUR VOL. 7. Contains material originally published in magazine form as FANTASTIC FOUR (Vol. 1) #61-71 and ANNUAL #5. First printing 2004. ISBN# 0-7851-1584-6. Published by MARVEL COMICS, a division of MARVEL ENTERTAINMENT GROUP, INC. OFFICE OF PUBLICATION: 10 East 40th Street, New York, NY 10016. Copyright © 1967, 1968 and 2004 Marvel Characters, Inc. All rights reserved. $49.99 per copy in the U.S. and $80.00 in Canada (GST #R127032852); Canadian Agreement #40668537. All characters featured in this issue and the distinctive names and likenesses thereof, and all related indicia are trademarks of Marvel Characters, Inc. No similarity between any of the names, characters, persons, and/or institutions in this magazine with those of any living or dead person or institution is intended, and any such similarity which may exist is purely coincidental. **Printed in Canada.** ALLEN LIPSON, Chief Executive Officer; AVI ARAD, Chief Creative Officer; GUI KARYO, President of Publishing and CIO; DAVID BOGART, Managing Editor; STAN LEE, Chairman Emeritus. For information regarding advertising in Marvel Comics or on Marvel.com, please contact Russell Brown, Executive Vice President, Consumer Products, Promotions and Media Sales at rbrown@marvel.com or 212-576-8561.

10 9 8 7 6 5 4 3 2 1

MARVEL MASTERWORKS
CREDITS

THE
FANTASTIC FOUR
Nos. 61-71 & ANNUAL No. 5

Writers: **Stan Lee**
Jack Kirby (Annual No. 5)

Penciler: **Jack Kirby**

Inkers: Joe Sinnott
Frank Giacoia (Annual No. 5)

Letterers: Art Simek (Nos. 64-70, Annual No. 5)
Sam Rosen (Nos. 61-63, 71, Annual No. 5)
L.P. Gregory (Annual No. 5)

Color Reconstruction: All Thumbs Creative

Art Reconstruction: Pond Scum
All Thumbs Creative

Special Thanks: Tom Brevoort, Tony Fornaro, Arthur
Fuchs, the Richard Howell/Carol Kalish
Collection, Ralph Macchio, Simon
Powell, Jeff Sharpe & Philippe Queveau

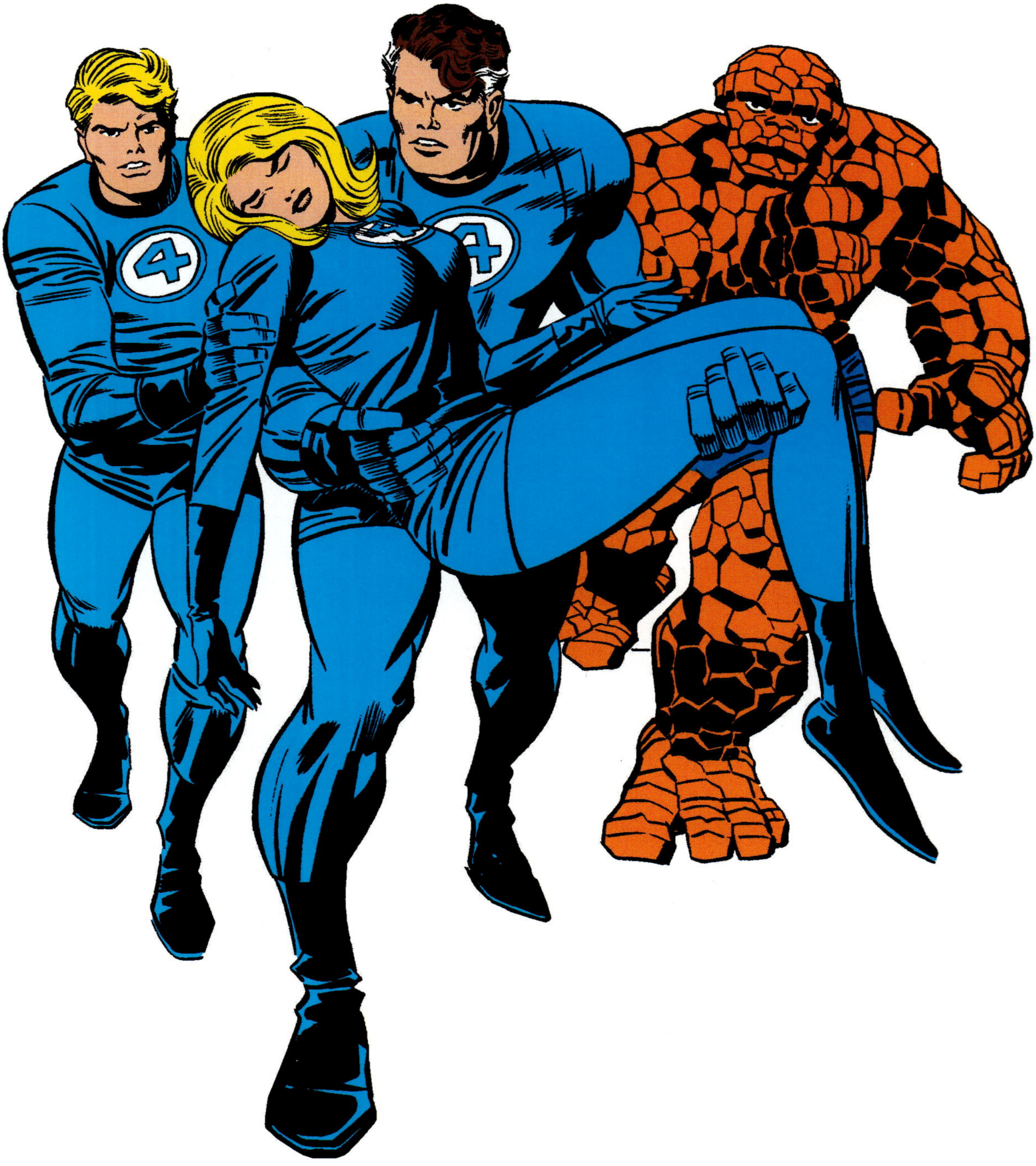

MARVEL MASTERWORKS
CONTENTS

INTRODUCTION
BY JOE SINNOTT

Looking back through *The Fantastic Four* issues #61-71, it is needless to say that these were more than just a great series of comic books. Starting at issue #44, Stan, Jack and I turned out a run that we were very proud to have created together back during the 1960s.

Some of my favorite covers I did with Jack were created during this period. Many were special favorites. Numbers 61, 65, 66, 67 and 69 especially stand out, but to pin it down to one cover, I would have to select #69. I wish Sue was included in it, but it has all the elements of a truly great cover. First of all, I was always partial to white backgrounds, the composition was flawless with a great city down-shot by Jack, and the craggy bricks and falling debris topped it all off. Jack always amazed me with the detailed buildings he created. No one else could ever do them quite like he could! On the cover to #69 the crumbling rocks, bricks and other types of debris fascinated me. If that wasn't enough, I especially liked it when the Human Torch would flame on and fly over the city—this cover had it all!

As great as Jack's compositions were on his covers, I always felt that his splash pages were even better! Just take a look at the splash pages in these issues! #61, 62, 63, 64, 65, 67, 70...just fantastic (pardon the pun)! Jack was the master of extraordinary machines. One of his most outstanding devices appeared on the splash page of issue #64. You can imagine just how long it took me to ink this panel. I must have lost money on that page, spending so much time with all that intricate "Kirby Tech," but it was well worth the satisfaction of completing such a page with Jack. Those splash pages were always much anticipated by the fans.

I was always careful to give full attention to detail in backgrounds that Jack created, as the visual aspect of them was so important to give dimension and reality to the comic-book pages. To embellish the pages in these issues I used a #3 Winsor Newton series #7 brush, a Hunt #102 pen, a compass, waterproof India ink and a ruler. I never used a French curve—but looking back I wish that I had. It would have made things a lot easier on some of those outstanding machines Jack created! Another aspect of Jack's work that always seems to be mentioned by fans is the "Kirby Krackle." We used it to great effect countless times and it sure was part of the Kirby identity. For the record, I used different size speedball pens to embellish and more clearly define what Jack intended with his powerful "krackle" scenes. For an extra treat check out the original version of the #65 cover packed with "Kirby Krackle" and included as a special bonus in this volume.

As you can tell by now, I haven't commented on the Fantastic Four storylines in these issues. Stan was certainly at his writing peak during this period, and Jack and I were privileged to be given such great material to illustrate. Many comic readers put these stories in their rightful place at the top of great achievements in the comic field.

The '60s are a period in comic history that will never be duplicated. In my humble opinion *The Fantastic Four* was the best comic of this era. These books by Stan, Jack and me were some of the most satisfying work I ever had the pleasure of doing, and I am proud to have been part of these books. I have a hard time expressing in words the great feeling of achievement and satisfaction that working on these books gave me. I am pleased that all the fans have appreciated the efforts that we put into these issues of *Fantastic Four*.

Joltin' Joe Sinnott

2004

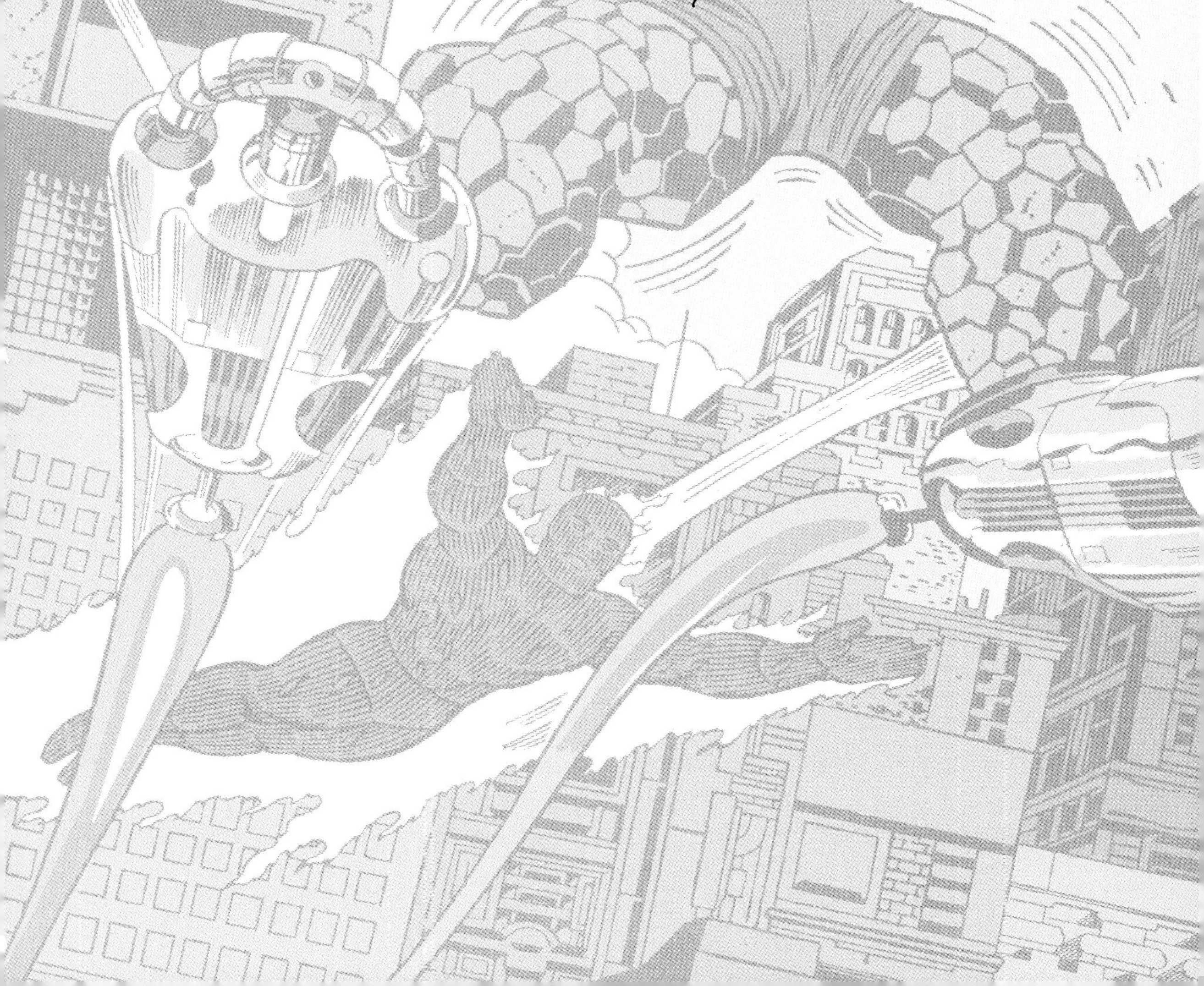

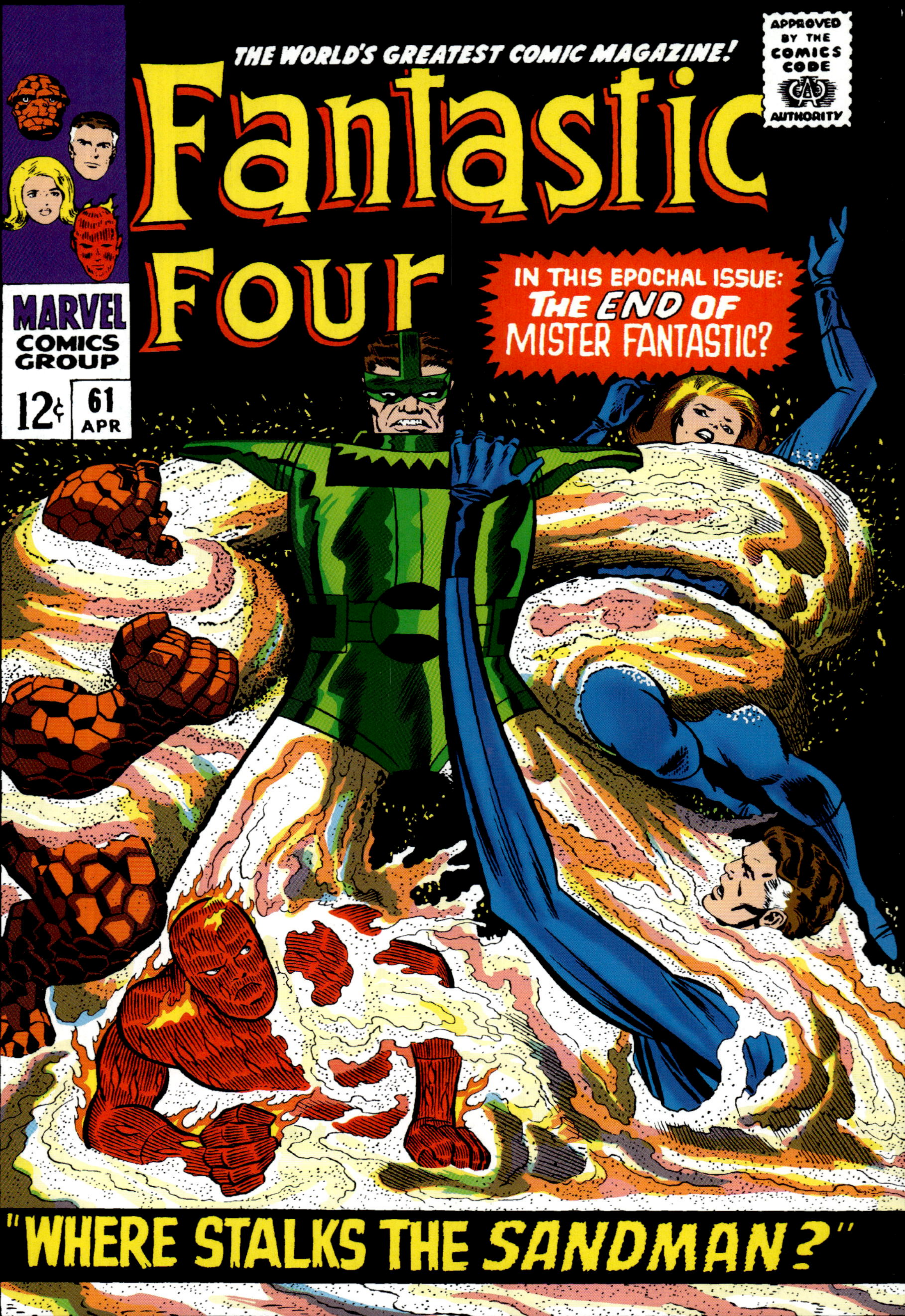
THE WORLD'S GREATEST COMIC MAGAZINE!
Fantastic Four
APPROVED BY THE COMICS CODE AUTHORITY
MARVEL COMICS GROUP
12¢
61 APR
IN THIS EPOCHAL ISSUE: THE END OF MISTER FANTASTIC?
"WHERE STALKS THE SANDMAN?"

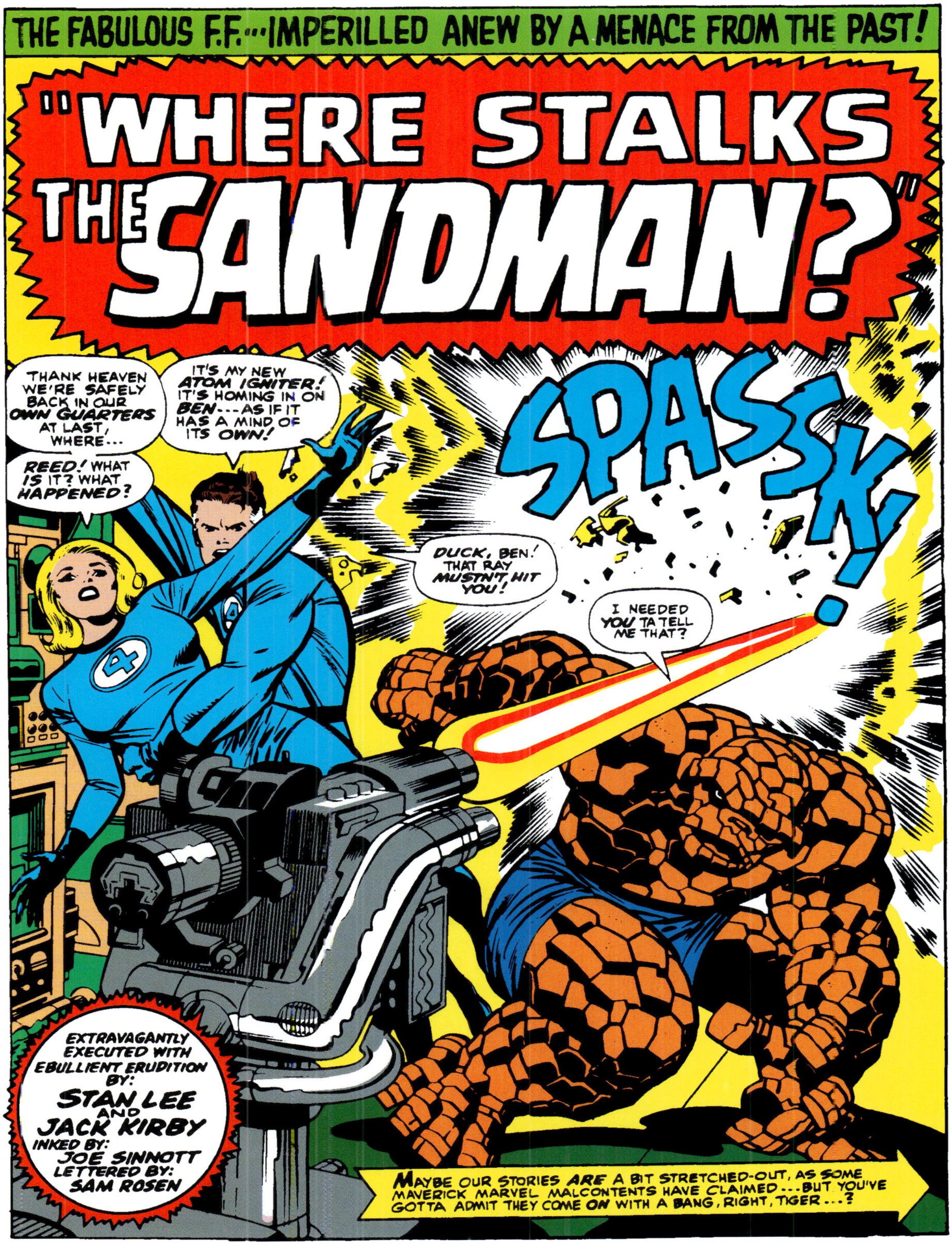
THE FABULOUS F.F.... IMPERILLED ANEW BY A MENACE FROM THE PAST!
"WHERE STALKS THE SANDMAN?"
THANK HEAVEN WE'RE SAFELY BACK IN OUR OWN QUARTERS AT LAST, WHERE...
REED! WHAT IS IT? WHAT HAPPENED?
IT'S MY NEW ATOM IGNITER! IT'S HOMING IN ON BEN--- AS IF IT HAS A MIND OF ITS OWN!
SPASSK!
DUCK, BEN! THAT RAY MUSTN'T HIT YOU!
I NEEDED YOU TA TELL ME THAT?
EXTRAVAGANTLY EXECUTED WITH EBULLIENT ERUDITION BY: STAN LEE AND JACK KIRBY INKED BY: JOE SINNOTT LETTERED BY: SAM ROSEN
MAYBE OUR STORIES ARE A BIT STRETCHED-OUT, AS SOME MAVERICK MARVEL MALCONTENTS HAVE CLAIMED... BUT YOU'VE GOTTA ADMIT THEY COME ON WITH A BANG, RIGHT, TIGER...?

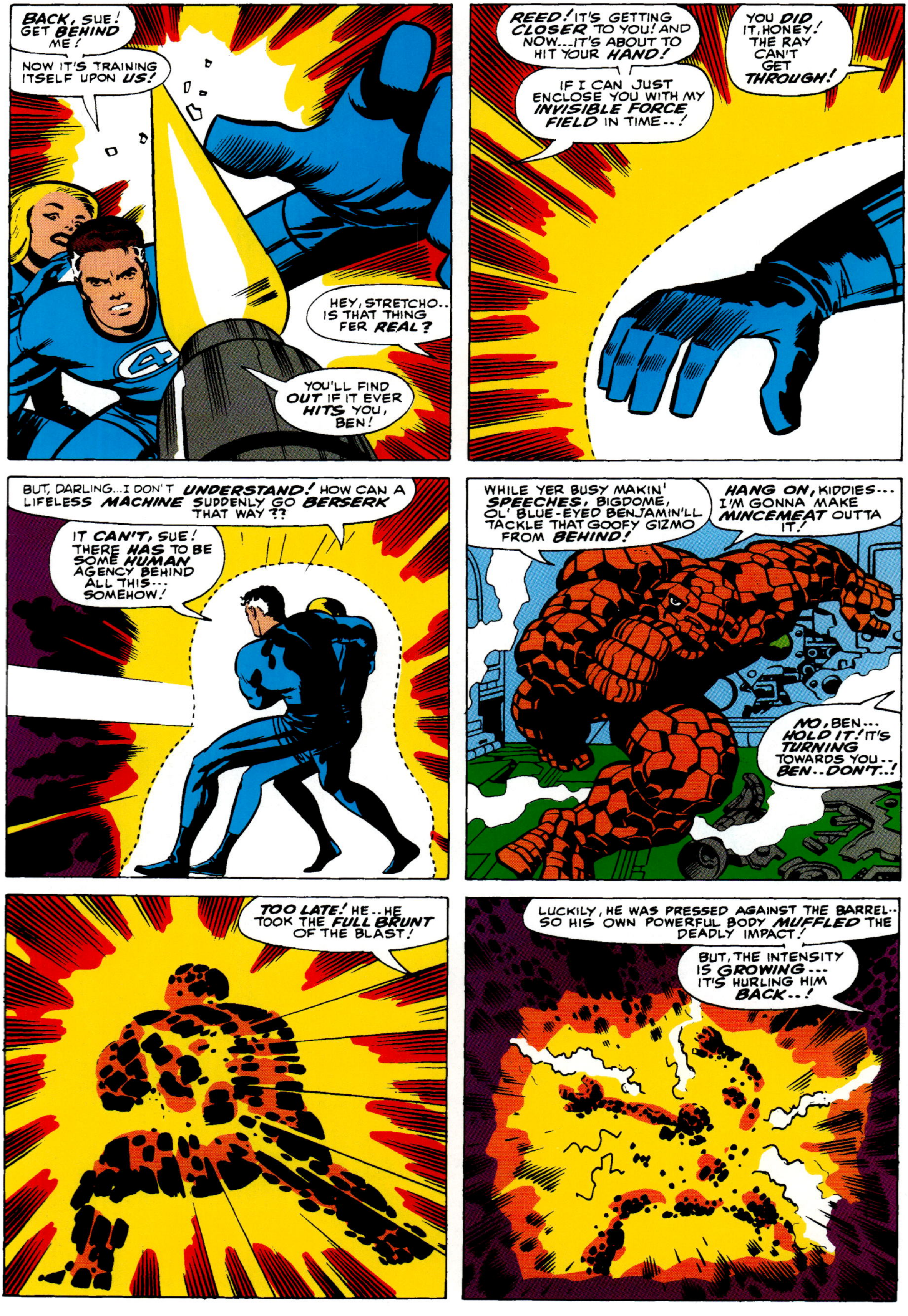

BACK, SUE! GET BEHIND ME!
NOW IT'S TRAINING ITSELF UPON US!
HEY, STRETCHO.. IS THAT THING FER REAL?
YOU'LL FIND OUT IF IT EVER HITS YOU, BEN!
REED! IT'S GETTING CLOSER TO YOU! AND NOW...IT'S ABOUT TO HIT YOUR HAND!
IF I CAN JUST ENCLOSE YOU WITH MY INVISIBLE FORCE FIELD IN TIME--!
YOU DID IT, HONEY! THE RAY CAN'T GET THROUGH!
BUT, DARLING...I DON'T UNDERSTAND! HOW CAN A LIFELESS MACHINE SUDDENLY GO BERSERK THAT WAY??
IT CAN'T, SUE! THERE HAS TO BE SOME HUMAN AGENCY BEHIND ALL THIS--- SOMEHOW!
WHILE YER BUSY MAKIN' SPEECHES, BIGDOME, OL' BLUE-EYED BENJAMIN'LL TACKLE THAT GOOFY GIZMO FROM BEHIND!
HANG ON, KIDDIES--- I'M GONNA MAKE MINCEMEAT OUTTA IT!
NO, BEN--- HOLD IT! IT'S TURNING TOWARDS YOU--! BEN--DON'T--!
TOO LATE! HE--HE TOOK THE FULL BRUNT OF THE BLAST!
LUCKILY, HE WAS PRESSED AGAINST THE BARREL-- SO HIS OWN POWERFUL BODY MUFFLED THE DEADLY IMPACT!
BUT, THE INTENSITY IS GROWING--- IT'S HURLING HIM BACK--!

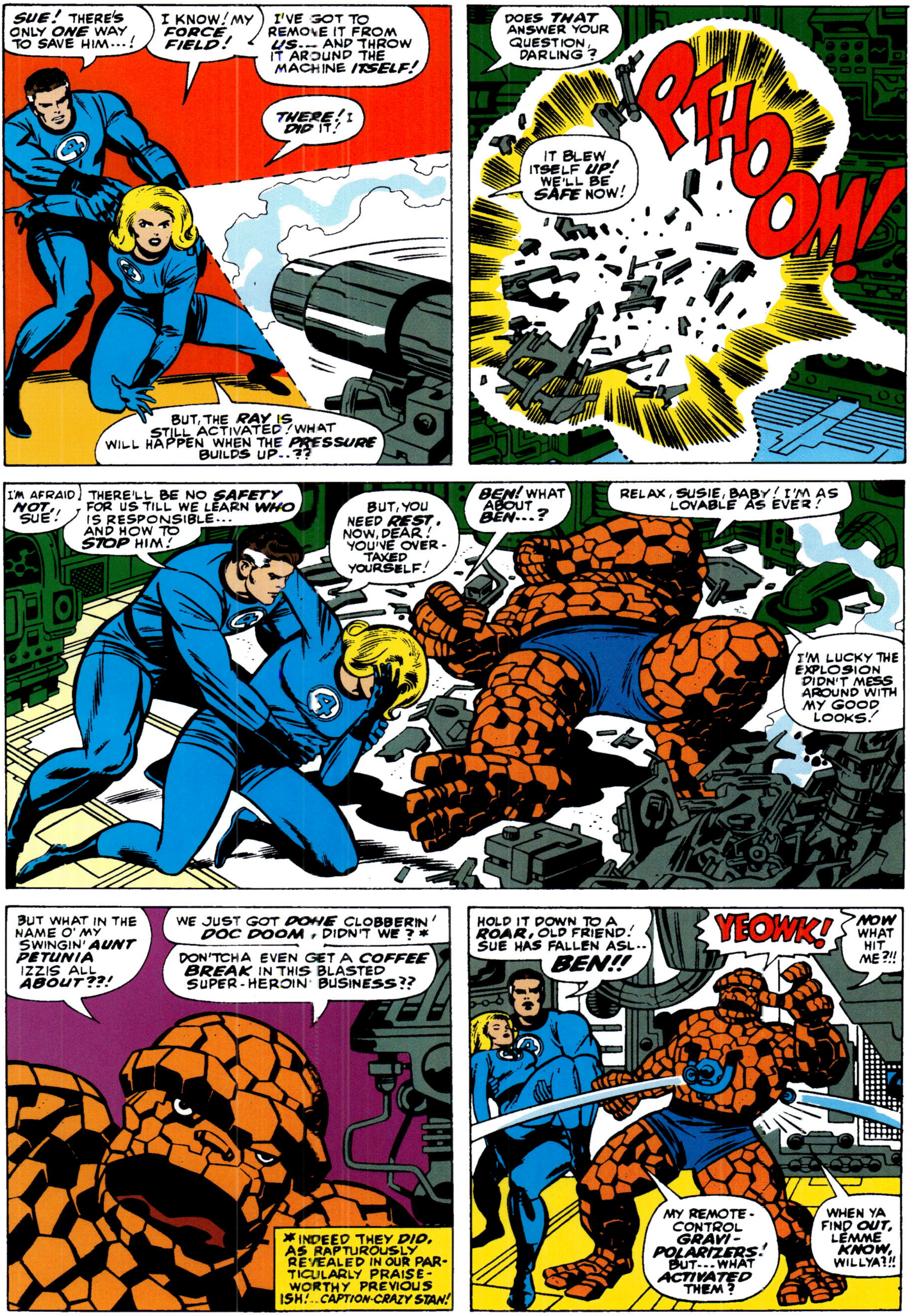
SUE! THERE'S ONLY ONE WAY TO SAVE HIM...!
I KNOW! MY FORCE FIELD!
I'VE GOT TO REMOVE IT FROM US... AND THROW IT AROUND THE MACHINE ITSELF!
THERE! I DID IT!
BUT, THE RAY IS STILL ACTIVATED! WHAT WILL HAPPEN WHEN THE PRESSURE BUILDS UP..??
DOES THAT ANSWER YOUR QUESTION, DARLING?
PTHOOOM!
IT BLEW ITSELF UP! WE'LL BE SAFE NOW!
I'M AFRAID NOT, SUE!
THERE'LL BE NO SAFETY FOR US TILL WE LEARN WHO IS RESPONSIBLE... AND HOW TO STOP HIM!
BUT, YOU NEED REST, NOW, DEAR! YOU'VE OVER-TAXED YOURSELF!
BEN! WHAT ABOUT BEN...?
RELAX, SUSIE, BABY! I'M AS LOVABLE AS EVER!
I'M LUCKY THE EXPLOSION DIDN'T MESS AROUND WITH MY GOOD LOOKS!
BUT WHAT IN THE NAME O' MY SWINGIN' AUNT PETUNIA IZZIS ALL ABOUT??!
WE JUST GOT DONE CLOBBERIN' DOC DOOM, DIDN'T WE? *
DON'TCHA EVEN GET A COFFEE BREAK IN THIS BLASTED SUPER-HEROIN' BUSINESS??
*INDEED THEY DID, AS RAPTUROUSLY REVEALED IN OUR PARTICULARLY PRAISE-WORTHY PREVIOUS ISH!...CAPTION-CRAZY STAN!
HOLD IT DOWN TO A ROAR, OLD FRIEND! SUE HAS FALLEN ASL-- BEN!!
YEOWK!
NOW WHAT HIT ME?!!
MY REMOTE-CONTROL GRAVI-POLARIZERS! BUT... WHAT ACTIVATED THEM?
WHEN YA FIND OUT, LEMME KNOW, WILLYA?!!

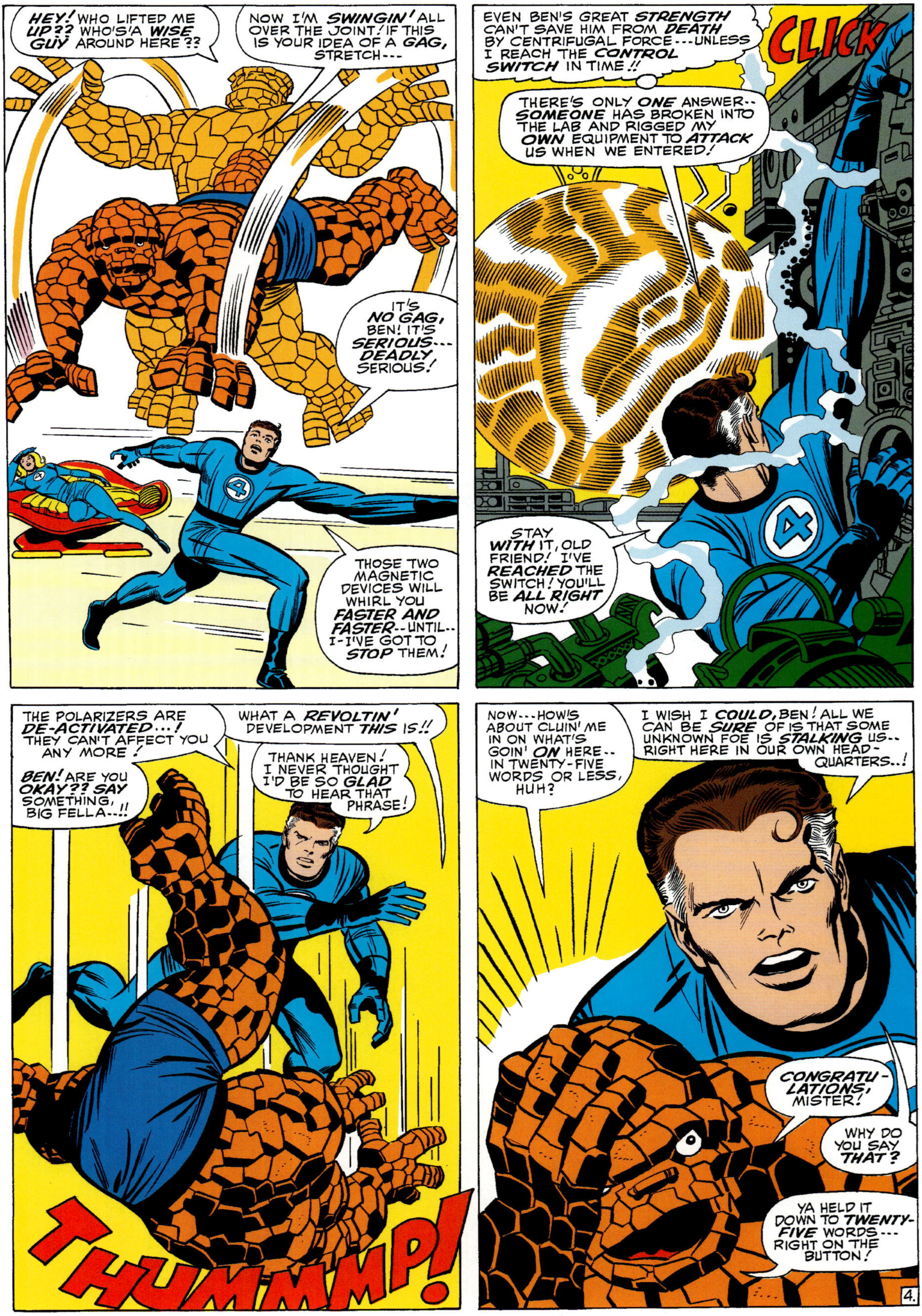
HEY! WHO LIFTED ME UP?? WHO'S'A WISE GUY AROUND HERE??
NOW I'M SWINGIN' ALL OVER THE JOINT! IF THIS IS YOUR IDEA OF A GAG, STRETCH---
IT'S NO GAG, BEN! IT'S SERIOUS--- DEADLY SERIOUS!
THOSE TWO MAGNETIC DEVICES WILL WHIRL YOU FASTER AND FASTER--UNTIL-- I-I'VE GOT TO STOP THEM!
EVEN BEN'S GREAT STRENGTH CAN'T SAVE HIM FROM DEATH BY CENTRIFUGAL FORCE---UNLESS I REACH THE CONTROL SWITCH IN TIME!!
CLICK
THERE'S ONLY ONE ANSWER-- SOMEONE HAS BROKEN INTO THE LAB AND RIGGED MY OWN EQUIPMENT TO ATTACK US WHEN WE ENTERED!
STAY WITH IT, OLD FRIEND! I'VE REACHED THE SWITCH! YOU'LL BE ALL RIGHT NOW!
THE POLARIZERS ARE DE-ACTIVATED...! THEY CAN'T AFFECT YOU ANY MORE!
BEN! ARE YOU OKAY?? SAY SOMETHING, BIG FELLA--!!
WHAT A REVOLTIN' DEVELOPMENT THIS IS!!
THANK HEAVEN! I NEVER THOUGHT I'D BE SO GLAD TO HEAR THAT PHRASE!
THUMMMP!
NOW---HOW'S ABOUT CLUIN' ME IN ON WHAT'S GOIN' ON HERE-- IN TWENTY-FIVE WORDS OR LESS, HUH?
I WISH I COULD, BEN! ALL WE CAN BE SURE OF IS THAT SOME UNKNOWN FOE IS STALKING US-- RIGHT HERE IN OUR OWN HEAD-QUARTERS--!
CONGRATU-LATIONS, MISTER!
WHY DO YOU SAY THAT?
YA HELD IT DOWN TO TWENTY-FIVE WORDS--- RIGHT ON THE BUTTON!
4.

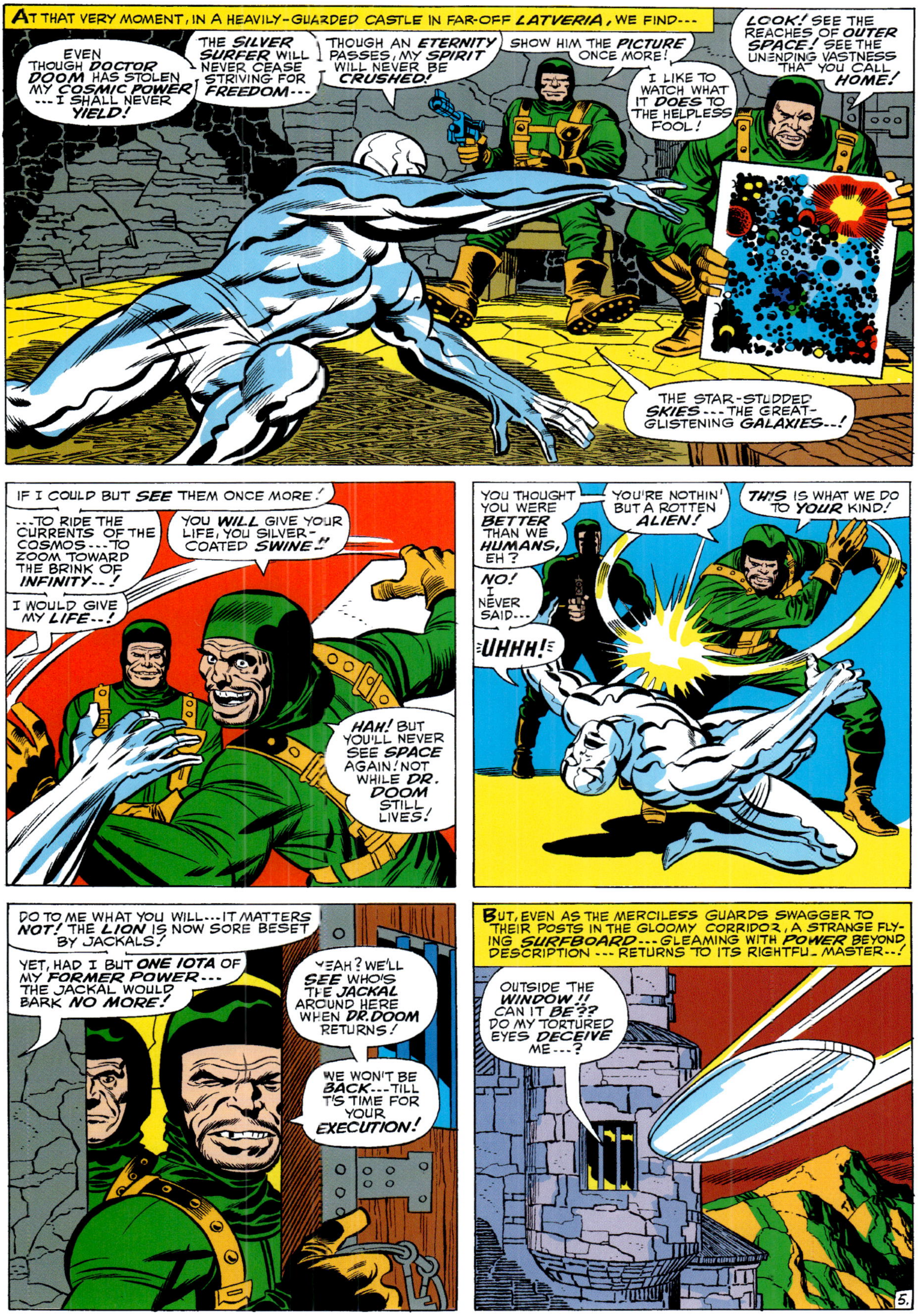

AT THAT VERY MOMENT, IN A HEAVILY-GUARDED CASTLE IN FAR-OFF LATVERIA, WE FIND---
EVEN THOUGH DOCTOR DOOM HAS STOLEN MY COSMIC POWER --- I SHALL NEVER YIELD!
THE SILVER SURFER WILL NEVER CEASE STRIVING FOR FREEDOM---
THOUGH AN ETERNITY PASSES, MY SPIRIT WILL NEVER BE CRUSHED!
SHOW HIM THE PICTURE ONCE MORE!
I LIKE TO WATCH WHAT IT DOES TO THE HELPLESS FOOL!
LOOK! SEE THE REACHES OF OUTER SPACE! SEE THE UNENDING VASTNESS THAT YOU CALL HOME!
THE STAR-STUDDED SKIES --- THE GREAT-GLISTENING GALAXIES--!
IF I COULD BUT SEE THEM ONCE MORE!
---TO RIDE THE CURRENTS OF THE COSMOS---TO ZOOM TOWARD THE BRINK OF INFINITY--!
I WOULD GIVE MY LIFE--!
YOU WILL GIVE YOUR LIFE, YOU SILVER-COATED SWINE!!
HAH! BUT YOU'LL NEVER SEE SPACE AGAIN! NOT WHILE DR. DOOM STILL LIVES!
YOU THOUGHT YOU WERE BETTER THAN WE HUMANS, EH?
YOU'RE NOTHIN' BUT A ROTTEN ALIEN!
THIS IS WHAT WE DO TO YOUR KIND!
NO! I NEVER SAID---
UHHH!
DO TO ME WHAT YOU WILL---IT MATTERS NOT! THE LION IS NOW SORE BESET BY JACKALS!
YET, HAD I BUT ONE IOTA OF MY FORMER POWER--- THE JACKAL WOULD BARK NO MORE!
YEAH? WE'LL SEE WHO'S THE JACKAL AROUND HERE WHEN DR. DOOM RETURNS!
WE WON'T BE BACK---TILL IT'S TIME FOR YOUR EXECUTION!
BUT, EVEN AS THE MERCILESS GUARDS SWAGGER TO THEIR POSTS IN THE GLOOMY CORRIDOR, A STRANGE FLYING SURFBOARD---GLEAMING WITH POWER BEYOND DESCRIPTION---RETURNS TO ITS RIGHTFUL MASTER--!
OUTSIDE THE WINDOW!! CAN IT BE?? DO MY TORTURED EYES DECEIVE ME---?
5.

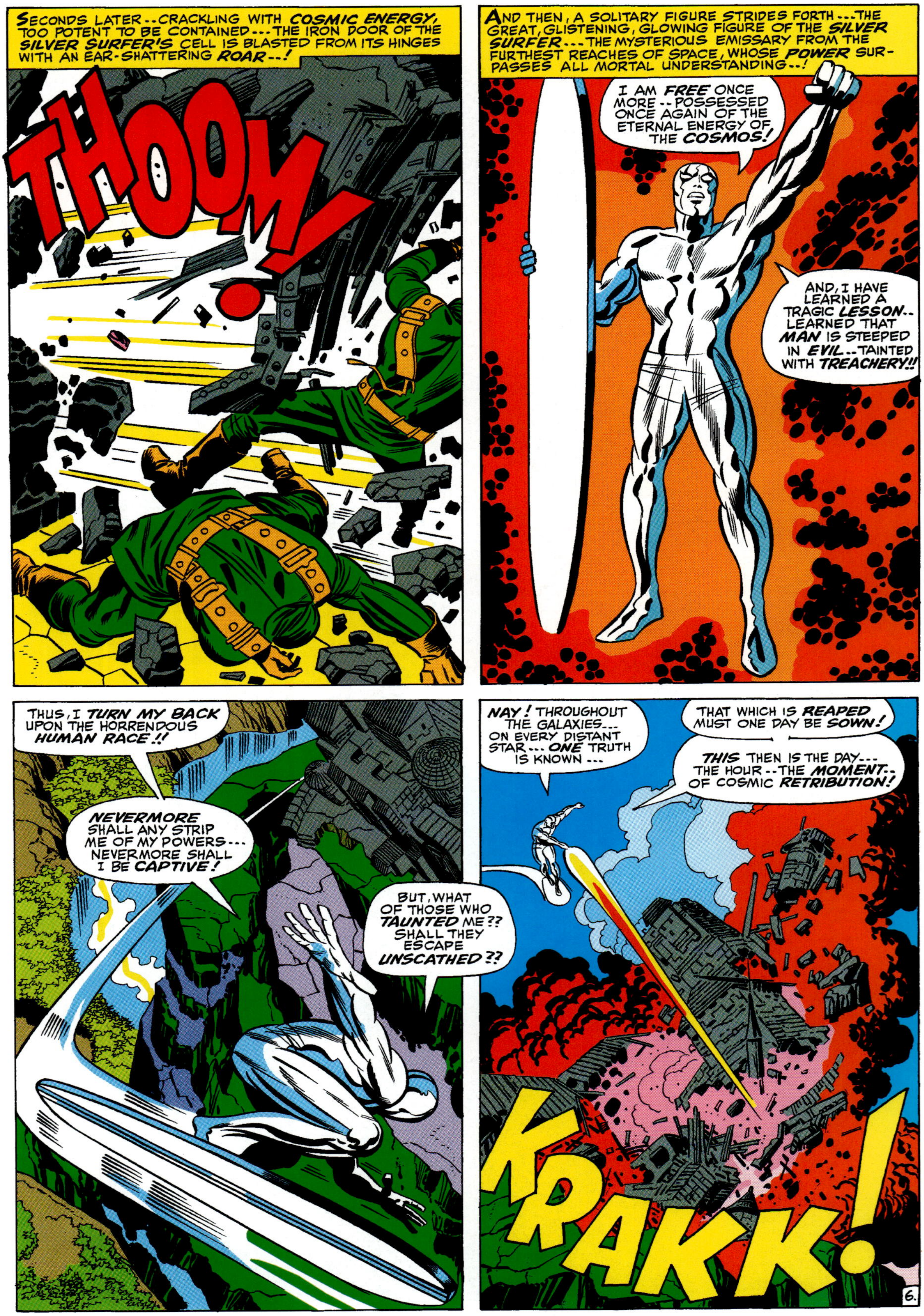
SECONDS LATER--CRACKLING WITH COSMIC ENERGY, TOO POTENT TO BE CONTAINED---THE IRON DOOR OF THE SILVER SURFER'S CELL IS BLASTED FROM ITS HINGES WITH AN EAR-SHATTERING ROAR--!
THOOM!
AND THEN, A SOLITARY FIGURE STRIDES FORTH---THE GREAT, GLISTENING, GLOWING FIGURE OF THE SILVER SURFER---THE MYSTERIOUS EMISSARY FROM THE FURTHEST REACHES OF SPACE, WHOSE POWER SURPASSES ALL MORTAL UNDERSTANDING--!
I AM FREE ONCE MORE--POSSESSED ONCE AGAIN OF THE ETERNAL ENERGY OF THE COSMOS!
AND, I HAVE LEARNED A TRAGIC LESSON-- LEARNED THAT MAN IS STEEPED IN EVIL--TAINTED WITH TREACHERY!!
THUS, I TURN MY BACK UPON THE HORRENDOUS HUMAN RACE!!
NEVERMORE SHALL ANY STRIP ME OF MY POWERS--- NEVERMORE SHALL I BE CAPTIVE!
BUT, WHAT OF THOSE WHO TAUNTED ME?? SHALL THEY ESCAPE UNSCATHED??
NAY! THROUGHOUT THE GALAXIES--- ON EVERY DISTANT STAR---ONE TRUTH IS KNOWN---
THAT WHICH IS REAPED MUST ONE DAY BE SOWN!
THIS THEN IS THE DAY--- THE HOUR--THE MOMENT-- OF COSMIC RETRIBUTION!
KRAKK!
6.

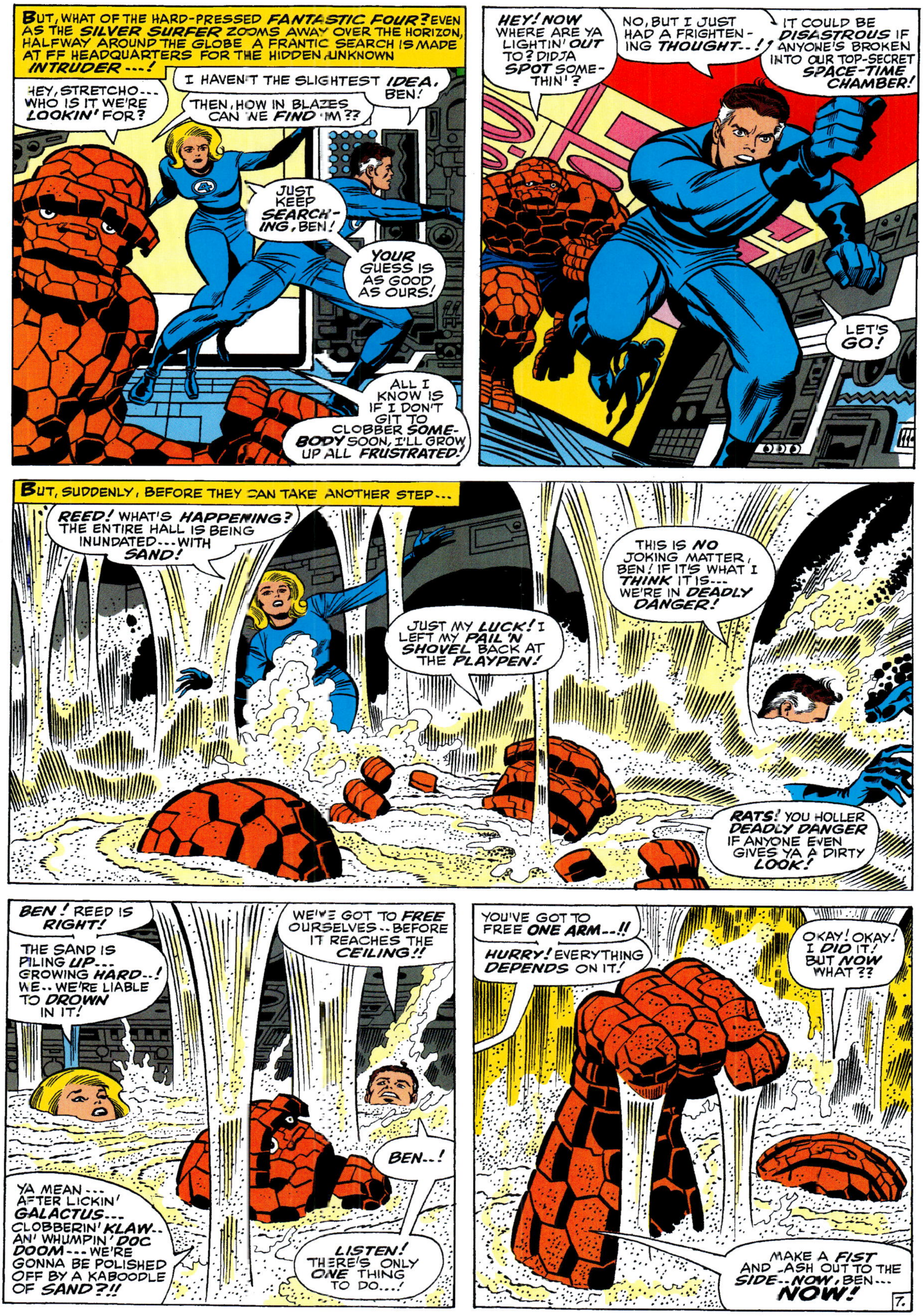

BUT, WHAT OF THE HARD-PRESSED FANTASTIC FOUR? EVEN AS THE SILVER SURFER ZOOMS AWAY OVER THE HORIZON, HALFWAY AROUND THE GLOBE A FRANTIC SEARCH IS MADE AT FF HEADQUARTERS FOR THE HIDDEN UNKNOWN INTRUDER---!
HEY, STRETCHO--- WHO IS IT WE'RE LOOKIN' FOR?
I HAVEN'T THE SLIGHTEST IDEA, BEN!
THEN, HOW IN BLAZES CAN WE FIND 'IM??
JUST KEEP SEARCH-ING, BEN!
YOUR GUESS IS AS GOOD AS OURS!
ALL I KNOW IS IF I DON'T GIT TO CLOBBER SOME-BODY SOON, I'LL GROW UP ALL FRUSTRATED!
HEY! NOW WHERE ARE YA LIGHTIN' OUT TO? DIDJA SPOT SOME-THIN'?
NO, BUT I JUST HAD A FRIGHTEN-ING THOUGHT--!
IT COULD BE DISASTROUS IF ANYONE'S BROKEN INTO OUR TOP-SECRET SPACE-TIME CHAMBER!
LET'S GO!
BUT, SUDDENLY, BEFORE THEY CAN TAKE ANOTHER STEP---
REED! WHAT'S HAPPENING? THE ENTIRE HALL IS BEING INUNDATED---WITH SAND!
THIS IS NO JOKING MATTER, BEN! IF IT'S WHAT I THINK IT IS--- WE'RE IN DEADLY DANGER!
JUST MY LUCK! I LEFT MY PAIL 'N SHOVEL BACK AT THE PLAYPEN!
RATS! YOU HOLLER DEADLY DANGER IF ANYONE EVEN GIVES YA A DIRTY LOOK!
BEN! REED IS RIGHT!
THE SAND IS PILING UP--- GROWING HARD--! WE--WE'RE LIABLE TO DROWN IN IT!
WE'VE GOT TO FREE OURSELVES--BEFORE IT REACHES THE CEILING!!
BEN--!
YA MEAN--- AFTER LICKIN' GALACTUS--- CLOBBERIN' KLAW-- AN' WHUMPIN' DOC DOOM---WE'RE GONNA BE POLISHED OFF BY A KABOODLE OF SAND?!!
LISTEN! THERE'S ONLY ONE THING TO DO---!
YOU'VE GOT TO FREE ONE ARM--!!
HURRY! EVERYTHING DEPENDS ON IT!
OKAY! OKAY! I DID IT! BUT NOW WHAT??
MAKE A FIST AND LASH OUT TO THE SIDE--NOW, BEN--- NOW!
7.

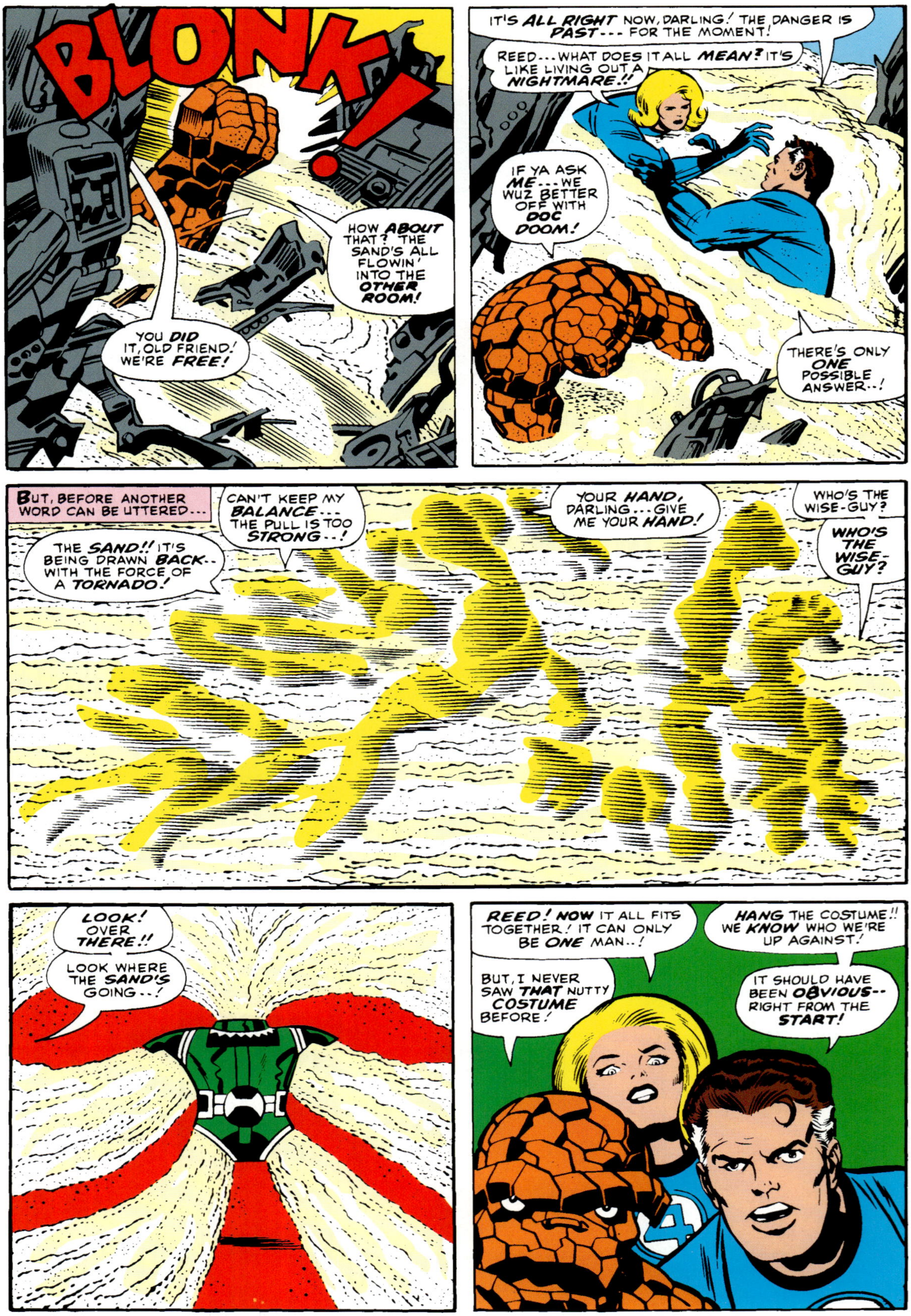
BLONK!
HOW ABOUT THAT? THE SAND'S ALL FLOWIN' INTO THE OTHER ROOM!
YOU DID IT, OLD FRIEND! WE'RE FREE!
IT'S ALL RIGHT NOW, DARLING! THE DANGER IS PAST--- FOR THE MOMENT!
REED... WHAT DOES IT ALL MEAN? IT'S LIKE LIVING OUT A NIGHTMARE!!
IF YA ASK ME... WE WUZ BETTER OFF WITH DOC DOOM!
THERE'S ONLY ONE POSSIBLE ANSWER..!
BUT, BEFORE ANOTHER WORD CAN BE UTTERED...
THE SAND!! IT'S BEING DRAWN BACK-- WITH THE FORCE OF A TORNADO!
CAN'T KEEP MY BALANCE... THE PULL IS TOO STRONG..!
YOUR HAND, DARLING... GIVE ME YOUR HAND!
WHO'S THE WISE-GUY?
WHO'S THE WISE-GUY?
LOOK! OVER THERE!!
LOOK WHERE THE SAND'S GOING..!
REED! NOW IT ALL FITS TOGETHER! IT CAN ONLY BE ONE MAN..!
BUT, I NEVER SAW THAT NUTTY COSTUME BEFORE!
HANG THE COSTUME!! WE KNOW WHO WE'RE UP AGAINST!
IT SHOULD HAVE BEEN OBVIOUS-- RIGHT FROM THE START!

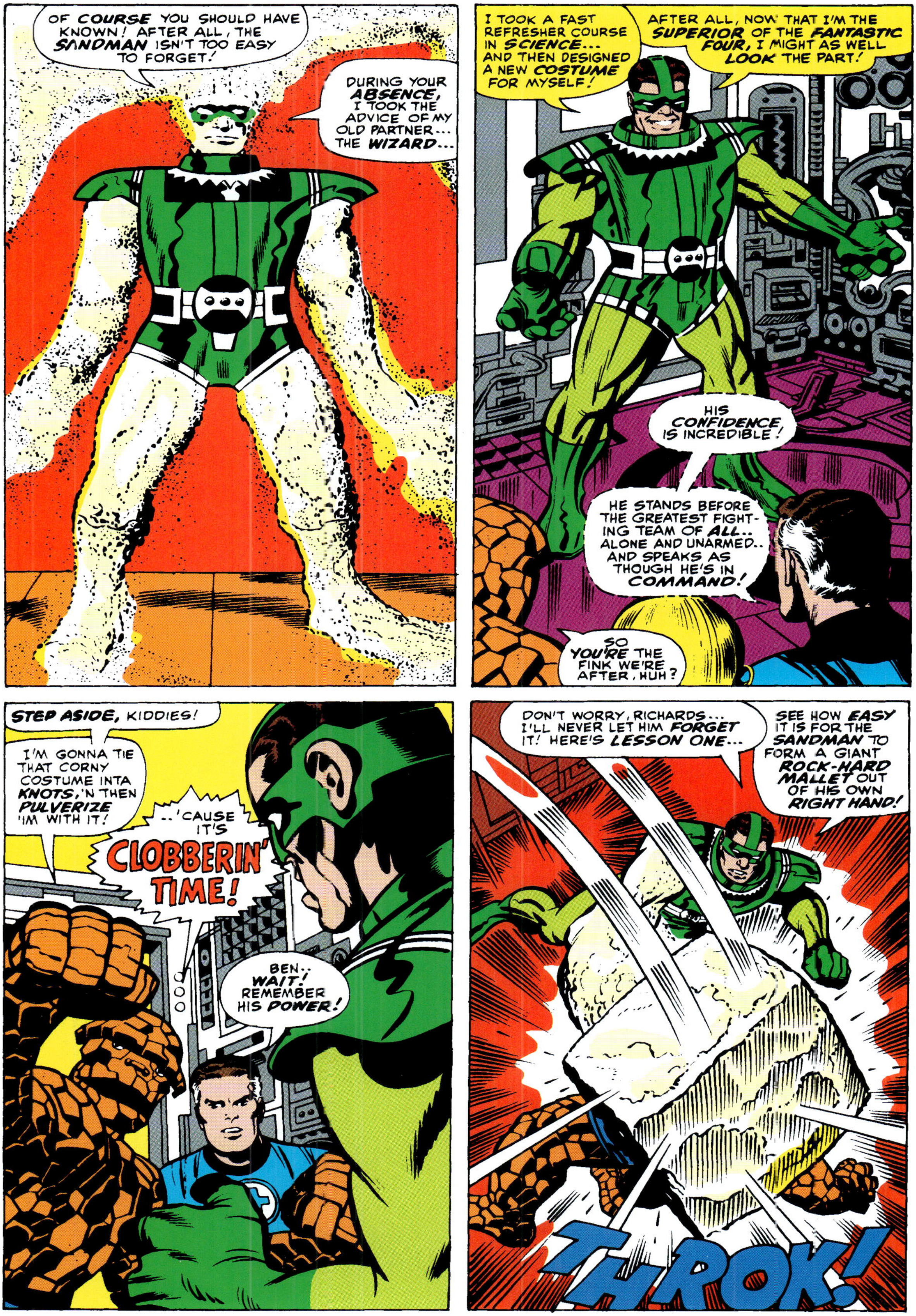
OF COURSE YOU SHOULD HAVE KNOWN! AFTER ALL, THE SANDMAN ISN'T TOO EASY TO FORGET!
DURING YOUR ABSENCE, I TOOK THE ADVICE OF MY OLD PARTNER... THE WIZARD...
I TOOK A FAST REFRESHER COURSE IN SCIENCE... AND THEN DESIGNED A NEW COSTUME FOR MYSELF!
AFTER ALL, NOW THAT I'M THE SUPERIOR OF THE FANTASTIC FOUR, I MIGHT AS WELL LOOK THE PART!
HIS CONFIDENCE IS INCREDIBLE!
HE STANDS BEFORE THE GREATEST FIGHTING TEAM OF ALL.. ALONE AND UNARMED.. AND SPEAKS AS THOUGH HE'S IN COMMAND!
SO YOU'RE THE FINK WE'RE AFTER, HUH?
STEP ASIDE, KIDDIES!
I'M GONNA TIE THAT CORNY COSTUME INTA KNOTS, 'N THEN PULVERIZE 'IM WITH IT!
..'CAUSE IT'S
CLOBBERIN' TIME!
BEN.. WAIT! REMEMBER HIS POWER!
DON'T WORRY, RICHARDS... I'LL NEVER LET HIM FORGET IT! HERE'S LESSON ONE...
SEE HOW EASY IT IS FOR THE SANDMAN TO FORM A GIANT ROCK-HARD MALLET OUT OF HIS OWN RIGHT HAND!
THROK!

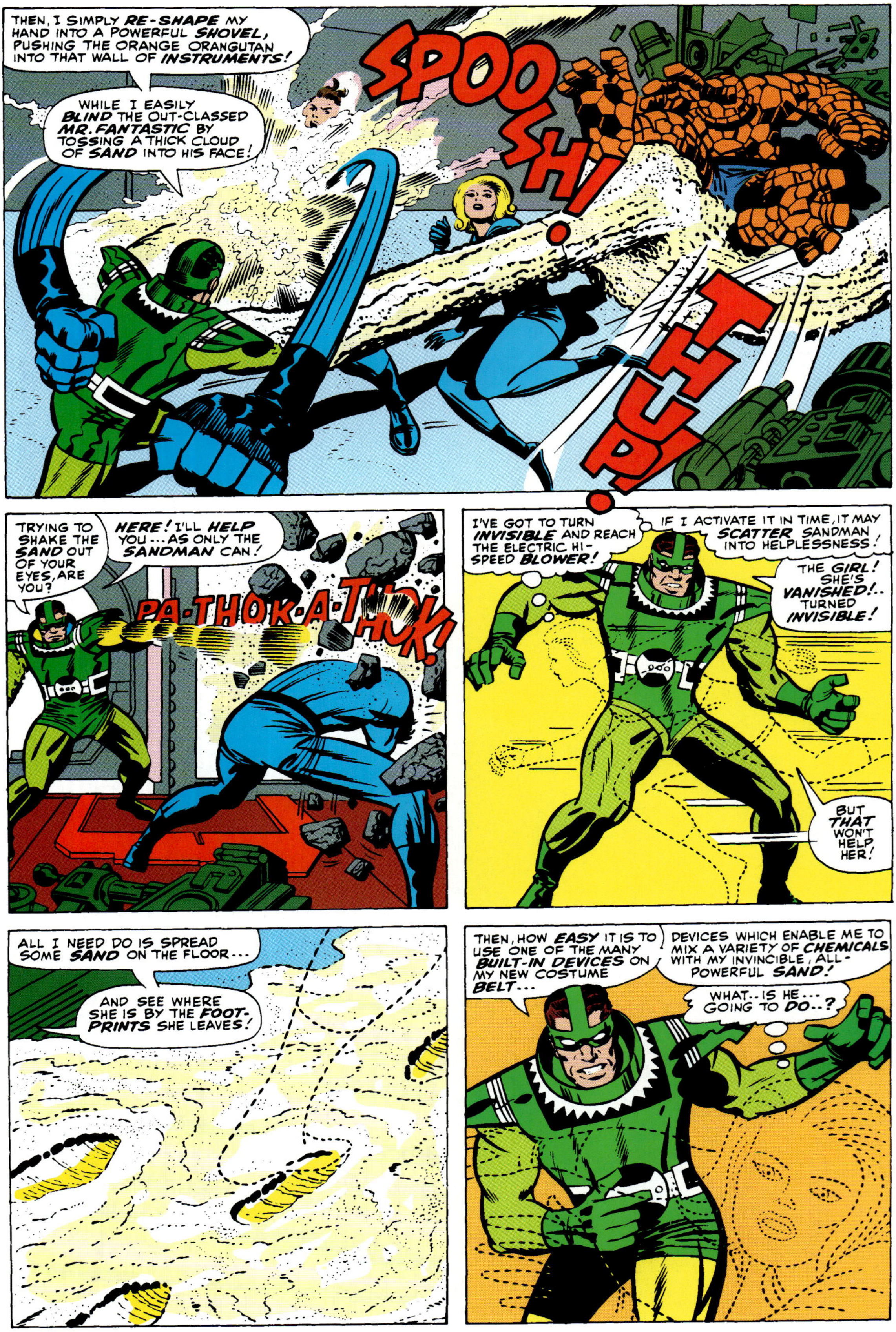
THEN, I SIMPLY RE-SHAPE MY HAND INTO A POWERFUL SHOVEL, PUSHING THE ORANGE ORANGUTAN INTO THAT WALL OF INSTRUMENTS!
WHILE I EASILY BLIND THE OUT-CLASSED MR. FANTASTIC BY TOSSING A THICK CLOUD OF SAND INTO HIS FACE!
SPOOSH!
THUP!
TRYING TO SHAKE THE SAND OUT OF YOUR EYES, ARE YOU?
HERE! I'LL HELP YOU... AS ONLY THE SANDMAN CAN!
PA-THOK-A-THOK!
I'VE GOT TO TURN INVISIBLE AND REACH THE ELECTRIC HI-SPEED BLOWER!
IF I ACTIVATE IT IN TIME, IT MAY SCATTER SANDMAN INTO HELPLESSNESS!
THE GIRL! SHE'S VANISHED!.. TURNED INVISIBLE!
BUT THAT WON'T HELP HER!
ALL I NEED DO IS SPREAD SOME SAND ON THE FLOOR...
AND SEE WHERE SHE IS BY THE FOOT-PRINTS SHE LEAVES!
THEN, HOW EASY IT IS TO USE ONE OF THE MANY BUILT-IN DEVICES ON MY NEW COSTUME BELT...
DEVICES WHICH ENABLE ME TO MIX A VARIETY OF CHEMICALS WITH MY INVINCIBLE, ALL-POWERFUL SAND!
WHAT--IS HE--- GOING TO DO--?

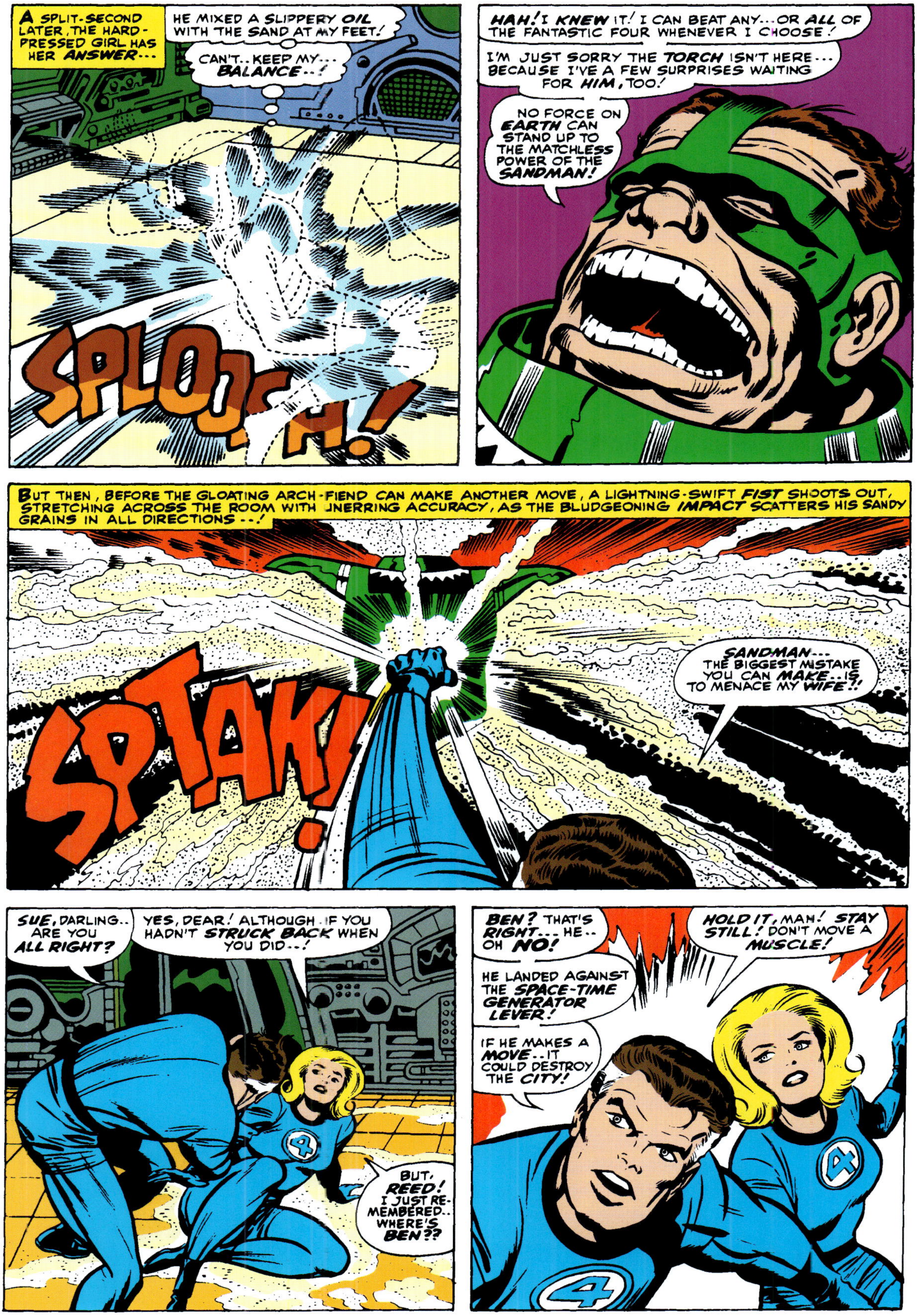
A SPLIT-SECOND LATER, THE HARD-PRESSED GIRL HAS HER ANSWER...
HE MIXED A SLIPPERY OIL WITH THE SAND AT MY FEET!
CAN'T.. KEEP MY... BALANCE..!
SPLOOSH!
HAH! I KNEW IT! I CAN BEAT ANY...OR ALL OF THE FANTASTIC FOUR WHENEVER I CHOOSE!
I'M JUST SORRY THE TORCH ISN'T HERE... BECAUSE I'VE A FEW SURPRISES WAITING FOR HIM, TOO!
NO FORCE ON EARTH CAN STAND UP TO THE MATCHLESS POWER OF THE SANDMAN!
BUT THEN, BEFORE THE GLOATING ARCH-FIEND CAN MAKE ANOTHER MOVE, A LIGHTNING-SWIFT FIST SHOOTS OUT, STRETCHING ACROSS THE ROOM WITH UNERRING ACCURACY, AS THE BLUDGEONING IMPACT SCATTERS HIS SANDY GRAINS IN ALL DIRECTIONS..!
SPTAK!
SANDMAN... THE BIGGEST MISTAKE YOU CAN MAKE.. IS TO MENACE MY WIFE!!
SUE, DARLING.. ARE YOU ALL RIGHT?
YES, DEAR! ALTHOUGH IF YOU HADN'T STRUCK BACK WHEN YOU DID..!
BUT, REED! I JUST RE-MEMBERED.. WHERE'S BEN??
BEN? THAT'S RIGHT... HE.. OH NO!
HE LANDED AGAINST THE SPACE-TIME GENERATOR LEVER!
IF HE MAKES A MOVE..IT COULD DESTROY THE CITY!
HOLD IT, MAN! STAY STILL! DON'T MOVE A MUSCLE!

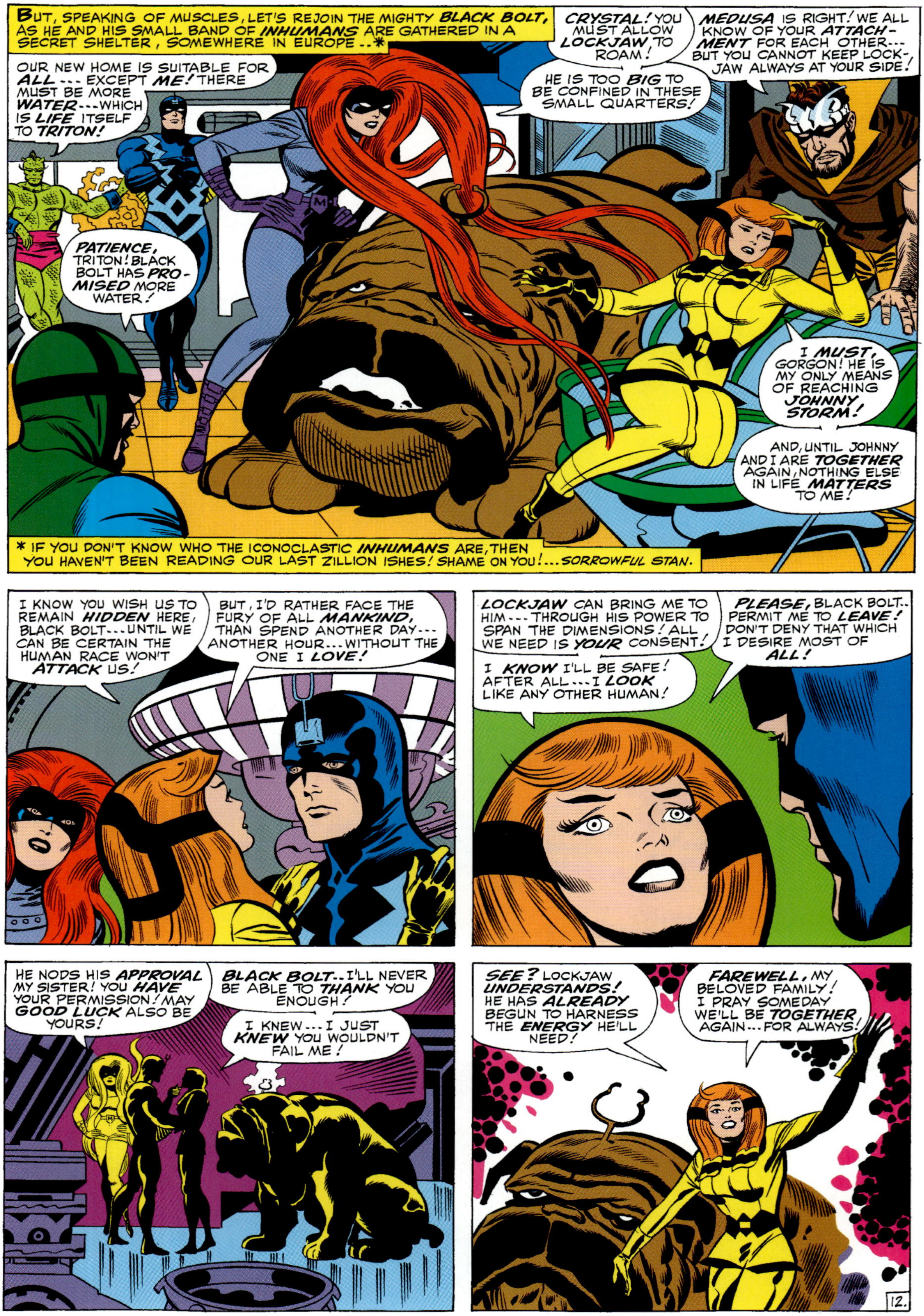

BUT, SPEAKING OF MUSCLES, LET'S REJOIN THE MIGHTY BLACK BOLT, AS HE AND HIS SMALL BAND OF INHUMANS ARE GATHERED IN A SECRET SHELTER, SOMEWHERE IN EUROPE--*
OUR NEW HOME IS SUITABLE FOR ALL--- EXCEPT ME! THERE MUST BE MORE WATER---WHICH IS LIFE ITSELF TO TRITON!
PATIENCE, TRITON! BLACK BOLT HAS PROMISED MORE WATER!
CRYSTAL! YOU MUST ALLOW LOCKJAW TO ROAM!
HE IS TOO BIG TO BE CONFINED IN THESE SMALL QUARTERS!
MEDUSA IS RIGHT! WE ALL KNOW OF YOUR ATTACHMENT FOR EACH OTHER--- BUT YOU CANNOT KEEP LOCKJAW ALWAYS AT YOUR SIDE!
I MUST, GORGON! HE IS MY ONLY MEANS OF REACHING JOHNNY STORM!
AND, UNTIL JOHNNY AND I ARE TOGETHER AGAIN, NOTHING ELSE IN LIFE MATTERS TO ME!
* IF YOU DON'T KNOW WHO THE ICONOCLASTIC INHUMANS ARE, THEN YOU HAVEN'T BEEN READING OUR LAST ZILLION ISHES! SHAME ON YOU!... SORROWFUL STAN.
I KNOW YOU WISH US TO REMAIN HIDDEN HERE, BLACK BOLT---UNTIL WE CAN BE CERTAIN THE HUMAN RACE WON'T ATTACK US!
BUT, I'D RATHER FACE THE FURY OF ALL MANKIND, THAN SPEND ANOTHER DAY--- ANOTHER HOUR--- WITHOUT THE ONE I LOVE!
LOCKJAW CAN BRING ME TO HIM--- THROUGH HIS POWER TO SPAN THE DIMENSIONS! ALL WE NEED IS YOUR CONSENT!
I KNOW I'LL BE SAFE! AFTER ALL--- I LOOK LIKE ANY OTHER HUMAN!
PLEASE, BLACK BOLT.. PERMIT ME TO LEAVE! DON'T DENY THAT WHICH I DESIRE MOST OF ALL!
HE NODS HIS APPROVAL MY SISTER! YOU HAVE YOUR PERMISSION! MAY GOOD LUCK ALSO BE YOURS!
BLACK BOLT.. I'LL NEVER BE ABLE TO THANK YOU ENOUGH!
I KNEW--- I JUST KNEW YOU WOULDN'T FAIL ME!
SEE? LOCKJAW UNDERSTANDS! HE HAS ALREADY BEGUN TO HARNESS THE ENERGY HE'LL NEED!
FAREWELL, MY BELOVED FAMILY! I PRAY SOMEDAY WE'LL BE TOGETHER AGAIN--- FOR ALWAYS!
12.

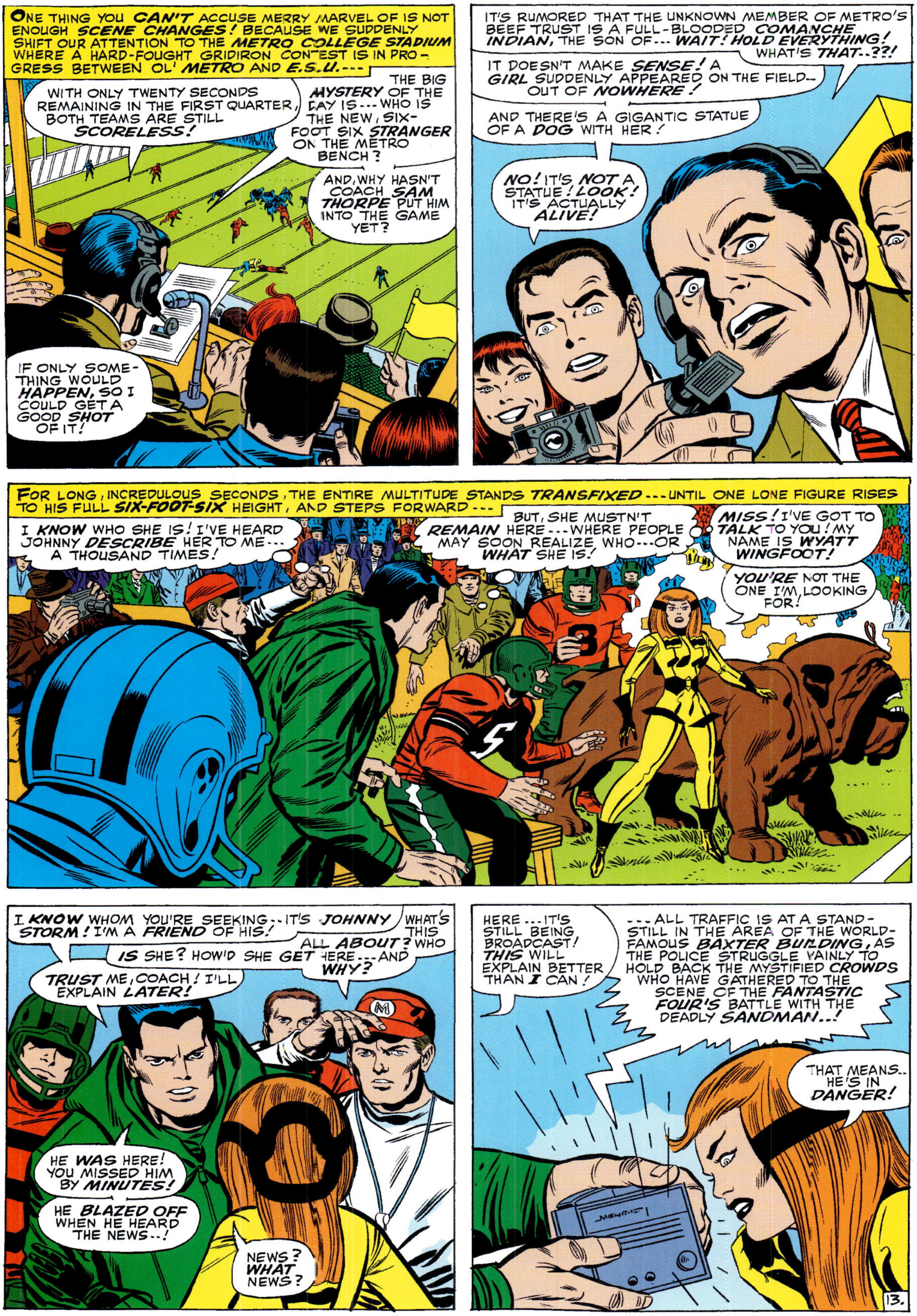
ONE THING YOU CAN'T ACCUSE MERRY MARVEL OF IS NOT ENOUGH SCENE CHANGES! BECAUSE WE SUDDENLY SHIFT OUR ATTENTION TO THE METRO COLLEGE STADIUM WHERE A HARD-FOUGHT GRIDIRON CONTEST IS IN PROGRESS BETWEEN OL' METRO AND E.S.U.---
WITH ONLY TWENTY SECONDS REMAINING IN THE FIRST QUARTER, BOTH TEAMS ARE STILL SCORELESS!
THE BIG MYSTERY OF THE DAY IS --- WHO IS THE NEW, SIX-FOOT SIX STRANGER ON THE METRO BENCH?
AND, WHY HASN'T COACH SAM THORPE PUT HIM INTO THE GAME YET?
IF ONLY SOMETHING WOULD HAPPEN, SO I COULD GET A GOOD SHOT OF IT!
IT'S RUMORED THAT THE UNKNOWN MEMBER OF METRO'S BEEF TRUST IS A FULL-BLOODED COMANCHE INDIAN, THE SON OF --- WAIT! HOLD EVERYTHING! WHAT'S THAT--??!
IT DOESN'T MAKE SENSE! A GIRL SUDDENLY APPEARED ON THE FIELD-- OUT OF NOWHERE!
AND THERE'S A GIGANTIC STATUE OF A DOG WITH HER!
NO! IT'S NOT A STATUE! LOOK! IT'S ACTUALLY ALIVE!
FOR LONG, INCREDULOUS SECONDS, THE ENTIRE MULTITUDE STANDS TRANSFIXED --- UNTIL ONE LONE FIGURE RISES TO HIS FULL SIX-FOOT-SIX HEIGHT, AND STEPS FORWARD ---
I KNOW WHO SHE IS! I'VE HEARD JOHNNY DESCRIBE HER TO ME --- A THOUSAND TIMES!
BUT, SHE MUSTN'T REMAIN HERE --- WHERE PEOPLE MAY SOON REALIZE WHO --- OR WHAT SHE IS!
MISS! I'VE GOT TO TALK TO YOU! MY NAME IS WYATT WINGFOOT!
YOU'RE NOT THE ONE I'M LOOKING FOR!
I KNOW WHOM YOU'RE SEEKING -- IT'S JOHNNY STORM! I'M A FRIEND OF HIS!
WHAT'S THIS ALL ABOUT? WHO IS SHE? HOW'D SHE GET HERE --- AND WHY?
TRUST ME, COACH! I'LL EXPLAIN LATER!
HE WAS HERE! YOU MISSED HIM BY MINUTES!
HE BLAZED OFF WHEN HE HEARD THE NEWS--!
NEWS? WHAT NEWS?
HERE --- IT'S STILL BEING BROADCAST! THIS WILL EXPLAIN BETTER THAN I CAN!
--- ALL TRAFFIC IS AT A STANDSTILL IN THE AREA OF THE WORLD-FAMOUS BAXTER BUILDING, AS THE POLICE STRUGGLE VAINLY TO HOLD BACK THE MYSTIFIED CROWDS WHO HAVE GATHERED TO THE SCENE OF THE FANTASTIC FOUR'S BATTLE WITH THE DEADLY SANDMAN...!
THAT MEANS.. HE'S IN DANGER!
13.

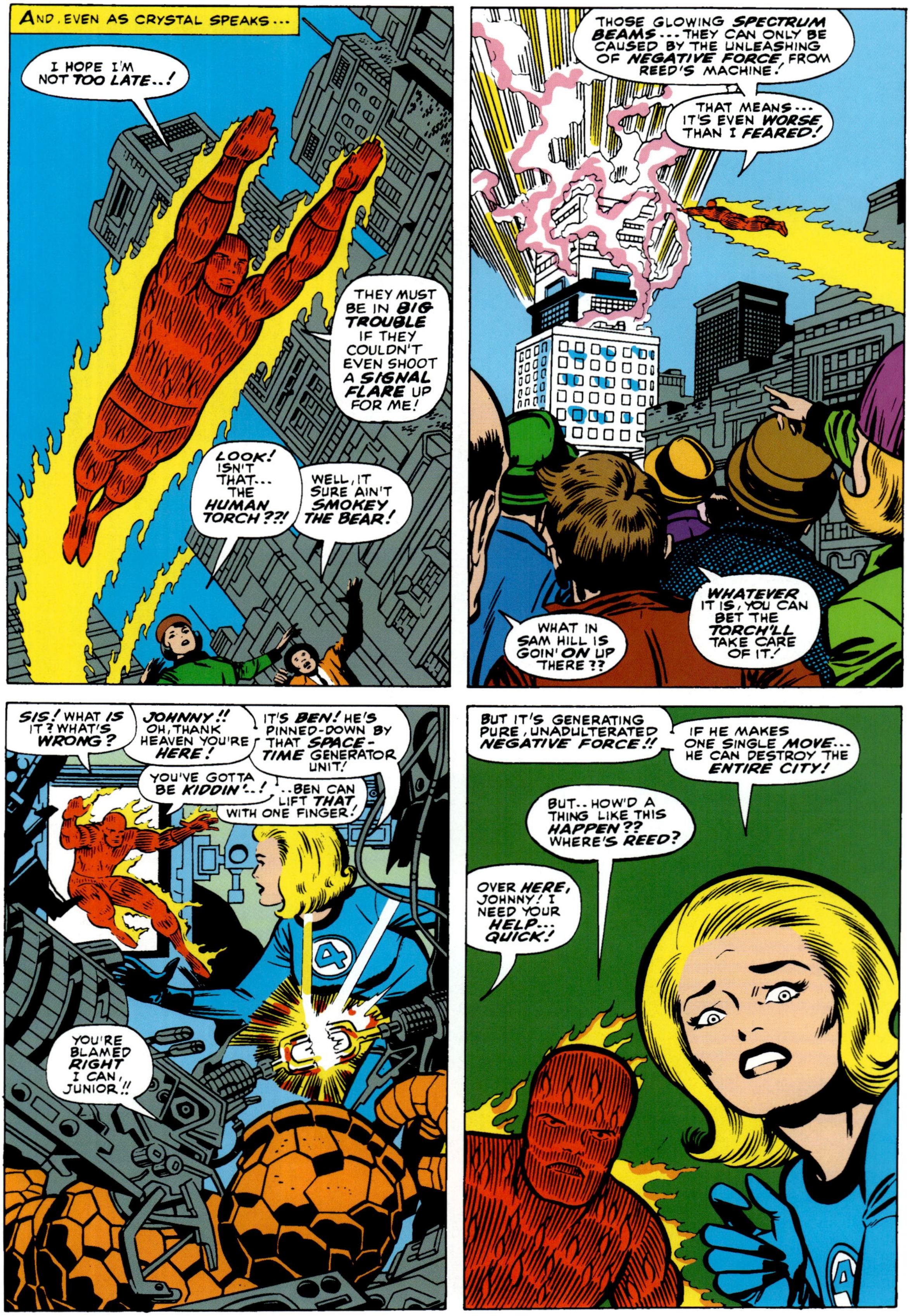

AND, EVEN AS CRYSTAL SPEAKS...
I HOPE I'M NOT TOO LATE..!
THEY MUST BE IN BIG TROUBLE IF THEY COULDN'T EVEN SHOOT A SIGNAL FLARE UP FOR ME!
LOOK! ISN'T THAT... THE HUMAN TORCH??!
WELL, IT SURE AIN'T SMOKEY THE BEAR!
THOSE GLOWING SPECTRUM BEAMS--- THEY CAN ONLY BE CAUSED BY THE UNLEASHING OF NEGATIVE FORCE, FROM REED'S MACHINE!
THAT MEANS--- IT'S EVEN WORSE THAN I FEARED!
WHAT IN SAM HILL IS GOIN' ON UP THERE??
WHATEVER IT IS, YOU CAN BET THE TORCH'LL TAKE CARE OF IT!
SIS! WHAT IS IT? WHAT'S WRONG?
JOHNNY!! OH, THANK HEAVEN YOU'RE HERE!
IT'S BEN! HE'S PINNED-DOWN BY THAT SPACE-TIME GENERATOR UNIT!
YOU'VE GOTTA BE KIDDIN'..!
..BEN CAN LIFT THAT WITH ONE FINGER!
YOU'RE BLAMED RIGHT I CAN, JUNIOR!!
BUT IT'S GENERATING PURE, UNADULTERATED NEGATIVE FORCE!!
IF HE MAKES ONE SINGLE MOVE... HE CAN DESTROY THE ENTIRE CITY!
BUT.. HOW'D A THING LIKE THIS HAPPEN?? WHERE'S REED?
OVER HERE, JOHNNY! I NEED YOUR HELP... QUICK!

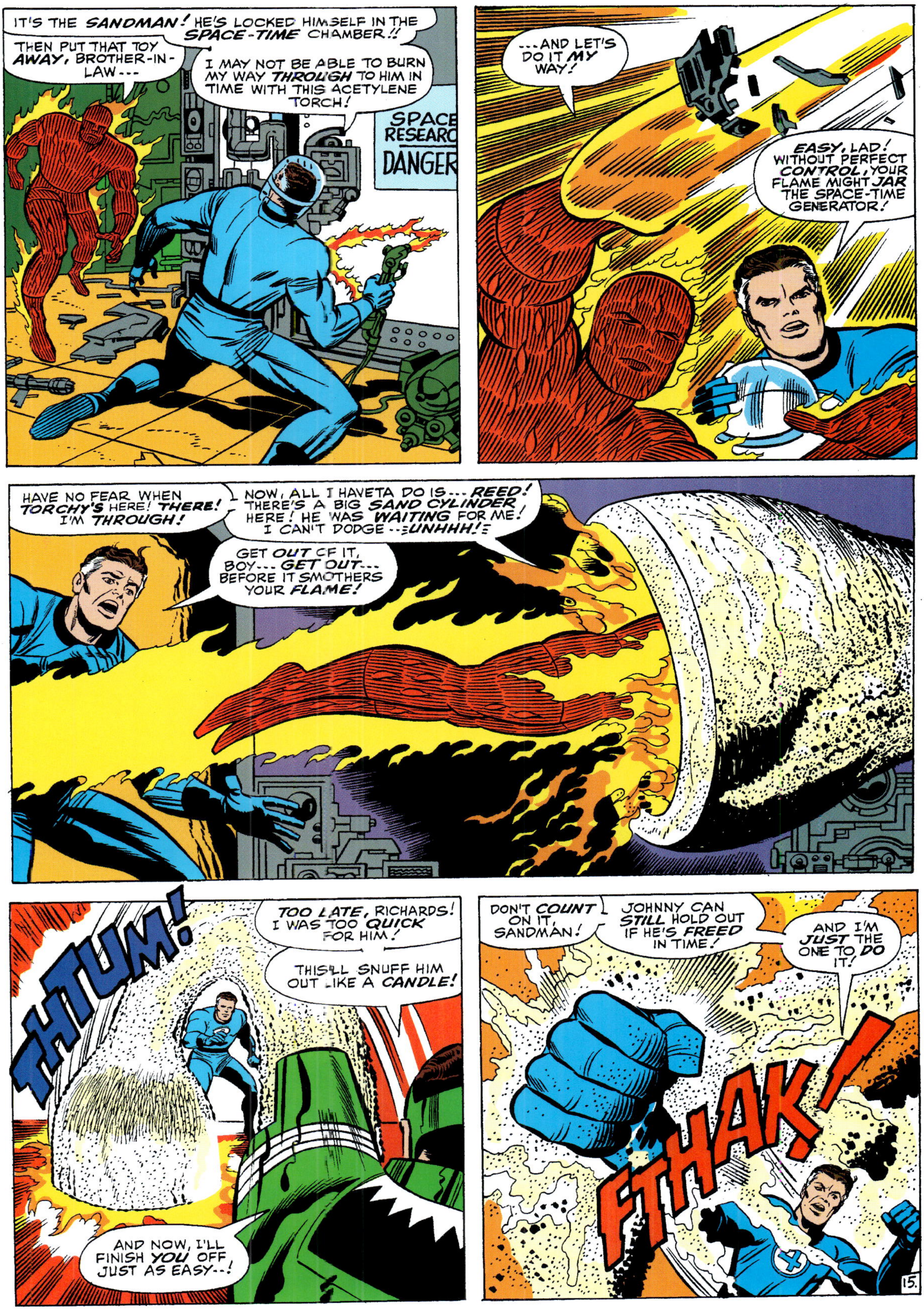
IT'S THE SANDMAN! HE'S LOCKED HIMSELF IN THE SPACE-TIME CHAMBER!!
THEN PUT THAT TOY AWAY, BROTHER-IN-LAW---
I MAY NOT BE ABLE TO BURN MY WAY THROUGH TO HIM IN TIME WITH THIS ACETYLENE TORCH!
SPACE RESEARC
DANGER
---AND LET'S DO IT MY WAY!
EASY, LAD! WITHOUT PERFECT CONTROL, YOUR FLAME MIGHT JAR THE SPACE-TIME GENERATOR!
HAVE NO FEAR WHEN TORCHY'S HERE! THERE! I'M THROUGH!
NOW, ALL I HAVETA DO IS--- REED! THERE'S A BIG SAND CYLINDER HERE! HE WAS WAITING FOR ME! I CAN'T DODGE ---UNHHH!
GET OUT OF IT, BOY--- GET OUT--- BEFORE IT SMOTHERS YOUR FLAME!
THTUM!
TOO LATE, RICHARDS! I WAS TOO QUICK FOR HIM!
THIS'LL SNUFF HIM OUT LIKE A CANDLE!
AND NOW, I'LL FINISH YOU OFF JUST AS EASY--!
DON'T COUNT ON IT, SANDMAN!
JOHNNY CAN STILL HOLD OUT IF HE'S FREED IN TIME!
AND I'M JUST THE ONE TO DO IT!
FTHAK!
15.

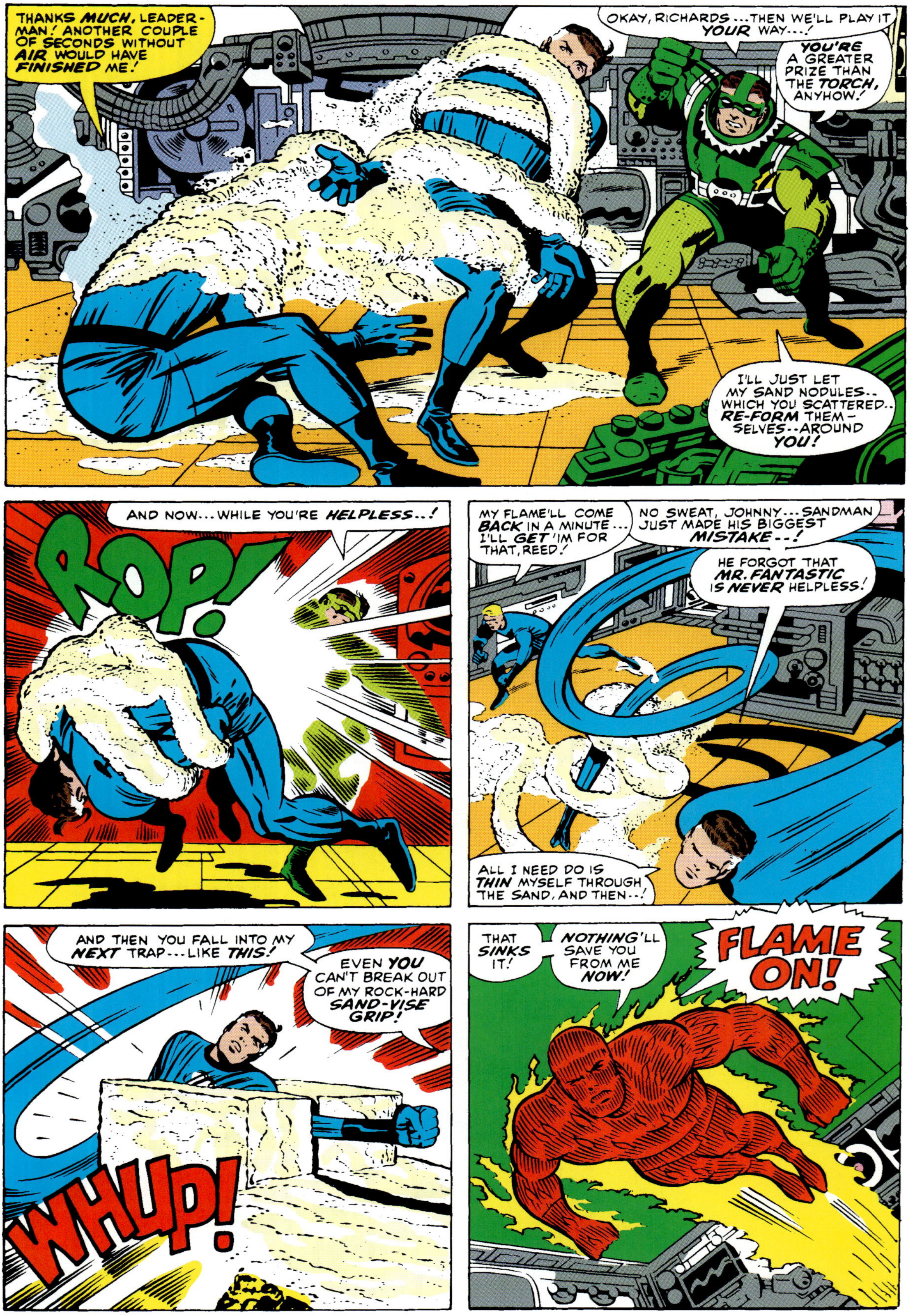
THANKS MUCH, LEADER-MAN! ANOTHER COUPLE OF SECONDS WITHOUT AIR WOULD HAVE FINISHED ME!
OKAY, RICHARDS...THEN WE'LL PLAY IT YOUR WAY...!
YOU'RE A GREATER PRIZE THAN THE TORCH, ANYHOW!
I'LL JUST LET MY SAND NODULES.. WHICH YOU SCATTERED.. RE-FORM THEM-SELVES--AROUND YOU!
AND NOW...WHILE YOU'RE HELPLESS..!
ROP!
MY FLAME'LL COME BACK IN A MINUTE... I'LL GET 'IM FOR THAT, REED!
NO SWEAT, JOHNNY...SANDMAN JUST MADE HIS BIGGEST MISTAKE--!
HE FORGOT THAT MR. FANTASTIC IS NEVER HELPLESS!
ALL I NEED DO IS THIN MYSELF THROUGH THE SAND, AND THEN--!
AND THEN YOU FALL INTO MY NEXT TRAP---LIKE THIS!
EVEN YOU CAN'T BREAK OUT OF MY ROCK-HARD SAND-VISE GRIP!
WHUP!
THAT SINKS IT!
NOTHING'LL SAVE YOU FROM ME NOW!
FLAME ON!

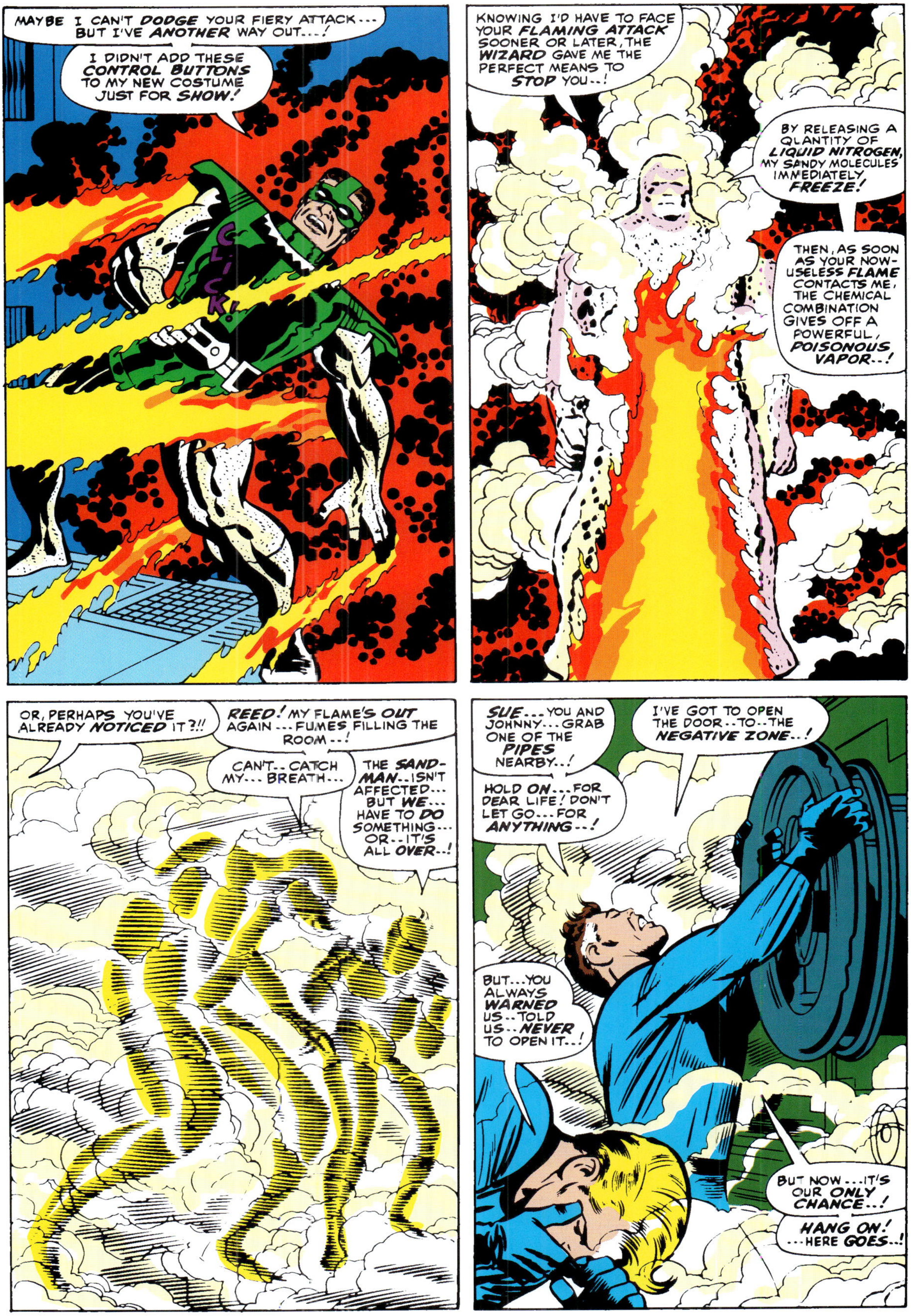
MAYBE I CAN'T DODGE YOUR FIERY ATTACK... BUT I'VE ANOTHER WAY OUT...!
I DIDN'T ADD THESE CONTROL BUTTONS TO MY NEW COSTUME JUST FOR SHOW!
CLICK!
KNOWING I'D HAVE TO FACE YOUR FLAMING ATTACK SOONER OR LATER, THE WIZARD GAVE ME THE PERFECT MEANS TO STOP YOU..!
BY RELEASING A QUANTITY OF LIQUID NITROGEN, MY SANDY MOLECULES IMMEDIATELY FREEZE!
THEN, AS SOON AS YOUR NOW-USELESS FLAME CONTACTS ME, THE CHEMICAL COMBINATION GIVES OFF A POWERFUL, POISONOUS VAPOR..!
OR, PERHAPS YOU'VE ALREADY NOTICED IT?!!
REED! MY FLAME'S OUT AGAIN... FUMES FILLING THE ROOM..!
CAN'T.. CATCH MY... BREATH...
THE SANDMAN.. ISN'T AFFECTED... BUT WE... HAVE TO DO SOMETHING... OR.. IT'S ALL OVER..!
SUE... YOU AND JOHNNY... GRAB ONE OF THE PIPES NEARBY..!
HOLD ON... FOR DEAR LIFE! DON'T LET GO... FOR ANYTHING..!
I'VE GOT TO OPEN THE DOOR.. TO.. THE NEGATIVE ZONE..!
BUT... YOU ALWAYS WARNED US.. TOLD US.. NEVER TO OPEN IT..!
BUT NOW... IT'S OUR ONLY CHANCE..!
HANG ON! ...HERE GOES..!

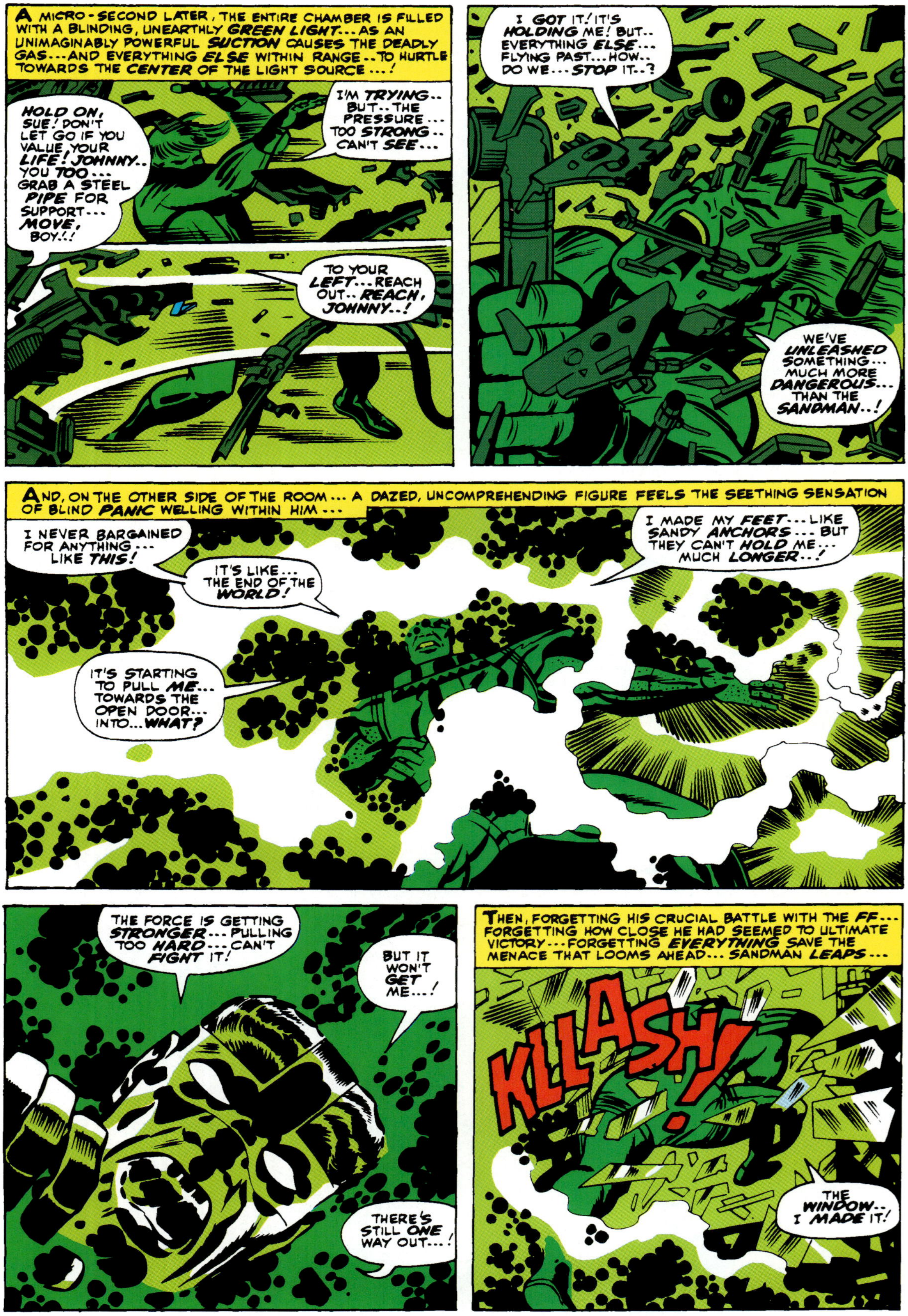

A MICRO-SECOND LATER, THE ENTIRE CHAMBER IS FILLED WITH A BLINDING, UNEARTHLY GREEN LIGHT... AS AN UNIMAGINABLY POWERFUL SUCTION CAUSES THE DEADLY GAS... AND EVERYTHING ELSE WITHIN RANGE.. TO HURTLE TOWARDS THE CENTER OF THE LIGHT SOURCE...!
HOLD ON, SUE! DON'T LET GO IF YOU VALUE YOUR LIFE! JOHNNY.. YOU TOO... GRAB A STEEL PIPE FOR SUPPORT... MOVE, BOY..!
I'M TRYING.. BUT.. THE PRESSURE... TOO STRONG.. CAN'T SEE...
TO YOUR LEFT... REACH OUT.. REACH, JOHNNY..!
I GOT IT! IT'S HOLDING ME! BUT.. EVERYTHING ELSE... FLYING PAST... HOW.. DO WE... STOP IT..?
WE'VE UNLEASHED SOMETHING... MUCH MORE DANGEROUS... THAN THE SANDMAN..!
AND, ON THE OTHER SIDE OF THE ROOM... A DAZED, UNCOMPREHENDING FIGURE FEELS THE SEETHING SENSATION OF BLIND PANIC WELLING WITHIN HIM...
I NEVER BARGAINED FOR ANYTHING... LIKE THIS!
IT'S LIKE... THE END OF THE WORLD!
I MADE MY FEET... LIKE SANDY ANCHORS... BUT THEY CAN'T HOLD ME... MUCH LONGER..!
IT'S STARTING TO PULL ME... TOWARDS THE OPEN DOOR... INTO... WHAT?
THE FORCE IS GETTING STRONGER... PULLING TOO HARD... CAN'T FIGHT IT!
BUT IT WON'T GET ME...!
THERE'S STILL ONE WAY OUT...!
THEN, FORGETTING HIS CRUCIAL BATTLE WITH THE FF... FORGETTING HOW CLOSE HE HAD SEEMED TO ULTIMATE VICTORY... FORGETTING EVERYTHING SAVE THE MENACE THAT LOOMS AHEAD... SANDMAN LEAPS...
KLLASH!
THE WINDOW.. I MADE IT!

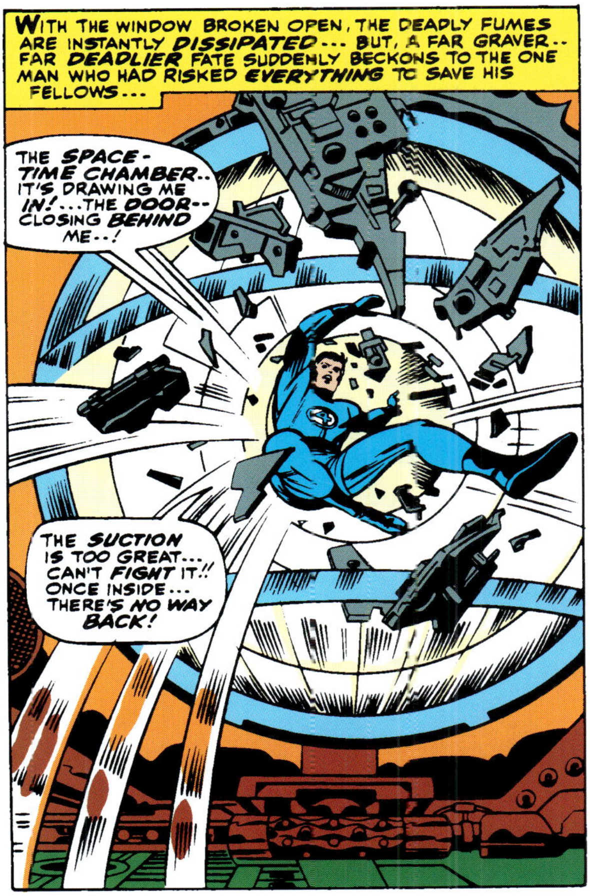
WITH THE WINDOW BROKEN OPEN, THE DEADLY FUMES ARE INSTANTLY DISSIPATED... BUT, A FAR GRAVER.. FAR DEADLIER FATE SUDDENLY BECKONS TO THE ONE MAN WHO HAD RISKED EVERYTHING TO SAVE HIS FELLOWS...
THE SPACE-TIME CHAMBER.. IT'S DRAWING ME IN!... THE DOOR-- CLOSING BEHIND ME..!
THE SUCTION IS TOO GREAT... CAN'T FIGHT IT!! ONCE INSIDE... THERE'S NO WAY BACK!

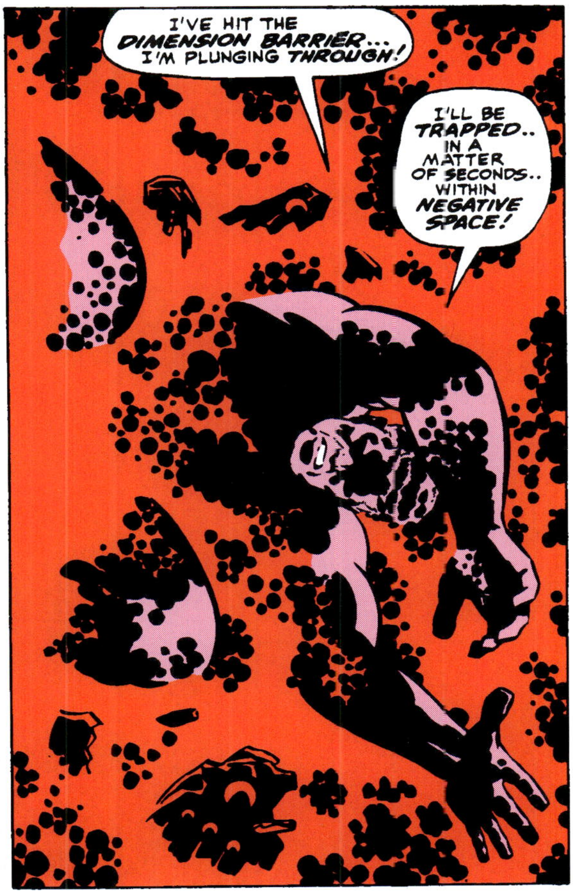
I'VE HIT THE DIMENSION BARRIER... I'M PLUNGING THROUGH!
I'LL BE TRAPPED.. IN A MATTER OF SECONDS.. WITHIN NEGATIVE SPACE!

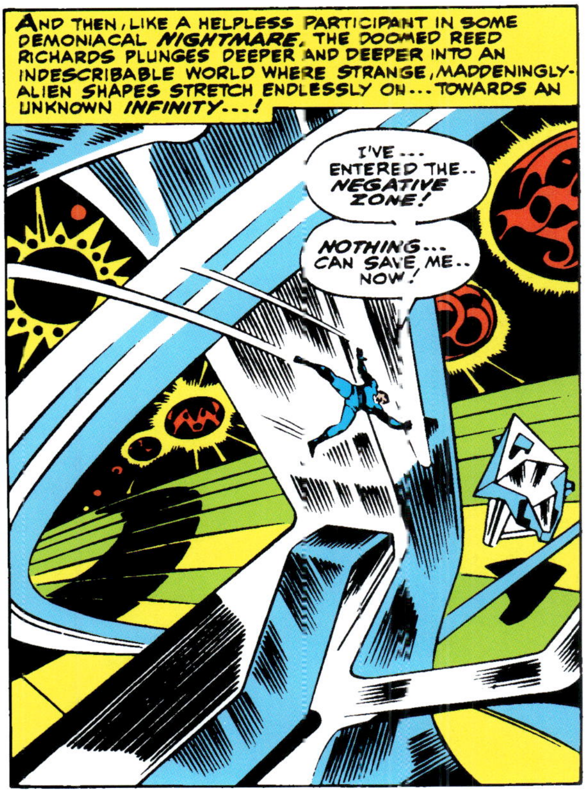
AND THEN, LIKE A HELPLESS PARTICIPANT IN SOME DEMONIACAL NIGHTMARE, THE DOOMED REED RICHARDS PLUNGES DEEPER AND DEEPER INTO AN INDESCRIBABLE WORLD WHERE STRANGE, MADDENINGLY-ALIEN SHAPES STRETCH ENDLESSLY ON... TOWARDS AN UNKNOWN INFINITY...!
I'VE... ENTERED THE.. NEGATIVE ZONE!
NOTHING... CAN SAVE ME.. NOW!

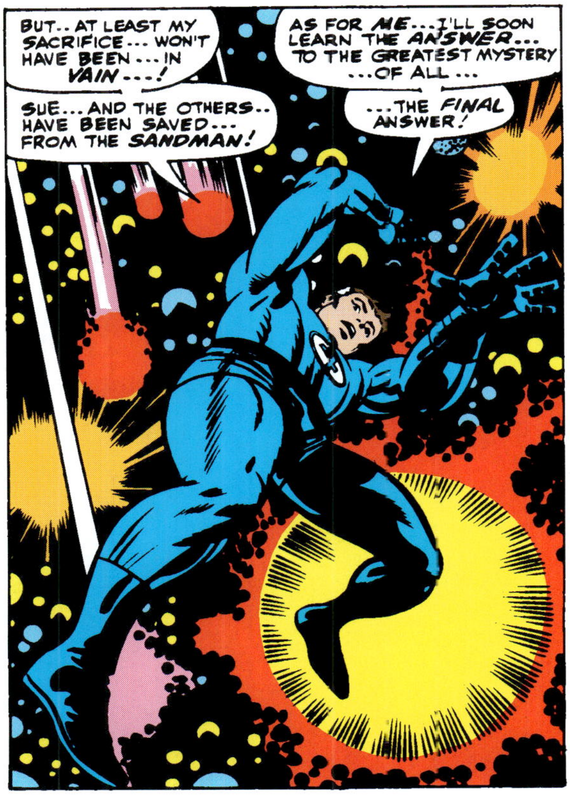
BUT.. AT LEAST MY SACRIFICE... WON'T HAVE BEEN... IN VAIN...!
SUE... AND THE OTHERS.. HAVE BEEN SAVED... FROM THE SANDMAN!
AS FOR ME...I'LL SOON LEARN THE ANSWER... TO THE GREATEST MYSTERY ...OF ALL...
...THE FINAL ANSWER!

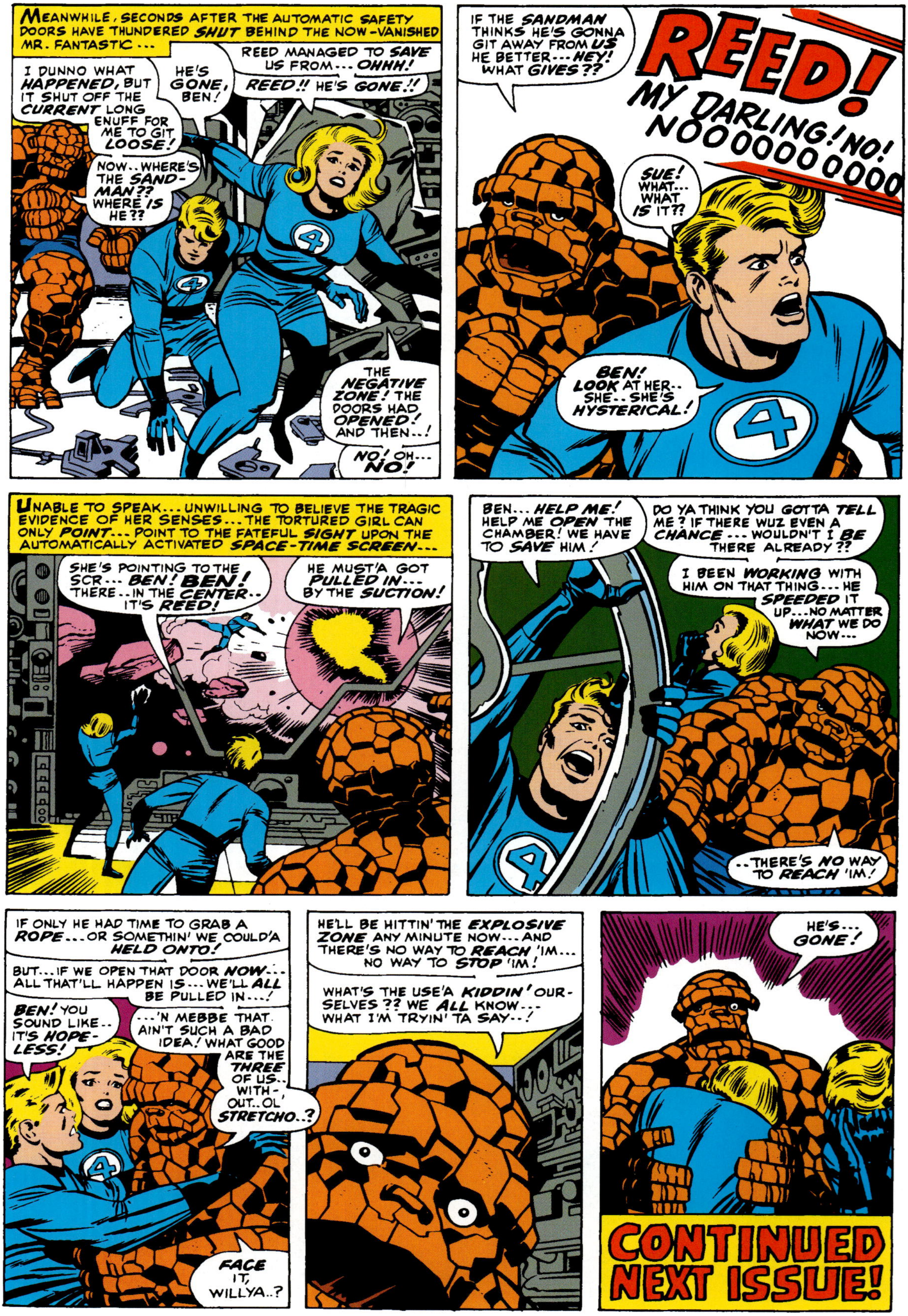
MEANWHILE, SECONDS AFTER THE AUTOMATIC SAFETY DOORS HAVE THUNDERED SHUT BEHIND THE NOW-VANISHED MR. FANTASTIC ...
I DUNNO WHAT HAPPENED, BUT IT SHUT OFF THE CURRENT LONG ENUFF FOR ME TO GIT LOOSE!
HE'S GONE, BEN!
REED MANAGED TO SAVE US FROM--- OHHH!
REED!! HE'S GONE!!
NOW..WHERE'S THE SAND-MAN?? WHERE IS HE??
THE NEGATIVE ZONE! THE DOORS HAD OPENED! AND THEN..!
NO! OH--- NO!
IF THE SANDMAN THINKS HE'S GONNA GIT AWAY FROM US HE BETTER--- HEY! WHAT GIVES??
REED! MY DARLING! NO! NOOOOOOOOOO
SUE! WHAT--- WHAT IS IT??
BEN! LOOK AT HER-- SHE--SHE'S HYSTERICAL!
UNABLE TO SPEAK... UNWILLING TO BELIEVE THE TRAGIC EVIDENCE OF HER SENSES... THE TORTURED GIRL CAN ONLY POINT... POINT TO THE FATEFUL SIGHT UPON THE AUTOMATICALLY ACTIVATED SPACE-TIME SCREEN---
SHE'S POINTING TO THE SCR--- BEN! BEN! THERE..IN THE CENTER.. IT'S REED!
HE MUST'A GOT PULLED IN--- BY THE SUCTION!
BEN... HELP ME! HELP ME OPEN THE CHAMBER! WE HAVE TO SAVE HIM!
DO YA THINK YOU GOTTA TELL ME? IF THERE WUZ EVEN A CHANCE--- WOULDN'T I BE THERE ALREADY??
I BEEN WORKING WITH HIM ON THAT THING--- HE SPEEDED IT UP...NO MATTER WHAT WE DO NOW---
..THERE'S NO WAY TO REACH 'IM!
IF ONLY HE HAD TIME TO GRAB A ROPE...OR SOMETHIN' WE COULD'A HELD ONTO!
BUT...IF WE OPEN THAT DOOR NOW... ALL THAT'LL HAPPEN IS---WE'LL ALL BE PULLED IN...!
BEN! YOU SOUND LIKE.. IT'S HOPE-LESS!
...'N MEBBE THAT AIN'T SUCH A BAD IDEA! WHAT GOOD ARE THE THREE OF US.. WITH-OUT..OL' STRETCHO..?
FACE IT, WILLYA..?
HE'LL BE HITTIN' THE EXPLOSIVE ZONE ANY MINUTE NOW--- AND THERE'S NO WAY TO REACH 'IM... NO WAY TO STOP 'IM!
WHAT'S THE USE'A KIDDIN' OUR-SELVES?? WE ALL KNOW--- WHAT I'M TRYIN' TA SAY--!
HE'S--- GONE!
CONTINUED NEXT ISSUE!

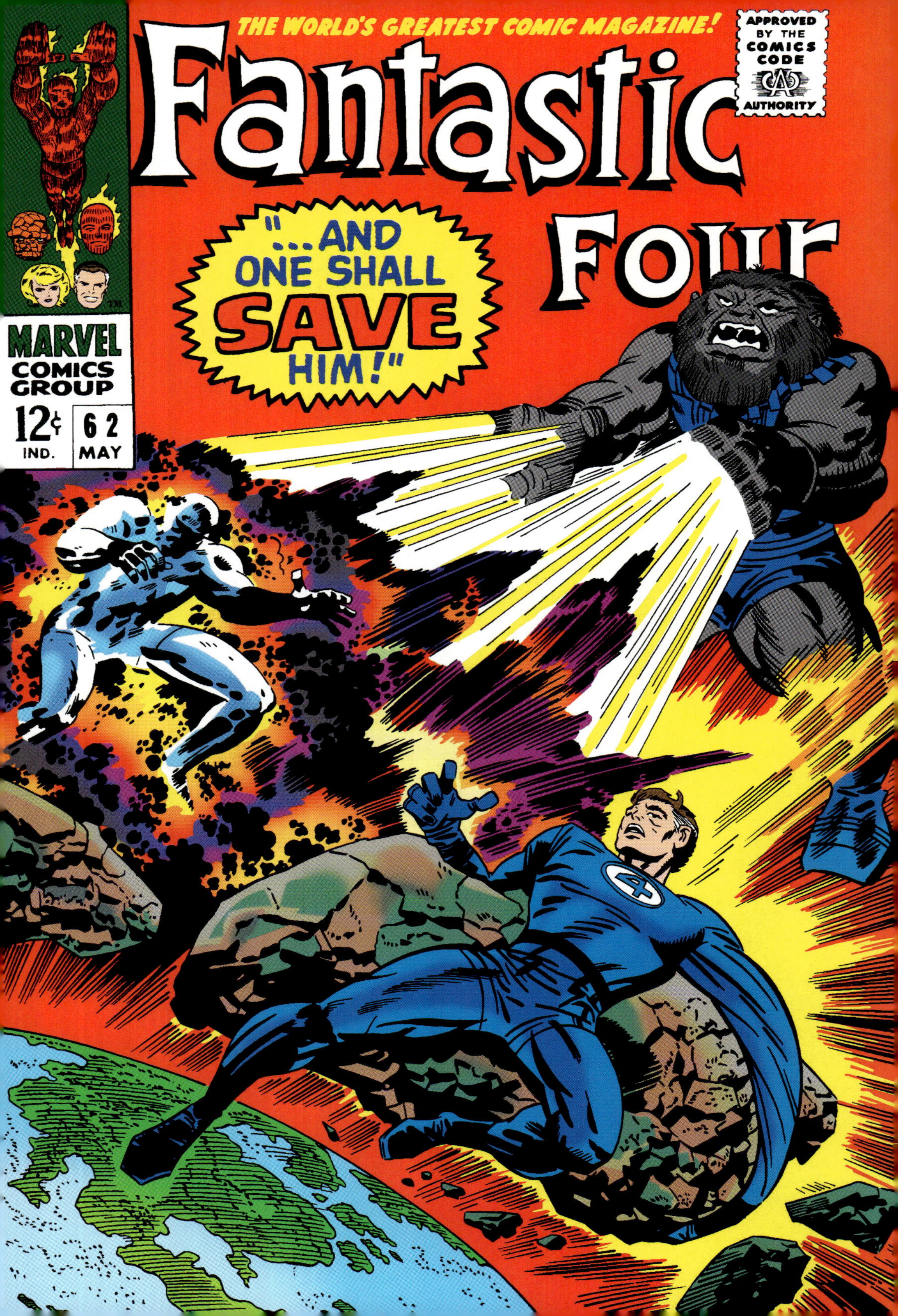
THE WORLD'S GREATEST COMIC MAGAZINE!
Fantastic Four
APPROVED BY THE COMICS CODE AUTHORITY
MARVEL COMICS GROUP
12¢ IND.
62 MAY
"...AND ONE SHALL SAVE HIM!"

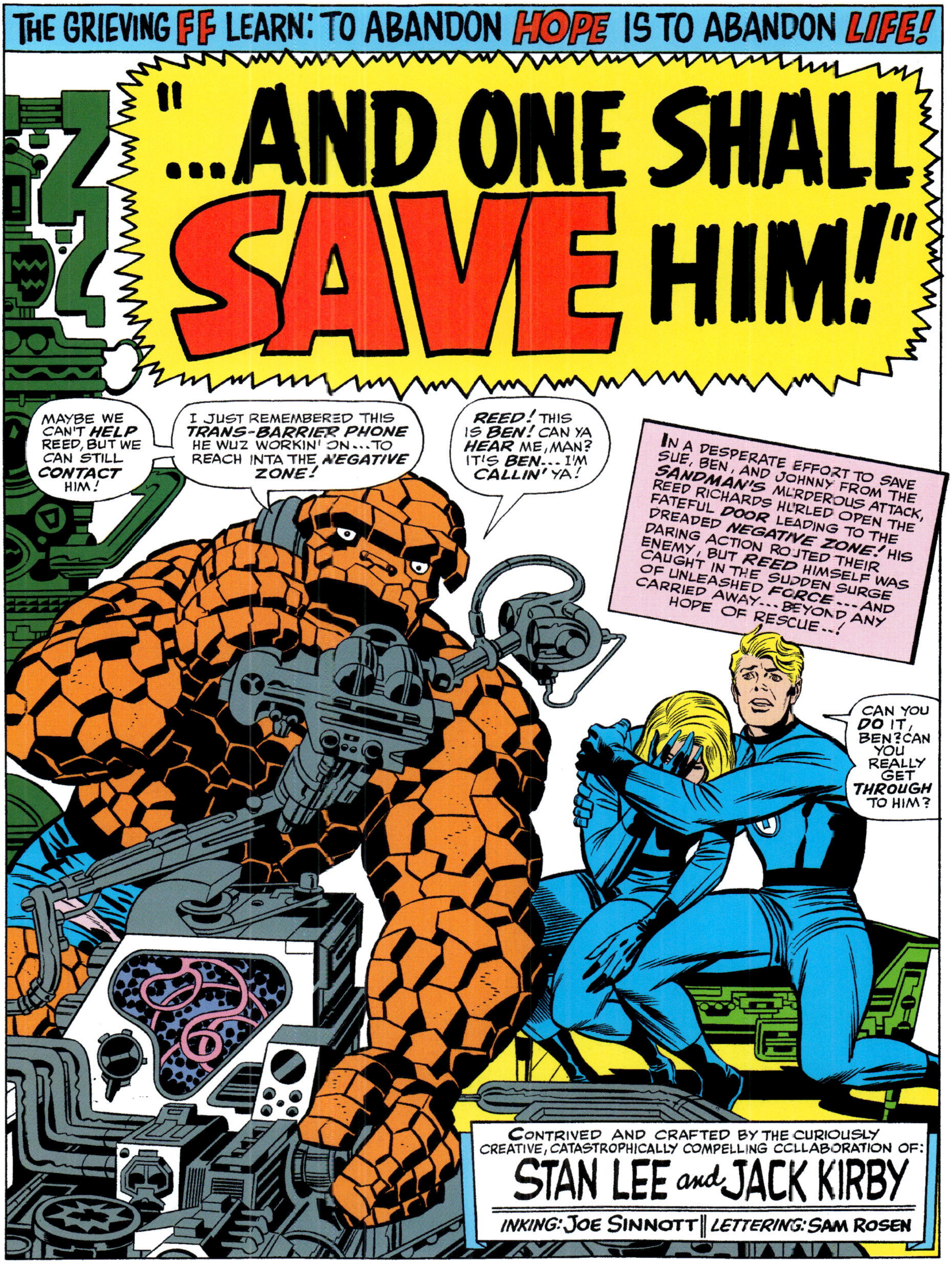
THE GRIEVING FF LEARN: TO ABANDON HOPE IS TO ABANDON LIFE!
"...AND ONE SHALL SAVE HIM!"
MAYBE WE CAN'T HELP REED, BUT WE CAN STILL CONTACT HIM!
I JUST REMEMBERED THIS TRANS-BARRIER PHONE HE WUZ WORKIN' ON... TO REACH INTA THE NEGATIVE ZONE!
REED! THIS IS BEN! CAN YA HEAR ME, MAN? IT'S BEN... I'M CALLIN' YA!
IN A DESPERATE EFFORT TO SAVE SUE, BEN, AND JOHNNY FROM THE SANDMAN'S MURDEROUS ATTACK, REED RICHARDS HURLED OPEN THE FATEFUL DOOR LEADING TO THE DREADED NEGATIVE ZONE! HIS DARING ACTION ROUTED THEIR ENEMY, BUT REED HIMSELF WAS CAUGHT IN THE SUDDEN SURGE OF UNLEASHED FORCE... AND CARRIED AWAY... BEYOND ANY HOPE OF RESCUE...!
CAN YOU DO IT, BEN? CAN YOU REALLY GET THROUGH TO HIM?
CONTRIVED AND CRAFTED BY THE CURIOUSLY CREATIVE, CATASTROPHICALLY COMPELLING COLLABORATION OF:
STAN LEE and JACK KIRBY
INKING: JOE SINNOTT || LETTERING: SAM ROSEN

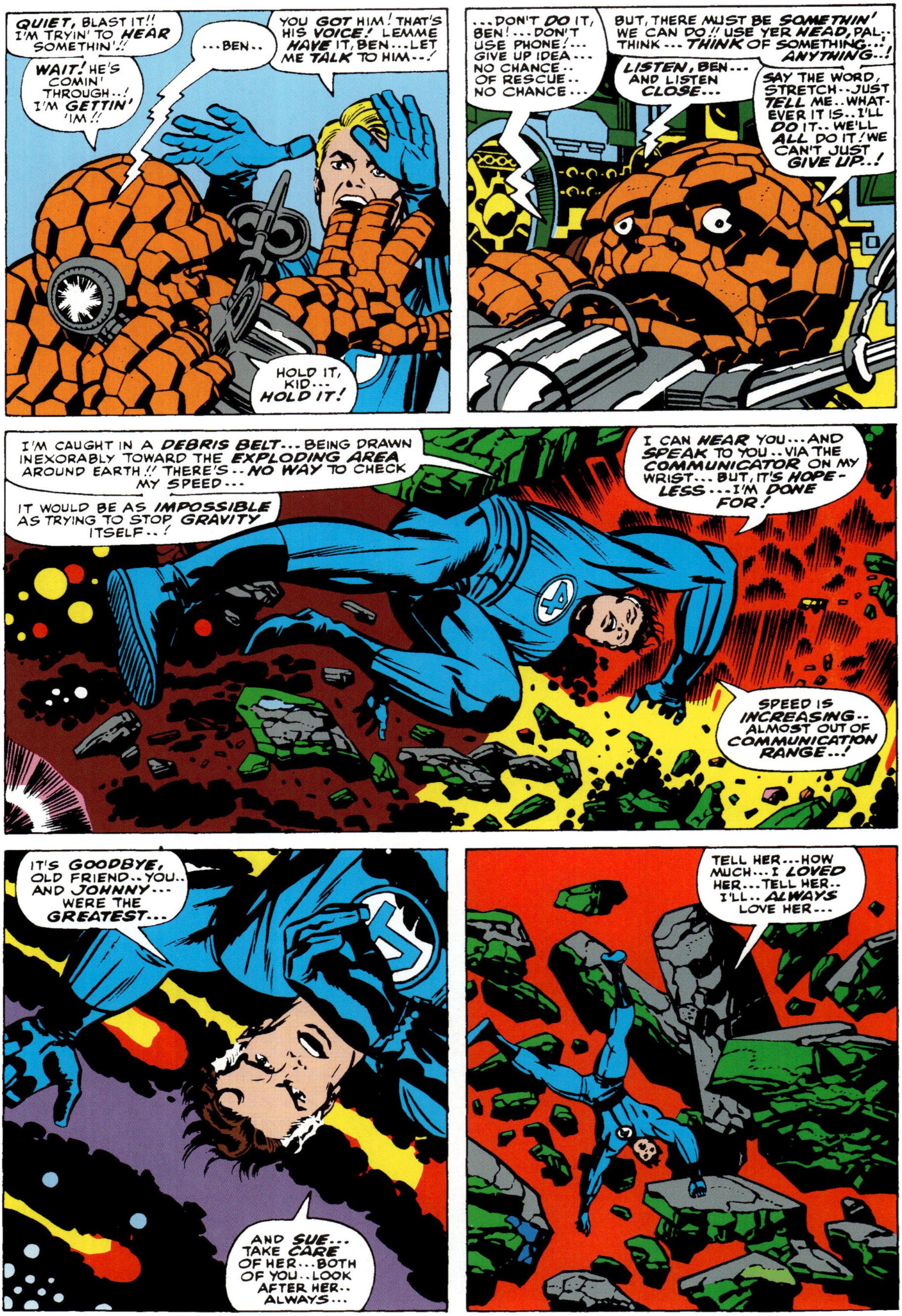
QUIET, BLAST IT!! I'M TRYIN' TO HEAR SOMETHIN'!!
WAIT! HE'S COMIN' THROUGH..! I'M GETTIN' 'IM!!
...BEN..
YOU GOT HIM! THAT'S HIS VOICE! LEMME HAVE IT, BEN...LET ME TALK TO HIM..!
HOLD IT, KID... HOLD IT!
...DON'T DO IT, BEN!...DON'T USE PHONE!... GIVE UP IDEA... NO CHANCE.. OF RESCUE.. NO CHANCE...
BUT, THERE MUST BE SOMETHIN' WE CAN DO!! USE YER HEAD, PAL.. THINK... THINK OF SOMETHING..! ANYTHING..!
LISTEN, BEN... AND LISTEN CLOSE...
SAY THE WORD, STRETCH.. JUST TELL ME.. WHAT-EVER IT IS.. I'LL DO IT.. WE'LL ALL DO IT! WE CAN'T JUST GIVE UP..!
I'M CAUGHT IN A DEBRIS BELT... BEING DRAWN INEXORABLY TOWARD THE EXPLODING AREA AROUND EARTH!! THERE'S.. NO WAY TO CHECK MY SPEED...
IT WOULD BE AS IMPOSSIBLE AS TRYING TO STOP GRAVITY ITSELF..!
I CAN HEAR YOU... AND SPEAK TO YOU.. VIA THE COMMUNICATOR ON MY WRIST... BUT, IT'S HOPE-LESS... I'M DONE FOR!
SPEED IS INCREASING.. ALMOST OUT OF COMMUNICATION RANGE..!
IT'S GOODBYE, OLD FRIEND.. YOU.. AND JOHNNY... WERE THE GREATEST...
AND SUE... TAKE CARE OF HER... BOTH OF YOU.. LOOK AFTER HER.. ALWAYS...
TELL HER... HOW MUCH... I LOVED HER... TELL HER.. I'LL.. ALWAYS LOVE HER...

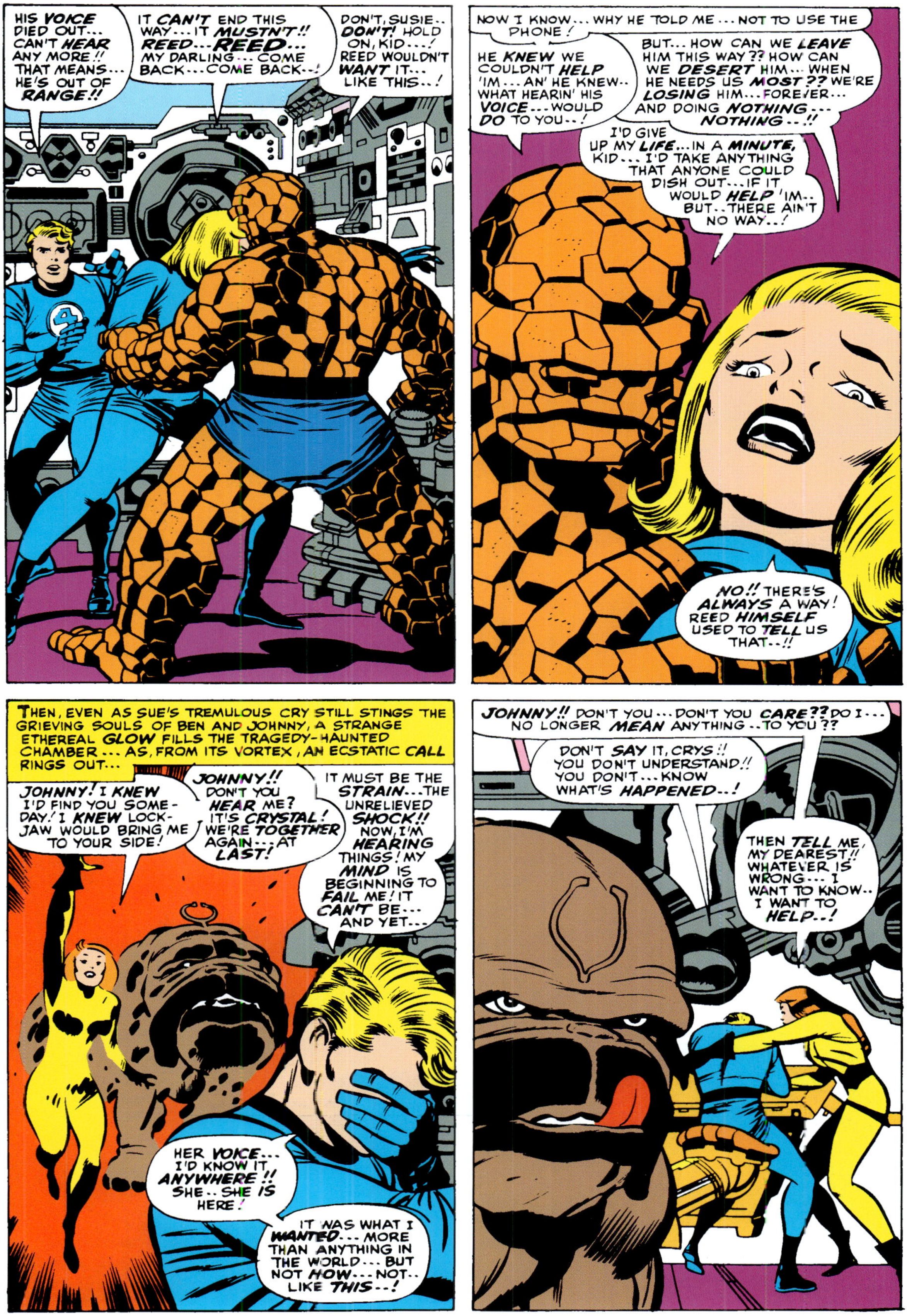
HIS VOICE DIED OUT... CAN'T HEAR ANY MORE!! THAT MEANS... HE'S OUT OF RANGE!!
IT CAN'T END THIS WAY... IT MUSTN'T!! REED... REED... MY DARLING... COME BACK... COME BACK...!
DON'T, SUSIE.. DON'T! HOLD ON, KID...! REED WOULDN'T WANT IT... LIKE THIS..!
NOW I KNOW... WHY HE TOLD ME... NOT TO USE THE PHONE!
HE KNEW WE COULDN'T HELP 'IM... AN' HE KNEW.. WHAT HEARIN' HIS VOICE... WOULD DO TO YOU..!
BUT... HOW CAN WE LEAVE HIM THIS WAY?? HOW CAN WE DESERT HIM... WHEN HE NEEDS US MOST?? WE'RE LOSING HIM... FOREVER... AND DOING NOTHING... NOTHING..!!
I'D GIVE UP MY LIFE... IN A MINUTE, KID... I'D TAKE ANYTHING THAT ANYONE COULD DISH OUT... IF IT WOULD HELP 'IM.. BUT.. THERE AIN'T NO WAY..!
NO!! THERE'S ALWAYS A WAY! REED HIMSELF USED TO TELL US THAT..!!
THEN, EVEN AS SUE'S TREMULOUS CRY STILL STINGS THE GRIEVING SOULS OF BEN AND JOHNNY, A STRANGE ETHEREAL GLOW FILLS THE TRAGEDY-HAUNTED CHAMBER... AS, FROM ITS VORTEX, AN ECSTATIC CALL RINGS OUT...
JOHNNY! I KNEW I'D FIND YOU SOME-DAY! I KNEW LOCK-JAW WOULD BRING ME TO YOUR SIDE!
JOHNNY!! DON'T YOU HEAR ME? IT'S CRYSTAL! WE'RE TOGETHER AGAIN... AT LAST!
IT MUST BE THE STRAIN... THE UNRELIEVED SHOCK!! NOW, I'M HEARING THINGS! MY MIND IS BEGINNING TO FAIL ME! IT CAN'T BE... AND YET...
HER VOICE... I'D KNOW IT ANYWHERE!! SHE.. SHE IS HERE!
IT WAS WHAT I WANTED... MORE THAN ANYTHING IN THE WORLD... BUT NOT HOW... NOT.. LIKE THIS..!
JOHNNY!! DON'T YOU... DON'T YOU CARE?? DO I... NO LONGER MEAN ANYTHING.. TO YOU??
DON'T SAY IT, CRYS!! YOU DON'T UNDERSTAND!! YOU DON'T... KNOW WHAT'S HAPPENED..!
THEN TELL ME, MY DEAREST!! WHATEVER IS WRONG... I WANT TO KNOW.. I WANT TO HELP..!

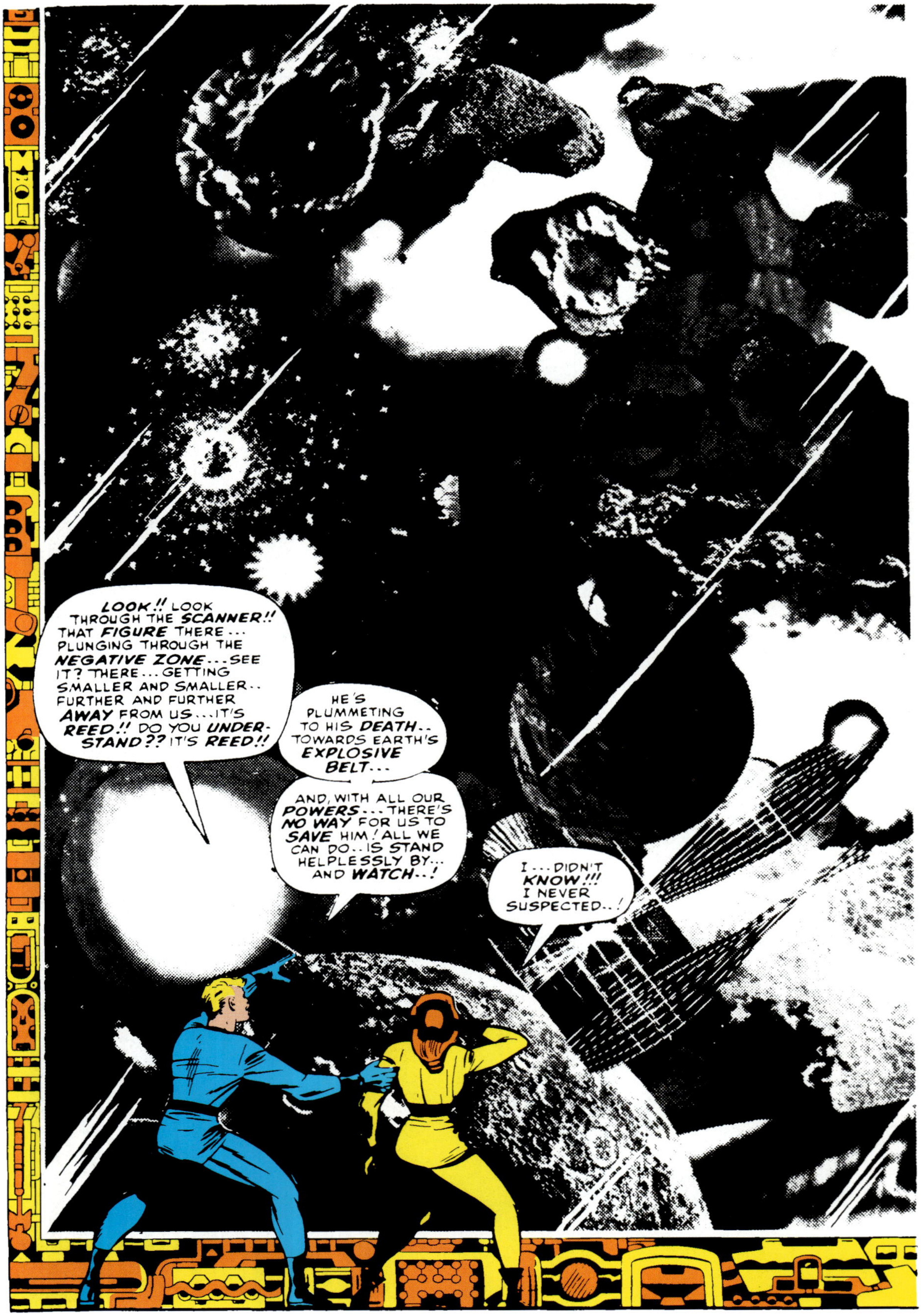

LOOK!! LOOK THROUGH THE SCANNER!! THAT FIGURE THERE... PLUNGING THROUGH THE NEGATIVE ZONE... SEE IT? THERE... GETTING SMALLER AND SMALLER.. FURTHER AND FURTHER AWAY FROM US... IT'S REED!! DO YOU UNDERSTAND?? IT'S REED!!
HE'S PLUMMETING TO HIS DEATH.. TOWARDS EARTH'S EXPLOSIVE BELT...
AND, WITH ALL OUR POWERS... THERE'S NO WAY FOR US TO SAVE HIM! ALL WE CAN DO.. IS STAND HELPLESSLY BY... AND WATCH..!
I... DIDN'T KNOW!!! I NEVER SUSPECTED..!

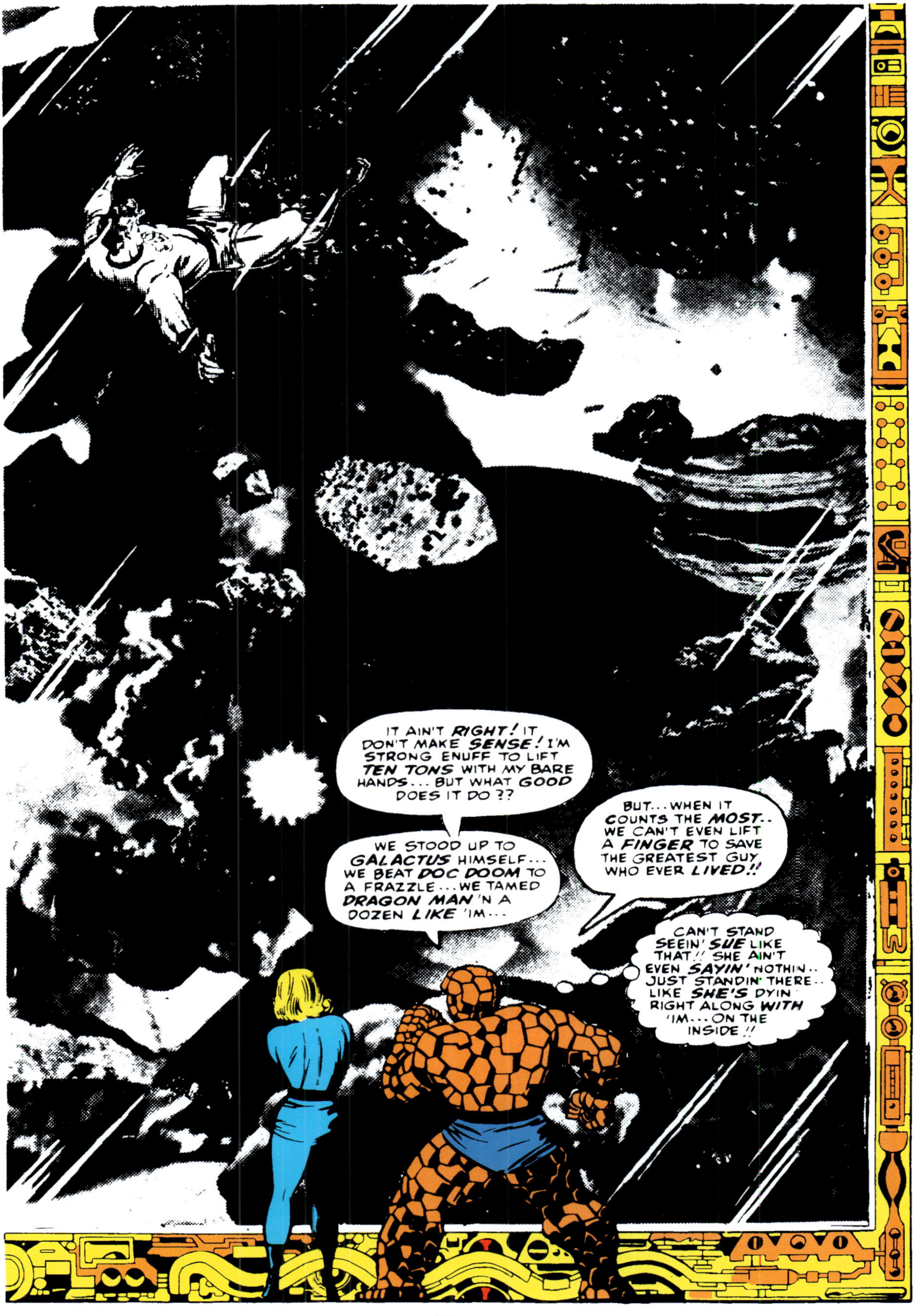
IT AIN'T RIGHT! IT DON'T MAKE SENSE! I'M STRONG ENUFF TO LIFT TEN TONS WITH MY BARE HANDS... BUT WHAT GOOD DOES IT DO ??
WE STOOD UP TO GALACTUS HIMSELF... WE BEAT DOC DOOM TO A FRAZZLE... WE TAMED DRAGON MAN 'N A DOZEN LIKE 'IM...
BUT... WHEN IT COUNTS THE MOST.. WE CAN'T EVEN LIFT A FINGER TO SAVE THE GREATEST GUY WHO EVER LIVED!!
CAN'T STAND SEEIN' SUE LIKE THAT!! SHE AIN'T EVEN SAYIN' NOTHIN.. JUST STANDIN' THERE.. LIKE SHE'S DYIN' RIGHT ALONG WITH 'IM... ON THE INSIDE!!

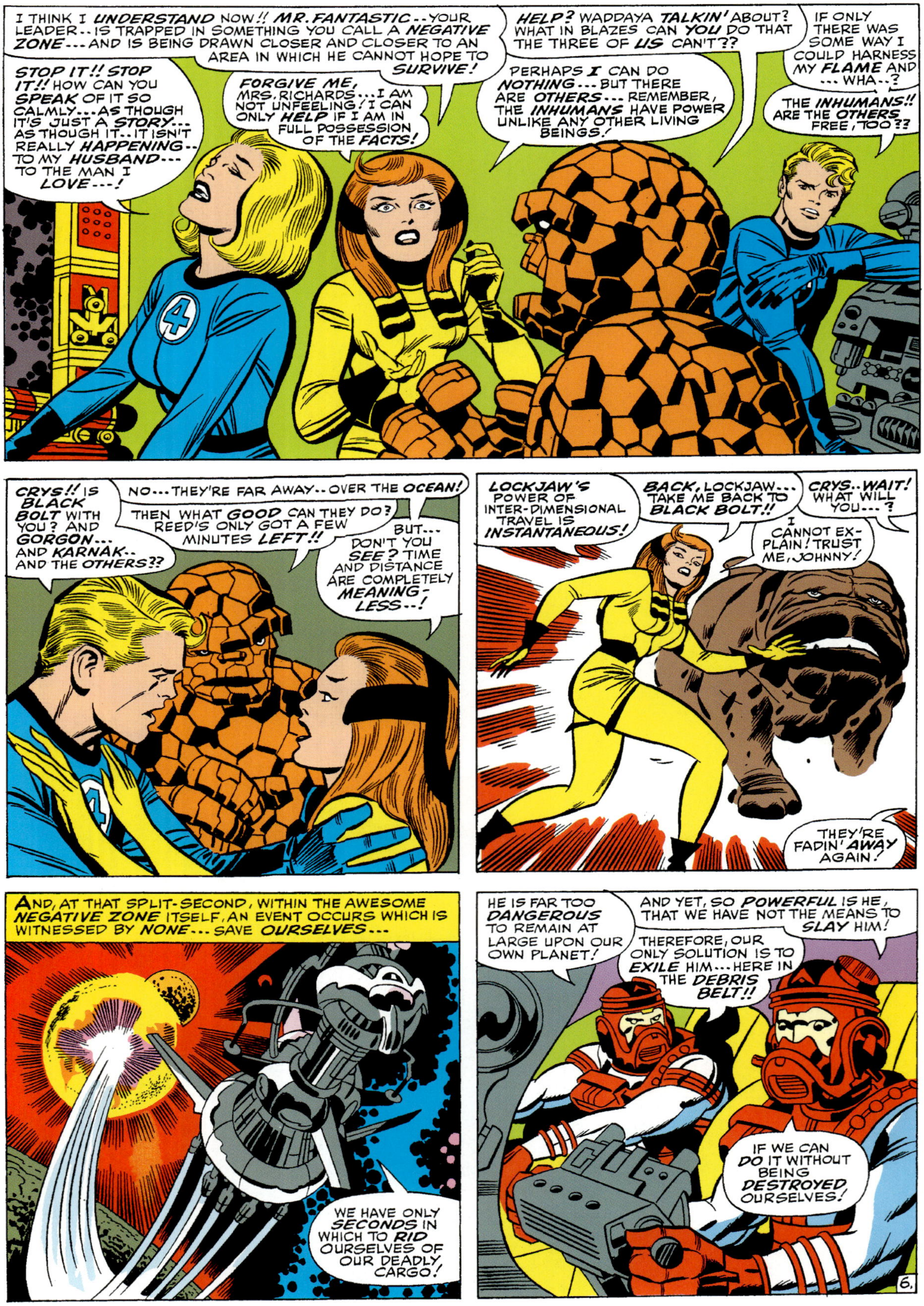
I THINK I UNDERSTAND NOW!! MR. FANTASTIC--YOUR LEADER--IS TRAPPED IN SOMETHING YOU CALL A NEGATIVE ZONE---AND IS BEING DRAWN CLOSER AND CLOSER TO AN AREA IN WHICH HE CANNOT HOPE TO SURVIVE!
STOP IT!! STOP IT!! HOW CAN YOU SPEAK OF IT SO CALMLY---AS THOUGH IT'S JUST A STORY---AS THOUGH IT--IT ISN'T REALLY HAPPENING--TO MY HUSBAND---TO THE MAN I LOVE---!
FORGIVE ME, MRS. RICHARDS---I AM NOT UNFEELING! I CAN ONLY HELP IF I AM IN FULL POSSESSION OF THE FACTS!
HELP? WADDAYA TALKIN' ABOUT? WHAT IN BLAZES CAN YOU DO THAT THE THREE OF US CAN'T??
PERHAPS I CAN DO NOTHING---BUT THERE ARE OTHERS---REMEMBER, THE INHUMANS HAVE POWER UNLIKE ANY OTHER LIVING BEINGS!
IF ONLY THERE WAS SOME WAY I COULD HARNESS MY FLAME AND ---WHA--?
THE INHUMANS!! ARE THE OTHERS FREE, TOO??
CRYS!! IS BLACK BOLT WITH YOU? AND GORGON---AND KARNAK--AND THE OTHERS??
NO---THEY'RE FAR AWAY--OVER THE OCEAN!
THEN WHAT GOOD CAN THEY DO? REED'S ONLY GOT A FEW MINUTES LEFT!!
BUT---DON'T YOU SEE? TIME AND DISTANCE ARE COMPLETELY MEANING-LESS--!
LOCKJAW'S POWER OF INTER-DIMENSIONAL TRAVEL IS INSTANTANEOUS!
BACK, LOCKJAW---TAKE ME BACK TO BLACK BOLT!!
CRYS--WAIT! WHAT WILL YOU---?
I CANNOT EXPLAIN! TRUST ME, JOHNNY!
THEY'RE FADIN' AWAY AGAIN!
AND, AT THAT SPLIT-SECOND, WITHIN THE AWESOME NEGATIVE ZONE ITSELF, AN EVENT OCCURS WHICH IS WITNESSED BY NONE---SAVE OURSELVES---
WE HAVE ONLY SECONDS IN WHICH TO RID OURSELVES OF OUR DEADLY CARGO!
HE IS FAR TOO DANGEROUS TO REMAIN AT LARGE UPON OUR OWN PLANET!
AND YET, SO POWERFUL IS HE, THAT WE HAVE NOT THE MEANS TO SLAY HIM!
THEREFORE, OUR ONLY SOLUTION IS TO EXILE HIM---HERE IN THE DEBRIS BELT!!
IF WE CAN DO IT WITHOUT BEING DESTROYED OURSELVES!
6.

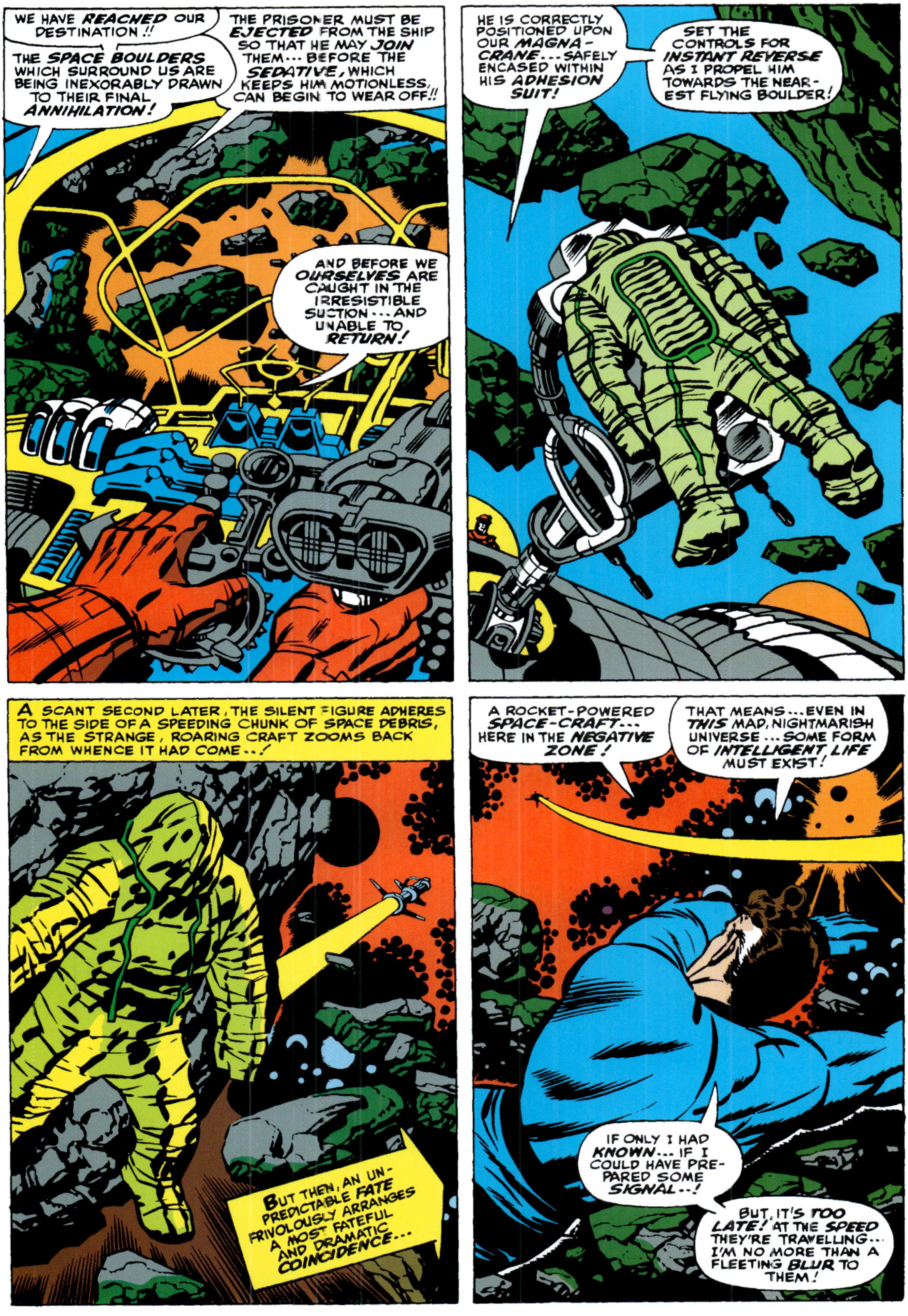
WE HAVE REACHED OUR DESTINATION!!
THE SPACE BOULDERS WHICH SURROUND US ARE BEING INEXORABLY DRAWN TO THEIR FINAL ANNIHILATION!
THE PRISONER MUST BE EJECTED FROM THE SHIP SO THAT HE MAY JOIN THEM... BEFORE THE SEDATIVE, WHICH KEEPS HIM MOTIONLESS, CAN BEGIN TO WEAR OFF!!
AND BEFORE WE OURSELVES ARE CAUGHT IN THE IRRESISTIBLE SUCTION... AND UNABLE TO RETURN!
HE IS CORRECTLY POSITIONED UPON OUR MAGNA-CRANE... SAFELY ENCASED WITHIN HIS ADHESION SUIT!
SET THE CONTROLS FOR INSTANT REVERSE AS I PROPEL HIM TOWARDS THE NEAREST FLYING BOULDER!
A SCANT SECOND LATER, THE SILENT FIGURE ADHERES TO THE SIDE OF A SPEEDING CHUNK OF SPACE DEBRIS, AS THE STRANGE, ROARING CRAFT ZOOMS BACK FROM WHENCE IT HAD COME..!
BUT THEN, AN UNPREDICTABLE FATE FRIVOLOUSLY ARRANGES A MOST FATEFUL AND DRAMATIC COINCIDENCE...
A ROCKET-POWERED SPACE-CRAFT... HERE IN THE NEGATIVE ZONE!
THAT MEANS... EVEN IN THIS MAD, NIGHTMARISH UNIVERSE... SOME FORM OF INTELLIGENT LIFE MUST EXIST!
IF ONLY I HAD KNOWN... IF I COULD HAVE PREPARED SOME SIGNAL..!
BUT, IT'S TOO LATE! AT THE SPEED THEY'RE TRAVELLING... I'M NO MORE THAN A FLEETING BLUR TO THEM!

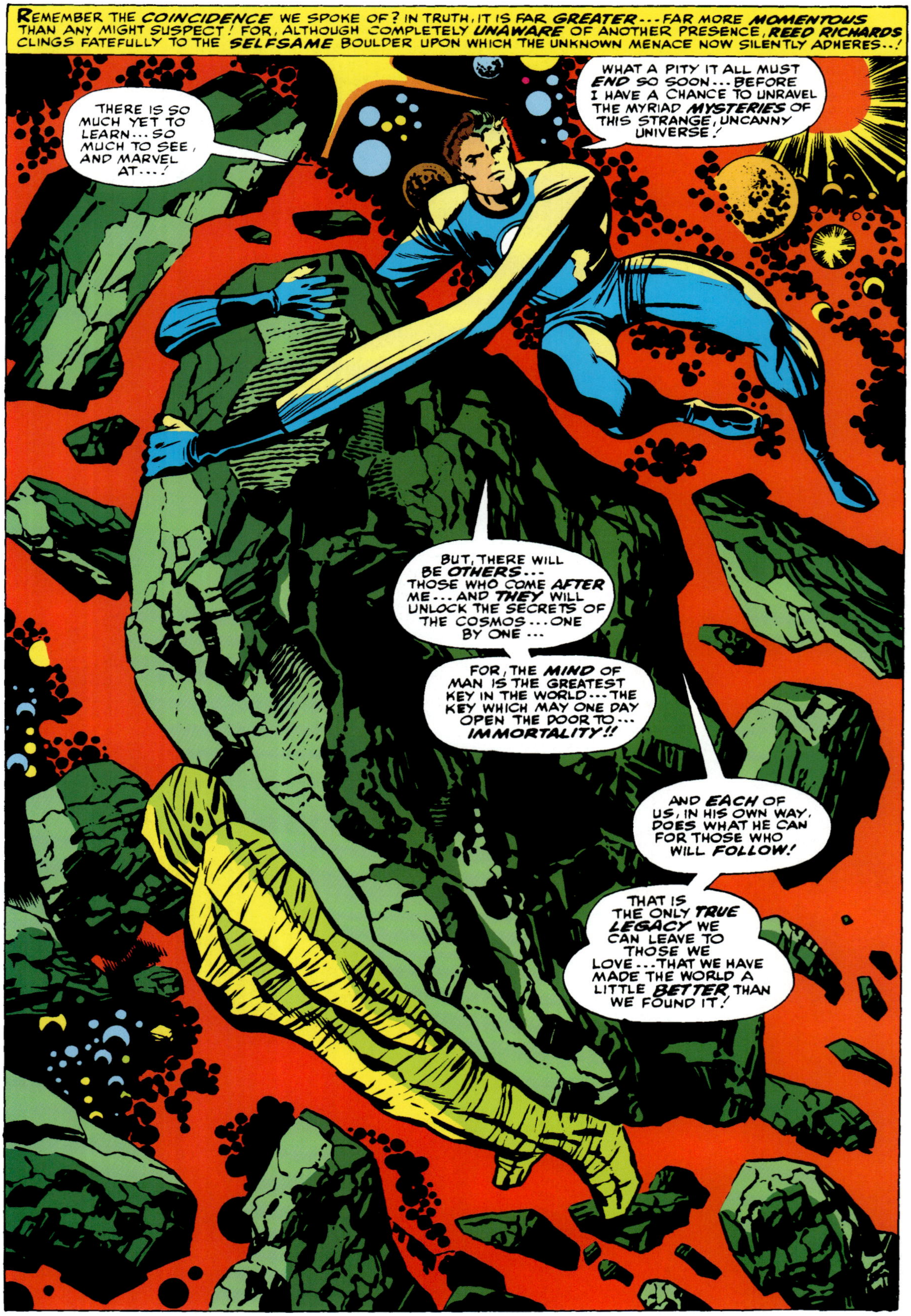
REMEMBER THE COINCIDENCE WE SPOKE OF? IN TRUTH, IT IS FAR GREATER--- FAR MORE MOMENTOUS THAN ANY MIGHT SUSPECT! FOR, ALTHOUGH COMPLETELY UNAWARE OF ANOTHER PRESENCE, REED RICHARDS CLINGS FATEFULLY TO THE SELFSAME BOULDER UPON WHICH THE UNKNOWN MENACE NOW SILENTLY ADHERES..!
THERE IS SO MUCH YET TO LEARN... SO MUCH TO SEE, AND MARVEL AT...!
WHAT A PITY IT ALL MUST END SO SOON... BEFORE I HAVE A CHANCE TO UNRAVEL THE MYRIAD MYSTERIES OF THIS STRANGE, UNCANNY UNIVERSE!
BUT, THERE WILL BE OTHERS... THOSE WHO COME AFTER ME... AND THEY WILL UNLOCK THE SECRETS OF THE COSMOS... ONE BY ONE...
FOR, THE MIND OF MAN IS THE GREATEST KEY IN THE WORLD... THE KEY WHICH MAY ONE DAY OPEN THE DOOR TO... IMMORTALITY!!
AND EACH OF US, IN HIS OWN WAY, DOES WHAT HE CAN FOR THOSE WHO WILL FOLLOW!
THAT IS THE ONLY TRUE LEGACY WE CAN LEAVE TO THOSE WE LOVE... THAT WE HAVE MADE THE WORLD A LITTLE BETTER THAN WE FOUND IT!

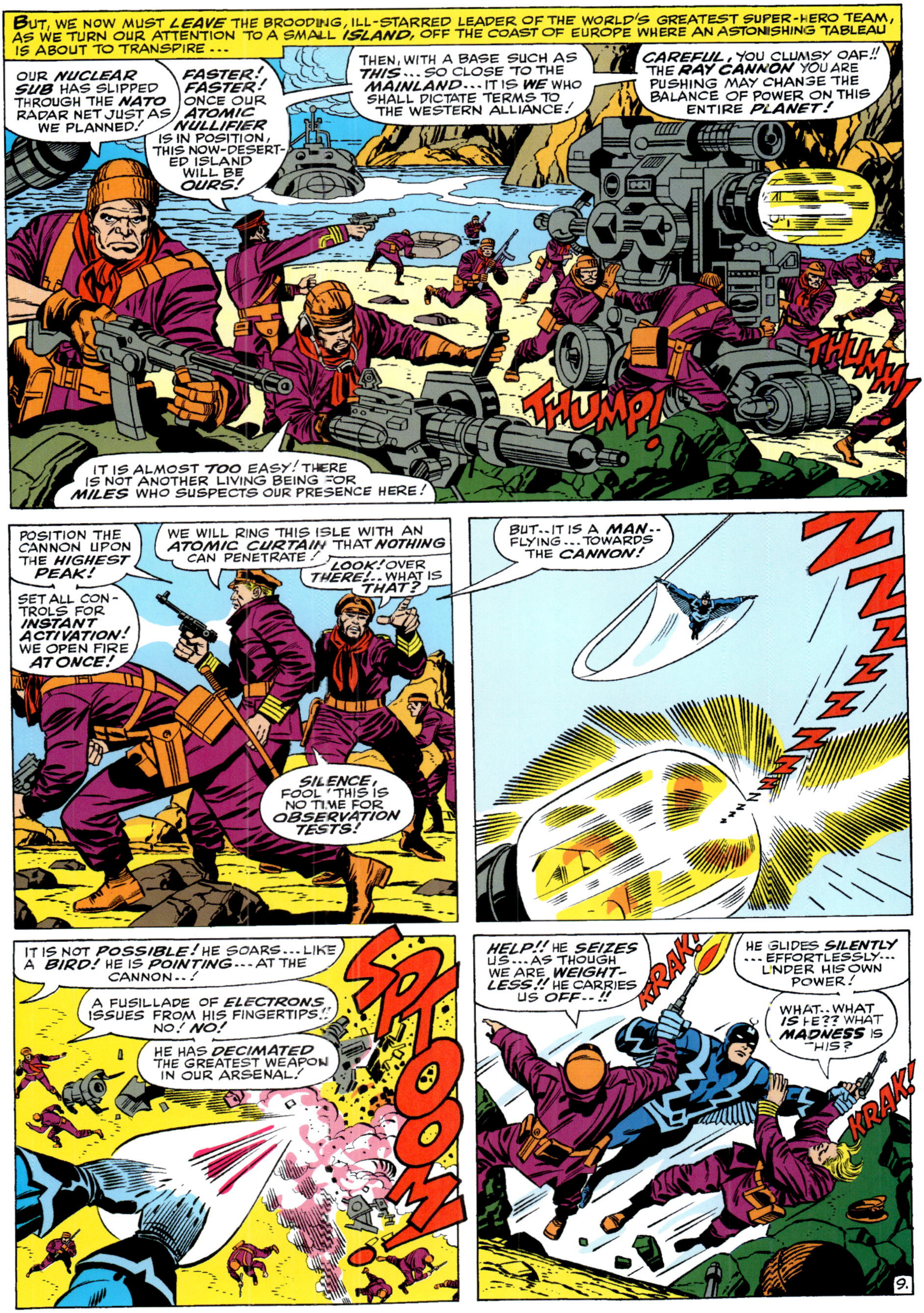
BUT, WE NOW MUST LEAVE THE BROODING, ILL-STARRED LEADER OF THE WORLD'S GREATEST SUPER-HERO TEAM, AS WE TURN OUR ATTENTION TO A SMALL ISLAND, OFF THE COAST OF EUROPE WHERE AN ASTONISHING TABLEAU IS ABOUT TO TRANSPIRE ...
OUR NUCLEAR SUB HAS SLIPPED THROUGH THE NATO RADAR NET JUST AS WE PLANNED!
FASTER! FASTER! ONCE OUR ATOMIC NULLIFIER IS IN POSITION, THIS NOW-DESERTED ISLAND WILL BE OURS!
THEN, WITH A BASE SUCH AS THIS... SO CLOSE TO THE MAINLAND... IT IS WE WHO SHALL DICTATE TERMS TO THE WESTERN ALLIANCE!
CAREFUL, YOU CLUMSY OAF!! THE RAY CANNON YOU ARE PUSHING MAY CHANGE THE BALANCE OF POWER ON THIS ENTIRE PLANET!
THUMP!
THUMM!
IT IS ALMOST TOO EASY! THERE IS NOT ANOTHER LIVING BEING FOR MILES WHO SUSPECTS OUR PRESENCE HERE!
POSITION THE CANNON UPON THE HIGHEST PEAK!
SET ALL CONTROLS FOR INSTANT ACTIVATION! WE OPEN FIRE AT ONCE!
WE WILL RING THIS ISLE WITH AN ATOMIC CURTAIN THAT NOTHING CAN PENETRATE!
LOOK! OVER THERE!.. WHAT IS THAT?
SILENCE, FOOL! THIS IS NO TIME FOR OBSERVATION TESTS!
BUT..IT IS A MAN.. FLYING... TOWARDS THE CANNON!
ZZZZZZZZZ
IT IS NOT POSSIBLE! HE SOARS... LIKE A BIRD! HE IS POINTING... AT THE CANNON..!
A FUSILLADE OF ELECTRONS ISSUES FROM HIS FINGERTIPS!! NO! NO!
HE HAS DECIMATED THE GREATEST WEAPON IN OUR ARSENAL!
SPTOOOM!
HELP!! HE SEIZES US... AS THOUGH WE ARE WEIGHTLESS!! HE CARRIES US OFF--!!
KRAK!
HE GLIDES SILENTLY ... EFFORTLESSLY... UNDER HIS OWN POWER!
WHAT.. WHAT IS HE?? WHAT MADNESS IS THIS?
KRAK!
9.

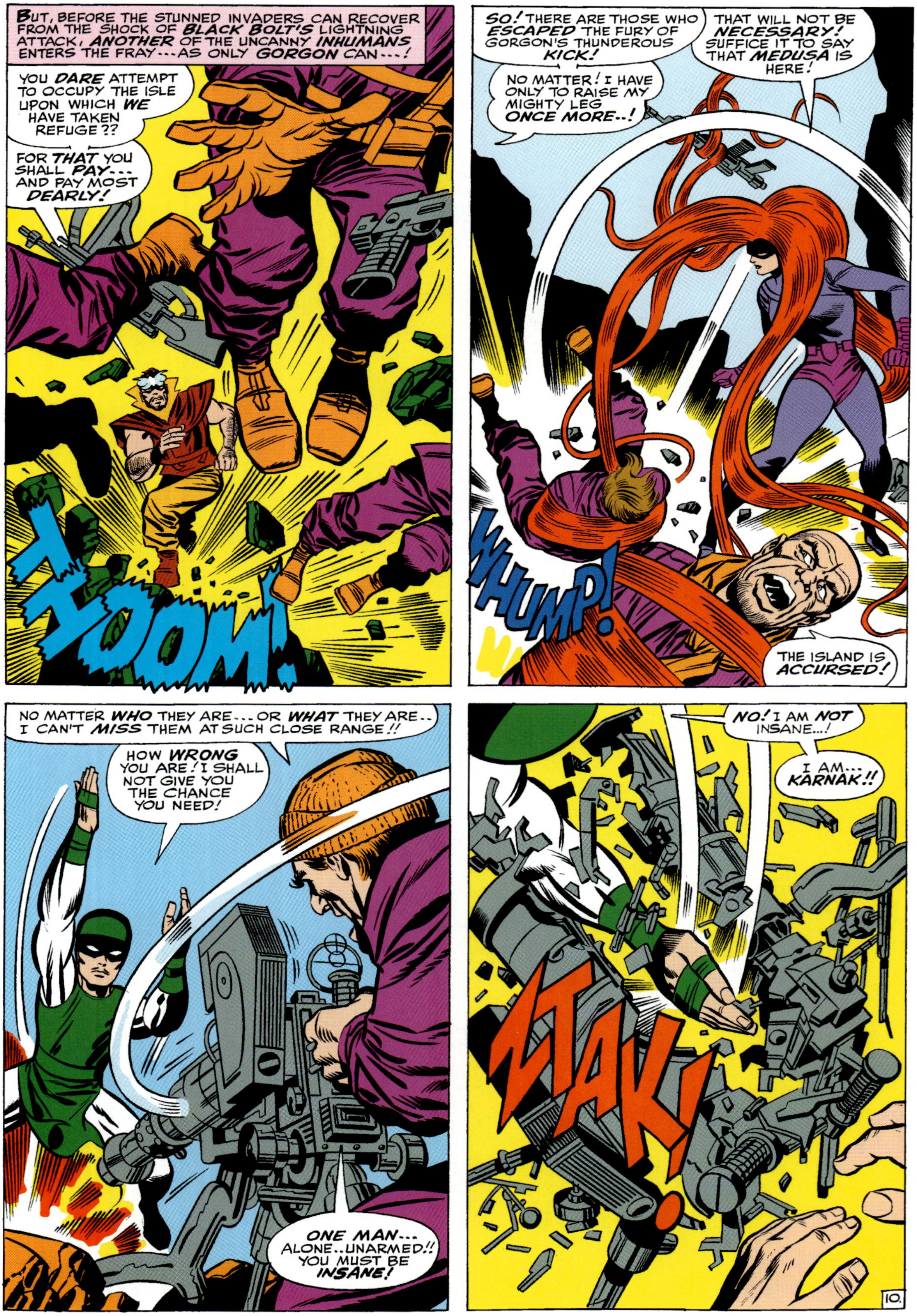

BUT, BEFORE THE STUNNED INVADERS CAN RECOVER FROM THE SHOCK OF BLACK BOLT'S LIGHTNING ATTACK, ANOTHER OF THE UNCANNY INHUMANS ENTERS THE FRAY--AS ONLY GORGON CAN--!
YOU DARE ATTEMPT TO OCCUPY THE ISLE UPON WHICH WE HAVE TAKEN REFUGE ??
FOR THAT YOU SHALL PAY--AND PAY MOST DEARLY!
THOOM!
SO! THERE ARE THOSE WHO ESCAPED THE FURY OF GORGON'S THUNDEROUS KICK!
NO MATTER! I HAVE ONLY TO RAISE MY MIGHTY LEG ONCE MORE--!
THAT WILL NOT BE NECESSARY! SUFFICE IT TO SAY THAT MEDUSA IS HERE!
WHUMP!
THE ISLAND IS ACCURSED!
NO MATTER WHO THEY ARE--OR WHAT THEY ARE-- I CAN'T MISS THEM AT SUCH CLOSE RANGE!!
HOW WRONG YOU ARE! I SHALL NOT GIVE YOU THE CHANCE YOU NEED!
ONE MAN--ALONE--UNARMED!! YOU MUST BE INSANE!
NO! I AM NOT INSANE...!
I AM... KARNAK!!
TAK!
10.

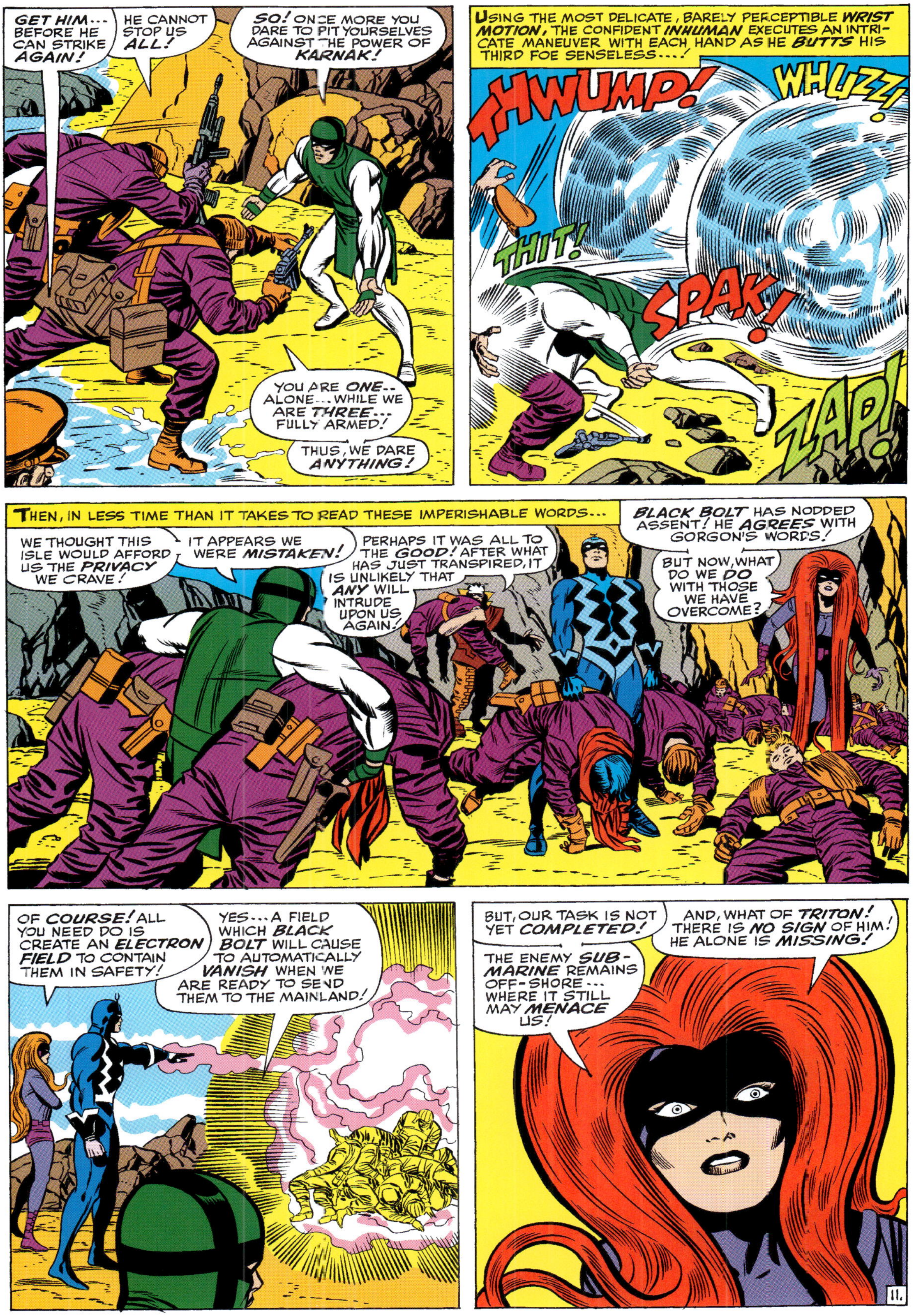
GET HIM--- BEFORE HE CAN STRIKE AGAIN!
HE CANNOT STOP US ALL!
SO! ONCE MORE YOU DARE TO PIT YOURSELVES AGAINST THE POWER OF KARNAK!
YOU ARE ONE-- ALONE--- WHILE WE ARE THREE--- FULLY ARMED!
THUS, WE DARE ANYTHING!
USING THE MOST DELICATE, BARELY PERCEPTIBLE WRIST MOTION, THE CONFIDENT INHUMAN EXECUTES AN INTRICATE MANEUVER WITH EACH HAND AS HE BUTTS HIS THIRD FOE SENSELESS---!
THWUMP!
WHUZZ!
THIT!
SPAK!
ZAP!
THEN, IN LESS TIME THAN IT TAKES TO READ THESE IMPERISHABLE WORDS---
WE THOUGHT THIS ISLE WOULD AFFORD US THE PRIVACY WE CRAVE!
IT APPEARS WE WERE MISTAKEN!
PERHAPS IT WAS ALL TO THE GOOD! AFTER WHAT HAS JUST TRANSPIRED, IT IS UNLIKELY THAT ANY WILL INTRUDE UPON US AGAIN!
BLACK BOLT HAS NODDED ASSENT! HE AGREES WITH GORGON'S WORDS!
BUT NOW, WHAT DO WE DO WITH THOSE WE HAVE OVERCOME?
OF COURSE! ALL YOU NEED DO IS CREATE AN ELECTRON FIELD TO CONTAIN THEM IN SAFETY!
YES--- A FIELD WHICH BLACK BOLT WILL CAUSE TO AUTOMATICALLY VANISH WHEN WE ARE READY TO SEND THEM TO THE MAINLAND!
BUT, OUR TASK IS NOT YET COMPLETED!
AND, WHAT OF TRITON! THERE IS NO SIGN OF HIM! HE ALONE IS MISSING!
THE ENEMY SUB-MARINE REMAINS OFF-SHORE--- WHERE IT STILL MAY MENACE US!
11.

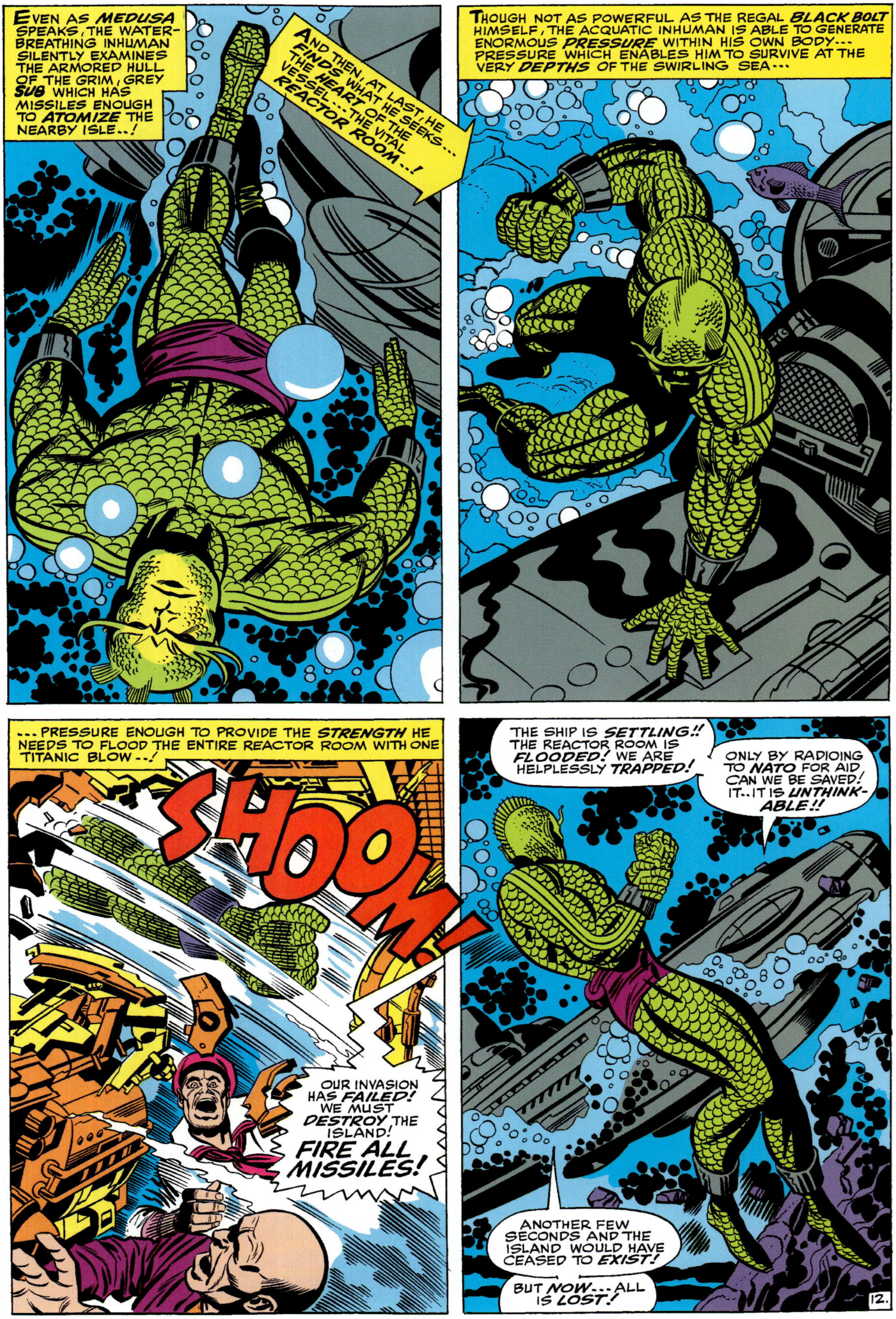
EVEN AS MEDUSA SPEAKS, THE WATER-BREATHING INHUMAN SILENTLY EXAMINES THE ARMORED HULL OF THE GRIM, GREY SUB WHICH HAS MISSILES ENOUGH TO ATOMIZE THE NEARBY ISLE..!
AND THEN, AT LAST, HE FINDS WHAT HE SEEKS... THE HEART OF THE VESSEL... THE VITAL REACTOR ROOM..!
THOUGH NOT AS POWERFUL AS THE REGAL BLACK BOLT HIMSELF, THE ACQUATIC INHUMAN IS ABLE TO GENERATE ENORMOUS PRESSURE WITHIN HIS OWN BODY--- PRESSURE WHICH ENABLES HIM TO SURVIVE AT THE VERY DEPTHS OF THE SWIRLING SEA---
---PRESSURE ENOUGH TO PROVIDE THE STRENGTH HE NEEDS TO FLOOD THE ENTIRE REACTOR ROOM WITH ONE TITANIC BLOW--!
SHOOM!
OUR INVASION HAS FAILED! WE MUST DESTROY THE ISLAND! FIRE ALL MISSILES!
THE SHIP IS SETTLING!! THE REACTOR ROOM IS FLOODED! WE ARE HELPLESSLY TRAPPED!
ONLY BY RADIOING TO NATO FOR AID CAN WE BE SAVED! IT..IT IS UNTHINKABLE!!
ANOTHER FEW SECONDS AND THE ISLAND WOULD HAVE CEASED TO EXIST!
BUT NOW... ALL IS LOST!
12.

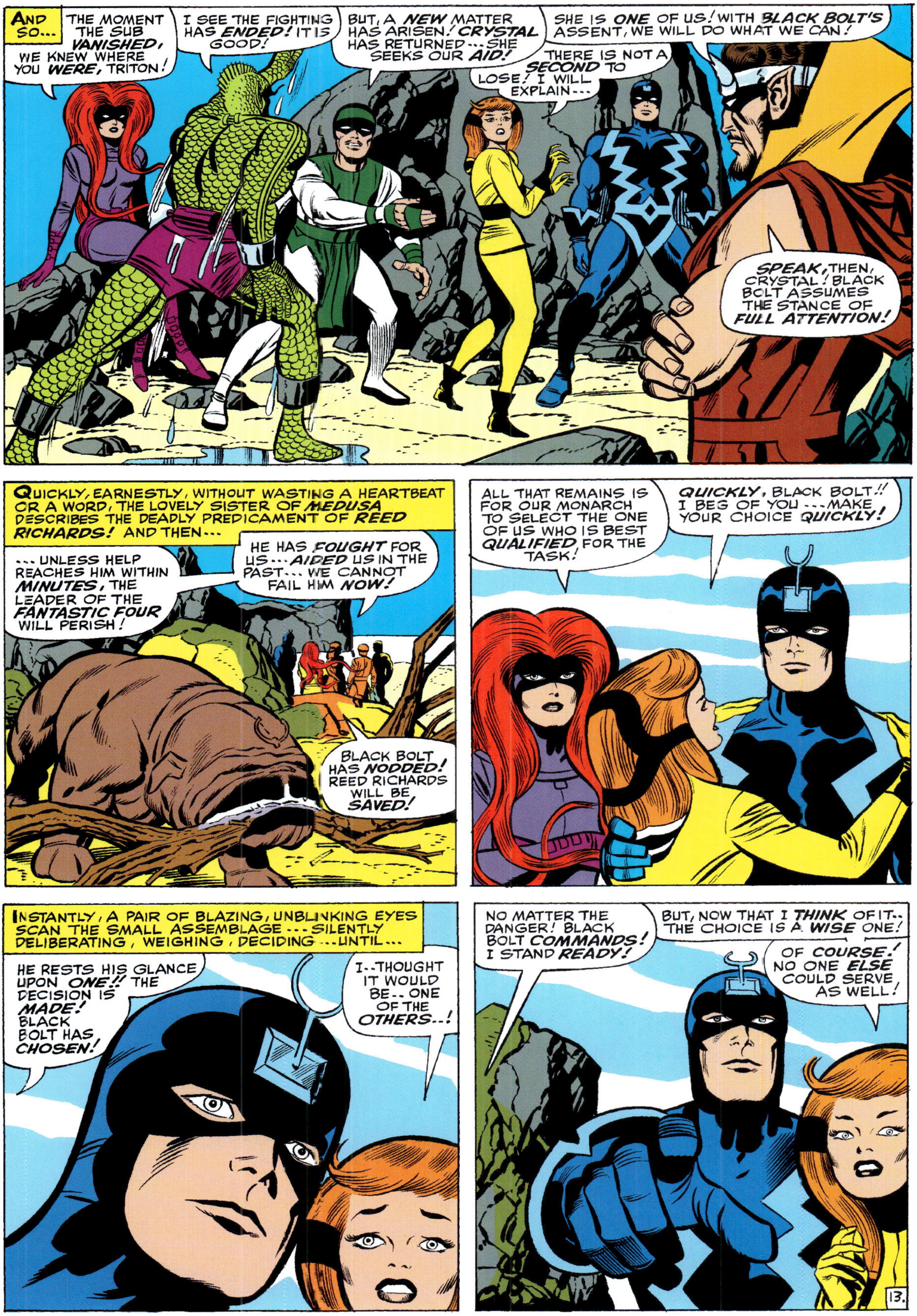
AND SO...
THE MOMENT THE SUB VANISHED, WE KNEW WHERE YOU WERE, TRITON!
I SEE THE FIGHTING HAS ENDED! IT IS GOOD!
BUT, A NEW MATTER HAS ARISEN! CRYSTAL HAS RETURNED--- SHE SEEKS OUR AID!
SHE IS ONE OF US! WITH BLACK BOLT'S ASSENT, WE WILL DO WHAT WE CAN!
THERE IS NOT A SECOND TO LOSE! I WILL EXPLAIN---
SPEAK, THEN, CRYSTAL! BLACK BOLT ASSUMES THE STANCE OF FULL ATTENTION!
QUICKLY, EARNESTLY, WITHOUT WASTING A HEARTBEAT OR A WORD, THE LOVELY SISTER OF MEDUSA DESCRIBES THE DEADLY PREDICAMENT OF REED RICHARDS! AND THEN---
---UNLESS HELP REACHES HIM WITHIN MINUTES, THE LEADER OF THE FANTASTIC FOUR WILL PERISH!
HE HAS FOUGHT FOR US---AIDED US IN THE PAST--- WE CANNOT FAIL HIM NOW!
BLACK BOLT HAS NODDED! REED RICHARDS WILL BE SAVED!
ALL THAT REMAINS IS FOR OUR MONARCH TO SELECT THE ONE OF US WHO IS BEST QUALIFIED FOR THE TASK!
QUICKLY, BLACK BOLT!! I BEG OF YOU ---MAKE YOUR CHOICE QUICKLY!
INSTANTLY, A PAIR OF BLAZING, UNBLINKING EYES SCAN THE SMALL ASSEMBLAGE --- SILENTLY DELIBERATING, WEIGHING, DECIDING --- UNTIL...
HE RESTS HIS GLANCE UPON ONE!! THE DECISION IS MADE! BLACK BOLT HAS CHOSEN!
I--THOUGHT IT WOULD BE-- ONE OF THE OTHERS--!
NO MATTER THE DANGER! BLACK BOLT COMMANDS! I STAND READY!
BUT, NOW THAT I THINK OF IT-- THE CHOICE IS A WISE ONE!
OF COURSE! NO ONE ELSE COULD SERVE AS WELL!
13.

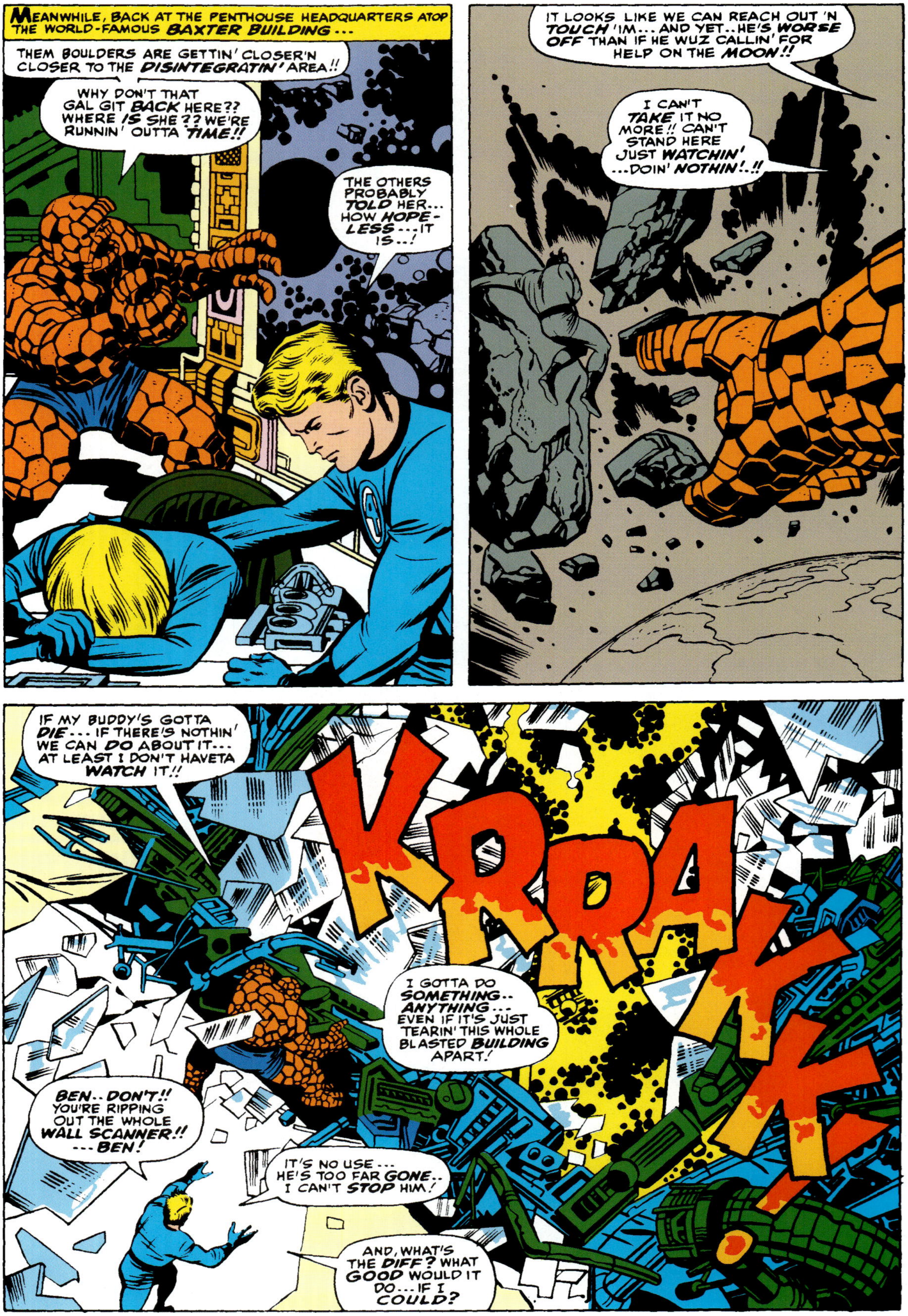

MEANWHILE, BACK AT THE PENTHOUSE HEADQUARTERS ATOP THE WORLD-FAMOUS BAXTER BUILDING...
THEM BOULDERS ARE GETTIN' CLOSER'N CLOSER TO THE DISINTEGRATIN' AREA!!
WHY DON'T THAT GAL GIT BACK HERE?? WHERE IS SHE?? WE'RE RUNNIN' OUTTA TIME!!
THE OTHERS PROBABLY TOLD HER... HOW HOPE-LESS...IT IS..!
IT LOOKS LIKE WE CAN REACH OUT 'N TOUCH 'IM... AND YET..HE'S WORSE OFF THAN IF HE WUZ CALLIN' FOR HELP ON THE MOON!!
I CAN'T TAKE IT NO MORE!! CAN'T STAND HERE JUST WATCHIN' ...DOIN' NOTHIN'..!!
IF MY BUDDY'S GOTTA DIE... IF THERE'S NOTHIN' WE CAN DO ABOUT IT... AT LEAST I DON'T HAVETA WATCH IT!!
KRRAKK
I GOTTA DO SOMETHING.. ANYTHING... EVEN IF IT'S JUST TEARIN' THIS WHOLE BLASTED BUILDING APART!
BEN..DON'T!! YOU'RE RIPPING OUT THE WHOLE WALL SCANNER!! ...BEN!
IT'S NO USE... HE'S TOO FAR GONE.. I CAN'T STOP HIM!
AND, WHAT'S THE DIFF? WHAT GOOD WOULD IT DO...IF I COULD?

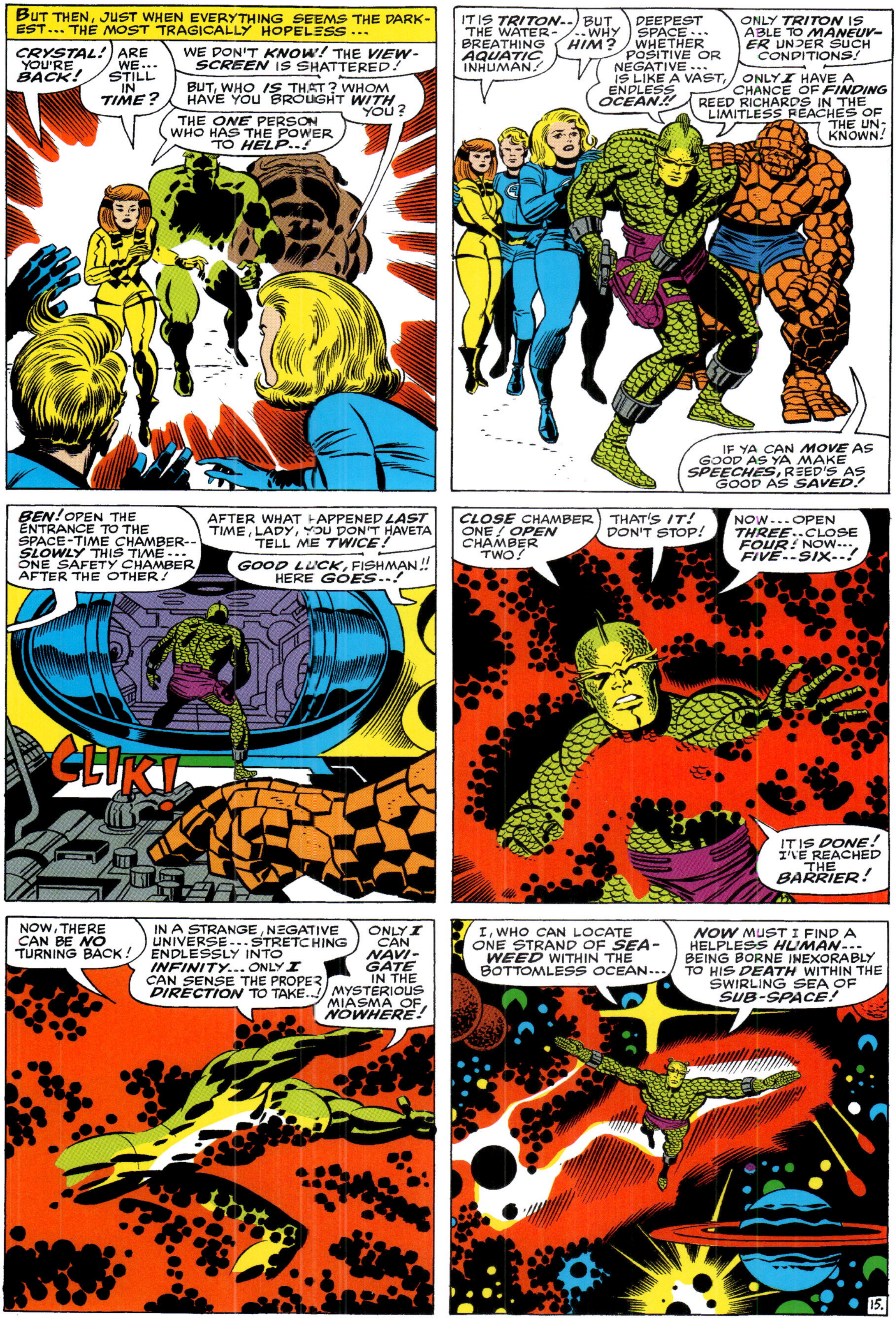

BUT THEN, JUST WHEN EVERYTHING SEEMS THE DARKEST--- THE MOST TRAGICALLY HOPELESS ---
CRYSTAL! YOU'RE BACK!
ARE WE--- STILL IN TIME?
WE DON'T KNOW! THE VIEW-SCREEN IS SHATTERED!
BUT, WHO IS THAT? WHOM HAVE YOU BROUGHT WITH YOU?
THE ONE PERSON WHO HAS THE POWER TO HELP--!
IT IS TRITON-- THE WATER-BREATHING AQUATIC INHUMAN!
BUT --WHY HIM?
DEEPEST SPACE--- WHETHER POSITIVE OR NEGATIVE--- IS LIKE A VAST, ENDLESS OCEAN!!
ONLY TRITON IS ABLE TO MANEUVER UNDER SUCH CONDITIONS!
ONLY I HAVE A CHANCE OF FINDING REED RICHARDS IN THE LIMITLESS REACHES OF THE UNKNOWN!
IF YA CAN MOVE AS GOOD AS YA MAKE SPEECHES, REED'S AS GOOD AS SAVED!
BEN! OPEN THE ENTRANCE TO THE SPACE-TIME CHAMBER-- SLOWLY THIS TIME--- ONE SAFETY CHAMBER AFTER THE OTHER!
AFTER WHAT HAPPENED LAST TIME, LADY, YOU DON'T HAVETA TELL ME TWICE!
GOOD LUCK, FISHMAN!! HERE GOES--!
CLIK!
CLOSE CHAMBER ONE! OPEN CHAMBER TWO!
THAT'S IT! DON'T STOP!
NOW--- OPEN THREE--CLOSE FOUR! NOW--- FIVE--SIX--!
IT IS DONE! I'VE REACHED THE BARRIER!
NOW, THERE CAN BE NO TURNING BACK!
IN A STRANGE, NEGATIVE UNIVERSE--- STRETCHING ENDLESSLY INTO INFINITY--- ONLY I CAN SENSE THE PROPER DIRECTION TO TAKE--!
ONLY I CAN NAVIGATE IN THE MYSTERIOUS MIASMA OF NOWHERE!
I, WHO CAN LOCATE ONE STRAND OF SEA-WEED WITHIN THE BOTTOMLESS OCEAN---
NOW MUST I FIND A HELPLESS HUMAN--- BEING BORNE INEXORABLY TO HIS DEATH WITHIN THE SWIRLING SEA OF SUB-SPACE!
15.

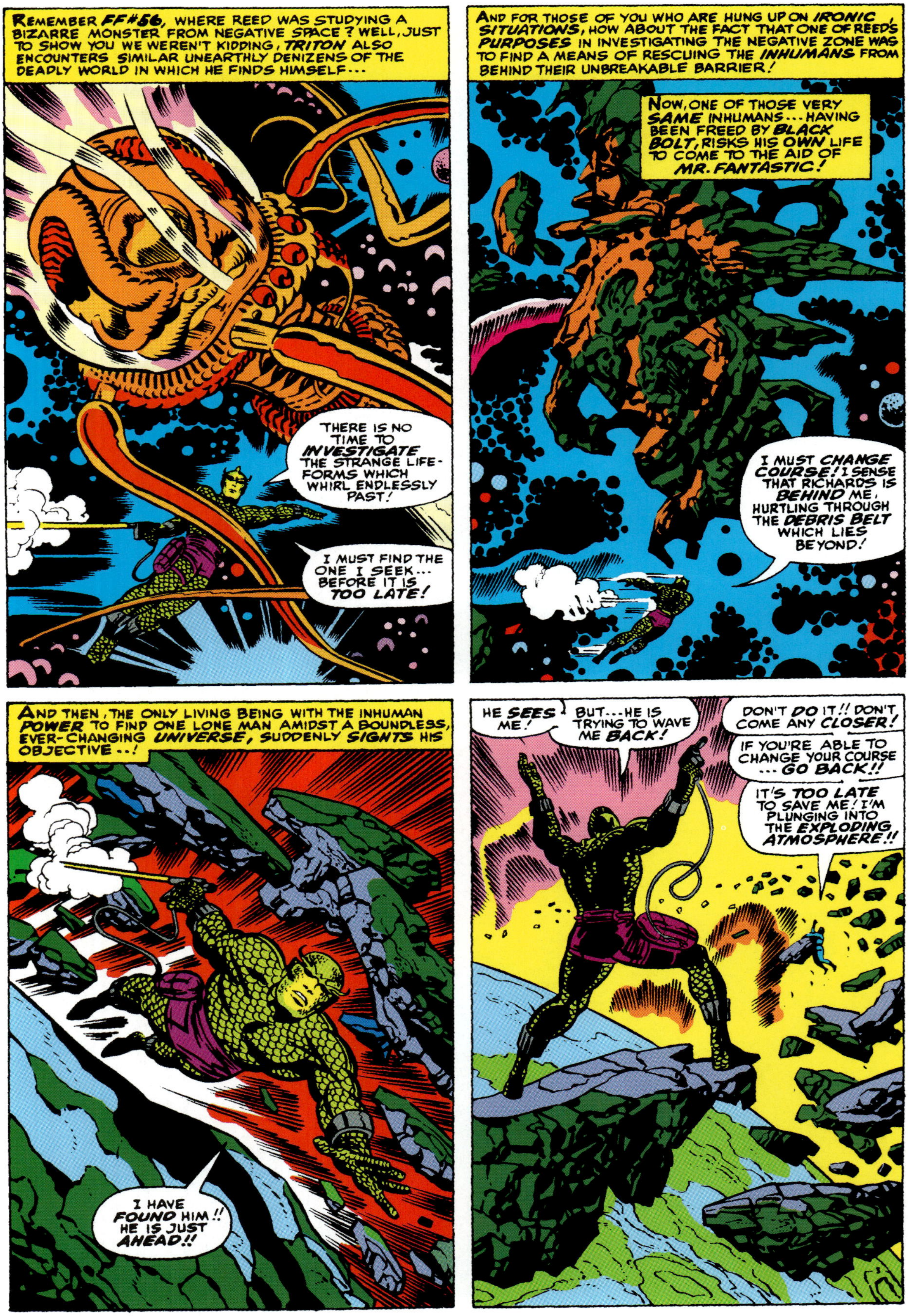
REMEMBER FF#56, WHERE REED WAS STUDYING A BIZARRE MONSTER FROM NEGATIVE SPACE? WELL, JUST TO SHOW YOU WE WEREN'T KIDDING, TRITON ALSO ENCOUNTERS SIMILAR UNEARTHLY DENIZENS OF THE DEADLY WORLD IN WHICH HE FINDS HIMSELF---
THERE IS NO TIME TO INVESTIGATE THE STRANGE LIFE-FORMS WHICH WHIRL ENDLESSLY PAST!
I MUST FIND THE ONE I SEEK--- BEFORE IT IS TOO LATE!
AND FOR THOSE OF YOU WHO ARE HUNG UP ON IRONIC SITUATIONS, HOW ABOUT THE FACT THAT ONE OF REED'S PURPOSES IN INVESTIGATING THE NEGATIVE ZONE WAS TO FIND A MEANS OF RESCUING THE INHUMANS FROM BEHIND THEIR UNBREAKABLE BARRIER!
NOW, ONE OF THOSE VERY SAME INHUMANS--- HAVING BEEN FREED BY BLACK BOLT, RISKS HIS OWN LIFE TO COME TO THE AID OF MR. FANTASTIC!
I MUST CHANGE COURSE! I SENSE THAT RICHARDS IS BEHIND ME, HURTLING THROUGH THE DEBRIS BELT WHICH LIES BEYOND!
AND THEN, THE ONLY LIVING BEING WITH THE INHUMAN POWER TO FIND ONE LONE MAN AMIDST A BOUNDLESS, EVER-CHANGING UNIVERSE, SUDDENLY SIGHTS HIS OBJECTIVE--!
I HAVE FOUND HIM!! HE IS JUST AHEAD!!
HE SEES ME!
BUT---HE IS TRYING TO WAVE ME BACK!
DON'T DO IT!! DON'T COME ANY CLOSER!
IF YOU'RE ABLE TO CHANGE YOUR COURSE ---GO BACK!!
IT'S TOO LATE TO SAVE ME! I'M PLUNGING INTO THE EXPLODING ATMOSPHERE!!

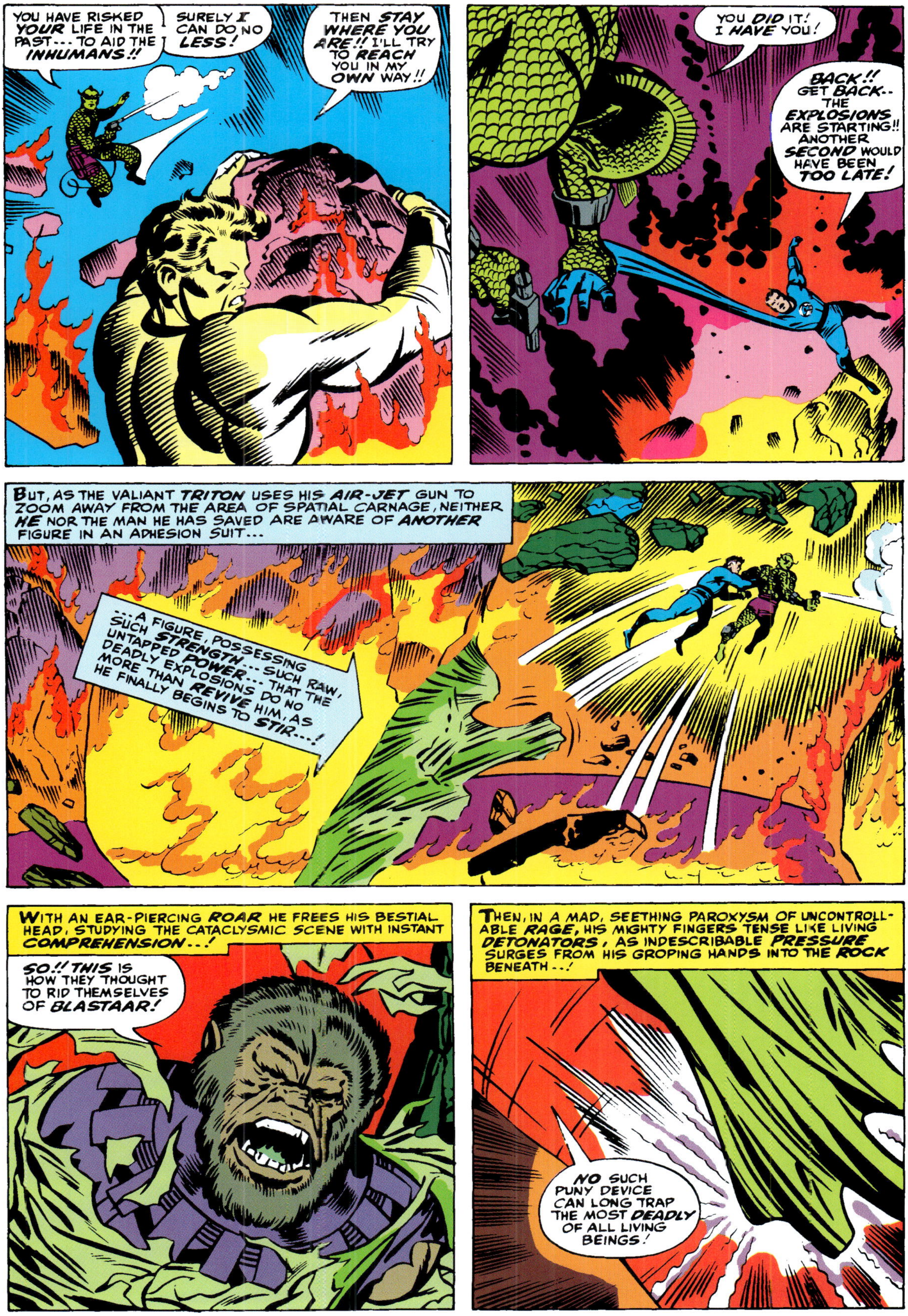
YOU HAVE RISKED YOUR LIFE IN THE PAST--- TO AID THE INHUMANS!!
SURELY I CAN DO NO LESS!
THEN STAY WHERE YOU ARE!! I'LL TRY TO REACH YOU IN MY OWN WAY!!
YOU DID IT! I HAVE YOU!
BACK!! GET BACK-- THE EXPLOSIONS ARE STARTING!! ANOTHER SECOND WOULD HAVE BEEN TOO LATE!
BUT, AS THE VALIANT TRITON USES HIS AIR-JET GUN TO ZOOM AWAY FROM THE AREA OF SPATIAL CARNAGE, NEITHER HE NOR THE MAN HE HAS SAVED ARE AWARE OF ANOTHER FIGURE IN AN ADHESION SUIT...
...A FIGURE, POSSESSING SUCH STRENGTH-- SUCH RAW, UNTAPPED POWER-- THAT THE DEADLY EXPLOSIONS DO NO MORE THAN REVIVE HIM, AS HE FINALLY BEGINS TO STIR...!
WITH AN EAR-PIERCING ROAR HE FREES HIS BESTIAL HEAD, STUDYING THE CATACLYSMIC SCENE WITH INSTANT COMPREHENSION...!
SO!! THIS IS HOW THEY THOUGHT TO RID THEMSELVES OF BLASTAAR!
THEN, IN A MAD, SEETHING PAROXYSM OF UNCONTROLL-ABLE RAGE, HIS MIGHTY FINGERS TENSE LIKE LIVING DETONATORS, AS INDESCRIBABLE PRESSURE SURGES FROM HIS GROPING HANDS INTO THE ROCK BENEATH...!
NO SUCH PUNY DEVICE CAN LONG TRAP THE MOST DEADLY OF ALL LIVING BEINGS!

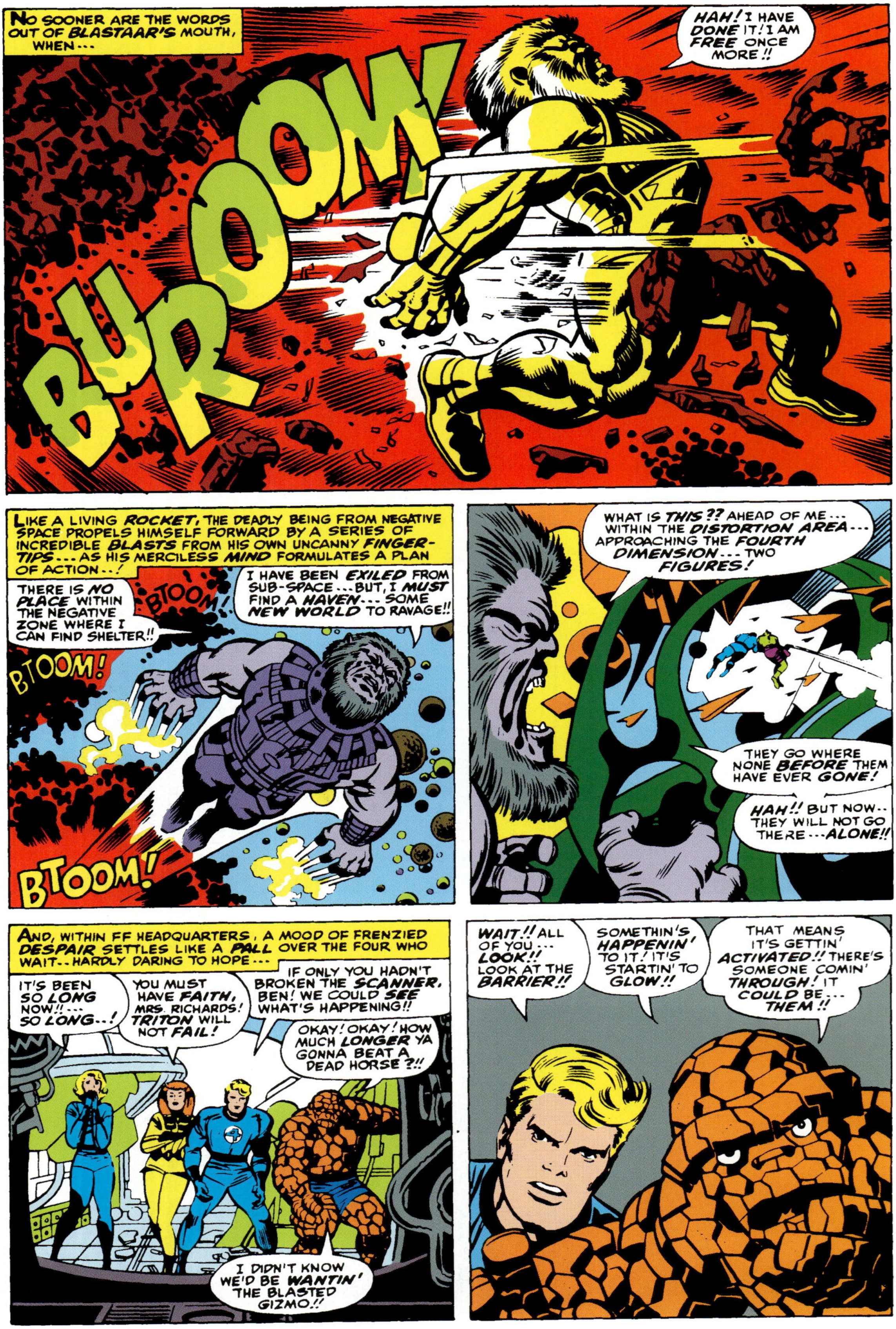
NO SOONER ARE THE WORDS OUT OF BLASTAAR'S MOUTH, WHEN ---
HAH! I HAVE DONE IT! I AM FREE ONCE MORE!!
BUROOOM!
LIKE A LIVING ROCKET, THE DEADLY BEING FROM NEGATIVE SPACE PROPELS HIMSELF FORWARD BY A SERIES OF INCREDIBLE BLASTS FROM HIS OWN UNCANNY FINGER-TIPS --- AS HIS MERCILESS MIND FORMULATES A PLAN OF ACTION --!
THERE IS NO PLACE WITHIN THE NEGATIVE ZONE WHERE I CAN FIND SHELTER!!
BTOOM!
I HAVE BEEN EXILED FROM SUB-SPACE --- BUT, I MUST FIND A HAVEN --- SOME NEW WORLD TO RAVAGE!!
BTOOM!
BTOOM!
WHAT IS THIS?? AHEAD OF ME --- WITHIN THE DISTORTION AREA --- APPROACHING THE FOURTH DIMENSION --- TWO FIGURES!
THEY GO WHERE NONE BEFORE THEM HAVE EVER GONE!
HAH!! BUT NOW -- THEY WILL NOT GO THERE --- ALONE!!
AND, WITHIN FF HEADQUARTERS, A MOOD OF FRENZIED DESPAIR SETTLES LIKE A PALL OVER THE FOUR WHO WAIT -- HARDLY DARING TO HOPE ---
IT'S BEEN SO LONG NOW!! --- SO LONG --!
YOU MUST HAVE FAITH, MRS. RICHARDS! TRITON WILL NOT FAIL!
IF ONLY YOU HADN'T BROKEN THE SCANNER, BEN! WE COULD SEE WHAT'S HAPPENING!!
OKAY! OKAY! HOW MUCH LONGER YA GONNA BEAT A DEAD HORSE?!!
I DIDN'T KNOW WE'D BE WANTIN' THE BLASTED GIZMO!!
WAIT!! ALL OF YOU --- LOOK!! LOOK AT THE BARRIER!!
SOMETHIN'S HAPPENIN' TO IT! IT'S STARTIN' TO GLOW!!
THAT MEANS IT'S GETTIN' ACTIVATED!! THERE'S SOMEONE COMIN' THROUGH! IT COULD BE --- THEM!!

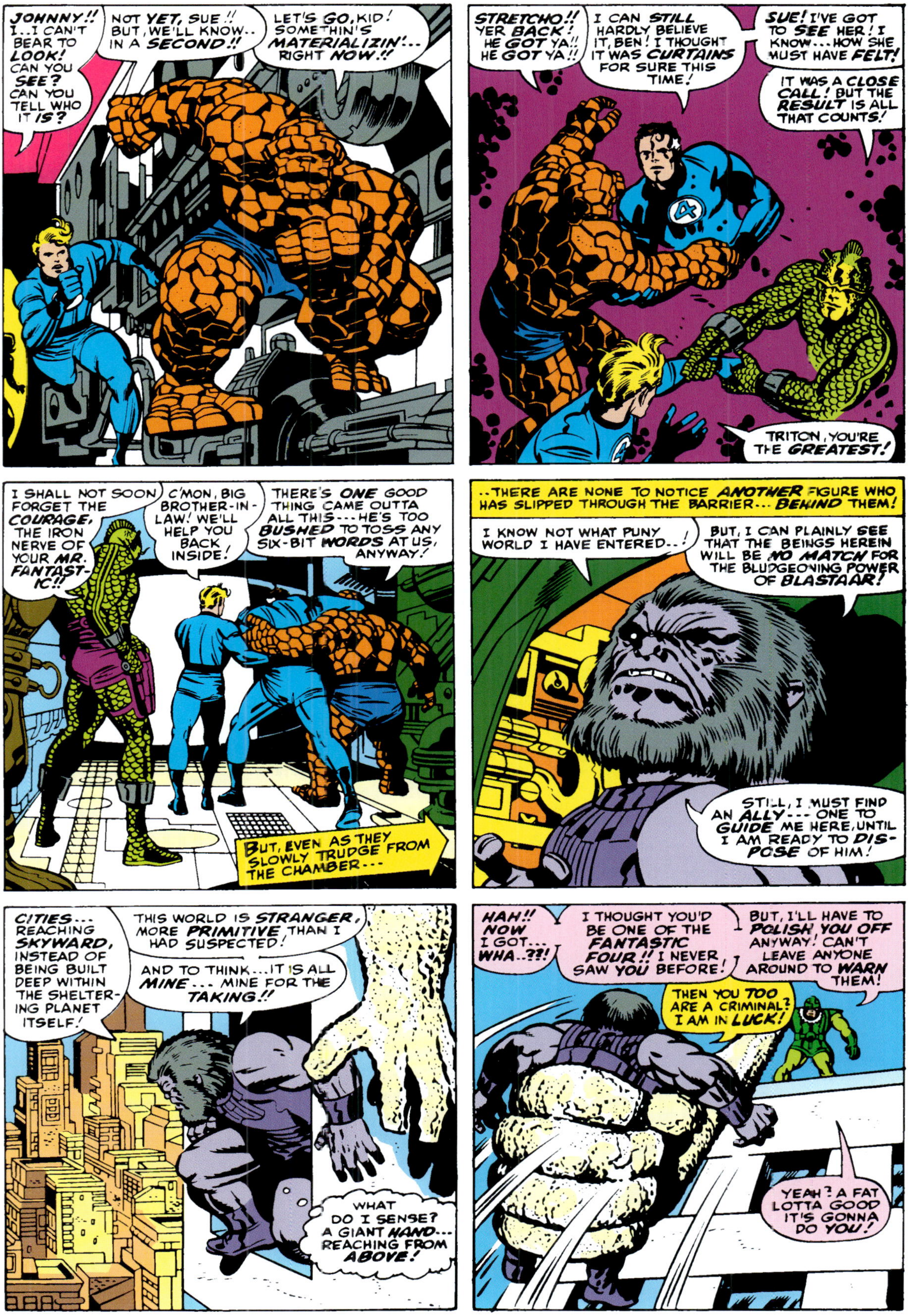
JOHNNY!! I..I CAN'T BEAR TO LOOK! CAN YOU SEE? CAN YOU TELL WHO IT IS?
NOT YET, SUE!! BUT, WE'LL KNOW.. IN A SECOND!!
LET'S GO, KID! SOMETHIN'S MATERIALIZIN'... RIGHT NOW!!
STRETCHO!! YER BACK! HE GOT YA!! HE GOT YA!!
I CAN STILL HARDLY BELIEVE IT, BEN! I THOUGHT IT WAS CURTAINS FOR SURE THIS TIME!
SUE! I'VE GOT TO SEE HER! I KNOW... HOW SHE MUST HAVE FELT!
IT WAS A CLOSE CALL! BUT THE RESULT IS ALL THAT COUNTS!
TRITON, YOU'RE THE GREATEST!
I SHALL NOT SOON FORGET THE COURAGE, THE IRON NERVE OF YOUR MR. FANTASTIC!!
C'MON, BIG BROTHER-IN-LAW! WE'LL HELP YOU BACK INSIDE!
THERE'S ONE GOOD THING CAME OUTTA ALL THIS--- HE'S TOO BUSHED TO TOSS ANY SIX-BIT WORDS AT US, ANYWAY!
BUT, EVEN AS THEY SLOWLY TRUDGE FROM THE CHAMBER---
..THERE ARE NONE TO NOTICE ANOTHER FIGURE WHO HAS SLIPPED THROUGH THE BARRIER... BEHIND THEM!
I KNOW NOT WHAT PUNY WORLD I HAVE ENTERED..!
BUT, I CAN PLAINLY SEE THAT THE BEINGS HEREIN WILL BE NO MATCH FOR THE BLUDGEONING POWER OF BLASTAAR!
STILL, I MUST FIND AN ALLY--- ONE TO GUIDE ME HERE, UNTIL I AM READY TO DISPOSE OF HIM!
CITIES... REACHING SKYWARD, INSTEAD OF BEING BUILT DEEP WITHIN THE SHELTERING PLANET ITSELF!
THIS WORLD IS STRANGER, MORE PRIMITIVE THAN I HAD SUSPECTED!
AND TO THINK... IT IS ALL MINE... MINE FOR THE TAKING!!
WHAT DO I SENSE? A GIANT HAND... REACHING FROM ABOVE!
HAH!! NOW I GOT... WHA..??!
I THOUGHT YOU'D BE ONE OF THE FANTASTIC FOUR!! I NEVER SAW YOU BEFORE!
BUT, I'LL HAVE TO POLISH YOU OFF ANYWAY! CAN'T LEAVE ANYONE AROUND TO WARN THEM!
THEN YOU TOO ARE A CRIMINAL? I AM IN LUCK!
YEAH? A FAT LOTTA GOOD IT'S GONNA DO YOU!

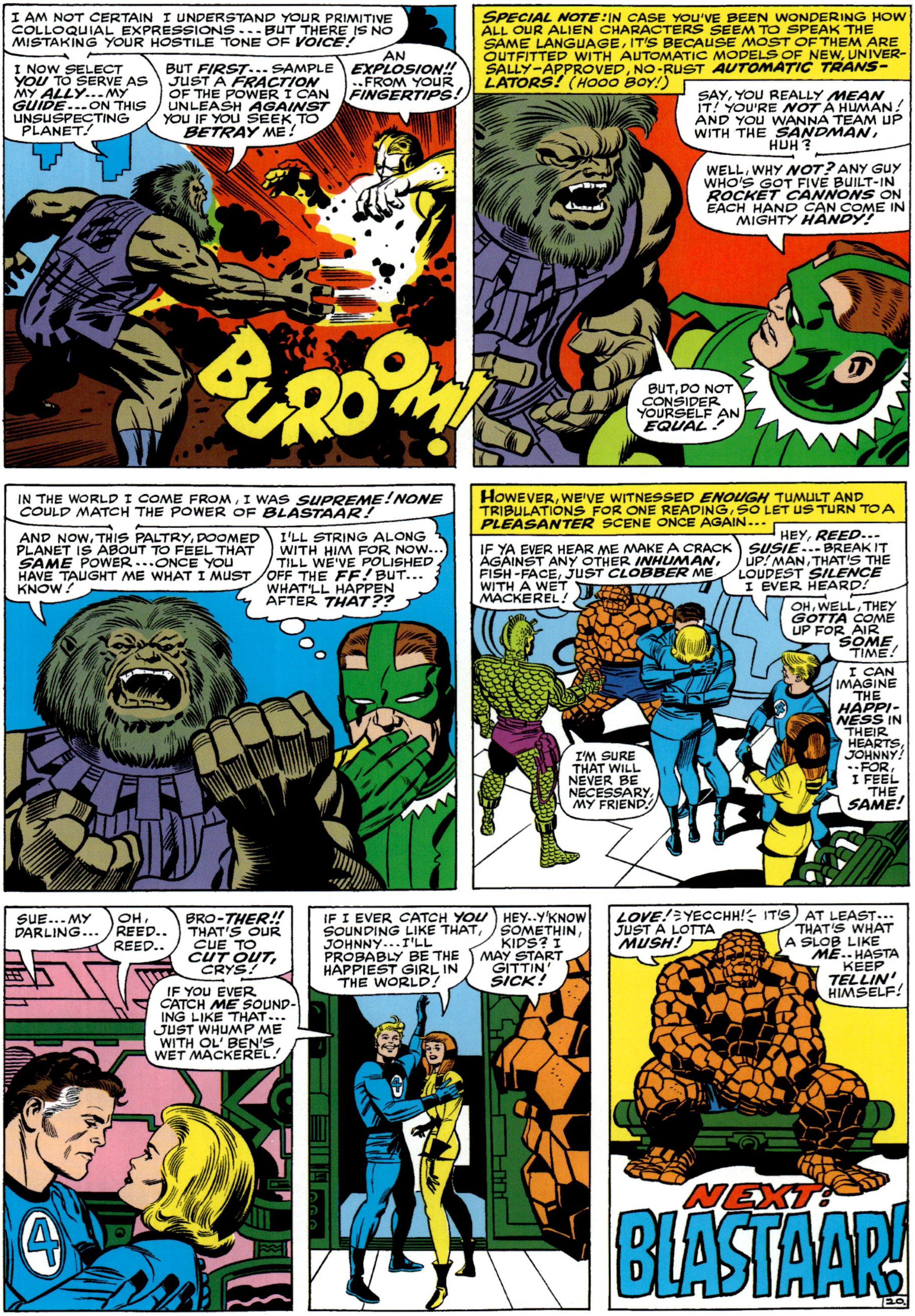
I AM NOT CERTAIN I UNDERSTAND YOUR PRIMITIVE COLLOQUIAL EXPRESSIONS--- BUT THERE IS NO MISTAKING YOUR HOSTILE TONE OF VOICE!
I NOW SELECT YOU TO SERVE AS MY ALLY---MY GUIDE---ON THIS UNSUSPECTING PLANET!
BUT FIRST--- SAMPLE JUST A FRACTION OF THE POWER I CAN UNLEASH AGAINST YOU IF YOU SEEK TO BETRAY ME!
AN EXPLOSION!! ..FROM YOUR FINGERTIPS!
BUROOM!
SPECIAL NOTE: IN CASE YOU'VE BEEN WONDERING HOW ALL OUR ALIEN CHARACTERS SEEM TO SPEAK THE SAME LANGUAGE, IT'S BECAUSE MOST OF THEM ARE OUTFITTED WITH AUTOMATIC MODELS OF NEW, UNIVERSALLY-APPROVED, NO-RUST AUTOMATIC TRANSLATORS! (Hooo Boy!)
SAY, YOU REALLY MEAN IT! YOU'RE NOT A HUMAN! AND YOU WANNA TEAM UP WITH THE SANDMAN, HUH?
WELL, WHY NOT? ANY GUY WHO'S GOT FIVE BUILT-IN ROCKET CANNONS ON EACH HAND CAN COME IN MIGHTY HANDY!
BUT, DO NOT CONSIDER YOURSELF AN EQUAL!
IN THE WORLD I COME FROM, I WAS SUPREME! NONE COULD MATCH THE POWER OF BLASTAAR!
AND NOW, THIS PALTRY, DOOMED PLANET IS ABOUT TO FEEL THAT SAME POWER---ONCE YOU HAVE TAUGHT ME WHAT I MUST KNOW!
I'LL STRING ALONG WITH HIM FOR NOW... TILL WE'VE POLISHED OFF THE FF! BUT--- WHAT'LL HAPPEN AFTER THAT??
HOWEVER, WE'VE WITNESSED ENOUGH TUMULT AND TRIBULATIONS FOR ONE READING, SO LET US TURN TO A PLEASANTER SCENE ONCE AGAIN---
IF YA EVER HEAR ME MAKE A CRACK AGAINST ANY OTHER INHUMAN, FISH-FACE, JUST CLOBBER ME WITH A WET MACKEREL!
HEY, REED--- SUSIE---BREAK IT UP! MAN, THAT'S THE LOUDEST SILENCE I EVER HEARD!
OH, WELL, THEY GOTTA COME UP FOR AIR SOME TIME!
I CAN IMAGINE THE HAPPINESS IN THEIR HEARTS, JOHNNY! --FOR, I FEEL THE SAME!
I'M SURE THAT WILL NEVER BE NECESSARY, MY FRIEND!
SUE---MY DARLING---
OH, REED.. REED..
BRO-THER!! THAT'S OUR CUE TO CUT OUT, CRYS!
IF YOU EVER CATCH ME SOUNDING LIKE THAT--- JUST WHUMP ME WITH OL' BEN'S WET MACKEREL!
IF I EVER CATCH YOU SOUNDING LIKE THAT, JOHNNY---I'LL PROBABLY BE THE HAPPIEST GIRL IN THE WORLD!
HEY..Y'KNOW SOMETHIN, KIDS? I MAY START GITTIN' SICK!
LOVE! YECCHH! IT'S JUST A LOTTA MUSH!
AT LEAST--- THAT'S WHAT A SLOB LIKE ME..HASTA KEEP TELLIN' HIMSELF!
NEXT: BLASTAAR!
20.

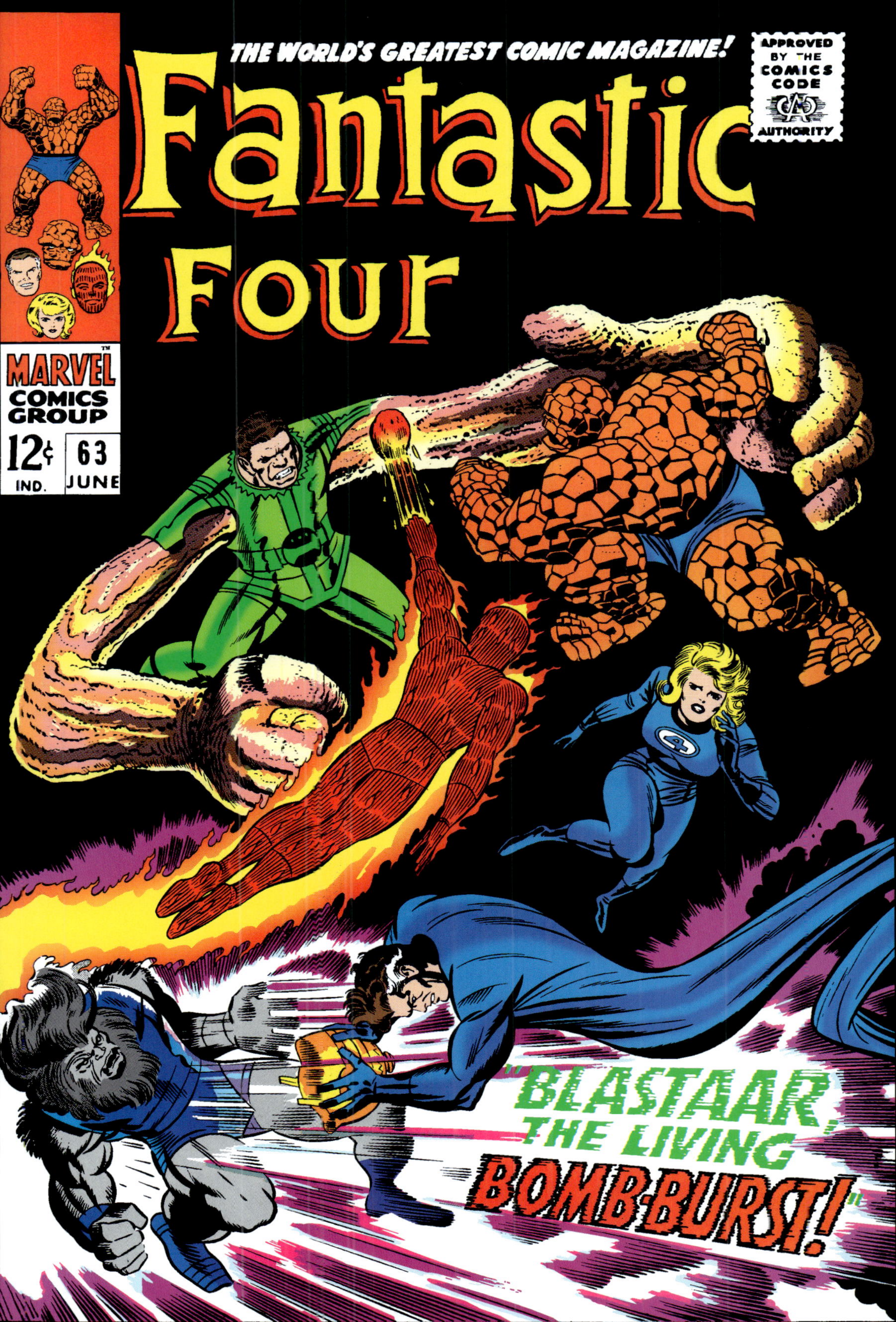
THE WORLD'S GREATEST COMIC MAGAZINE!
Fantastic Four
APPROVED BY THE COMICS CODE AUTHORITY
MARVEL COMICS GROUP
12¢ IND.
63 JUNE
"BLASTAAR, THE LIVING BOMB-BURST!"

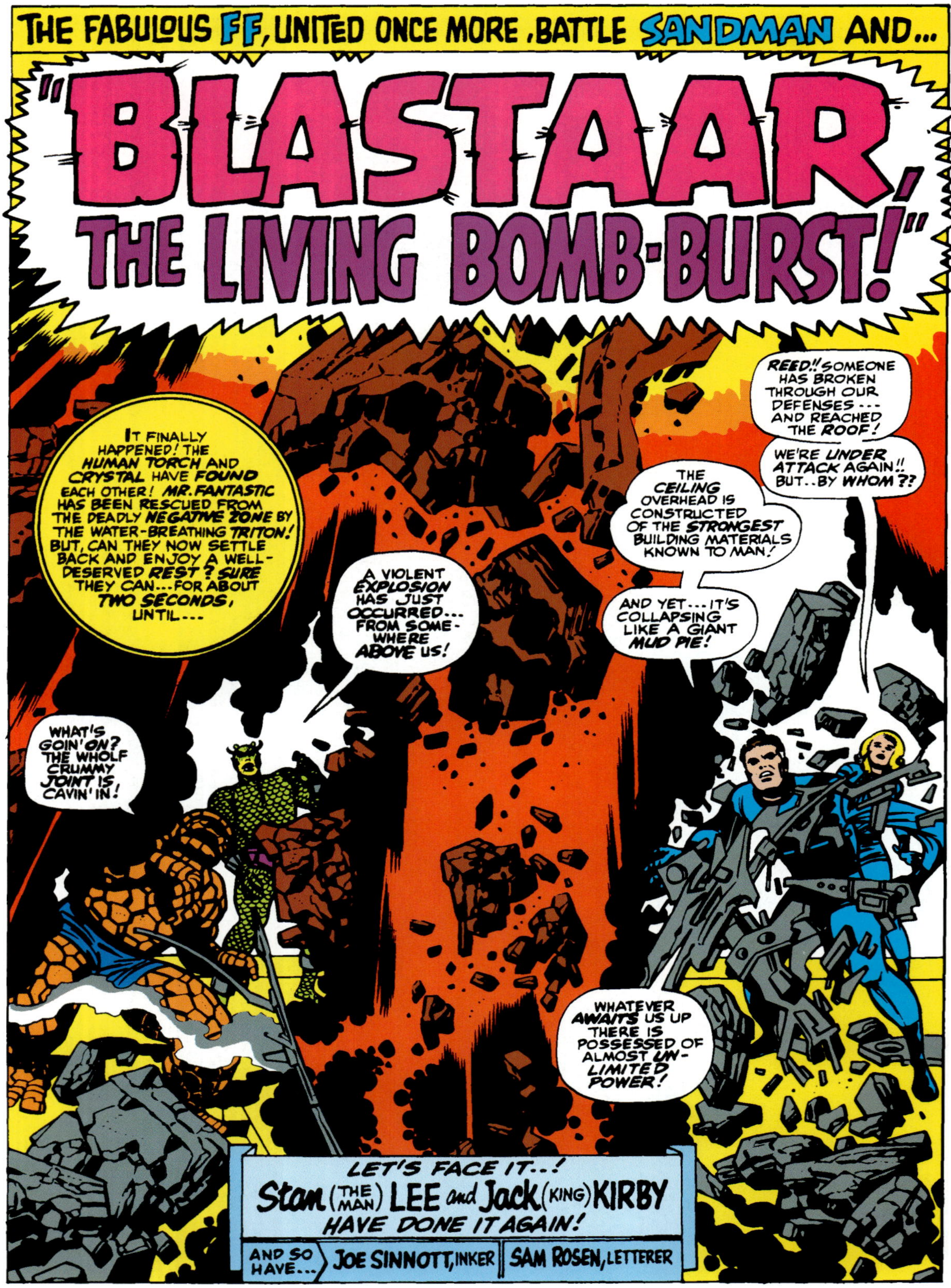
THE FABULOUS FF, UNITED ONCE MORE, BATTLE SANDMAN AND...
"BLASTAAR, THE LIVING BOMB-BURST!"
IT FINALLY HAPPENED! THE HUMAN TORCH AND CRYSTAL HAVE FOUND EACH OTHER! MR. FANTASTIC HAS BEEN RESCUED FROM THE DEADLY NEGATIVE ZONE BY THE WATER-BREATHING TRITON! BUT, CAN THEY NOW SETTLE BACK AND ENJOY A WELL-DESERVED REST? SURE THEY CAN... FOR ABOUT TWO SECONDS, UNTIL...
A VIOLENT EXPLOSION HAS JUST OCCURRED... FROM SOME-WHERE ABOVE US!
THE CEILING OVERHEAD IS CONSTRUCTED OF THE STRONGEST BUILDING MATERIALS KNOWN TO MAN!
AND YET... IT'S COLLAPSING LIKE A GIANT MUD PIE!
REED!! SOMEONE HAS BROKEN THROUGH OUR DEFENSES --- AND REACHED THE ROOF!
WE'RE UNDER ATTACK AGAIN!! BUT.. BY WHOM??
WHAT'S GOIN' ON? THE WHOLF CRUMMY JOINT IS CAVIN' IN!
WHATEVER AWAITS US UP THERE IS POSSESSED OF ALMOST UN-LIMITED POWER!
LET'S FACE IT..! Stan (THE MAN) LEE and Jack (KING) KIRBY HAVE DONE IT AGAIN!
AND SO HAVE... JOE SINNOTT, INKER SAM ROSEN, LETTERER

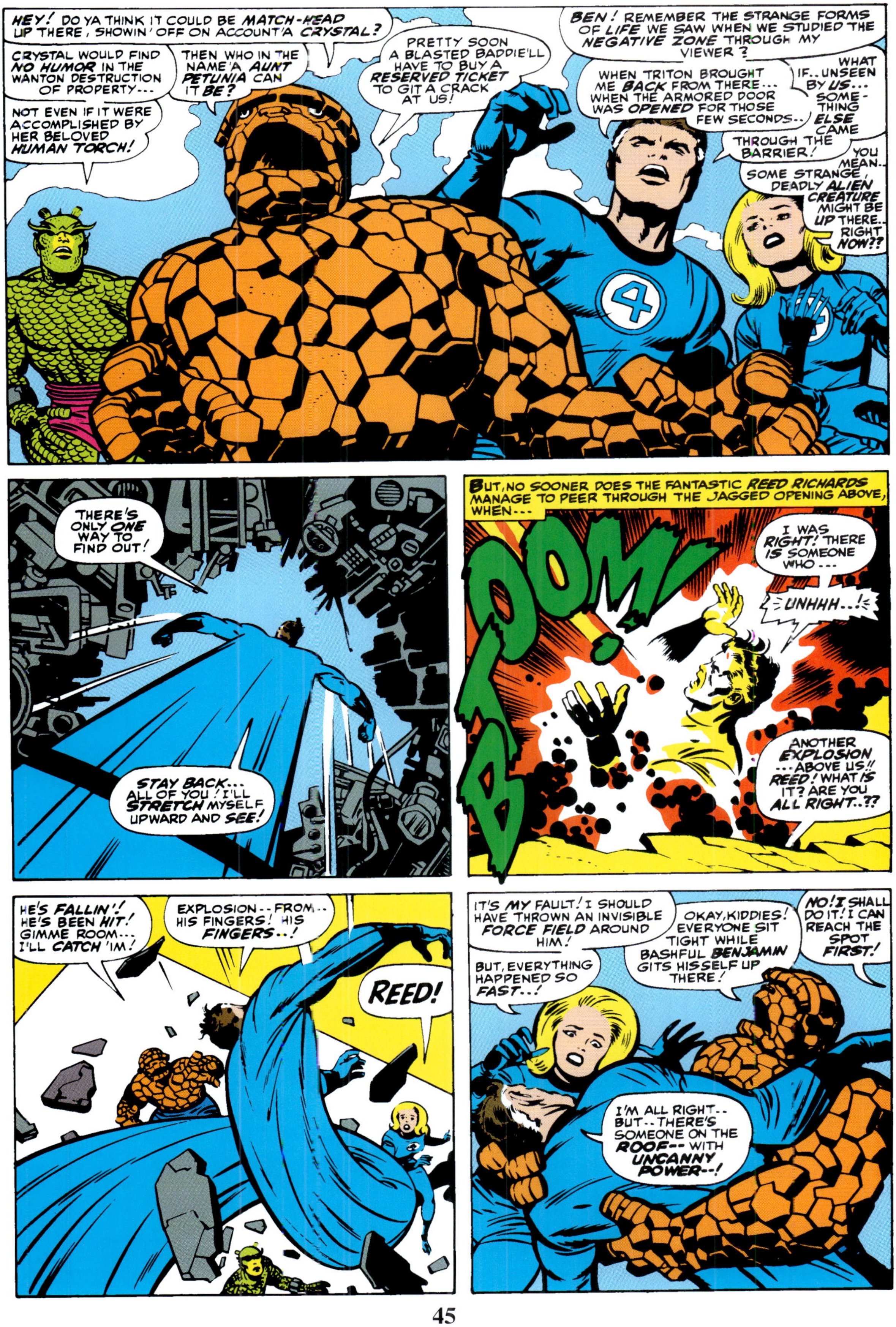
HEY! DO YA THINK IT COULD BE MATCH-HEAD UP THERE, SHOWIN' OFF ON ACCOUNT'A CRYSTAL?
CRYSTAL WOULD FIND NO HUMOR IN THE WANTON DESTRUCTION OF PROPERTY---
NOT EVEN IF IT WERE ACCOMPLISHED BY HER BELOVED HUMAN TORCH!
THEN WHO IN THE NAME'A AUNT PETUNIA CAN IT BE?
PRETTY SOON A BLASTED BADDIE'LL HAVE TO BUY A RESERVED TICKET TO GIT A CRACK AT US!
BEN! REMEMBER THE STRANGE FORMS OF LIFE WE SAW WHEN WE STUDIED THE NEGATIVE ZONE THROUGH MY VIEWER?
WHEN TRITON BROUGHT ME BACK FROM THERE--- WHEN THE ARMORED DOOR WAS OPENED FOR THOSE FEW SECONDS--
WHAT IF.. UNSEEN BY US... SOME-THING ELSE CAME THROUGH THE BARRIER!
YOU MEAN.. SOME STRANGE, DEADLY ALIEN CREATURE MIGHT BE UP THERE.. RIGHT NOW??
THERE'S ONLY ONE WAY TO FIND OUT!
STAY BACK... ALL OF YOU! I'LL STRETCH MYSELF UPWARD AND SEE!
BUT, NO SOONER DOES THE FANTASTIC REED RICHARDS MANAGE TO PEER THROUGH THE JAGGED OPENING ABOVE, WHEN---
BTOOM!
I WAS RIGHT! THERE IS SOMEONE WHO ---
UNHHH..!
ANOTHER EXPLOSION ... ABOVE US!! REED! WHAT IS IT? ARE YOU ALL RIGHT..??
HE'S FALLIN'! HE'S BEEN HIT! GIMME ROOM... I'LL CATCH 'IM!
EXPLOSION--FROM-- HIS FINGERS! HIS FINGERS--!
REED!
IT'S MY FAULT! I SHOULD HAVE THROWN AN INVISIBLE FORCE FIELD AROUND HIM!
BUT, EVERYTHING HAPPENED SO FAST--!
OKAY, KIDDIES! EVERYONE SIT TIGHT WHILE BASHFUL BENJAMIN GITS HISSELF UP THERE!
NO! I SHALL DO IT! I CAN REACH THE SPOT FIRST!
I'M ALL RIGHT-- BUT--THERE'S SOMEONE ON THE ROOF-- WITH UNCANNY POWER--!

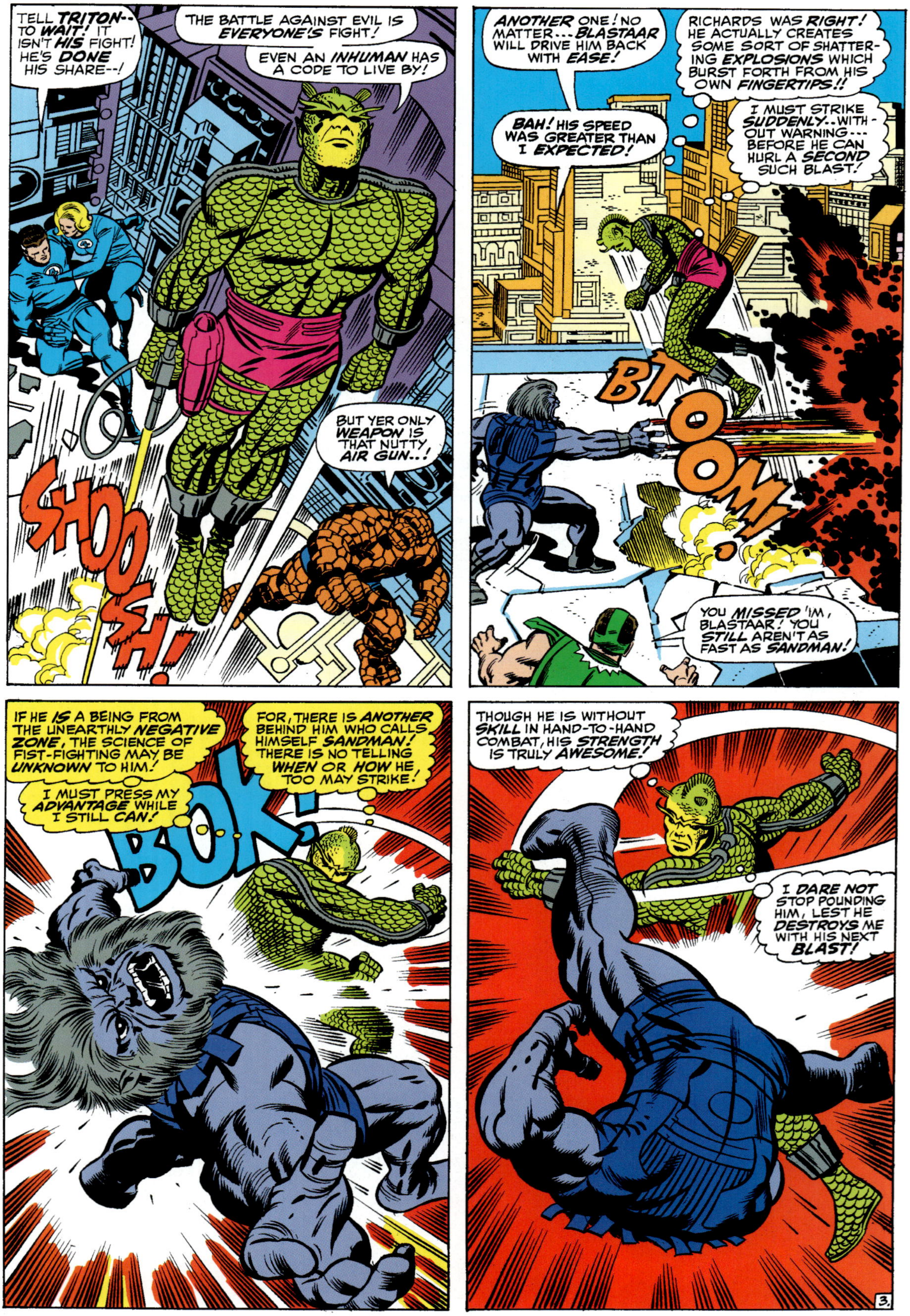
TELL TRITON--TO WAIT! IT ISN'T HIS FIGHT! HE'S DONE HIS SHARE--!
THE BATTLE AGAINST EVIL IS EVERYONE'S FIGHT!
EVEN AN INHUMAN HAS A CODE TO LIVE BY!
BUT YER ONLY WEAPON IS THAT NUTTY AIR GUN..!
SHOOOSH!
ANOTHER ONE! NO MATTER... BLASTAAR WILL DRIVE HIM BACK WITH EASE!
RICHARDS WAS RIGHT! HE ACTUALLY CREATES SOME SORT OF SHATTERING EXPLOSIONS WHICH BURST FORTH FROM HIS OWN FINGERTIPS!!
BAH! HIS SPEED WAS GREATER THAN I EXPECTED!
I MUST STRIKE SUDDENLY..WITHOUT WARNING--- BEFORE HE CAN HURL A SECOND SUCH BLAST!
BTOOOM!
YOU MISSED 'IM, BLASTAAR! YOU STILL AREN'T AS FAST AS SANDMAN!
IF HE IS A BEING FROM THE UNEARTHLY NEGATIVE ZONE, THE SCIENCE OF FIST-FIGHTING MAY BE UNKNOWN TO HIM!
FOR, THERE IS ANOTHER BEHIND HIM WHO CALLS HIMSELF SANDMAN! THERE IS NO TELLING WHEN OR HOW HE TOO MAY STRIKE!
I MUST PRESS MY ADVANTAGE WHILE I STILL CAN!
BOK!
THOUGH HE IS WITHOUT SKILL IN HAND-TO-HAND COMBAT, HIS STRENGTH IS TRULY AWESOME!
I DARE NOT STOP POUNDING HIM, LEST HE DESTROYS ME WITH HIS NEXT BLAST!
3

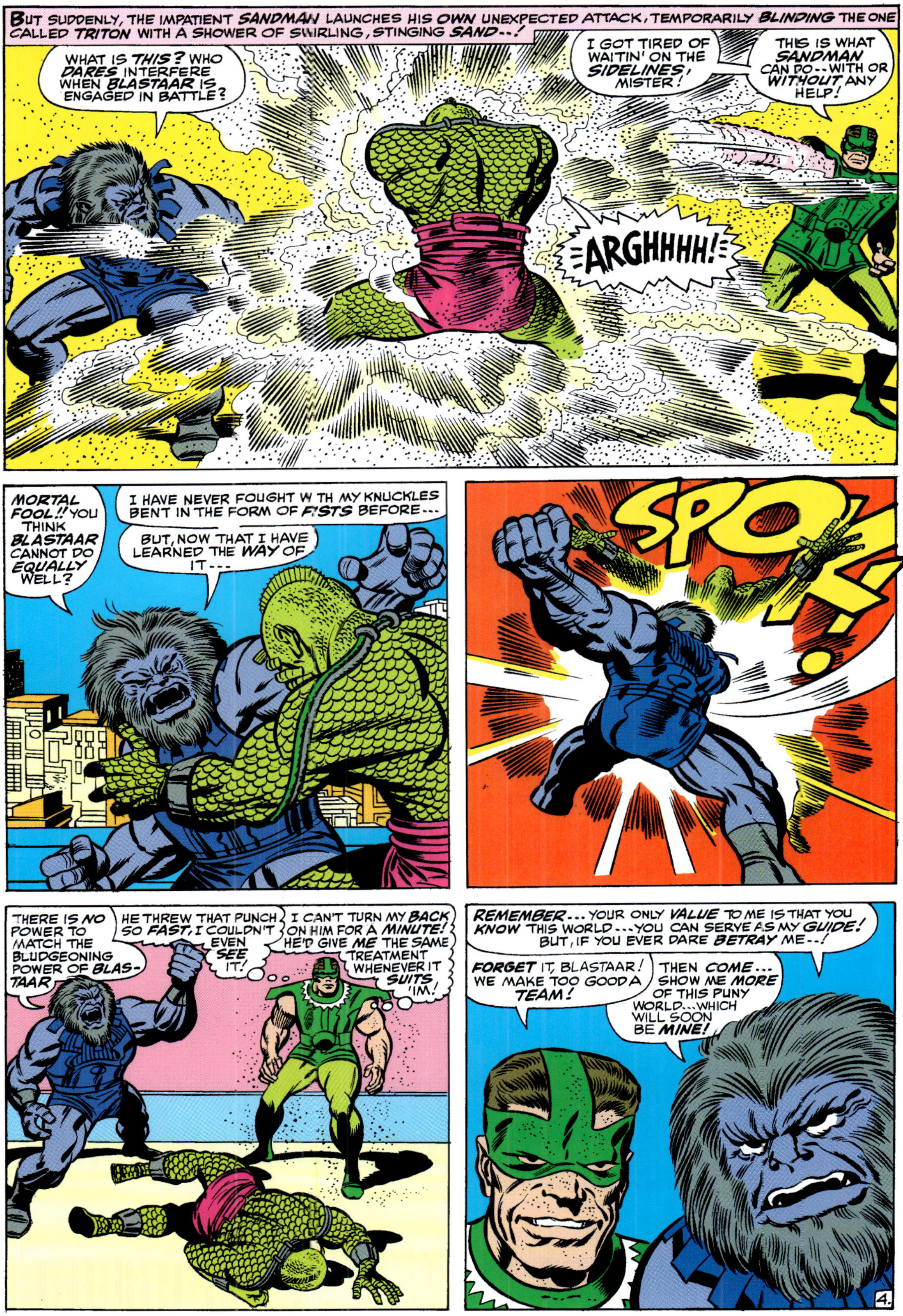

BUT SUDDENLY, THE IMPATIENT SANDMAN LAUNCHES HIS OWN UNEXPECTED ATTACK, TEMPORARILY BLINDING THE ONE CALLED TRITON WITH A SHOWER OF SWIRLING, STINGING SAND--!
WHAT IS THIS? WHO DARES INTERFERE WHEN BLASTAAR IS ENGAGED IN BATTLE?
I GOT TIRED OF WAITIN' ON THE SIDELINES, MISTER!
THIS IS WHAT SANDMAN CAN DO--WITH OR WITHOUT ANY HELP!
ARGHHHH!
MORTAL FOOL!! YOU THINK BLASTAAR CANNOT DO EQUALLY WELL?
I HAVE NEVER FOUGHT WITH MY KNUCKLES BENT IN THE FORM OF FISTS BEFORE---
BUT, NOW THAT I HAVE LEARNED THE WAY OF IT---
SPOK!
THERE IS NO POWER TO MATCH THE BLUDGEONING POWER OF BLASTAAR
HE THREW THAT PUNCH SO FAST, I COULDN'T EVEN SEE IT!
I CAN'T TURN MY BACK ON HIM FOR A MINUTE! HE'D GIVE ME THE SAME TREATMENT WHENEVER IT SUITS 'IM!
REMEMBER... YOUR ONLY VALUE TO ME IS THAT YOU KNOW THIS WORLD... YOU CAN SERVE AS MY GUIDE! BUT, IF YOU EVER DARE BETRAY ME--!
FORGET IT, BLASTAAR! WE MAKE TOO GOOD A TEAM!
THEN COME... SHOW ME MORE OF THIS PUNY WORLD... WHICH WILL SOON BE MINE!
4.

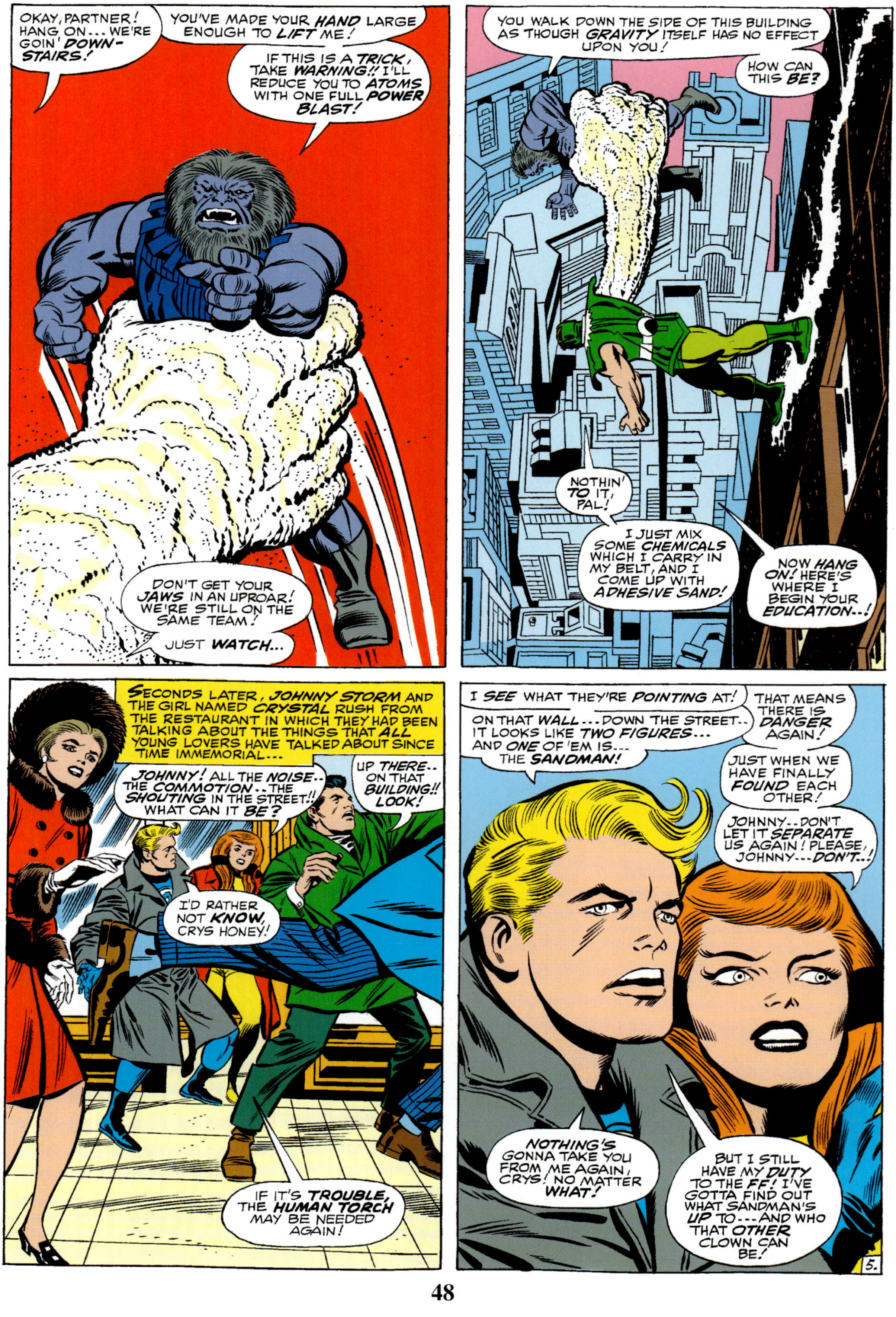

OKAY, PARTNER! HANG ON... WE'RE GOIN' DOWN-STAIRS!
YOU'VE MADE YOUR HAND LARGE ENOUGH TO LIFT ME!
IF THIS IS A TRICK, TAKE WARNING!! I'LL REDUCE YOU TO ATOMS WITH ONE FULL POWER BLAST!
DON'T GET YOUR JAWS IN AN UPROAR! WE'RE STILL ON THE SAME TEAM!
JUST WATCH...
YOU WALK DOWN THE SIDE OF THIS BUILDING AS THOUGH GRAVITY ITSELF HAS NO EFFECT UPON YOU!
HOW CAN THIS BE?
NOTHIN' TO IT, PAL!
I JUST MIX SOME CHEMICALS WHICH I CARRY IN MY BELT, AND I COME UP WITH ADHESIVE SAND!
NOW HANG ON! HERE'S WHERE I BEGIN YOUR EDUCATION..!
SECONDS LATER, JOHNNY STORM AND THE GIRL NAMED CRYSTAL RUSH FROM THE RESTAURANT IN WHICH THEY HAD BEEN TALKING ABOUT THE THINGS THAT ALL YOUNG LOVERS HAVE TALKED ABOUT SINCE TIME IMMEMORIAL...
JOHNNY! ALL THE NOISE.. THE COMMOTION.. THE SHOUTING IN THE STREET!! WHAT CAN IT BE?
UP THERE.. ON THAT BUILDING!! LOOK!
I'D RATHER NOT KNOW, CRYS HONEY!
IF IT'S TROUBLE, THE HUMAN TORCH MAY BE NEEDED AGAIN!
I SEE WHAT THEY'RE POINTING AT!
ON THAT WALL... DOWN THE STREET.. IT LOOKS LIKE TWO FIGURES... AND ONE OF 'EM IS... THE SANDMAN!
THAT MEANS THERE IS DANGER AGAIN!
JUST WHEN WE HAVE FINALLY FOUND EACH OTHER!
JOHNNY.. DON'T LET IT SEPARATE US AGAIN! PLEASE, JOHNNY... DON'T..!
NOTHING'S GONNA TAKE YOU FROM ME AGAIN, CRYS! NO MATTER WHAT!
BUT I STILL HAVE MY DUTY TO THE FF! I'VE GOTTA FIND OUT WHAT SANDMAN'S UP TO... AND WHO THAT OTHER CLOWN CAN BE!
5.

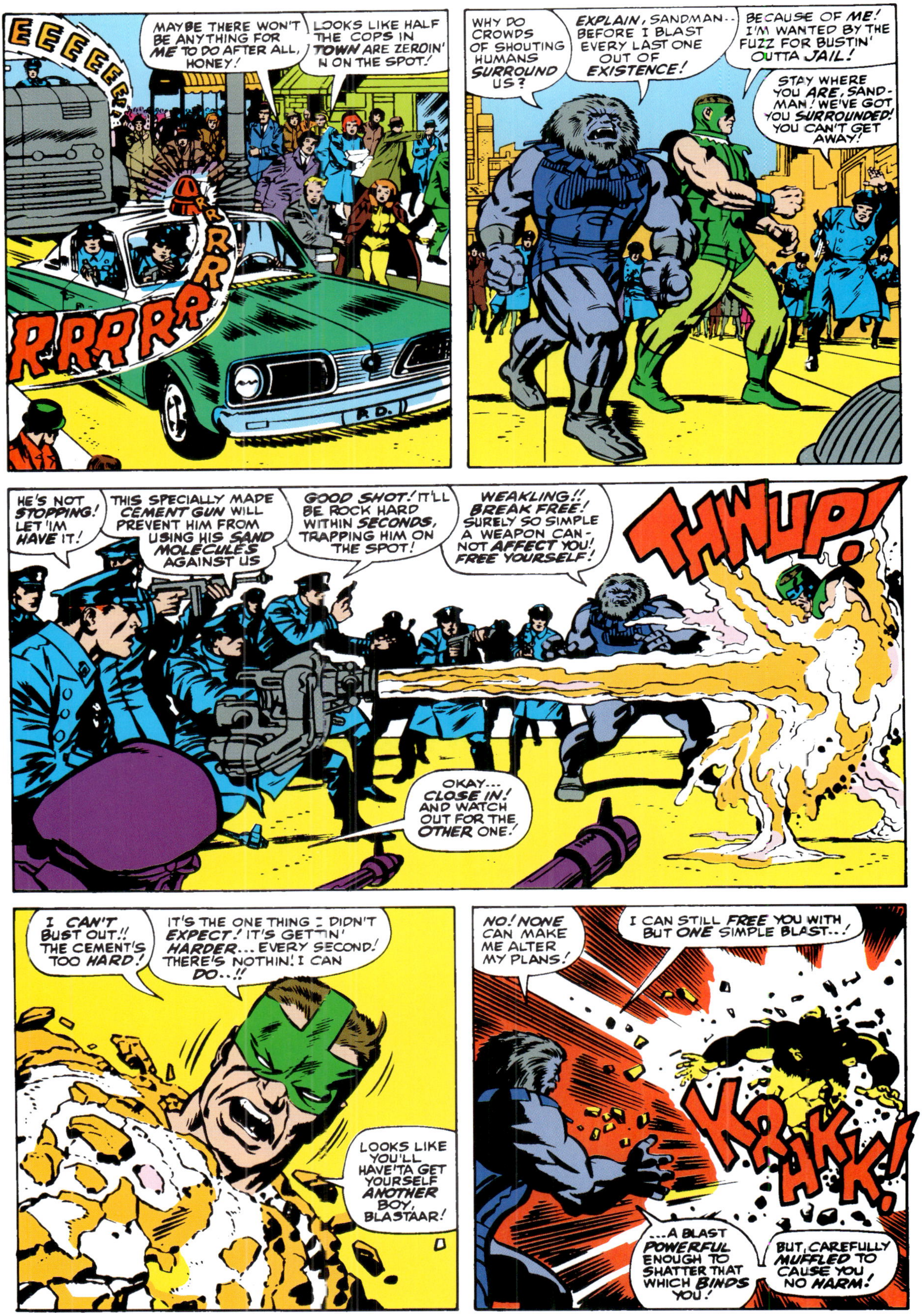
EEEEEEE
MAYBE THERE WON'T BE ANYTHING FOR ME TO DO AFTER ALL, HONEY!
LOOKS LIKE HALF THE COPS IN TOWN ARE ZEROIN' IN ON THE SPOT!
RRRRRRRRR
R.D.
WHY DO CROWDS OF SHOUTING HUMANS SURROUND US?
EXPLAIN, SANDMAN-- BEFORE I BLAST EVERY LAST ONE OUT OF EXISTENCE!
BECAUSE OF ME! I'M WANTED BY THE FUZZ FOR BUSTIN' OUTTA JAIL!
STAY WHERE YOU ARE, SANDMAN! WE'VE GOT YOU SURROUNDED! YOU CAN'T GET AWAY!
HE'S NOT STOPPING! LET 'IM HAVE IT!
THIS SPECIALLY MADE CEMENT GUN WILL PREVENT HIM FROM USING HIS SAND MOLECULES AGAINST US
GOOD SHOT! IT'LL BE ROCK HARD WITHIN SECONDS, TRAPPING HIM ON THE SPOT!
WEAKLING!! BREAK FREE! SURELY SO SIMPLE A WEAPON CANNOT AFFECT YOU! FREE YOURSELF!
THWUP!
OKAY... CLOSE IN! AND WATCH OUT FOR THE OTHER ONE!
I CAN'T BUST OUT!! THE CEMENT'S TOO HARD!
IT'S THE ONE THING I DIDN'T EXPECT! IT'S GETTIN' HARDER... EVERY SECOND! THERE'S NOTHIN' I CAN DO..!!
LOOKS LIKE YOU'LL HAVE'TA GET YOURSELF ANOTHER BOY, BLASTAAR!
NO! NONE CAN MAKE ME ALTER MY PLANS!
I CAN STILL FREE YOU WITH BUT ONE SIMPLE BLAST...!
KRAKK!
...A BLAST POWERFUL ENOUGH TO SHATTER THAT WHICH BINDS YOU!
BUT, CAREFULLY MUFFLED TO CAUSE YOU NO HARM!

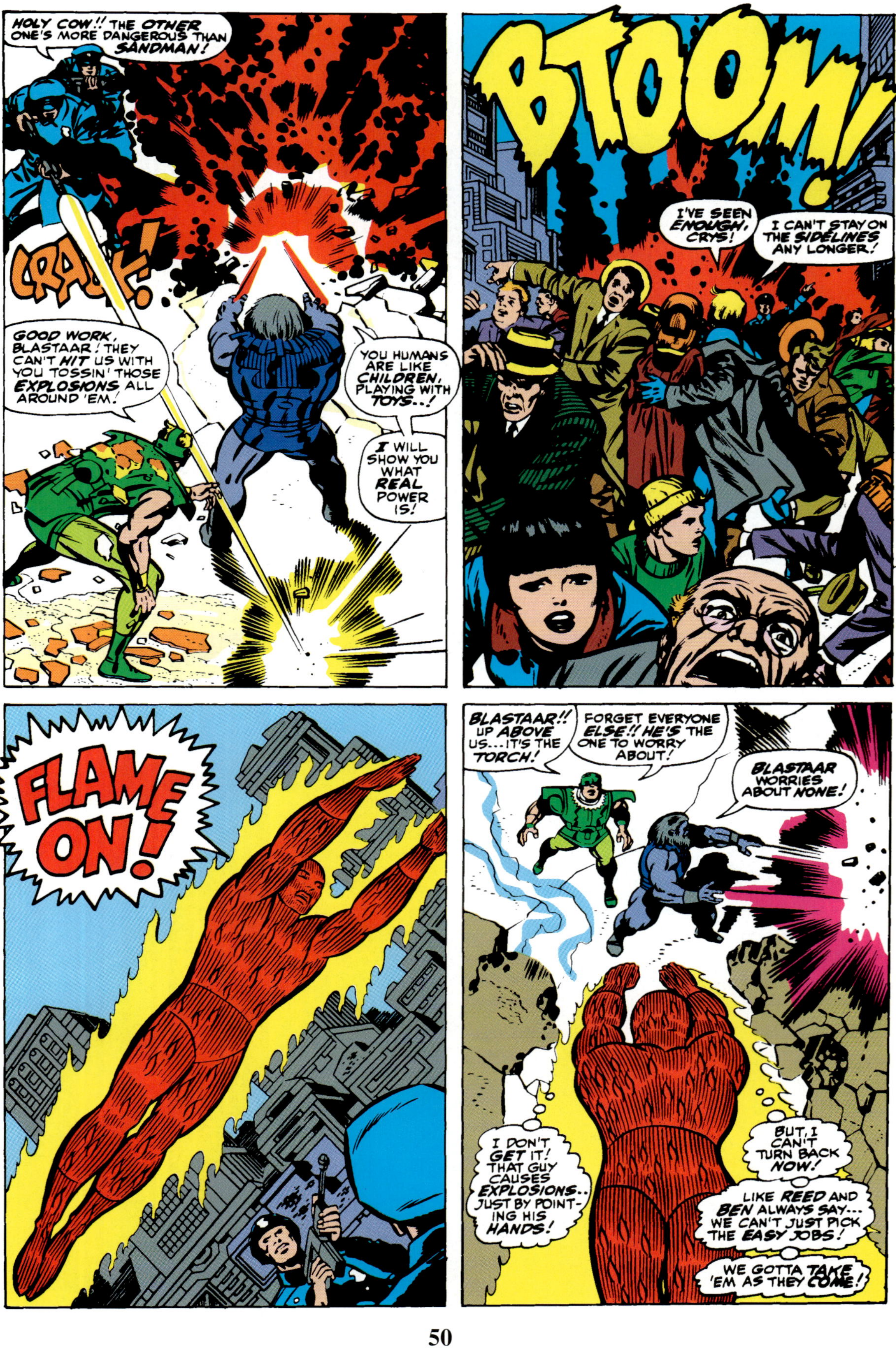
HOLY COW!! THE OTHER ONE'S MORE DANGEROUS THAN SANDMAN!
CRACK!
GOOD WORK, BLASTAAR! THEY CAN'T HIT US WITH YOU TOSSIN' THOSE EXPLOSIONS ALL AROUND 'EM!
YOU HUMANS ARE LIKE CHILDREN, PLAYING WITH TOYS..!
I WILL SHOW YOU WHAT REAL POWER IS!
BTOOM!
I'VE SEEN ENOUGH, CRYS!
I CAN'T STAY ON THE SIDELINES ANY LONGER!
FLAME ON!
BLASTAAR!! UP ABOVE US... IT'S THE TORCH!
FORGET EVERYONE ELSE!! HE'S THE ONE TO WORRY ABOUT!
BLASTAAR WORRIES ABOUT NONE!
I DON'T GET IT! THAT GUY CAUSES EXPLOSIONS.. JUST BY POINTING HIS HANDS!
BUT, I CAN'T TURN BACK NOW!
LIKE REED AND BEN ALWAYS SAY... WE CAN'T JUST PICK THE EASY JOBS!
WE GOTTA TAKE 'EM AS THEY COME!

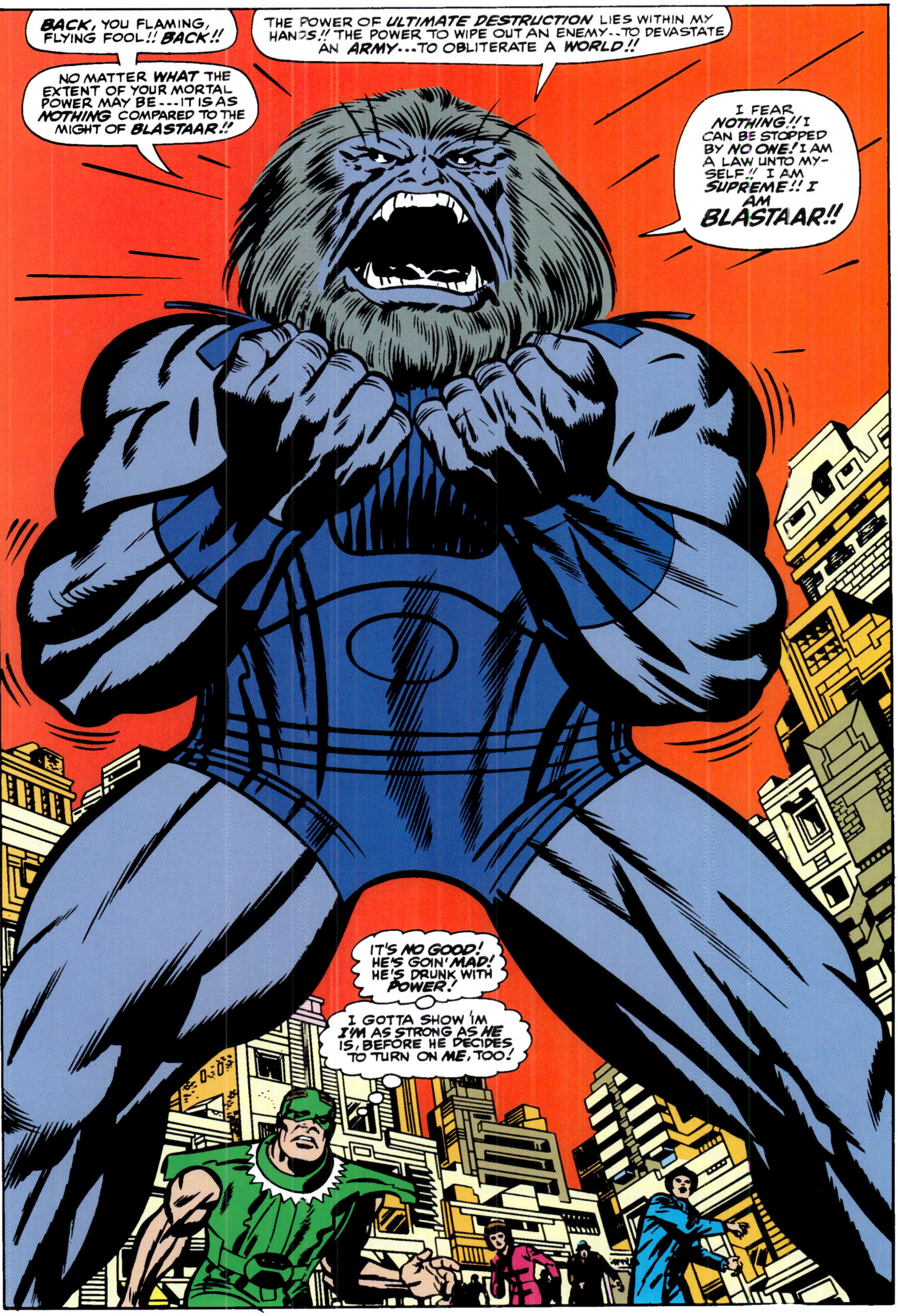
BACK, YOU FLAMING, FLYING FOOL!! BACK!!
NO MATTER WHAT THE EXTENT OF YOUR MORTAL POWER MAY BE---IT IS AS NOTHING COMPARED TO THE MIGHT OF BLASTAAR!!
THE POWER OF ULTIMATE DESTRUCTION LIES WITHIN MY HANDS!! THE POWER TO WIPE OUT AN ENEMY--TO DEVASTATE AN ARMY...TO OBLITERATE A WORLD!!
I FEAR NOTHING!! I CAN BE STOPPED BY NO ONE! I AM A LAW UNTO MYSELF!! I AM SUPREME!! I AM BLASTAAR!!
IT'S NO GOOD! HE'S GOIN' MAD! HE'S DRUNK WITH POWER!
I GOTTA SHOW 'IM I'M AS STRONG AS HE IS, BEFORE HE DECIDES TO TURN ON ME, TOO!

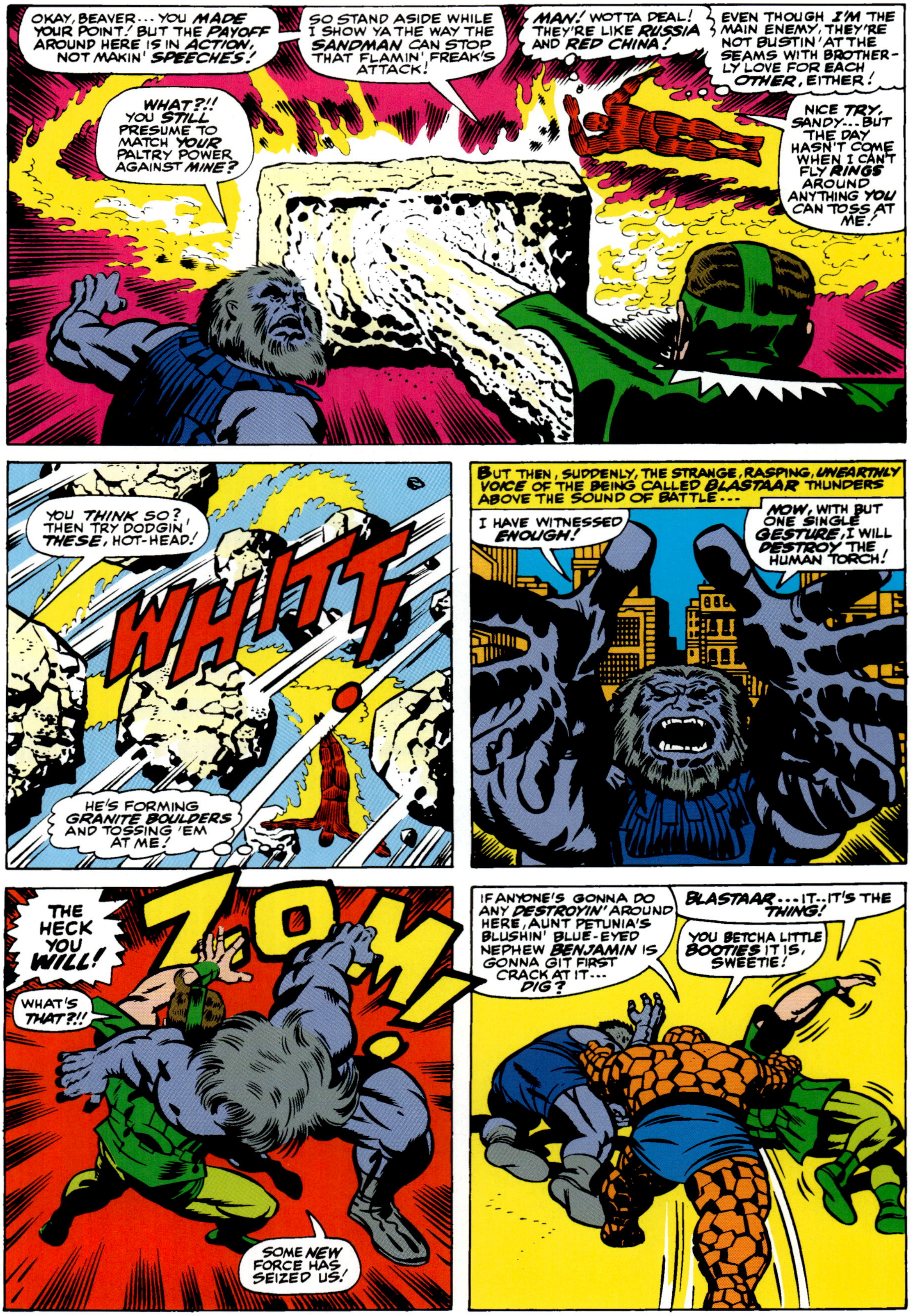
OKAY, BEAVER... YOU MADE YOUR POINT! BUT THE PAYOFF AROUND HERE IS IN ACTION, NOT MAKIN' SPEECHES!
SO STAND ASIDE WHILE I SHOW YA THE WAY THE SANDMAN CAN STOP THAT FLAMIN' FREAK'S ATTACK!
WHAT?!! YOU STILL PRESUME TO MATCH YOUR PALTRY POWER AGAINST MINE?
MAN! WOTTA DEAL! THEY'RE LIKE RUSSIA AND RED CHINA!
EVEN THOUGH I'M THE MAIN ENEMY, THEY'RE NOT BUSTIN' AT THE SEAMS WITH BROTHERLY LOVE FOR EACH OTHER, EITHER!
NICE TRY, SANDY... BUT THE DAY HASN'T COME WHEN I CAN'T FLY RINGS AROUND ANYTHING YOU CAN TOSS AT ME!
YOU THINK SO? THEN TRY DODGIN' THESE, HOT-HEAD!
WHITT!
HE'S FORMING GRANITE BOULDERS AND TOSSING 'EM AT ME!
BUT THEN, SUDDENLY, THE STRANGE, RASPING, UNEARTHLY VOICE OF THE BEING CALLED BLASTAAR THUNDERS ABOVE THE SOUND OF BATTLE...
I HAVE WITNESSED ENOUGH!
NOW, WITH BUT ONE SINGLE GESTURE, I WILL DESTROY THE HUMAN TORCH!
THE HECK YOU WILL!
ZOOM!
WHAT'S THAT?!!
SOME NEW FORCE HAS SEIZED US!
IF ANYONE'S GONNA DO ANY DESTROYIN' AROUND HERE, AUNT PETUNIA'S BLUSHIN' BLUE-EYED NEPHEW BENJAMIN IS GONNA GIT FIRST CRACK AT IT... DIG?
BLASTAAR... IT.. IT'S THE THING!
YOU BETCHA LITTLE BOOTIES IT IS, SWEETIE!

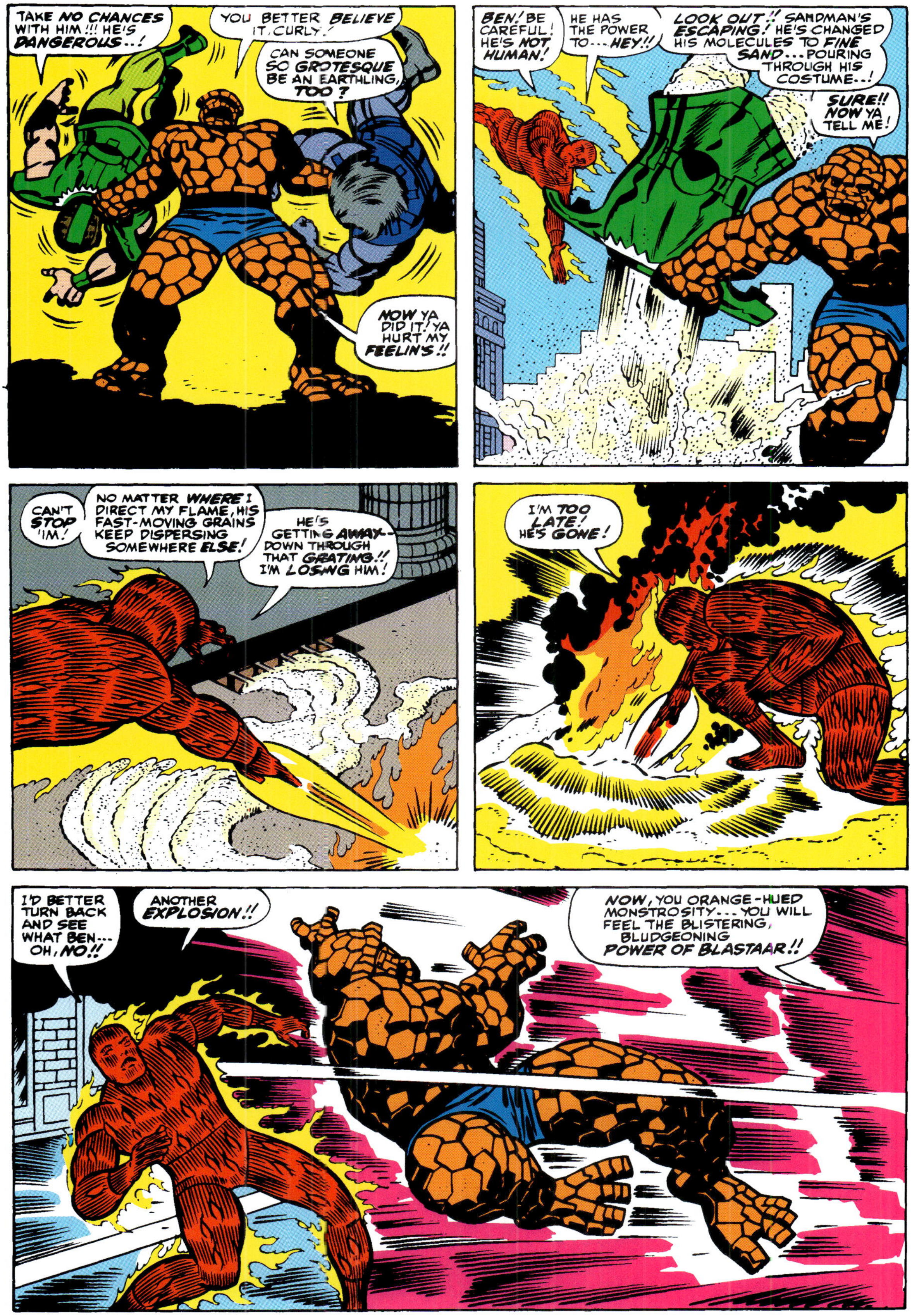
TAKE NO CHANCES WITH HIM!!! HE'S DANGEROUS..!
YOU BETTER BELIEVE IT, CURLY!
CAN SOMEONE SO GROTESQUE BE AN EARTHLING, TOO?
NOW YA DID IT! YA HURT MY FEELIN'S!!
BEN! BE CAREFUL! HE'S NOT HUMAN!
HE HAS THE POWER TO...HEY!!
LOOK OUT!! SANDMAN'S ESCAPING! HE'S CHANGED HIS MOLECULES TO FINE SAND...POURING THROUGH HIS COSTUME..!
SURE!! NOW YA TELL ME!
CAN'T STOP 'IM!
NO MATTER WHERE I DIRECT MY FLAME, HIS FAST-MOVING GRAINS KEEP DISPERSING SOMEWHERE ELSE!
HE'S GETTING AWAY--DOWN THROUGH THAT GRATING!! I'M LOSING HIM!
I'M TOO LATE! HE'S GONE!
I'D BETTER TURN BACK AND SEE WHAT BEN... OH, NO!!
ANOTHER EXPLOSION!!
NOW, YOU ORANGE-HUED MONSTROSITY... YOU WILL FEEL THE BLISTERING, BLUDGEONING POWER OF BLASTAAR!!

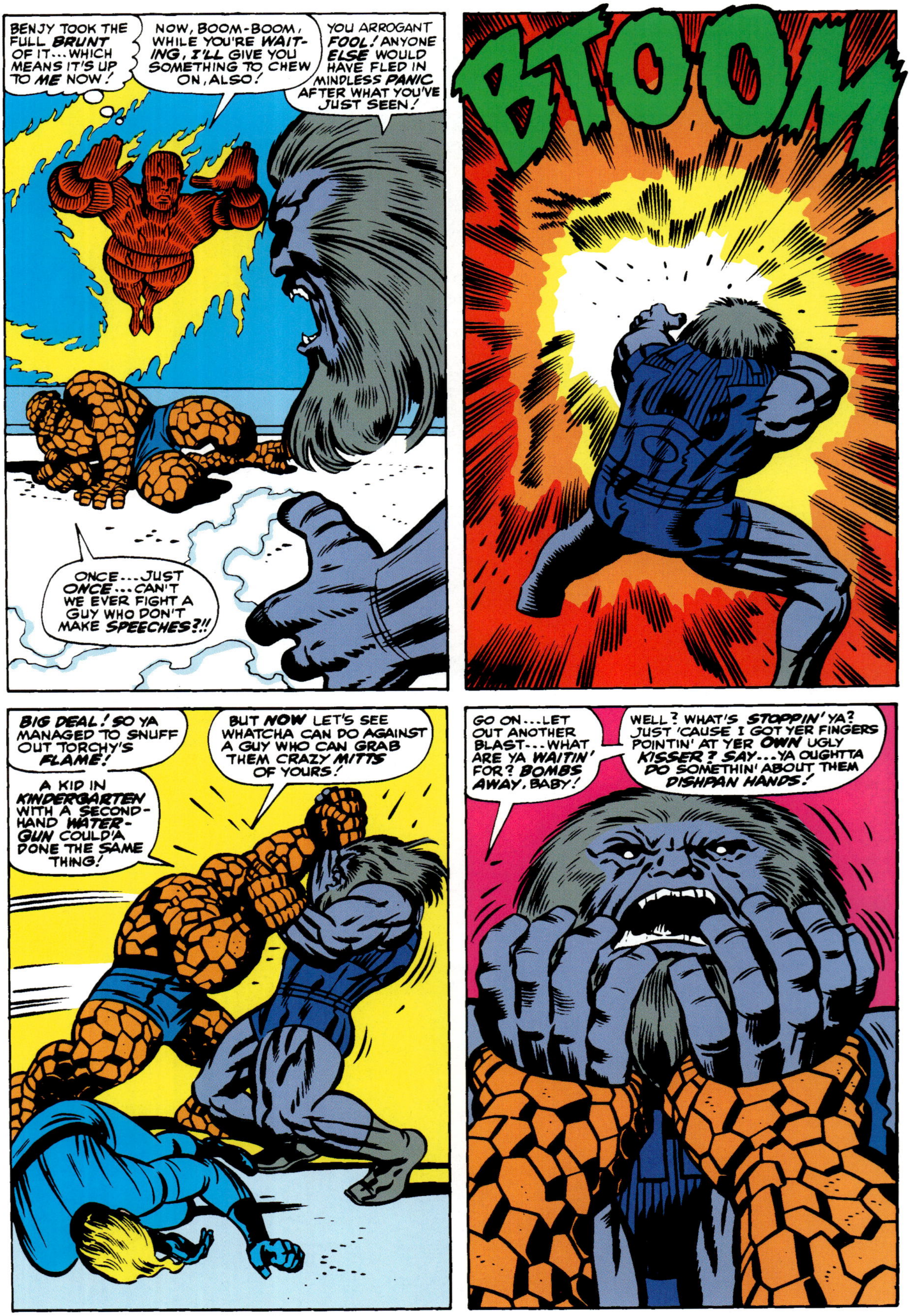
BENJY TOOK THE FULL BRUNT OF IT... WHICH MEANS IT'S UP TO ME NOW!
NOW, BOOM-BOOM, WHILE YOU'RE WAIT-ING, I'LL GIVE YOU SOMETHING TO CHEW ON, ALSO!
YOU ARROGANT FOOL! ANYONE ELSE WOULD HAVE FLED IN MINDLESS PANIC AFTER WHAT YOU'VE JUST SEEN!
ONCE...JUST ONCE...CAN'T WE EVER FIGHT A GUY WHO DON'T MAKE SPEECHES?!!
BTOOM
BIG DEAL! SO YA MANAGED TO SNUFF OUT TORCHY'S FLAME!
A KID IN KINDERGARTEN WITH A SECOND-HAND WATER-GUN COULD'A DONE THE SAME THING!
BUT NOW LET'S SEE WHATCHA CAN DO AGAINST A GUY WHO CAN GRAB THEM CRAZY MITTS OF YOURS!
GO ON...LET OUT ANOTHER BLAST...WHAT ARE YA WAITIN' FOR? BOMBS AWAY, BABY!
WELL? WHAT'S STOPPIN' YA? JUST 'CAUSE I GOT YER FINGERS POINTIN' AT YER OWN UGLY KISSER? SAY...YA OUGHTTA DO SOMETHIN' ABOUT THEM DISHPAN HANDS!

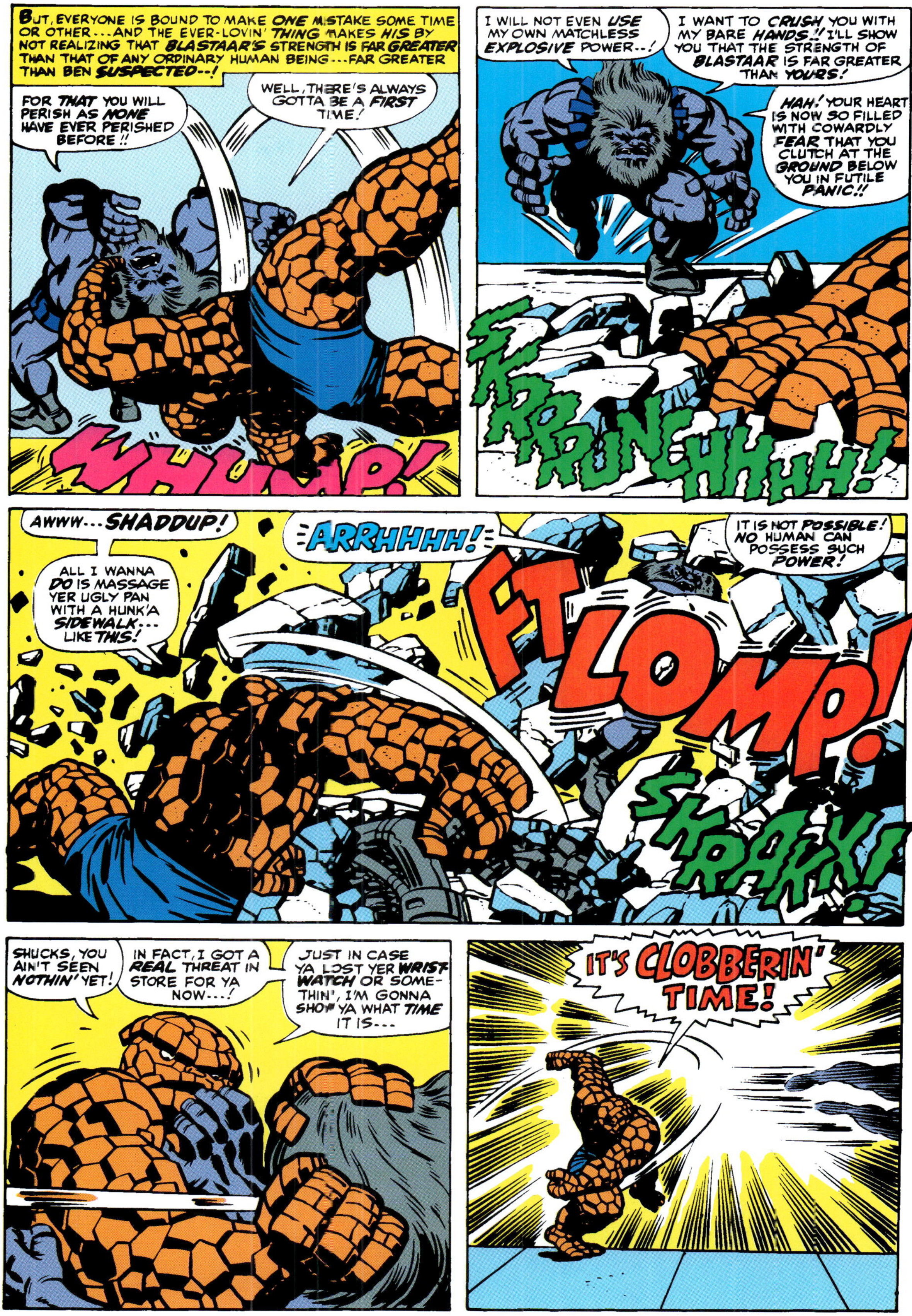
BUT, EVERYONE IS BOUND TO MAKE ONE MISTAKE SOME TIME OR OTHER...AND THE EVER-LOVIN' THING MAKES HIS BY NOT REALIZING THAT BLASTAAR'S STRENGTH IS FAR GREATER THAN THAT OF ANY ORDINARY HUMAN BEING...FAR GREATER THAN BEN SUSPECTED--!
FOR THAT YOU WILL PERISH AS NONE HAVE EVER PERISHED BEFORE!!
WELL, THERE'S ALWAYS GOTTA BE A FIRST TIME!
WHUMP!
I WILL NOT EVEN USE MY OWN MATCHLESS EXPLOSIVE POWER--!
I WANT TO CRUSH YOU WITH MY BARE HANDS!! I'LL SHOW YOU THAT THE STRENGTH OF BLASTAAR IS FAR GREATER THAN YOURS!
HAH! YOUR HEART IS NOW SO FILLED WITH COWARDLY FEAR THAT YOU CLUTCH AT THE GROUND BELOW YOU IN FUTILE PANIC!!
KRRRUNCHHHHH!
AWWW...SHADDUP!
ALL I WANNA DO IS MASSAGE YER UGLY PAN WITH A HUNK'A SIDEWALK...LIKE THIS!
ARRHHHH!
IT IS NOT POSSIBLE! NO HUMAN CAN POSSESS SUCH POWER!
FTLOMP!
SKRAKK!
SHUCKS, YOU AIN'T SEEN NOTHIN' YET!
IN FACT, I GOT A REAL THREAT IN STORE FOR YA NOW---!
JUST IN CASE YA LOST YER WRIST WATCH OR SOMETHIN', I'M GONNA SHOW YA WHAT TIME IT IS---
IT'S CLOBBERIN' TIME!

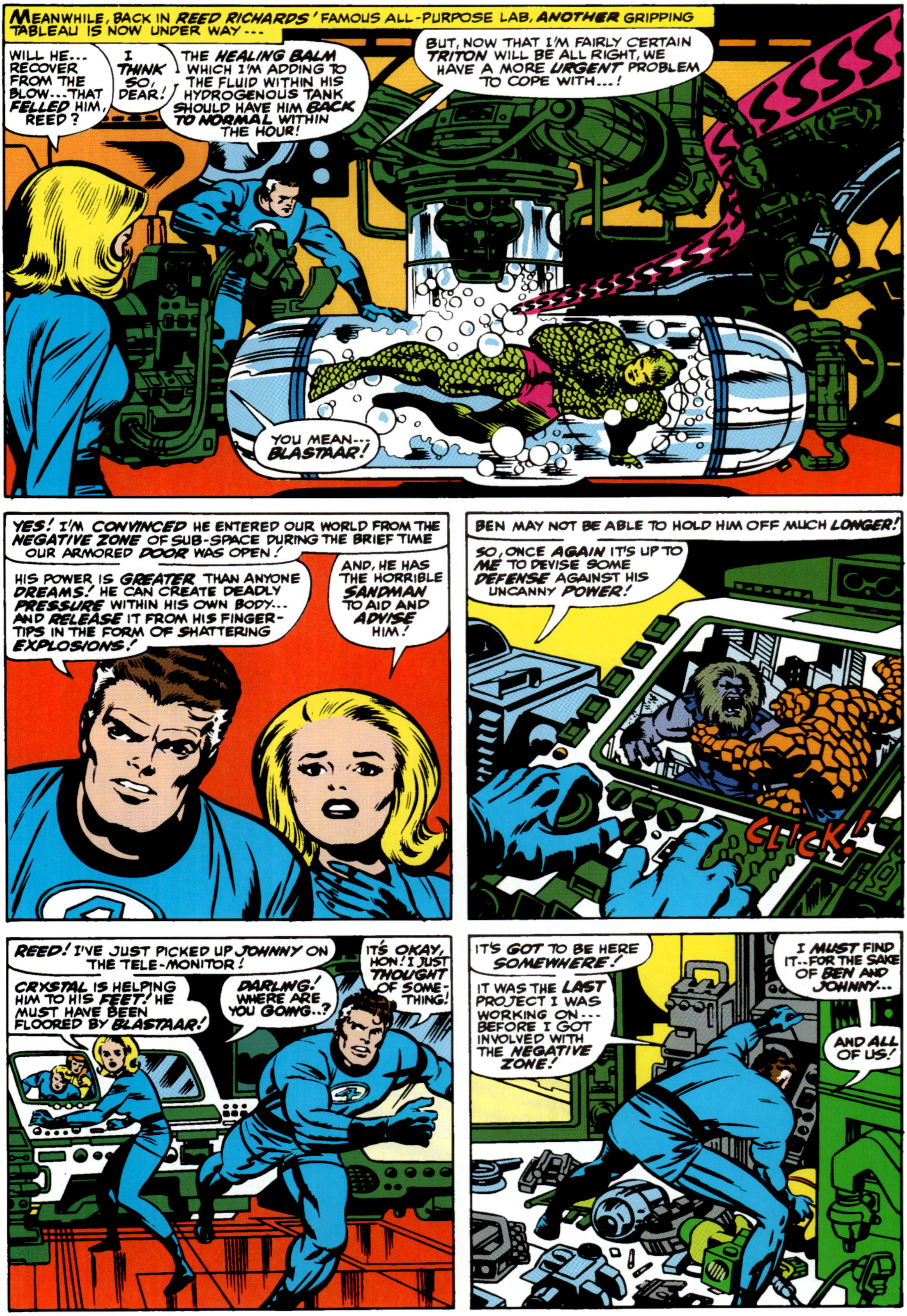
MEANWHILE, BACK IN REED RICHARDS' FAMOUS ALL-PURPOSE LAB, ANOTHER GRIPPING TABLEAU IS NOW UNDER WAY---
WILL HE... RECOVER FROM THE BLOW---THAT FELLED HIM, REED?
I THINK SO, DEAR!
THE HEALING BALM WHICH I'M ADDING TO THE FLUID WITHIN HIS HYDROGENOUS TANK SHOULD HAVE HIM BACK TO NORMAL WITHIN THE HOUR!
BUT, NOW THAT I'M FAIRLY CERTAIN TRITON WILL BE ALL RIGHT, WE HAVE A MORE URGENT PROBLEM TO COPE WITH...!
YOU MEAN--- BLASTAAR!
YES! I'M CONVINCED HE ENTERED OUR WORLD FROM THE NEGATIVE ZONE OF SUB-SPACE DURING THE BRIEF TIME OUR ARMORED DOOR WAS OPEN!
HIS POWER IS GREATER THAN ANYONE DREAMS! HE CAN CREATE DEADLY PRESSURE WITHIN HIS OWN BODY... AND RELEASE IT FROM HIS FINGER-TIPS IN THE FORM OF SHATTERING EXPLOSIONS!
AND, HE HAS THE HORRIBLE SANDMAN TO AID AND ADVISE HIM!
BEN MAY NOT BE ABLE TO HOLD HIM OFF MUCH LONGER!
SO, ONCE AGAIN IT'S UP TO ME TO DEVISE SOME DEFENSE AGAINST HIS UNCANNY POWER!
CLICK!
REED! I'VE JUST PICKED UP JOHNNY ON THE TELE-MONITOR!
CRYSTAL IS HELPING HIM TO HIS FEET! HE MUST HAVE BEEN FLOORED BY BLASTAAR!
DARLING! WHERE ARE YOU GOING..?
IT'S OKAY, HON! I JUST THOUGHT OF SOME-THING!
IT'S GOT TO BE HERE SOMEWHERE!
IT WAS THE LAST PROJECT I WAS WORKING ON--- BEFORE I GOT INVOLVED WITH THE NEGATIVE ZONE!
I MUST FIND IT..FOR THE SAKE OF BEN AND JOHNNY...
AND ALL OF US!

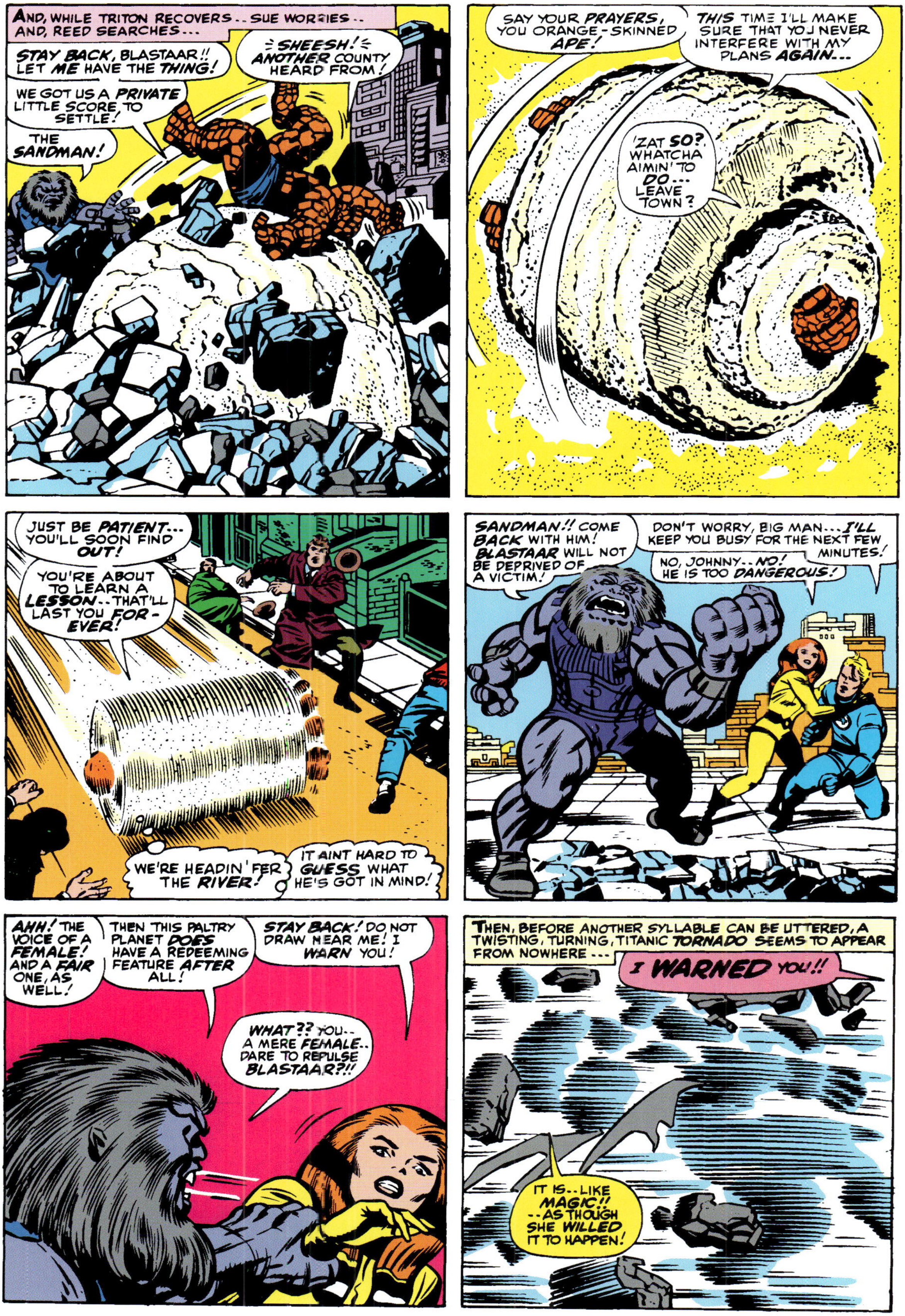
AND, WHILE TRITON RECOVERS.. SUE WORRIES.. AND, REED SEARCHES...
STAY BACK, BLASTAAR!! LET ME HAVE THE THING!
WE GOT US A PRIVATE LITTLE SCORE TO SETTLE!
SHEESH! ANOTHER COUNTY HEARD FROM!
THE SANDMAN!
SAY YOUR PRAYERS, YOU ORANGE-SKINNED APE!
THIS TIME I'LL MAKE SURE THAT YOU NEVER INTERFERE WITH MY PLANS AGAIN...
'ZAT SO? WHATCHA AIMIN' TO DO... LEAVE TOWN?
JUST BE PATIENT... YOU'LL SOON FIND OUT!
YOU'RE ABOUT TO LEARN A LESSON..THAT'LL LAST YOU FOR-EVER!
WE'RE HEADIN' FER THE RIVER!
IT AINT HARD TO GUESS WHAT HE'S GOT IN MIND!
SANDMAN!! COME BACK WITH HIM! BLASTAAR WILL NOT BE DEPRIVED OF A VICTIM!
DON'T WORRY, BIG MAN...I'LL KEEP YOU BUSY FOR THE NEXT FEW MINUTES!
NO, JOHNNY..NO! HE IS TOO DANGEROUS!
AHH! THE VOICE OF A FEMALE! AND A FAIR ONE, AS WELL!
THEN THIS PALTRY PLANET DOES HAVE A REDEEMING FEATURE AFTER ALL!
STAY BACK! DO NOT DRAW NEAR ME! I WARN YOU!
WHAT?? YOU.. A MERE FEMALE.. DARE TO REPULSE BLASTAAR?!!
THEN, BEFORE ANOTHER SYLLABLE CAN BE UTTERED, A TWISTING, TURNING, TITANIC TORNADO SEEMS TO APPEAR FROM NOWHERE...
I WARNED YOU!!
IT IS..LIKE MAGIC!! --AS THOUGH SHE WILLED IT TO HAPPEN!

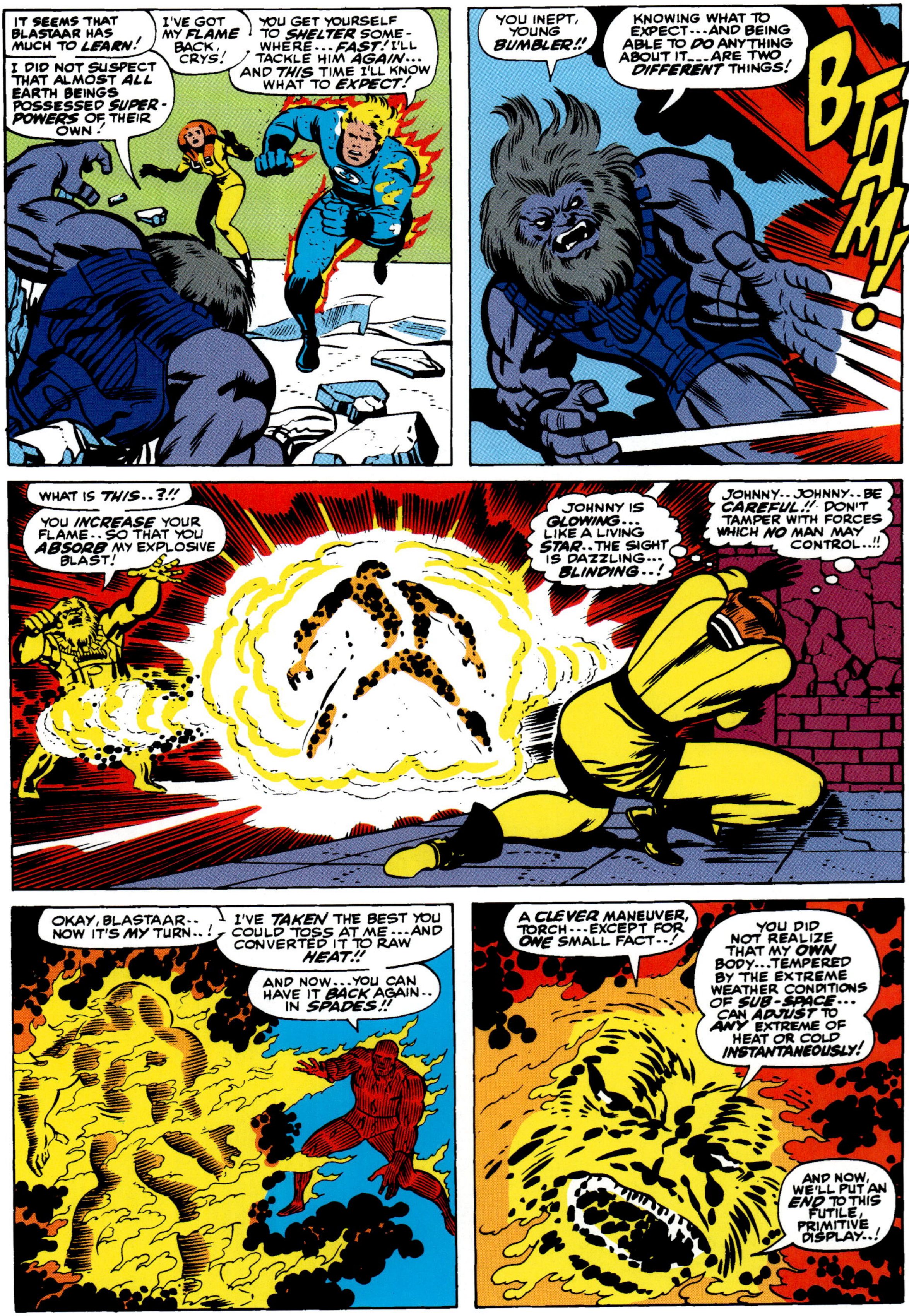
IT SEEMS THAT BLASTAAR HAS MUCH TO LEARN!
I DID NOT SUSPECT THAT ALMOST ALL EARTH BEINGS POSSESSED SUPER-POWERS OF THEIR OWN!
I'VE GOT MY FLAME BACK, CRYS!
YOU GET YOURSELF TO SHELTER SOME-WHERE...FAST! I'LL TACKLE HIM AGAIN...AND THIS TIME I'LL KNOW WHAT TO EXPECT!
YOU INEPT, YOUNG BUMBLER!!
KNOWING WHAT TO EXPECT...AND BEING ABLE TO DO ANYTHING ABOUT IT...ARE TWO DIFFERENT THINGS!
BTAM!
WHAT IS THIS..?!!
YOU INCREASE YOUR FLAME..SO THAT YOU ABSORB MY EXPLOSIVE BLAST!
JOHNNY IS GLOWING...LIKE A LIVING STAR..THE SIGHT IS DAZZLING...BLINDING..!
JOHNNY..JOHNNY..BE CAREFUL!! DON'T TAMPER WITH FORCES WHICH NO MAN MAY CONTROL..!!
OKAY, BLASTAAR..NOW IT'S MY TURN..!
I'VE TAKEN THE BEST YOU COULD TOSS AT ME...AND CONVERTED IT TO RAW HEAT!!
AND NOW...YOU CAN HAVE IT BACK AGAIN..IN SPADES!!
A CLEVER MANEUVER, TORCH...EXCEPT FOR ONE SMALL FACT..!
YOU DID NOT REALIZE THAT MY OWN BODY...TEMPERED BY THE EXTREME WEATHER CONDITIONS OF SUB-SPACE...CAN ADJUST TO ANY EXTREME OF HEAT OR COLD INSTANTANEOUSLY!
AND NOW, WE'LL PUT AN END TO THIS FUTILE, PRIMITIVE DISPLAY..!

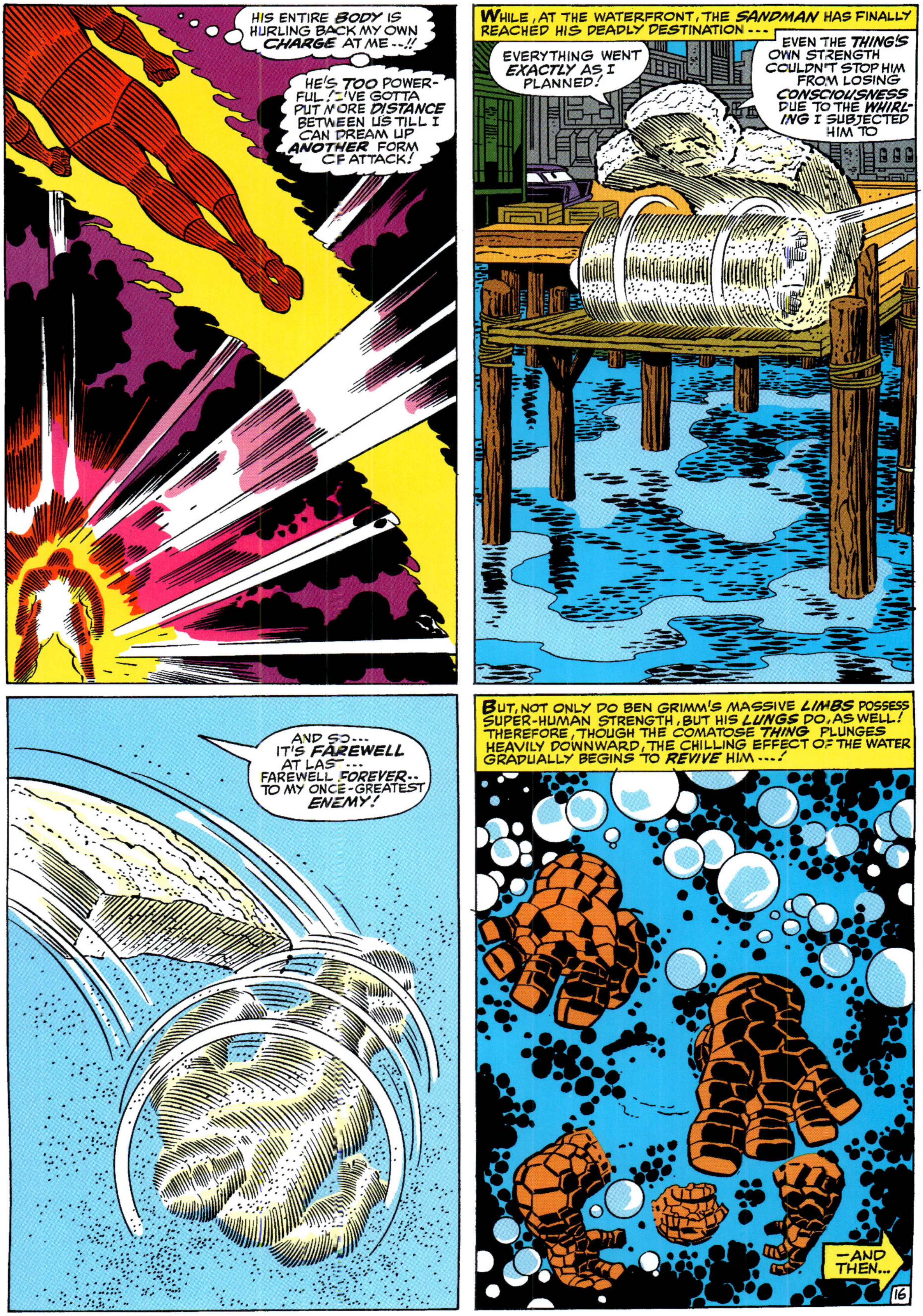
HIS ENTIRE BODY IS HURLING BACK MY OWN CHARGE AT ME--!!
HE'S TOO POWERFUL! I'VE GOTTA PUT MORE DISTANCE BETWEEN US TILL I CAN DREAM UP ANOTHER FORM OF ATTACK!
WHILE, AT THE WATERFRONT, THE SANDMAN HAS FINALLY REACHED HIS DEADLY DESTINATION---
EVERYTHING WENT EXACTLY AS I PLANNED!
EVEN THE THING'S OWN STRENGTH COULDN'T STOP HIM FROM LOSING CONSCIOUSNESS DUE TO THE WHIRLING I SUBJECTED HIM TO
AND SO--- IT'S FAREWELL AT LAST--- FAREWELL FOREVER-- TO MY ONCE-GREATEST ENEMY!
BUT, NOT ONLY DO BEN GRIMM'S MASSIVE LIMBS POSSESS SUPER-HUMAN STRENGTH, BUT HIS LUNGS DO, AS WELL! THEREFORE, THOUGH THE COMATOSE THING PLUNGES HEAVILY DOWNWARD, THE CHILLING EFFECT OF THE WATER GRADUALLY BEGINS TO REVIVE HIM---!
—AND THEN...
16

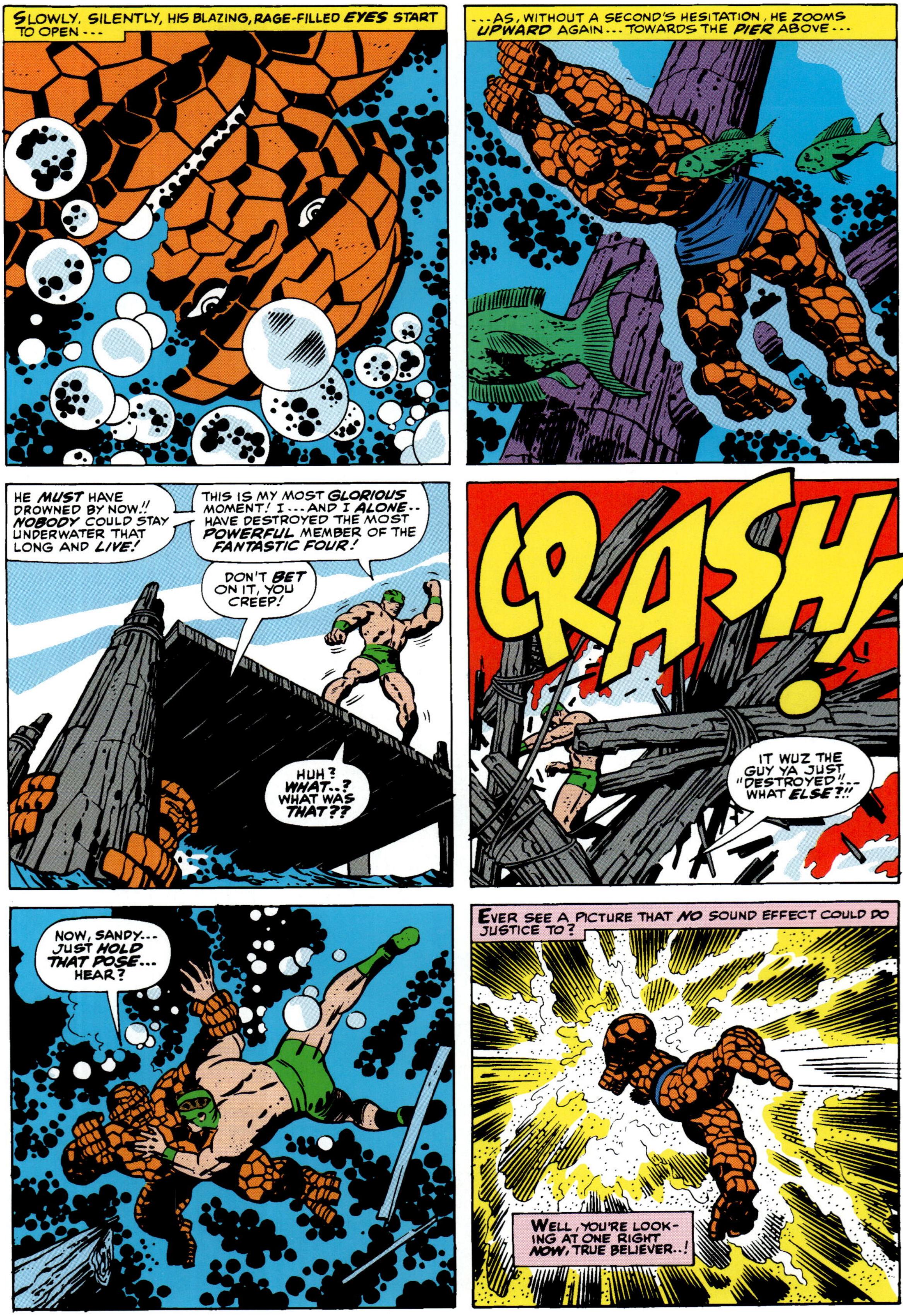
SLOWLY, SILENTLY, HIS BLAZING, RAGE-FILLED EYES START TO OPEN ---
---AS, WITHOUT A SECOND'S HESITATION, HE ZOOMS UPWARD AGAIN--- TOWARDS THE PIER ABOVE---
HE MUST HAVE DROWNED BY NOW!! NOBODY COULD STAY UNDERWATER THAT LONG AND LIVE!
THIS IS MY MOST GLORIOUS MOMENT! I---AND I ALONE-- HAVE DESTROYED THE MOST POWERFUL MEMBER OF THE FANTASTIC FOUR!
DON'T BET ON IT, YOU CREEP!
HUH? WHAT--? WHAT WAS THAT??
CRASH!
IT WUZ THE GUY YA JUST "DESTROYED!"-- WHAT ELSE?!!
NOW, SANDY--- JUST HOLD THAT POSE--- HEAR?
EVER SEE A PICTURE THAT NO SOUND EFFECT COULD DO JUSTICE TO?
WELL, YOU'RE LOOKING AT ONE RIGHT NOW, TRUE BELIEVER--!

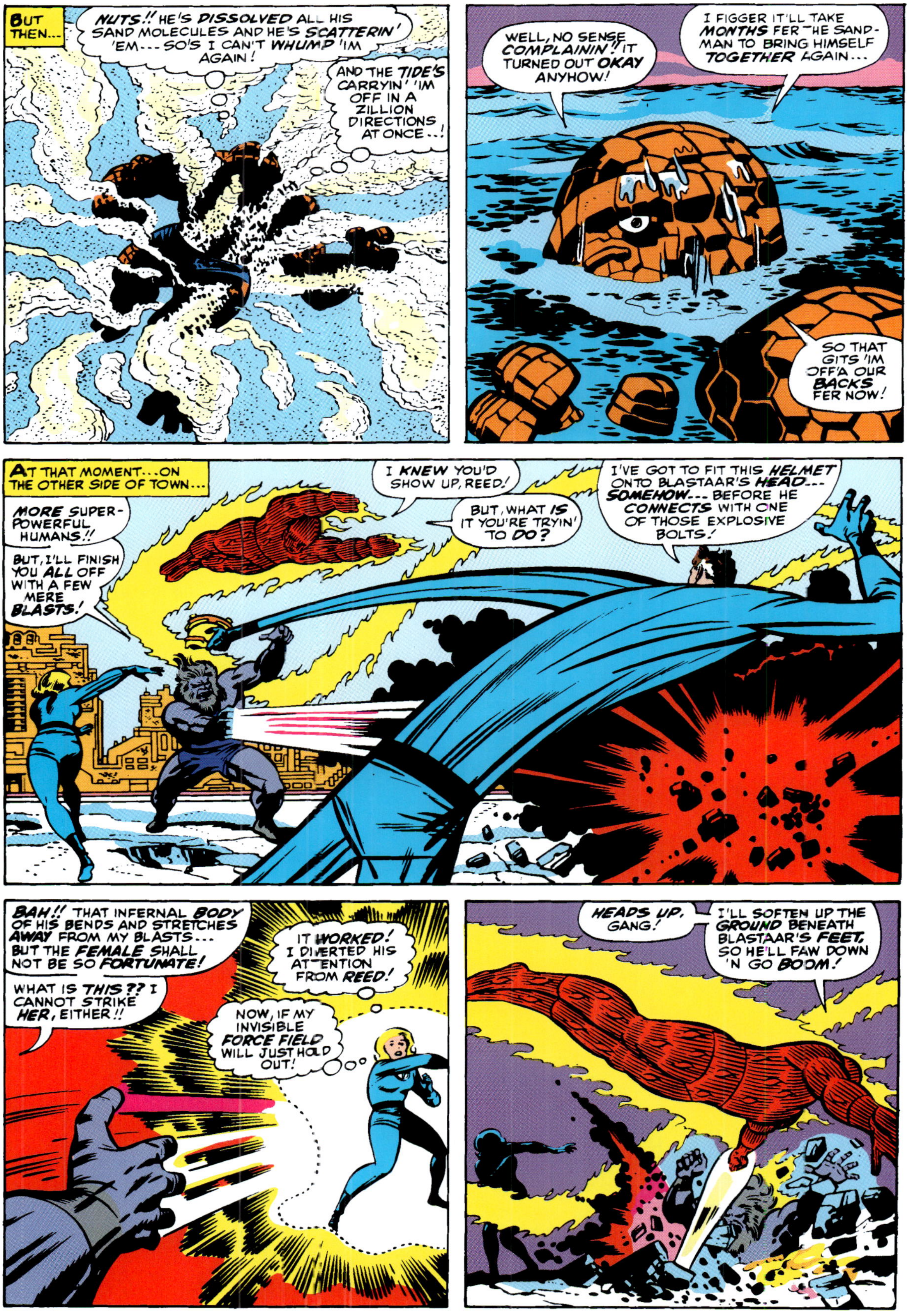
BUT THEN...
NUTS!! HE'S DISSOLVED ALL HIS SAND MOLECULES AND HE'S SCATTERIN' 'EM--- SO'S I CAN'T WHUMP 'IM AGAIN!
AND THE TIDE'S CARRYIN' 'IM OFF IN A ZILLION DIRECTIONS AT ONCE--!
WELL, NO SENSE COMPLAININ'! IT TURNED OUT OKAY ANYHOW!
I FIGGER IT'LL TAKE MONTHS FER THE SAND-MAN TO BRING HIMSELF TOGETHER AGAIN...
SO THAT GITS 'IM OFF'A OUR BACKS FER NOW!
AT THAT MOMENT...ON THE OTHER SIDE OF TOWN...
MORE SUPER-POWERFUL HUMANS!!
BUT, I'LL FINISH YOU ALL OFF WITH A FEW MERE BLASTS!
I KNEW YOU'D SHOW UP, REED!
BUT, WHAT IS IT YOU'RE TRYIN' TO DO?
I'VE GOT TO FIT THIS HELMET ONTO BLASTAAR'S HEAD--- SOMEHOW--- BEFORE HE CONNECTS WITH ONE OF THOSE EXPLOSIVE BOLTS!
BAH!! THAT INFERNAL BODY OF HIS BENDS AND STRETCHES AWAY FROM MY BLASTS... BUT THE FEMALE SHALL NOT BE SO FORTUNATE!
WHAT IS THIS?? I CANNOT STRIKE HER, EITHER!!
IT WORKED! I DIVERTED HIS ATTENTION FROM REED!
NOW, IF MY INVISIBLE FORCE FIELD WILL JUST HOLD OUT!
HEADS UP, GANG!
I'LL SOFTEN UP THE GROUND BENEATH BLASTAAR'S FEET, SO HE'LL FAW DOWN 'N GO BOOM!

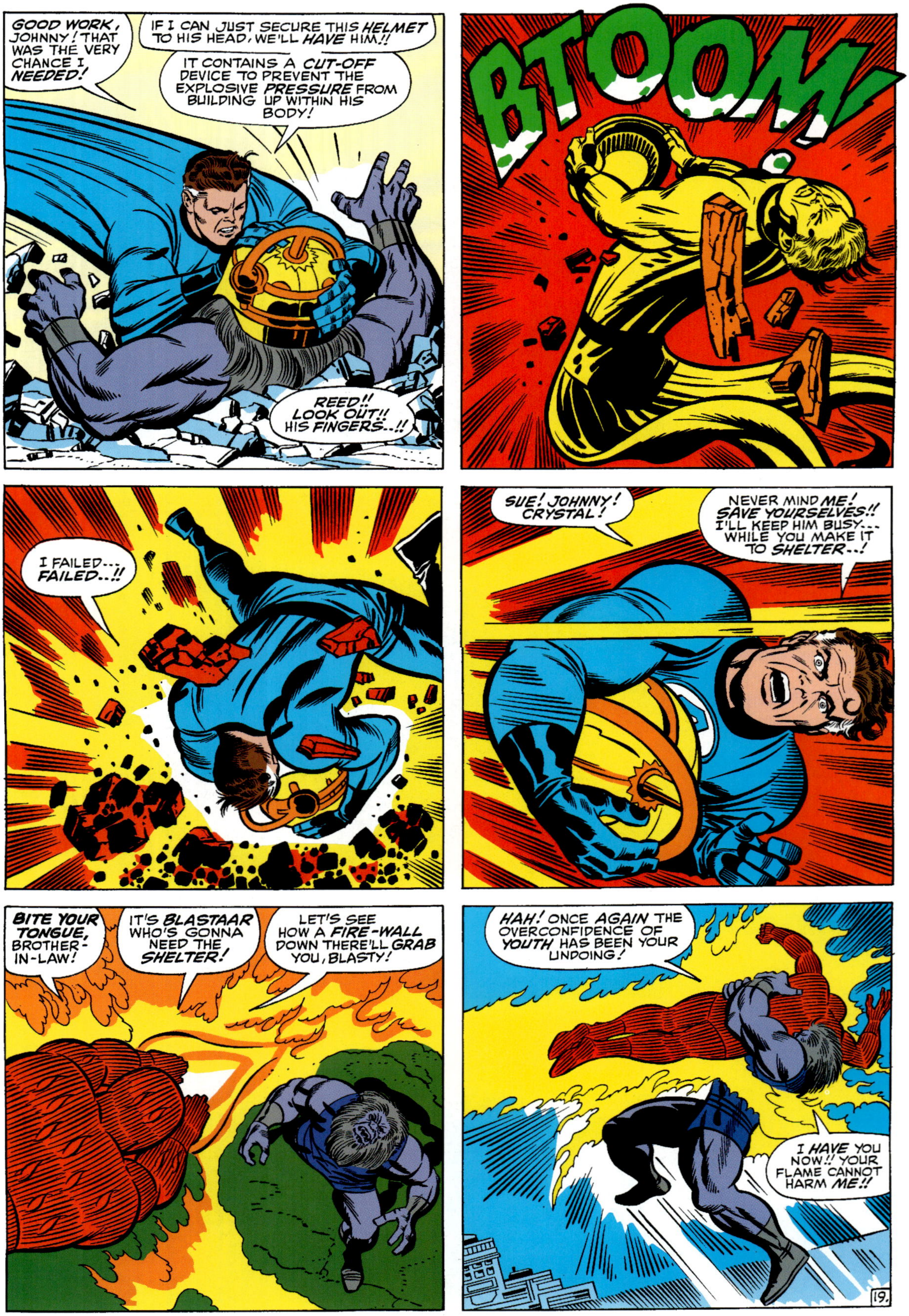
GOOD WORK, JOHNNY! THAT WAS THE VERY CHANCE I NEEDED!
IF I CAN JUST SECURE THIS HELMET TO HIS HEAD, WE'LL HAVE HIM!!
IT CONTAINS A CUT-OFF DEVICE TO PREVENT THE EXPLOSIVE PRESSURE FROM BUILDING UP WITHIN HIS BODY!
REED!! LOOK OUT!! HIS FINGERS..!!
BTOOM!
I FAILED... FAILED..!!
SUE! JOHNNY! CRYSTAL!
NEVER MIND ME! SAVE YOURSELVES!! I'LL KEEP HIM BUSY... WHILE YOU MAKE IT TO SHELTER..!
BITE YOUR TONGUE, BROTHER-IN-LAW!
IT'S BLASTAAR WHO'S GONNA NEED THE SHELTER!
LET'S SEE HOW A FIRE-WALL DOWN THERE'LL GRAB YOU, BLASTY!
HAH! ONCE AGAIN THE OVERCONFIDENCE OF YOUTH HAS BEEN YOUR UNDOING!
I HAVE YOU NOW!! YOUR FLAME CANNOT HARM ME!!
19.

I AM NOT SOME PUNY *HUMAN* WHO CAN BE DRIVEN OFF BY THE POWER OF *FIRE!* I...AM... *BLASTAAR!*

THANKS TO *JOHNNY,* I'VE A *SECOND CHANCE!!*

AND *THIS* TIME-- I'LL *MAKE* IT!

THWUPP!

THERE! BY *CUTTING* OFF THE *PRESSURE BUILD-UP* IN YOUR BODY-- YOU BECOME AS *VULNERABLE* AS *ANY* MAN!

NO! NO--- YOU *CAN'T!* YOU *CAN'T!!*

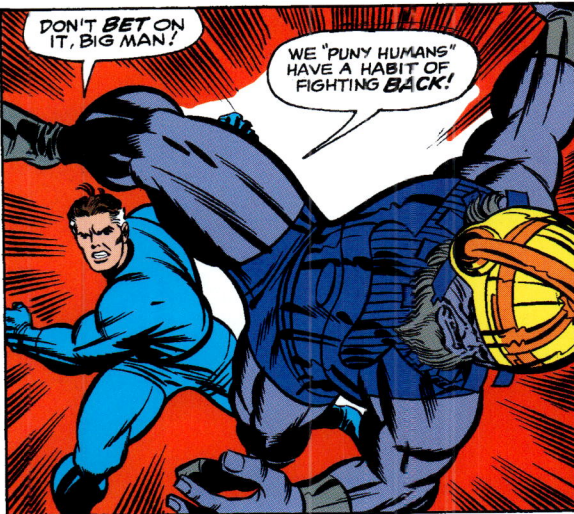

DON'T *BET* ON IT, BIG MAN!

WE "PUNY HUMANS" HAVE A HABIT OF FIGHTING *BACK!*

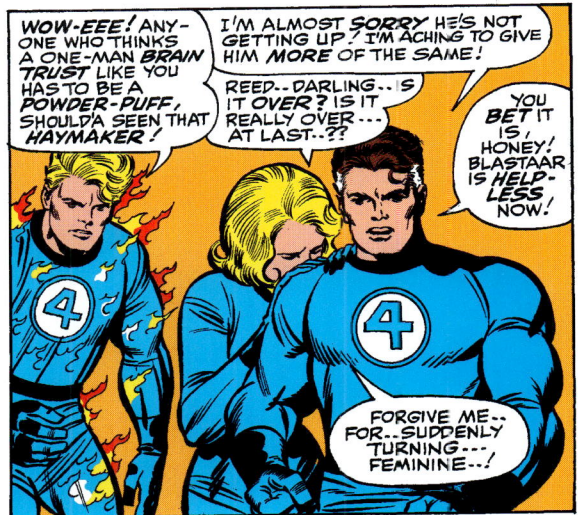

WOW-EEE! ANY-ONE WHO THINKS A ONE-MAN *BRAIN TRUST* LIKE YOU HAS TO BE A *POWDER-PUFF,* SHOULD'A SEEN THAT *HAYMAKER!*

I'M ALMOST *SORRY* HE'S NOT GETTING UP! I'M ACHING TO GIVE HIM *MORE* OF THE SAME!

REED--DARLING-- IS IT *OVER?* IS IT REALLY OVER--- AT *LAST--??*

YOU *BET* IT IS, *HONEY!* BLASTAAR IS *HELP-LESS* NOW!

FORGIVE ME-- FOR--SUDDENLY TURNING--- *FEMININE--!*

NONSENSE, DEAREST! YOU DID YOUR *SHARE* ...WHEN IT *COUNTED!*

NOW, MUCH AS I WANT TO *STUDY* BLASTAAR... WE'VE GOT TO GET HIM *BACK*-- BACK TO THE *NEGATIVE ZONE*...TO HIS OWN WORLD!

WHAT *GIVES,* STRETCHO? LOOKS LIKE I MISSED ALL THE *FUN!*

YOU'RE *ALONE!* WHAT HAPPENED TO *SAND-MAN?*

HE'S *KAPUT* FER A WHILE! I'D'A BEEN HERE *SOONER,* BUT YA CAN NEVER FIND A *CAB* WHEN YA NEED ONE!

BEN, WE'VE GOT TO TAKE BLASTAAR BACK--TO THE *SUB-SPACE* LAB!

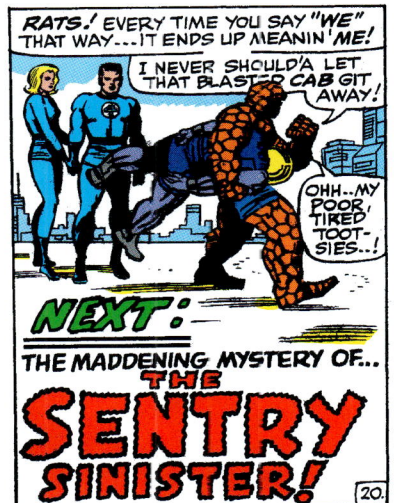

RATS! EVERY TIME YOU SAY *"WE"* THAT WAY---IT ENDS UP MEANIN' *ME!* I NEVER SHOULD'A LET THAT BLASTED *CAB* GIT AWAY!

OHH--MY POOR, TIRED TOOT-SIES--!

NEXT:

THE MADDENING MYSTERY OF...

THE SENTRY SINISTER!

20.

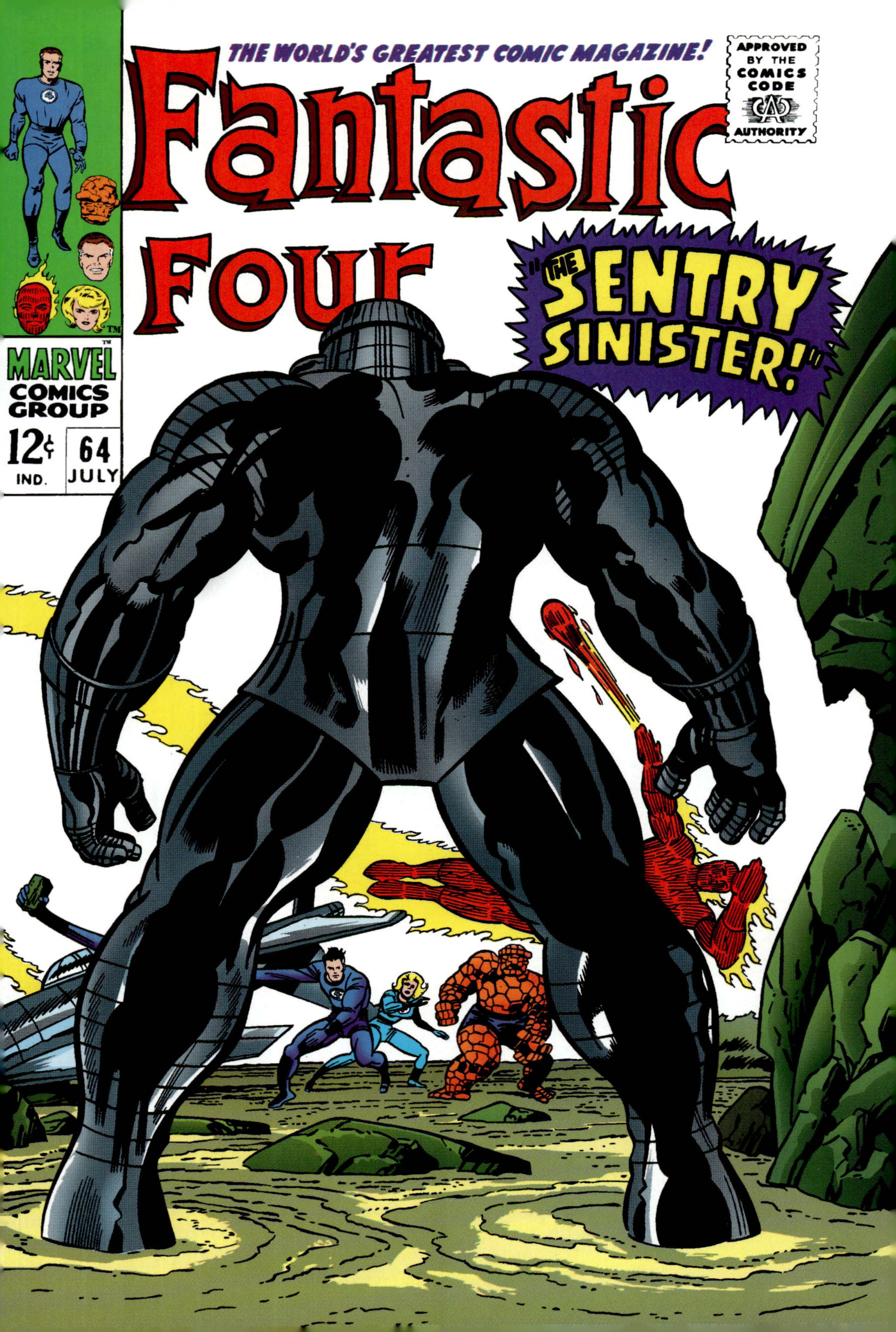
THE WORLD'S GREATEST COMIC MAGAZINE!
Fantastic Four
APPROVED BY THE COMICS CODE AUTHORITY
MARVEL COMICS GROUP
12¢ IND.
64 JULY
"THE SENTRY SINISTER!"

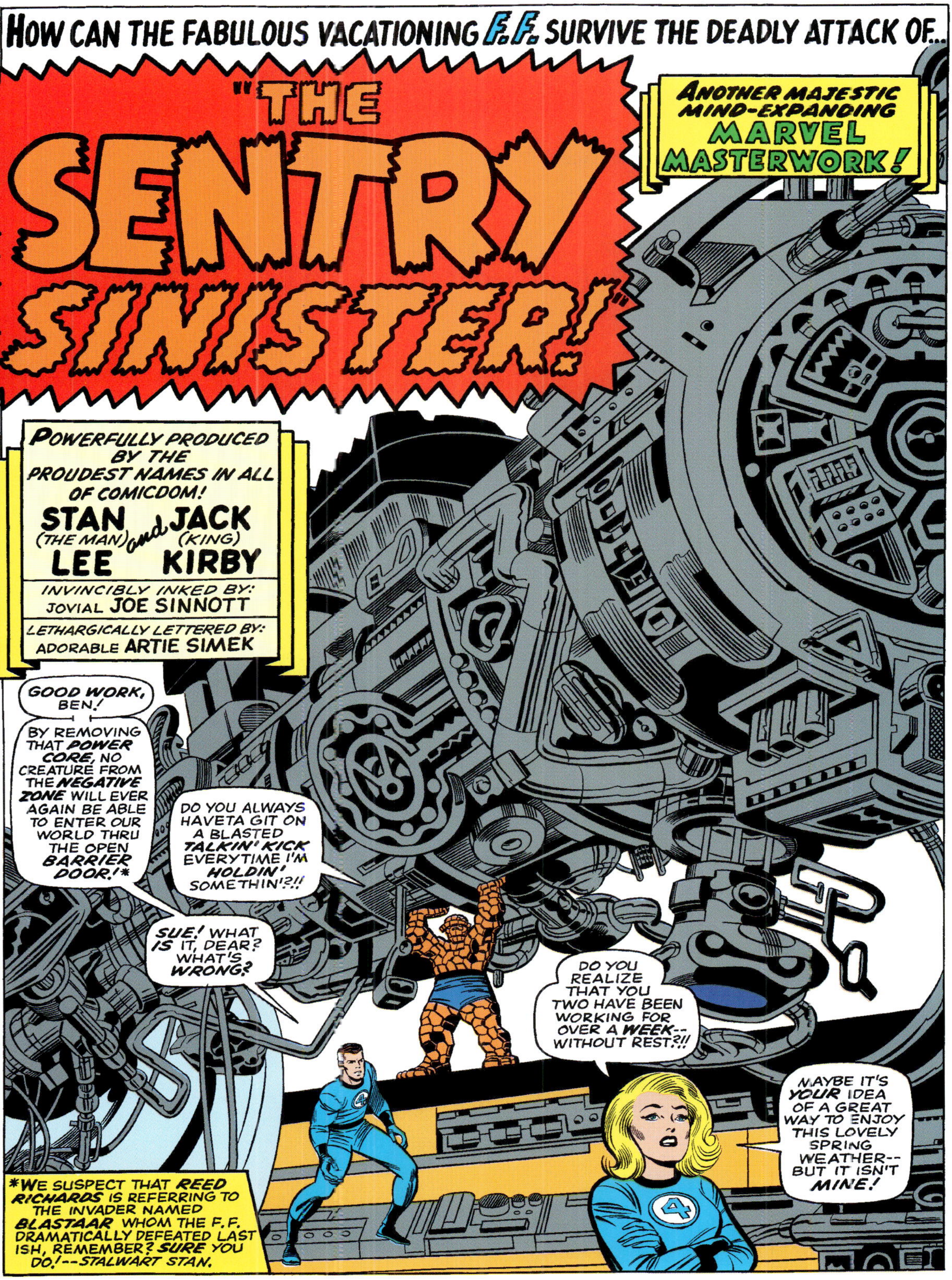

HOW CAN THE FABULOUS VACATIONING F.F. SURVIVE THE DEADLY ATTACK OF...
"THE SENTRY SINISTER!"
ANOTHER MAJESTIC MIND-EXPANDING MARVEL MASTERWORK!
POWERFULLY PRODUCED BY THE PROUDEST NAMES IN ALL OF COMICDOM! STAN (THE MAN) LEE and JACK (KING) KIRBY
INVINCIBLY INKED BY: JOVIAL JOE SINNOTT
LETHARGICALLY LETTERED BY: ADORABLE ARTIE SIMEK
GOOD WORK, BEN!
BY REMOVING THAT POWER CORE, NO CREATURE FROM THE NEGATIVE ZONE WILL EVER AGAIN BE ABLE TO ENTER OUR WORLD THRU THE OPEN BARRIER DOOR!*
DO YOU ALWAYS HAVETA GIT ON A BLASTED TALKIN' KICK EVERYTIME I'M HOLDIN' SOMETHIN'?!!
SUE! WHAT IS IT, DEAR? WHAT'S WRONG?
DO YOU REALIZE THAT YOU TWO HAVE BEEN WORKING FOR OVER A WEEK-- WITHOUT REST?!!
MAYBE IT'S YOUR IDEA OF A GREAT WAY TO ENJOY THIS LOVELY SPRING WEATHER-- BUT IT ISN'T MINE!
*WE SUSPECT THAT REED RICHARDS IS REFERRING TO THE INVADER NAMED BLASTAAR WHOM THE F.F. DRAMATICALLY DEFEATED LAST ISH, REMEMBER? SURE YOU DO!--STALWART STAN.

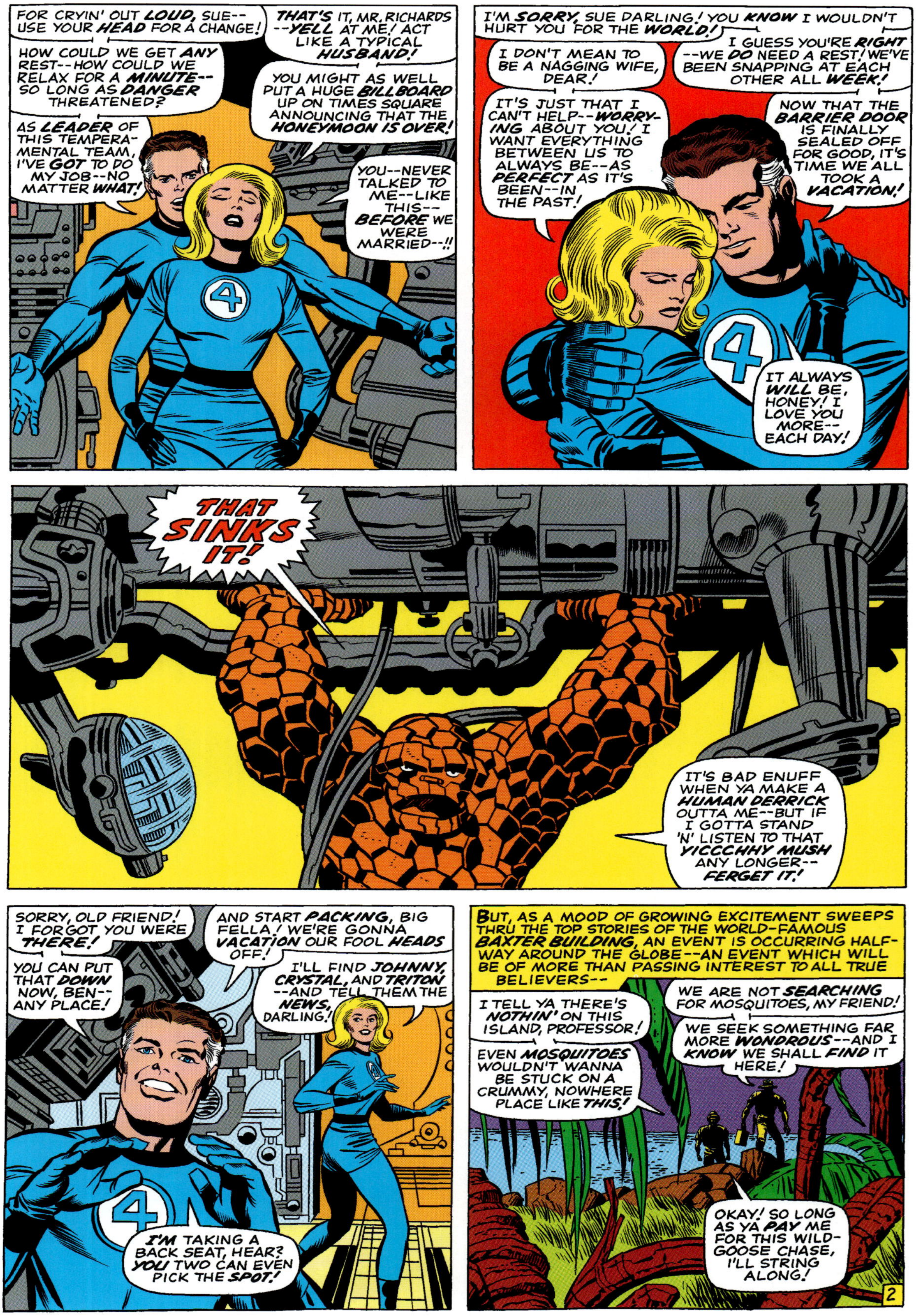
FOR CRYIN' OUT LOUD, SUE-- USE YOUR HEAD FOR A CHANGE!
HOW COULD WE GET ANY REST--HOW COULD WE RELAX FOR A MINUTE-- SO LONG AS DANGER THREATENED?
AS LEADER OF THIS TEMPERAMENTAL TEAM, I'VE GOT TO DO MY JOB--NO MATTER WHAT!
THAT'S IT, MR. RICHARDS --YELL AT ME! ACT LIKE A TYPICAL HUSBAND!
YOU MIGHT AS WELL PUT A HUGE BILLBOARD UP ON TIMES SQUARE ANNOUNCING THAT THE HONEYMOON IS OVER!
YOU--NEVER TALKED TO ME--LIKE THIS-- BEFORE WE WERE MARRIED--!!
I'M SORRY, SUE DARLING! YOU KNOW I WOULDN'T HURT YOU FOR THE WORLD!
I DON'T MEAN TO BE A NAGGING WIFE, DEAR!
IT'S JUST THAT I CAN'T HELP--WORRYING ABOUT YOU! I WANT EVERYTHING BETWEEN US TO ALWAYS BE--AS PERFECT AS IT'S BEEN--IN THE PAST!
I GUESS YOU'RE RIGHT --WE DO NEED A REST! WE'VE BEEN SNAPPING AT EACH OTHER ALL WEEK!
NOW THAT THE BARRIER DOOR IS FINALLY SEALED OFF FOR GOOD, IT'S TIME WE ALL TOOK A VACATION!
IT ALWAYS WILL BE, HONEY! I LOVE YOU MORE-- EACH DAY!
THAT SINKS IT!
IT'S BAD ENUFF WHEN YA MAKE A HUMAN DERRICK OUTTA ME--BUT IF I GOTTA STAND 'N' LISTEN TO THAT YICCCHHY MUSH ANY LONGER-- FERGET IT!
SORRY, OLD FRIEND! I FORGOT YOU WERE THERE!
YOU CAN PUT THAT DOWN NOW, BEN-- ANY PLACE!
AND START PACKING, BIG FELLA! WE'RE GONNA VACATION OUR FOOL HEADS OFF!
I'LL FIND JOHNNY, CRYSTAL, AND TRITON --AND TELL THEM THE NEWS, DARLING!
I'M TAKING A BACK SEAT, HEAR? YOU! TWO CAN EVEN PICK THE SPOT!
BUT, AS A MOOD OF GROWING EXCITEMENT SWEEPS THRU THE TOP STORIES OF THE WORLD-FAMOUS BAXTER BUILDING, AN EVENT IS OCCURRING HALF-WAY AROUND THE GLOBE--AN EVENT WHICH WILL BE OF MORE THAN PASSING INTEREST TO ALL TRUE BELIEVERS--
I TELL YA THERE'S NOTHIN' ON THIS ISLAND, PROFESSOR!
EVEN MOSQUITOES WOULDN'T WANNA BE STUCK ON A CRUMMY, NOWHERE PLACE LIKE THIS!
WE ARE NOT SEARCHING FOR MOSQUITOES, MY FRIEND!
WE SEEK SOMETHING FAR MORE WONDROUS--AND I KNOW WE SHALL FIND IT HERE!
OKAY! SO LONG AS YA PAY ME FOR THIS WILD-GOOSE CHASE, I'LL STRING ALONG!
2

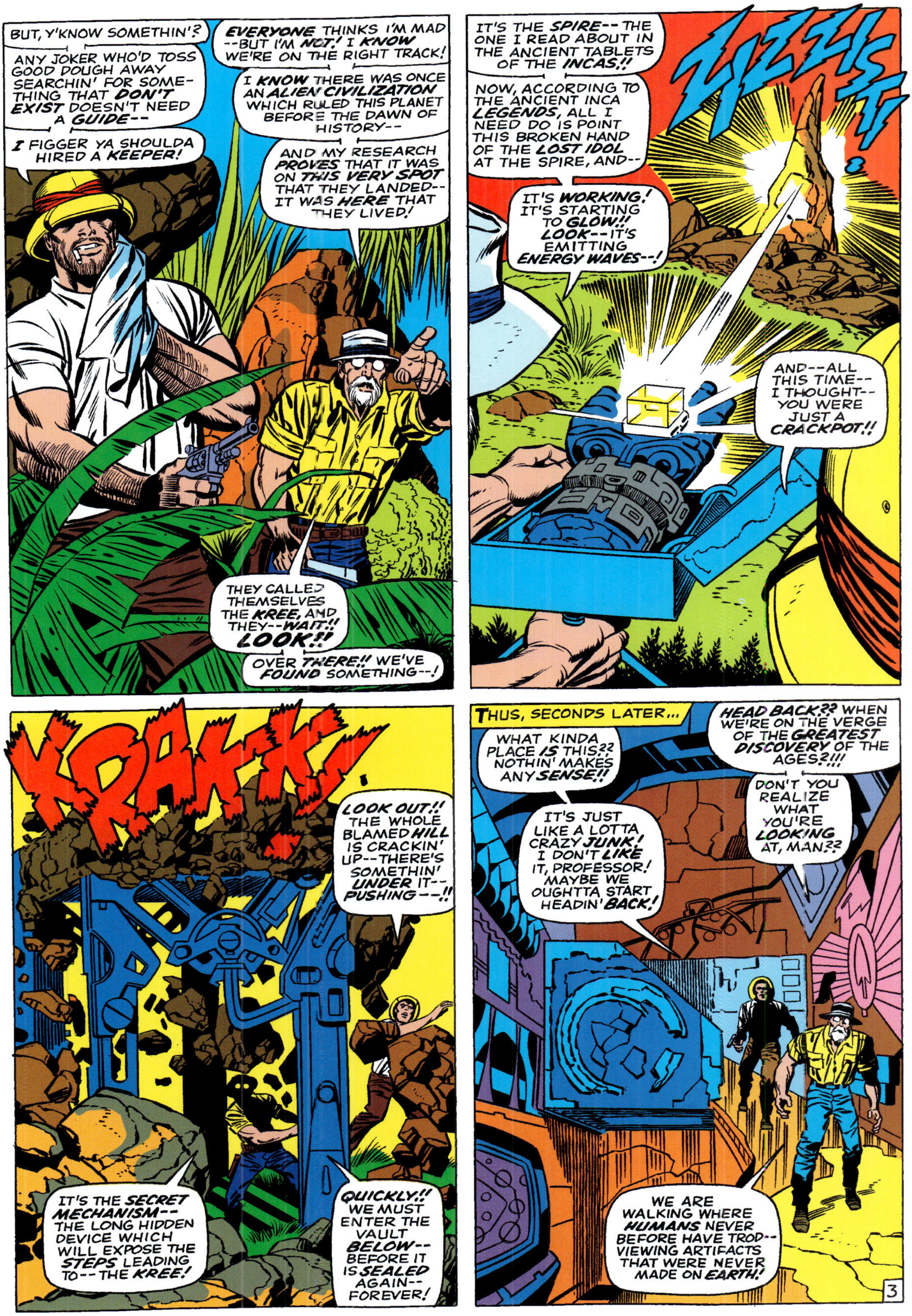
BUT, Y'KNOW SOMETHIN'?
ANY JOKER WHO'D TOSS GOOD DOUGH AWAY SEARCHIN' FOR SOMETHING THAT DON'T EXIST DOESN'T NEED A GUIDE--
I FIGGER YA SHOULDA HIRED A KEEPER!
EVERYONE THINKS I'M MAD --BUT I'M NOT! I KNOW WE'RE ON THE RIGHT TRACK!
I KNOW THERE WAS ONCE AN ALIEN CIVILIZATION WHICH RULED THIS PLANET BEFORE THE DAWN OF HISTORY--
AND MY RESEARCH PROVES THAT IT WAS ON THIS VERY SPOT THAT THEY LANDED-- IT WAS HERE THAT THEY LIVED!
THEY CALLED THEMSELVES THE KREE, AND THEY--WAIT!! LOOK!!
OVER THERE!! WE'VE FOUND SOMETHING--!
IT'S THE SPIRE-- THE ONE I READ ABOUT IN THE ANCIENT TABLETS OF THE INCAS!!
NOW, ACCORDING TO THE ANCIENT INCA LEGENDS, ALL I NEED DO IS POINT THIS BROKEN HAND OF THE LOST IDOL AT THE SPIRE, AND--
ZZZZISST!
IT'S WORKING! IT'S STARTING TO GLOW!! LOOK--IT'S EMITTING ENERGY WAVES--!
AND--ALL THIS TIME-- I THOUGHT-- YOU WERE JUST A CRACKPOT!!
KRAKK!
LOOK OUT!! THE WHOLE BLAMED HILL IS CRACKIN' UP--THERE'S SOMETHIN' UNDER IT-- PUSHING--!!
IT'S THE SECRET MECHANISM-- THE LONG HIDDEN DEVICE WHICH WILL EXPOSE THE STEPS LEADING TO-- THE KREE!
QUICKLY!! WE MUST ENTER THE VAULT BELOW-- BEFORE IT IS SEALED AGAIN-- FOREVER!
THUS, SECONDS LATER...
WHAT KINDA PLACE IS THIS?? NOTHIN' MAKES ANY SENSE!!
HEAD BACK?? WHEN WE'RE ON THE VERGE OF THE GREATEST DISCOVERY OF THE AGES?!!!
IT'S JUST LIKE A LOTTA CRAZY JUNK! I DON'T LIKE IT, PROFESSOR! MAYBE WE OUGHTTA START HEADIN' BACK!
DON'T YOU REALIZE WHAT YOU'RE LOOKING AT, MAN??
WE ARE WALKING WHERE HUMANS NEVER BEFORE HAVE TROD-- VIEWING ARTIFACTS THAT WERE NEVER MADE ON EARTH!
3

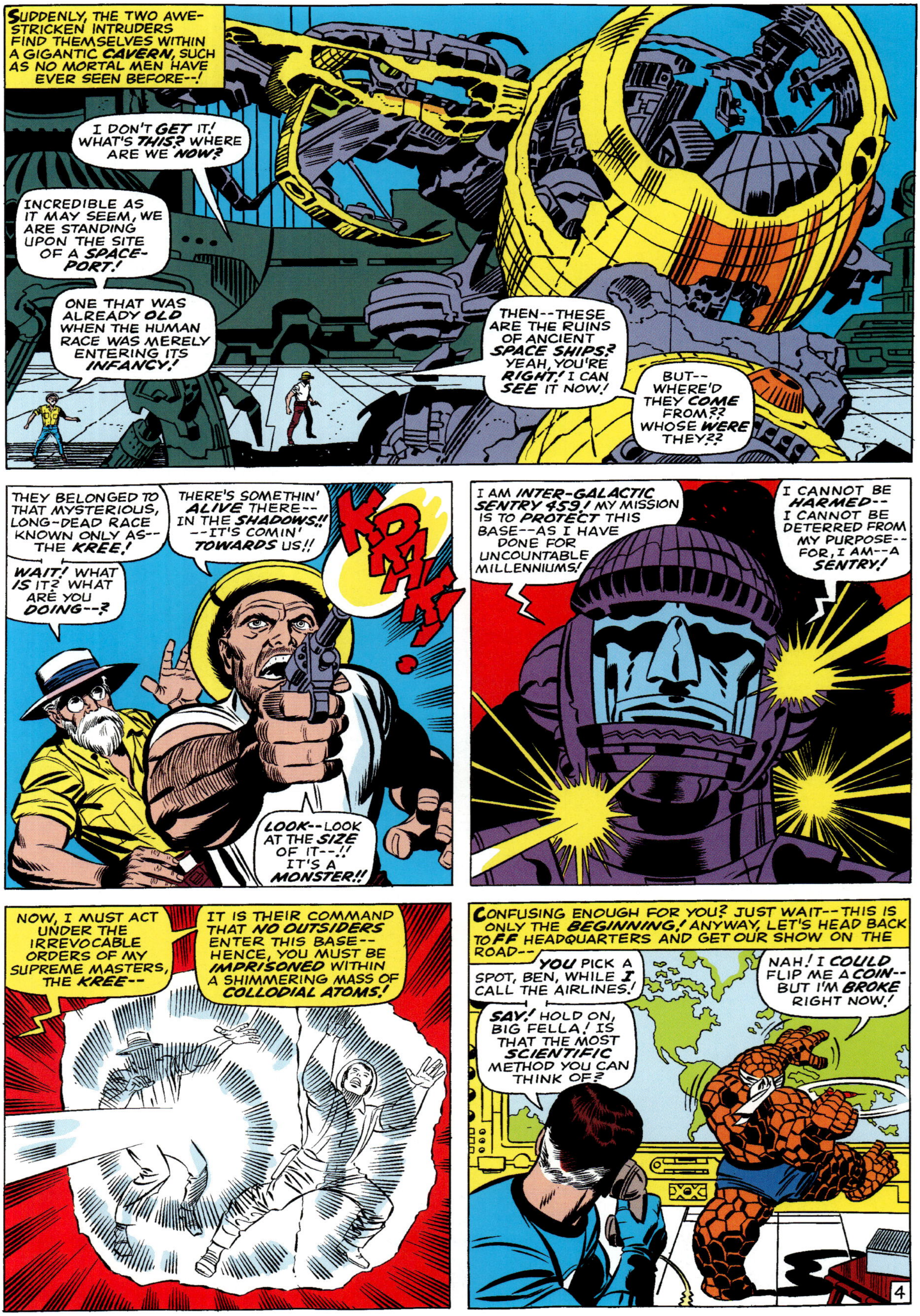
SUDDENLY, THE TWO AWE-STRICKEN INTRUDERS FIND THEMSELVES WITHIN A GIGANTIC CAVERN, SUCH AS NO MORTAL MEN HAVE EVER SEEN BEFORE--!
I DON'T GET IT! WHAT'S THIS? WHERE ARE WE NOW?
INCREDIBLE AS IT MAY SEEM, WE ARE STANDING UPON THE SITE OF A SPACE-PORT!
ONE THAT WAS ALREADY OLD WHEN THE HUMAN RACE WAS MERELY ENTERING ITS INFANCY!
THEN--THESE ARE THE RUINS OF ANCIENT SPACE SHIPS? YEAH, YOU'RE RIGHT! I CAN SEE IT NOW!
BUT--WHERE'D THEY COME FROM?? WHOSE WERE THEY??
THEY BELONGED TO THAT MYSTERIOUS, LONG-DEAD RACE KNOWN ONLY AS--THE KREE!
THERE'S SOMETHIN' ALIVE THERE-- IN THE SHADOWS!! --IT'S COMIN' TOWARDS US!!
KRAK!
WAIT! WHAT IS IT? WHAT ARE YOU DOING--?
LOOK--LOOK AT THE SIZE OF IT--!! IT'S A MONSTER!!
I AM INTER-GALACTIC SENTRY 459! MY MISSION IS TO PROTECT THIS BASE--AS I HAVE DONE FOR UNCOUNTABLE MILLENNIUMS!
I CANNOT BE HARMED-- I CANNOT BE DETERRED FROM MY PURPOSE-- FOR, I AM--A SENTRY!
NOW, I MUST ACT UNDER THE IRREVOCABLE ORDERS OF MY SUPREME MASTERS, THE KREE--
IT IS THEIR COMMAND THAT NO OUTSIDERS ENTER THIS BASE-- HENCE, YOU MUST BE IMPRISONED WITHIN A SHIMMERING MASS OF COLLODIAL ATOMS!
CONFUSING ENOUGH FOR YOU? JUST WAIT--THIS IS ONLY THE BEGINNING! ANYWAY, LET'S HEAD BACK TO FF HEADQUARTERS AND GET OUR SHOW ON THE ROAD--
YOU PICK A SPOT, BEN, WHILE I CALL THE AIRLINES!
NAH! I COULD FLIP ME A COIN-- BUT I'M BROKE RIGHT NOW!
SAY! HOLD ON, BIG FELLA! IS THAT THE MOST SCIENTIFIC METHOD YOU CAN THINK OF?
4

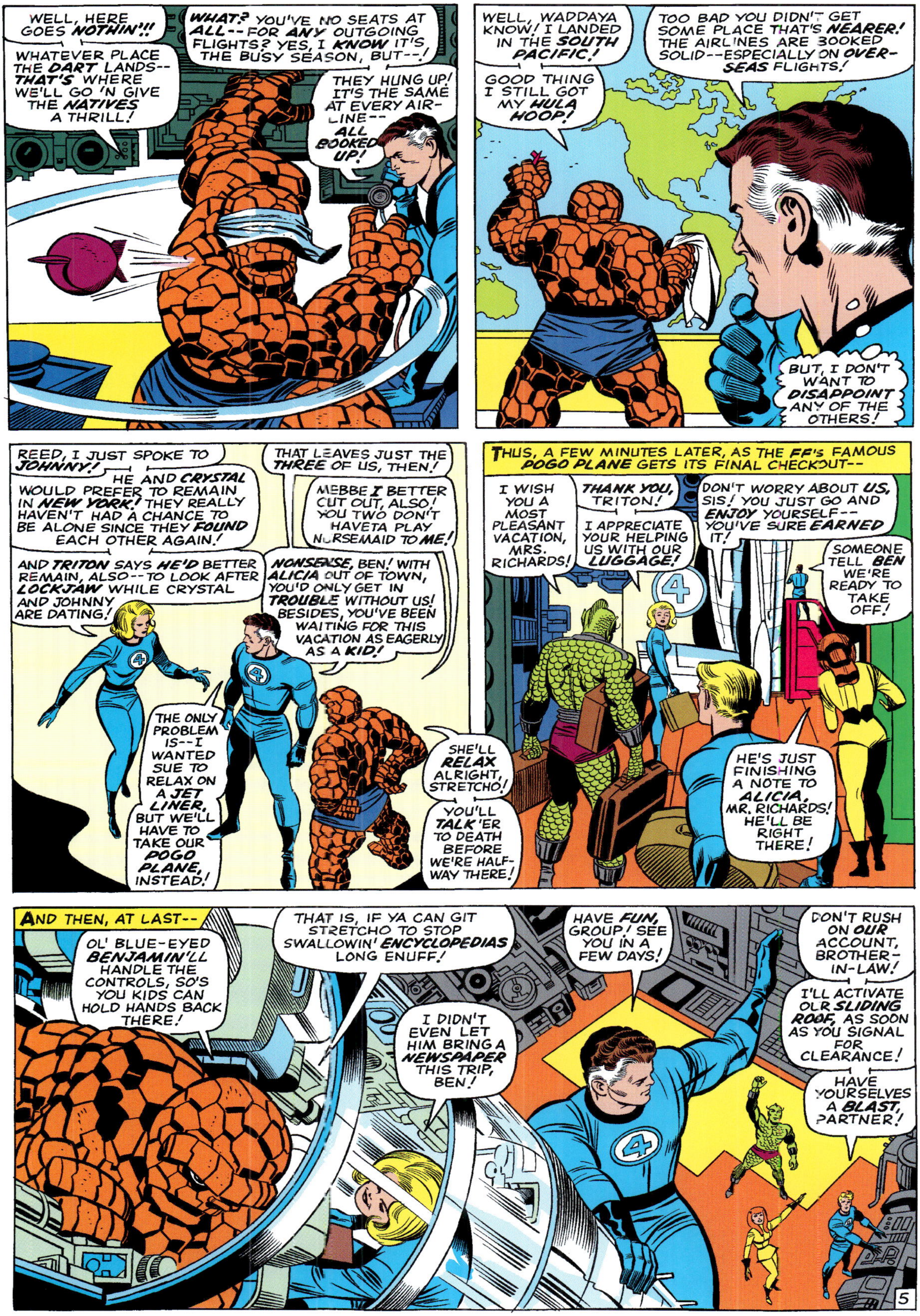
WELL, HERE GOES NOTHIN'!!
WHATEVER PLACE THE DART LANDS-- THAT'S WHERE WE'LL GO 'N GIVE THE NATIVES A THRILL!
WHAT? YOU'VE NO SEATS AT ALL--FOR ANY OUTGOING FLIGHTS? YES, I KNOW IT'S THE BUSY SEASON, BUT--!
THEY HUNG UP! IT'S THE SAME AT EVERY AIR-LINE-- ALL BOOKED UP!
WELL, WADDAYA KNOW! I LANDED IN THE SOUTH PACIFIC!
GOOD THING I STILL GOT MY HULA HOOP!
TOO BAD YOU DIDN'T GET SOME PLACE THAT'S NEARER! THE AIRLINES ARE BOOKED SOLID--ESPECIALLY ON OVER-SEAS FLIGHTS!
BUT, I DON'T WANT TO DISAPPOINT ANY OF THE OTHERS!
REED, I JUST SPOKE TO JOHNNY!
HE AND CRYSTAL WOULD PREFER TO REMAIN IN NEW YORK! THEY REALLY HAVEN'T HAD A CHANCE TO BE ALONE SINCE THEY FOUND EACH OTHER AGAIN!
AND TRITON SAYS HE'D BETTER REMAIN, ALSO--TO LOOK AFTER LOCKJAW WHILE CRYSTAL AND JOHNNY ARE DATING!
THAT LEAVES JUST THE THREE OF US, THEN!
MEBBE I BETTER CUT OUT, ALSO! YOU TWO DON'T HAVETA PLAY NURSEMAID TO ME!
NONSENSE, BEN! WITH ALICIA OUT OF TOWN, YOU'D ONLY GET IN TROUBLE WITHOUT US! BESIDES, YOU'VE BEEN WAITING FOR THIS VACATION AS EAGERLY AS A KID!
THE ONLY PROBLEM IS--I WANTED SUE TO RELAX ON A JET LINER, BUT WE'LL HAVE TO TAKE OUR POGO PLANE, INSTEAD!
SHE'LL RELAX ALRIGHT, STRETCHO!
YOU'LL TALK 'ER TO DEATH BEFORE WE'RE HALF-WAY THERE!
THUS, A FEW MINUTES LATER, AS THE FF's FAMOUS POGO PLANE GETS ITS FINAL CHECKOUT--
I WISH YOU A MOST PLEASANT VACATION, MRS. RICHARDS!
THANK YOU, TRITON!
I APPRECIATE YOUR HELPING US WITH OUR LUGGAGE!
DON'T WORRY ABOUT US, SIS! YOU JUST GO AND ENJOY YOURSELF-- YOU'VE SURE EARNED IT!
SOMEONE TELL BEN WE'RE READY TO TAKE OFF!
HE'S JUST FINISHING A NOTE TO ALICIA, MR. RICHARDS! HE'LL BE RIGHT THERE!
AND THEN, AT LAST--
OL' BLUE-EYED BENJAMIN'LL HANDLE THE CONTROLS, SO'S YOU KIDS CAN HOLD HANDS BACK THERE!
THAT IS, IF YA CAN GIT STRETCHO TO STOP SWALLOWIN' ENCYCLOPEDIAS LONG ENUFF!
I DIDN'T EVEN LET HIM BRING A NEWSPAPER THIS TRIP, BEN!
HAVE FUN, GROUP! SEE YOU IN A FEW DAYS!
DON'T RUSH ON OUR ACCOUNT, BROTHER-IN-LAW!
I'LL ACTIVATE OUR SLIDING ROOF, AS SOON AS YOU SIGNAL FOR CLEARANCE!
HAVE YOURSELVES A BLAST, PARTNER!
5

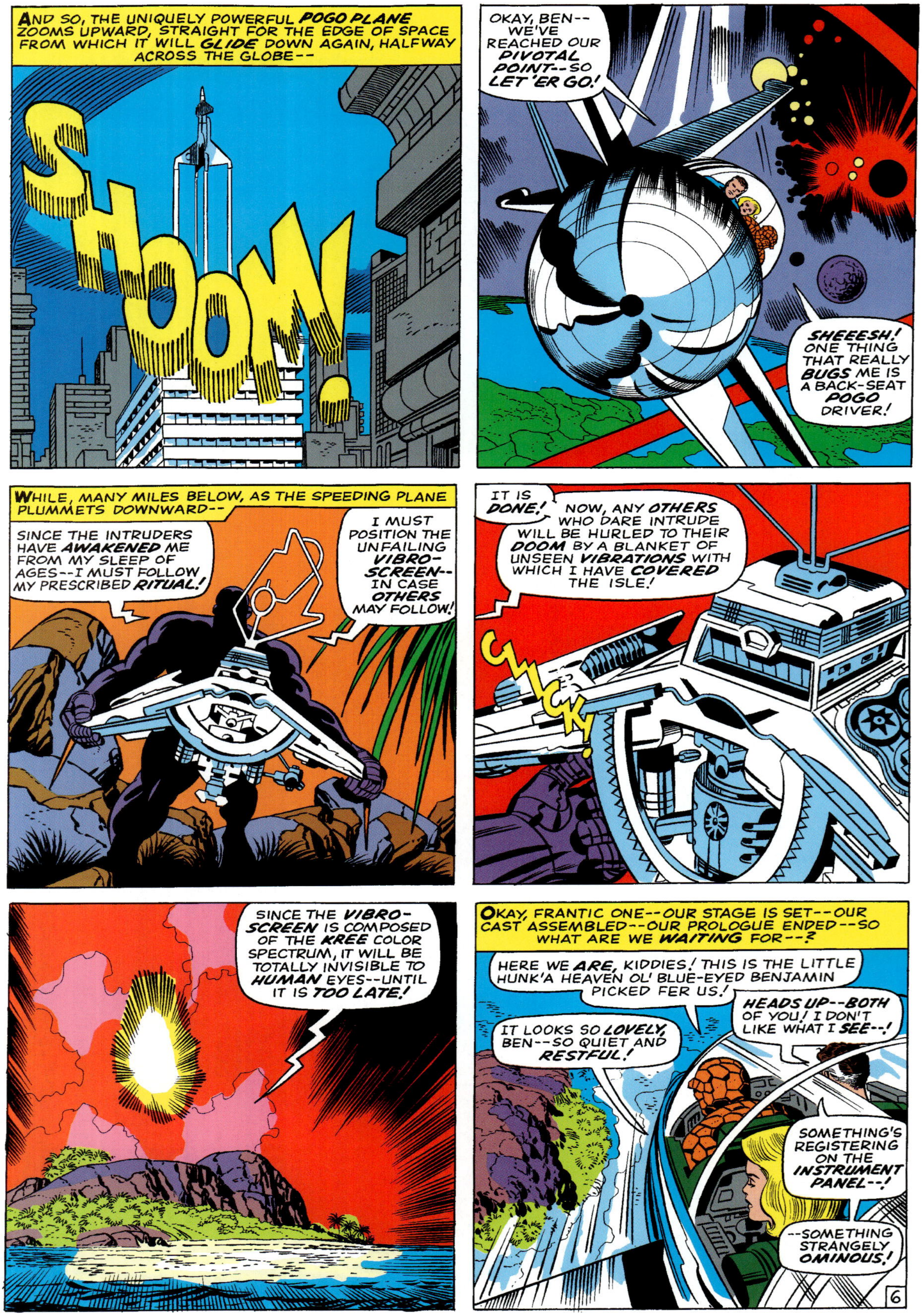
AND SO, THE UNIQUELY POWERFUL POGO PLANE ZOOMS UPWARD, STRAIGHT FOR THE EDGE OF SPACE FROM WHICH IT WILL GLIDE DOWN AGAIN, HALFWAY ACROSS THE GLOBE--
SHOOM!
OKAY, BEN--WE'VE REACHED OUR PIVOTAL POINT--SO LET 'ER GO!
SHEEESH! ONE THING THAT REALLY BUGS ME IS A BACK-SEAT POGO DRIVER!
WHILE, MANY MILES BELOW, AS THE SPEEDING PLANE PLUMMETS DOWNWARD--
SINCE THE INTRUDERS HAVE AWAKENED ME FROM MY SLEEP OF AGES--I MUST FOLLOW MY PRESCRIBED RITUAL!
I MUST POSITION THE UNFAILING VIBRO-SCREEN--IN CASE OTHERS MAY FOLLOW!
IT IS DONE!
NOW, ANY OTHERS WHO DARE INTRUDE WILL BE HURLED TO THEIR DOOM BY A BLANKET OF UNSEEN VIBRATIONS WITH WHICH I HAVE COVERED THE ISLE!
CLICK!
SINCE THE VIBRO-SCREEN IS COMPOSED OF THE KREE COLOR SPECTRUM, IT WILL BE TOTALLY INVISIBLE TO HUMAN EYES--UNTIL IT IS TOO LATE!
OKAY, FRANTIC ONE--OUR STAGE IS SET--OUR CAST ASSEMBLED--OUR PROLOGUE ENDED--SO WHAT ARE WE WAITING FOR--?
HERE WE ARE, KIDDIES! THIS IS THE LITTLE HUNK'A HEAVEN OL' BLUE-EYED BENJAMIN PICKED FER US!
IT LOOKS SO LOVELY, BEN--SO QUIET AND RESTFUL!
HEADS UP--BOTH OF YOU! I DON'T LIKE WHAT I SEE--!
SOMETHING'S REGISTERING ON THE INSTRUMENT PANEL--!
--SOMETHING STRANGELY OMINOUS!
6

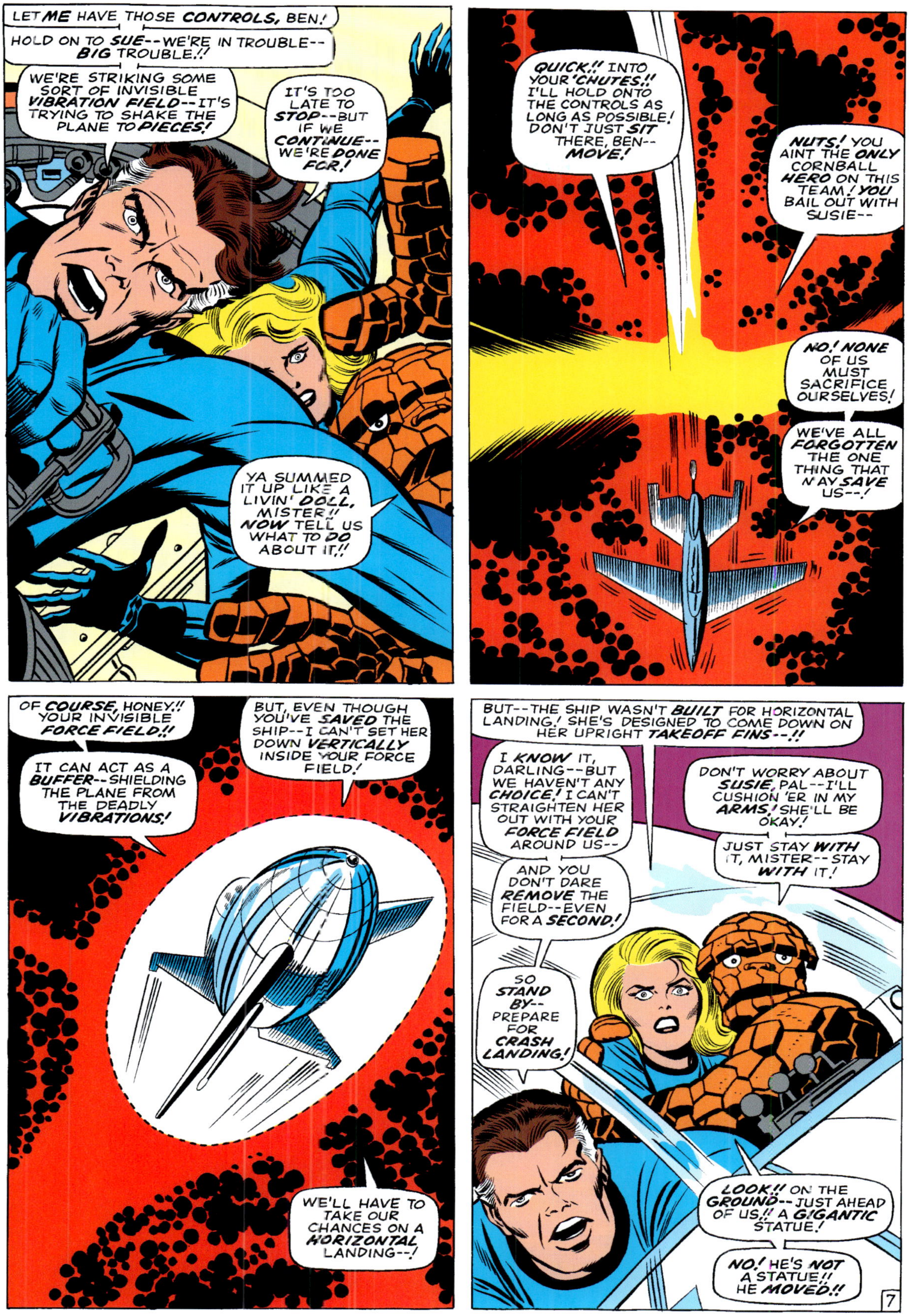
LET ME HAVE THOSE CONTROLS, BEN!
HOLD ON TO SUE--WE'RE IN TROUBLE--BIG TROUBLE!!
WE'RE STRIKING SOME SORT OF INVISIBLE VIBRATION FIELD--IT'S TRYING TO SHAKE THE PLANE TO PIECES!
IT'S TOO LATE TO STOP--BUT IF WE CONTINUE--WE'RE DONE FOR!
YA SUMMED IT UP LIKE A LIVIN' DOLL, MISTER!! NOW TELL US WHAT TO DO ABOUT IT!!
QUICK!! INTO YOUR 'CHUTES!! I'LL HOLD ONTO THE CONTROLS AS LONG AS POSSIBLE! DON'T JUST SIT THERE, BEN--MOVE!
NUTS! YOU AINT THE ONLY CORNBALL HERO ON THIS TEAM! YOU BAIL OUT WITH SUSIE--
NO! NONE OF US MUST SACRIFICE OURSELVES!
WE'VE ALL FORGOTTEN THE ONE THING THAT MAY SAVE US--!
OF COURSE, HONEY!! YOUR INVISIBLE FORCE FIELD!!
IT CAN ACT AS A BUFFER--SHIELDING THE PLANE FROM THE DEADLY VIBRATIONS!
BUT, EVEN THOUGH YOU'VE SAVED THE SHIP--I CAN'T SET HER DOWN VERTICALLY INSIDE YOUR FORCE FIELD!
WE'LL HAVE TO TAKE OUR CHANCES ON A HORIZONTAL LANDING--!
BUT--THE SHIP WASN'T BUILT FOR HORIZONTAL LANDING! SHE'S DESIGNED TO COME DOWN ON HER UPRIGHT TAKEOFF FINS--!!
I KNOW IT, DARLING--BUT WE HAVEN'T ANY CHOICE! I CAN'T STRAIGHTEN HER OUT WITH YOUR FORCE FIELD AROUND US--
AND YOU DON'T DARE REMOVE THE FIELD--EVEN FOR A SECOND!
SO STAND BY--PREPARE FOR CRASH LANDING!
DON'T WORRY ABOUT SUSIE, PAL--I'LL CUSHION 'ER IN MY ARMS! SHE'LL BE OKAY!
JUST STAY WITH IT, MISTER--STAY WITH IT!
LOOK!! ON THE GROUND--JUST AHEAD OF US!! A GIGANTIC STATUE!
NO! HE'S NOT A STATUE!! HE MOVED!!
7

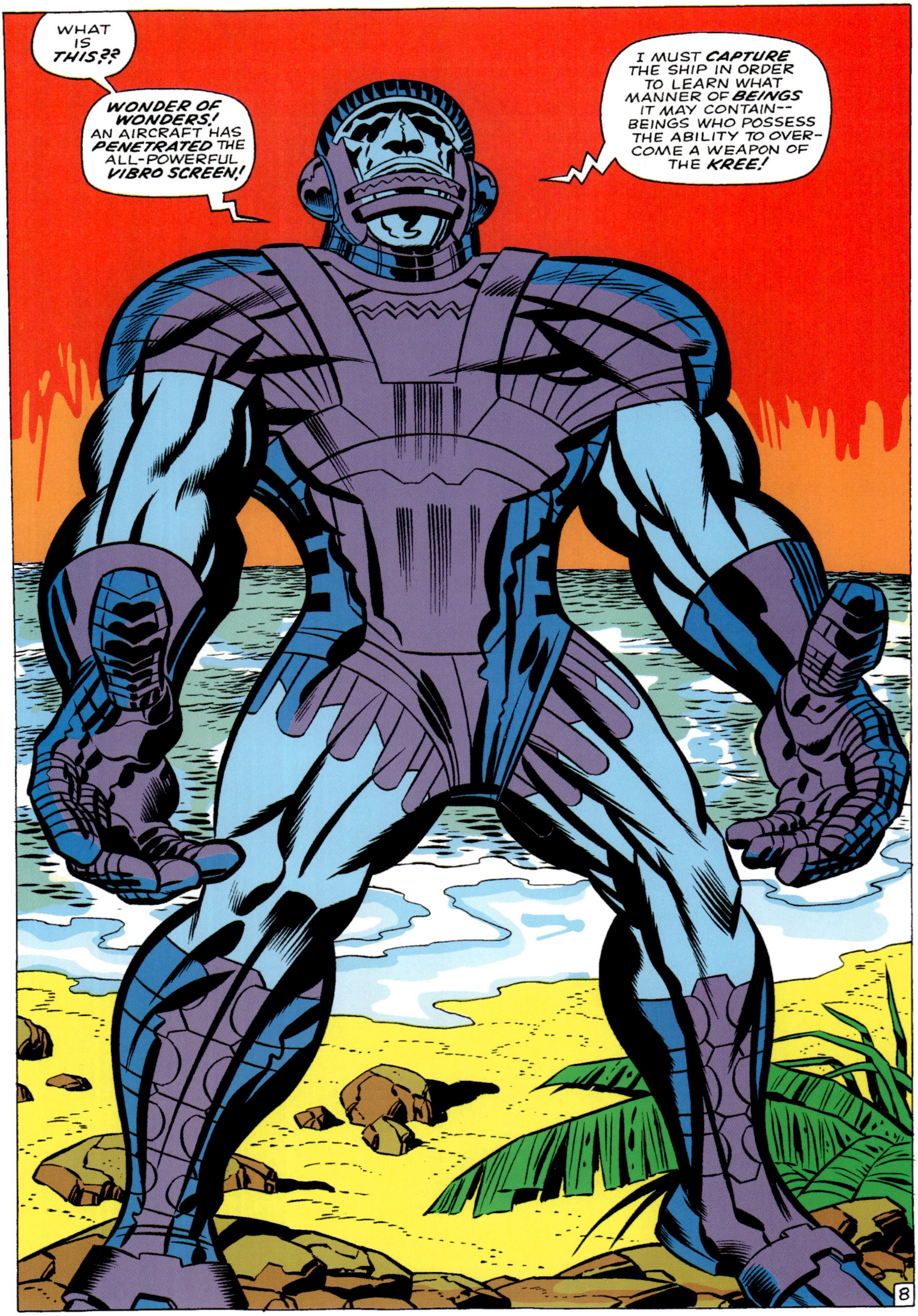
WHAT IS THIS??
WONDER OF WONDERS! AN AIRCRAFT HAS PENETRATED THE ALL-POWERFUL VIBRO SCREEN!
I MUST CAPTURE THE SHIP IN ORDER TO LEARN WHAT MANNER OF BEINGS IT MAY CONTAIN-- BEINGS WHO POSSESS THE ABILITY TO OVER-COME A WEAPON OF THE KREE!
8

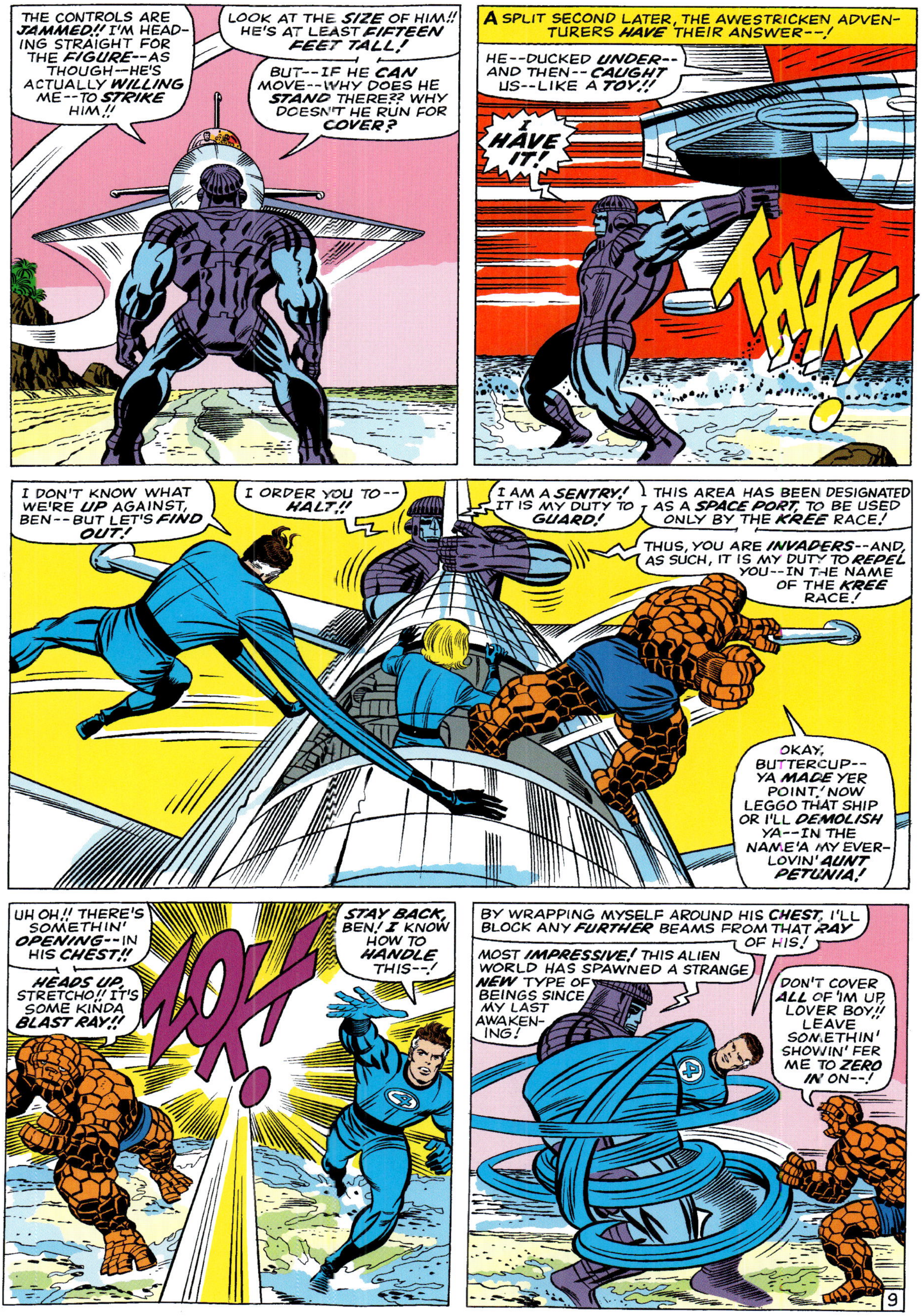
THE CONTROLS ARE JAMMED!! I'M HEADING STRAIGHT FOR THE FIGURE--AS THOUGH--HE'S ACTUALLY WILLING ME--TO STRIKE HIM!!
LOOK AT THE SIZE OF HIM!! HE'S AT LEAST FIFTEEN FEET TALL!
BUT--IF HE CAN MOVE--WHY DOES HE STAND THERE?? WHY DOESN'T HE RUN FOR COVER?
A SPLIT SECOND LATER, THE AWESTRICKEN ADVENTURERS HAVE THEIR ANSWER--!
HE--DUCKED UNDER--AND THEN--CAUGHT US--LIKE A TOY!!
I HAVE IT!
THAK!
I DON'T KNOW WHAT WE'RE UP AGAINST, BEN--BUT LET'S FIND OUT!
I ORDER YOU TO--HALT!!
I AM A SENTRY! IT IS MY DUTY TO GUARD!
THIS AREA HAS BEEN DESIGNATED AS A SPACE PORT, TO BE USED ONLY BY THE KREE RACE!
THUS, YOU ARE INVADERS--AND, AS SUCH, IT IS MY DUTY TO REPEL YOU--IN THE NAME OF THE KREE RACE!
OKAY, BUTTERCUP--YA MADE YER POINT! NOW LEGGO THAT SHIP OR I'LL DEMOLISH YA--IN THE NAME'A MY EVER-LOVIN' AUNT PETUNIA!
UH OH!! THERE'S SOMETHIN' OPENING--IN HIS CHEST!!
HEADS UP, STRETCHO!! IT'S SOME KINDA BLAST RAY!!
ZOK!
STAY BACK, BEN! I KNOW HOW TO HANDLE THIS--!
BY WRAPPING MYSELF AROUND HIS CHEST, I'LL BLOCK ANY FURTHER BEAMS FROM THAT RAY OF HIS!
MOST IMPRESSIVE! THIS ALIEN WORLD HAS SPAWNED A STRANGE NEW TYPE OF BEINGS SINCE MY LAST AWAKENING!
DON'T COVER ALL OF 'IM UP, LOVER BOY!! LEAVE SOMETHIN' SHOWIN' FER ME TO ZERO IN ON--!
9

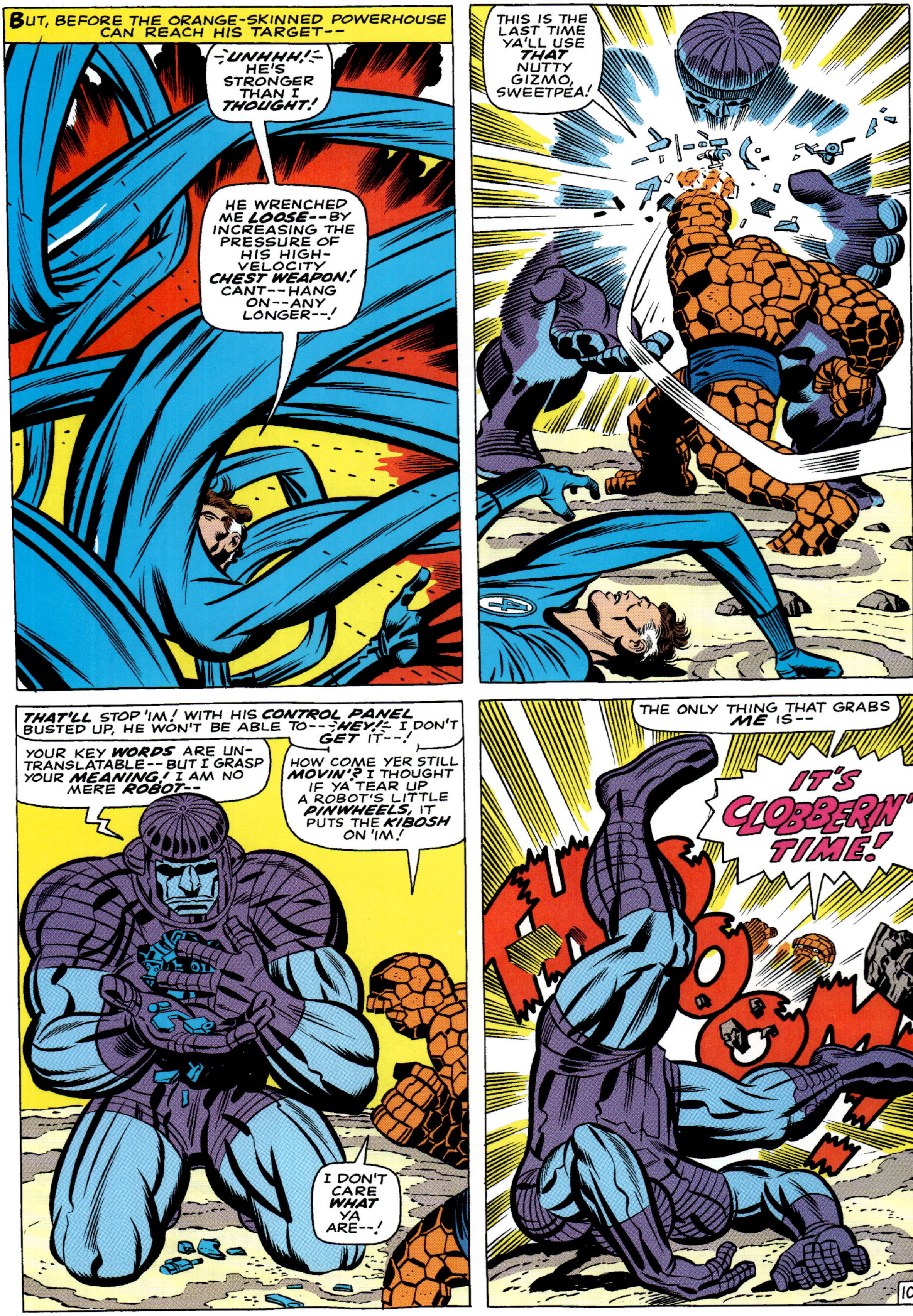
BUT, BEFORE THE ORANGE-SKINNED POWERHOUSE CAN REACH HIS TARGET--
-UNHHH!- HE'S STRONGER THAN I THOUGHT!
HE WRENCHED ME LOOSE--BY INCREASING THE PRESSURE OF HIS HIGH-VELOCITY CHEST WEAPON! CANT--HANG ON--ANY LONGER--!
THIS IS THE LAST TIME YA'LL USE THAT NUTTY GIZMO, SWEETPEA!
THAT'LL STOP 'IM! WITH HIS CONTROL PANEL BUSTED UP, HE WON'T BE ABLE TO-- HEY! I DON'T GET IT--!
YOUR KEY WORDS ARE UNTRANSLATABLE--BUT I GRASP YOUR MEANING! I AM NO MERE ROBOT--
HOW COME YER STILL MOVIN'? I THOUGHT IF YA TEAR UP A ROBOT'S LITTLE PINWHEELS, IT PUTS THE KIBOSH ON 'IM!
I DON'T CARE WHAT YA ARE--!
THE ONLY THING THAT GRABS ME IS--
IT'S CLOBBERIN' TIME!
THOOM
10

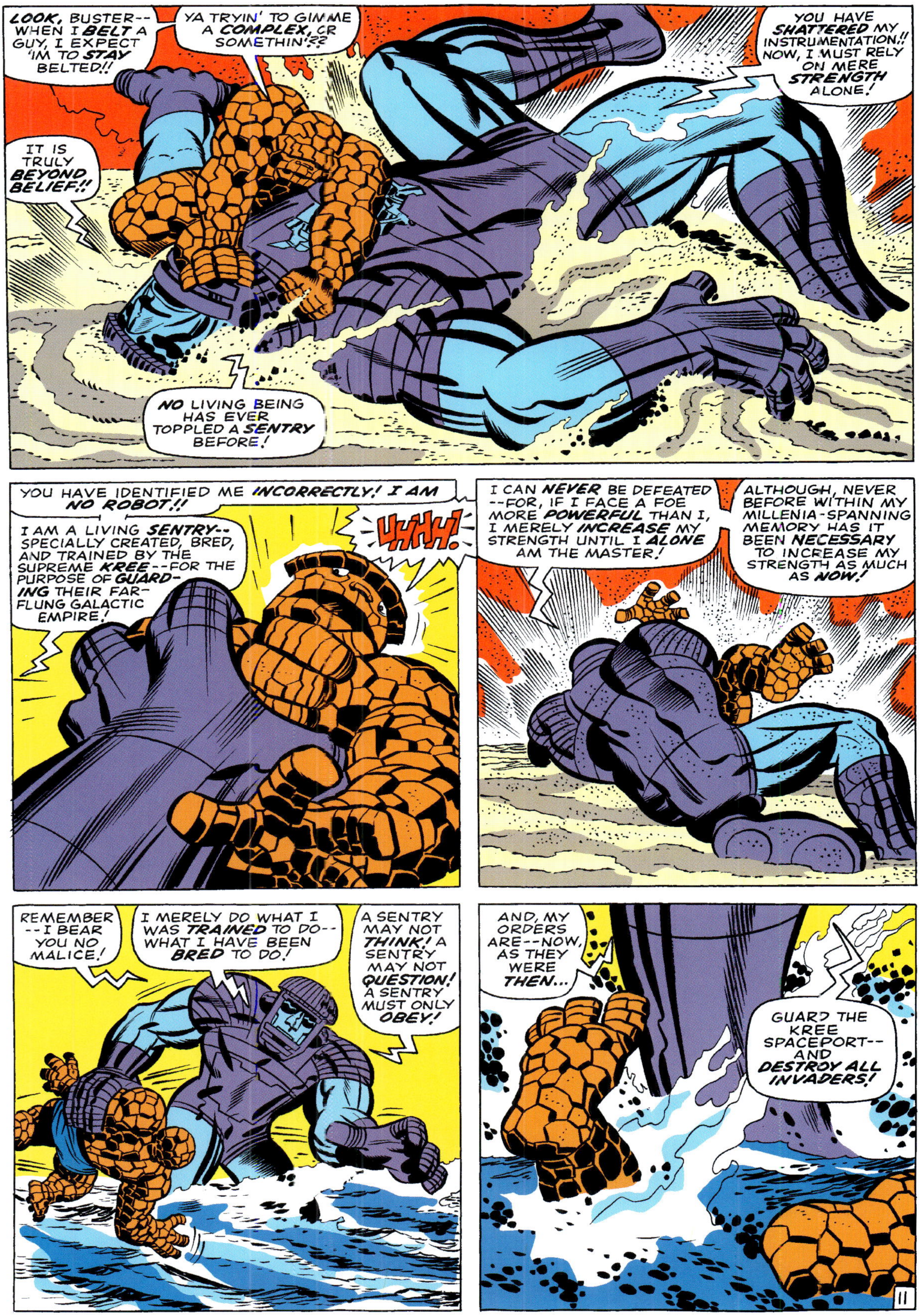

LOOK, BUSTER-- WHEN I BELT A GUY, I EXPECT 'IM TO STAY BELTED!!
YA TRYIN' TO GIMME A COMPLEX, OR SOMETHIN'??
YOU HAVE SHATTERED MY INSTRUMENTATION!! NOW, I MUST RELY ON MERE STRENGTH ALONE!
IT IS TRULY BEYOND BELIEF!!
NO LIVING BEING HAS EVER TOPPLED A SENTRY BEFORE!
YOU HAVE IDENTIFIED ME INCORRECTLY! I AM NO ROBOT!!
I AM A LIVING SENTRY-- SPECIALLY CREATED, BRED, AND TRAINED BY THE SUPREME KREE--FOR THE PURPOSE OF GUARD-ING THEIR FAR-FLUNG GALACTIC EMPIRE!
UHHH!
I CAN NEVER BE DEFEATED --FOR, IF I FACE A FOE MORE POWERFUL THAN I, I MERELY INCREASE MY STRENGTH UNTIL I ALONE AM THE MASTER!
ALTHOUGH, NEVER BEFORE WITHIN MY MILLENIA-SPANNING MEMORY HAS IT BEEN NECESSARY TO INCREASE MY STRENGTH AS MUCH AS NOW!
REMEMBER --I BEAR YOU NO MALICE!
I MERELY DO WHAT I WAS TRAINED TO DO-- WHAT I HAVE BEEN BRED TO DO!
A SENTRY MAY NOT THINK! A SENTRY MAY NOT QUESTION! A SENTRY MUST ONLY OBEY!
AND, MY ORDERS ARE--NOW, AS THEY WERE THEN...
GUARD THE KREE SPACEPORT-- AND DESTROY ALL INVADERS!
11

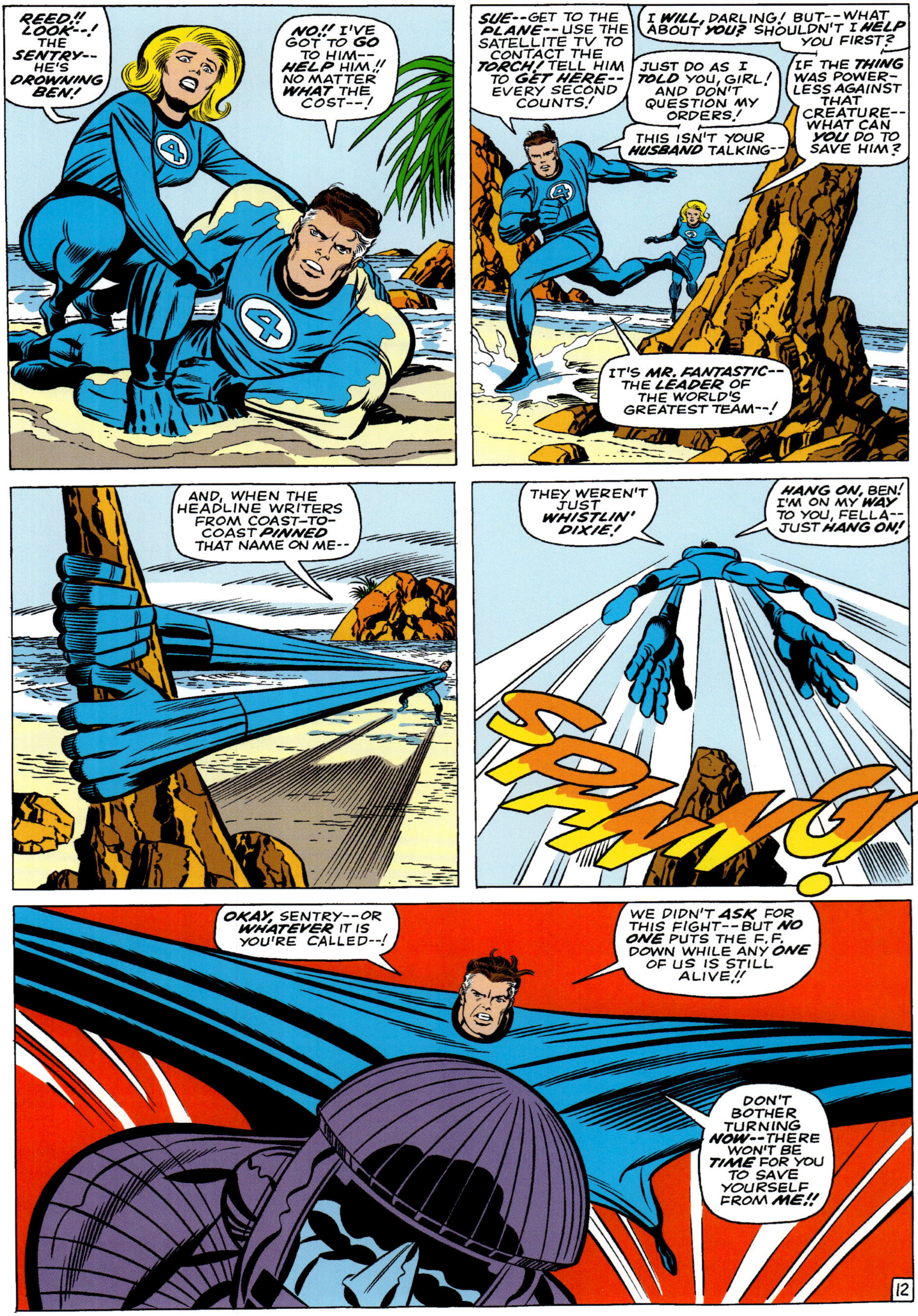
REED!! LOOK--! THE SENTRY--HE'S DROWNING BEN!
NO!! I'VE GOT TO GO TO HIM--HELP HIM!! NO MATTER WHAT THE COST--!
SUE--GET TO THE PLANE--USE THE SATELLITE TV TO CONTACT THE TORCH! TELL HIM TO GET HERE--EVERY SECOND COUNTS!
I WILL, DARLING! BUT--WHAT ABOUT YOU? SHOULDN'T I HELP YOU FIRST?
IF THE THING WAS POWERLESS AGAINST THAT CREATURE--WHAT CAN YOU DO TO SAVE HIM?
JUST DO AS I TOLD YOU, GIRL! AND DON'T QUESTION MY ORDERS!
THIS ISN'T YOUR HUSBAND TALKING--
IT'S MR. FANTASTIC--THE LEADER OF THE WORLD'S GREATEST TEAM--!
AND, WHEN THE HEADLINE WRITERS FROM COAST-TO-COAST PINNED THAT NAME ON ME--
THEY WEREN'T JUST WHISTLIN' DIXIE!
HANG ON, BEN! I'M ON MY WAY TO YOU, FELLA--JUST HANG ON!
SPANG!
OKAY, SENTRY--OR WHATEVER IT IS YOU'RE CALLED--!
WE DIDN'T ASK FOR THIS FIGHT--BUT NO ONE PUTS THE F.F. DOWN WHILE ANY ONE OF US IS STILL ALIVE!!
DON'T BOTHER TURNING NOW--THERE WON'T BE TIME FOR YOU TO SAVE YOURSELF FROM ME!!
12

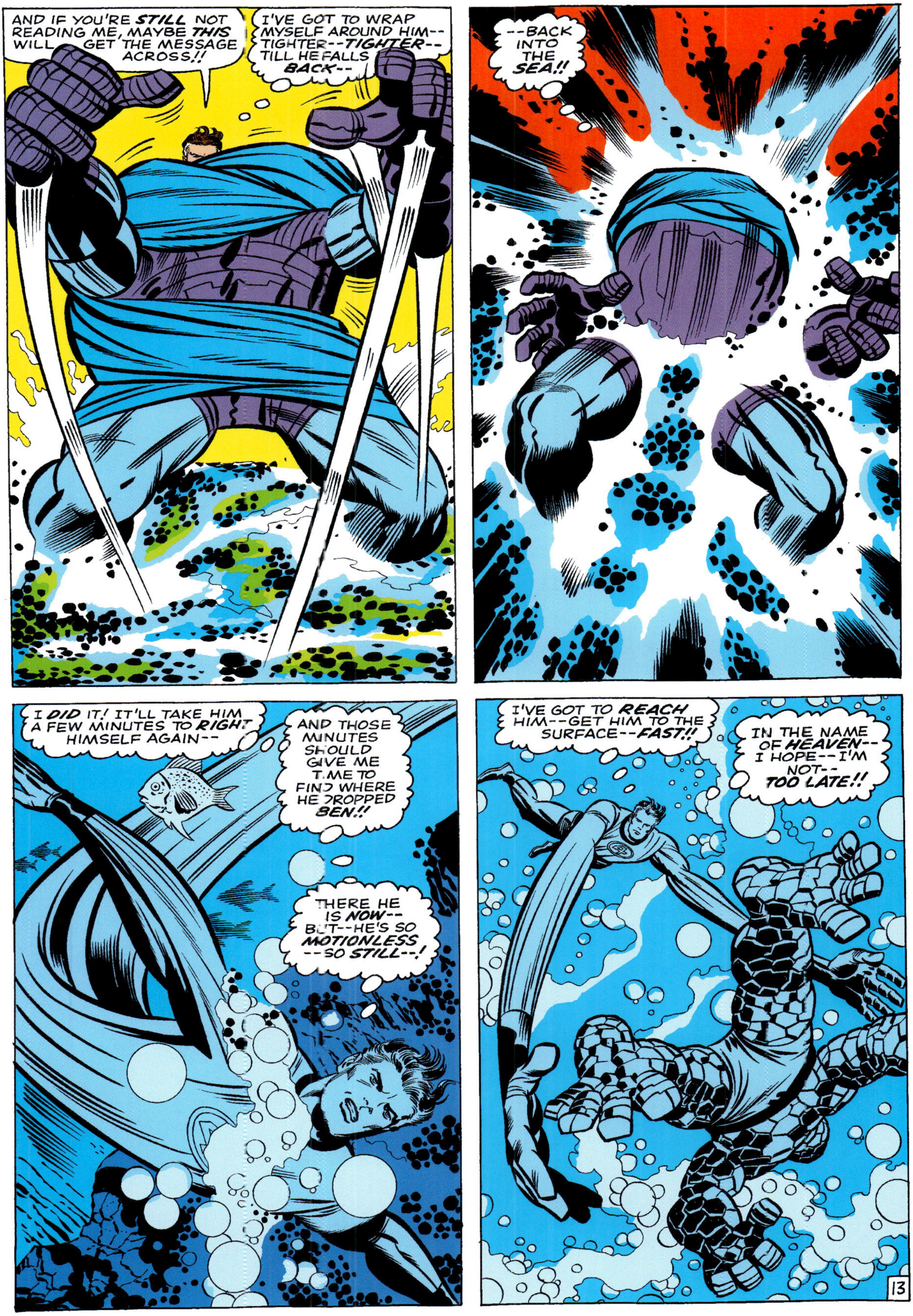
AND IF YOU'RE STILL NOT READING ME, MAYBE THIS WILL GET THE MESSAGE ACROSS!!
I'VE GOT TO WRAP MYSELF AROUND HIM-- TIGHTER--TIGHTER-- TILL HE FALLS BACK--
--BACK INTO THE SEA!!
I DID IT! IT'LL TAKE HIM A FEW MINUTES TO RIGHT HIMSELF AGAIN--
AND THOSE MINUTES SHOULD GIVE ME TIME TO FIND WHERE HE DROPPED BEN!!
THERE HE IS NOW-- BUT--HE'S SO MOTIONLESS --SO STILL--!
I'VE GOT TO REACH HIM--GET HIM TO THE SURFACE--FAST!!
IN THE NAME OF HEAVEN-- I HOPE--I'M NOT-- TOO LATE!!
13

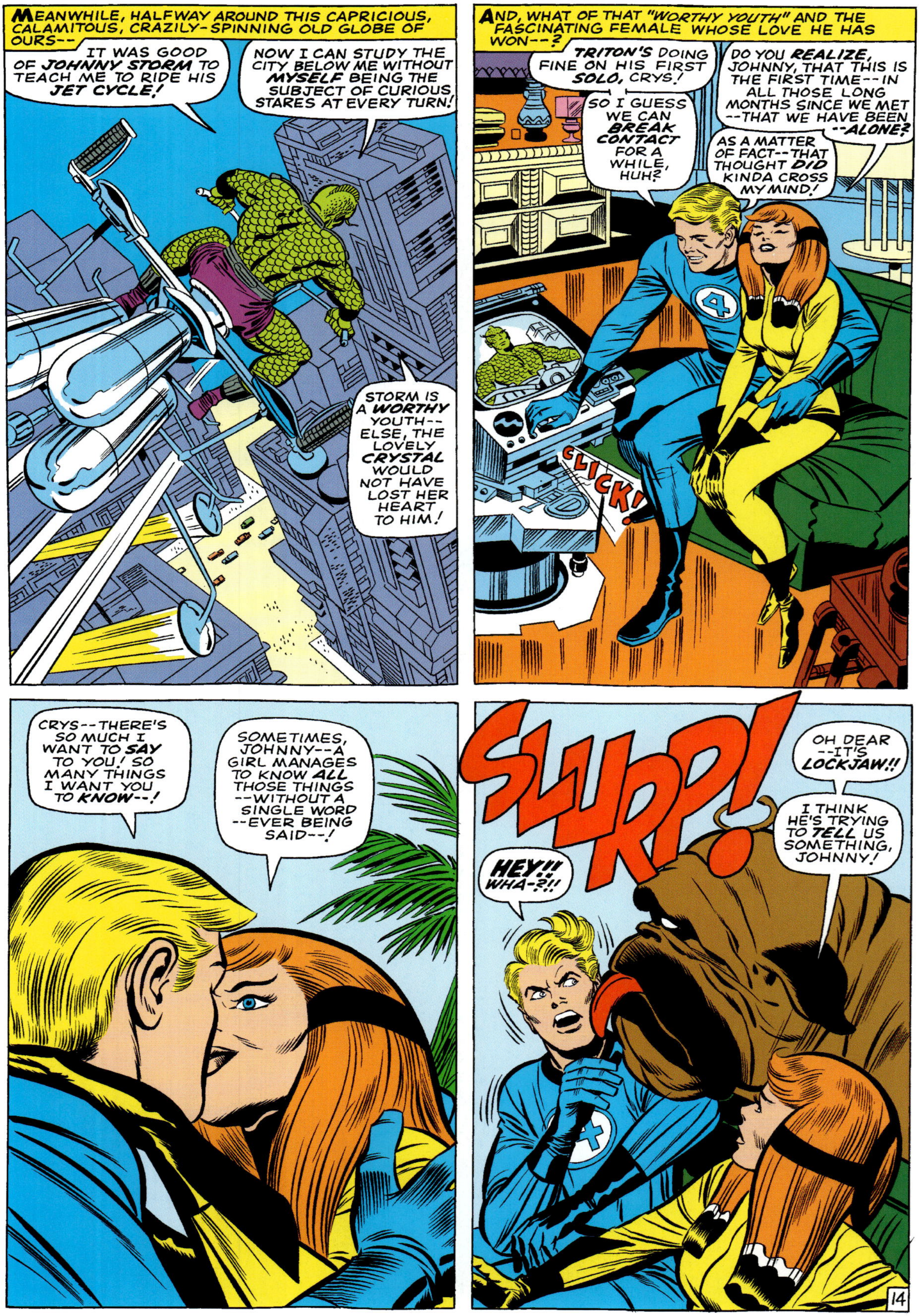

MEANWHILE, HALFWAY AROUND THIS CAPRICIOUS, CALAMITOUS, CRAZILY-SPINNING OLD GLOBE OF OURS--
IT WAS GOOD OF JOHNNY STORM TO TEACH ME TO RIDE HIS JET CYCLE!
NOW I CAN STUDY THE CITY BELOW ME WITHOUT MYSELF BEING THE SUBJECT OF CURIOUS STARES AT EVERY TURN!
STORM IS A WORTHY YOUTH-- ELSE, THE LOVELY CRYSTAL WOULD NOT HAVE LOST HER HEART TO HIM!
AND, WHAT OF THAT "WORTHY YOUTH" AND THE FASCINATING FEMALE WHOSE LOVE HE HAS WON--?
TRITON'S DOING FINE ON HIS FIRST SOLO, CRYS!
SO I GUESS WE CAN BREAK CONTACT FOR A WHILE, HUH?
DO YOU REALIZE, JOHNNY, THAT THIS IS THE FIRST TIME--IN ALL THOSE LONG MONTHS SINCE WE MET --THAT WE HAVE BEEN --ALONE?
AS A MATTER OF FACT--THAT THOUGHT DID KINDA CROSS MY MIND!
CLICK!
CRYS--THERE'S SO MUCH I WANT TO SAY TO YOU! SO MANY THINGS I WANT YOU TO KNOW--!
SOMETIMES, JOHNNY--A GIRL MANAGES TO KNOW ALL THOSE THINGS --WITHOUT A SINGLE WORD --EVER BEING SAID--!
SLURP!
HEY!! WHA-?!!
OH DEAR --IT'S LOCKJAW!!
I THINK HE'S TRYING TO TELL US SOMETHING, JOHNNY!
14

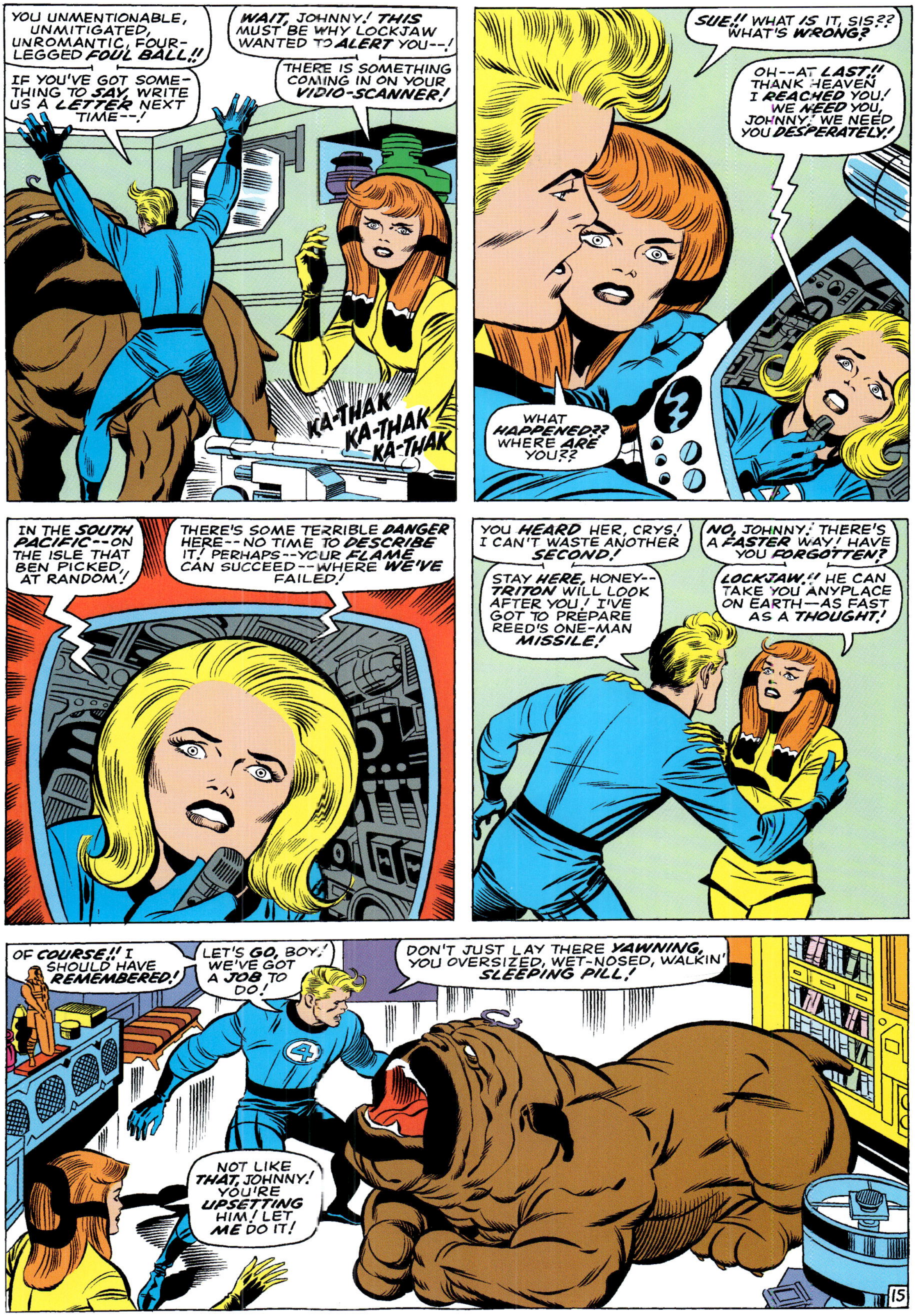

YOU UNMENTIONABLE, UNMITIGATED, UNROMANTIC, FOUR-LEGGED FOUL BALL!!
IF YOU'VE GOT SOME-THING TO SAY, WRITE US A LETTER NEXT TIME--!
WAIT, JOHNNY! THIS MUST BE WHY LOCKJAW WANTED TO ALERT YOU--!
THERE IS SOMETHING COMING IN ON YOUR VIDIO-SCANNER!
KA-THAK KA-THAK KA-THAK
SUE!! WHAT IS IT, SIS?? WHAT'S WRONG?
OH--AT LAST!! THANK HEAVEN I REACHED YOU! WE NEED YOU, JOHNNY! WE NEED YOU DESPERATELY!
WHAT HAPPENED?? WHERE ARE YOU??
IN THE SOUTH PACIFIC--ON THE ISLE THAT BEN PICKED, AT RANDOM!
THERE'S SOME TERRIBLE DANGER HERE--NO TIME TO DESCRIBE IT! PERHAPS--YOUR FLAME CAN SUCCEED--WHERE WE'VE FAILED!
YOU HEARD HER, CRYS! I CAN'T WASTE ANOTHER SECOND!
STAY HERE, HONEY--TRITON WILL LOOK AFTER YOU! I'VE GOT TO PREPARE REED'S ONE-MAN MISSILE!
NO, JOHNNY! THERE'S A FASTER WAY! HAVE YOU FORGOTTEN?
LOCKJAW!! HE CAN TAKE YOU ANYPLACE ON EARTH—AS FAST AS A THOUGHT!
OF COURSE!! I SHOULD HAVE REMEMBERED!
LET'S GO, BOY! WE'VE GOT A JOB TO DO!
DON'T JUST LAY THERE YAWNING, YOU OVERSIZED, WET-NOSED, WALKIN' SLEEPING PILL!
NOT LIKE THAT, JOHNNY! YOU'RE UPSETTING HIM! LET ME DO IT!
15

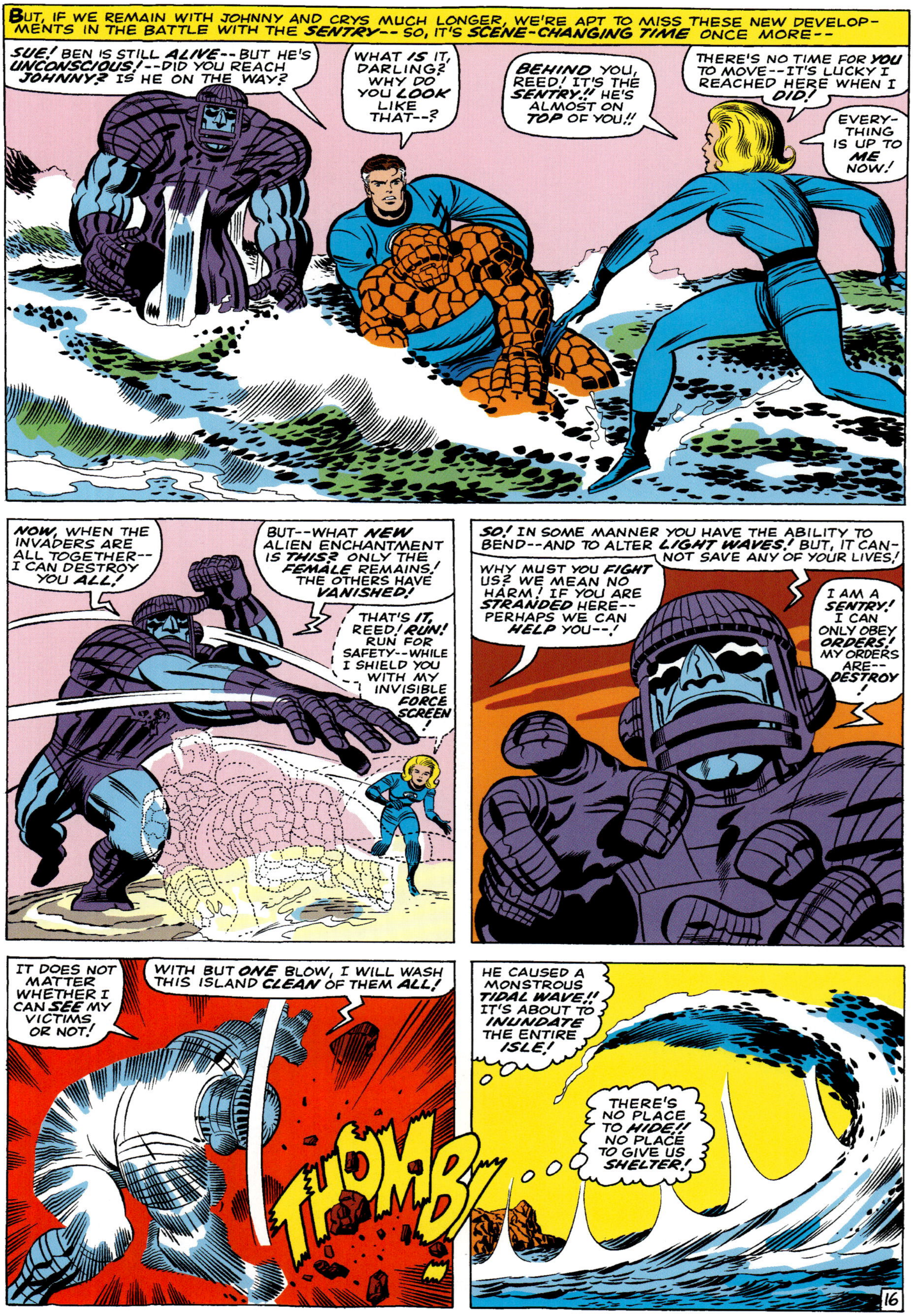
BUT, IF WE REMAIN WITH JOHNNY AND CRYS MUCH LONGER, WE'RE APT TO MISS THESE NEW DEVELOPMENTS IN THE BATTLE WITH THE SENTRY-- SO, IT'S SCENE-CHANGING TIME ONCE MORE--
SUE! BEN IS STILL ALIVE--BUT HE'S UNCONSCIOUS!--DID YOU REACH JOHNNY? IS HE ON THE WAY?
WHAT IS IT, DARLING? WHY DO YOU LOOK LIKE THAT--?
BEHIND YOU, REED! IT'S THE SENTRY!! HE'S ALMOST ON TOP OF YOU!!
THERE'S NO TIME FOR YOU TO MOVE--IT'S LUCKY I REACHED HERE WHEN I DID!
EVERY-THING IS UP TO ME NOW!
NOW, WHEN THE INVADERS ARE ALL TOGETHER-- I CAN DESTROY YOU ALL!
BUT--WHAT NEW ALIEN ENCHANTMENT IS THIS? ONLY THE FEMALE REMAINS! THE OTHERS HAVE VANISHED!
THAT'S IT, REED! RUN! RUN FOR SAFETY--WHILE I SHIELD YOU WITH MY INVISIBLE FORCE SCREEN!
SO! IN SOME MANNER YOU HAVE THE ABILITY TO BEND--AND TO ALTER LIGHT WAVES! BUT, IT CANNOT SAVE ANY OF YOUR LIVES!
WHY MUST YOU FIGHT US? WE MEAN NO HARM! IF YOU ARE STRANDED HERE-- PERHAPS WE CAN HELP YOU--!
I AM A SENTRY! I CAN ONLY OBEY ORDERS! MY ORDERS ARE--DESTROY!
IT DOES NOT MATTER WHETHER I CAN SEE MY VICTIMS OR NOT!
WITH BUT ONE BLOW, I WILL WASH THIS ISLAND CLEAN OF THEM ALL!
THOOM-B!
HE CAUSED A MONSTROUS TIDAL WAVE!! IT'S ABOUT TO INUNDATE THE ENTIRE ISLE!
THERE'S NO PLACE TO HIDE!! NO PLACE TO GIVE US SHELTER!
16

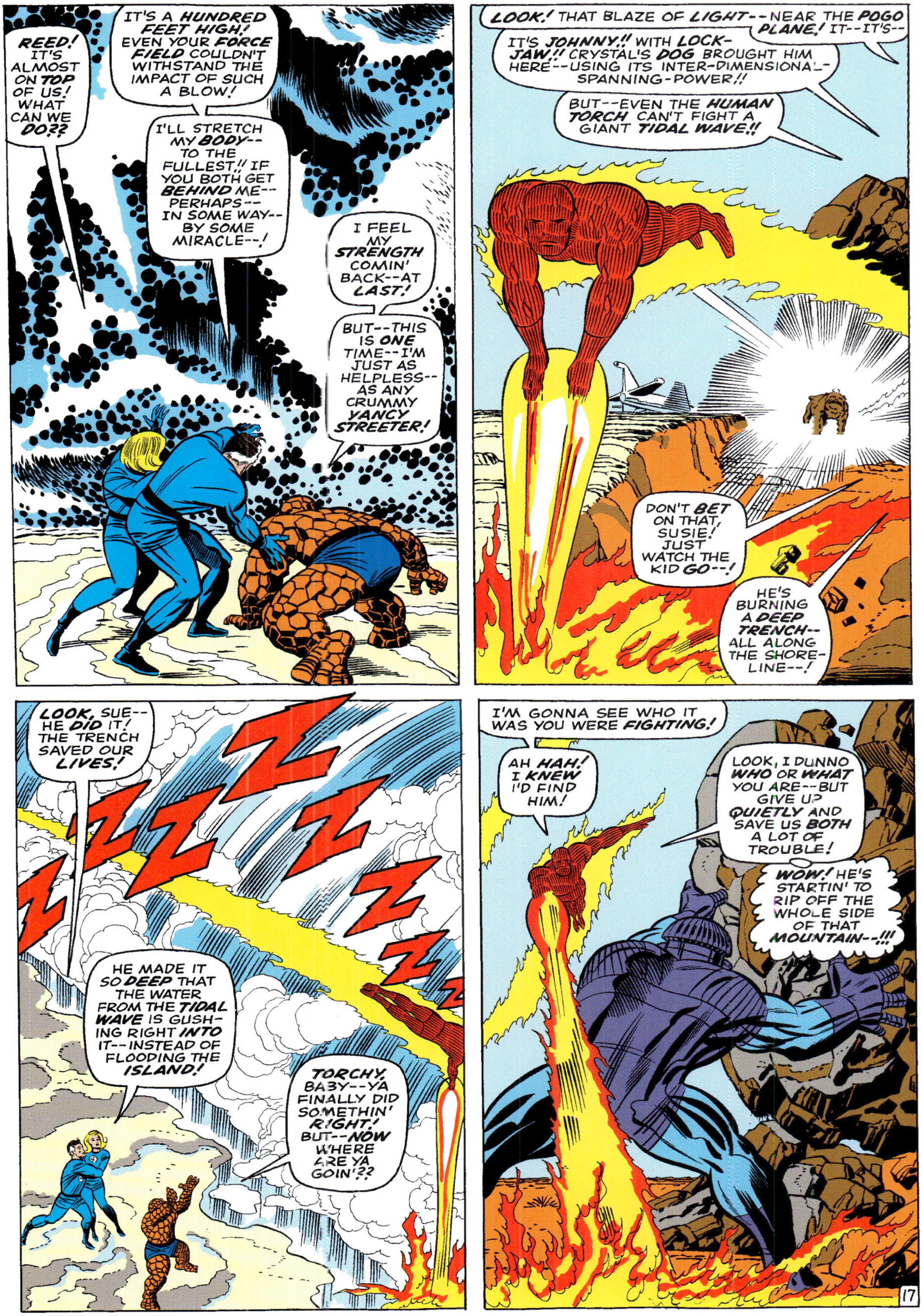
REED! IT'S ALMOST ON TOP OF US! WHAT CAN WE DO??
IT'S A HUNDRED FEET HIGH! EVEN YOUR FORCE FIELD COULDN'T WITHSTAND THE IMPACT OF SUCH A BLOW!
I'LL STRETCH MY BODY-- TO THE FULLEST!! IF YOU BOTH GET BEHIND ME-- PERHAPS-- IN SOME WAY-- BY SOME MIRACLE--!
I FEEL MY STRENGTH COMIN' BACK--AT LAST!
BUT--THIS IS ONE TIME--I'M JUST AS HELPLESS-- AS ANY CRUMMY YANCY STREETER!
LOOK! THAT BLAZE OF LIGHT--NEAR THE POGO PLANE! IT--IT'S--
IT'S JOHNNY!! WITH LOCK-JAW!! CRYSTAL'S DOG BROUGHT HIM HERE--USING ITS INTER-DIMENSIONAL-SPANNING-POWER!!
BUT--EVEN THE HUMAN TORCH CAN'T FIGHT A GIANT TIDAL WAVE!!
DON'T BET ON THAT, SUSIE! JUST WATCH THE KID GO--!
HE'S BURNING A DEEP TRENCH-- ALL ALONG THE SHORE-LINE--!
LOOK, SUE-- HE DID IT! THE TRENCH SAVED OUR LIVES!
HE MADE IT SO DEEP THAT THE WATER FROM THE TIDAL WAVE IS GUSH-ING RIGHT INTO IT--INSTEAD OF FLOODING THE ISLAND!
TORCHY, BABY--YA FINALLY DID SOMETHIN' RIGHT! BUT--NOW WHERE ARE YA GOIN'??
I'M GONNA SEE WHO IT WAS YOU WERE FIGHTING!
AH HAH! I KNEW I'D FIND HIM!
LOOK, I DUNNO WHO OR WHAT YOU ARE--BUT GIVE UP QUIETLY AND SAVE US BOTH A LOT OF TROUBLE!
WOW! HE'S STARTIN' TO RIP OFF THE WHOLE SIDE OF THAT MOUNTAIN--!!!
17

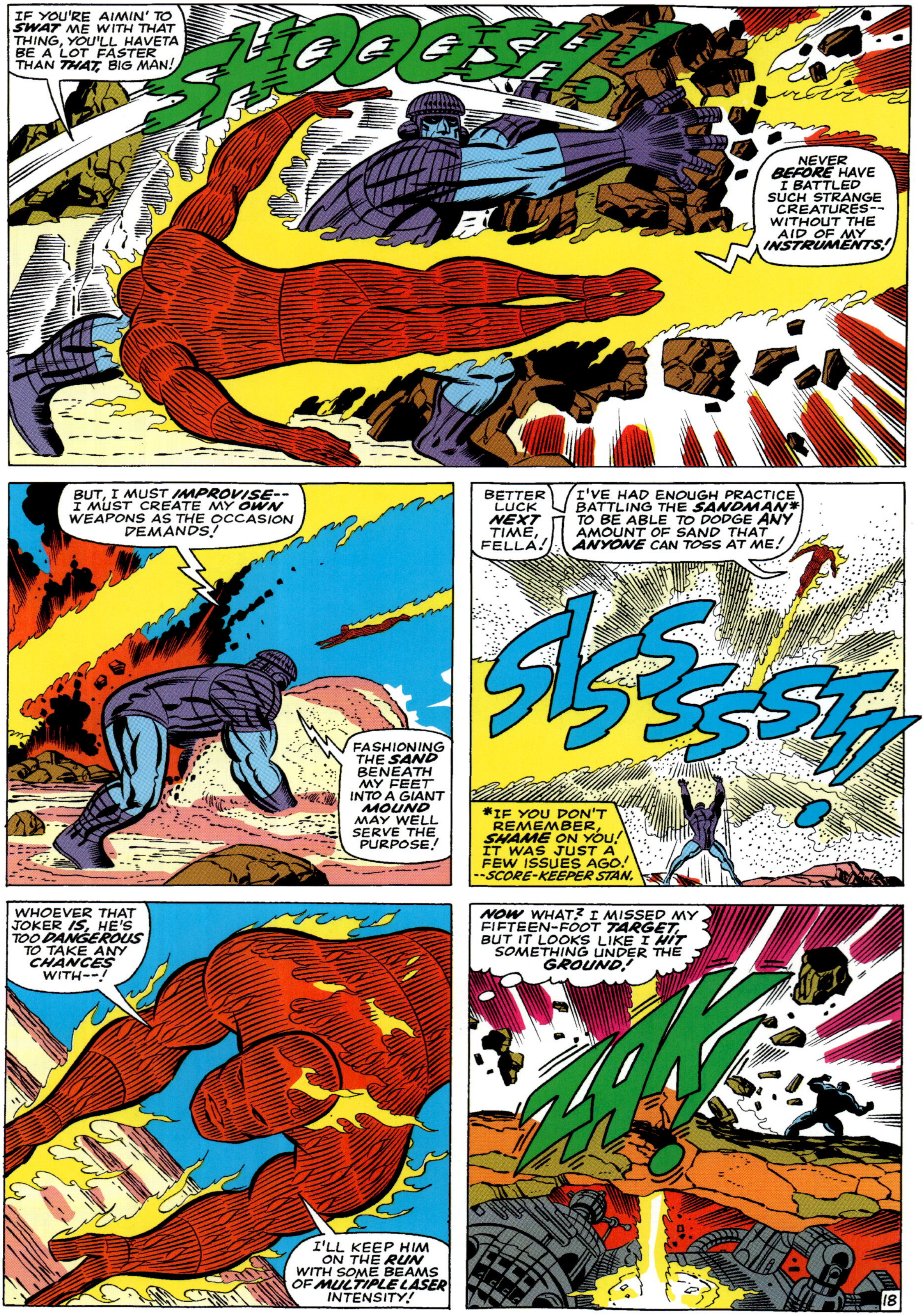
IF YOU'RE AIMIN' TO SWAT ME WITH THAT THING, YOU'LL HAVETA BE A LOT FASTER THAN THAT, BIG MAN!
SHOOOSH!
NEVER BEFORE HAVE I BATTLED SUCH STRANGE CREATURES-- WITHOUT THE AID OF MY INSTRUMENTS!
BUT, I MUST IMPROVISE-- I MUST CREATE MY OWN WEAPONS AS THE OCCASION DEMANDS!
FASHIONING THE SAND BENEATH MY FEET INTO A GIANT MOUND MAY WELL SERVE THE PURPOSE!
BETTER LUCK NEXT TIME, FELLA!
I'VE HAD ENOUGH PRACTICE BATTLING THE SANDMAN* TO BE ABLE TO DODGE ANY AMOUNT OF SAND THAT ANYONE CAN TOSS AT ME!
SISSSSST!!
*IF YOU DON'T REMEMBER, SHAME ON YOU! IT WAS JUST A FEW ISSUES AGO! --SCORE-KEEPER STAN.
WHOEVER THAT JOKER IS, HE'S TOO DANGEROUS TO TAKE ANY CHANCES WITH--!
I'LL KEEP HIM ON THE RUN WITH SOME BEAMS OF MULTIPLE LASER INTENSITY!
NOW WHAT? I MISSED MY FIFTEEN-FOOT TARGET, BUT IT LOOKS LIKE I HIT SOMETHING UNDER THE GROUND!
ZAK!
18

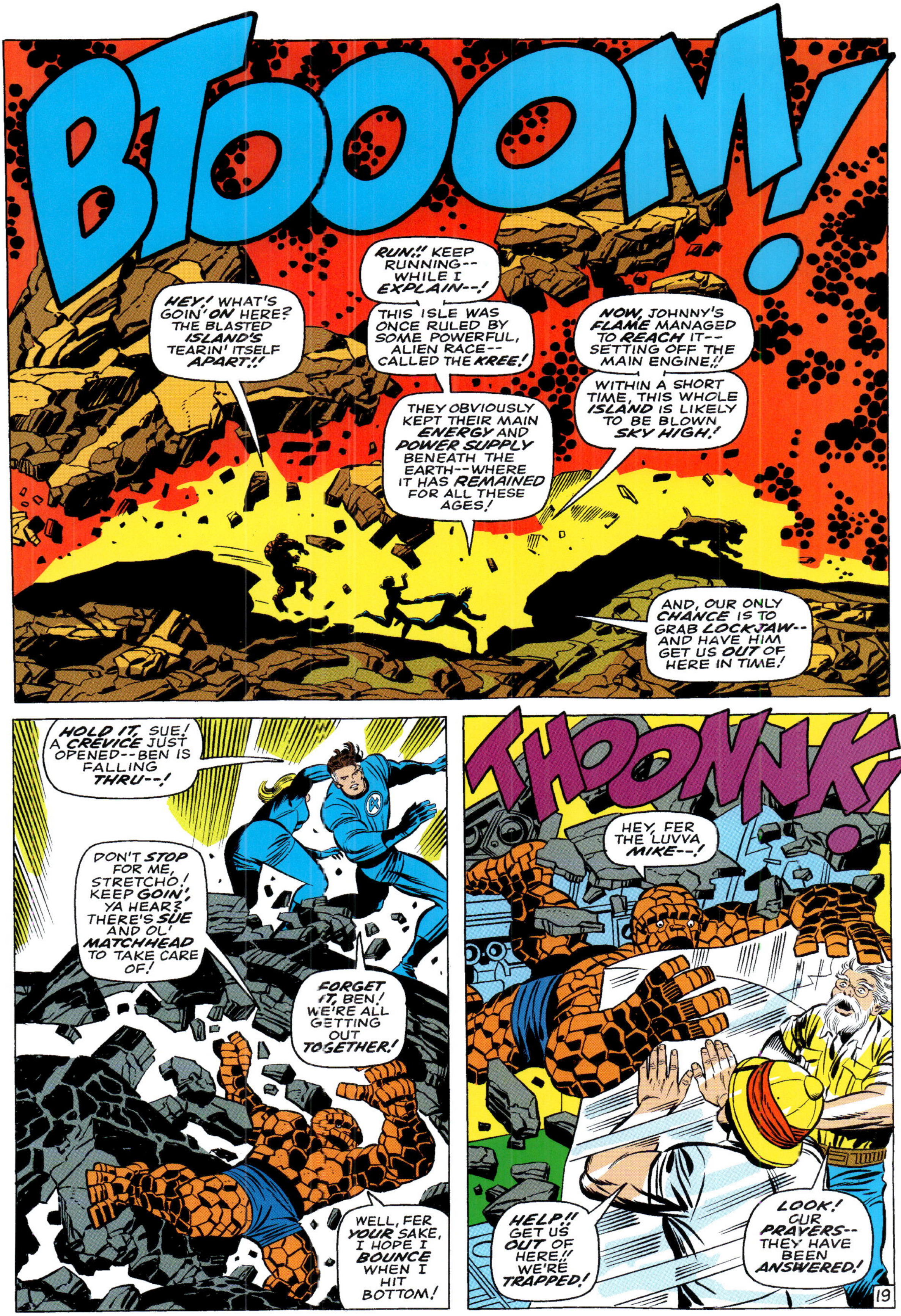
BTOOOM!
HEY! WHAT'S GOIN' ON HERE? THE BLASTED ISLAND'S TEARIN' ITSELF APART!!
RUN!! KEEP RUNNING-- WHILE I EXPLAIN--!
THIS ISLE WAS ONCE RULED BY SOME POWERFUL, ALIEN RACE-- CALLED THE KREE!
THEY OBVIOUSLY KEPT THEIR MAIN ENERGY AND POWER SUPPLY BENEATH THE EARTH--WHERE IT HAS REMAINED FOR ALL THESE AGES!
NOW, JOHNNY'S FLAME MANAGED TO REACH IT-- SETTING OFF THE MAIN ENGINE!!
WITHIN A SHORT TIME, THIS WHOLE ISLAND IS LIKELY TO BE BLOWN SKY HIGH!
AND, OUR ONLY CHANCE IS TO GRAB LOCKJAW-- AND HAVE HIM GET US OUT OF HERE IN TIME!
HOLD IT, SUE! A CREVICE JUST OPENED--BEN IS FALLING THRU--!
DON'T STOP FOR ME, STRETCHO! KEEP GOIN', YA HEAR? THERE'S SUE AND OL' MATCHHEAD TO TAKE CARE OF!
FORGET IT, BEN! WE'RE ALL GETTING OUT TOGETHER!
WELL, FER YOUR SAKE, I HOPE I BOUNCE WHEN I HIT BOTTOM!
THOONNK!
HEY, FER THE LUVVA MIKE--!
HELP!! GET US OUT OF HERE!! WE'RE TRAPPED!
LOOK! OUR PRAYERS-- THEY HAVE BEEN ANSWERED!
19

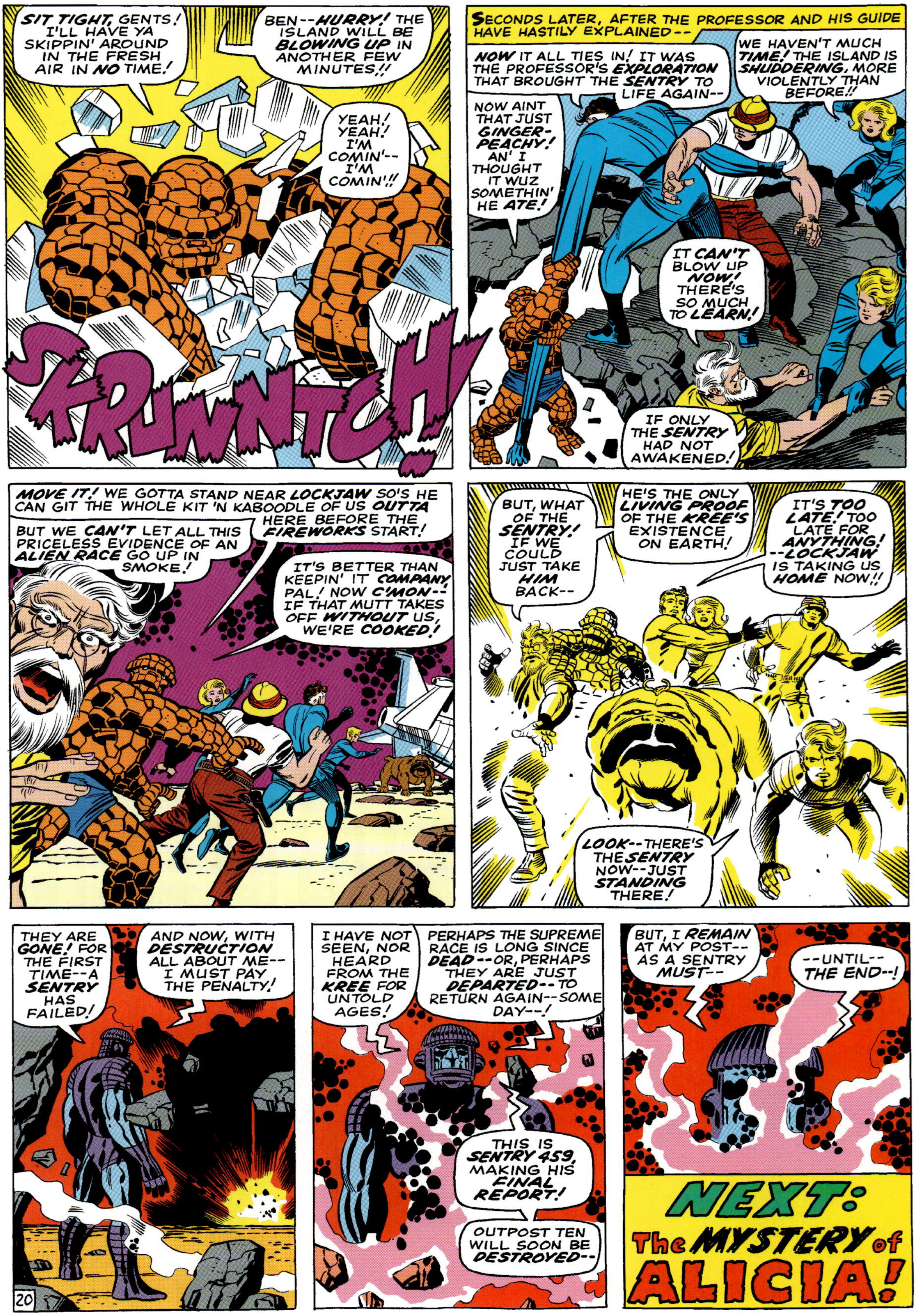
SIT TIGHT, GENTS! I'LL HAVE YA SKIPPIN' AROUND IN THE FRESH AIR IN NO TIME!
BEN--HURRY! THE ISLAND WILL BE BLOWING UP IN ANOTHER FEW MINUTES!!
YEAH! YEAH! I'M COMIN'-- I'M COMIN'!!
SKRUNNTCH!
SECONDS LATER, AFTER THE PROFESSOR AND HIS GUIDE HAVE HASTILY EXPLAINED--
NOW IT ALL TIES IN! IT WAS THE PROFESSOR'S EXPLORATION THAT BROUGHT THE SENTRY TO LIFE AGAIN--
WE HAVEN'T MUCH TIME! THE ISLAND IS SHUDDERING, MORE VIOLENTLY THAN BEFORE!!
NOW AINT THAT JUST GINGER-PEACHY! AN' I THOUGHT IT WUZ SOMETHIN' HE ATE!
IT CAN'T BLOW UP NOW! THERE'S SO MUCH TO LEARN!
IF ONLY THE SENTRY HAD NOT AWAKENED!
MOVE IT! WE GOTTA STAND NEAR LOCKJAW SO'S HE CAN GIT THE WHOLE KIT 'N KABOODLE OF US OUTTA HERE BEFORE THE FIREWORKS START!
BUT WE CAN'T LET ALL THIS PRICELESS EVIDENCE OF AN ALIEN RACE GO UP IN SMOKE!
IT'S BETTER THAN KEEPIN' IT COMPANY, PAL! NOW C'MON-- IF THAT MUTT TAKES OFF WITHOUT US, WE'RE COOKED!
BUT, WHAT OF THE SENTRY! IF WE COULD JUST TAKE HIM BACK--
HE'S THE ONLY LIVING PROOF OF THE KREE'S EXISTENCE ON EARTH!
IT'S TOO LATE! TOO LATE FOR ANYTHING! --LOCKJAW IS TAKING US HOME NOW!!
LOOK--THERE'S THE SENTRY NOW--JUST STANDING THERE!
THEY ARE GONE! FOR THE FIRST TIME--A SENTRY HAS FAILED!
AND NOW, WITH DESTRUCTION ALL ABOUT ME-- I MUST PAY THE PENALTY!
20
I HAVE NOT SEEN, NOR HEARD FROM THE KREE FOR UNTOLD AGES!
PERHAPS THE SUPREME RACE IS LONG SINCE DEAD--OR, PERHAPS THEY ARE JUST DEPARTED--TO RETURN AGAIN--SOME DAY--!
THIS IS SENTRY 459, MAKING HIS FINAL REPORT!
OUTPOST TEN WILL SOON BE DESTROYED--
BUT, I REMAIN AT MY POST-- AS A SENTRY MUST--
--UNTIL-- THE END--!
NEXT: The MYSTERY of ALICIA!

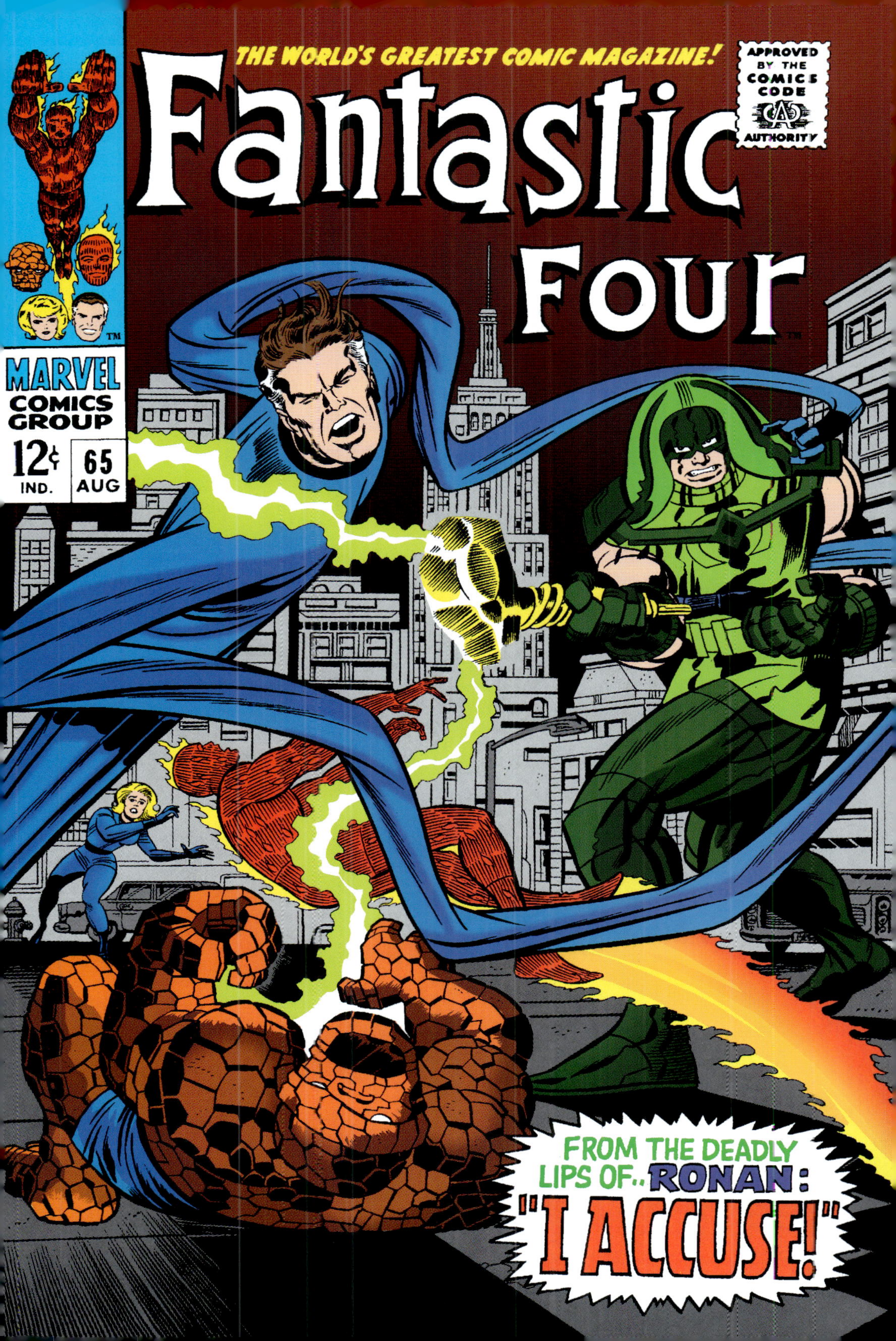
THE WORLD'S GREATEST COMIC MAGAZINE!
APPROVED BY THE COMICS CODE AUTHORITY
Fantastic Four
MARVEL COMICS GROUP
12¢ IND.
65 AUG
FROM THE DEADLY LIPS OF.. RONAN:
"I ACCUSE!"

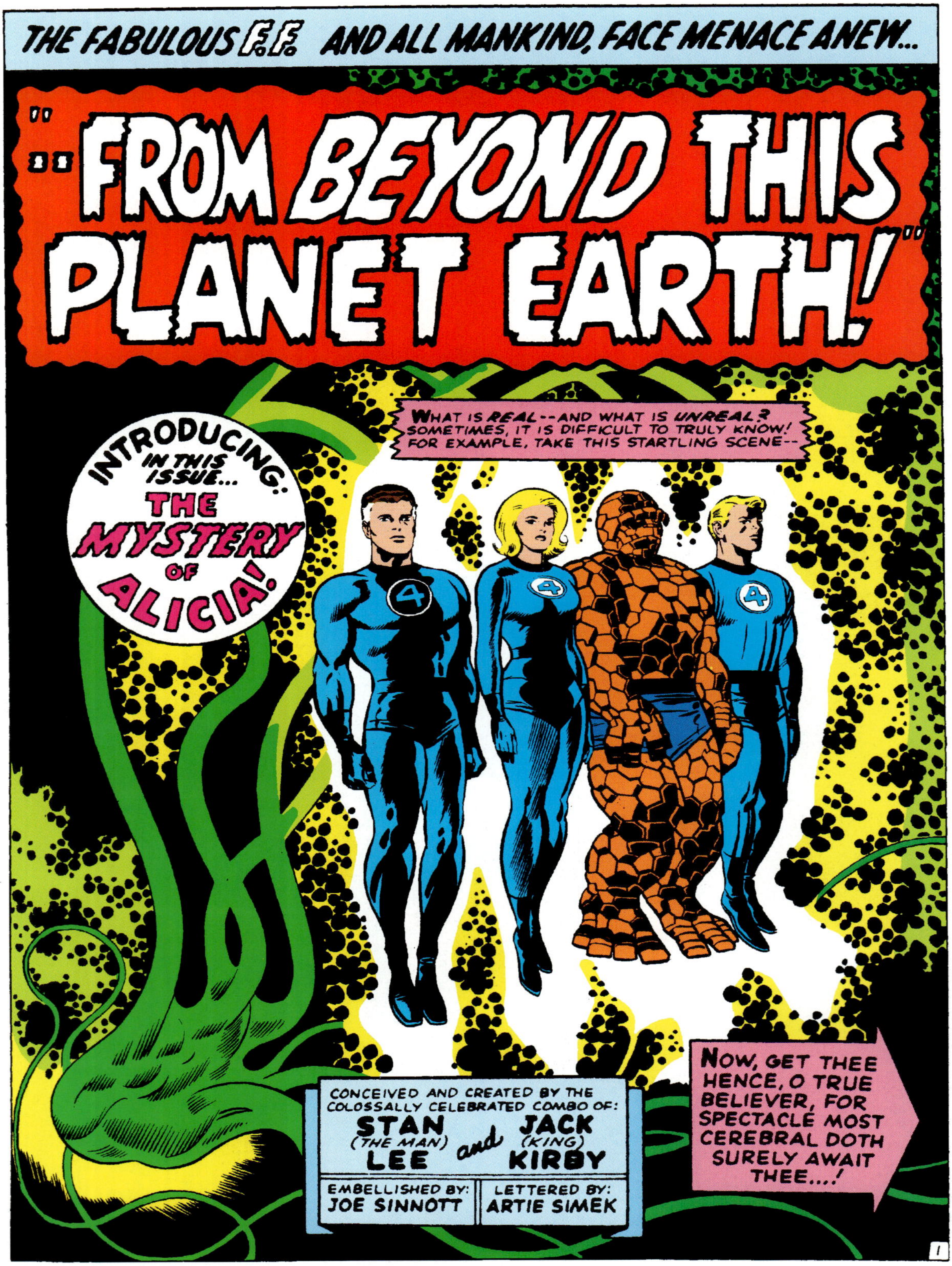
THE FABULOUS F.F. AND ALL MANKIND, FACE MENACE ANEW...
"--FROM BEYOND THIS PLANET EARTH!"
WHAT IS REAL--AND WHAT IS UNREAL? SOMETIMES, IT IS DIFFICULT TO TRULY KNOW! FOR EXAMPLE, TAKE THIS STARTLING SCENE--
INTRODUCING: IN THIS ISSUE... THE MYSTERY OF ALICIA!
CONCEIVED AND CREATED BY THE COLOSSALLY CELEBRATED COMBO OF: STAN (THE MAN) LEE and JACK (KING) KIRBY
EMBELLISHED BY: JOE SINNOTT
LETTERED BY: ARTIE SIMEK
NOW, GET THEE HENCE, O TRUE BELIEVER, FOR SPECTACLE MOST CEREBRAL DOTH SURELY AWAIT THEE...!
1

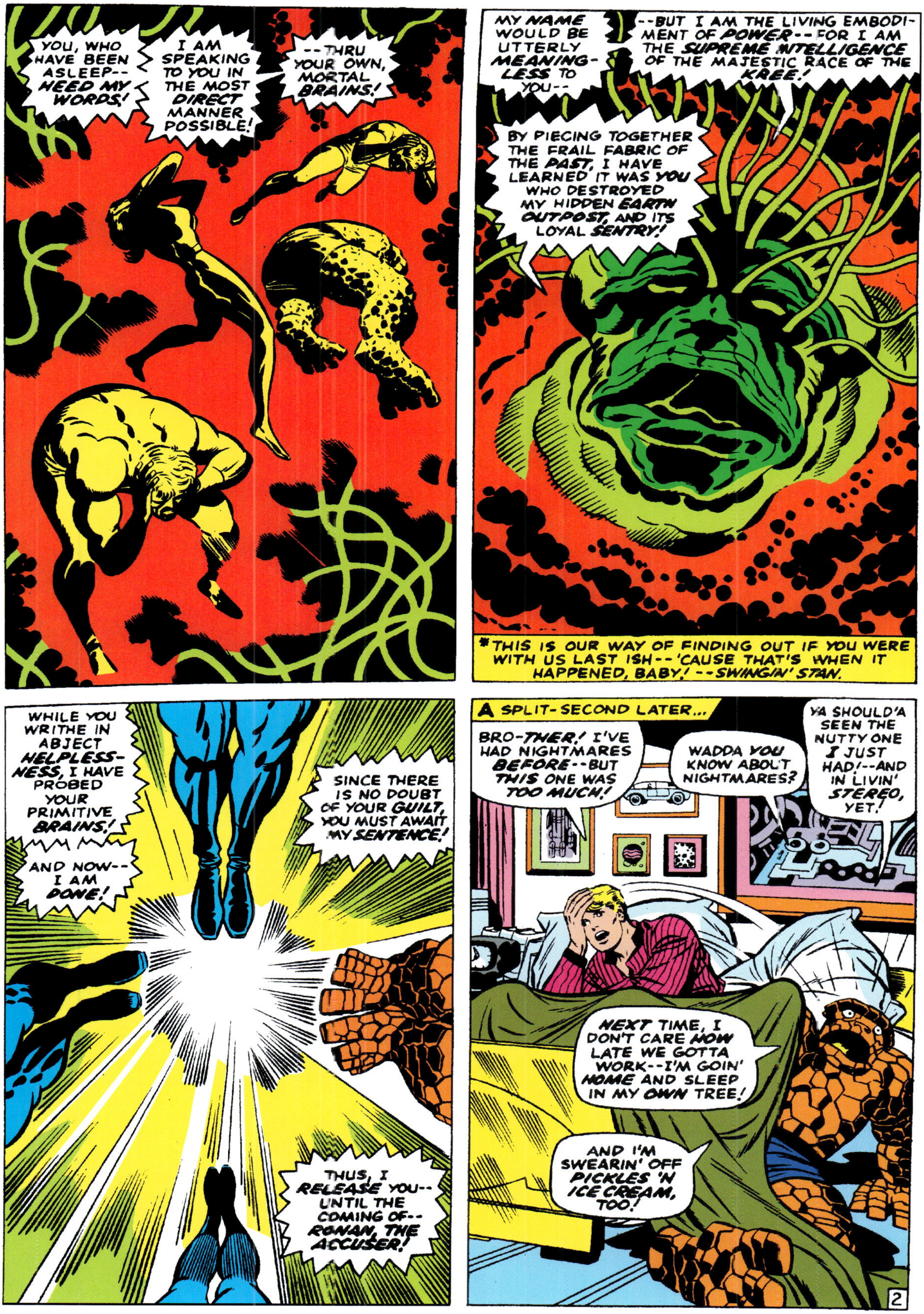
YOU, WHO HAVE BEEN ASLEEP-- HEED MY WORDS!
I AM SPEAKING TO YOU IN THE MOST DIRECT MANNER POSSIBLE!
--THRU YOUR OWN, MORTAL BRAINS!
MY NAME WOULD BE UTTERLY MEANING-LESS TO YOU--
--BUT I AM THE LIVING EMBODI-MENT OF POWER--FOR I AM THE SUPREME INTELLIGENCE OF THE MAJESTIC RACE OF THE KREE!
BY PIECING TOGETHER THE FRAIL FABRIC OF THE PAST, I HAVE LEARNED IT WAS YOU WHO DESTROYED MY HIDDEN EARTH OUTPOST, AND ITS LOYAL SENTRY!
*THIS IS OUR WAY OF FINDING OUT IF YOU WERE WITH US LAST ISH--'CAUSE THAT'S WHEN IT HAPPENED, BABY! --SWINGIN' STAN.
WHILE YOU WRITHE IN ABJECT HELPLESS-NESS, I HAVE PROBED YOUR PRIMITIVE BRAINS!
AND NOW-- I AM DONE!
SINCE THERE IS NO DOUBT OF YOUR GUILT, YOU MUST AWAIT MY SENTENCE!
THUS, I RELEASE YOU-- UNTIL THE COMING OF-- RONAN, THE ACCUSER!
A SPLIT-SECOND LATER...
BRO-THER! I'VE HAD NIGHTMARES BEFORE--BUT THIS ONE WAS TOO MUCH!
WADDA YOU KNOW ABOUT NIGHTMARES?
YA SHOULD'A SEEN THE NUTTY ONE I JUST HAD!--AND IN LIVIN' STEREO, YET!
NEXT TIME, I DON'T CARE HOW LATE WE GOTTA WORK--I'M GOIN' HOME AND SLEEP IN MY OWN TREE!
AND I'M SWEARIN' OFF PICKLES 'N ICE CREAM, TOO!
2

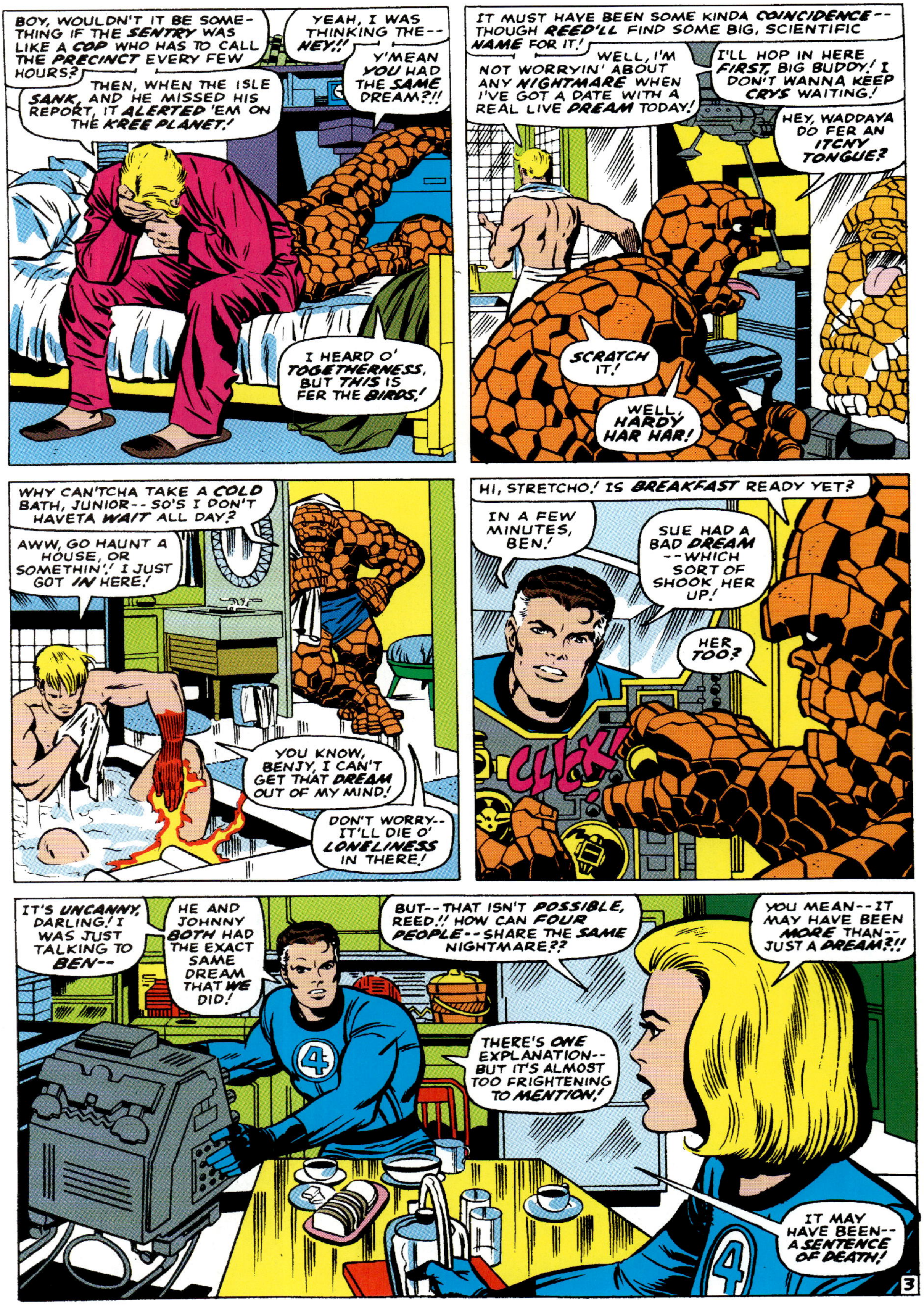
BOY, WOULDN'T IT BE SOMETHING IF THE SENTRY WAS LIKE A COP WHO HAS TO CALL THE PRECINCT EVERY FEW HOURS?
THEN, WHEN THE ISLE SANK, AND HE MISSED HIS REPORT, IT ALERTED 'EM ON THE KREE PLANET!
YEAH, I WAS THINKING THE-- HEY!!
Y'MEAN YOU HAD THE SAME DREAM?!!
I HEARD O' TOGETHERNESS, BUT THIS IS FER THE BIRDS!
IT MUST HAVE BEEN SOME KINDA COINCIDENCE-- THOUGH REED'LL FIND SOME BIG, SCIENTIFIC NAME FOR IT!
WELL, I'M NOT WORRYIN' ABOUT ANY NIGHTMARE WHEN I'VE GOT A DATE WITH A REAL LIVE DREAM TODAY!
I'LL HOP IN HERE FIRST, BIG BUDDY! I DON'T WANNA KEEP CRYS WAITING!
HEY, WADDAYA DO FER AN ITCHY TONGUE?
SCRATCH IT!
WELL, HARDY HAR HAR!
WHY CAN'TCHA TAKE A COLD BATH, JUNIOR-- SO'S I DON'T HAVETA WAIT ALL DAY?
AWW, GO HAUNT A HOUSE, OR SOMETHIN'! I JUST GOT IN HERE!
YOU KNOW, BENJY, I CAN'T GET THAT DREAM OUT OF MY MIND!
DON'T WORRY-- IT'LL DIE O' LONELINESS IN THERE!
HI, STRETCHO! IS BREAKFAST READY YET?
IN A FEW MINUTES, BEN!
SUE HAD A BAD DREAM --WHICH SORT OF SHOOK HER UP!
HER TOO?
CLICK!
IT'S UNCANNY, DARLING! I WAS JUST TALKING TO BEN--
HE AND JOHNNY BOTH HAD THE EXACT SAME DREAM THAT WE DID!
BUT--THAT ISN'T POSSIBLE, REED!! HOW CAN FOUR PEOPLE--SHARE THE SAME NIGHTMARE??
YOU MEAN--IT MAY HAVE BEEN MORE THAN-- JUST A DREAM?!!
THERE'S ONE EXPLANATION-- BUT IT'S ALMOST TOO FRIGHTENING TO MENTION!
IT MAY HAVE BEEN-- A SENTENCE OF DEATH!
3

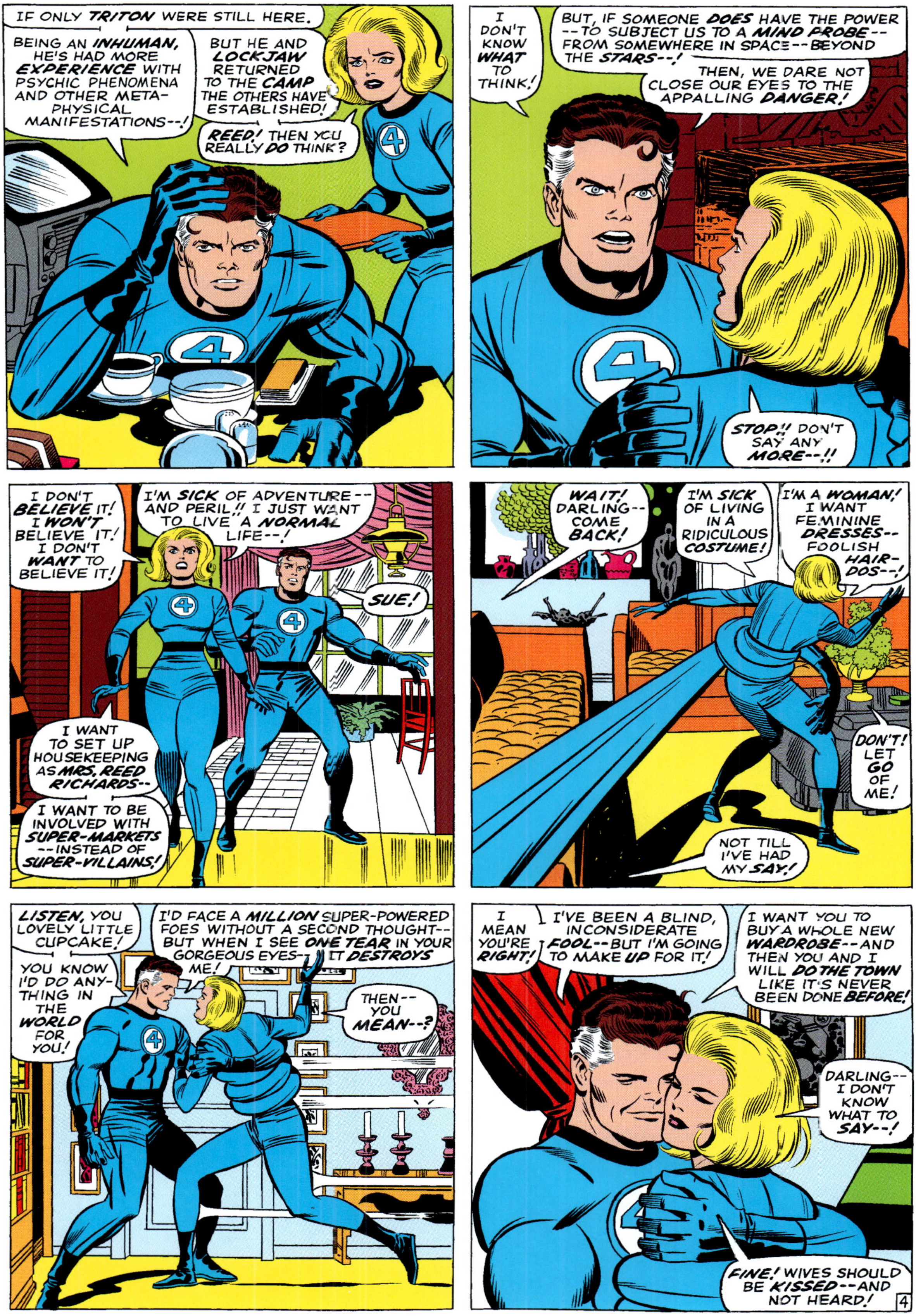
IF ONLY TRITON WERE STILL HERE.
BEING AN INHUMAN, HE'S HAD MORE EXPERIENCE WITH PSYCHIC PHENOMENA AND OTHER META-PHYSICAL MANIFESTATIONS--!
BUT HE AND LOCKJAW RETURNED TO THE CAMP THE OTHERS HAVE ESTABLISHED!
REED! THEN YOU REALLY DO THINK?
I DON'T KNOW WHAT TO THINK!
BUT, IF SOMEONE DOES HAVE THE POWER --TO SUBJECT US TO A MIND PROBE-- FROM SOMEWHERE IN SPACE--BEYOND THE STARS--!
THEN, WE DARE NOT CLOSE OUR EYES TO THE APPALLING DANGER!
STOP!! DON'T SAY ANY MORE--!!
I DON'T BELIEVE IT! I WON'T BELIEVE IT! I DON'T WANT TO BELIEVE IT!
I'M SICK OF ADVENTURE-- AND PERIL!! I JUST WANT TO LIVE A NORMAL LIFE--!
SUE!
I WANT TO SET UP HOUSEKEEPING AS MRS. REED RICHARDS--
I WANT TO BE INVOLVED WITH SUPER-MARKETS --INSTEAD OF SUPER-VILLAINS!
WAIT! DARLING-- COME BACK!
I'M SICK OF LIVING IN A RIDICULOUS COSTUME!
I'M A WOMAN! I WANT FEMININE DRESSES-- FOOLISH HAIR-DOS--!
DON'T! LET GO OF ME!
NOT TILL I'VE HAD MY SAY!
LISTEN, YOU LOVELY LITTLE CUPCAKE!
YOU KNOW I'D DO ANY-THING IN THE WORLD FOR YOU!
I'D FACE A MILLION SUPER-POWERED FOES WITHOUT A SECOND THOUGHT-- BUT WHEN I SEE ONE TEAR IN YOUR GORGEOUS EYES-- IT DESTROYS ME!
THEN-- YOU MEAN--?
I MEAN YOU'RE RIGHT!
I'VE BEEN A BLIND, INCONSIDERATE FOOL--BUT I'M GOING TO MAKE UP FOR IT!
I WANT YOU TO BUY A WHOLE NEW WARDROBE--AND THEN YOU AND I WILL DO THE TOWN LIKE IT'S NEVER BEEN DONE BEFORE!
DARLING-- I DON'T KNOW WHAT TO SAY--!
FINE! WIVES SHOULD BE KISSED--AND NOT HEARD!
4

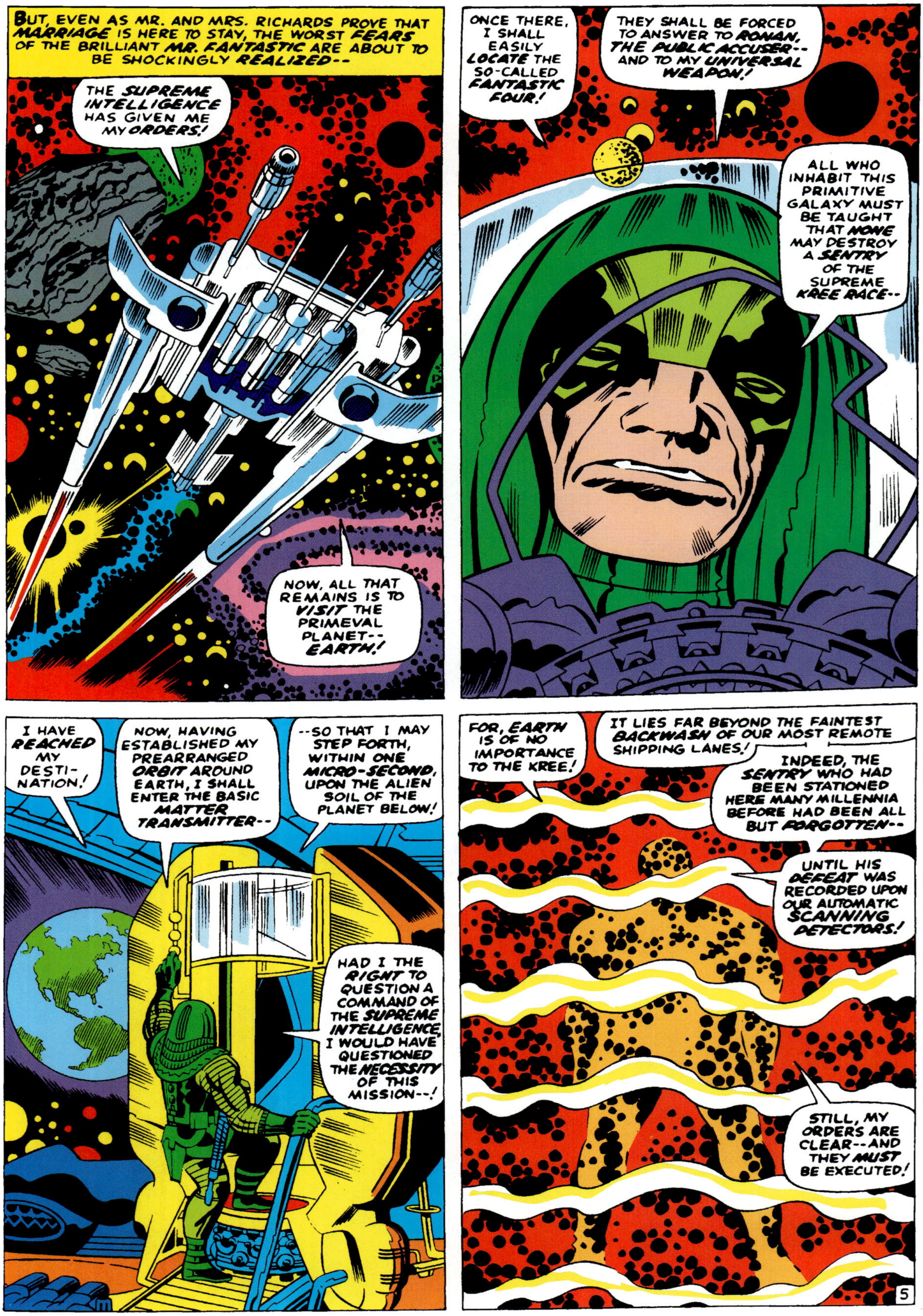
BUT, EVEN AS MR. AND MRS. RICHARDS PROVE THAT MARRIAGE IS HERE TO STAY, THE WORST FEARS OF THE BRILLIANT MR. FANTASTIC ARE ABOUT TO BE SHOCKINGLY REALIZED--
THE SUPREME INTELLIGENCE HAS GIVEN ME MY ORDERS!
NOW, ALL THAT REMAINS IS TO VISIT THE PRIMEVAL PLANET-- EARTH!
ONCE THERE, I SHALL EASILY LOCATE THE SO-CALLED FANTASTIC FOUR!
THEY SHALL BE FORCED TO ANSWER TO RONAN, THE PUBLIC ACCUSER-- AND TO MY UNIVERSAL WEAPON!
ALL WHO INHABIT THIS PRIMITIVE GALAXY MUST BE TAUGHT THAT NONE MAY DESTROY A SENTRY OF THE SUPREME KREE RACE--
I HAVE REACHED MY DESTI-NATION!
NOW, HAVING ESTABLISHED MY PREARRANGED ORBIT AROUND EARTH, I SHALL ENTER THE BASIC MATTER TRANSMITTER--
--SO THAT I MAY STEP FORTH, WITHIN ONE MICRO-SECOND, UPON THE ALIEN SOIL OF THE PLANET BELOW!
HAD I THE RIGHT TO QUESTION A COMMAND OF THE SUPREME INTELLIGENCE, I WOULD HAVE QUESTIONED THE NECESSITY OF THIS MISSION--!
FOR, EARTH IS OF NO IMPORTANCE TO THE KREE!
IT LIES FAR BEYOND THE FAINTEST BACKWASH OF OUR MOST REMOTE SHIPPING LANES!
INDEED, THE SENTRY WHO HAD BEEN STATIONED HERE MANY MILLENNIA BEFORE HAD BEEN ALL BUT FORGOTTEN--
UNTIL HIS DEFEAT WAS RECORDED UPON OUR AUTOMATIC SCANNING DETECTORS!
STILL, MY ORDERS ARE CLEAR--AND THEY MUST BE EXECUTED!
5

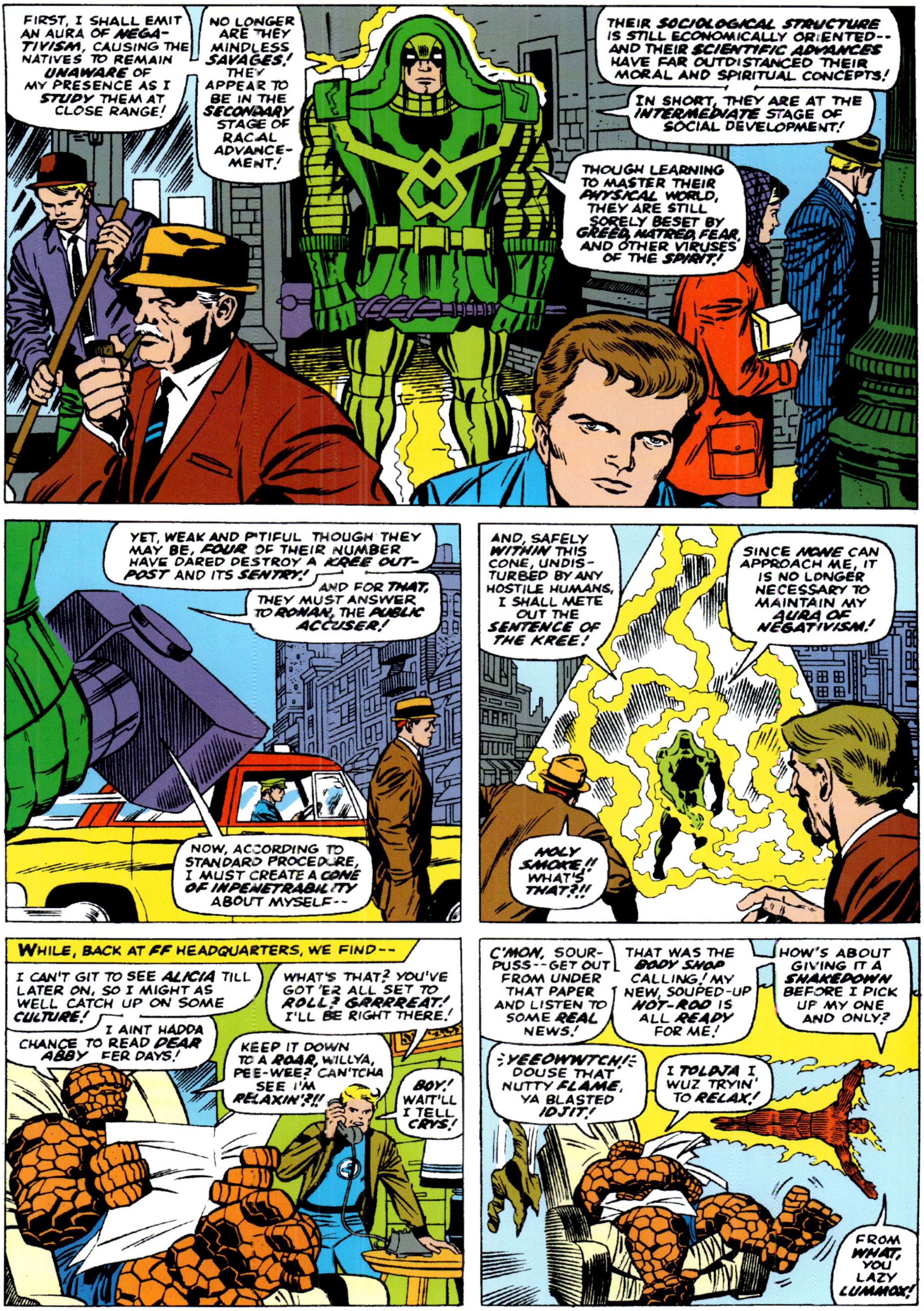
FIRST, I SHALL EMIT AN AURA OF NEGATIVISM, CAUSING THE NATIVES TO REMAIN UNAWARE OF MY PRESENCE AS I STUDY THEM AT CLOSE RANGE!
NO LONGER ARE THEY MINDLESS SAVAGES! THEY APPEAR TO BE IN THE SECONDARY STAGE OF RACIAL ADVANCEMENT!
THEIR SOCIOLOGICAL STRUCTURE IS STILL ECONOMICALLY ORIENTED-- AND THEIR SCIENTIFIC ADVANCES HAVE FAR OUTDISTANCED THEIR MORAL AND SPIRITUAL CONCEPTS!
IN SHORT, THEY ARE AT THE INTERMEDIATE STAGE OF SOCIAL DEVELOPMENT!
THOUGH LEARNING TO MASTER THEIR PHYSICAL WORLD, THEY ARE STILL SORELY BESET BY GREED, HATRED, FEAR, AND OTHER VIRUSES OF THE SPIRIT!
YET, WEAK AND PITIFUL THOUGH THEY MAY BE, FOUR OF THEIR NUMBER HAVE DARED DESTROY A KREE OUTPOST AND ITS SENTRY!
AND FOR THAT, THEY MUST ANSWER TO RONAN, THE PUBLIC ACCUSER!
NOW, ACCORDING TO STANDARD PROCEDURE, I MUST CREATE A CONE OF INPENETRABILITY ABOUT MYSELF--
AND, SAFELY WITHIN THIS CONE, UNDISTURBED BY ANY HOSTILE HUMANS, I SHALL METE OUT THE SENTENCE OF THE KREE!
SINCE NONE CAN APPROACH ME, IT IS NO LONGER NECESSARY TO MAINTAIN MY AURA OF NEGATIVISM!
HOLY SMOKE!! WHAT'S THAT?!!
WHILE, BACK AT FF HEADQUARTERS, WE FIND--
I CAN'T GIT TO SEE ALICIA TILL LATER ON, SO I MIGHT AS WELL CATCH UP ON SOME CULTURE!
I AINT HADDA CHANCE TO READ DEAR ABBY FER DAYS!
WHAT'S THAT? YOU'VE GOT 'ER ALL SET TO ROLL? GRRRREAT! I'LL BE RIGHT THERE!
KEEP IT DOWN TO A ROAR, WILLYA, PEE-WEE? CAN'TCHA SEE I'M RELAXIN'?!!
BOY! WAIT'LL I TELL CRYS!
C'MON, SOURPUSS--GET OUT FROM UNDER THAT PAPER AND LISTEN TO SOME REAL NEWS!
THAT WAS THE BODY SHOP CALLING! MY NEW, SOUPED-UP HOT-ROD IS ALL READY FOR ME!
HOW'S ABOUT GIVING IT A SHAKEDOWN BEFORE I PICK UP MY ONE AND ONLY?
YEEOWWTCH! DOUSE THAT NUTTY FLAME, YA BLASTED IDJIT!
I TOLDJA I WUZ TRYIN' TO RELAX!
FROM WHAT, YOU LAZY LUMMOX!

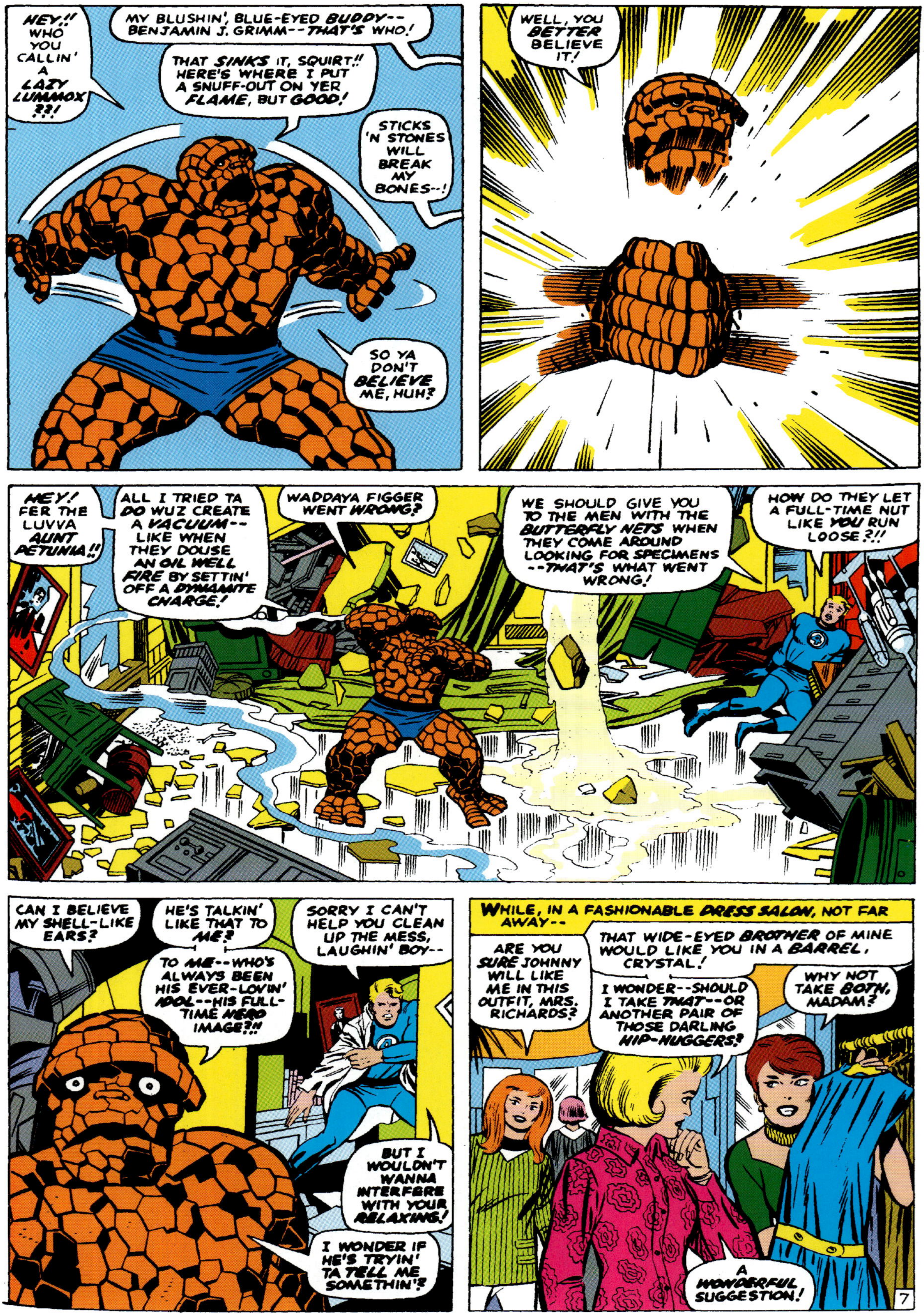
HEY!! WHO YOU CALLIN' A LAZY LUMMOX ??!
MY BLUSHIN', BLUE-EYED BUDDY-- BENJAMIN J. GRIMM--THAT'S WHO!
THAT SINKS IT, SQUIRT!! HERE'S WHERE I PUT A SNUFF-OUT ON YER FLAME, BUT GOOD!
STICKS 'N STONES WILL BREAK MY BONES--!
SO YA DON'T BELIEVE ME, HUH?
WELL, YOU BETTER BELIEVE IT!
HEY! FER THE LUVVA AUNT PETUNIA!!
ALL I TRIED TA DO WUZ CREATE A VACUUM-- LIKE WHEN THEY DOUSE AN OIL WELL FIRE BY SETTIN' OFF A DYNAMITE CHARGE!
WADDAYA FIGGER WENT WRONG?
WE SHOULD GIVE YOU TO THE MEN WITH THE BUTTERFLY NETS WHEN THEY COME AROUND LOOKING FOR SPECIMENS --THAT'S WHAT WENT WRONG!
HOW DO THEY LET A FULL-TIME NUT LIKE YOU RUN LOOSE?!!
CAN I BELIEVE MY SHELL-LIKE EARS?
HE'S TALKIN' LIKE THAT TO ME?
TO ME--WHO'S ALWAYS BEEN HIS EVER-LOVIN' IDOL--HIS FULL-TIME HERO IMAGE?!!
SORRY I CAN'T HELP YOU CLEAN UP THE MESS, LAUGHIN' BOY--
BUT I WOULDN'T WANNA INTERFERE WITH YOUR RELAXING!
I WONDER IF HE'S TRYIN' TA TELL ME SOMETHIN'?
WHILE, IN A FASHIONABLE DRESS SALON, NOT FAR AWAY--
ARE YOU SURE JOHNNY WILL LIKE ME IN THIS OUTFIT, MRS. RICHARDS?
THAT WIDE-EYED BROTHER OF MINE WOULD LIKE YOU IN A BARREL, CRYSTAL!
I WONDER--SHOULD I TAKE THAT--OR ANOTHER PAIR OF THOSE DARLING HIP-HUGGERS?
WHY NOT TAKE BOTH, MADAM?
A WONDERFUL SUGGESTION!
7

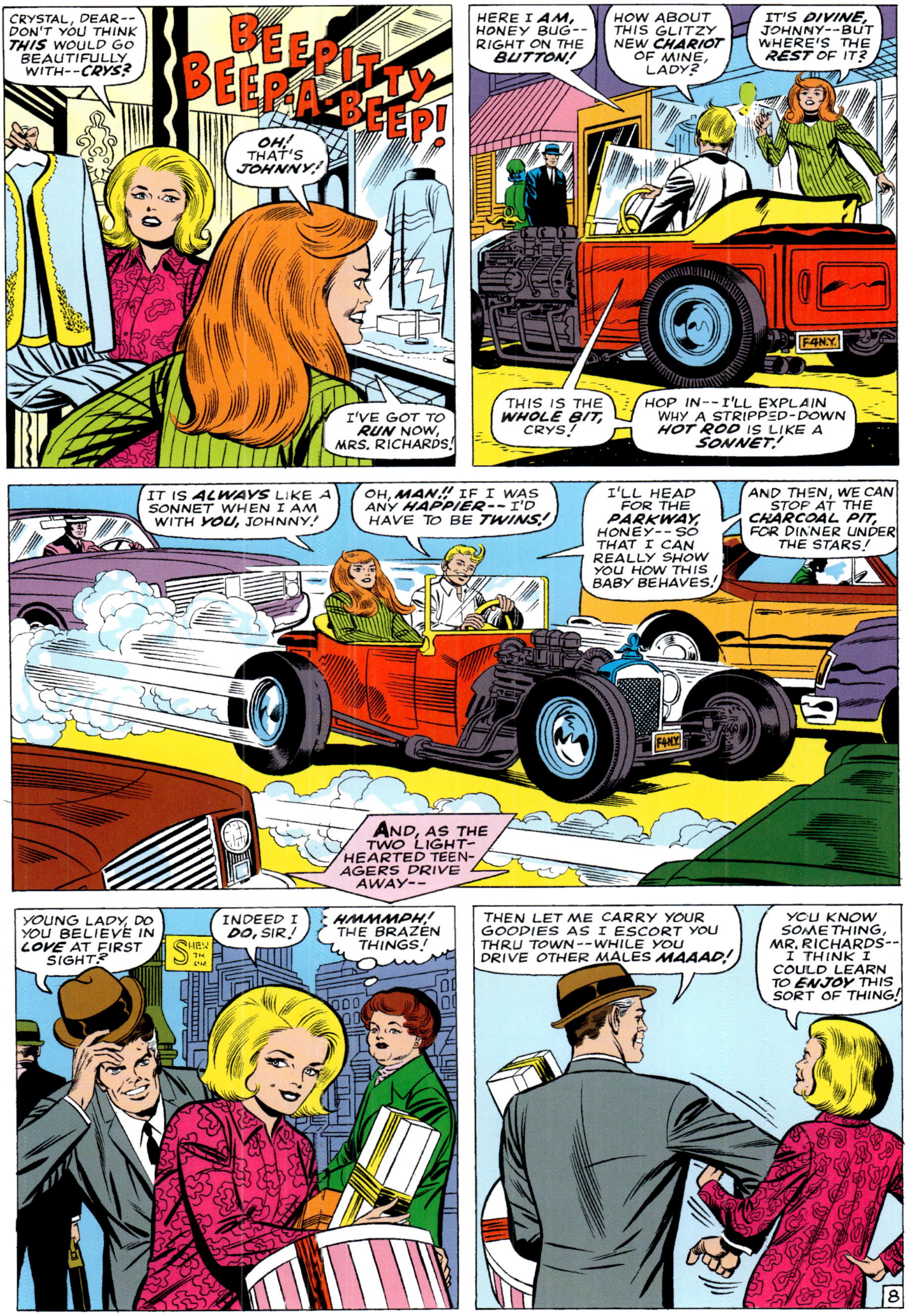
CRYSTAL, DEAR-- DON'T YOU THINK THIS WOULD GO BEAUTIFULLY WITH--CRYS?
BEEP BEEP-PITTY BEEP-A-BEEP!
OH! THAT'S JOHNNY!
I'VE GOT TO RUN NOW, MRS. RICHARDS!
HERE I AM, HONEY BUG-- RIGHT ON THE BUTTON!
HOW ABOUT THIS GLITZY NEW CHARIOT OF MINE, LADY?
IT'S DIVINE, JOHNNY--BUT WHERE'S THE REST OF IT?
F4N.Y.
THIS IS THE WHOLE BIT, CRYS!
HOP IN--I'LL EXPLAIN WHY A STRIPPED-DOWN HOT ROD IS LIKE A SONNET!
IT IS ALWAYS LIKE A SONNET WHEN I AM WITH YOU, JOHNNY!
OH, MAN!! IF I WAS ANY HAPPIER--I'D HAVE TO BE TWINS!
I'LL HEAD FOR THE PARKWAY, HONEY--SO THAT I CAN REALLY SHOW YOU HOW THIS BABY BEHAVES!
AND THEN, WE CAN STOP AT THE CHARCOAL PIT, FOR DINNER UNDER THE STARS!
F4N.Y.
AND, AS THE TWO LIGHT-HEARTED TEEN-AGERS DRIVE AWAY--
YOUNG LADY, DO YOU BELIEVE IN LOVE AT FIRST SIGHT?
INDEED I DO, SIR!
HMMMPH! THE BRAZEN THINGS!
THEN LET ME CARRY YOUR GOODIES AS I ESCORT YOU THRU TOWN--WHILE YOU DRIVE OTHER MALES MAAAD!
YOU KNOW SOMETHING, MR. RICHARDS-- I THINK I COULD LEARN TO ENJOY THIS SORT OF THING!
8

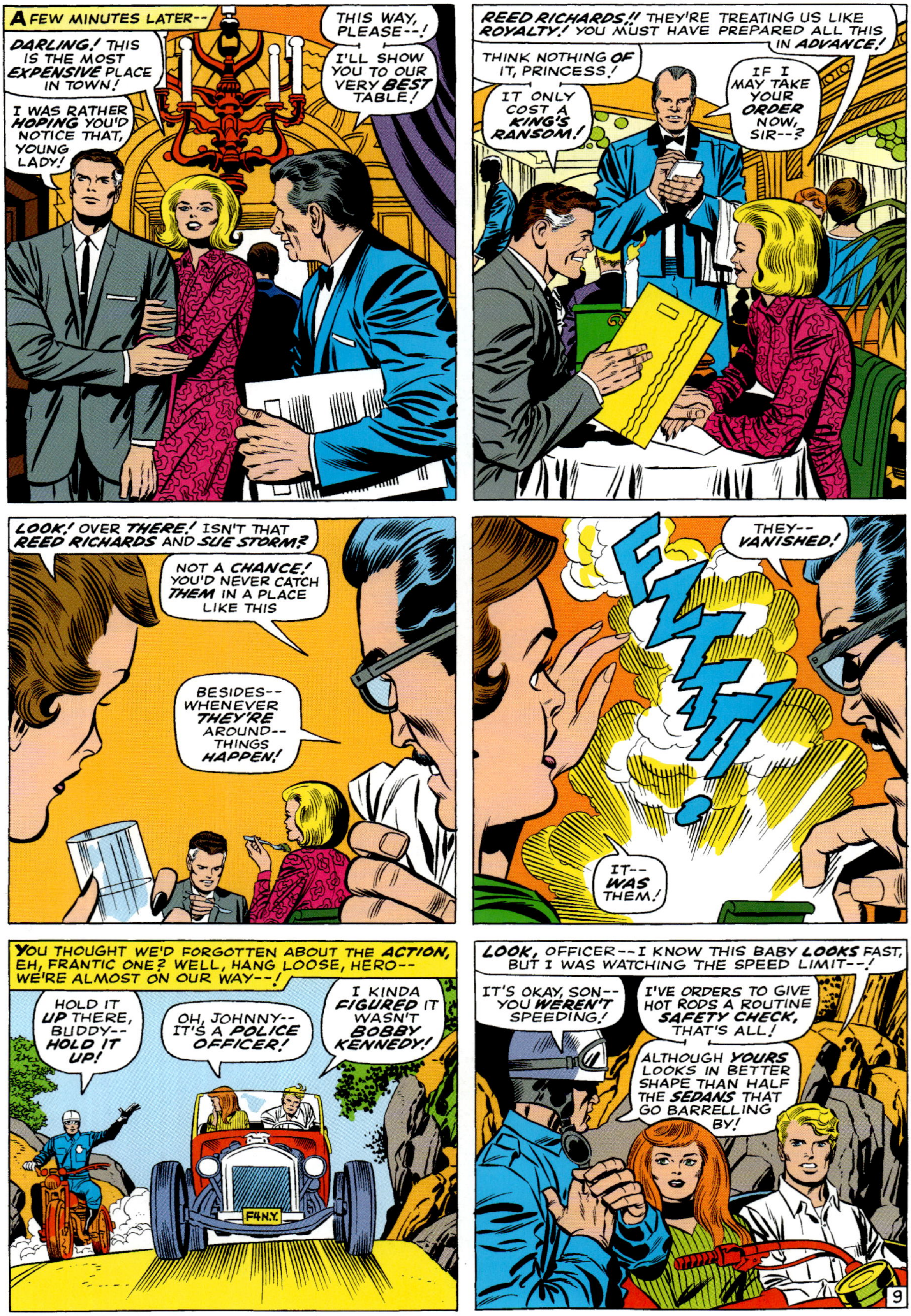
A FEW MINUTES LATER--
DARLING! THIS IS THE MOST EXPENSIVE PLACE IN TOWN!
I WAS RATHER HOPING YOU'D NOTICE THAT, YOUNG LADY!
THIS WAY, PLEASE--!
I'LL SHOW YOU TO OUR VERY BEST TABLE!
REED RICHARDS!! THEY'RE TREATING US LIKE ROYALTY! YOU MUST HAVE PREPARED ALL THIS IN ADVANCE!
THINK NOTHING OF IT, PRINCESS!
IT ONLY COST A KING'S RANSOM!
IF I MAY TAKE YOUR ORDER NOW, SIR--?
LOOK! OVER THERE! ISN'T THAT REED RICHARDS AND SUE STORM?
NOT A CHANCE! YOU'D NEVER CATCH THEM IN A PLACE LIKE THIS
BESIDES-- WHENEVER THEY'RE AROUND-- THINGS HAPPEN!
FZZTTT!
THEY-- VANISHED!
IT-- WAS THEM!
YOU THOUGHT WE'D FORGOTTEN ABOUT THE ACTION, EH, FRANTIC ONE? WELL, HANG LOOSE, HERO-- WE'RE ALMOST ON OUR WAY--!
HOLD IT UP THERE, BUDDY-- HOLD IT UP!
OH, JOHNNY-- IT'S A POLICE OFFICER!
I KINDA FIGURED IT WASN'T BOBBY KENNEDY!
F4N.Y.
LOOK, OFFICER--I KNOW THIS BABY LOOKS FAST, BUT I WAS WATCHING THE SPEED LIMIT--!
IT'S OKAY, SON-- YOU WEREN'T SPEEDING!
I'VE ORDERS TO GIVE HOT RODS A ROUTINE SAFETY CHECK, THAT'S ALL!
ALTHOUGH YOURS LOOKS IN BETTER SHAPE THAN HALF THE SEDANS THAT GO BARRELLING BY!
9

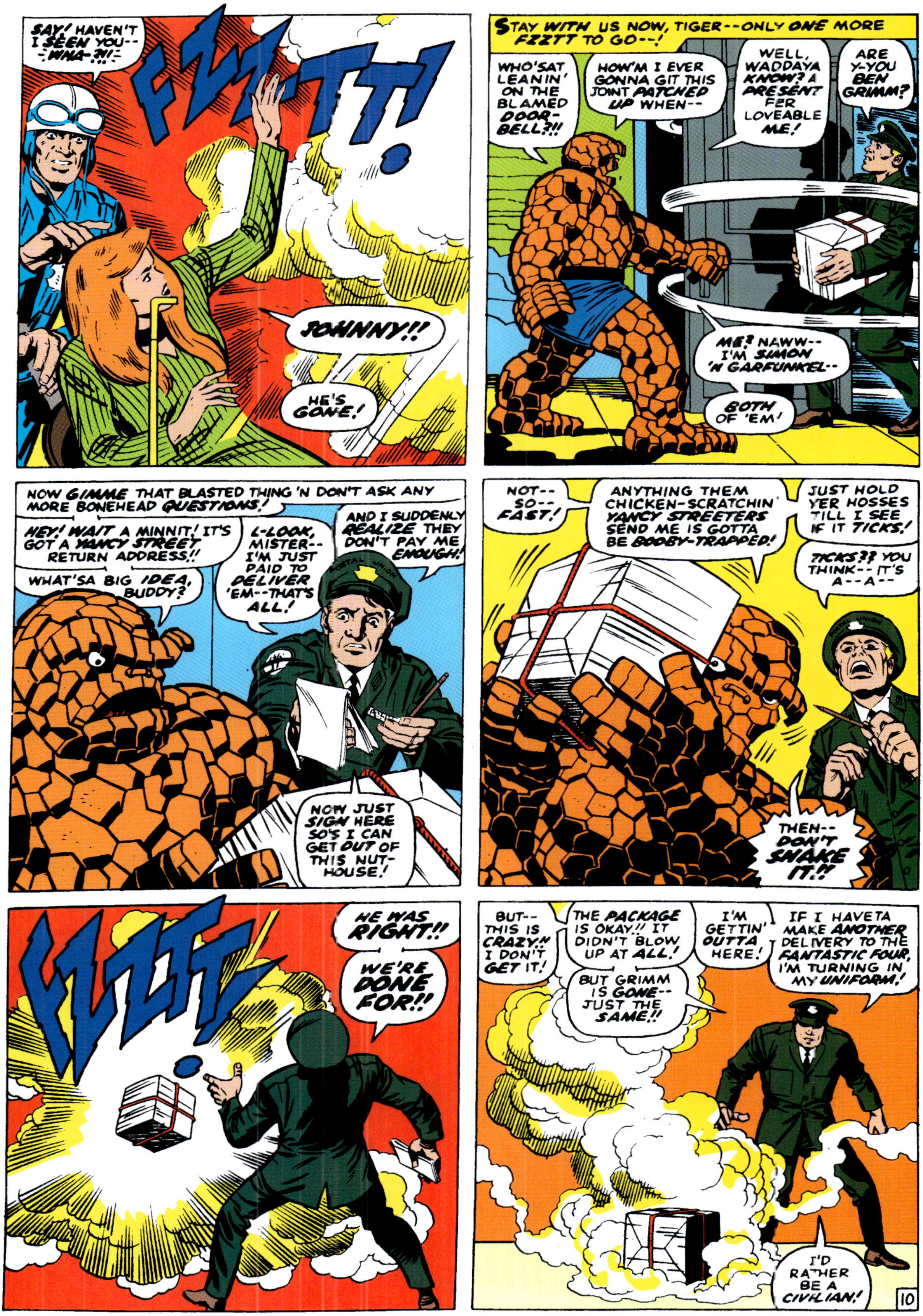
SAY! HAVEN'T I SEEN YOU-- -WHA-?!!-
FZZ-TT!
JOHNNY!!
HE'S GONE!
STAY WITH US NOW, TIGER--ONLY ONE MORE FZZTT TO GO--!
WHO'SAT LEANIN' ON THE BLAMED DOOR-BELL?!!
HOW'M I EVER GONNA GIT THIS JOINT PATCHED UP WHEN--
WELL, WADDAYA KNOW? A PRESENT FER LOVEABLE ME!
ARE Y-YOU BEN GRIMM?
ME? NAWW-- I'M SIMON 'N GARFUNKEL--
BOTH OF 'EM!
NOW GIMME THAT BLASTED THING 'N DON'T ASK ANY MORE BONEHEAD QUESTIONS!
HEY! WAIT A MINNIT! IT'S GOT A YANCY STREET RETURN ADDRESS!!
WHAT'SA BIG IDEA, BUDDY?
L-LOOK, MISTER-- I'M JUST PAID TO DELIVER 'EM--THAT'S ALL!
AND I SUDDENLY REALIZE THEY DON'T PAY ME ENOUGH!
NOW JUST SIGN HERE SO'S I CAN GET OUT OF THIS NUT-HOUSE!
NOT-- SO-- FAST!
ANYTHING THEM CHICKEN-SCRATCHIN' YANCY STREETERS SEND ME IS GOTTA BE BOOBY-TRAPPED!
JUST HOLD YER HOSSES TILL I SEE IF IT TICKS!
TICKS?? YOU THINK-- IT'S A--A--
THEN-- DON'T SHAKE IT!!
FZZTT!
HE WAS RIGHT!!
WE'RE DONE FOR!!
BUT-- THIS IS CRAZY!! I DON'T GET IT!
THE PACKAGE IS OKAY!! IT DIDN'T BLOW UP AT ALL!
BUT GRIMM IS GONE-- JUST THE SAME!!
I'M GETTIN' OUTTA HERE!
IF I HAVETA MAKE ANOTHER DELIVERY TO THE FANTASTIC FOUR, I'M TURNING IN MY UNIFORM!
I'D RATHER BE A CIVILIAN!
10

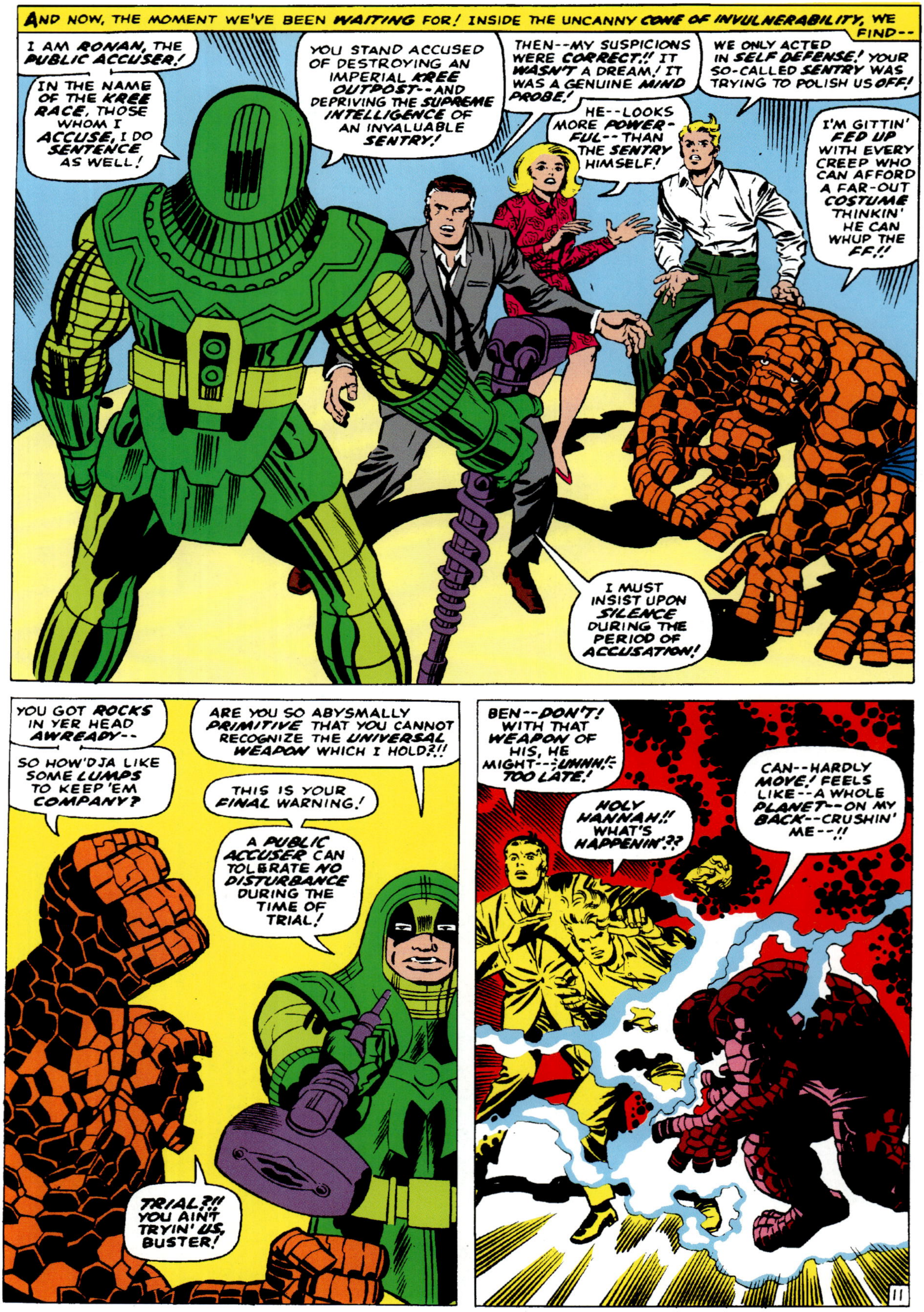
AND NOW, THE MOMENT WE'VE BEEN WAITING FOR! INSIDE THE UNCANNY CONE OF INVULNERABILITY, WE FIND--
I AM RONAN, THE PUBLIC ACCUSER!
IN THE NAME OF THE KREE RACE, THOSE WHOM I ACCUSE, I DO SENTENCE AS WELL!
YOU STAND ACCUSED OF DESTROYING AN IMPERIAL KREE OUTPOST--AND DEPRIVING THE SUPREME INTELLIGENCE OF AN INVALUABLE SENTRY!
THEN--MY SUSPICIONS WERE CORRECT!! IT WASN'T A DREAM! IT WAS A GENUINE MIND PROBE!
HE--LOOKS MORE POWER-FUL--THAN THE SENTRY HIMSELF!
WE ONLY ACTED IN SELF DEFENSE! YOUR SO-CALLED SENTRY WAS TRYING TO POLISH US OFF!
I'M GITTIN' FED UP WITH EVERY CREEP WHO CAN AFFORD A FAR-OUT COSTUME THINKIN' HE CAN WHUP THE FF!!
I MUST INSIST UPON SILENCE DURING THE PERIOD OF ACCUSATION!
YOU GOT ROCKS IN YER HEAD AWREADY--
SO HOW'DJA LIKE SOME LUMPS TO KEEP 'EM COMPANY?
ARE YOU SO ABYSMALLY PRIMITIVE THAT YOU CANNOT RECOGNIZE THE UNIVERSAL WEAPON WHICH I HOLD?!!
THIS IS YOUR FINAL WARNING!
A PUBLIC ACCUSER CAN TOLERATE NO DISTURBANCE DURING THE TIME OF TRIAL!
TRIAL?!! YOU AIN'T TRYIN' US, BUSTER!
BEN--DON'T! WITH THAT WEAPON OF HIS, HE MIGHT--UNNH!--TOO LATE!
HOLY HANNAH!! WHAT'S HAPPENIN'??
CAN--HARDLY MOVE! FEELS LIKE--A WHOLE PLANET--ON MY BACK--CRUSHIN' ME--!!
11

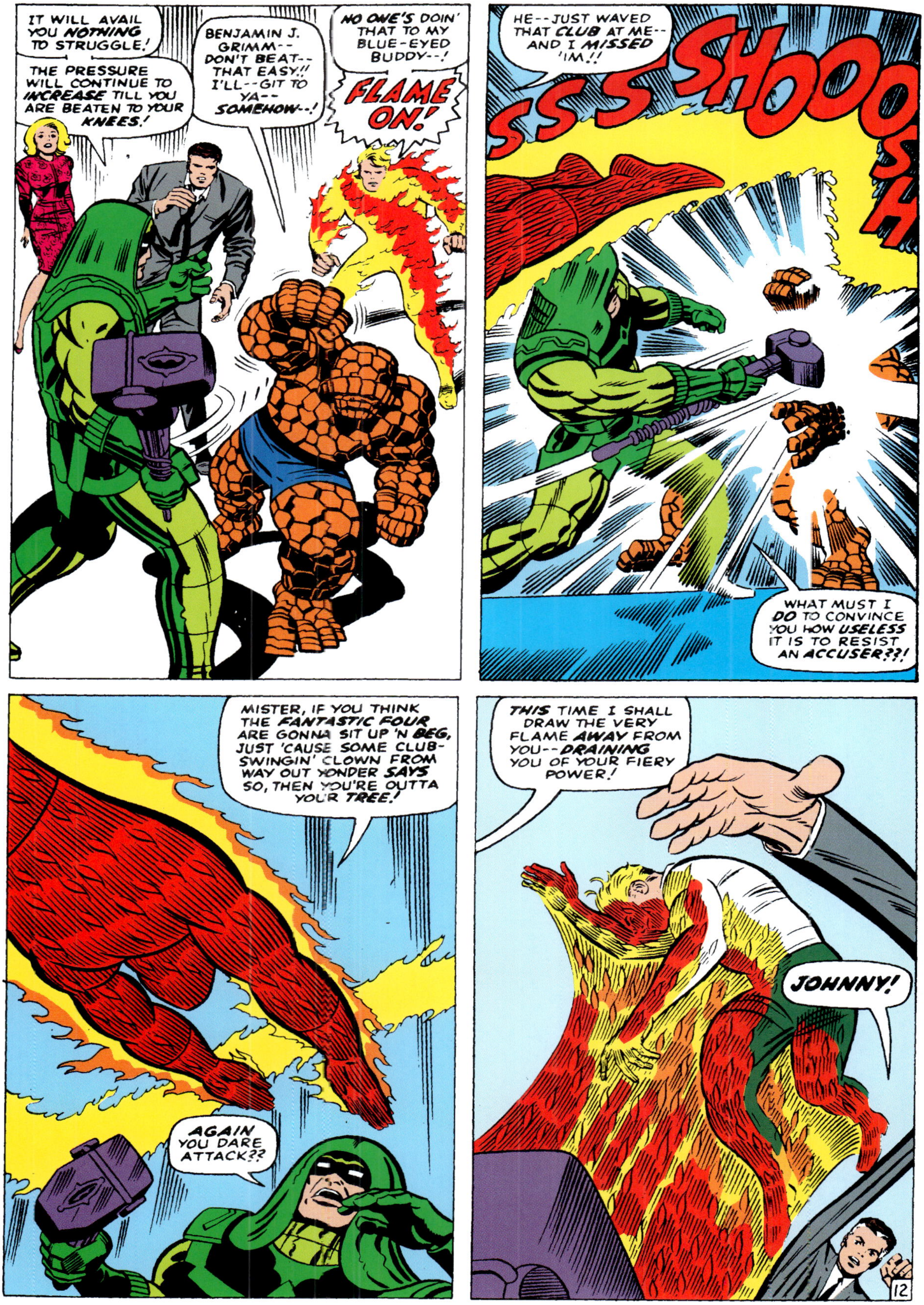
IT WILL AVAIL YOU NOTHING TO STRUGGLE!
THE PRESSURE WILL CONTINUE TO INCREASE TILL YOU ARE BEATEN TO YOUR KNEES!
BENJAMIN J. GRIMM-- DON'T BEAT-- THAT EASY!! I'LL--GIT TO YA-- SOMEHOW--!
NO ONE'S DOIN' THAT TO MY BLUE-EYED BUDDY--!
FLAME ON!
HE--JUST WAVED THAT CLUB AT ME-- AND I MISSED 'IM!!
SSS SHOOOSH
WHAT MUST I DO TO CONVINCE YOU HOW USELESS IT IS TO RESIST AN ACCUSER??!
MISTER, IF YOU THINK THE FANTASTIC FOUR ARE GONNA SIT UP 'N BEG, JUST 'CAUSE SOME CLUB-SWINGIN' CLOWN FROM WAY OUT YONDER SAYS SO, THEN YOU'RE OUTTA YOUR TREE!
AGAIN YOU DARE ATTACK??
THIS TIME I SHALL DRAW THE VERY FLAME AWAY FROM YOU--DRAINING YOU OF YOUR FIERY POWER!
JOHNNY!
12

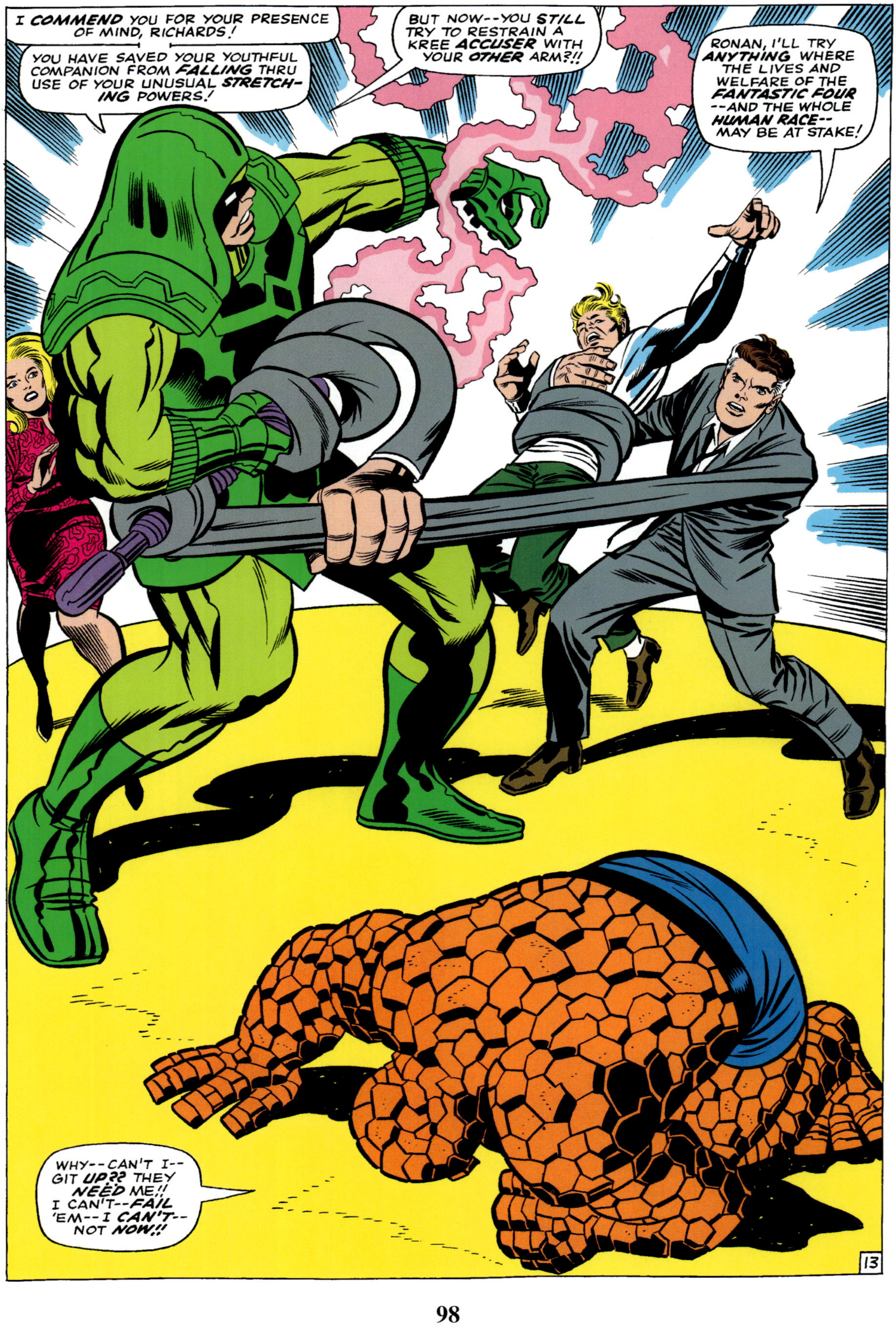
I COMMEND YOU FOR YOUR PRESENCE OF MIND, RICHARDS!
YOU HAVE SAVED YOUR YOUTHFUL COMPANION FROM FALLING THRU USE OF YOUR UNUSUAL STRETCHING POWERS!
BUT NOW--YOU STILL TRY TO RESTRAIN A KREE ACCUSER WITH YOUR OTHER ARM?!!
RONAN, I'LL TRY ANYTHING WHERE THE LIVES AND WELFARE OF THE FANTASTIC FOUR --AND THE WHOLE HUMAN RACE-- MAY BE AT STAKE!
WHY--CAN'T I-- GIT UP?? THEY NEED ME!! I CAN'T--FAIL 'EM--I CAN'T-- NOT NOW!!
13

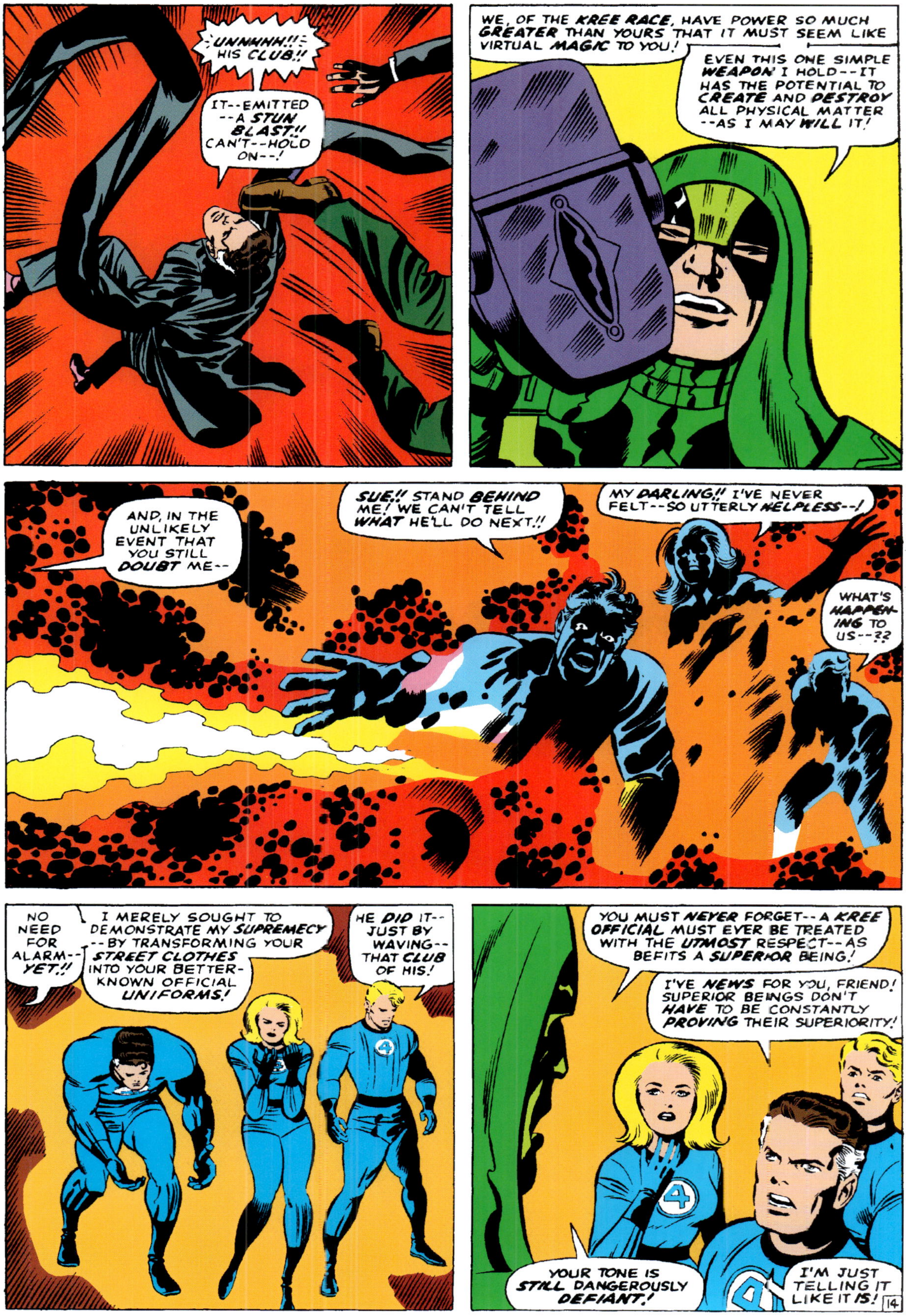
UNNHHH!! HIS CLUB!!
IT--EMITTED --A STUN BLAST!! CAN'T--HOLD ON--!
WE, OF THE KREE RACE, HAVE POWER SO MUCH GREATER THAN YOURS THAT IT MUST SEEM LIKE VIRTUAL MAGIC TO YOU!
EVEN THIS ONE SIMPLE WEAPON I HOLD--IT HAS THE POTENTIAL TO CREATE AND DESTROY ALL PHYSICAL MATTER --AS I MAY WILL IT!
AND, IN THE UNLIKELY EVENT THAT YOU STILL DOUBT ME--
SUE!! STAND BEHIND ME! WE CAN'T TELL WHAT HE'LL DO NEXT!!
MY DARLING!! I'VE NEVER FELT--SO UTTERLY HELPLESS--!
WHAT'S HAPPEN-ING TO US--??
NO NEED FOR ALARM--YET!!
I MERELY SOUGHT TO DEMONSTRATE MY SUPREMECY --BY TRANSFORMING YOUR STREET CLOTHES INTO YOUR BETTER-KNOWN OFFICIAL UNIFORMS!
HE DID IT-- JUST BY WAVING-- THAT CLUB OF HIS!
YOU MUST NEVER FORGET--A KREE OFFICIAL MUST EVER BE TREATED WITH THE UTMOST RESPECT--AS BEFITS A SUPERIOR BEING!
I'VE NEWS FOR YOU, FRIEND! SUPERIOR BEINGS DON'T HAVE TO BE CONSTANTLY PROVING THEIR SUPERIORITY!
YOUR TONE IS STILL DANGEROUSLY DEFIANT!
I'M JUST TELLING IT LIKE IT IS!
14

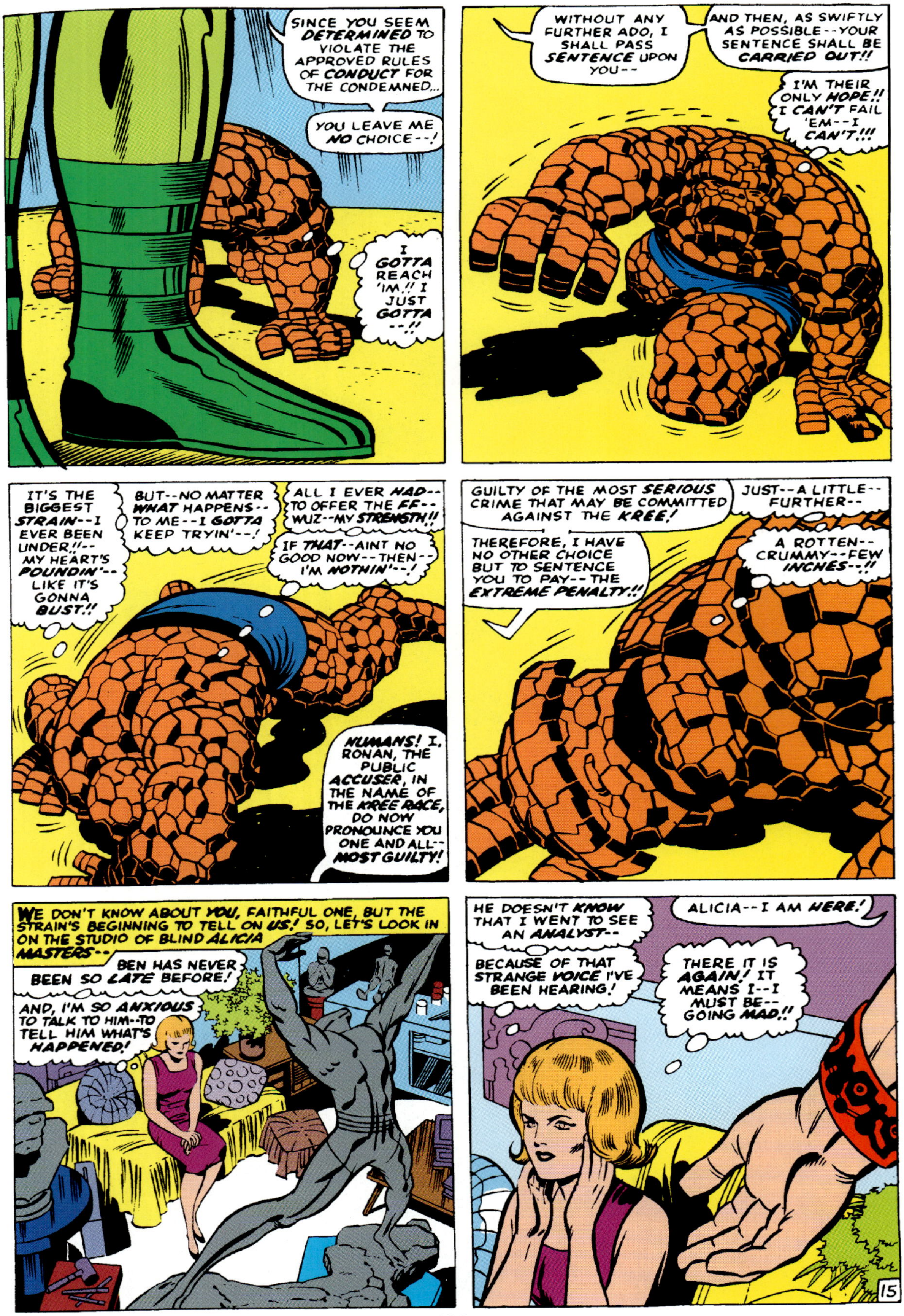
SINCE YOU SEEM DETERMINED TO VIOLATE THE APPROVED RULES OF CONDUCT FOR THE CONDEMNED...
YOU LEAVE ME NO CHOICE--!
I GOTTA REACH 'IM!! I JUST GOTTA--!!
WITHOUT ANY FURTHER ADO, I SHALL PASS SENTENCE UPON YOU--
AND THEN, AS SWIFTLY AS POSSIBLE--YOUR SENTENCE SHALL BE CARRIED OUT!!
I'M THEIR ONLY HOPE!! I CAN'T FAIL 'EM--I CAN'T!!!
IT'S THE BIGGEST STRAIN--I EVER BEEN UNDER!!--MY HEART'S POUNDIN'--LIKE IT'S GONNA BUST!!
BUT--NO MATTER WHAT HAPPENS--TO ME--I GOTTA KEEP TRYIN'--!
ALL I EVER HAD--TO OFFER THE FF--WUZ--MY STRENGTH!!
IF THAT--AINT NO GOOD NOW--THEN--I'M NOTHIN'--!
HUMANS! I, RONAN, THE PUBLIC ACCUSER, IN THE NAME OF THE KREE RACE, DO NOW PRONOUNCE YOU ONE AND ALL--MOST GUILTY!
GUILTY OF THE MOST SERIOUS CRIME THAT MAY BE COMMITTED AGAINST THE KREE!
THEREFORE, I HAVE NO OTHER CHOICE BUT TO SENTENCE YOU TO PAY--THE EXTREME PENALTY!!
JUST--A LITTLE--FURTHER--
A ROTTEN--CRUMMY--FEW INCHES--!!
WE DON'T KNOW ABOUT YOU, FAITHFUL ONE, BUT THE STRAIN'S BEGINNING TO TELL ON US! SO, LET'S LOOK IN ON THE STUDIO OF BLIND ALICIA MASTERS--
BEN HAS NEVER BEEN SO LATE BEFORE!
AND, I'M SO ANXIOUS TO TALK TO HIM--TO TELL HIM WHAT'S HAPPENED!
HE DOESN'T KNOW THAT I WENT TO SEE AN ANALYST--
BECAUSE OF THAT STRANGE VOICE I'VE BEEN HEARING!
ALICIA--I AM HERE!
THERE IT IS AGAIN! IT MEANS I--I MUST BE--GOING MAD!!
15

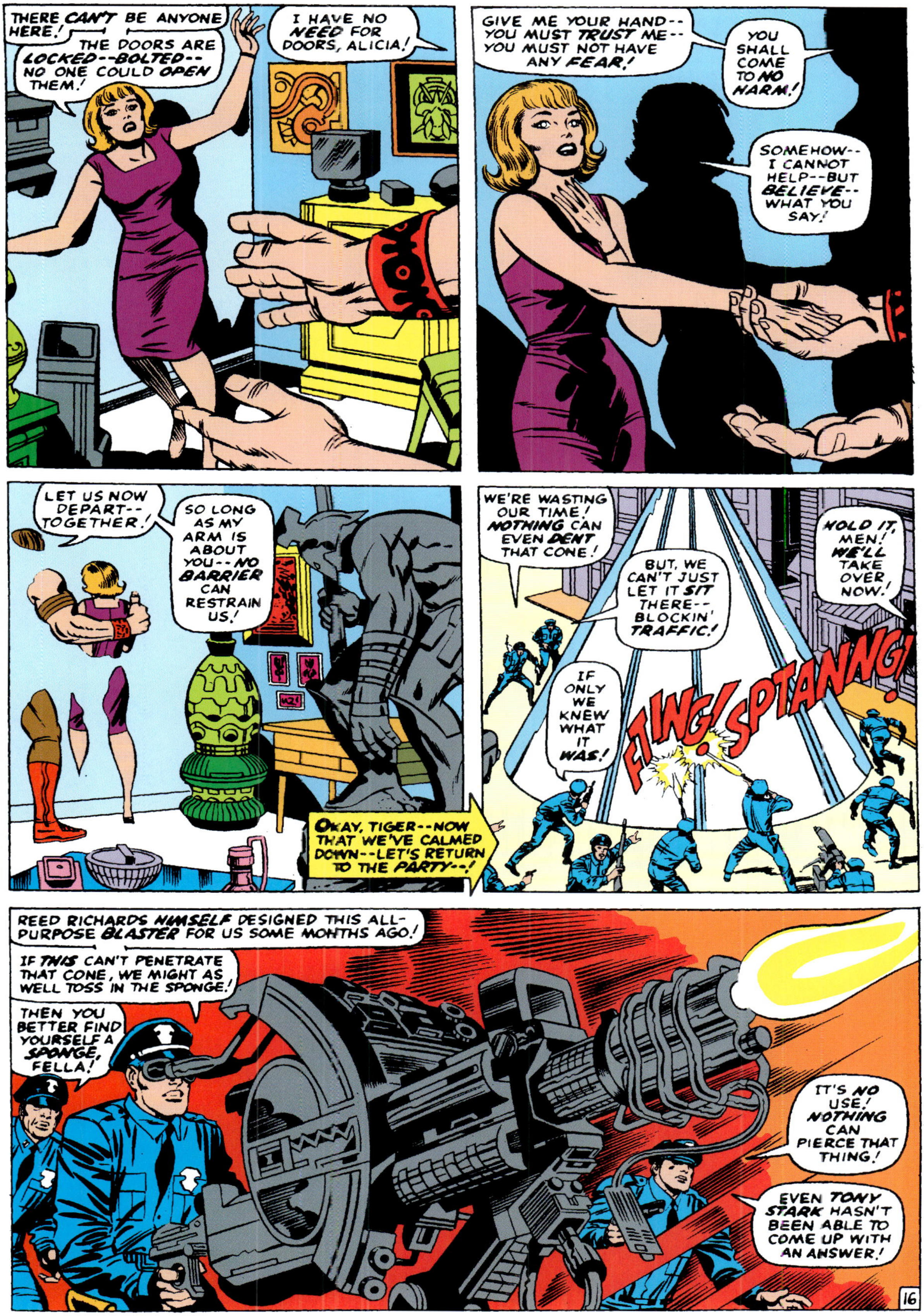
THERE CAN'T BE ANYONE HERE!
THE DOORS ARE LOCKED--BOLTED--NO ONE COULD OPEN THEM!
I HAVE NO NEED FOR DOORS, ALICIA!
GIVE ME YOUR HAND--YOU MUST TRUST ME--YOU MUST NOT HAVE ANY FEAR!
YOU SHALL COME TO NO HARM!
SOMEHOW--I CANNOT HELP--BUT BELIEVE--WHAT YOU SAY!
LET US NOW DEPART--TOGETHER!
SO LONG AS MY ARM IS ABOUT YOU--NO BARRIER CAN RESTRAIN US!
OKAY, TIGER--NOW THAT WE'VE CALMED DOWN--LET'S RETURN TO THE PARTY--!
WE'RE WASTING OUR TIME! NOTHING CAN EVEN DENT THAT CONE!
BUT, WE CAN'T JUST LET IT SIT THERE--BLOCKIN' TRAFFIC!
HOLD IT, MEN! WE'LL TAKE OVER NOW!
IF ONLY WE KNEW WHAT IT WAS!
FTING! SPTANNG!
REED RICHARDS HIMSELF DESIGNED THIS ALL-PURPOSE BLASTER FOR US SOME MONTHS AGO!
IF THIS CAN'T PENETRATE THAT CONE, WE MIGHT AS WELL TOSS IN THE SPONGE!
THEN YOU BETTER FIND YOURSELF A SPONGE, FELLA!
IT'S NO USE! NOTHING CAN PIERCE THAT THING!
EVEN TONY STARK HASN'T BEEN ABLE TO COME UP WITH AN ANSWER!
16

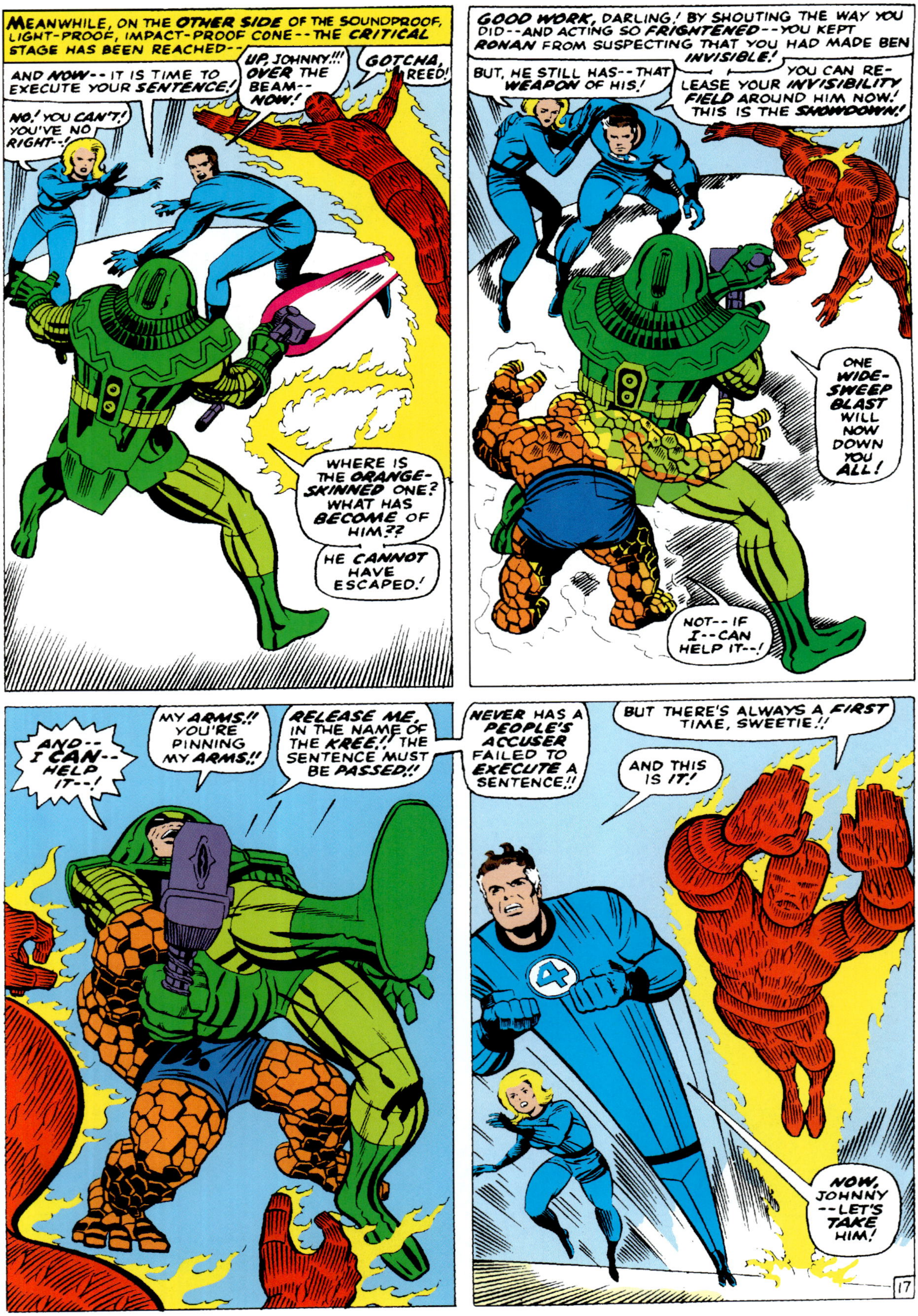

MEANWHILE, ON THE OTHER SIDE OF THE SOUNDPROOF, LIGHT-PROOF, IMPACT-PROOF CONE--THE CRITICAL STAGE HAS BEEN REACHED--
AND NOW-- IT IS TIME TO EXECUTE YOUR SENTENCE!
NO! YOU CAN'T! YOU'VE NO RIGHT--!
UP, JOHNNY!!! OVER THE BEAM-- NOW!
GOTCHA, REED!
WHERE IS THE ORANGE-SKINNED ONE? WHAT HAS BECOME OF HIM??
HE CANNOT HAVE ESCAPED!
GOOD WORK, DARLING! BY SHOUTING THE WAY YOU DID--AND ACTING SO FRIGHTENED--YOU KEPT RONAN FROM SUSPECTING THAT YOU HAD MADE BEN INVISIBLE!
BUT, HE STILL HAS--THAT WEAPON OF HIS!
YOU CAN RE-LEASE YOUR INVISIBILITY FIELD AROUND HIM NOW! THIS IS THE SHOWDOWN!
ONE WIDE-SWEEP BLAST WILL NOW DOWN YOU ALL!
NOT--IF I--CAN HELP IT--!
AND-- I CAN-- HELP IT--!
MY ARMS!! YOU'RE PINNING MY ARMS!!
RELEASE ME, IN THE NAME OF THE KREE!! THE SENTENCE MUST BE PASSED!!
NEVER HAS A PEOPLE'S ACCUSER FAILED TO EXECUTE A SENTENCE!!
BUT THERE'S ALWAYS A FIRST TIME, SWEETIE!!
AND THIS IS IT!
NOW, JOHNNY --LET'S TAKE HIM!
17

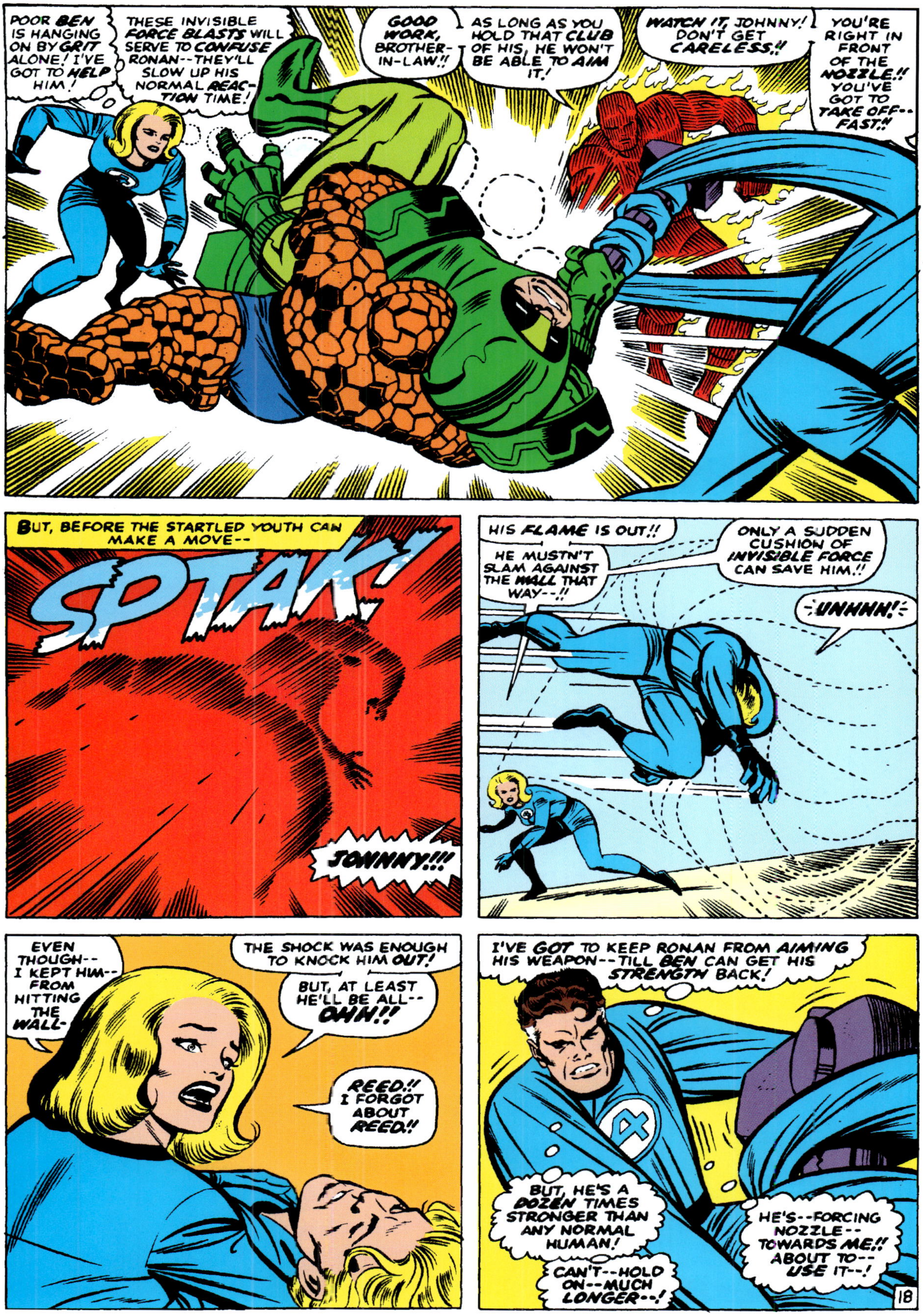
POOR BEN IS HANGING ON BY GRIT ALONE! I'VE GOT TO HELP HIM!
THESE INVISIBLE FORCE BLASTS WILL SERVE TO CONFUSE RONAN--THEY'LL SLOW UP HIS NORMAL REACTION TIME!
GOOD WORK, BROTHER-IN-LAW!!
AS LONG AS YOU HOLD THAT CLUB OF HIS, HE WON'T BE ABLE TO AIM IT!
WATCH IT, JOHNNY! DON'T GET CARELESS!!
YOU'RE RIGHT IN FRONT OF THE NOZZLE!! YOU'VE GOT TO TAKE OFF--FAST!!
BUT, BEFORE THE STARTLED YOUTH CAN MAKE A MOVE--
SPTAK!
JOHNNY!!!
HIS FLAME IS OUT!!
HE MUSTN'T SLAM AGAINST THE WALL THAT WAY--!!
ONLY A SUDDEN CUSHION OF INVISIBLE FORCE CAN SAVE HIM!!
UNHHH!
EVEN THOUGH--I KEPT HIM--FROM HITTING THE WALL--
THE SHOCK WAS ENOUGH TO KNOCK HIM OUT!
BUT, AT LEAST HE'LL BE ALL--OHH!!
REED!! I FORGOT ABOUT REED!!
I'VE GOT TO KEEP RONAN FROM AIMING HIS WEAPON--TILL BEN CAN GET HIS STRENGTH BACK!
BUT, HE'S A DOZEN TIMES STRONGER THAN ANY NORMAL HUMAN!
CAN'T--HOLD ON--MUCH LONGER--!
HE'S--FORCING NOZZLE--TOWARDS ME!! ABOUT TO--USE IT--!
18

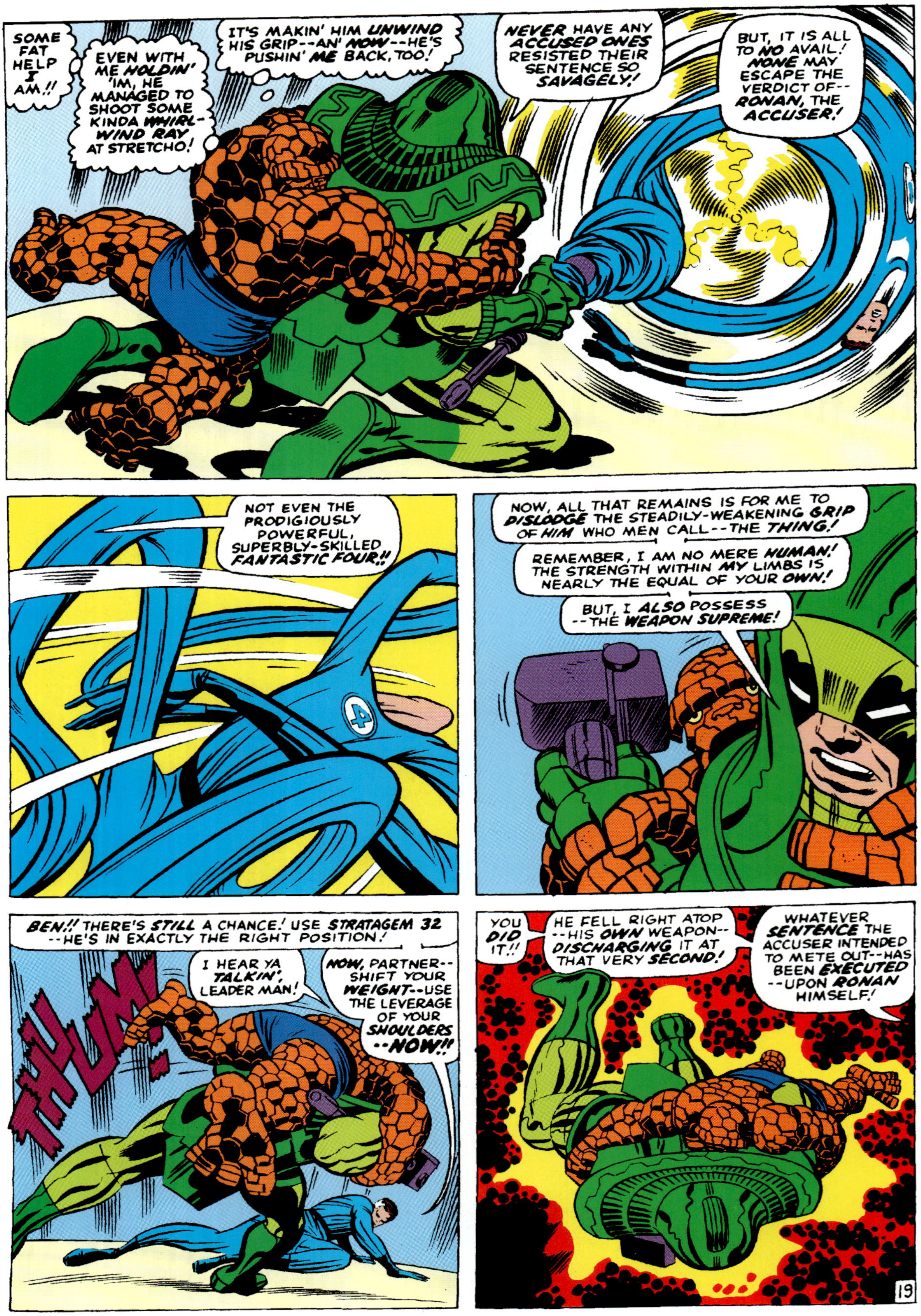

SOME FAT HELP I AM.!!
EVEN WITH ME HOLDIN' 'IM, HE MANAGED TO SHOOT SOME KINDA WHIRL-WIND RAY AT STRETCHO!
IT'S MAKIN' HIM UNWIND HIS GRIP--AN' NOW--HE'S PUSHIN' ME BACK, TOO!
NEVER HAVE ANY ACCUSED ONES RESISTED THEIR SENTENCE SO SAVAGELY!
BUT, IT IS ALL TO NO AVAIL! NONE MAY ESCAPE THE VERDICT OF--RONAN, THE ACCUSER!
NOT EVEN THE PRODIGIOUSLY POWERFUL, SUPERBLY-SKILLED FANTASTIC FOUR!!
NOW, ALL THAT REMAINS IS FOR ME TO DISLODGE THE STEADILY-WEAKENING GRIP OF HIM WHO MEN CALL--THE THING!
REMEMBER, I AM NO MERE HUMAN! THE STRENGTH WITHIN MY LIMBS IS NEARLY THE EQUAL OF YOUR OWN!
BUT, I ALSO POSSESS --THE WEAPON SUPREME!
BEN!! THERE'S STILL A CHANCE! USE STRATAGEM 32 --HE'S IN EXACTLY THE RIGHT POSITION!
I HEAR YA TALKIN', LEADER MAN!
NOW, PARTNER--SHIFT YOUR WEIGHT--USE THE LEVERAGE OF YOUR SHOULDERS --NOW!!
THUMM!
YOU DID IT!!
HE FELL RIGHT ATOP --HIS OWN WEAPON--DISCHARGING IT AT THAT VERY SECOND!
WHATEVER SENTENCE THE ACCUSER INTENDED TO METE OUT--HAS BEEN EXECUTED --UPON RONAN HIMSELF!
19

BUT THEN, SUDDENLY, *ANOTHER* EXPLOSION OCCURS--OF FAR GREATER *INTENSITY* THAN THE FIRST--!

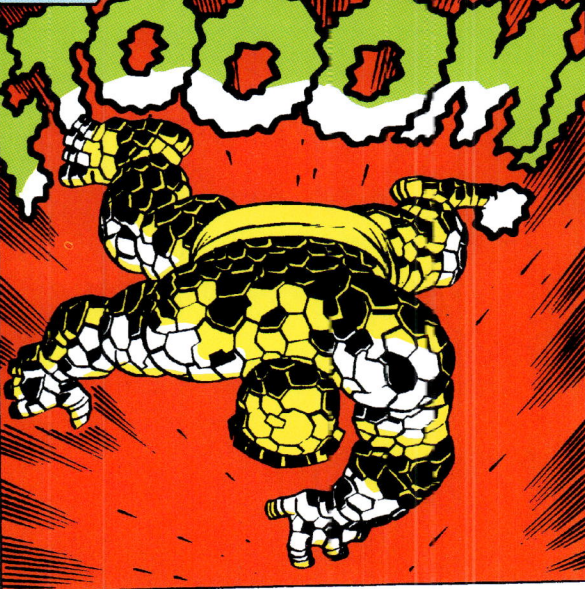

TOOOM!

AND, WHEN THE SMOKE CLEARS, THE MYSTERIOUS *CONE,* AND ITS ALIEN *OCCUPANT,* ARE *GONE!* NOTHING REMAINS, SAVE--

THE *FF!!* IT WAS *THEM* INSIDE!!

DON'T JUST *STAND* THERE! GET SOME *STRETCHERS!!* MOVE!

WHAT COULD'A DONE *THAT* TO THE *THING!!?*

THROW UP A *BARRICADE!* KEEP THOSE *CROWDS* BACK!

THE *ACCUSER'S* GONE--AN' HE TOOK HIS LITTLE STAR-HOPPIN' KIDDIE CAR *WITH 'IM!*

SUE! HOW'S *JOHNNY?* WILL THE LAD BE ALL RIGHT??

YES, DARLING! IT WAS ONLY THE SUDDEN *SHOCK* THAT FLOORED HIM!

STAND CLEAR, THERE! LET THOSE *SQUAD CARS* THRU!

O'MALLEY! GET THAT *ARTILLERY* BACK TO THE *PRECINCT!!*

I DON'T *GET* IT, STRETCH! HOW COME EVERYTHIN' *ENDED* SO FAST??

THERE MUST HAVE BEEN AN *AUTOMATIC ACTIVATOR* ON RONAN'S *ORBITING SHIP!*

¿YEAH? *NOW* SAY IT IN *ENGLISH!*

WITH THE *FAILURE* OF HIS MISSION, ALL TRACES OF HIS PRESENCE HERE WERE *REMOVED*--INSTANTANEOUSLY!

BUT, *RONAN* NO LONGER *MATTERS* TO US!

WHAT *DOES* MATTER IS--THE *KREE* NOW KNOW THEY ARE DEALING WITH AN *INTELLIGENT* RACE --AND A *FIGHTING* RACE!

AND I PRAY THAT SUCH KNOW-LEDGE WILL KEEP THEM FROM EVER *RETURNING!*

NEXT: THE MYSTERY DEEPENS!

20

105

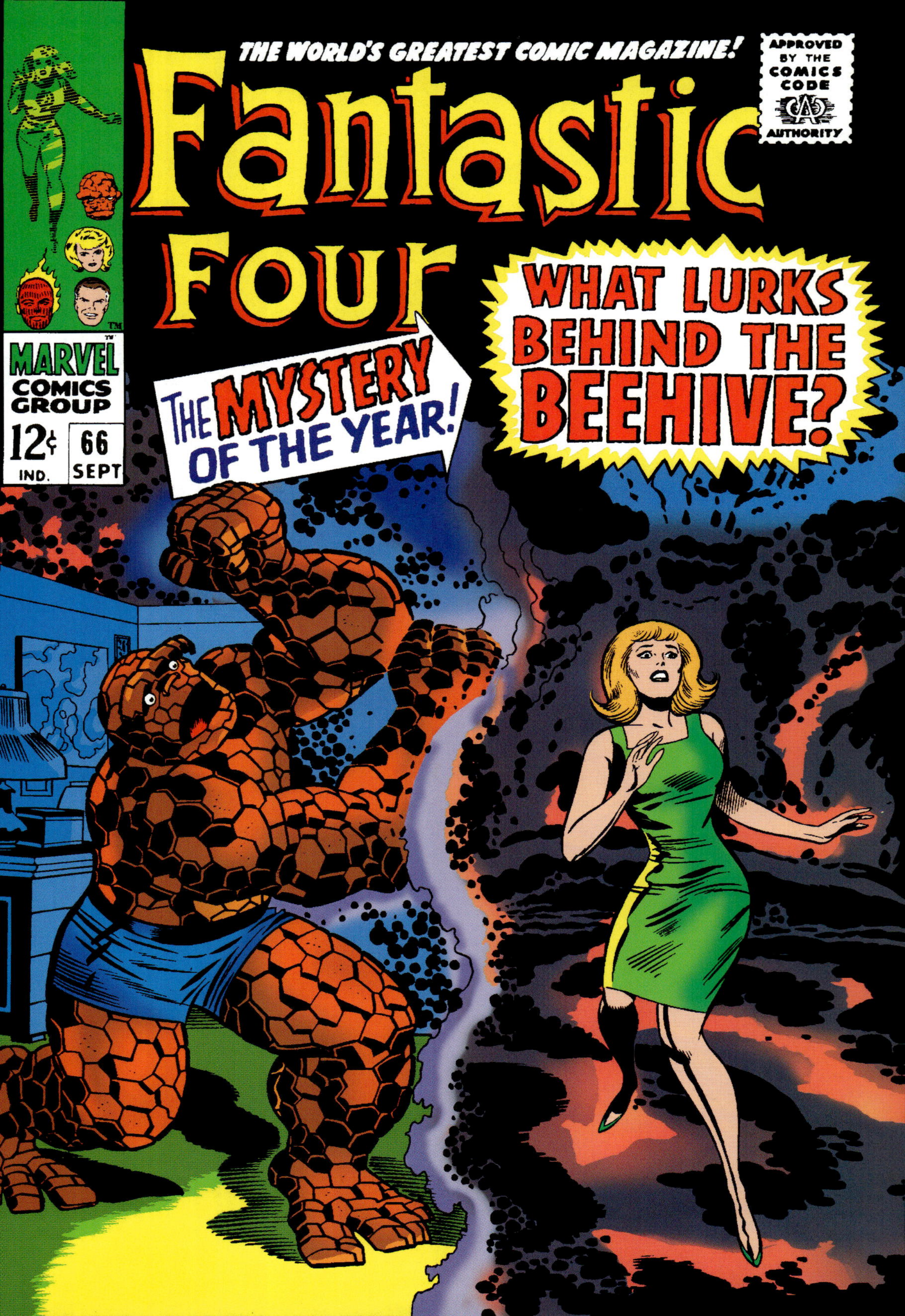
THE WORLD'S GREATEST COMIC MAGAZINE!
APPROVED BY THE COMICS CODE AUTHORITY
Fantastic Four
MARVEL COMICS GROUP
12¢ IND.
66 SEPT
THE MYSTERY OF THE YEAR!
WHAT LURKS BEHIND THE BEEHIVE?

TO SAVE ALICIA, THE FABULOUS FF MUST SOLVE THE DEADLY RIDDLE OF...
"WHAT LURKS BEHIND THE BEEHIVE?"
THAT'S STRANGE! ALICIA ISN'T HERE!
BUT WHY WOULD SHE LEAVE HER FRONT DOOR UNLOCKED WHEN SHE WENT OUT?
SHE PROBABLY JUST WENT SHOPPING!
I'M SURE SHE'LL BE BACK SOON!
NUTS! I BRING THE TWO OF YA WITH ME TO TELL HER THAT I HADDA BREAK OUR DATE YESTERDAY ON ACCOUNTA US FIGHTIN' THAT BLASTED KREE*--
'N NOW SHE AINT EVEN HERE TO LISTEN TO MY EVER-LOVIN' ALIBI!
A STRANGE WAY TO START AN ACTION-FILLED MYSTERY EPIC? JUST WAIT, FAITHFUL ONE! THE EXCITEMENT'S JUST AHEAD--
AIDED BY THE INKING OF JOVIAL JOE SINNOTT AND THE LETTERING OF ADORABLE ARTIE SIMEK
STAN (THE MAN) LEE and JACK (KING) KIRBY HAVE DONE IT AGAIN! BUT DON'T TAKE OUR WORD FOR IT! SEE FOR YOURSELF--
*TO BEN IT WAS ONLY YESTERDAY-- BUT TO US IT WAS A MONTH AGO, IN FF#65, REMEMBER?--SPECIFIC STAN.

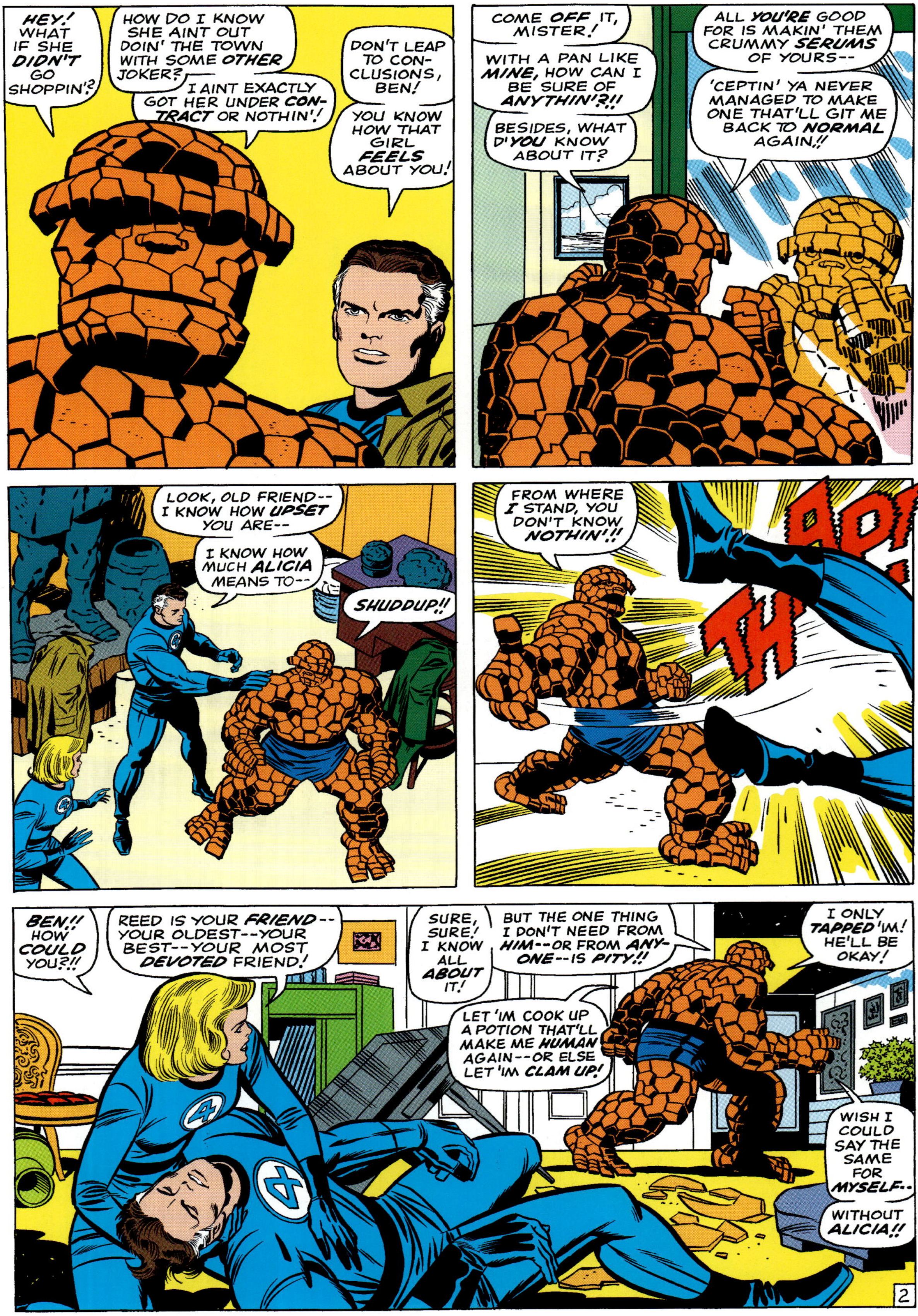
HEY! WHAT IF SHE DIDN'T GO SHOPPIN'?
HOW DO I KNOW SHE AINT OUT DOIN' THE TOWN WITH SOME OTHER JOKER?
I AINT EXACTLY GOT HER UNDER CONTRACT OR NOTHIN'!
DON'T LEAP TO CONCLUSIONS, BEN!
YOU KNOW HOW THAT GIRL FEELS ABOUT YOU!
COME OFF IT, MISTER!
WITH A PAN LIKE MINE, HOW CAN I BE SURE OF ANYTHIN'?!!
BESIDES, WHAT D'YOU KNOW ABOUT IT?
ALL YOU'RE GOOD FOR IS MAKIN' THEM CRUMMY SERUMS OF YOURS--
'CEPTIN' YA NEVER MANAGED TO MAKE ONE THAT'LL GIT ME BACK TO NORMAL AGAIN!!
LOOK, OLD FRIEND-- I KNOW HOW UPSET YOU ARE--
I KNOW HOW MUCH ALICIA MEANS TO--
SHUDDUP!!
FROM WHERE I STAND, YOU DON'T KNOW NOTHIN'!!
BEN!! HOW COULD YOU?!!
REED IS YOUR FRIEND-- YOUR OLDEST--YOUR BEST--YOUR MOST DEVOTED FRIEND!
SURE, SURE! I KNOW ALL ABOUT IT!
BUT THE ONE THING I DON'T NEED FROM HIM--OR FROM ANYONE--IS PITY!!
LET 'IM COOK UP A POTION THAT'LL MAKE ME HUMAN AGAIN--OR ELSE LET 'IM CLAM UP!
I ONLY TAPPED 'IM! HE'LL BE OKAY!
WISH I COULD SAY THE SAME FOR MYSELF--
WITHOUT ALICIA!!
2

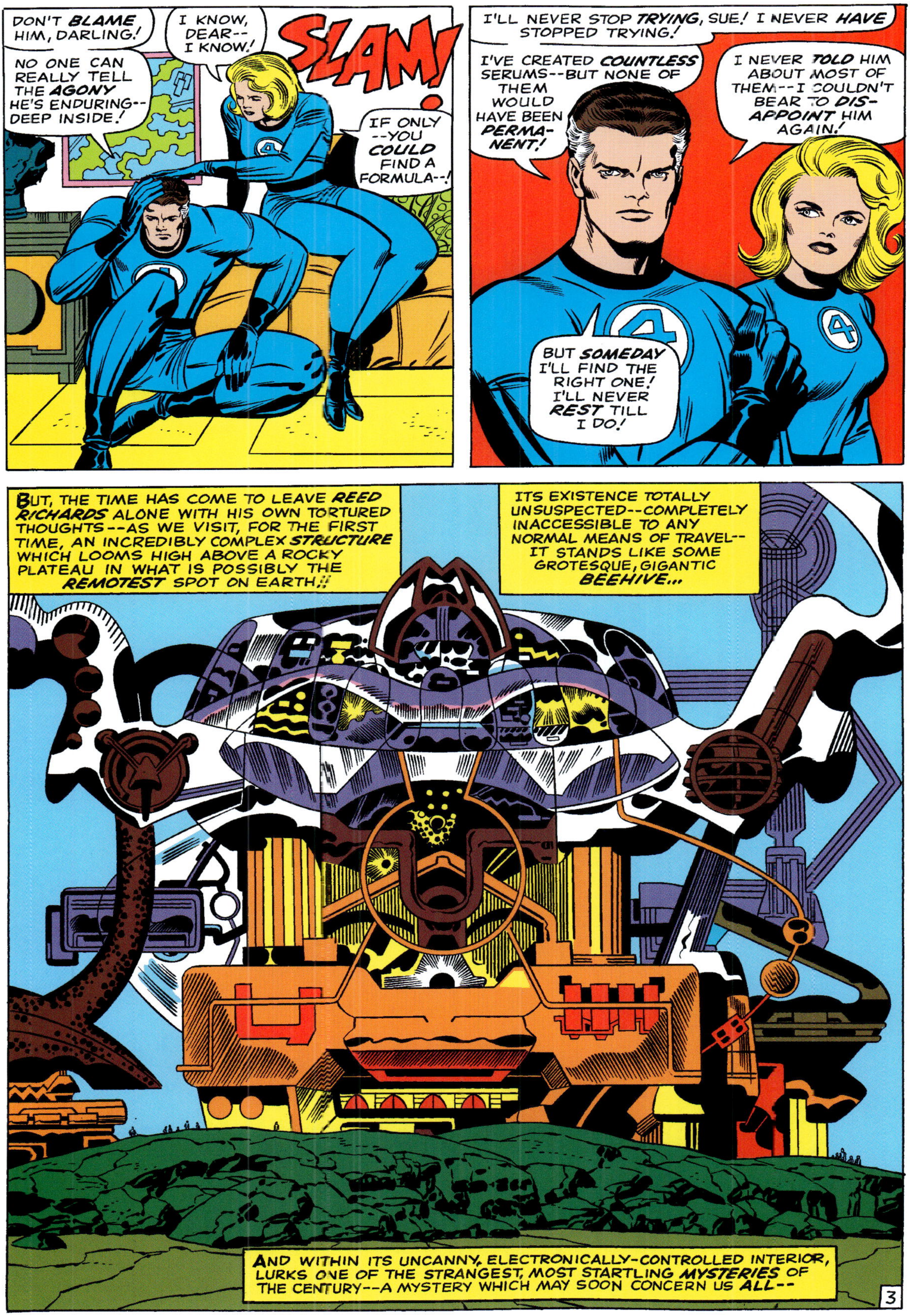
DON'T BLAME HIM, DARLING!
NO ONE CAN REALLY TELL THE AGONY HE'S ENDURING-- DEEP INSIDE!
I KNOW, DEAR-- I KNOW!
SLAM!
IF ONLY --YOU COULD FIND A FORMULA--!
I'LL NEVER STOP TRYING, SUE! I NEVER HAVE STOPPED TRYING!
I'VE CREATED COUNTLESS SERUMS--BUT NONE OF THEM WOULD HAVE BEEN PERMA-NENT!
I NEVER TOLD HIM ABOUT MOST OF THEM--I COULDN'T BEAR TO DIS-APPOINT HIM AGAIN!
BUT SOMEDAY I'LL FIND THE RIGHT ONE! I'LL NEVER REST TILL I DO!
BUT, THE TIME HAS COME TO LEAVE REED RICHARDS ALONE WITH HIS OWN TORTURED THOUGHTS--AS WE VISIT, FOR THE FIRST TIME, AN INCREDIBLY COMPLEX STRUCTURE WHICH LOOMS HIGH ABOVE A ROCKY PLATEAU IN WHAT IS POSSIBLY THE REMOTEST SPOT ON EARTH!!
ITS EXISTENCE TOTALLY UNSUSPECTED--COMPLETELY INACCESSIBLE TO ANY NORMAL MEANS OF TRAVEL-- IT STANDS LIKE SOME GROTESQUE, GIGANTIC BEEHIVE...
AND WITHIN ITS UNCANNY, ELECTRONICALLY-CONTROLLED INTERIOR, LURKS ONE OF THE STRANGEST, MOST STARTLING MYSTERIES OF THE CENTURY--A MYSTERY WHICH MAY SOON CONCERN US ALL--
3

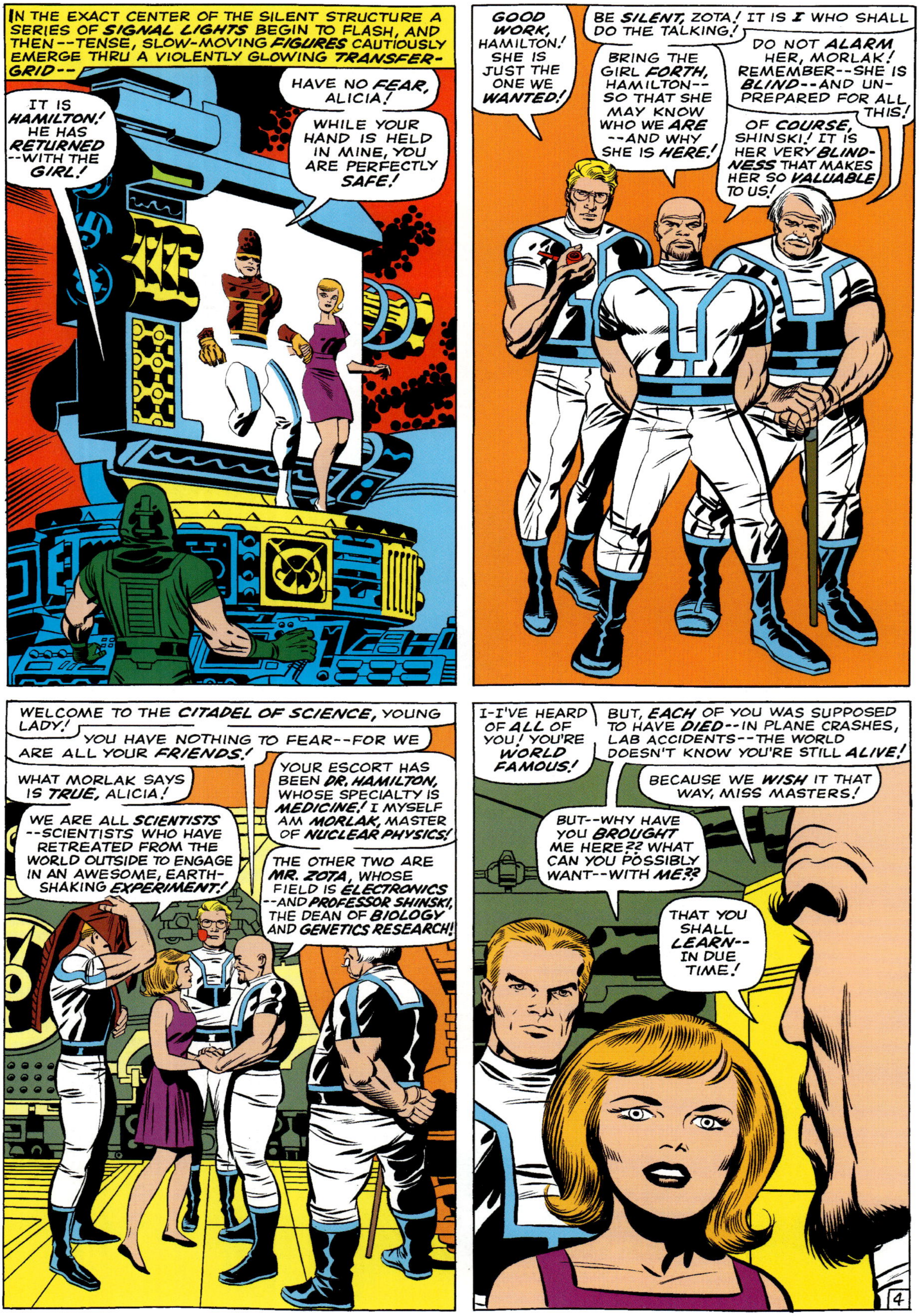
IN THE EXACT CENTER OF THE SILENT STRUCTURE A SERIES OF SIGNAL LIGHTS BEGIN TO FLASH, AND THEN--TENSE, SLOW-MOVING FIGURES CAUTIOUSLY EMERGE THRU A VIOLENTLY GLOWING TRANSFER-GRID--
IT IS HAMILTON! HE HAS RETURNED --WITH THE GIRL!
HAVE NO FEAR, ALICIA!
WHILE YOUR HAND IS HELD IN MINE, YOU ARE PERFECTLY SAFE!
GOOD WORK, HAMILTON! SHE IS JUST THE ONE WE WANTED!
BE SILENT, ZOTA! IT IS I WHO SHALL DO THE TALKING!
BRING THE GIRL FORTH, HAMILTON-- SO THAT SHE MAY KNOW WHO WE ARE --AND WHY SHE IS HERE!
DO NOT ALARM HER, MORLAK! REMEMBER--SHE IS BLIND--AND UNPREPARED FOR ALL THIS!
OF COURSE, SHINSKI! IT IS HER VERY BLINDNESS THAT MAKES HER SO VALUABLE TO US!
WELCOME TO THE CITADEL OF SCIENCE, YOUNG LADY!
YOU HAVE NOTHING TO FEAR--FOR WE ARE ALL YOUR FRIENDS!
WHAT MORLAK SAYS IS TRUE, ALICIA!
WE ARE ALL SCIENTISTS --SCIENTISTS WHO HAVE RETREATED FROM THE WORLD OUTSIDE TO ENGAGE IN AN AWESOME, EARTH-SHAKING EXPERIMENT!
YOUR ESCORT HAS BEEN DR. HAMILTON, WHOSE SPECIALTY IS MEDICINE! I MYSELF AM MORLAK, MASTER OF NUCLEAR PHYSICS!
THE OTHER TWO ARE MR. ZOTA, WHOSE FIELD IS ELECTRONICS --AND PROFESSOR SHINSKI, THE DEAN OF BIOLOGY AND GENETICS RESEARCH!
I-I'VE HEARD OF ALL OF YOU! YOU'RE WORLD FAMOUS!
BUT, EACH OF YOU WAS SUPPOSED TO HAVE DIED--IN PLANE CRASHES, LAB ACCIDENTS--THE WORLD DOESN'T KNOW YOU'RE STILL ALIVE!
BECAUSE WE WISH IT THAT WAY, MISS MASTERS!
BUT--WHY HAVE YOU BROUGHT ME HERE?? WHAT CAN YOU POSSIBLY WANT--WITH ME??
THAT YOU SHALL LEARN-- IN DUE TIME!
4

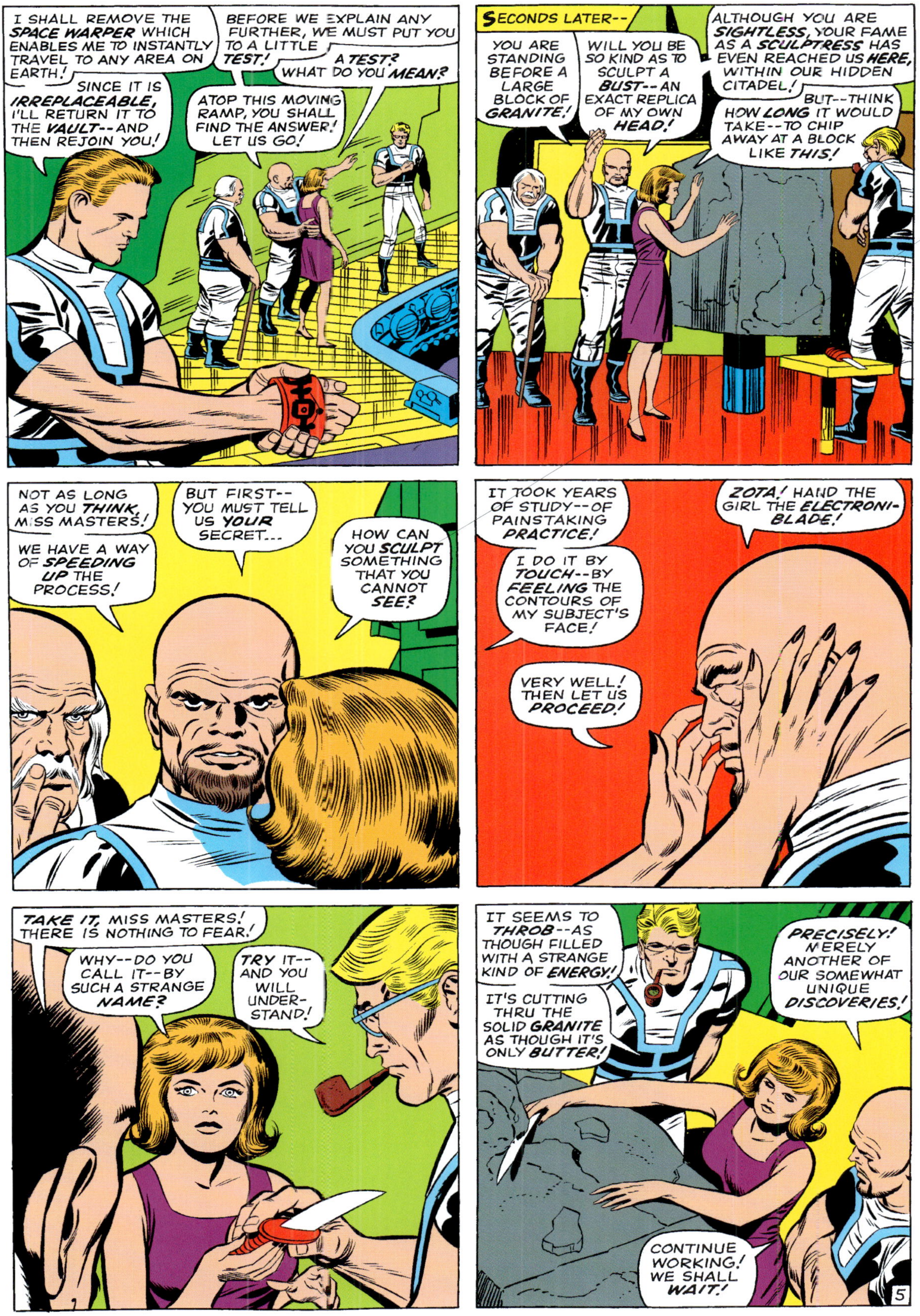
I SHALL REMOVE THE SPACE WARPER WHICH ENABLES ME TO INSTANTLY TRAVEL TO ANY AREA ON EARTH!
SINCE IT IS IRREPLACEABLE, I'LL RETURN IT TO THE VAULT--AND THEN REJOIN YOU!
BEFORE WE EXPLAIN ANY FURTHER, WE MUST PUT YOU TO A LITTLE TEST!
A TEST? WHAT DO YOU MEAN?
ATOP THIS MOVING RAMP, YOU SHALL FIND THE ANSWER! LET US GO!
SECONDS LATER--
YOU ARE STANDING BEFORE A LARGE BLOCK OF GRANITE!
WILL YOU BE SO KIND AS TO SCULPT A BUST--AN EXACT REPLICA OF MY OWN HEAD!
ALTHOUGH YOU ARE SIGHTLESS, YOUR FAME AS A SCULPTRESS HAS EVEN REACHED US HERE, WITHIN OUR HIDDEN CITADEL!
BUT--THINK HOW LONG IT WOULD TAKE--TO CHIP AWAY AT A BLOCK LIKE THIS!
NOT AS LONG AS YOU THINK, MISS MASTERS!
WE HAVE A WAY OF SPEEDING UP THE PROCESS!
BUT FIRST--YOU MUST TELL US YOUR SECRET...
HOW CAN YOU SCULPT SOMETHING THAT YOU CANNOT SEE?
IT TOOK YEARS OF STUDY--OF PAINSTAKING PRACTICE!
I DO IT BY TOUCH--BY FEELING THE CONTOURS OF MY SUBJECT'S FACE!
ZOTA! HAND THE GIRL THE ELECTRONI-BLADE!
VERY WELL! THEN LET US PROCEED!
TAKE IT, MISS MASTERS! THERE IS NOTHING TO FEAR!
WHY--DO YOU CALL IT--BY SUCH A STRANGE NAME?
TRY IT--AND YOU WILL UNDER-STAND!
IT SEEMS TO THROB--AS THOUGH FILLED WITH A STRANGE KIND OF ENERGY!
IT'S CUTTING THRU THE SOLID GRANITE AS THOUGH IT'S ONLY BUTTER!
PRECISELY! MERELY ANOTHER OF OUR SOMEWHAT UNIQUE DISCOVERIES!
CONTINUE WORKING! WE SHALL WAIT!
5

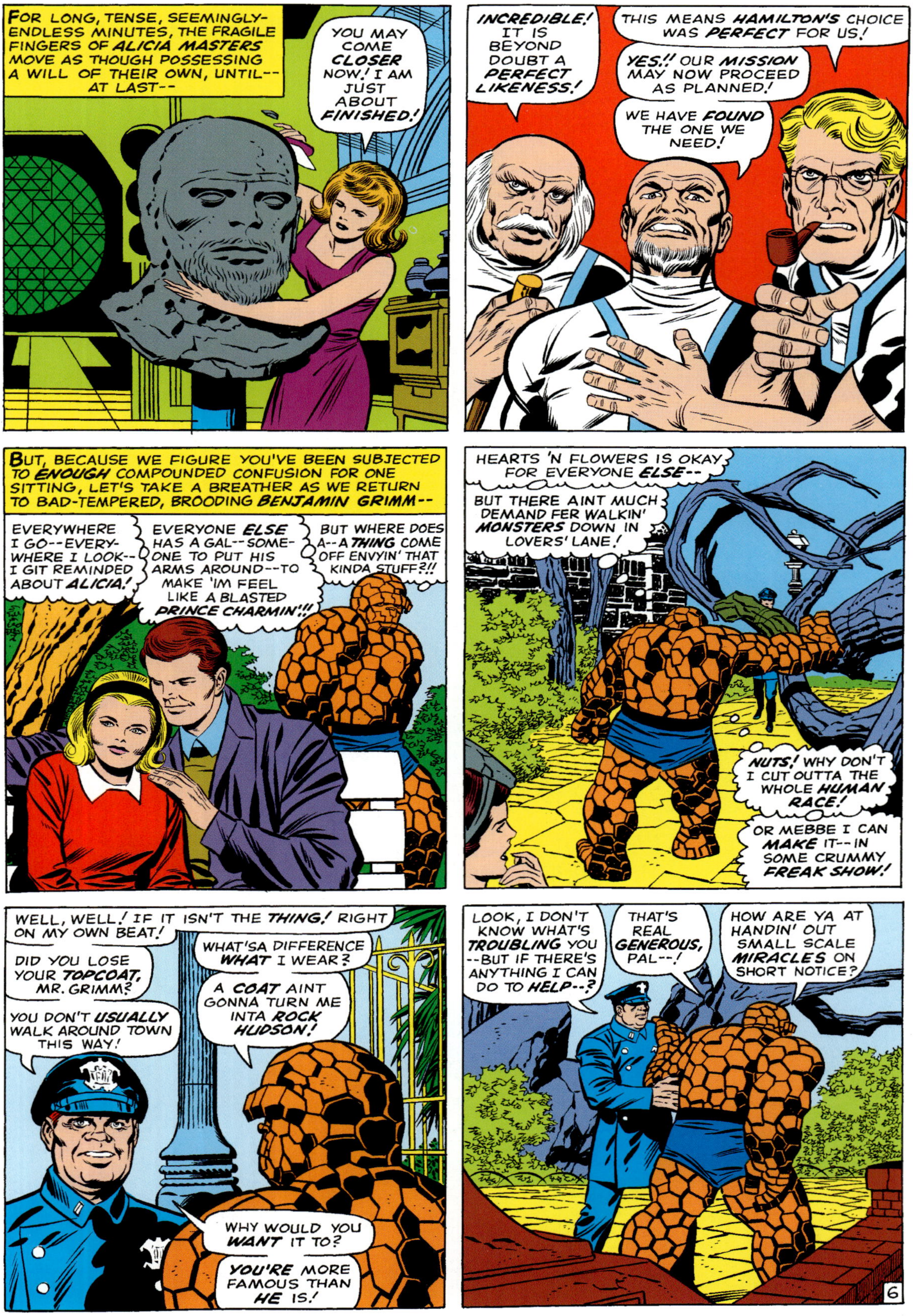
FOR LONG, TENSE, SEEMINGLY-ENDLESS MINUTES, THE FRAGILE FINGERS OF ALICIA MASTERS MOVE AS THOUGH POSSESSING A WILL OF THEIR OWN, UNTIL--AT LAST--
YOU MAY COME CLOSER NOW! I AM JUST ABOUT FINISHED!
INCREDIBLE! IT IS BEYOND DOUBT A PERFECT LIKENESS!
THIS MEANS HAMILTON'S CHOICE WAS PERFECT FOR US!
YES!! OUR MISSION MAY NOW PROCEED AS PLANNED!
WE HAVE FOUND THE ONE WE NEED!
BUT, BECAUSE WE FIGURE YOU'VE BEEN SUBJECTED TO ENOUGH COMPOUNDED CONFUSION FOR ONE SITTING, LET'S TAKE A BREATHER AS WE RETURN TO BAD-TEMPERED, BROODING BENJAMIN GRIMM--
EVERYWHERE I GO--EVERY-WHERE I LOOK--I GIT REMINDED ABOUT ALICIA!
EVERYONE ELSE HAS A GAL--SOME-ONE TO PUT HIS ARMS AROUND--TO MAKE 'IM FEEL LIKE A BLASTED PRINCE CHARMIN'!!
BUT WHERE DOES A--A THING COME OFF ENVYIN' THAT KINDA STUFF?!!
HEARTS 'N FLOWERS IS OKAY FOR EVERYONE ELSE--
BUT THERE AINT MUCH DEMAND FER WALKIN' MONSTERS DOWN IN LOVERS' LANE!
NUTS! WHY DON'T I CUT OUTTA THE WHOLE HUMAN RACE!
OR MEBBE I CAN MAKE IT--IN SOME CRUMMY FREAK SHOW!
WELL, WELL! IF IT ISN'T THE THING! RIGHT ON MY OWN BEAT!
DID YOU LOSE YOUR TOPCOAT, MR. GRIMM?
YOU DON'T USUALLY WALK AROUND TOWN THIS WAY!
WHAT'SA DIFFERENCE WHAT I WEAR?
A COAT AINT GONNA TURN ME INTA ROCK HUDSON!
WHY WOULD YOU WANT IT TO?
YOU'RE MORE FAMOUS THAN HE IS!
LOOK, I DON'T KNOW WHAT'S TROUBLING YOU--BUT IF THERE'S ANYTHING I CAN DO TO HELP--?
THAT'S REAL GENEROUS, PAL--!
HOW ARE YA AT HANDIN' OUT SMALL SCALE MIRACLES ON SHORT NOTICE?
6

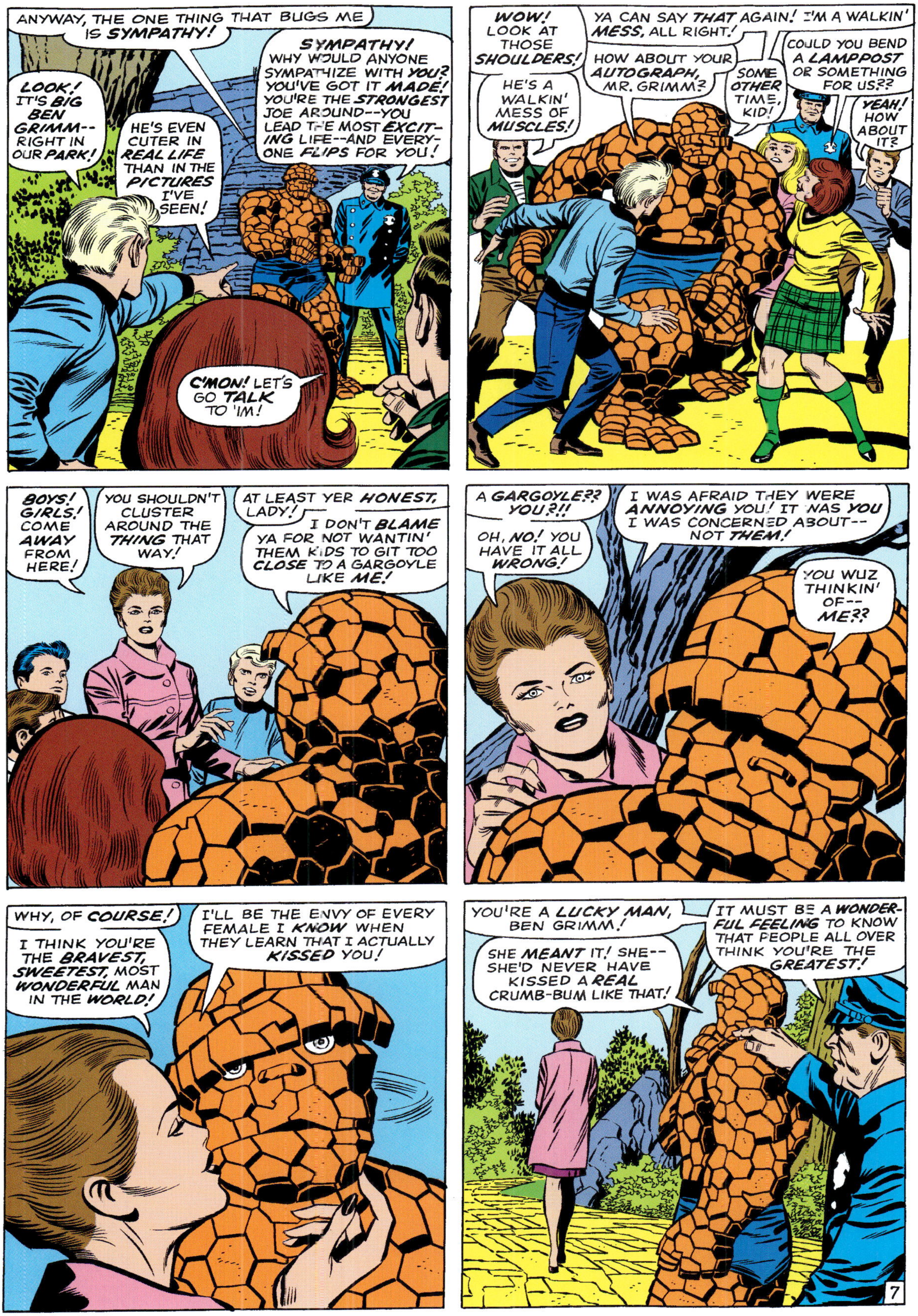
ANYWAY, THE ONE THING THAT BUGS ME IS SYMPATHY!
SYMPATHY! WHY WOULD ANYONE SYMPATHIZE WITH YOU? YOU'VE GOT IT MADE! YOU'RE THE STRONGEST JOE AROUND--YOU LEAD THE MOST EXCITING LIFE--AND EVERYONE FLIPS FOR YOU!
LOOK! IT'S BIG BEN GRIMM--RIGHT IN OUR PARK!
HE'S EVEN CUTER IN REAL LIFE THAN IN THE PICTURES I'VE SEEN!
C'MON! LET'S GO TALK TO 'IM!
WOW! LOOK AT THOSE SHOULDERS!
HE'S A WALKIN' MESS OF MUSCLES!
YA CAN SAY THAT AGAIN! I'M A WALKIN' MESS, ALL RIGHT!
HOW ABOUT YOUR AUTOGRAPH, MR. GRIMM?
SOME OTHER TIME, KID!
COULD YOU BEND A LAMPPOST OR SOMETHING FOR US??
YEAH! HOW ABOUT IT?
BOYS! GIRLS! COME AWAY FROM HERE!
YOU SHOULDN'T CLUSTER AROUND THE THING THAT WAY!
AT LEAST YER HONEST, LADY!
I DON'T BLAME YA FOR NOT WANTIN' THEM KIDS TO GIT TOO CLOSE TO A GARGOYLE LIKE ME!
A GARGOYLE?? YOU?!!
OH, NO! YOU HAVE IT ALL WRONG!
I WAS AFRAID THEY WERE ANNOYING YOU! IT WAS YOU I WAS CONCERNED ABOUT--NOT THEM!
YOU WUZ THINKIN' OF--ME??
WHY, OF COURSE!
I THINK YOU'RE THE BRAVEST, SWEETEST, MOST WONDERFUL MAN IN THE WORLD!
I'LL BE THE ENVY OF EVERY FEMALE I KNOW WHEN THEY LEARN THAT I ACTUALLY KISSED YOU!
YOU'RE A LUCKY MAN, BEN GRIMM!
SHE MEANT IT! SHE--SHE'D NEVER HAVE KISSED A REAL CRUMB-BUM LIKE THAT!
IT MUST BE A WONDERFUL FEELING TO KNOW THAT PEOPLE ALL OVER THINK YOU'RE THE GREATEST!
7

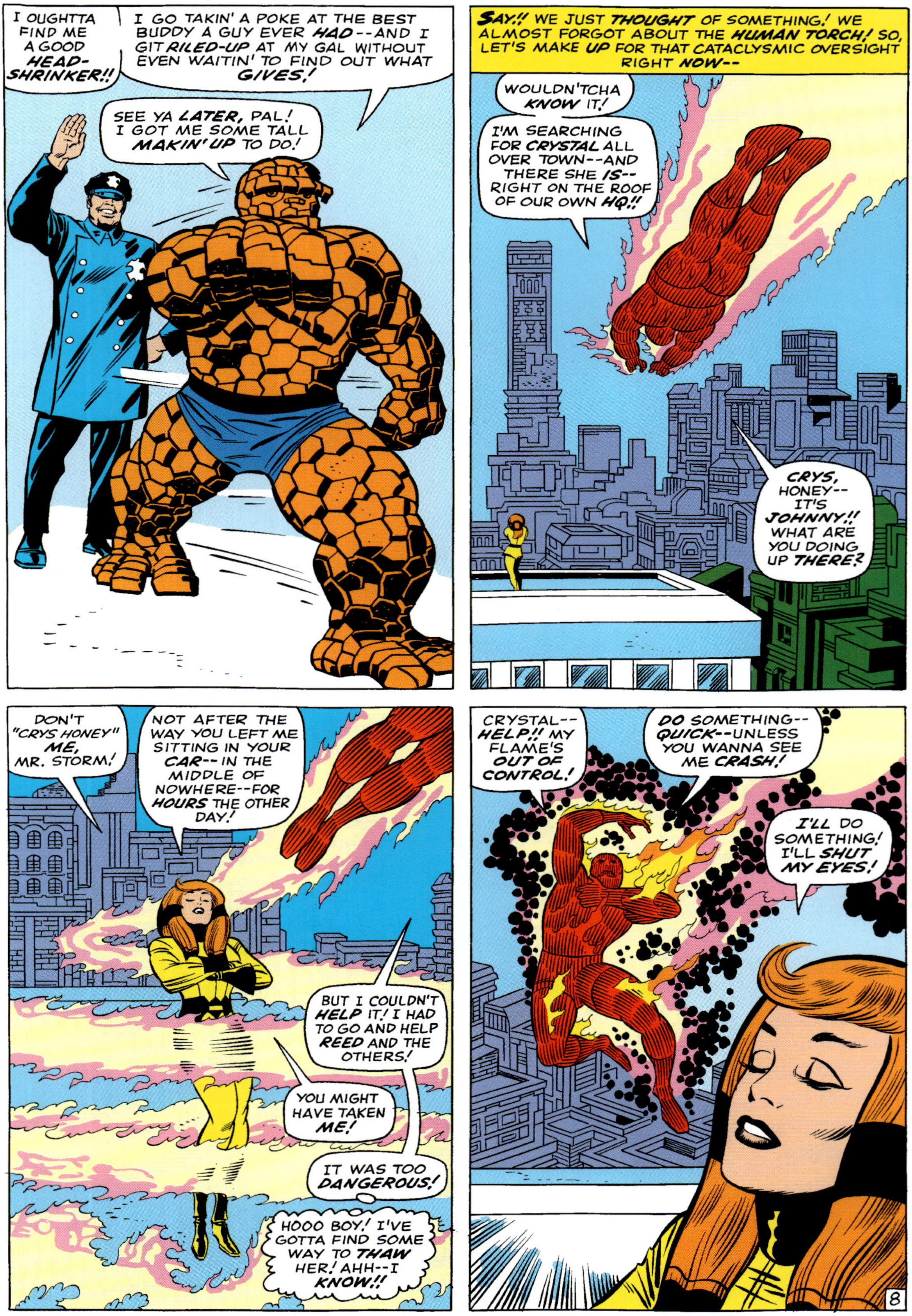
I OUGHTTA FIND ME A GOOD HEAD-SHRINKER!!
I GO TAKIN' A POKE AT THE BEST BUDDY A GUY EVER HAD--AND I GIT RILED-UP AT MY GAL WITHOUT EVEN WAITIN' TO FIND OUT WHAT GIVES!
SEE YA LATER, PAL! I GOT ME SOME TALL MAKIN' UP TO DO!
SAY!! WE JUST THOUGHT OF SOMETHING! WE ALMOST FORGOT ABOUT THE HUMAN TORCH! SO, LET'S MAKE UP FOR THAT CATACLYSMIC OVERSIGHT RIGHT NOW--
WOULDN'TCHA KNOW IT!
I'M SEARCHING FOR CRYSTAL ALL OVER TOWN--AND THERE SHE IS--RIGHT ON THE ROOF OF OUR OWN HQ!!
CRYS, HONEY--IT'S JOHNNY!! WHAT ARE YOU DOING UP THERE?
DON'T "CRYS HONEY" ME, MR. STORM!
NOT AFTER THE WAY YOU LEFT ME SITTING IN YOUR CAR--IN THE MIDDLE OF NOWHERE--FOR HOURS THE OTHER DAY!
BUT I COULDN'T HELP IT! I HAD TO GO AND HELP REED AND THE OTHERS!
YOU MIGHT HAVE TAKEN ME!
IT WAS TOO DANGEROUS!
HOOO BOY! I'VE GOTTA FIND SOME WAY TO THAW HER! AHH--I KNOW!!
CRYSTAL--HELP!! MY FLAME'S OUT OF CONTROL!
DO SOMETHING--QUICK--UNLESS YOU WANNA SEE ME CRASH!
I'LL DO SOMETHING! I'LL SHUT MY EYES!
8

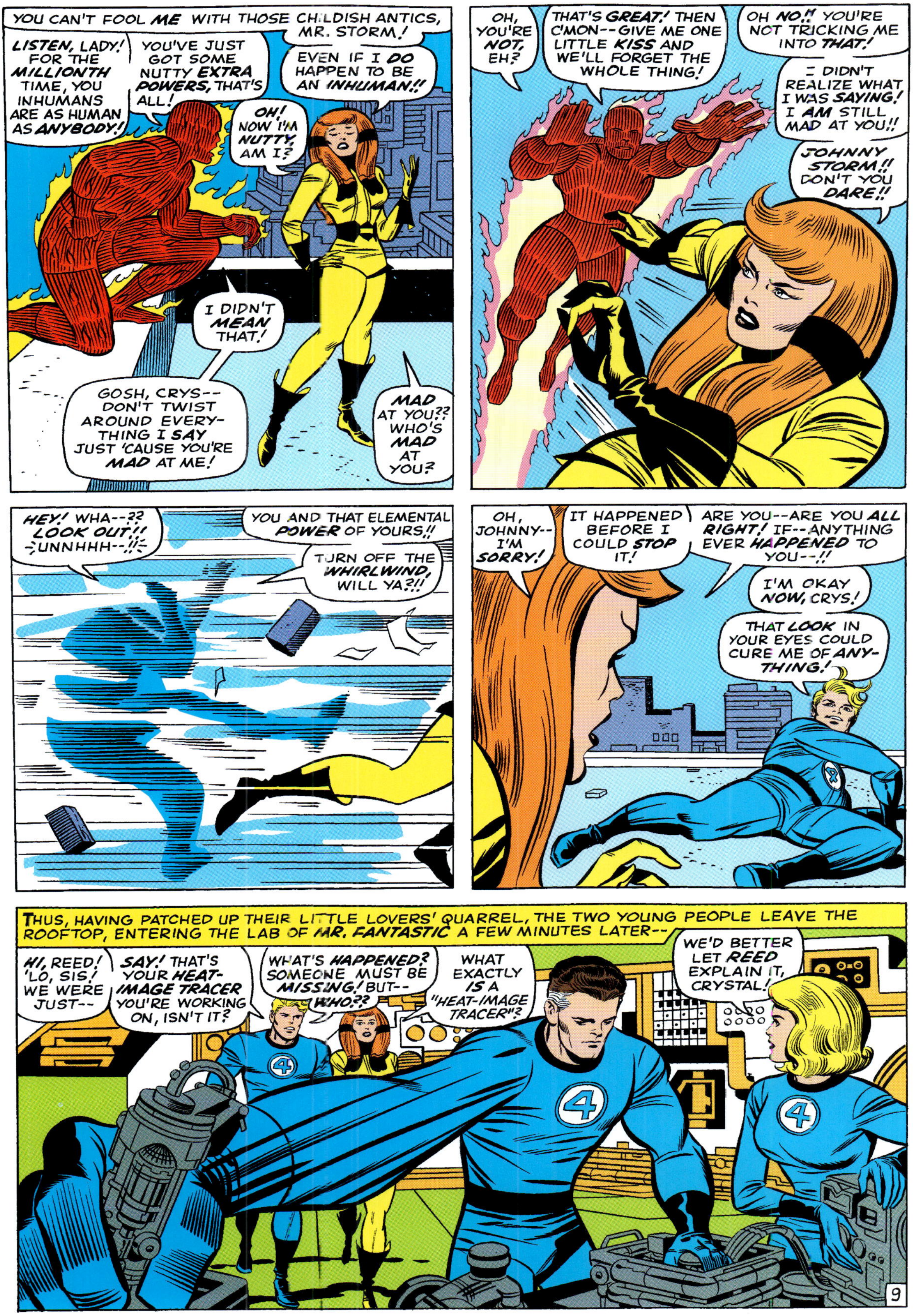
YOU CAN'T FOOL ME WITH THOSE CHILDISH ANTICS, MR. STORM!
LISTEN, LADY! FOR THE MILLIONTH TIME, YOU INHUMANS ARE AS HUMAN AS ANYBODY!
YOU'VE JUST GOT SOME NUTTY EXTRA POWERS, THAT'S ALL!
EVEN IF I DO HAPPEN TO BE AN INHUMAN!!
OH! NOW I'M NUTTY, AM I?
I DIDN'T MEAN THAT!
GOSH, CRYS-- DON'T TWIST AROUND EVERY-THING I SAY JUST 'CAUSE YOU'RE MAD AT ME!
MAD AT YOU?? WHO'S MAD AT YOU?
OH, YOU'RE NOT, EH?
THAT'S GREAT! THEN C'MON--GIVE ME ONE LITTLE KISS AND WE'LL FORGET THE WHOLE THING!
OH NO!! YOU'RE NOT TRICKING ME INTO THAT!
I DIDN'T REALIZE WHAT I WAS SAYING! I AM STILL MAD AT YOU!!
JOHNNY STORM!! DON'T YOU DARE!!
HEY! WHA--?? LOOK OUT!! UNNHHH--!!
YOU AND THAT ELEMENTAL POWER OF YOURS!!
TURN OFF THE WHIRLWIND, WILL YA?!!
OH, JOHNNY-- I'M SORRY!
IT HAPPENED BEFORE I COULD STOP IT!
ARE YOU--ARE YOU ALL RIGHT! IF--ANYTHING EVER HAPPENED TO YOU--!!
I'M OKAY NOW, CRYS!
THAT LOOK IN YOUR EYES COULD CURE ME OF ANY-THING!
THUS, HAVING PATCHED UP THEIR LITTLE LOVERS' QUARREL, THE TWO YOUNG PEOPLE LEAVE THE ROOFTOP, ENTERING THE LAB OF MR. FANTASTIC A FEW MINUTES LATER--
HI, REED! 'LO, SIS! WE WERE JUST--
SAY! THAT'S YOUR HEAT-IMAGE TRACER YOU'RE WORKING ON, ISN'T IT?
WHAT'S HAPPENED? SOMEONE MUST BE MISSING! BUT-- WHO??
WHAT EXACTLY IS A "HEAT-IMAGE TRACER"?
WE'D BETTER LET REED EXPLAIN IT, CRYSTAL!
9

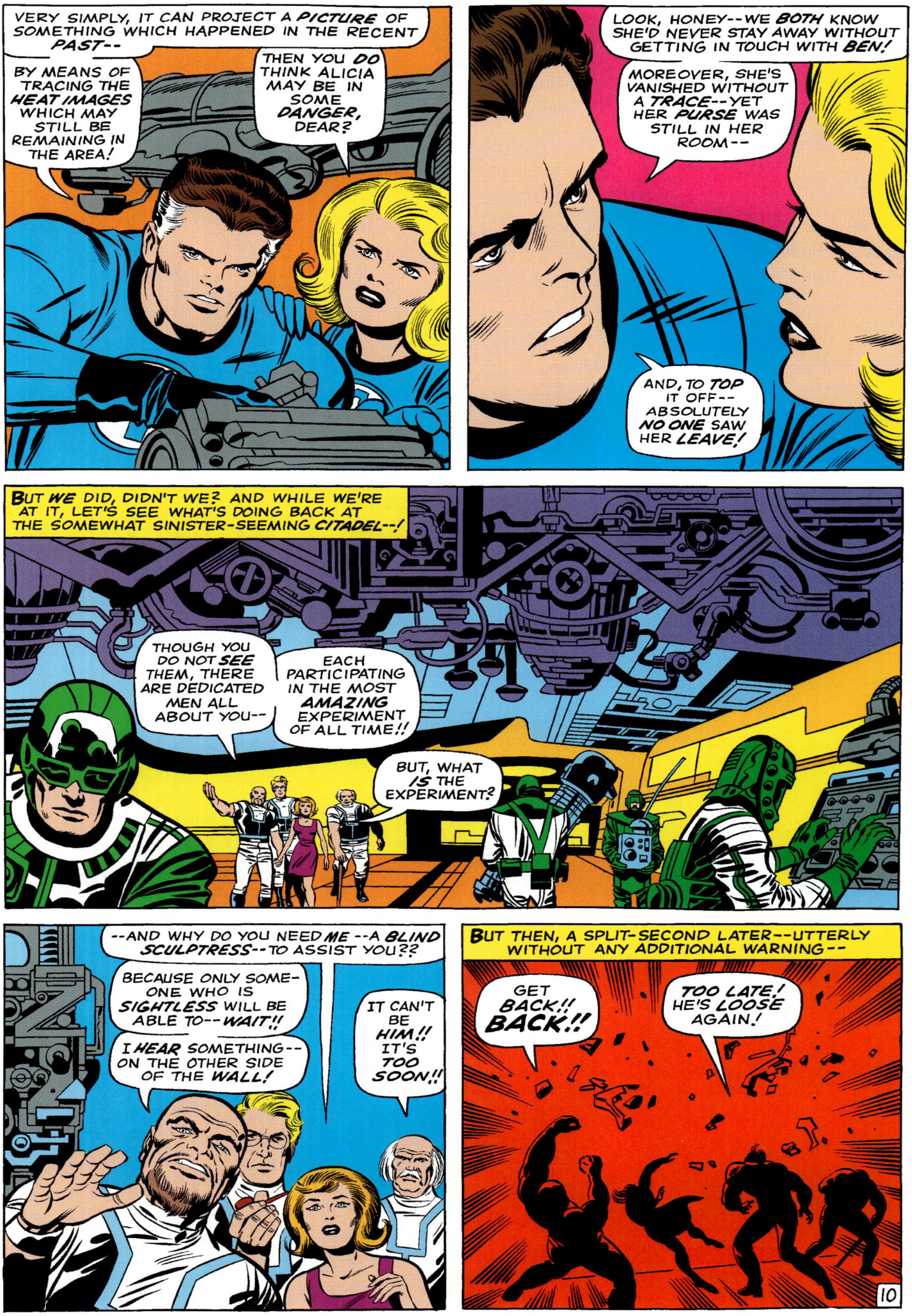

VERY SIMPLY, IT CAN PROJECT A PICTURE OF SOMETHING WHICH HAPPENED IN THE RECENT PAST--
BY MEANS OF TRACING THE HEAT IMAGES WHICH MAY STILL BE REMAINING IN THE AREA!
THEN YOU DO THINK ALICIA MAY BE IN SOME DANGER, DEAR?
LOOK, HONEY--WE BOTH KNOW SHE'D NEVER STAY AWAY WITHOUT GETTING IN TOUCH WITH BEN!
MOREOVER, SHE'S VANISHED WITHOUT A TRACE--YET HER PURSE WAS STILL IN HER ROOM--
AND, TO TOP IT OFF--ABSOLUTELY NO ONE SAW HER LEAVE!
BUT WE DID, DIDN'T WE? AND WHILE WE'RE AT IT, LET'S SEE WHAT'S DOING BACK AT THE SOMEWHAT SINISTER-SEEMING CITADEL--!
THOUGH YOU DO NOT SEE THEM, THERE ARE DEDICATED MEN ALL ABOUT YOU--
EACH PARTICIPATING IN THE MOST AMAZING EXPERIMENT OF ALL TIME!!
BUT, WHAT IS THE EXPERIMENT?
--AND WHY DO YOU NEED ME--A BLIND SCULPTRESS--TO ASSIST YOU??
BECAUSE ONLY SOME-ONE WHO IS SIGHTLESS WILL BE ABLE TO--WAIT!!
I HEAR SOMETHING--ON THE OTHER SIDE OF THE WALL!
IT CAN'T BE HIM!! IT'S TOO SOON!!
BUT THEN, A SPLIT-SECOND LATER--UTTERLY WITHOUT ANY ADDITIONAL WARNING--
GET BACK!! BACK!!
TOO LATE! HE'S LOOSE AGAIN!
10

11.

117

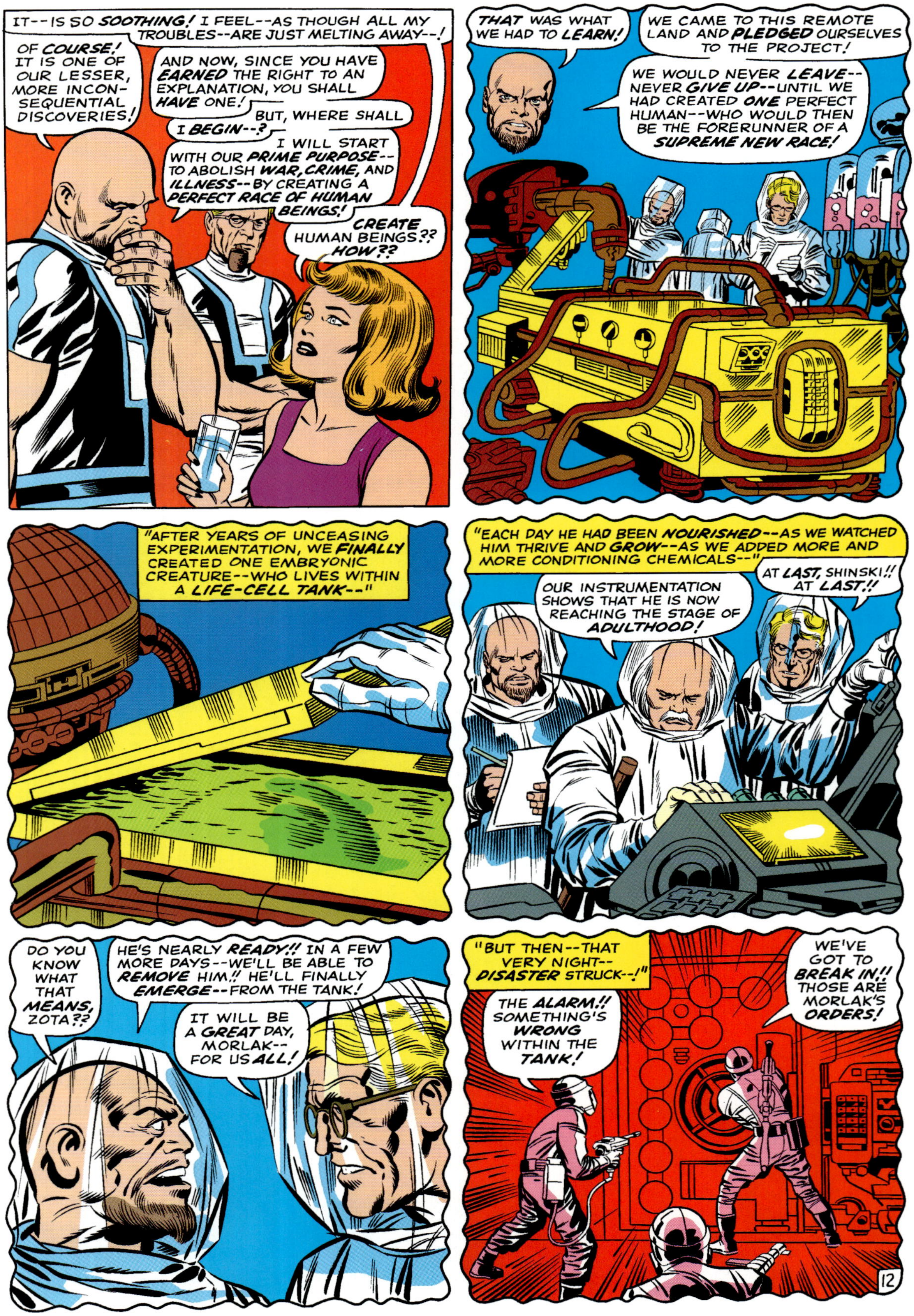

IT--IS SO SOOTHING! I FEEL--AS THOUGH ALL MY TROUBLES--ARE JUST MELTING AWAY--!
OF COURSE! IT IS ONE OF OUR LESSER, MORE INCON-SEQUENTIAL DISCOVERIES!
AND NOW, SINCE YOU HAVE EARNED THE RIGHT TO AN EXPLANATION, YOU SHALL HAVE ONE!
BUT, WHERE SHALL I BEGIN--?
I WILL START WITH OUR PRIME PURPOSE--TO ABOLISH WAR, CRIME, AND ILLNESS--BY CREATING A PERFECT RACE OF HUMAN BEINGS!
CREATE HUMAN BEINGS?? HOW??
THAT WAS WHAT WE HAD TO LEARN!
WE CAME TO THIS REMOTE LAND AND PLEDGED OURSELVES TO THE PROJECT!
WE WOULD NEVER LEAVE--NEVER GIVE UP--UNTIL WE HAD CREATED ONE PERFECT HUMAN--WHO WOULD THEN BE THE FORERUNNER OF A SUPREME NEW RACE!
"AFTER YEARS OF UNCEASING EXPERIMENTATION, WE FINALLY CREATED ONE EMBRYONIC CREATURE--WHO LIVES WITHIN A LIFE-CELL TANK--"
"EACH DAY HE HAD BEEN NOURISHED--AS WE WATCHED HIM THRIVE AND GROW--AS WE ADDED MORE AND MORE CONDITIONING CHEMICALS--"
OUR INSTRUMENTATION SHOWS THAT HE IS NOW REACHING THE STAGE OF ADULTHOOD!
AT LAST, SHINSKI!! AT LAST!!
DO YOU KNOW WHAT THAT MEANS, ZOTA??
HE'S NEARLY READY!! IN A FEW MORE DAYS--WE'LL BE ABLE TO REMOVE HIM!! HE'LL FINALLY EMERGE--FROM THE TANK!
IT WILL BE A GREAT DAY, MORLAK--FOR US ALL!
"BUT THEN--THAT VERY NIGHT--DISASTER STRUCK--!"
THE ALARM!! SOMETHING'S WRONG WITHIN THE TANK!
WE'VE GOT TO BREAK IN!! THOSE ARE MORLAK'S ORDERS!
12

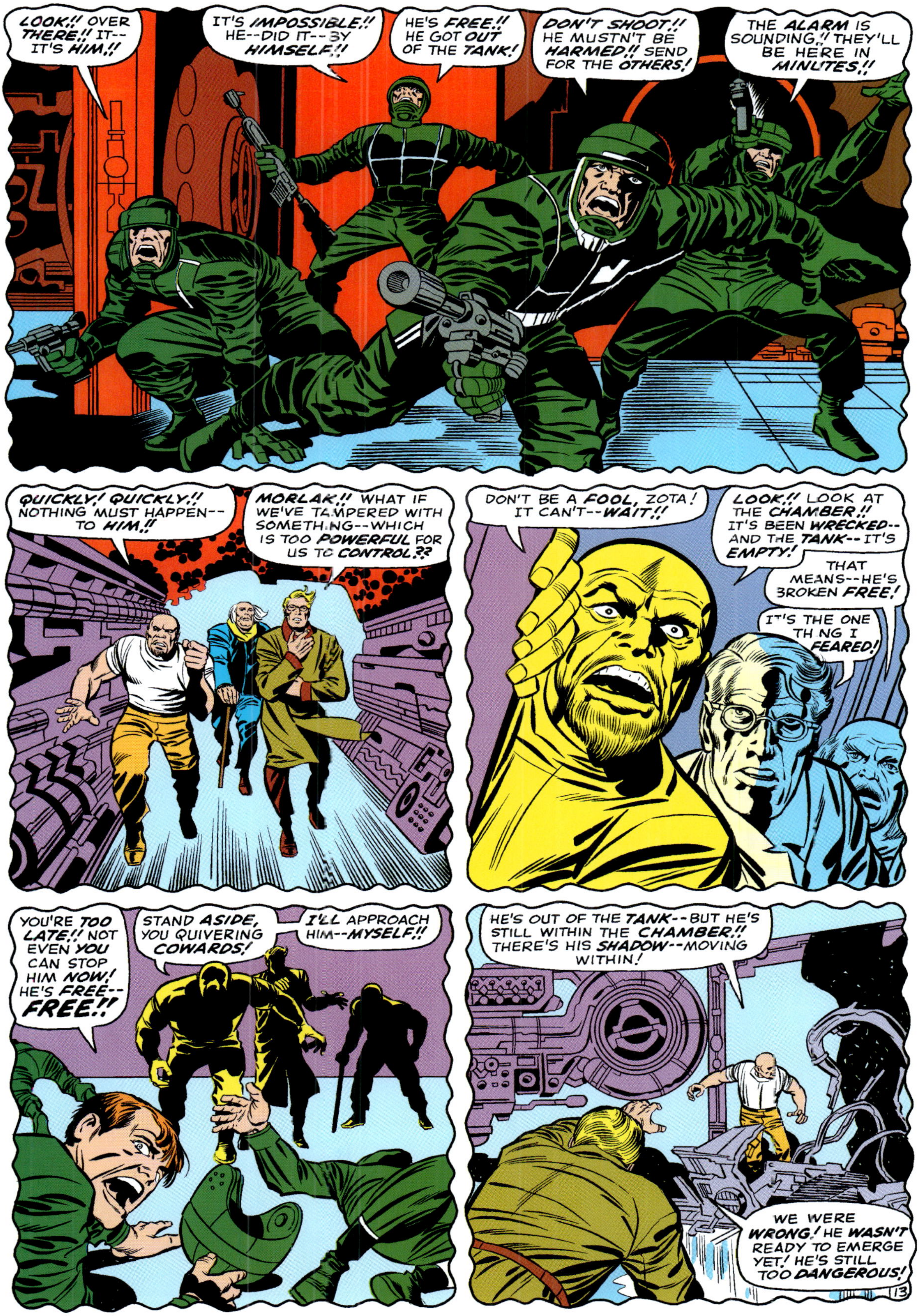
LOOK!! OVER THERE!! IT-- IT'S HIM!!
IT'S IMPOSSIBLE!! HE--DID IT--BY HIMSELF!!
HE'S FREE!! HE GOT OUT OF THE TANK!
DON'T SHOOT!! HE MUSTN'T BE HARMED!! SEND FOR THE OTHERS!
THE ALARM IS SOUNDING!! THEY'LL BE HERE IN MINUTES!!
QUICKLY! QUICKLY!! NOTHING MUST HAPPEN-- TO HIM!!
MORLAK!! WHAT IF WE'VE TAMPERED WITH SOMETHING--WHICH IS TOO POWERFUL FOR US TO CONTROL??
DON'T BE A FOOL, ZOTA! IT CAN'T--WAIT!!
LOOK!! LOOK AT THE CHAMBER!! IT'S BEEN WRECKED-- AND THE TANK--IT'S EMPTY!
THAT MEANS--HE'S BROKEN FREE!
IT'S THE ONE THING I FEARED!
YOU'RE TOO LATE!! NOT EVEN YOU CAN STOP HIM NOW! HE'S FREE-- FREE!!
STAND ASIDE, YOU QUIVERING COWARDS!
I'LL APPROACH HIM--MYSELF!!
HE'S OUT OF THE TANK--BUT HE'S STILL WITHIN THE CHAMBER!! THERE'S HIS SHADOW--MOVING WITHIN!
WE WERE WRONG! HE WASN'T READY TO EMERGE YET! HE'S STILL TOO DANGEROUS!
13

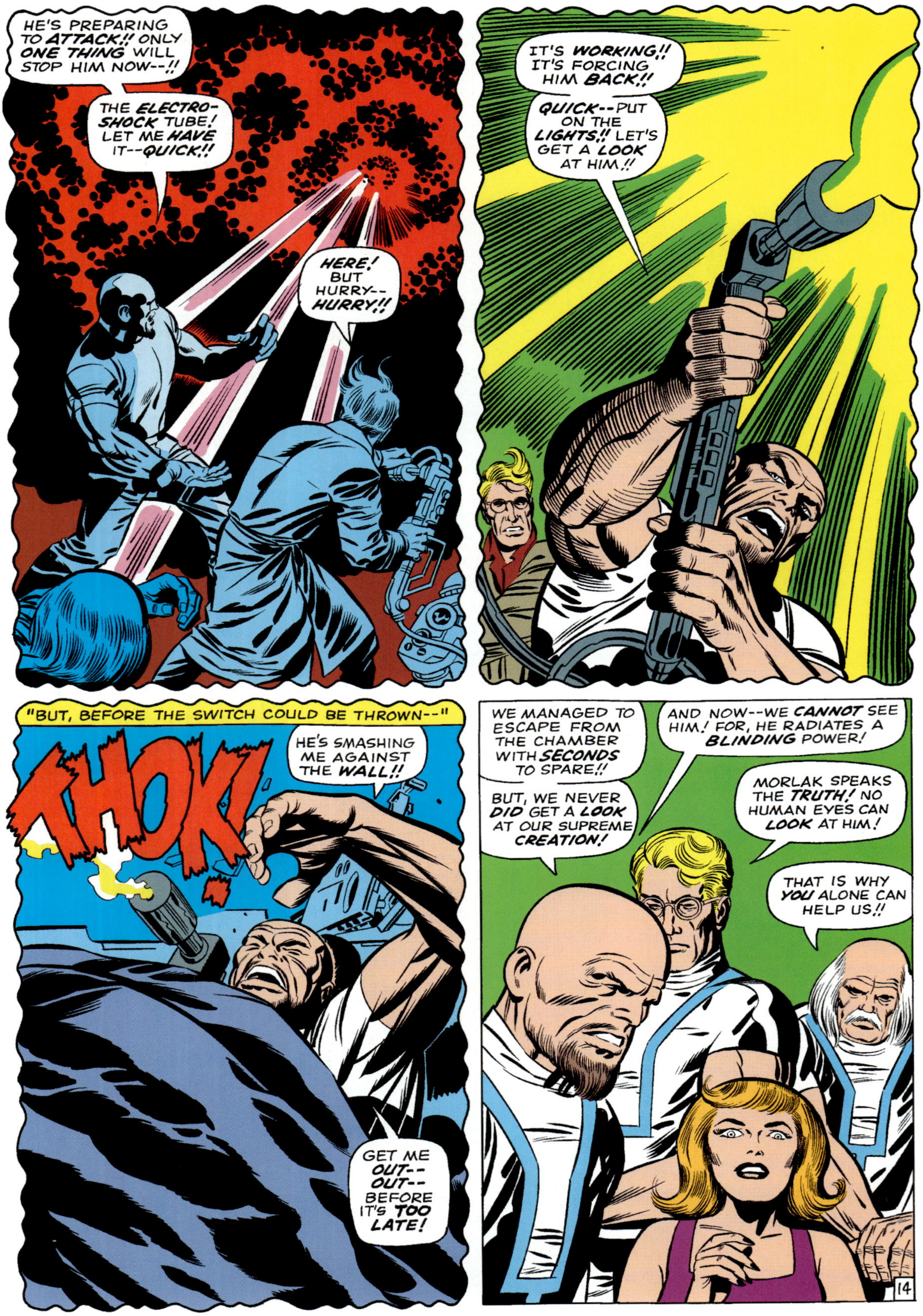
HE'S PREPARING TO ATTACK!! ONLY ONE THING WILL STOP HIM NOW--!!
THE ELECTRO-SHOCK TUBE! LET ME HAVE IT--QUICK!!
HERE! BUT HURRY--HURRY!!
IT'S WORKING!! IT'S FORCING HIM BACK!!
QUICK--PUT ON THE LIGHTS!! LET'S GET A LOOK AT HIM!!
"BUT, BEFORE THE SWITCH COULD BE THROWN--"
THOK!
HE'S SMASHING ME AGAINST THE WALL!!
GET ME OUT--OUT--BEFORE IT'S TOO LATE!
WE MANAGED TO ESCAPE FROM THE CHAMBER WITH SECONDS TO SPARE!!
BUT, WE NEVER DID GET A LOOK AT OUR SUPREME CREATION!
AND NOW--WE CANNOT SEE HIM! FOR, HE RADIATES A BLINDING POWER!
MORLAK SPEAKS THE TRUTH! NO HUMAN EYES CAN LOOK AT HIM!
THAT IS WHY YOU ALONE CAN HELP US!!
14

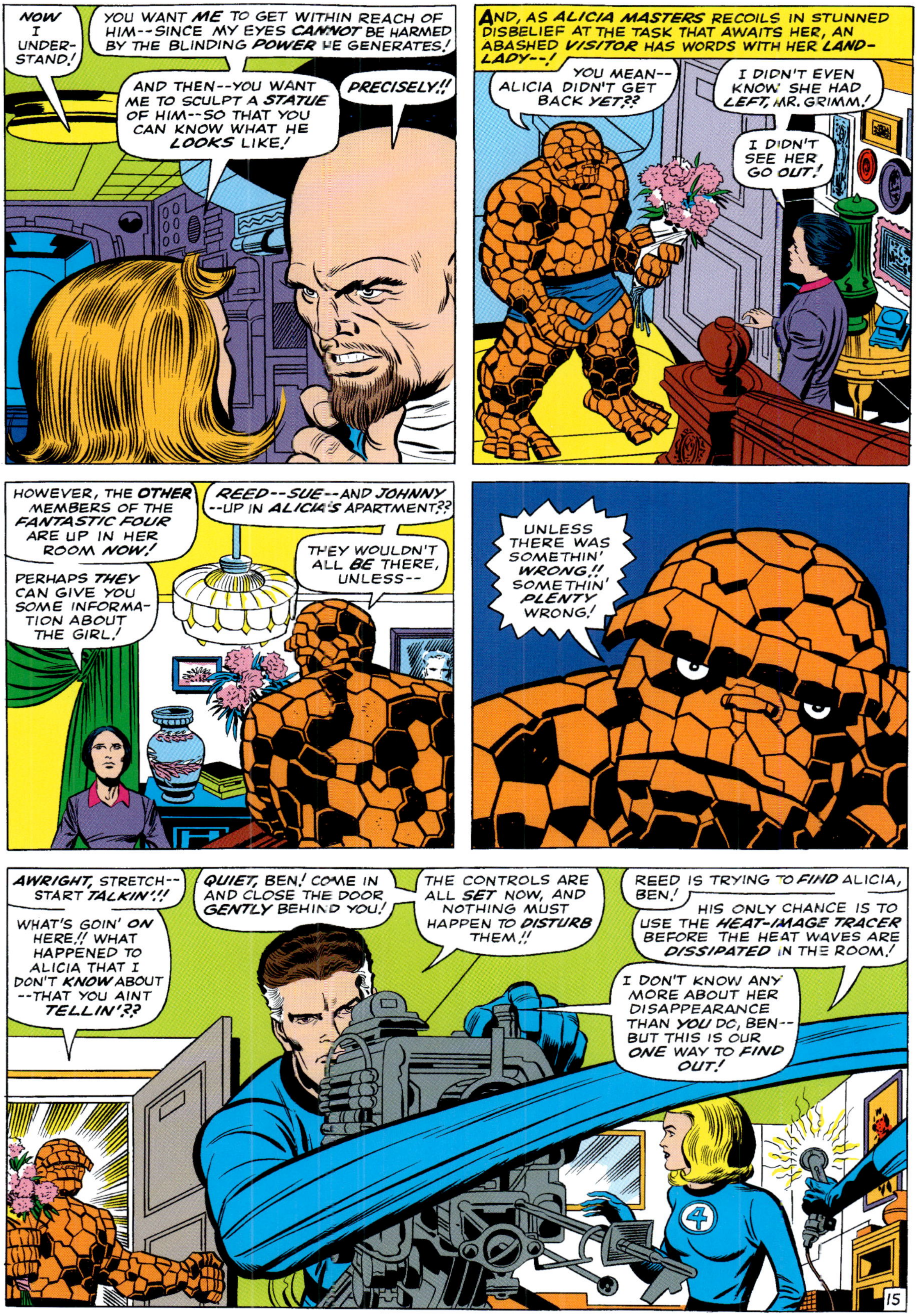
NOW I UNDER-STAND!
YOU WANT ME TO GET WITHIN REACH OF HIM--SINCE MY EYES CANNOT BE HARMED BY THE BLINDING POWER HE GENERATES!
AND THEN--YOU WANT ME TO SCULPT A STATUE OF HIM--SO THAT YOU CAN KNOW WHAT HE LOOKS LIKE!
PRECISELY!!
AND, AS ALICIA MASTERS RECOILS IN STUNNED DISBELIEF AT THE TASK THAT AWAITS HER, AN ABASHED VISITOR HAS WORDS WITH HER LAND-LADY--!
YOU MEAN-- ALICIA DIDN'T GET BACK YET??
I DIDN'T EVEN KNOW SHE HAD LEFT, MR. GRIMM!
I DIDN'T SEE HER GO OUT!
HOWEVER, THE OTHER MEMBERS OF THE FANTASTIC FOUR ARE UP IN HER ROOM NOW!
PERHAPS THEY CAN GIVE YOU SOME INFORMATION ABOUT THE GIRL!
REED--SUE--AND JOHNNY --UP IN ALICIA'S APARTMENT??
THEY WOULDN'T ALL BE THERE, UNLESS--
UNLESS THERE WAS SOMETHIN' WRONG!! SOMETHIN' PLENTY WRONG!
AWRIGHT, STRETCH-- START TALKIN'!!
WHAT'S GOIN' ON HERE!! WHAT HAPPENED TO ALICIA THAT I DON'T KNOW ABOUT --THAT YOU AINT TELLIN'??
QUIET, BEN! COME IN AND CLOSE THE DOOR GENTLY BEHIND YOU!
THE CONTROLS ARE ALL SET NOW, AND NOTHING MUST HAPPEN TO DISTURB THEM!!
REED IS TRYING TO FIND ALICIA, BEN!
HIS ONLY CHANCE IS TO USE THE HEAT-IMAGE TRACER BEFORE THE HEAT WAVES ARE DISSIPATED IN THE ROOM!
I DON'T KNOW ANY MORE ABOUT HER DISAPPEARANCE THAN YOU DO, BEN-- BUT THIS IS OUR ONE WAY TO FIND OUT!
15

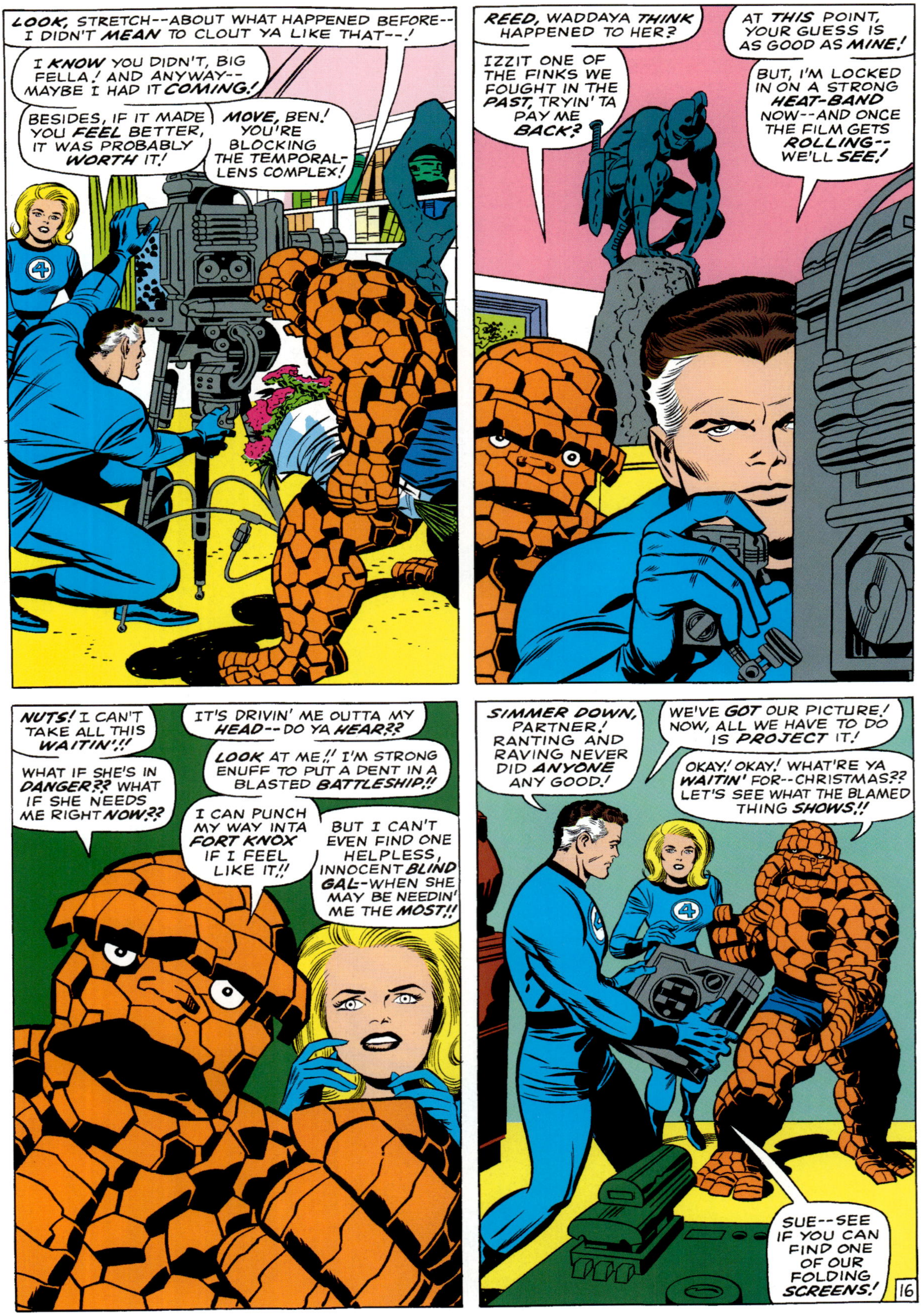
LOOK, STRETCH--ABOUT WHAT HAPPENED BEFORE--I DIDN'T MEAN TO CLOUT YA LIKE THAT--!
I KNOW YOU DIDN'T, BIG FELLA! AND ANYWAY--MAYBE I HAD IT COMING!
BESIDES, IF IT MADE YOU FEEL BETTER, IT WAS PROBABLY WORTH IT!
MOVE, BEN! YOU'RE BLOCKING THE TEMPORAL-LENS COMPLEX!
REED, WADDAYA THINK HAPPENED TO HER?
IZZIT ONE OF THE FINKS WE FOUGHT IN THE PAST, TRYIN' TA PAY ME BACK?
AT THIS POINT, YOUR GUESS IS AS GOOD AS MINE!
BUT, I'M LOCKED IN ON A STRONG HEAT-BAND NOW--AND ONCE THE FILM GETS ROLLING--WE'LL SEE!
NUTS! I CAN'T TAKE ALL THIS WAITIN'!!
WHAT IF SHE'S IN DANGER?? WHAT IF SHE NEEDS ME RIGHT NOW??
IT'S DRIVIN' ME OUTTA MY HEAD--DO YA HEAR??
LOOK AT ME!! I'M STRONG ENUFF TO PUT A DENT IN A BLASTED BATTLESHIP!!
I CAN PUNCH MY WAY INTA FORT KNOX IF I FEEL LIKE IT!!
BUT I CAN'T EVEN FIND ONE HELPLESS, INNOCENT BLIND GAL--WHEN SHE MAY BE NEEDIN' ME THE MOST!!
SIMMER DOWN, PARTNER! RANTING AND RAVING NEVER DID ANYONE ANY GOOD!
WE'VE GOT OUR PICTURE! NOW, ALL WE HAVE TO DO IS PROJECT IT!
OKAY! OKAY! WHAT'RE YA WAITIN' FOR--CHRISTMAS?? LET'S SEE WHAT THE BLAMED THING SHOWS!!
SUE--SEE IF YOU CAN FIND ONE OF OUR FOLDING SCREENS!
16

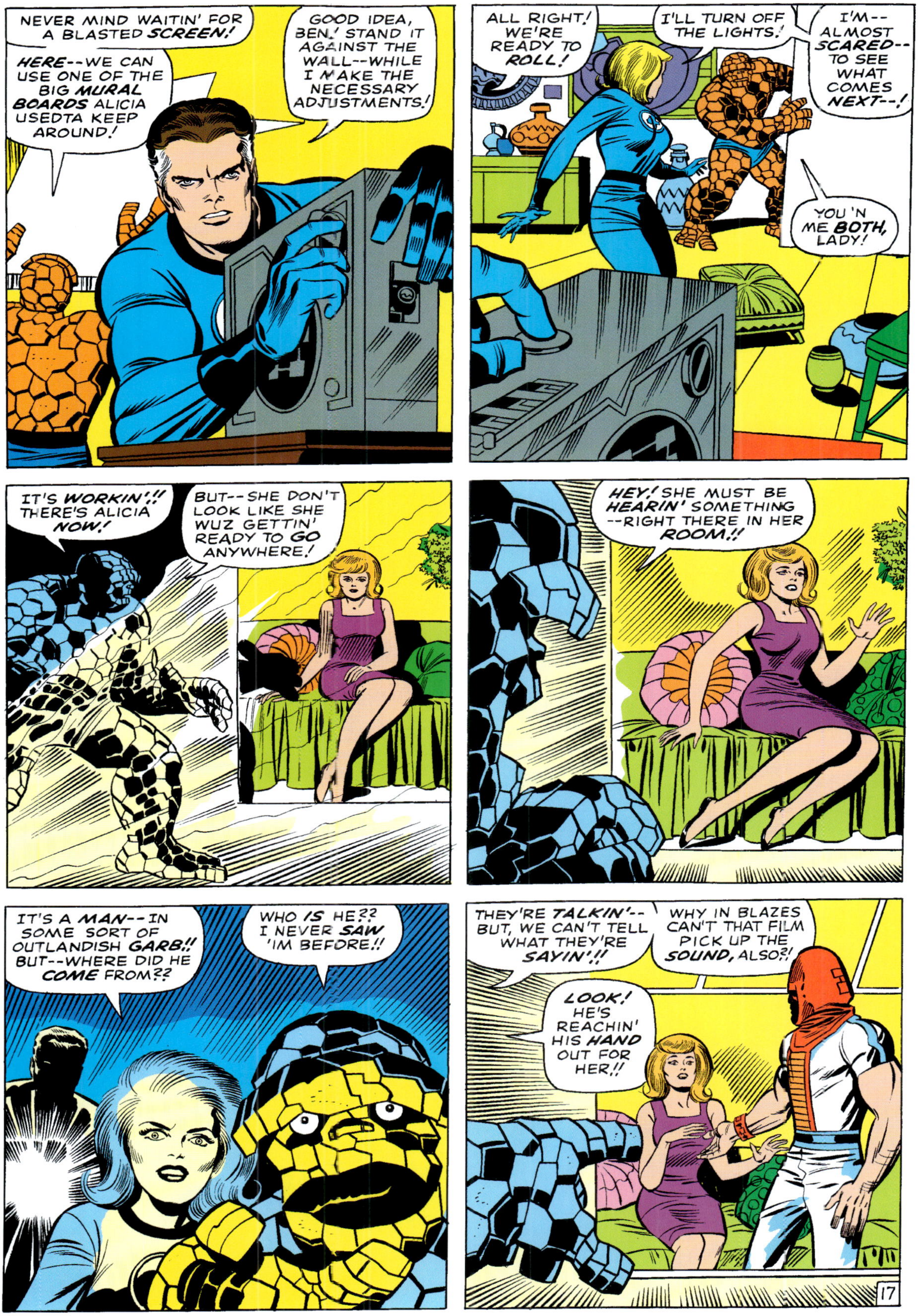

NEVER MIND WAITIN' FOR A BLASTED SCREEN!
HERE--WE CAN USE ONE OF THE BIG MURAL BOARDS ALICIA USEDTA KEEP AROUND!
GOOD IDEA, BEN! STAND IT AGAINST THE WALL--WHILE I MAKE THE NECESSARY ADJUSTMENTS!
ALL RIGHT! WE'RE READY TO ROLL!
I'LL TURN OFF THE LIGHTS!
I'M-- ALMOST SCARED-- TO SEE WHAT COMES NEXT--!
YOU 'N ME BOTH, LADY!
IT'S WORKIN'!! THERE'S ALICIA NOW!
BUT--SHE DON'T LOOK LIKE SHE WUZ GETTIN' READY TO GO ANYWHERE!
HEY! SHE MUST BE HEARIN' SOMETHING --RIGHT THERE IN HER ROOM!!
IT'S A MAN--IN SOME SORT OF OUTLANDISH GARB!! BUT--WHERE DID HE COME FROM??
WHO IS HE?? I NEVER SAW 'IM BEFORE!!
THEY'RE TALKIN'-- BUT, WE CAN'T TELL WHAT THEY'RE SAYIN'!!
WHY IN BLAZES CAN'T THAT FILM PICK UP THE SOUND, ALSO?!
LOOK! HE'S REACHIN' HIS HAND OUT FOR HER!!
17

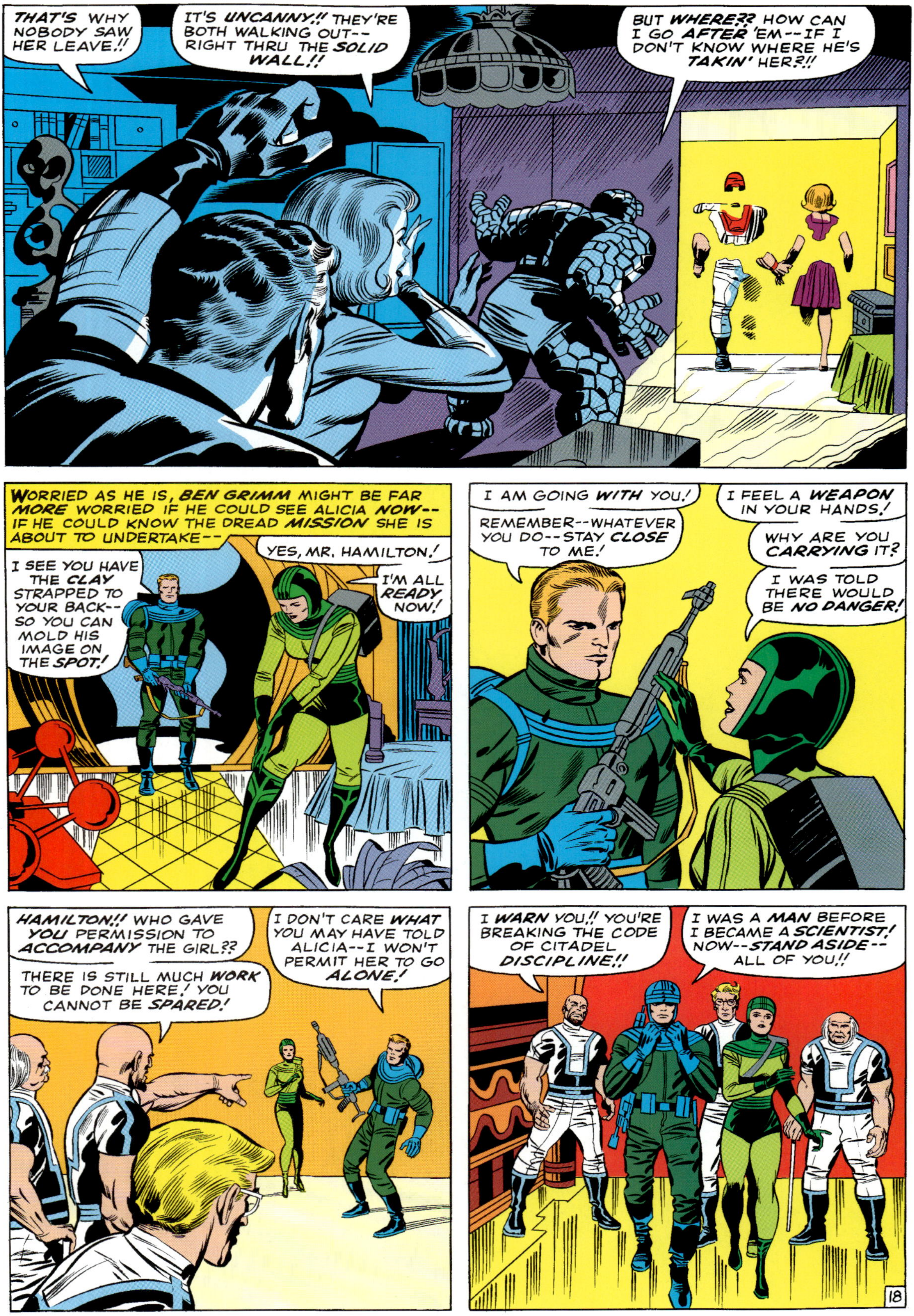
THAT'S WHY NOBODY SAW HER LEAVE.!!
IT'S UNCANNY.!! THEY'RE BOTH WALKING OUT-- RIGHT THRU THE SOLID WALL!!
BUT WHERE?? HOW CAN I GO AFTER 'EM--IF I DON'T KNOW WHERE HE'S TAKIN' HER?!!
WORRIED AS HE IS, BEN GRIMM MIGHT BE FAR MORE WORRIED IF HE COULD SEE ALICIA NOW-- IF HE COULD KNOW THE DREAD MISSION SHE IS ABOUT TO UNDERTAKE--
YES, MR. HAMILTON.!
I SEE YOU HAVE THE CLAY STRAPPED TO YOUR BACK-- SO YOU CAN MOLD HIS IMAGE ON THE SPOT.!
I'M ALL READY NOW.!
I AM GOING WITH YOU.!
REMEMBER--WHATEVER YOU DO--STAY CLOSE TO ME.!
I FEEL A WEAPON IN YOUR HANDS.!
WHY ARE YOU CARRYING IT?
I WAS TOLD THERE WOULD BE NO DANGER.!
HAMILTON!! WHO GAVE YOU PERMISSION TO ACCOMPANY THE GIRL??
THERE IS STILL MUCH WORK TO BE DONE HERE.! YOU CANNOT BE SPARED.!
I DON'T CARE WHAT YOU MAY HAVE TOLD ALICIA--I WON'T PERMIT HER TO GO ALONE.!
I WARN YOU.!! YOU'RE BREAKING THE CODE OF CITADEL DISCIPLINE!!
I WAS A MAN BEFORE I BECAME A SCIENTIST.! NOW--STAND ASIDE-- ALL OF YOU.!!
18

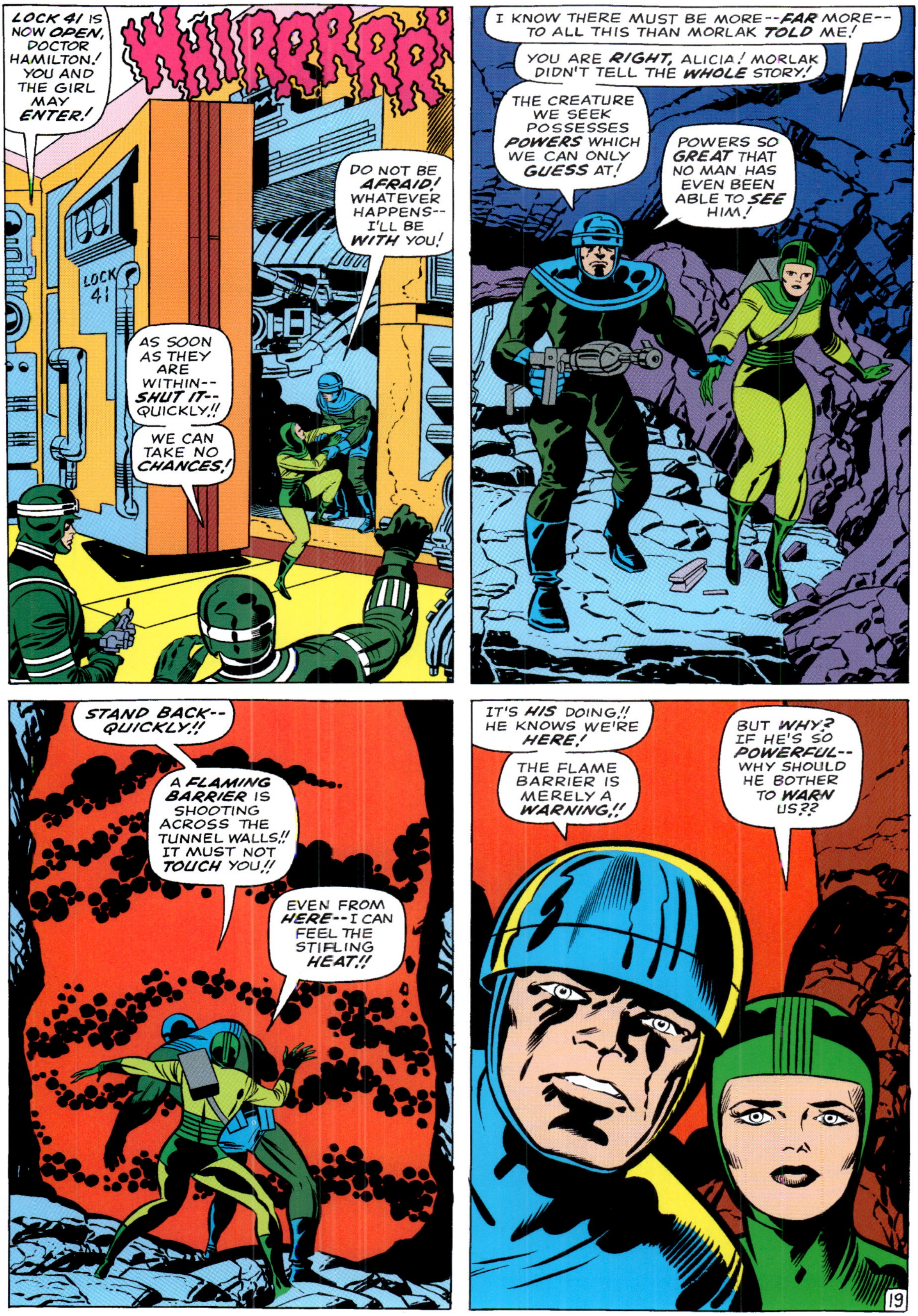
LOCK 41 IS NOW OPEN, DOCTOR HAMILTON! YOU AND THE GIRL MAY ENTER!
WHIRRRRR
DO NOT BE AFRAID! WHATEVER HAPPENS-- I'LL BE WITH YOU!
LOCK 41
AS SOON AS THEY ARE WITHIN-- SHUT IT-- QUICKLY!!
WE CAN TAKE NO CHANCES!
I KNOW THERE MUST BE MORE--FAR MORE-- TO ALL THIS THAN MORLAK TOLD ME!
YOU ARE RIGHT, ALICIA! MORLAK DIDN'T TELL THE WHOLE STORY!
THE CREATURE WE SEEK POSSESSES POWERS WHICH WE CAN ONLY GUESS AT!
POWERS SO GREAT THAT NO MAN HAS EVEN BEEN ABLE TO SEE HIM!
STAND BACK-- QUICKLY!!
A FLAMING BARRIER IS SHOOTING ACROSS THE TUNNEL WALLS!! IT MUST NOT TOUCH YOU!!
EVEN FROM HERE--I CAN FEEL THE STIFLING HEAT!!
IT'S HIS DOING!! HE KNOWS WE'RE HERE!
THE FLAME BARRIER IS MERELY A WARNING!!
BUT WHY? IF HE'S SO POWERFUL-- WHY SHOULD HE BOTHER TO WARN US??
19

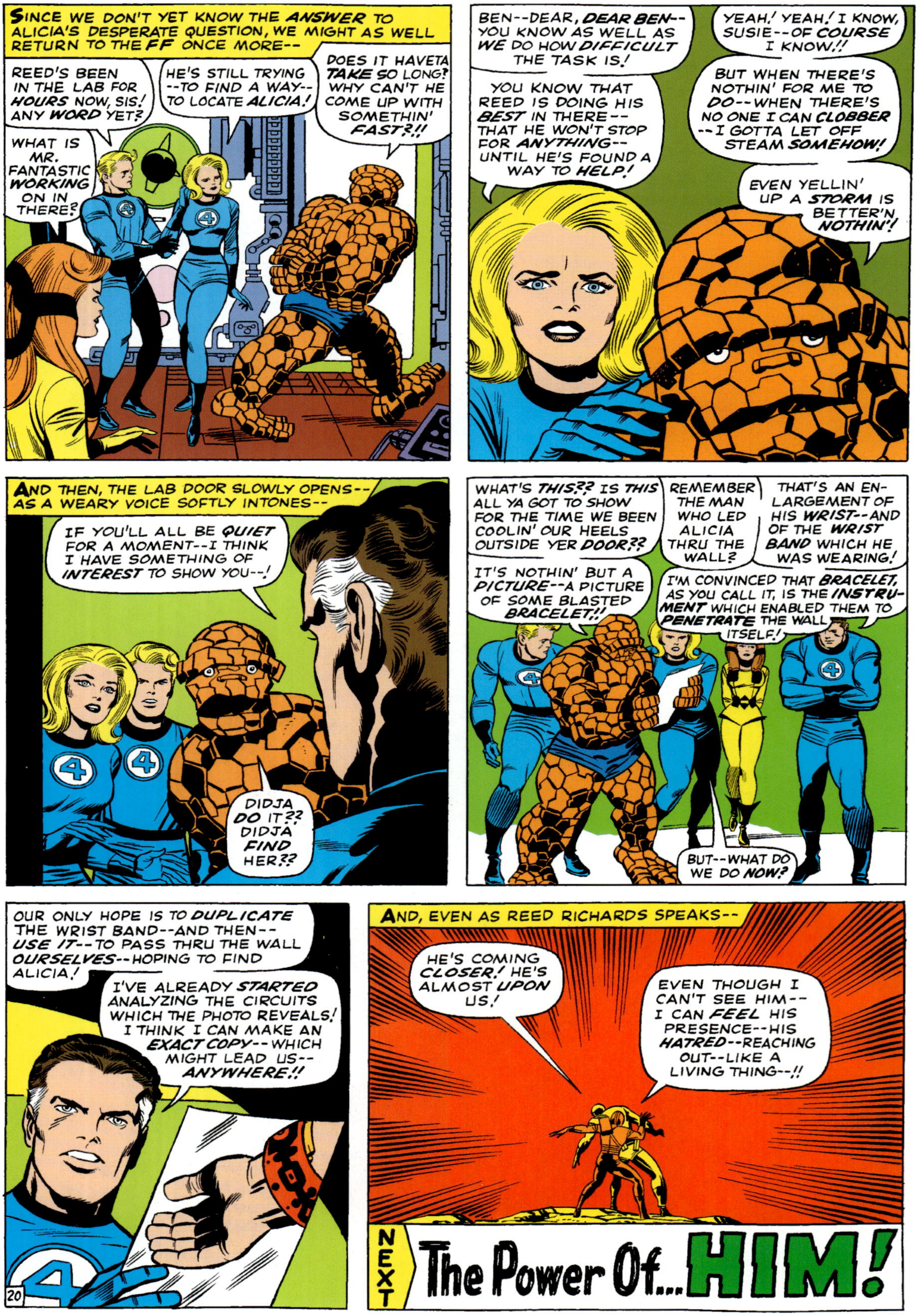
SINCE WE DON'T YET KNOW THE ANSWER TO ALICIA'S DESPERATE QUESTION, WE MIGHT AS WELL RETURN TO THE FF ONCE MORE--
REED'S BEEN IN THE LAB FOR HOURS NOW, SIS! ANY WORD YET?
HE'S STILL TRYING --TO FIND A WAY-- TO LOCATE ALICIA!
DOES IT HAVETA TAKE SO LONG? WHY CAN'T HE COME UP WITH SOMETHIN' FAST?!!
WHAT IS MR. FANTASTIC WORKING ON IN THERE?
BEN--DEAR, DEAR BEN-- YOU KNOW AS WELL AS WE DO HOW DIFFICULT THE TASK IS!
YOU KNOW THAT REED IS DOING HIS BEST IN THERE-- THAT HE WON'T STOP FOR ANYTHING-- UNTIL HE'S FOUND A WAY TO HELP!
YEAH! YEAH! I KNOW, SUSIE--OF COURSE I KNOW!!
BUT WHEN THERE'S NOTHIN' FOR ME TO DO--WHEN THERE'S NO ONE I CAN CLOBBER --I GOTTA LET OFF STEAM SOMEHOW!
EVEN YELLIN' UP A STORM IS BETTER'N NOTHIN'!
AND THEN, THE LAB DOOR SLOWLY OPENS-- AS A WEARY VOICE SOFTLY INTONES--
IF YOU'LL ALL BE QUIET FOR A MOMENT--I THINK I HAVE SOMETHING OF INTEREST TO SHOW YOU--!
DIDJA DO IT?? DIDJA FIND HER??
WHAT'S THIS?? IS THIS ALL YA GOT TO SHOW FOR THE TIME WE BEEN COOLIN' OUR HEELS OUTSIDE YER DOOR??
IT'S NOTHIN' BUT A PICTURE--A PICTURE OF SOME BLASTED BRACELET!!
REMEMBER THE MAN WHO LED ALICIA THRU THE WALL?
THAT'S AN ENLARGEMENT OF HIS WRIST--AND OF THE WRIST BAND WHICH HE WAS WEARING!
I'M CONVINCED THAT BRACELET, AS YOU CALL IT, IS THE INSTRUMENT WHICH ENABLED THEM TO PENETRATE THE WALL ITSELF!
BUT--WHAT DO WE DO NOW?
OUR ONLY HOPE IS TO DUPLICATE THE WRIST BAND--AND THEN-- USE IT--TO PASS THRU THE WALL OURSELVES--HOPING TO FIND ALICIA!
I'VE ALREADY STARTED ANALYZING THE CIRCUITS WHICH THE PHOTO REVEALS! I THINK I CAN MAKE AN EXACT COPY--WHICH MIGHT LEAD US-- ANYWHERE!!
20
AND, EVEN AS REED RICHARDS SPEAKS--
HE'S COMING CLOSER! HE'S ALMOST UPON US!
EVEN THOUGH I CAN'T SEE HIM-- I CAN FEEL HIS PRESENCE--HIS HATRED--REACHING OUT--LIKE A LIVING THING--!!
NEXT The Power Of...HIM!

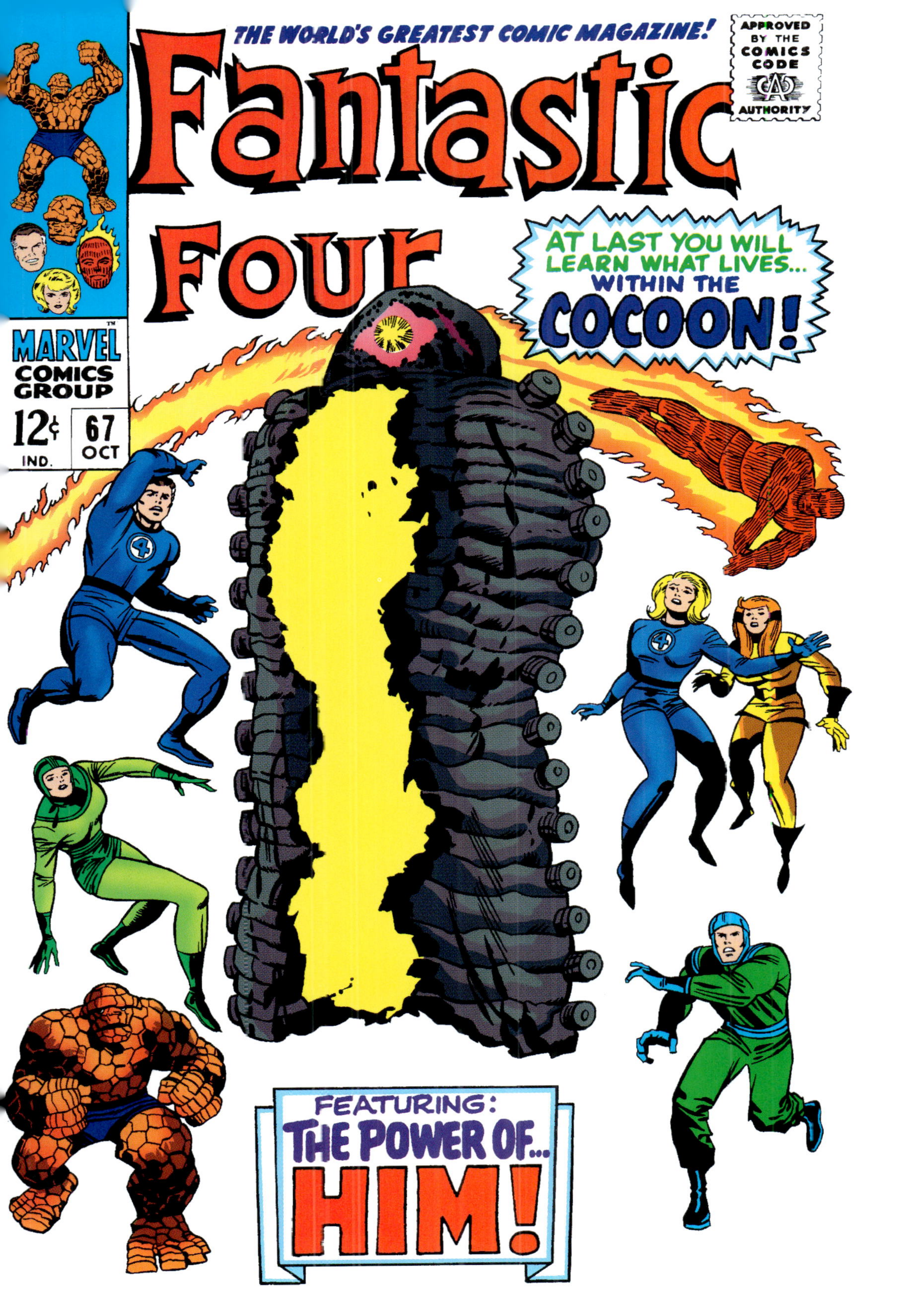
THE WORLD'S GREATEST COMIC MAGAZINE!
Fantastic Four
APPROVED BY THE COMICS CODE AUTHORITY
MARVEL COMICS GROUP
12¢ IND.
67 OCT
AT LAST YOU WILL LEARN WHAT LIVES... WITHIN THE COCOON!
FEATURING: THE POWER OF... HIM!

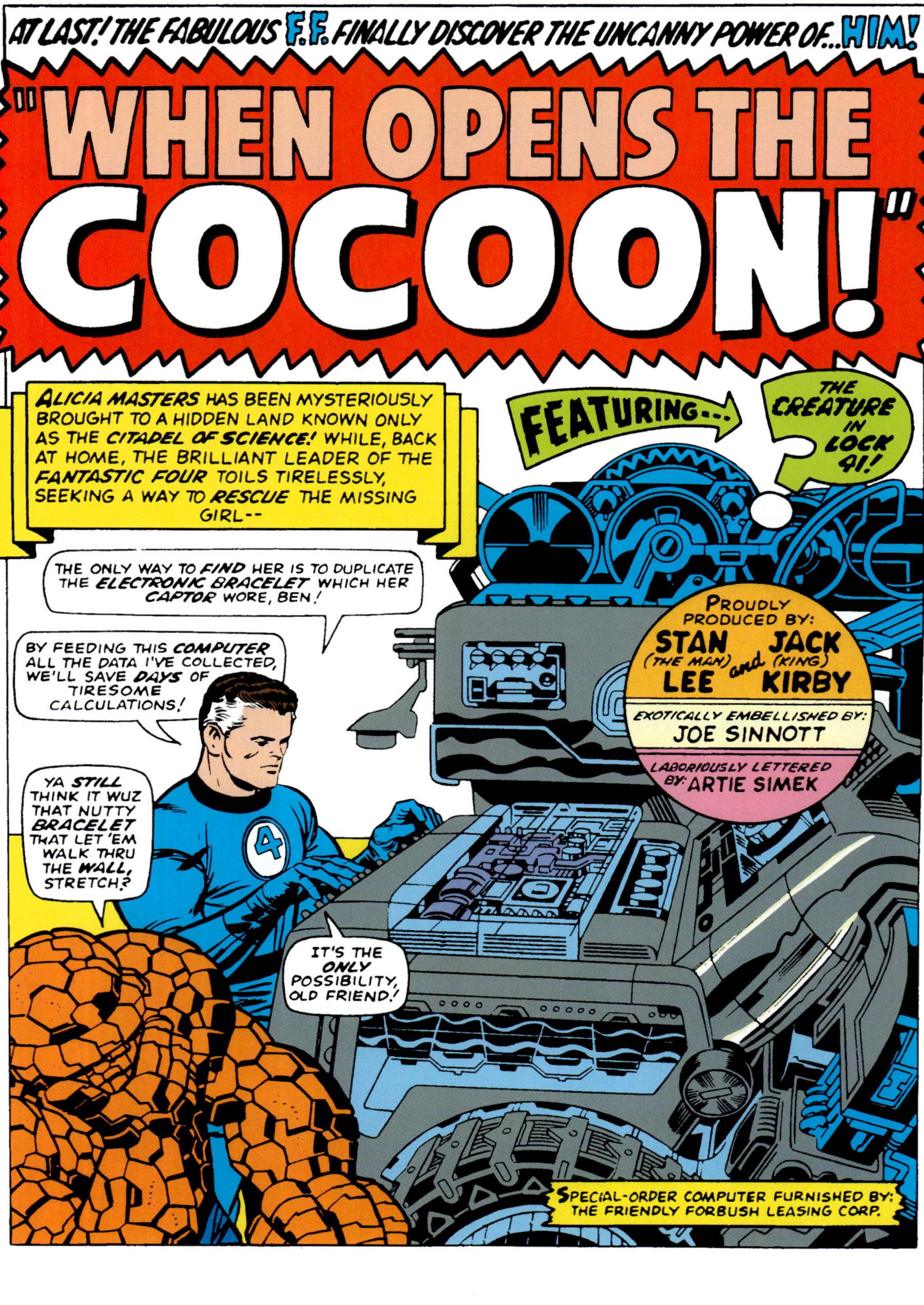

AT LAST! THE FABULOUS F.F. FINALLY DISCOVER THE UNCANNY POWER OF...HIM!
"WHEN OPENS THE COCOON!"
ALICIA MASTERS HAS BEEN MYSTERIOUSLY BROUGHT TO A HIDDEN LAND KNOWN ONLY AS THE CITADEL OF SCIENCE! WHILE, BACK AT HOME, THE BRILLIANT LEADER OF THE FANTASTIC FOUR TOILS TIRELESSLY, SEEKING A WAY TO RESCUE THE MISSING GIRL--
FEATURING...
THE CREATURE IN LOCK 41!
THE ONLY WAY TO FIND HER IS TO DUPLICATE THE ELECTRONIC BRACELET WHICH HER CAPTOR WORE, BEN.!
BY FEEDING THIS COMPUTER ALL THE DATA I'VE COLLECTED, WE'LL SAVE DAYS OF TIRESOME CALCULATIONS!
PROUDLY PRODUCED BY: STAN (THE MAN) LEE and JACK (KING) KIRBY
EXOTICALLY EMBELLISHED BY: JOE SINNOTT
LABORIOUSLY LETTERED BY: ARTIE SIMEK
YA STILL THINK IT WUZ THAT NUTTY BRACELET THAT LET 'EM WALK THRU THE WALL, STRETCH?
IT'S THE ONLY POSSIBILITY, OLD FRIEND!
SPECIAL-ORDER COMPUTER FURNISHED BY: THE FRIENDLY FORBUSH LEASING CORP.

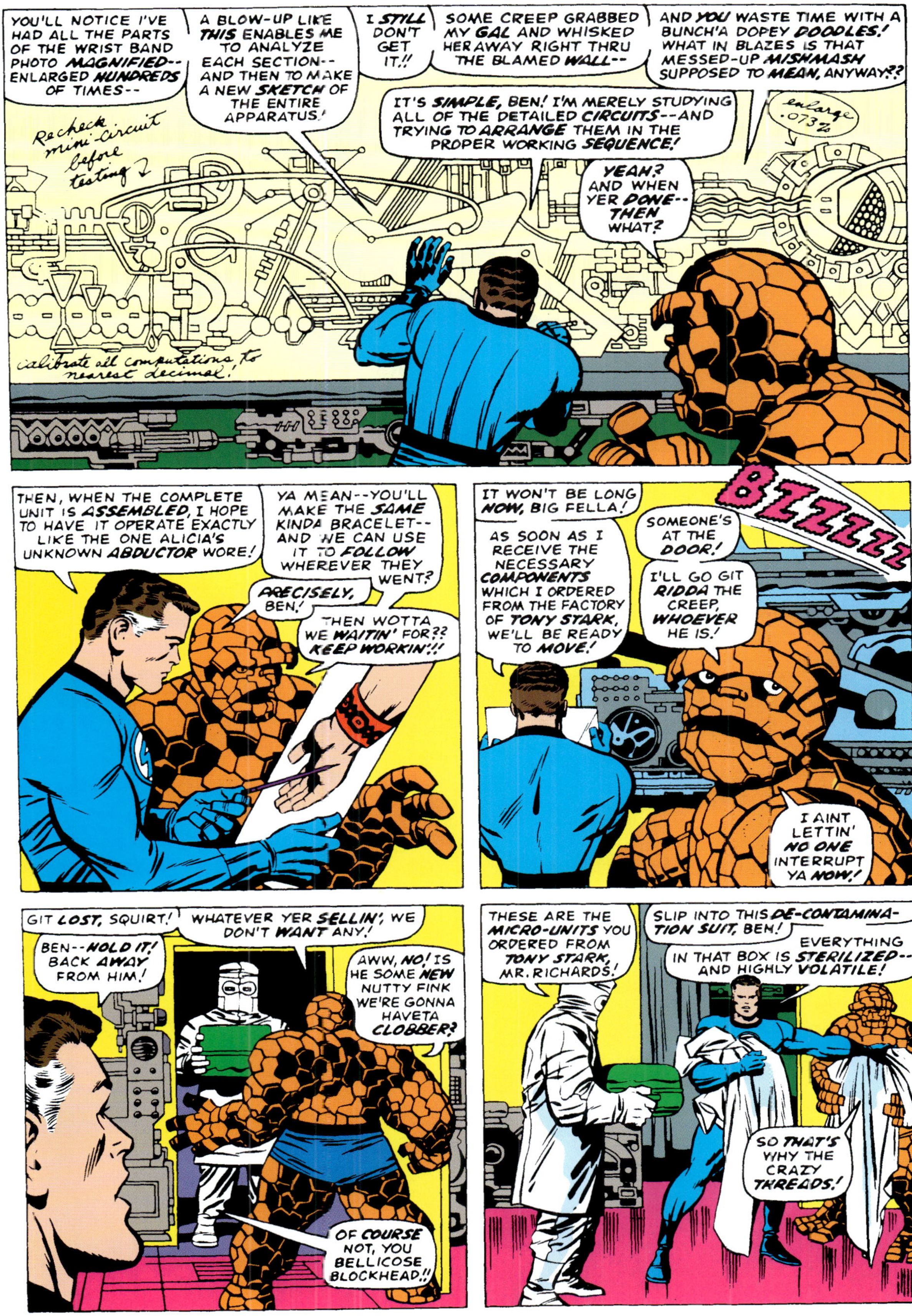
YOU'LL NOTICE I'VE HAD ALL THE PARTS OF THE WRIST BAND PHOTO MAGNIFIED-- ENLARGED HUNDREDS OF TIMES--
A BLOW-UP LIKE THIS ENABLES ME TO ANALYZE EACH SECTION-- AND THEN TO MAKE A NEW SKETCH OF THE ENTIRE APPARATUS!
I STILL DON'T GET IT.!!
SOME CREEP GRABBED MY GAL AND WHISKED HER AWAY RIGHT THRU THE BLAMED WALL--
AND YOU WASTE TIME WITH A BUNCH'A DOPEY DOODLES! WHAT IN BLAZES IS THAT MESSED-UP MISHMASH SUPPOSED TO MEAN, ANYWAY??
IT'S SIMPLE, BEN! I'M MERELY STUDYING ALL OF THE DETAILED CIRCUITS--AND TRYING TO ARRANGE THEM IN THE PROPER WORKING SEQUENCE!
YEAH? AND WHEN YER DONE-- THEN WHAT?
Recheck mini-circuit before testing
enlarge .073%
calibrate all computations to nearest decimal!
THEN, WHEN THE COMPLETE UNIT IS ASSEMBLED, I HOPE TO HAVE IT OPERATE EXACTLY LIKE THE ONE ALICIA'S UNKNOWN ABDUCTOR WORE!
YA MEAN--YOU'LL MAKE THE SAME KINDA BRACELET-- AND WE CAN USE IT TO FOLLOW WHEREVER THEY WENT?
PRECISELY, BEN!
THEN WOTTA WE WAITIN' FOR?? KEEP WORKIN'!!
IT WON'T BE LONG NOW, BIG FELLA!
AS SOON AS I RECEIVE THE NECESSARY COMPONENTS WHICH I ORDERED FROM THE FACTORY OF TONY STARK, WE'LL BE READY TO MOVE!
BZZZZZ
SOMEONE'S AT THE DOOR!
I'LL GO GIT RIDDA THE CREEP, WHOEVER HE IS!
I AINT LETTIN' NO ONE INTERRUPT YA NOW!
GIT LOST, SQUIRT!
WHATEVER YER SELLIN', WE DON'T WANT ANY!
BEN--HOLD IT! BACK AWAY FROM HIM!
AWW, NO! IS HE SOME NEW NUTTY FINK WE'RE GONNA HAVETA CLOBBER?
OF COURSE NOT, YOU BELLICOSE BLOCKHEAD!!
THESE ARE THE MICRO-UNITS YOU ORDERED FROM TONY STARK, MR. RICHARDS!
SLIP INTO THIS DE-CONTAMINATION SUIT, BEN!
EVERYTHING IN THAT BOX IS STERILIZED-- AND HIGHLY VOLATILE!
SO THAT'S WHY THE CRAZY THREADS!

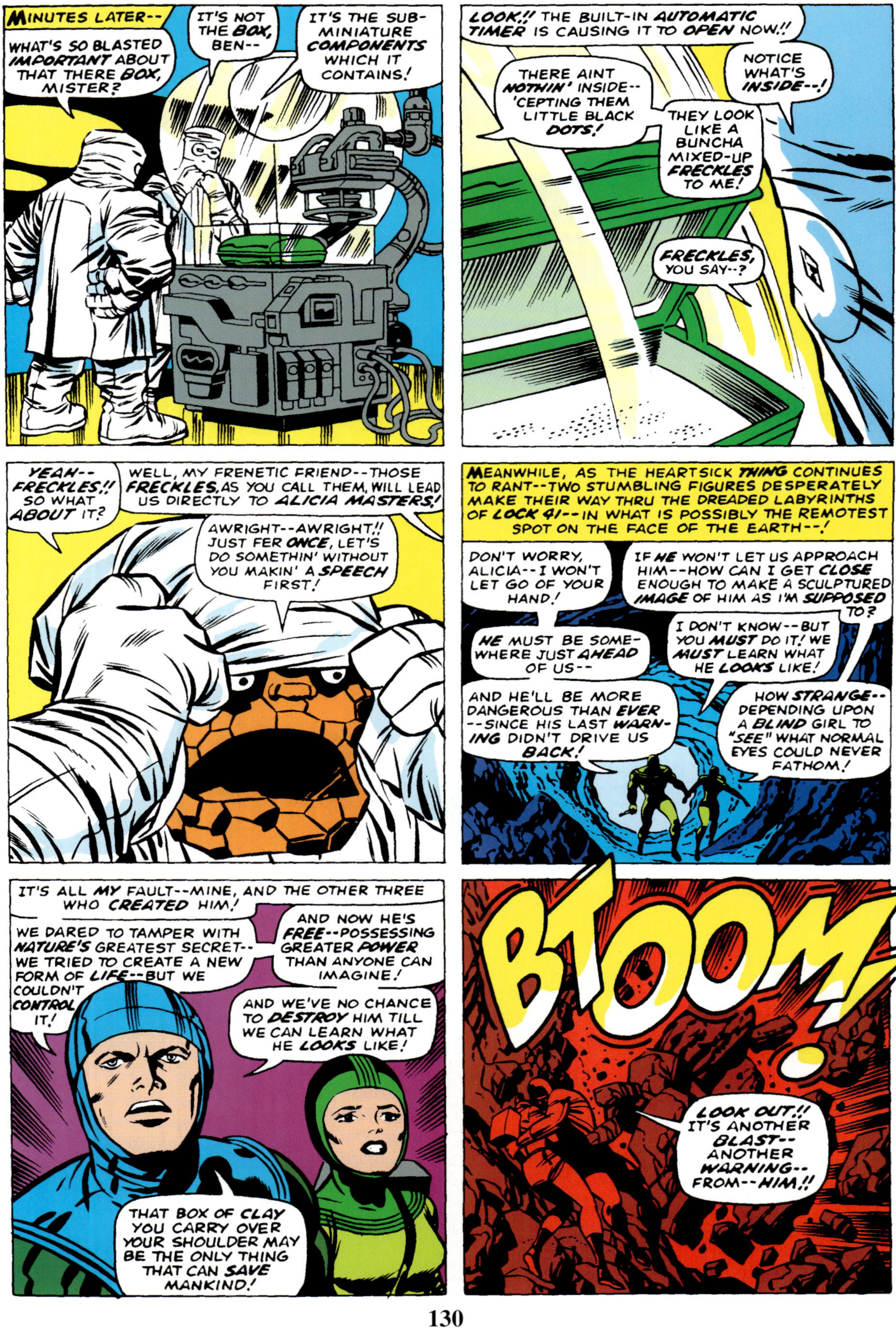
MINUTES LATER--
WHAT'S SO BLASTED IMPORTANT ABOUT THAT THERE BOX, MISTER?
IT'S NOT THE BOX, BEN--
IT'S THE SUB-MINIATURE COMPONENTS WHICH IT CONTAINS!
LOOK!! THE BUILT-IN AUTOMATIC TIMER IS CAUSING IT TO OPEN NOW!!
THERE AINT NOTHIN' INSIDE--'CEPTING THEM LITTLE BLACK DOTS!
NOTICE WHAT'S INSIDE--!
THEY LOOK LIKE A BUNCHA MIXED-UP FRECKLES TO ME!
FRECKLES, YOU SAY--?
YEAH--FRECKLES!! SO WHAT ABOUT IT?
WELL, MY FRENETIC FRIEND--THOSE FRECKLES, AS YOU CALL THEM, WILL LEAD US DIRECTLY TO ALICIA MASTERS!
AWRIGHT--AWRIGHT!! JUST FER ONCE, LET'S DO SOMETHIN' WITHOUT YOU MAKIN' A SPEECH FIRST!
MEANWHILE, AS THE HEARTSICK THING CONTINUES TO RANT--TWO STUMBLING FIGURES DESPERATELY MAKE THEIR WAY THRU THE DREADED LABYRINTHS OF LOCK 41--IN WHAT IS POSSIBLY THE REMOTEST SPOT ON THE FACE OF THE EARTH--!
DON'T WORRY, ALICIA--I WON'T LET GO OF YOUR HAND!
IF HE WON'T LET US APPROACH HIM--HOW CAN I GET CLOSE ENOUGH TO MAKE A SCULPTURED IMAGE OF HIM AS I'M SUPPOSED TO?
HE MUST BE SOMEWHERE JUST AHEAD OF US--
I DON'T KNOW--BUT YOU MUST DO IT! WE MUST LEARN WHAT HE LOOKS LIKE!
AND HE'LL BE MORE DANGEROUS THAN EVER--SINCE HIS LAST WARNING DIDN'T DRIVE US BACK!
HOW STRANGE--DEPENDING UPON A BLIND GIRL TO "SEE" WHAT NORMAL EYES COULD NEVER FATHOM!
IT'S ALL MY FAULT--MINE, AND THE OTHER THREE WHO CREATED HIM!
WE DARED TO TAMPER WITH NATURE'S GREATEST SECRET--WE TRIED TO CREATE A NEW FORM OF LIFE--BUT WE COULDN'T CONTROL IT!
AND NOW HE'S FREE--POSSESSING GREATER POWER THAN ANYONE CAN IMAGINE!
AND WE'VE NO CHANCE TO DESTROY HIM TILL WE CAN LEARN WHAT HE LOOKS LIKE!
THAT BOX OF CLAY YOU CARRY OVER YOUR SHOULDER MAY BE THE ONLY THING THAT CAN SAVE MANKIND!
BTOOM!
LOOK OUT!! IT'S ANOTHER BLAST--ANOTHER WARNING--FROM--HIM!!

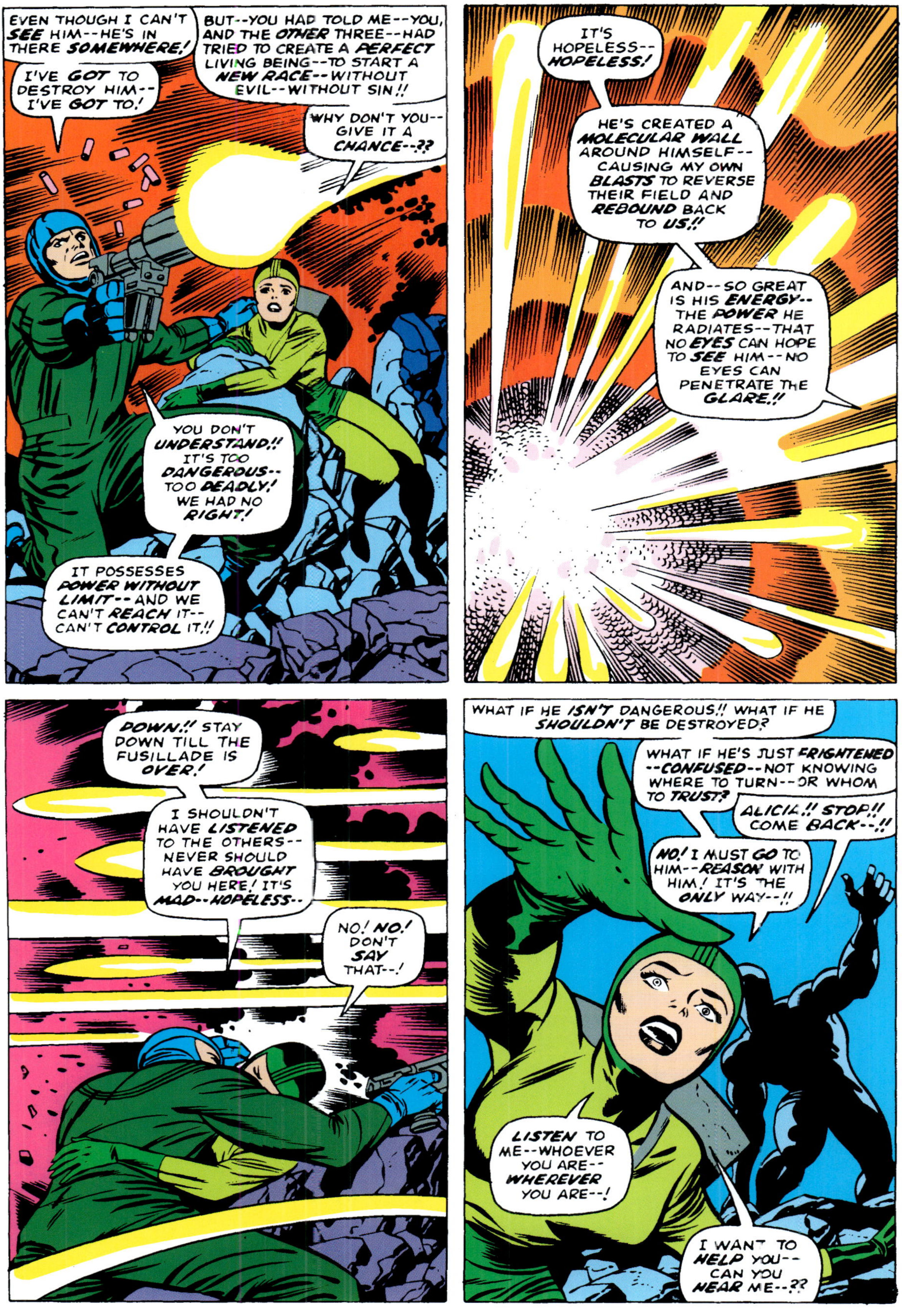
EVEN THOUGH I CAN'T SEE HIM--HE'S IN THERE SOMEWHERE!
I'VE GOT TO DESTROY HIM--I'VE GOT TO!
BUT--YOU HAD TOLD ME--YOU, AND THE OTHER THREE--HAD TRIED TO CREATE A PERFECT LIVING BEING--TO START A NEW RACE--WITHOUT EVIL--WITHOUT SIN!!
WHY DON'T YOU--GIVE IT A CHANCE--??
YOU DON'T UNDERSTAND!! IT'S TOO DANGEROUS--TOO DEADLY! WE HAD NO RIGHT!
IT POSSESSES POWER WITHOUT LIMIT--AND WE CAN'T REACH IT--CAN'T CONTROL IT!!
IT'S HOPELESS--HOPELESS!
HE'S CREATED A MOLECULAR WALL AROUND HIMSELF--CAUSING MY OWN BLASTS TO REVERSE THEIR FIELD AND REBOUND BACK TO US!!
AND--SO GREAT IS HIS ENERGY--THE POWER HE RADIATES--THAT NO EYES CAN HOPE TO SEE HIM--NO EYES CAN PENETRATE THE GLARE!!
DOWN!! STAY DOWN TILL THE FUSILLADE IS OVER!
I SHOULDN'T HAVE LISTENED TO THE OTHERS--NEVER SHOULD HAVE BROUGHT YOU HERE! IT'S MAD--HOPELESS--
NO! NO! DON'T SAY THAT--!
WHAT IF HE ISN'T DANGEROUS!! WHAT IF HE SHOULDN'T BE DESTROYED?
WHAT IF HE'S JUST FRIGHTENED--CONFUSED--NOT KNOWING WHERE TO TURN--OR WHOM TO TRUST?
ALICIA!! STOP!! COME BACK--!!
NO! I MUST GO TO HIM--REASON WITH HIM! IT'S THE ONLY WAY--!!
LISTEN TO ME--WHOEVER YOU ARE--WHEREVER YOU ARE--!
I WANT TO HELP YOU--CAN YOU HEAR ME--??

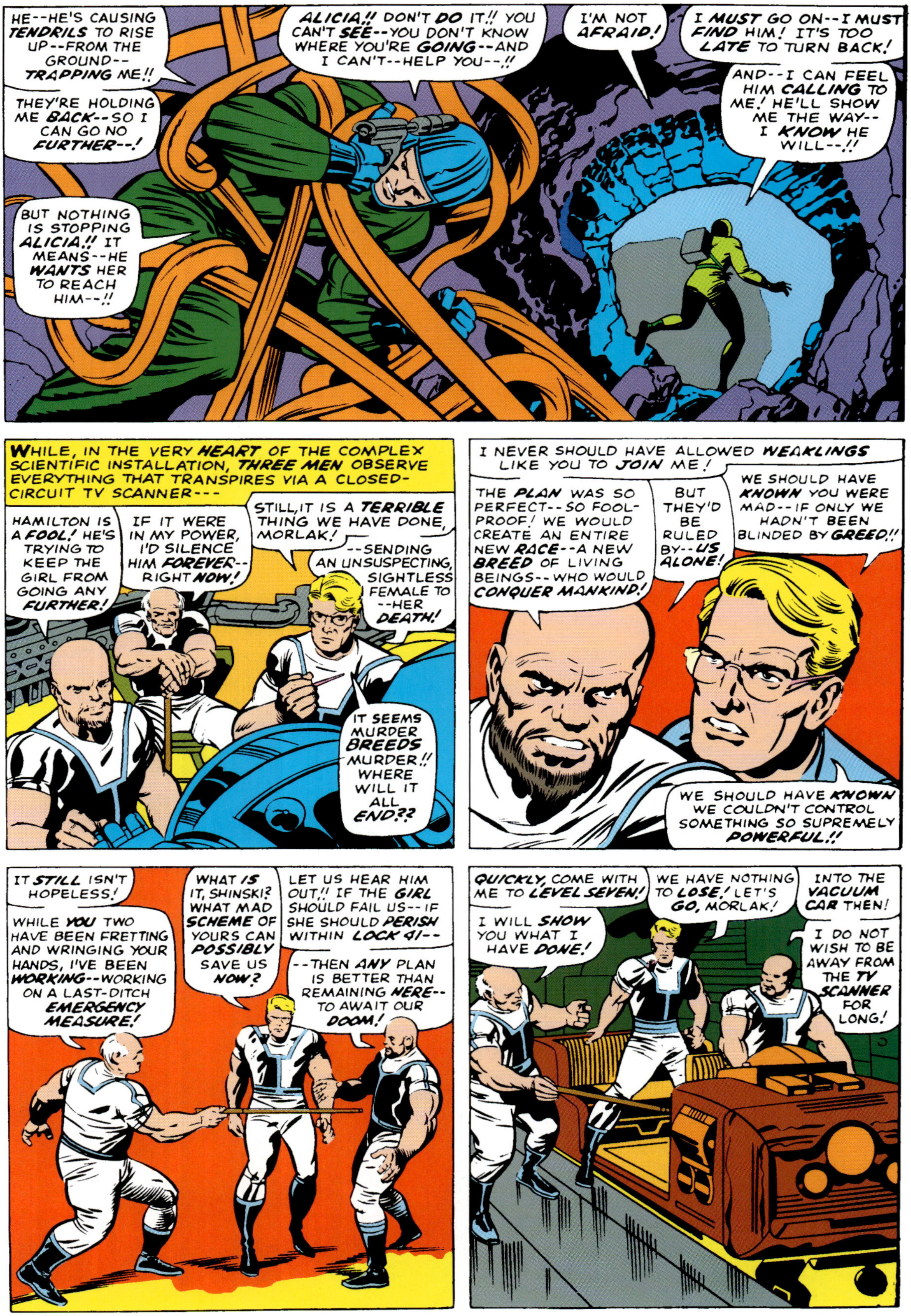
HE--HE'S CAUSING TENDRILS TO RISE UP--FROM THE GROUND--TRAPPING ME!!
THEY'RE HOLDING ME BACK--SO I CAN GO NO FURTHER--!
BUT NOTHING IS STOPPING ALICIA!! IT MEANS--HE WANTS HER TO REACH HIM--!!
ALICIA!! DON'T DO IT!! YOU CAN'T SEE--YOU DON'T KNOW WHERE YOU'RE GOING--AND I CAN'T--HELP YOU--!!
I'M NOT AFRAID!
I MUST GO ON--I MUST FIND HIM! IT'S TOO LATE TO TURN BACK!
AND--I CAN FEEL HIM CALLING TO ME! HE'LL SHOW ME THE WAY--I KNOW HE WILL--!!
WHILE, IN THE VERY HEART OF THE COMPLEX SCIENTIFIC INSTALLATION, THREE MEN OBSERVE EVERYTHING THAT TRANSPIRES VIA A CLOSED-CIRCUIT TV SCANNER---
HAMILTON IS A FOOL! HE'S TRYING TO KEEP THE GIRL FROM GOING ANY FURTHER!
IF IT WERE IN MY POWER, I'D SILENCE HIM FOREVER--RIGHT NOW!
STILL, IT IS A TERRIBLE THING WE HAVE DONE, MORLAK!
--SENDING AN UNSUSPECTING, SIGHTLESS FEMALE TO --HER DEATH!
IT SEEMS MURDER BREEDS MURDER!! WHERE WILL IT ALL END??
I NEVER SHOULD HAVE ALLOWED WEAKLINGS LIKE YOU TO JOIN ME!
THE PLAN WAS SO PERFECT--SO FOOL-PROOF! WE WOULD CREATE AN ENTIRE NEW RACE--A NEW BREED OF LIVING BEINGS--WHO WOULD CONQUER MANKIND!
BUT THEY'D BE RULED BY--US ALONE!
WE SHOULD HAVE KNOWN YOU WERE MAD--IF ONLY WE HADN'T BEEN BLINDED BY GREED!!
WE SHOULD HAVE KNOWN WE COULDN'T CONTROL SOMETHING SO SUPREMELY POWERFUL!!
IT STILL ISN'T HOPELESS!
WHILE YOU TWO HAVE BEEN FRETTING AND WRINGING YOUR HANDS, I'VE BEEN WORKING--WORKING ON A LAST-DITCH EMERGENCY MEASURE!
WHAT IS IT, SHINSKI? WHAT MAD SCHEME OF YOURS CAN POSSIBLY SAVE US NOW?
LET US HEAR HIM OUT!! IF THE GIRL SHOULD FAIL US--IF SHE SHOULD PERISH WITHIN LOCK 41--
--THEN ANY PLAN IS BETTER THAN REMAINING HERE--TO AWAIT OUR DOOM!
QUICKLY, COME WITH ME TO LEVEL SEVEN!
I WILL SHOW YOU WHAT I HAVE DONE!
WE HAVE NOTHING TO LOSE! LET'S GO, MORLAK!
INTO THE VACUUM CAR THEN!
I DO NOT WISH TO BE AWAY FROM THE TV SCANNER FOR LONG!

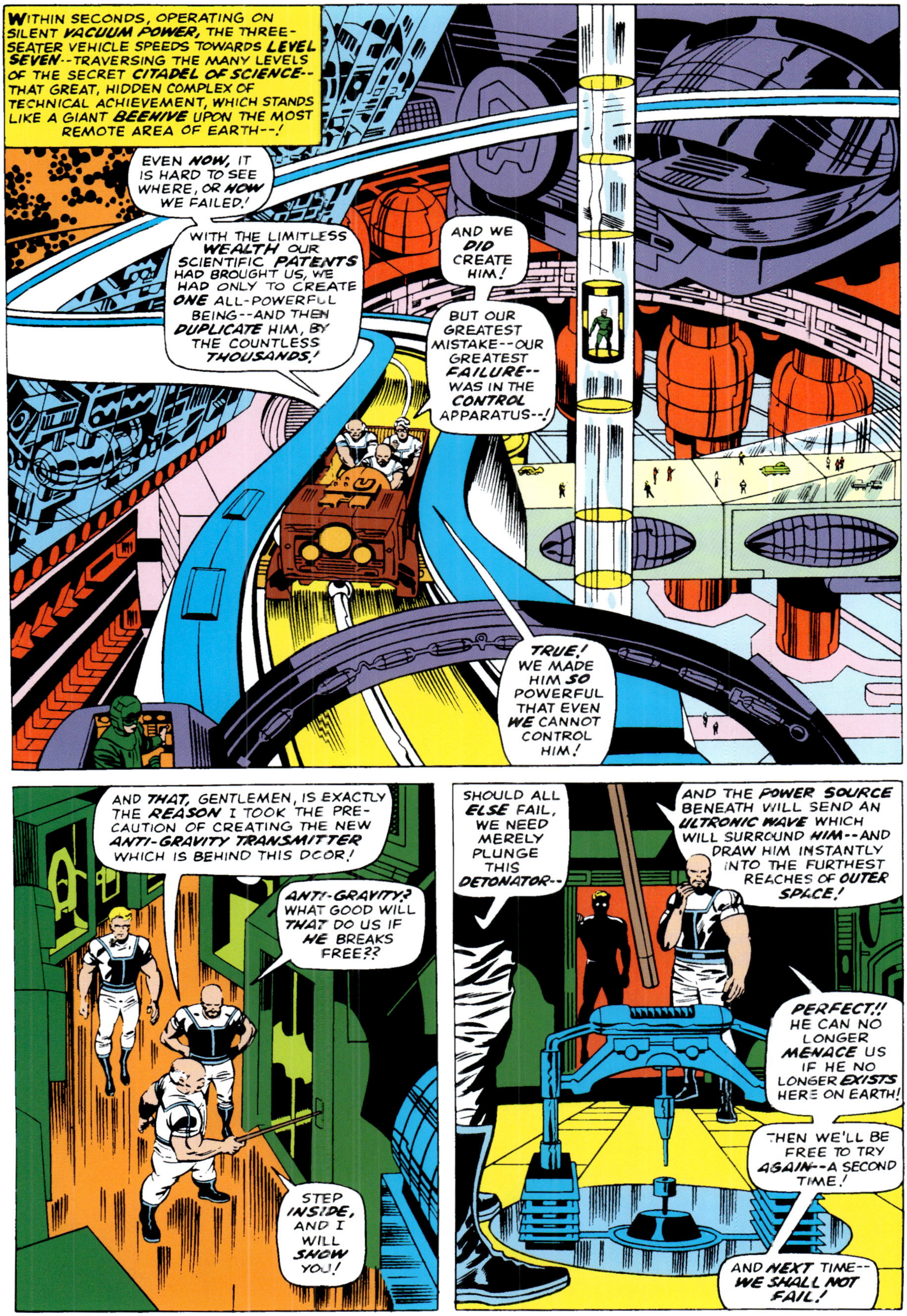
WITHIN SECONDS, OPERATING ON SILENT VACUUM POWER, THE THREE-SEATER VEHICLE SPEEDS TOWARDS LEVEL SEVEN--TRAVERSING THE MANY LEVELS OF THE SECRET CITADEL OF SCIENCE--THAT GREAT, HIDDEN COMPLEX OF TECHNICAL ACHIEVEMENT, WHICH STANDS LIKE A GIANT BEEHIVE UPON THE MOST REMOTE AREA OF EARTH--!
EVEN NOW, IT IS HARD TO SEE WHERE, OR HOW WE FAILED!
WITH THE LIMITLESS WEALTH OUR SCIENTIFIC PATENTS HAD BROUGHT US, WE HAD ONLY TO CREATE ONE ALL-POWERFUL BEING--AND THEN DUPLICATE HIM, BY THE COUNTLESS THOUSANDS!
AND WE DID CREATE HIM!
BUT OUR GREATEST MISTAKE--OUR GREATEST FAILURE--WAS IN THE CONTROL APPARATUS--!
TRUE! WE MADE HIM SO POWERFUL THAT EVEN WE CANNOT CONTROL HIM!
AND THAT, GENTLEMEN, IS EXACTLY THE REASON I TOOK THE PRE-CAUTION OF CREATING THE NEW ANTI-GRAVITY TRANSMITTER WHICH IS BEHIND THIS DOOR!
ANTI-GRAVITY? WHAT GOOD WILL THAT DO US IF HE BREAKS FREE??
STEP INSIDE, AND I WILL SHOW YOU!
SHOULD ALL ELSE FAIL, WE NEED MERELY PLUNGE THIS DETONATOR--
AND THE POWER SOURCE BENEATH WILL SEND AN ULTRONIC WAVE WHICH WILL SURROUND HIM--AND DRAW HIM INSTANTLY INTO THE FURTHEST REACHES OF OUTER SPACE!
PERFECT!! HE CAN NO LONGER MENACE US IF HE NO LONGER EXISTS HERE ON EARTH!
THEN WE'LL BE FREE TO TRY AGAIN--A SECOND TIME!
AND NEXT TIME--WE SHALL NOT FAIL!

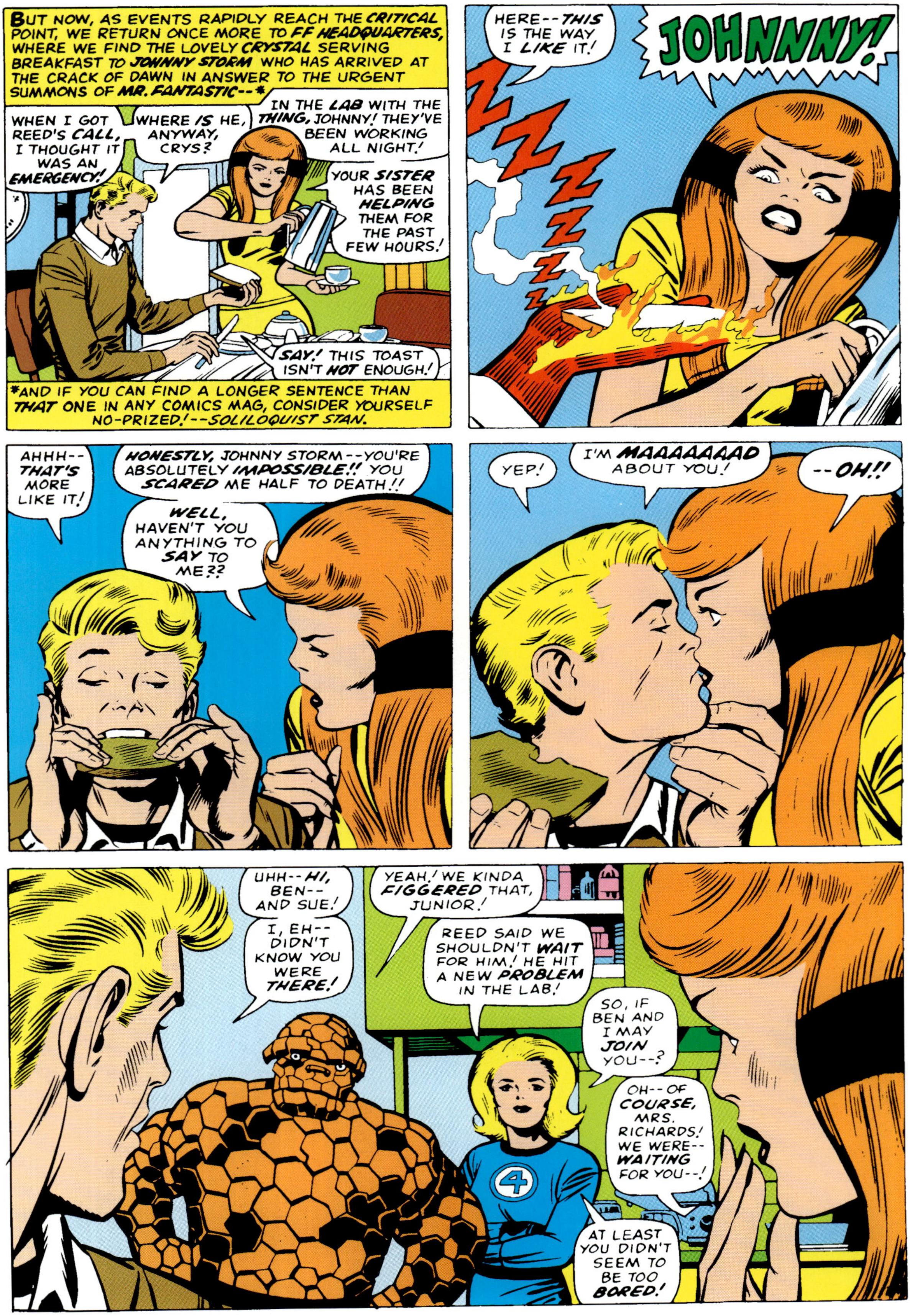
BUT NOW, AS EVENTS RAPIDLY REACH THE CRITICAL POINT, WE RETURN ONCE MORE TO FF HEADQUARTERS, WHERE WE FIND THE LOVELY CRYSTAL SERVING BREAKFAST TO JOHNNY STORM WHO HAS ARRIVED AT THE CRACK OF DAWN IN ANSWER TO THE URGENT SUMMONS OF MR. FANTASTIC--*
WHEN I GOT REED'S CALL, I THOUGHT IT WAS AN EMERGENCY!
WHERE IS HE, ANYWAY, CRYS?
IN THE LAB WITH THE THING, JOHNNY! THEY'VE BEEN WORKING ALL NIGHT!
YOUR SISTER HAS BEEN HELPING THEM FOR THE PAST FEW HOURS!
SAY! THIS TOAST ISN'T HOT ENOUGH!
*AND IF YOU CAN FIND A LONGER SENTENCE THAN THAT ONE IN ANY COMICS MAG, CONSIDER YOURSELF NO-PRIZED!--SOLILOQUIST STAN.
HERE--THIS IS THE WAY I LIKE IT!
JOHNNNY!
AHHH--THAT'S MORE LIKE IT!
HONESTLY, JOHNNY STORM--YOU'RE ABSOLUTELY IMPOSSIBLE!! YOU SCARED ME HALF TO DEATH!!
WELL, HAVEN'T YOU ANYTHING TO SAY TO ME??
YEP!
I'M MAAAAAAAAD ABOUT YOU!
--OH!!
UHH--HI, BEN--AND SUE!
I, EH--DIDN'T KNOW YOU WERE THERE!
YEAH! WE KINDA FIGGERED THAT, JUNIOR!
REED SAID WE SHOULDN'T WAIT FOR HIM! HE HIT A NEW PROBLEM IN THE LAB!
SO, IF BEN AND I MAY JOIN YOU--?
OH--OF COURSE, MRS. RICHARDS! WE WERE--WAITING FOR YOU--!
AT LEAST YOU DIDN'T SEEM TO BE TOO BORED!

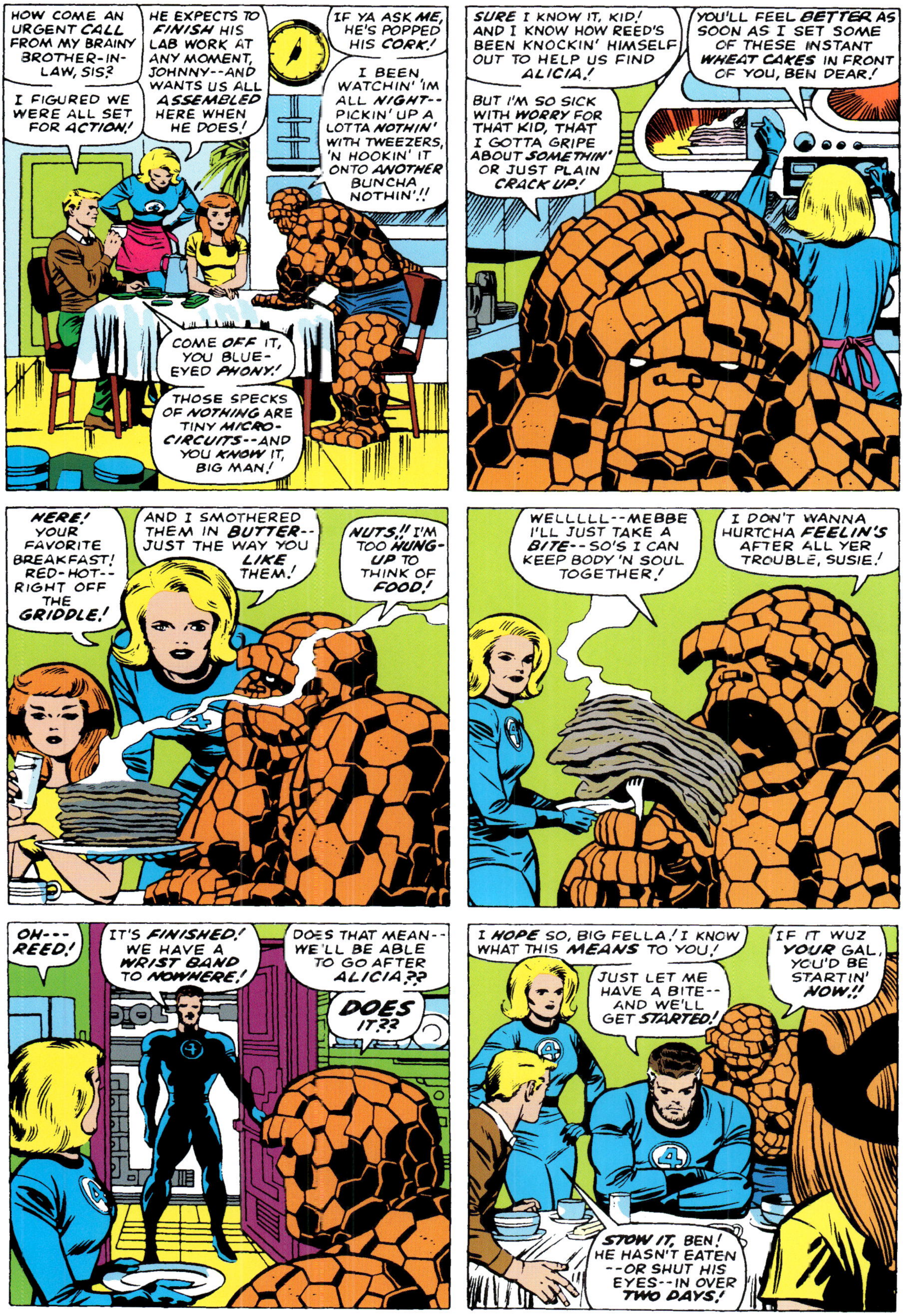
HOW COME AN URGENT CALL FROM MY BRAINY BROTHER-IN-LAW, SIS?
I FIGURED WE WERE ALL SET FOR ACTION!
HE EXPECTS TO FINISH HIS LAB WORK AT ANY MOMENT, JOHNNY--AND WANTS US ALL ASSEMBLED HERE WHEN HE DOES!
IF YA ASK ME, HE'S POPPED HIS CORK!
I BEEN WATCHIN' 'IM ALL NIGHT--PICKIN' UP A LOTTA NOTHIN' WITH TWEEZERS, 'N HOOKIN' IT ONTO ANOTHER BUNCHA NOTHIN'!!
COME OFF IT, YOU BLUE-EYED PHONY!
THOSE SPECKS OF NOTHING ARE TINY MICRO-CIRCUITS--AND YOU KNOW IT, BIG MAN!
SURE I KNOW IT, KID! AND I KNOW HOW REED'S BEEN KNOCKIN' HIMSELF OUT TO HELP US FIND ALICIA!
BUT I'M SO SICK WITH WORRY FOR THAT KID, THAT I GOTTA GRIPE ABOUT SOMETHIN' OR JUST PLAIN CRACK UP!
YOU'LL FEEL BETTER AS SOON AS I SET SOME OF THESE INSTANT WHEAT CAKES IN FRONT OF YOU, BEN DEAR!
HERE! YOUR FAVORITE BREAKFAST! RED-HOT--RIGHT OFF THE GRIDDLE!
AND I SMOTHERED THEM IN BUTTER--JUST THE WAY YOU LIKE THEM!
NUTS!! I'M TOO HUNG-UP TO THINK OF FOOD!
WELLLLL--MEBBE I'LL JUST TAKE A BITE--SO'S I CAN KEEP BODY 'N SOUL TOGETHER!
I DON'T WANNA HURTCHA FEELIN'S AFTER ALL YER TROUBLE, SUSIE!
OH---REED!
IT'S FINISHED! WE HAVE A WRIST BAND TO NOWHERE!
DOES THAT MEAN--WE'LL BE ABLE TO GO AFTER ALICIA??
DOES IT??
I HOPE SO, BIG FELLA! I KNOW WHAT THIS MEANS TO YOU!
JUST LET ME HAVE A BITE--AND WE'LL GET STARTED!
IF IT WUZ YOUR GAL, YOU'D BE STARTIN' NOW!!
STOW IT, BEN! HE HASN'T EATEN--OR SHUT HIS EYES--IN OVER TWO DAYS!

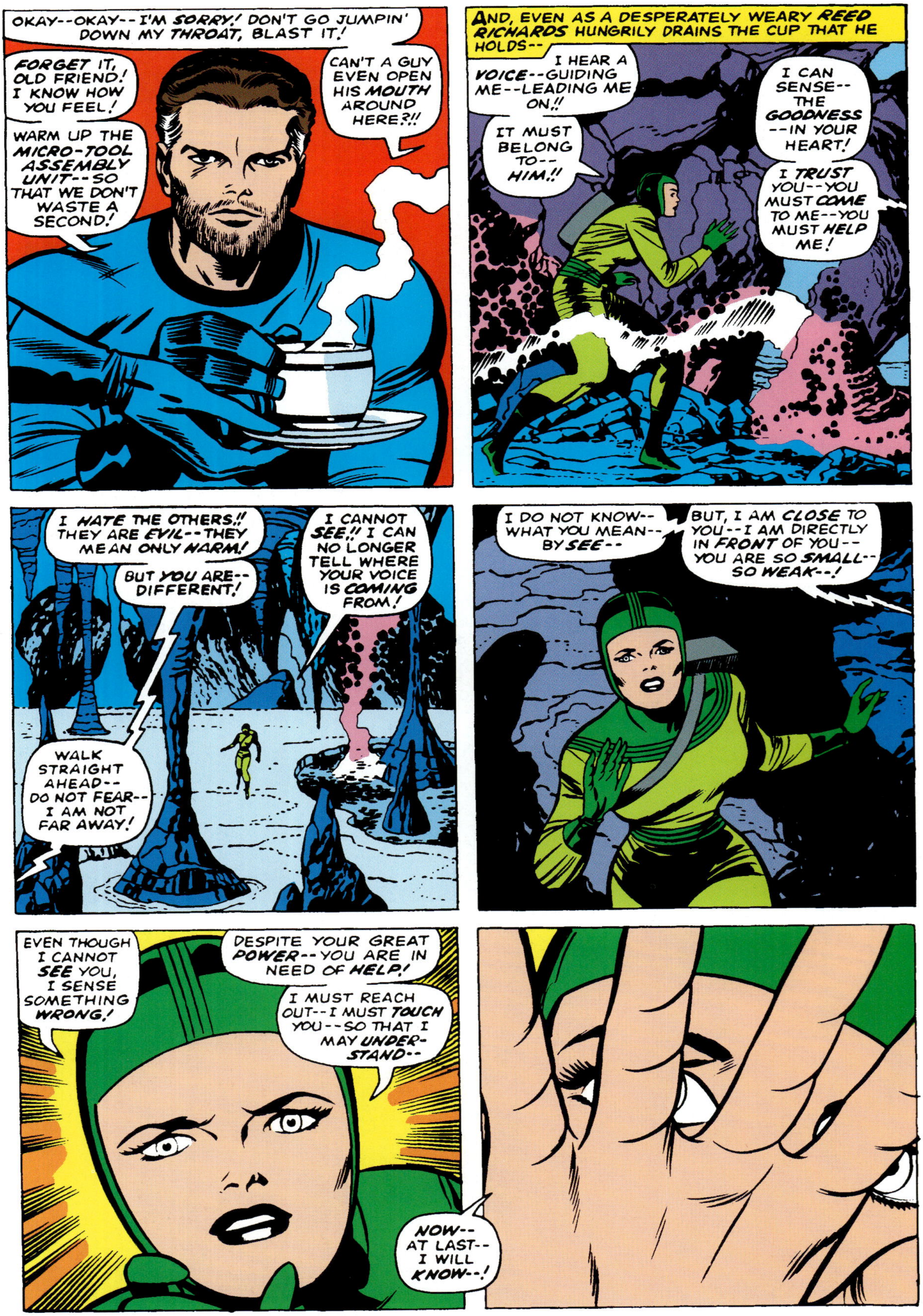

OKAY--OKAY--I'M SORRY! DON'T GO JUMPIN' DOWN MY THROAT, BLAST IT!
CAN'T A GUY EVEN OPEN HIS MOUTH AROUND HERE?!!
FORGET IT, OLD FRIEND! I KNOW HOW YOU FEEL!
WARM UP THE MICRO-TOOL ASSEMBLY UNIT--SO THAT WE DON'T WASTE A SECOND!
AND, EVEN AS A DESPERATELY WEARY REED RICHARDS HUNGRILY DRAINS THE CUP THAT HE HOLDS--
I HEAR A VOICE--GUIDING ME--LEADING ME ON!!
IT MUST BELONG TO--HIM!!
I CAN SENSE--THE GOODNESS--IN YOUR HEART!
I TRUST YOU--YOU MUST COME TO ME--YOU MUST HELP ME!
I HATE THE OTHERS!! THEY ARE EVIL--THEY MEAN ONLY HARM!
BUT YOU ARE--DIFFERENT!
I CANNOT SEE!! I CAN NO LONGER TELL WHERE YOUR VOICE IS COMING FROM!
WALK STRAIGHT AHEAD--DO NOT FEAR--I AM NOT FAR AWAY!
I DO NOT KNOW--WHAT YOU MEAN--BY SEE--
BUT, I AM CLOSE TO YOU--I AM DIRECTLY IN FRONT OF YOU--YOU ARE SO SMALL--SO WEAK--!
EVEN THOUGH I CANNOT SEE YOU, I SENSE SOMETHING WRONG!
DESPITE YOUR GREAT POWER--YOU ARE IN NEED OF HELP!
I MUST REACH OUT--I MUST TOUCH YOU--SO THAT I MAY UNDERSTAND--
NOW--AT LAST--I WILL KNOW--!

YOU--YOU HAVE NO FORM! YOU ARE ENCASED WITHIN SOMETHING--SOMETHING THAT TINGLES WITH LIFE-- AND YET IS NOT ALIVE--!
I AM ABOUT TO--BE BORN!
THAT WHICH YOU FEEL--IS MY COCOON! --IT IS SOON TO OPEN--AND THEN--
--THEN-- I SHALL EMERGE!!
BUT NOW-- A WEAKNESS-- OVERTAKES ME! --I AM SO ALONE --SO HELPLESS!!
DON'T BE AFRAID!! I WILL STAY WITH YOU!
I HAVE KNOWN ANOTHER LIKE YOU--ONE WHO IS ALSO POWERFUL --BUT WHO NEEDS UNDERSTANDING --AND COMPASSION!
FOR THE SAKE OF THE LOVE I FEEL FOR HIM-- I WILL NOT DESERT YOU!

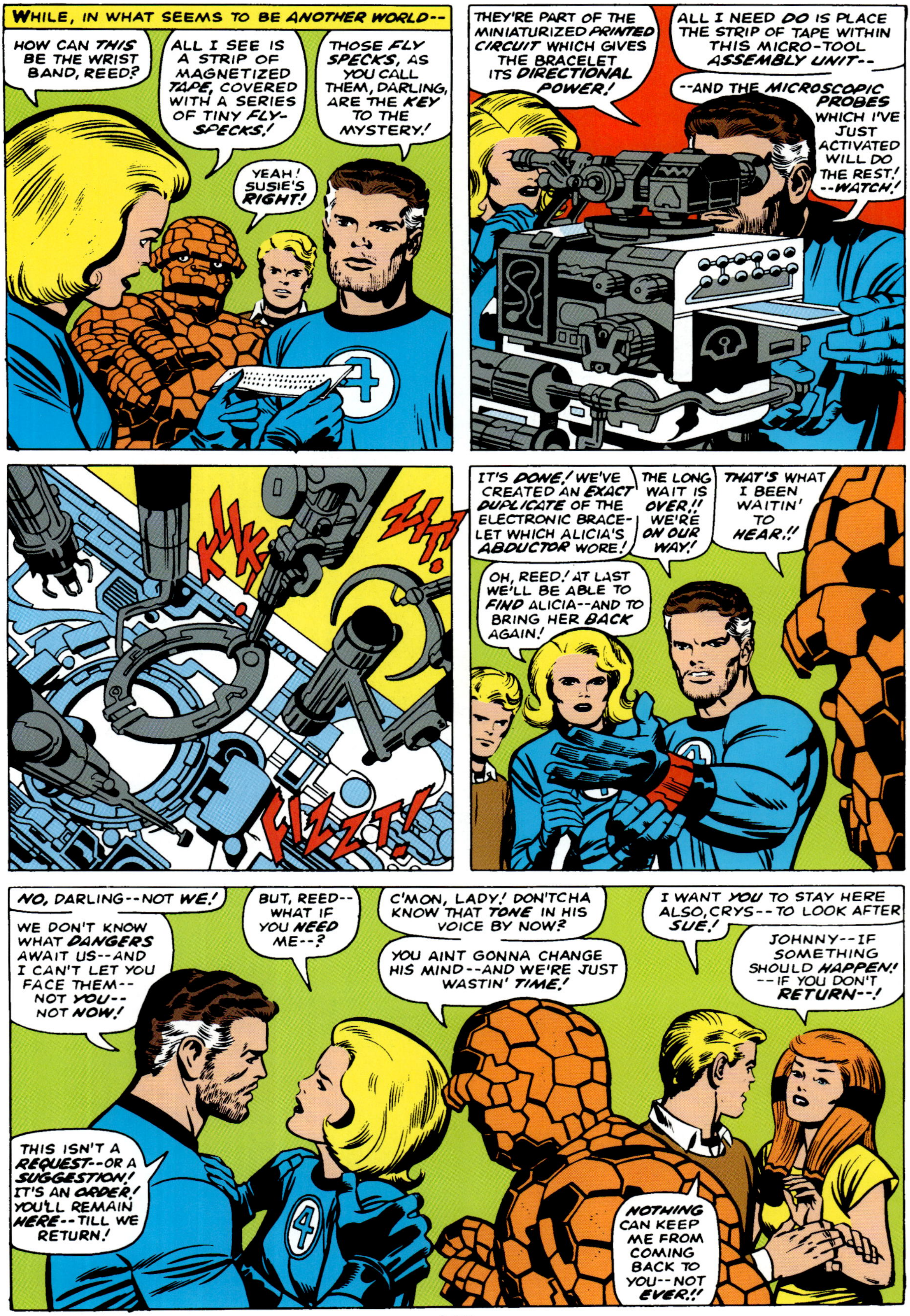
WHILE, IN WHAT SEEMS TO BE ANOTHER WORLD--
HOW CAN THIS BE THE WRIST BAND, REED?
ALL I SEE IS A STRIP OF MAGNETIZED TAPE, COVERED WITH A SERIES OF TINY FLY-SPECKS!
THOSE FLY SPECKS, AS YOU CALL THEM, DARLING, ARE THE KEY TO THE MYSTERY!
YEAH! SUSIE'S RIGHT!
THEY'RE PART OF THE MINIATURIZED PRINTED CIRCUIT WHICH GIVES THE BRACELET ITS DIRECTIONAL POWER!
ALL I NEED DO IS PLACE THE STRIP OF TAPE WITHIN THIS MICRO-TOOL ASSEMBLY UNIT--
--AND THE MICROSCOPIC PROBES WHICH I'VE JUST ACTIVATED WILL DO THE REST! --WATCH!
KLIK!
ZZIT!
FIZZZT!
IT'S DONE! WE'VE CREATED AN EXACT DUPLICATE OF THE ELECTRONIC BRACELET WHICH ALICIA'S ABDUCTOR WORE!
THE LONG WAIT IS OVER!! WE'RE ON OUR WAY!
THAT'S WHAT I BEEN WAITIN' TO HEAR!!
OH, REED! AT LAST WE'LL BE ABLE TO FIND ALICIA--AND TO BRING HER BACK AGAIN!
NO, DARLING--NOT WE!
WE DON'T KNOW WHAT DANGERS AWAIT US--AND I CAN'T LET YOU FACE THEM--NOT YOU--NOT NOW!
BUT, REED--WHAT IF YOU NEED ME--?
C'MON, LADY! DON'TCHA KNOW THAT TONE IN HIS VOICE BY NOW?
YOU AINT GONNA CHANGE HIS MIND--AND WE'RE JUST WASTIN' TIME!
I WANT YOU TO STAY HERE ALSO, CRYS--TO LOOK AFTER SUE!
JOHNNY--IF SOMETHING SHOULD HAPPEN! --IF YOU DON'T RETURN--!
THIS ISN'T A REQUEST--OR A SUGGESTION! IT'S AN ORDER! YOU'LL REMAIN HERE--TILL WE RETURN!
NOTHING CAN KEEP ME FROM COMING BACK TO YOU--NOT EVER!!

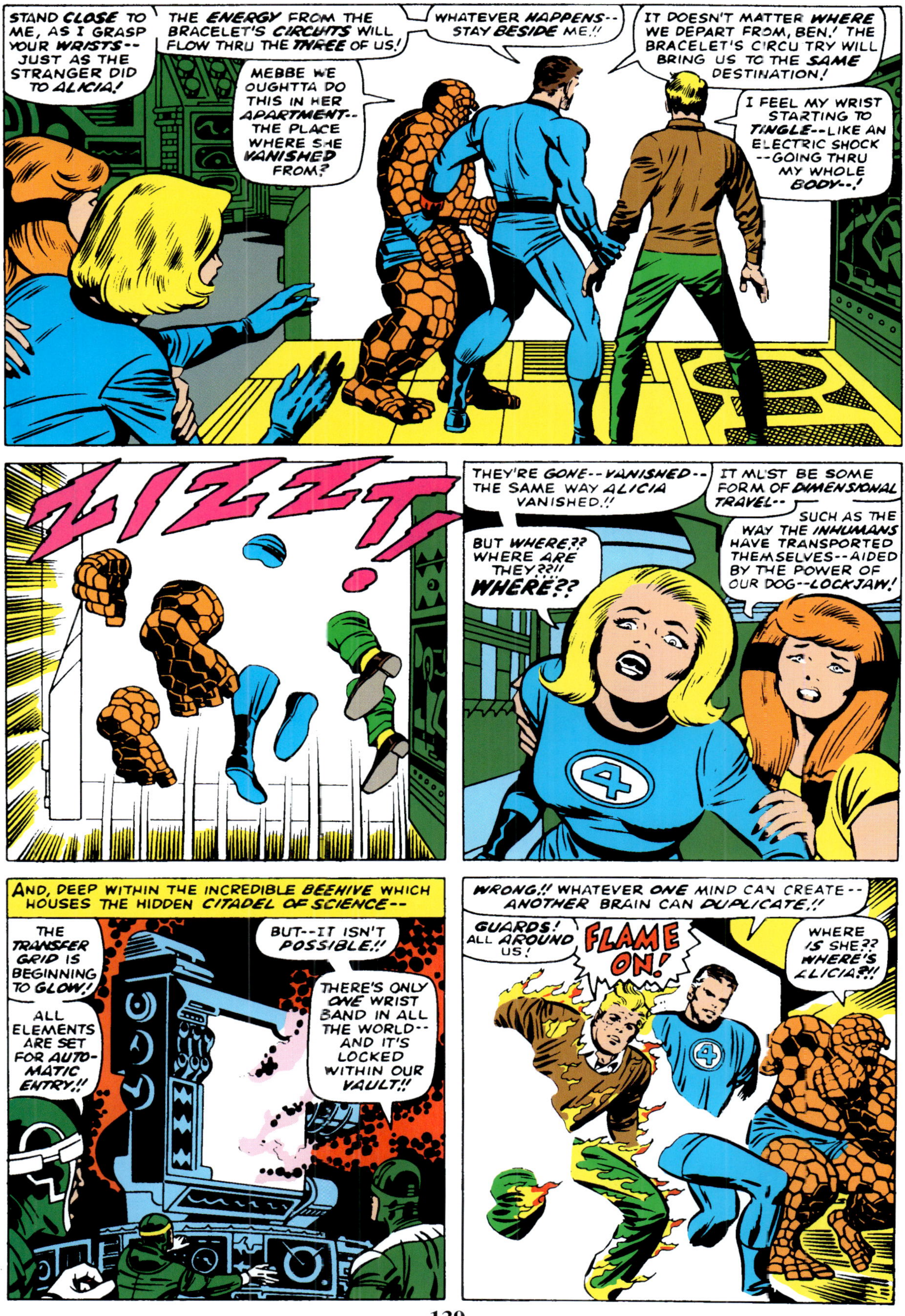

STAND CLOSE TO ME, AS I GRASP YOUR WRISTS--JUST AS THE STRANGER DID TO ALICIA!
THE ENERGY FROM THE BRACELET'S CIRCUITS WILL FLOW THRU THE THREE OF US!
WHATEVER HAPPENS--STAY BESIDE ME!!
IT DOESN'T MATTER WHERE WE DEPART FROM, BEN! THE BRACELET'S CIRCUITRY WILL BRING US TO THE SAME DESTINATION!
MEBBE WE OUGHTTA DO THIS IN HER APARTMENT--THE PLACE WHERE SHE VANISHED FROM?
I FEEL MY WRIST STARTING TO TINGLE--LIKE AN ELECTRIC SHOCK--GOING THRU MY WHOLE BODY--!
ZIZZT!
THEY'RE GONE--VANISHED--THE SAME WAY ALICIA VANISHED!!
BUT WHERE?? WHERE ARE THEY??!! WHERE??
IT MUST BE SOME FORM OF DIMENSIONAL TRAVEL--
SUCH AS THE WAY THE INHUMANS HAVE TRANSPORTED THEMSELVES--AIDED BY THE POWER OF OUR DOG--LOCKJAW!
AND, DEEP WITHIN THE INCREDIBLE BEEHIVE WHICH HOUSES THE HIDDEN CITADEL OF SCIENCE--
THE TRANSFER GRID IS BEGINNING TO GLOW!
ALL ELEMENTS ARE SET FOR AUTOMATIC ENTRY!!
BUT--IT ISN'T POSSIBLE!!
THERE'S ONLY ONE WRIST BAND IN ALL THE WORLD--AND IT'S LOCKED WITHIN OUR VAULT!!
WRONG!! WHATEVER ONE MIND CAN CREATE--ANOTHER BRAIN CAN DUPLICATE!!
GUARDS! ALL AROUND US!
FLAME ON!
WHERE IS SHE?? WHERE'S ALICIA?!!

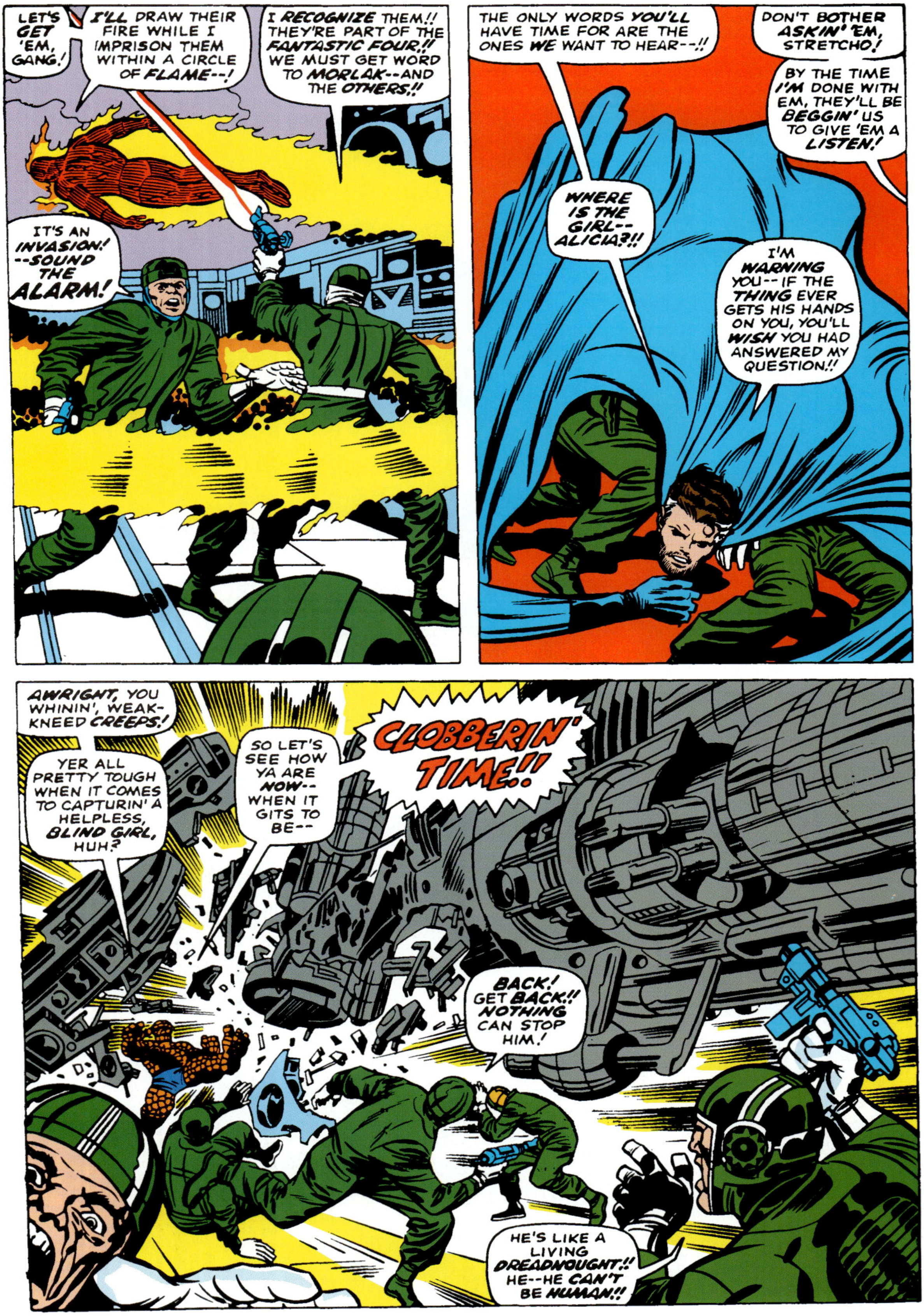
LET'S GET 'EM, GANG!
I'LL DRAW THEIR FIRE WHILE I IMPRISON THEM WITHIN A CIRCLE OF FLAME--!
I RECOGNIZE THEM!! THEY'RE PART OF THE FANTASTIC FOUR!! WE MUST GET WORD TO MORLAK--AND THE OTHERS!!
IT'S AN INVASION! --SOUND THE ALARM!
THE ONLY WORDS YOU'LL HAVE TIME FOR ARE THE ONES WE WANT TO HEAR--!!
DON'T BOTHER ASKIN' 'EM, STRETCHO!
BY THE TIME I'M DONE WITH EM, THEY'LL BE BEGGIN' US TO GIVE 'EM A LISTEN!
WHERE IS THE GIRL--ALICIA?!!
I'M WARNING YOU-- IF THE THING EVER GETS HIS HANDS ON YOU, YOU'LL WISH YOU HAD ANSWERED MY QUESTION!!
AWRIGHT, YOU WHININ', WEAK-KNEED CREEPS!
YER ALL PRETTY TOUGH WHEN IT COMES TO CAPTURIN' A HELPLESS, BLIND GIRL, HUH?
SO LET'S SEE HOW YA ARE NOW-- WHEN IT GITS TO BE--
CLOBBERIN' TIME!!
BACK! GET BACK!! NOTHING CAN STOP HIM!
HE'S LIKE A LIVING DREADNOUGHT!! HE--HE CAN'T BE HUMAN!!

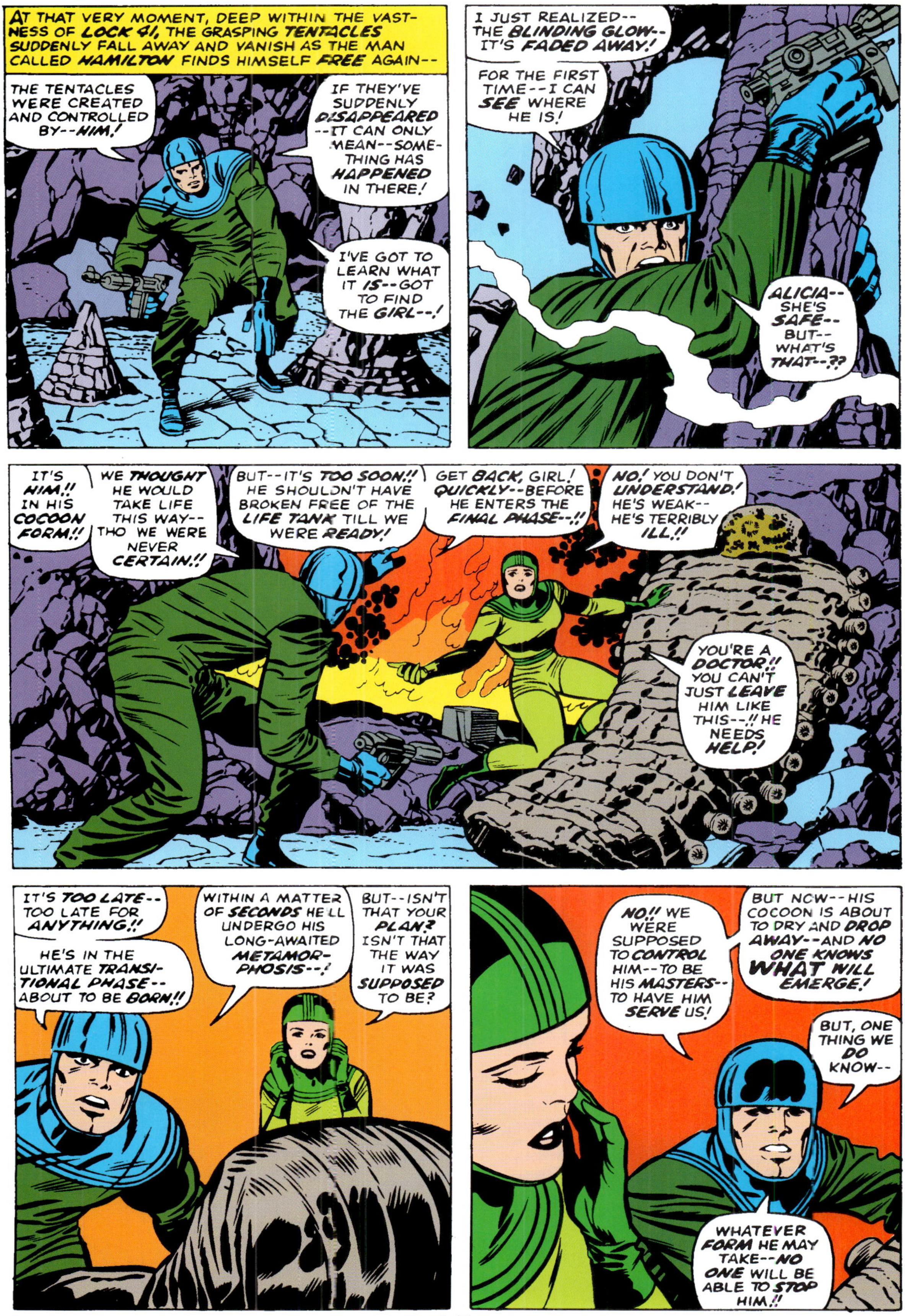
AT THAT VERY MOMENT, DEEP WITHIN THE VASTNESS OF LOCK 41, THE GRASPING TENTACLES SUDDENLY FALL AWAY AND VANISH AS THE MAN CALLED HAMILTON FINDS HIMSELF FREE AGAIN--
THE TENTACLES WERE CREATED AND CONTROLLED BY--HIM!
IF THEY'VE SUDDENLY DISAPPEARED--IT CAN ONLY MEAN--SOMETHING HAS HAPPENED IN THERE!
I'VE GOT TO LEARN WHAT IT IS--GOT TO FIND THE GIRL--!
I JUST REALIZED-- THE BLINDING GLOW-- IT'S FADED AWAY!
FOR THE FIRST TIME--I CAN SEE WHERE HE IS!
ALICIA-- SHE'S SAFE-- BUT-- WHAT'S THAT--??
IT'S HIM!! IN HIS COCOON FORM!!
WE THOUGHT HE WOULD TAKE LIFE THIS WAY-- THO WE WERE NEVER CERTAIN!!
BUT--IT'S TOO SOON!! HE SHOULDN'T HAVE BROKEN FREE OF THE LIFE TANK TILL WE WERE READY!
GET BACK, GIRL! QUICKLY--BEFORE HE ENTERS THE FINAL PHASE--!!
NO! YOU DON'T UNDERSTAND! HE'S WEAK-- HE'S TERRIBLY ILL!!
YOU'RE A DOCTOR!! YOU CAN'T JUST LEAVE HIM LIKE THIS--!! HE NEEDS HELP!
IT'S TOO LATE-- TOO LATE FOR ANYTHING!!
HE'S IN THE ULTIMATE TRANSITIONAL PHASE-- ABOUT TO BE BORN!!
WITHIN A MATTER OF SECONDS HE'LL UNDERGO HIS LONG-AWAITED METAMORPHOSIS--!
BUT--ISN'T THAT YOUR PLAN? ISN'T THAT THE WAY IT WAS SUPPOSED TO BE?
NO!! WE WERE SUPPOSED TO CONTROL HIM--TO BE HIS MASTERS-- TO HAVE HIM SERVE US!
BUT NOW--HIS COCOON IS ABOUT TO DRY AND DROP AWAY--AND NO ONE KNOWS WHAT WILL EMERGE!
BUT, ONE THING WE DO KNOW--
WHATEVER FORM HE MAY TAKE--NO ONE WILL BE ABLE TO STOP HIM!!

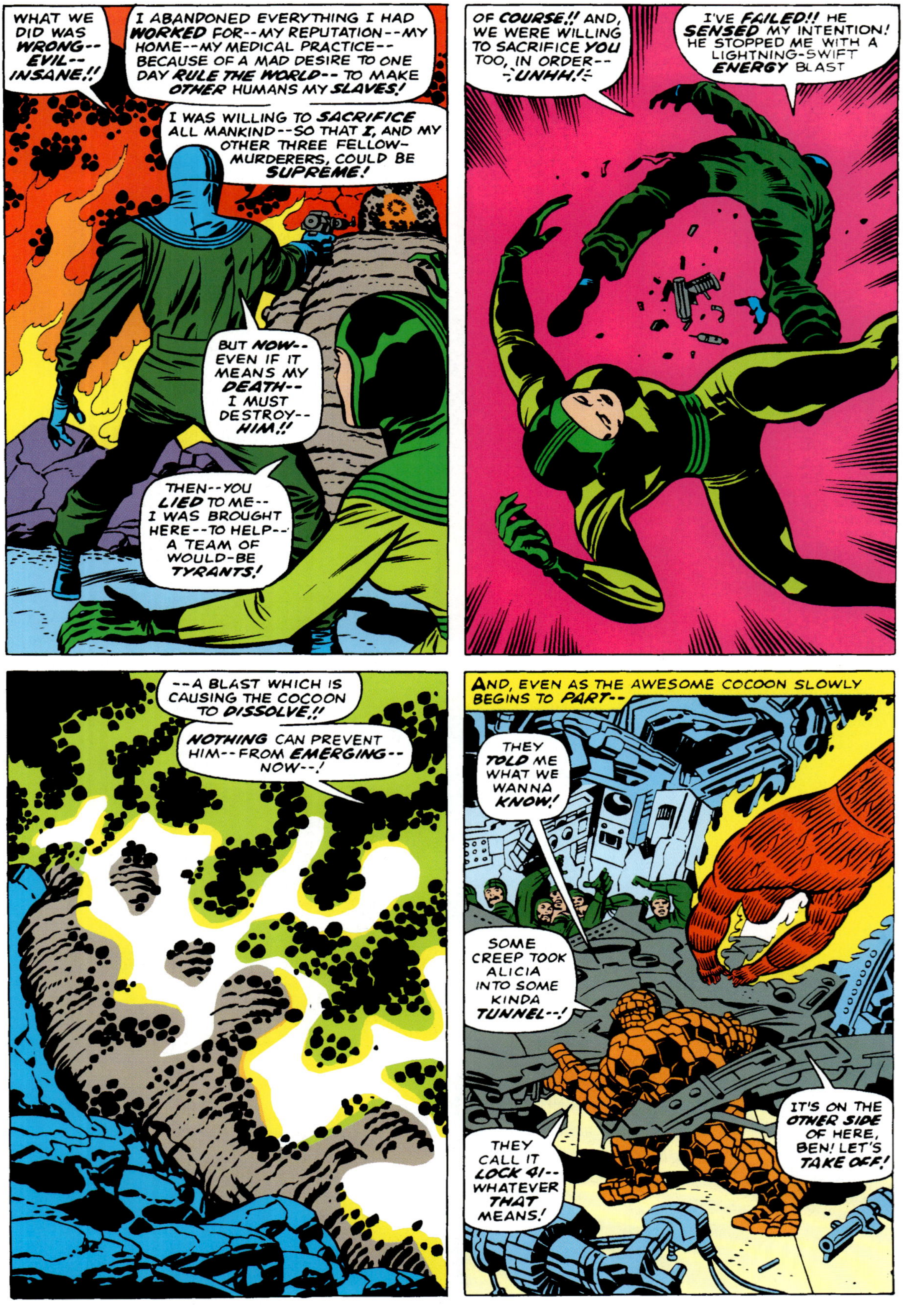
WHAT WE DID WAS WRONG-- EVIL-- INSANE!!
I ABANDONED EVERYTHING I HAD WORKED FOR--MY REPUTATION--MY HOME--MY MEDICAL PRACTICE--BECAUSE OF A MAD DESIRE TO ONE DAY RULE THE WORLD--TO MAKE OTHER HUMANS MY SLAVES!
I WAS WILLING TO SACRIFICE ALL MANKIND--SO THAT I, AND MY OTHER THREE FELLOW-MURDERERS, COULD BE SUPREME!
BUT NOW--EVEN IF IT MEANS MY DEATH--I MUST DESTROY--HIM!!
THEN--YOU LIED TO ME--I WAS BROUGHT HERE--TO HELP--A TEAM OF WOULD-BE TYRANTS!
OF COURSE!! AND, WE WERE WILLING TO SACRIFICE YOU TOO, IN ORDER-- UNHH!
I'VE FAILED!! HE SENSED MY INTENTION! HE STOPPED ME WITH A LIGHTNING-SWIFT ENERGY BLAST
--A BLAST WHICH IS CAUSING THE COCOON TO DISSOLVE!!
NOTHING CAN PREVENT HIM--FROM EMERGING--NOW--!
AND, EVEN AS THE AWESOME COCOON SLOWLY BEGINS TO PART--
THEY TOLD ME WHAT WE WANNA KNOW!
SOME CREEP TOOK ALICIA INTO SOME KINDA TUNNEL--!
THEY CALL IT LOCK 41--WHATEVER THAT MEANS!
IT'S ON THE OTHER SIDE OF HERE, BEN! LET'S TAKE OFF!

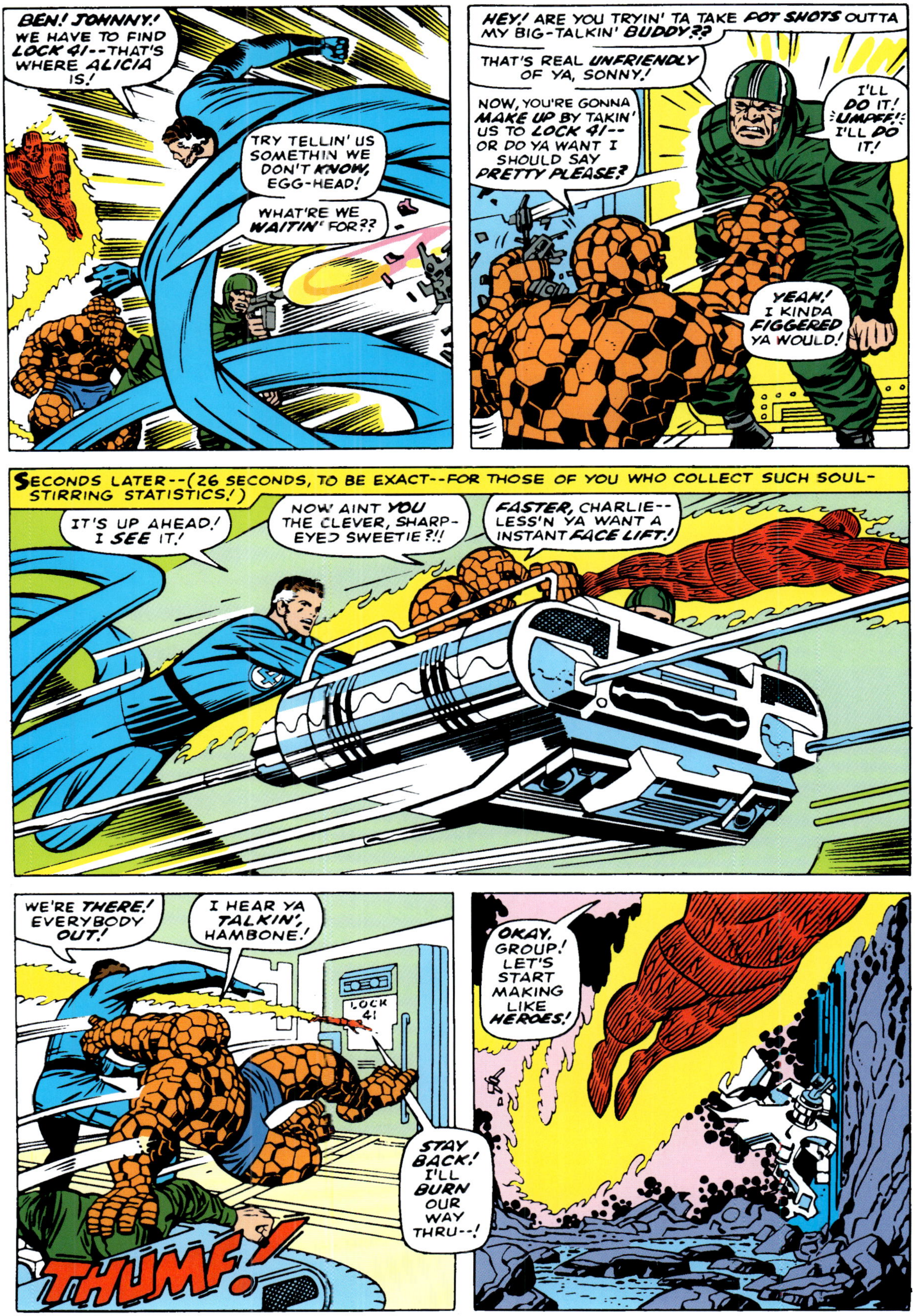
BEN! JOHNNY! WE HAVE TO FIND LOCK 41--THAT'S WHERE ALICIA IS!
TRY TELLIN' US SOMETHIN WE DON'T KNOW, EGG-HEAD!
WHAT'RE WE WAITIN' FOR??
HEY! ARE YOU TRYIN' TA TAKE POT SHOTS OUTTA MY BIG-TALKIN' BUDDY??
THAT'S REAL UNFRIENDLY OF YA, SONNY!
NOW, YOU'RE GONNA MAKE UP BY TAKIN' US TO LOCK 41-- OR DO YA WANT I SHOULD SAY PRETTY PLEASE?
I'LL DO IT! UMPF! I'LL DO IT!
YEAH! I KINDA FIGGERED YA WOULD!
SECONDS LATER--(26 SECONDS, TO BE EXACT--FOR THOSE OF YOU WHO COLLECT SUCH SOUL-STIRRING STATISTICS!)
IT'S UP AHEAD! I SEE IT!
NOW AINT YOU THE CLEVER, SHARP-EYED SWEETIE?!!
FASTER, CHARLIE-- LESS'N YA WANT A INSTANT FACE LIFT!
WE'RE THERE! EVERYBODY OUT!
I HEAR YA TALKIN', HAMBONE!
LOCK 41
STAY BACK! I'LL BURN OUR WAY THRU--!
THUMF!
OKAY, GROUP! LET'S START MAKING LIKE HEROES!

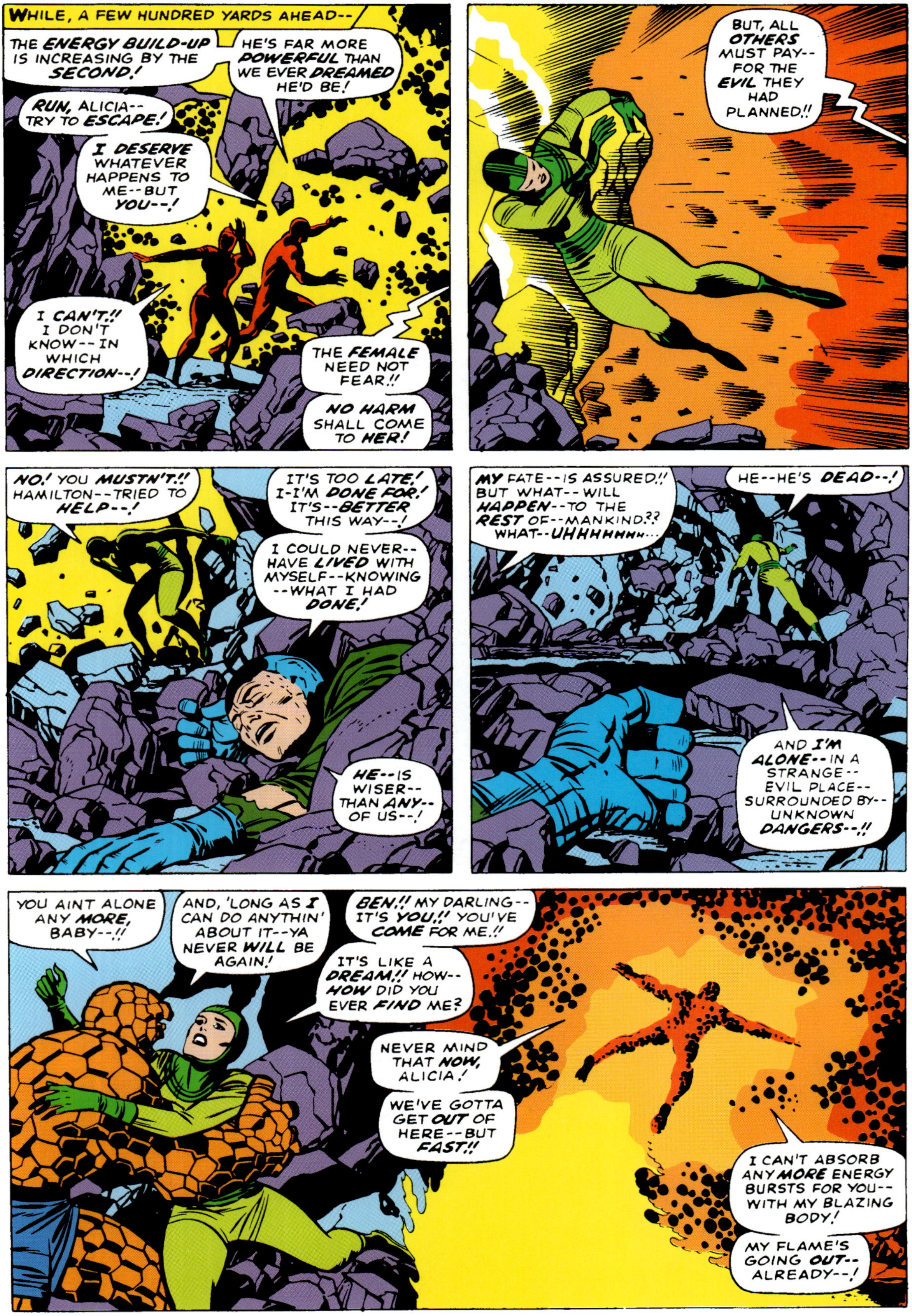
WHILE, A FEW HUNDRED YARDS AHEAD--
THE ENERGY BUILD-UP IS INCREASING BY THE SECOND!
HE'S FAR MORE POWERFUL THAN WE EVER DREAMED HE'D BE!
RUN, ALICIA-- TRY TO ESCAPE!
I DESERVE WHATEVER HAPPENS TO ME--BUT YOU--!
I CAN'T!! I DON'T KNOW--IN WHICH DIRECTION--!
THE FEMALE NEED NOT FEAR!!
NO HARM SHALL COME TO HER!
BUT, ALL OTHERS MUST PAY-- FOR THE EVIL THEY HAD PLANNED!!
NO! YOU MUSTN'T!! HAMILTON--TRIED TO HELP--!
IT'S TOO LATE! I-I'M DONE FOR! IT'S--BETTER THIS WAY--!
I COULD NEVER-- HAVE LIVED WITH MYSELF--KNOWING --WHAT I HAD DONE!
HE--IS WISER-- THAN ANY-- OF US--!
MY FATE--IS ASSURED!! BUT WHAT--WILL HAPPEN--TO THE REST OF--MANKIND?? WHAT--UHHHHHHH...
HE--HE'S DEAD--!
AND I'M ALONE--IN A STRANGE-- EVIL PLACE-- SURROUNDED BY-- UNKNOWN DANGERS--!!
YOU AINT ALONE ANY MORE, BABY--!!
AND, 'LONG AS I CAN DO ANYTHIN' ABOUT IT--YA NEVER WILL BE AGAIN!
BEN!! MY DARLING-- IT'S YOU!! YOU'VE COME FOR ME!!
IT'S LIKE A DREAM!! HOW-- HOW DID YOU EVER FIND ME?
NEVER MIND THAT NOW, ALICIA!
WE'VE GOTTA GET OUT OF HERE--BUT FAST!!
I CAN'T ABSORB ANY MORE ENERGY BURSTS FOR YOU-- WITH MY BLAZING BODY!
MY FLAME'S GOING OUT-- ALREADY--!

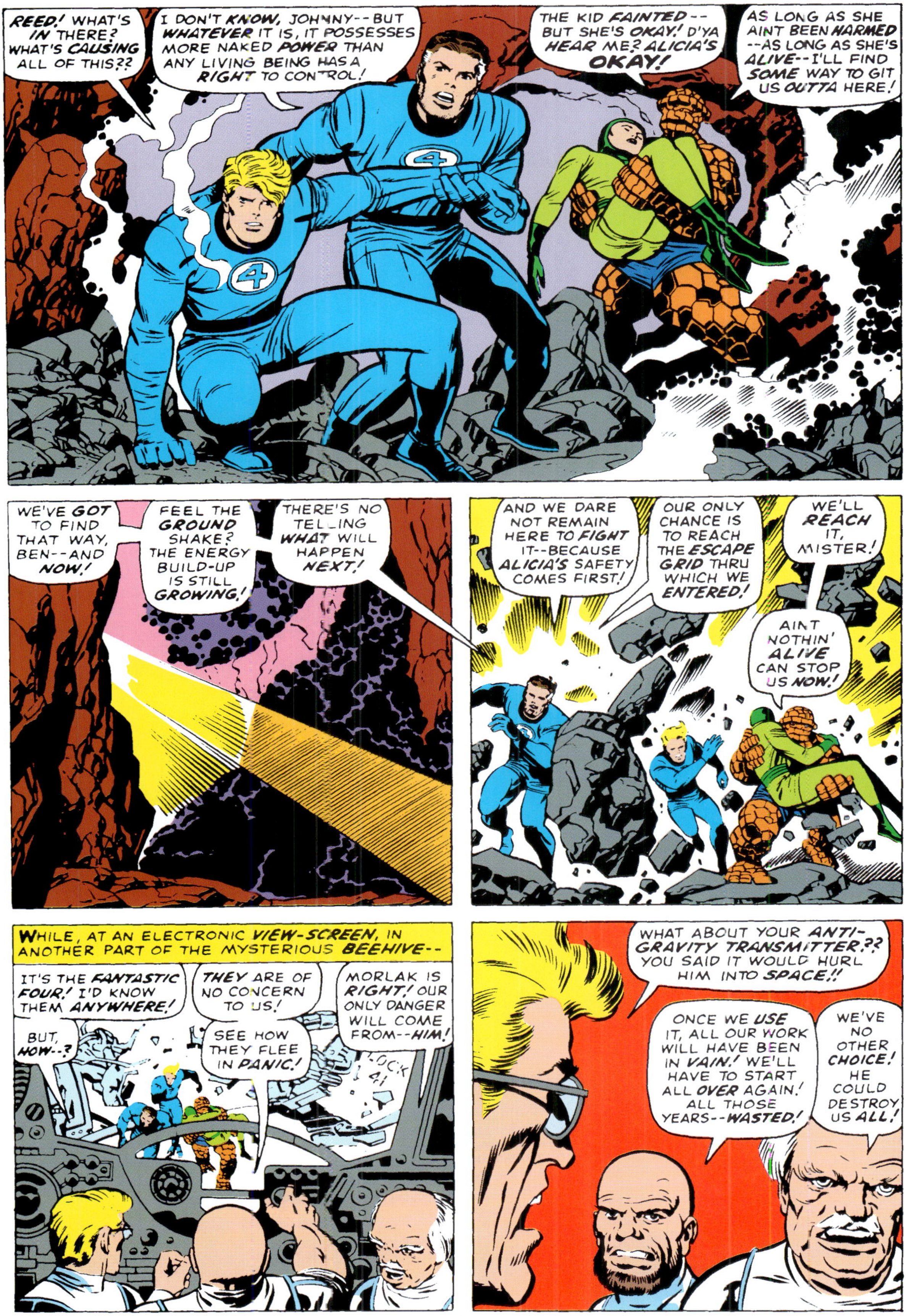
REED! WHAT'S IN THERE? WHAT'S CAUSING ALL OF THIS??
I DON'T KNOW, JOHNNY-- BUT WHATEVER IT IS, IT POSSESSES MORE NAKED POWER THAN ANY LIVING BEING HAS A RIGHT TO CONTROL!
THE KID FAINTED-- BUT SHE'S OKAY! D'YA HEAR ME? ALICIA'S OKAY!
AS LONG AS SHE AIN'T BEEN HARMED --AS LONG AS SHE'S ALIVE--I'LL FIND SOME WAY TO GIT US OUTTA HERE!
WE'VE GOT TO FIND THAT WAY, BEN--AND NOW!
FEEL THE GROUND SHAKE? THE ENERGY BUILD-UP IS STILL GROWING!
THERE'S NO TELLING WHAT WILL HAPPEN NEXT!
AND WE DARE NOT REMAIN HERE TO FIGHT IT--BECAUSE ALICIA'S SAFETY COMES FIRST!
OUR ONLY CHANCE IS TO REACH THE ESCAPE GRID THRU WHICH WE ENTERED!
WE'LL REACH IT, MISTER!
AIN'T NOTHIN' ALIVE CAN STOP US NOW!
WHILE, AT AN ELECTRONIC VIEW-SCREEN, IN ANOTHER PART OF THE MYSTERIOUS BEEHIVE--
IT'S THE FANTASTIC FOUR! I'D KNOW THEM ANYWHERE!
BUT, HOW--?
THEY ARE OF NO CONCERN TO US!
SEE HOW THEY FLEE IN PANIC!
MORLAK IS RIGHT! OUR ONLY DANGER WILL COME FROM--HIM!
WHAT ABOUT YOUR ANTI-GRAVITY TRANSMITTER?? YOU SAID IT WOULD HURL HIM INTO SPACE!!
ONCE WE USE IT, ALL OUR WORK WILL HAVE BEEN IN VAIN! WE'LL HAVE TO START ALL OVER AGAIN! ALL THOSE YEARS--WASTED!
WE'VE NO OTHER CHOICE! HE COULD DESTROY US ALL!

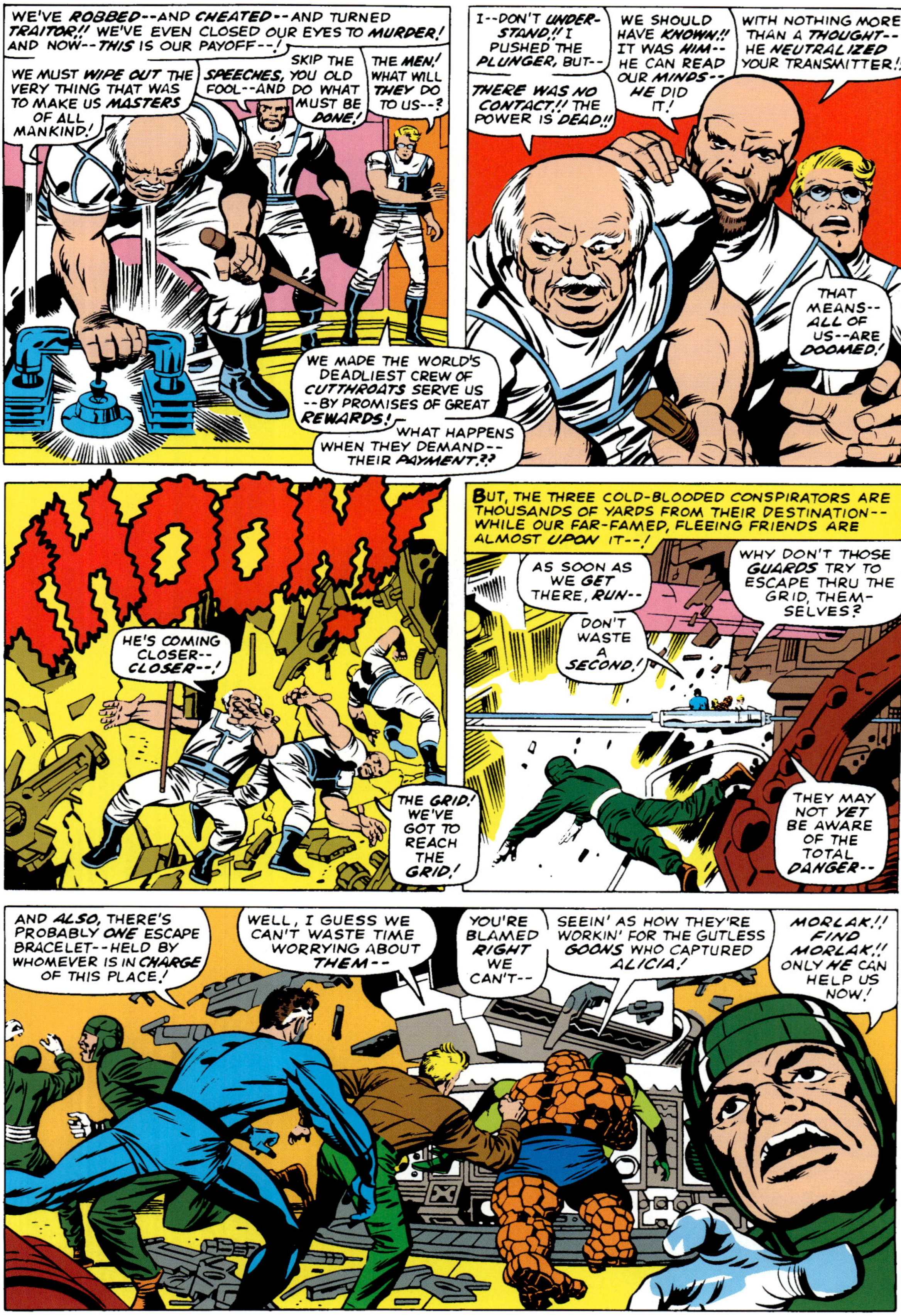

WE'VE ROBBED--AND CHEATED--AND TURNED TRAITOR!! WE'VE EVEN CLOSED OUR EYES TO MURDER! AND NOW--THIS IS OUR PAYOFF--!
WE MUST WIPE OUT THE VERY THING THAT WAS TO MAKE US MASTERS OF ALL MANKIND!
SKIP THE SPEECHES, YOU OLD FOOL--AND DO WHAT MUST BE DONE!
THE MEN! WHAT WILL THEY DO TO US--?
WE MADE THE WORLD'S DEADLIEST CREW OF CUTTHROATS SERVE US --BY PROMISES OF GREAT REWARDS!
WHAT HAPPENS WHEN THEY DEMAND--THEIR PAYMENT??
I--DON'T UNDERSTAND!! I PUSHED THE PLUNGER, BUT--
THERE WAS NO CONTACT!! THE POWER IS DEAD!!
WE SHOULD HAVE KNOWN!! IT WAS HIM--HE CAN READ OUR MINDS--HE DID IT!
WITH NOTHING MORE THAN A THOUGHT--HE NEUTRALIZED YOUR TRANSMITTER!!
THAT MEANS--ALL OF US--ARE DOOMED!
WHOOM!
HE'S COMING CLOSER--CLOSER--!
THE GRID! WE'VE GOT TO REACH THE GRID!
BUT, THE THREE COLD-BLOODED CONSPIRATORS ARE THOUSANDS OF YARDS FROM THEIR DESTINATION--WHILE OUR FAR-FAMED, FLEEING FRIENDS ARE ALMOST UPON IT--!
AS SOON AS WE GET THERE, RUN--
DON'T WASTE A SECOND!
WHY DON'T THOSE GUARDS TRY TO ESCAPE THRU THE GRID, THEMSELVES?
THEY MAY NOT YET BE AWARE OF THE TOTAL DANGER--
AND ALSO, THERE'S PROBABLY ONE ESCAPE BRACELET--HELD BY WHOMEVER IS IN CHARGE OF THIS PLACE!
WELL, I GUESS WE CAN'T WASTE TIME WORRYING ABOUT THEM--
YOU'RE BLAMED RIGHT WE CAN'T--
SEEIN' AS HOW THEY'RE WORKIN' FOR THE GUTLESS GOONS WHO CAPTURED ALICIA!
MORLAK!! FIND MORLAK!! ONLY HE CAN HELP US NOW!

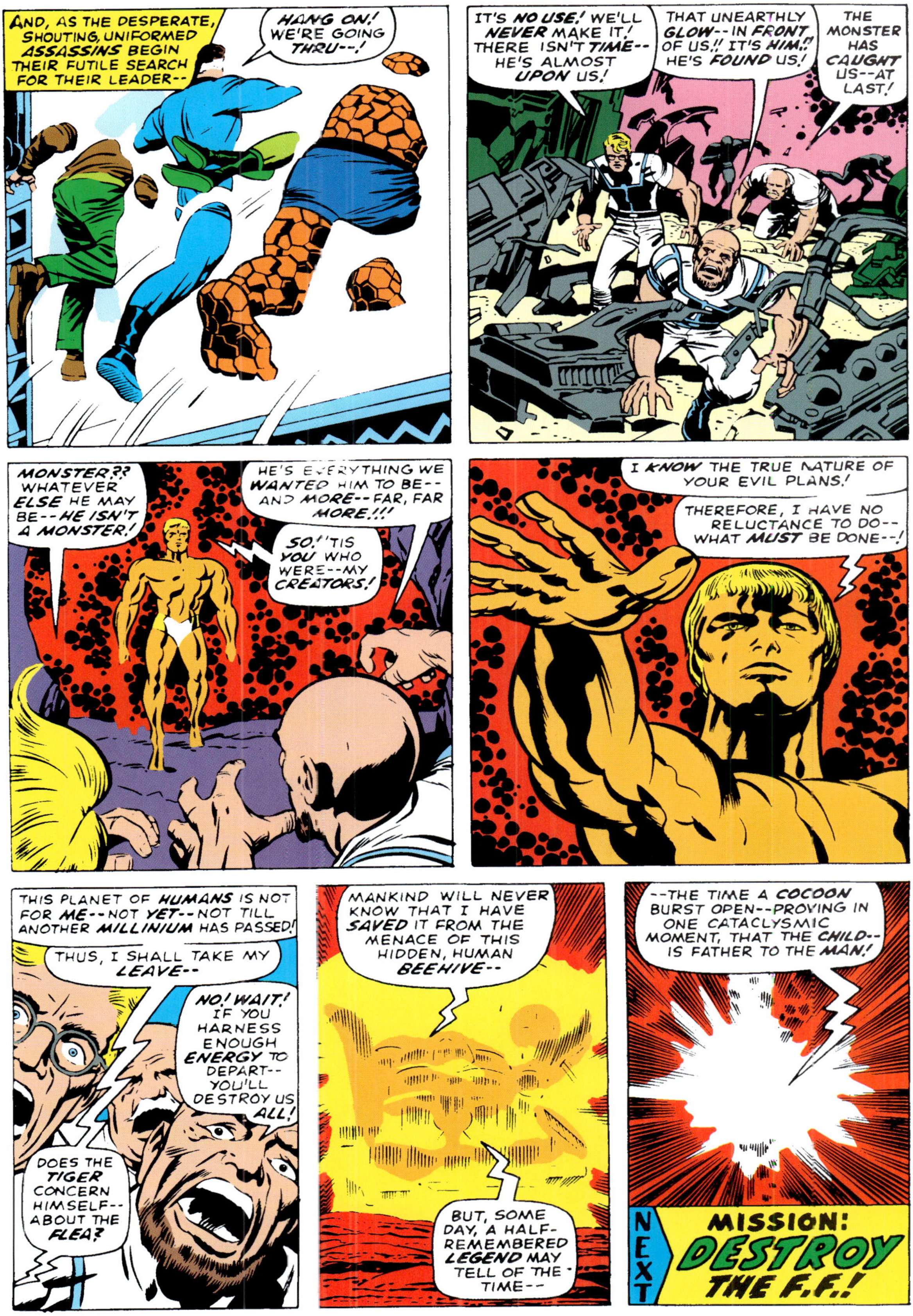

AND, AS THE DESPERATE, SHOUTING, UNIFORMED ASSASSINS BEGIN THEIR FUTILE SEARCH FOR THEIR LEADER--
HANG ON! WE'RE GOING THRU--!
IT'S NO USE! WE'LL NEVER MAKE IT! THERE ISN'T TIME-- HE'S ALMOST UPON US!
THAT UNEARTHLY GLOW-- IN FRONT OF US!! IT'S HIM!! HE'S FOUND US!
THE MONSTER HAS CAUGHT US--AT LAST!
MONSTER?? WHATEVER ELSE HE MAY BE--HE ISN'T A MONSTER!
HE'S EVERYTHING WE WANTED HIM TO BE-- AND MORE--FAR, FAR MORE!!!
SO! 'TIS YOU WHO WERE--MY CREATORS!
I KNOW THE TRUE NATURE OF YOUR EVIL PLANS!
THEREFORE, I HAVE NO RELUCTANCE TO DO-- WHAT MUST BE DONE--!
THIS PLANET OF HUMANS IS NOT FOR ME--NOT YET--NOT TILL ANOTHER MILLINIUM HAS PASSED!
THUS, I SHALL TAKE MY LEAVE--
NO! WAIT! IF YOU HARNESS ENOUGH ENERGY TO DEPART-- YOU'LL DESTROY US ALL!
DOES THE TIGER CONCERN HIMSELF-- ABOUT THE FLEA?
MANKIND WILL NEVER KNOW THAT I HAVE SAVED IT FROM THE MENACE OF THIS HIDDEN, HUMAN BEEHIVE--
BUT, SOME DAY, A HALF-REMEMBERED LEGEND MAY TELL OF THE TIME--
--THE TIME A COCOON BURST OPEN--PROVING IN ONE CATACLYSMIC MOMENT, THAT THE CHILD-- IS FATHER TO THE MAN!
NEXT
MISSION: DESTROY THE F.F.!

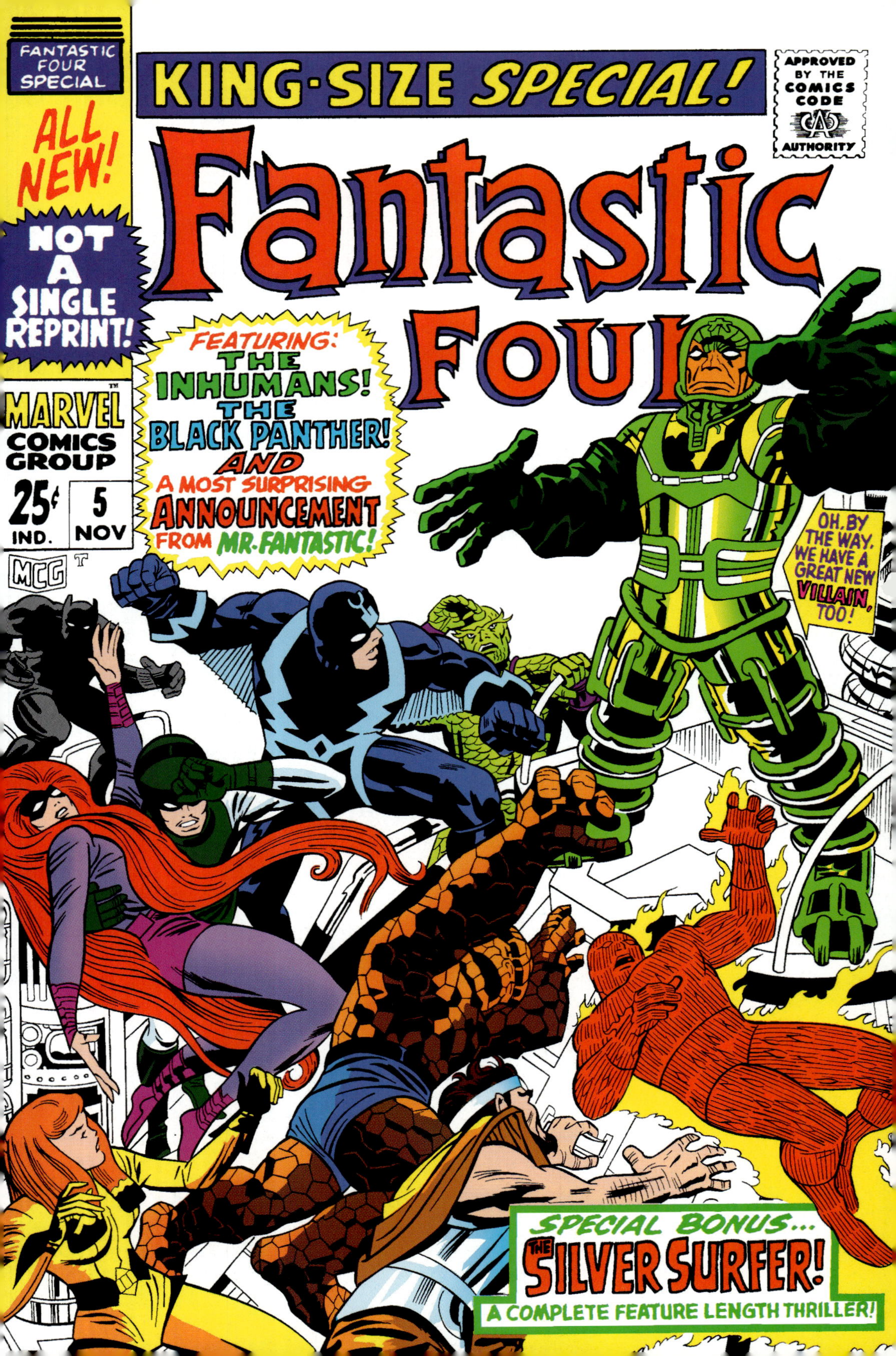
FANTASTIC FOUR SPECIAL
KING-SIZE SPECIAL!
APPROVED BY THE COMICS CODE AUTHORITY
ALL NEW!
NOT A SINGLE REPRINT!
Fantastic Four
FEATURING: THE INHUMANS! THE BLACK PANTHER! AND A MOST SURPRISING ANNOUNCEMENT FROM MR. FANTASTIC!
MARVEL COMICS GROUP
25¢ IND.
5 NOV
MCG
OH, BY THE WAY, WE HAVE A GREAT NEW VILLAIN, TOO!
SPECIAL BONUS... THE SILVER SURFER!
A COMPLETE FEATURE LENGTH THRILLER!

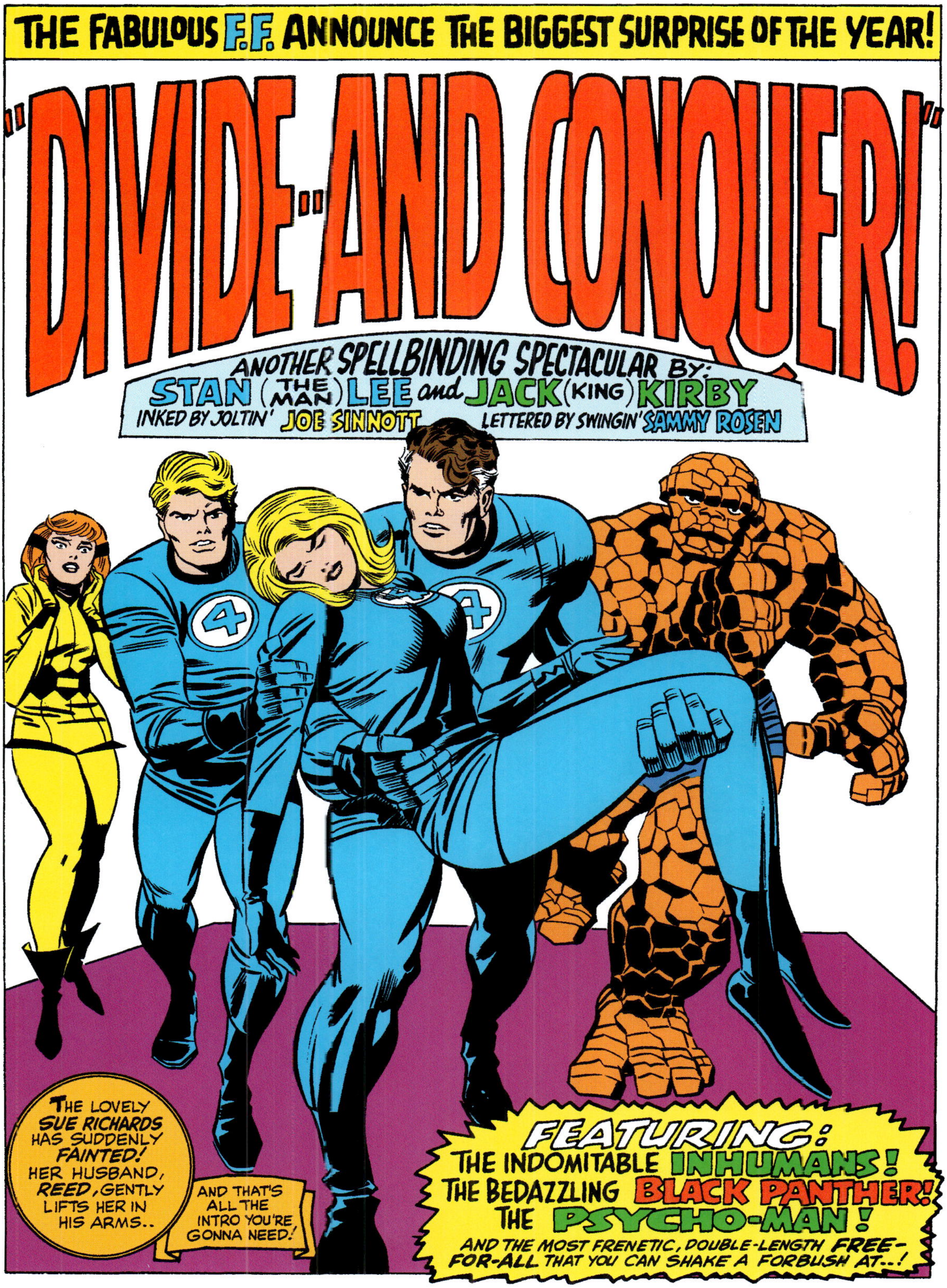

THE FABULOUS F.F. ANNOUNCE THE BIGGEST SURPRISE OF THE YEAR!
"DIVIDE--AND CONQUER!"
ANOTHER SPELLBINDING SPECTACULAR BY:
STAN (THE MAN) LEE and JACK (KING) KIRBY
INKED BY JOLTIN' JOE SINNOTT LETTERED BY SWINGIN' SAMMY ROSEN
THE LOVELY SUE RICHARDS HAS SUDDENLY FAINTED! HER HUSBAND, REED, GENTLY LIFTS HER IN HIS ARMS..
AND THAT'S ALL THE INTRO YOU'RE GONNA NEED!
FEATURING:
THE INDOMITABLE INHUMANS!
THE BEDAZZLING BLACK PANTHER!
THE PSYCHO-MAN!
AND THE MOST FRENETIC, DOUBLE-LENGTH FREE-FOR-ALL THAT YOU CAN SHAKE A FORBUSH AT..!

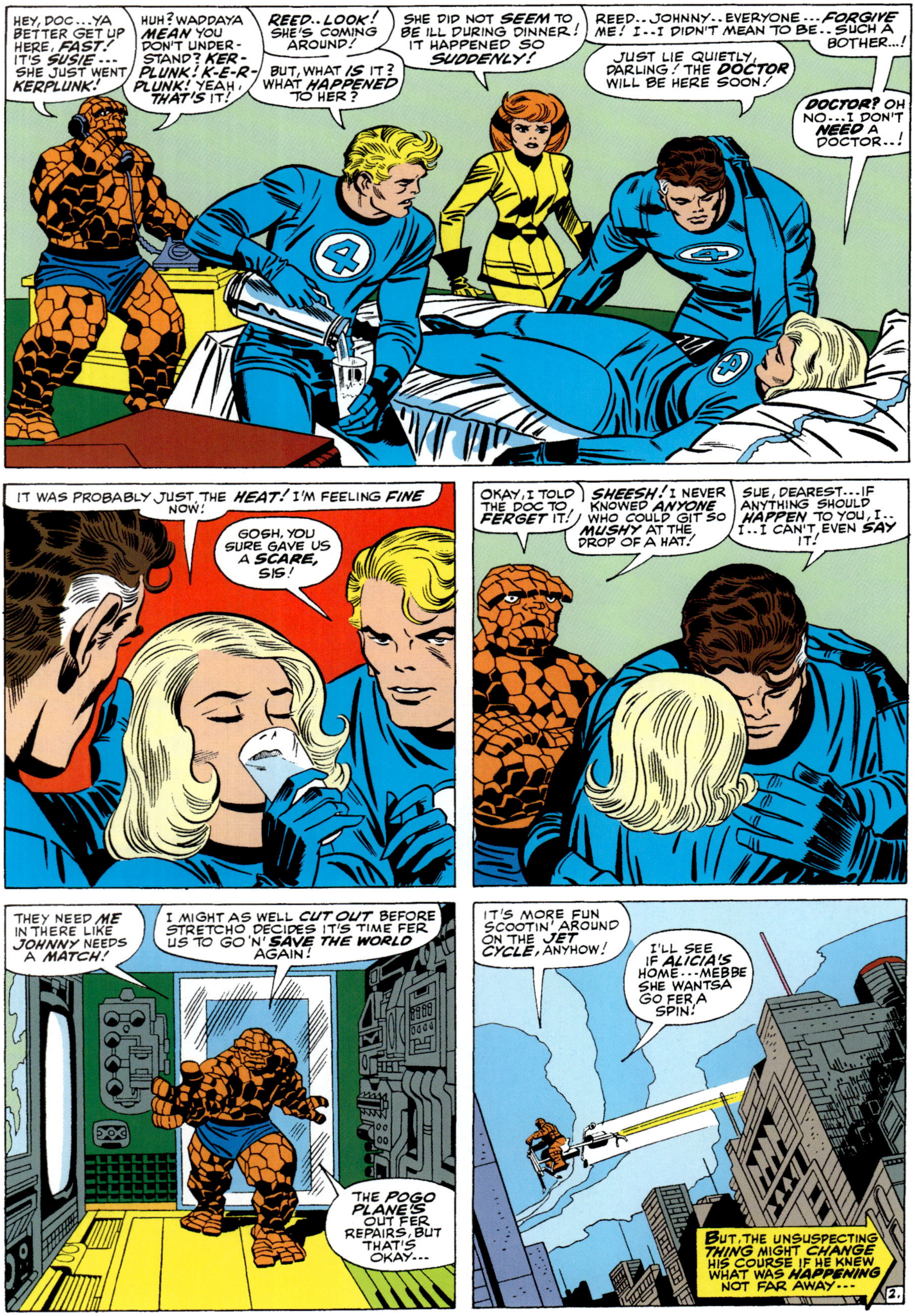
HEY, DOC...YA BETTER GET UP HERE, FAST! IT'S SUSIE--- SHE JUST WENT KERPLUNK!
HUH? WADDAYA MEAN YOU DON'T UNDER-STAND? KER-PLUNK! K-E-R-PLUNK! YEAH, THAT'S IT!
REED..LOOK! SHE'S COMING AROUND!
BUT, WHAT IS IT? WHAT HAPPENED TO HER?
SHE DID NOT SEEM TO BE ILL DURING DINNER! IT HAPPENED SO SUDDENLY!
REED..JOHNNY..EVERYONE---FORGIVE ME! I--I DIDN'T MEAN TO BE..SUCH A BOTHER...!
JUST LIE QUIETLY, DARLING! THE DOCTOR WILL BE HERE SOON!
DOCTOR? OH NO---I DON'T NEED A DOCTOR..!
IT WAS PROBABLY JUST THE HEAT! I'M FEELING FINE NOW!
GOSH, YOU SURE GAVE US A SCARE, SIS!
OKAY, I TOLD THE DOC TO FERGET IT!
SHEESH! I NEVER KNOWED ANYONE WHO COULD GIT SO MUSHY AT THE DROP OF A HAT!
SUE, DEAREST---IF ANYTHING SHOULD HAPPEN TO YOU, I.. I..I CAN'T EVEN SAY IT!
THEY NEED ME IN THERE LIKE JOHNNY NEEDS A MATCH!
I MIGHT AS WELL CUT OUT BEFORE STRETCHO DECIDES IT'S TIME FER US TO GO 'N' SAVE THE WORLD AGAIN!
THE POGO PLANE'S OUT FER REPAIRS, BUT THAT'S OKAY---
IT'S MORE FUN SCOOTIN' AROUND ON THE JET CYCLE, ANYHOW!
I'LL SEE IF ALICIA'S HOME---MEBBE SHE WANTSA GO FER A SPIN!
BUT, THE UNSUSPECTING THING MIGHT CHANGE HIS COURSE IF HE KNEW WHAT WAS HAPPENING NOT FAR AWAY---
2.

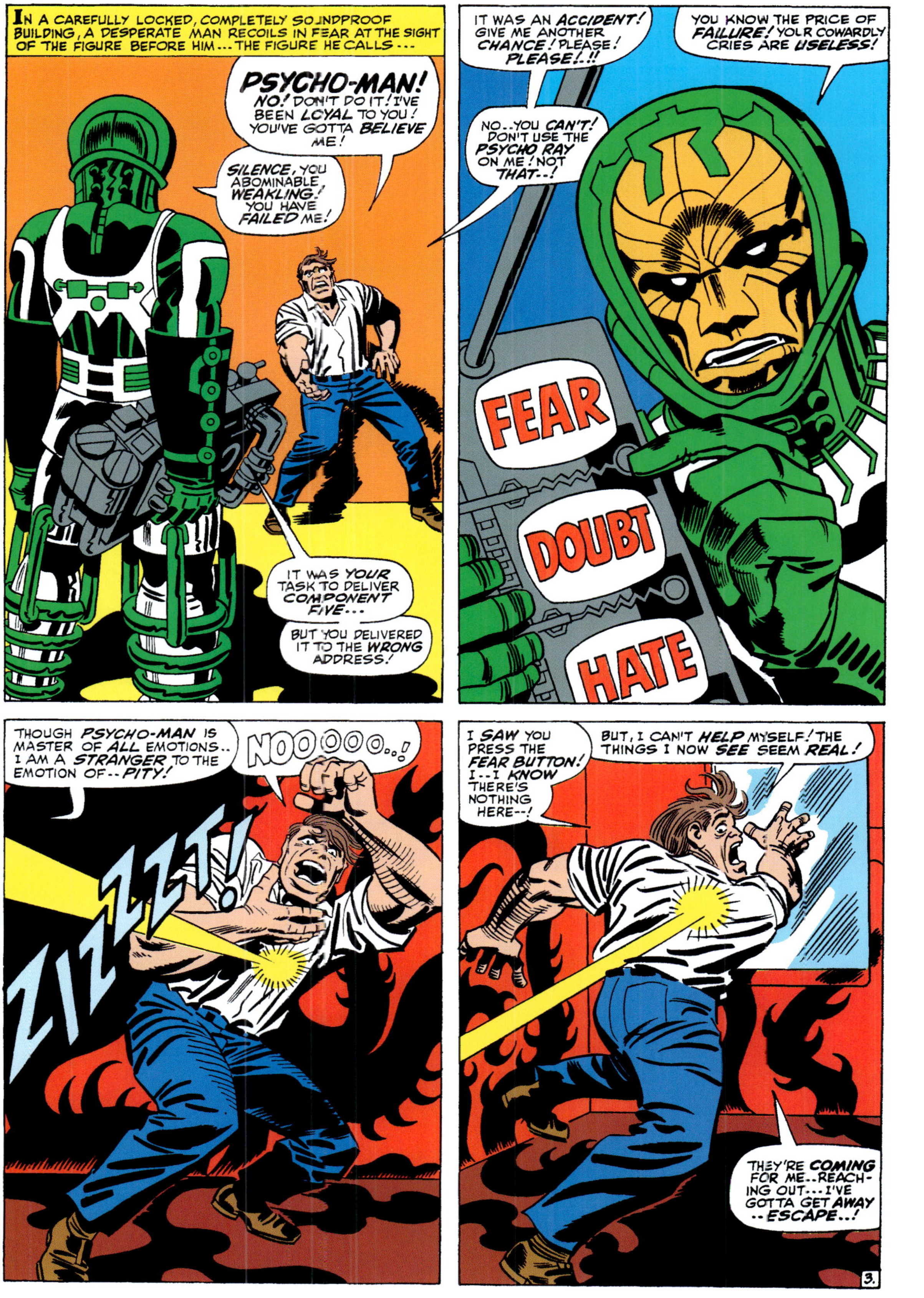

IN A CAREFULLY LOCKED, COMPLETELY SOUNDPROOF BUILDING, A DESPERATE MAN RECOILS IN FEAR AT THE SIGHT OF THE FIGURE BEFORE HIM... THE FIGURE HE CALLS...
PSYCHO-MAN! NO! DON'T DO IT! I'VE BEEN LOYAL TO YOU! YOU'VE GOTTA BELIEVE ME!
SILENCE, YOU ABOMINABLE WEAKLING! YOU HAVE FAILED ME!
IT WAS YOUR TASK TO DELIVER COMPONENT FIVE...
BUT YOU DELIVERED IT TO THE WRONG ADDRESS!
IT WAS AN ACCIDENT! GIVE ME ANOTHER CHANCE! PLEASE! PLEASE!..!!
YOU KNOW THE PRICE OF FAILURE! YOUR COWARDLY CRIES ARE USELESS!
NO..YOU CAN'T! DON'T USE THE PSYCHO RAY ON ME! NOT THAT--!
FEAR
DOUBT
HATE
THOUGH PSYCHO-MAN IS MASTER OF ALL EMOTIONS.. I AM A STRANGER TO THE EMOTION OF--PITY!
NOOOOOO..!
ZIZZZZT!
I SAW YOU PRESS THE FEAR BUTTON! I--I KNOW THERE'S NOTHING HERE--!
BUT, I CAN'T HELP MYSELF! THE THINGS I NOW SEE SEEM REAL!
THEY'RE COMING FOR ME..REACHING OUT...I'VE GOTTA GET AWAY ..ESCAPE..!
3.

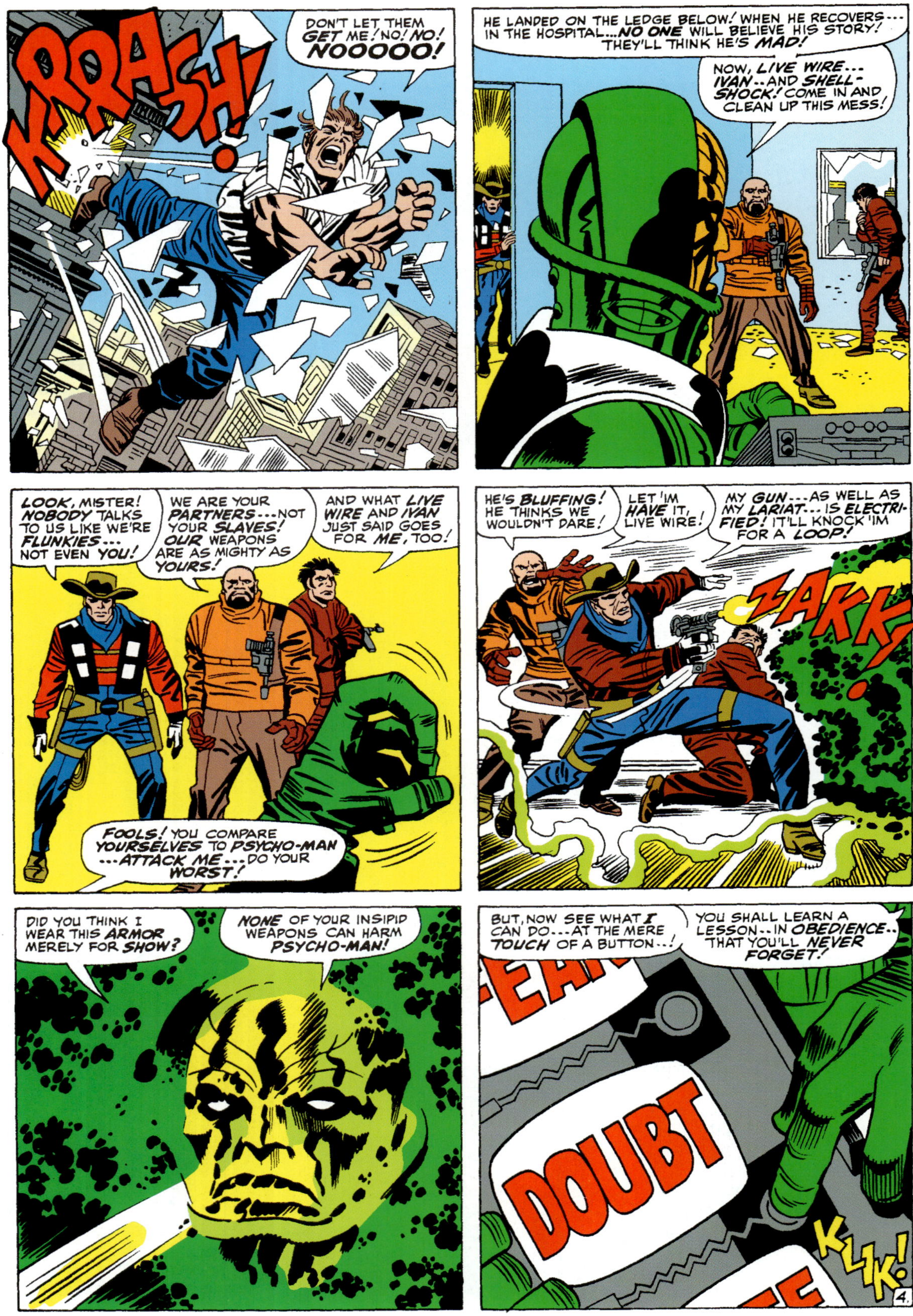
K-RRASH!
DON'T LET THEM GET ME! NO! NO! NOOOOO!
HE LANDED ON THE LEDGE BELOW! WHEN HE RECOVERS... IN THE HOSPITAL...NO ONE WILL BELIEVE HIS STORY! THEY'LL THINK HE'S MAD!
NOW, LIVE WIRE... IVAN..AND SHELL-SHOCK! COME IN AND CLEAN UP THIS MESS!
LOOK, MISTER! NOBODY TALKS TO US LIKE WE'RE FLUNKIES... NOT EVEN YOU!
WE ARE YOUR PARTNERS...NOT YOUR SLAVES! OUR WEAPONS ARE AS MIGHTY AS YOURS!
AND WHAT LIVE WIRE AND IVAN JUST SAID GOES FOR ME, TOO!
FOOLS! YOU COMPARE YOURSELVES TO PSYCHO-MAN ...ATTACK ME...DO YOUR WORST!
HE'S BLUFFING! HE THINKS WE WOULDN'T DARE!
LET 'IM HAVE IT, LIVE WIRE!
MY GUN...AS WELL AS MY LARIAT...IS ELECTRIFIED! IT'LL KNOCK 'IM FOR A LOOP!
ZAKK!
DID YOU THINK I WEAR THIS ARMOR MERELY FOR SHOW?
NONE OF YOUR INSIPID WEAPONS CAN HARM PSYCHO-MAN!
BUT, NOW SEE WHAT I CAN DO...AT THE MERE TOUCH OF A BUTTON..!
YOU SHALL LEARN A LESSON..IN OBEDIENCE.. THAT YOU'LL NEVER FORGET!
DOUBT
KLIK!
4.

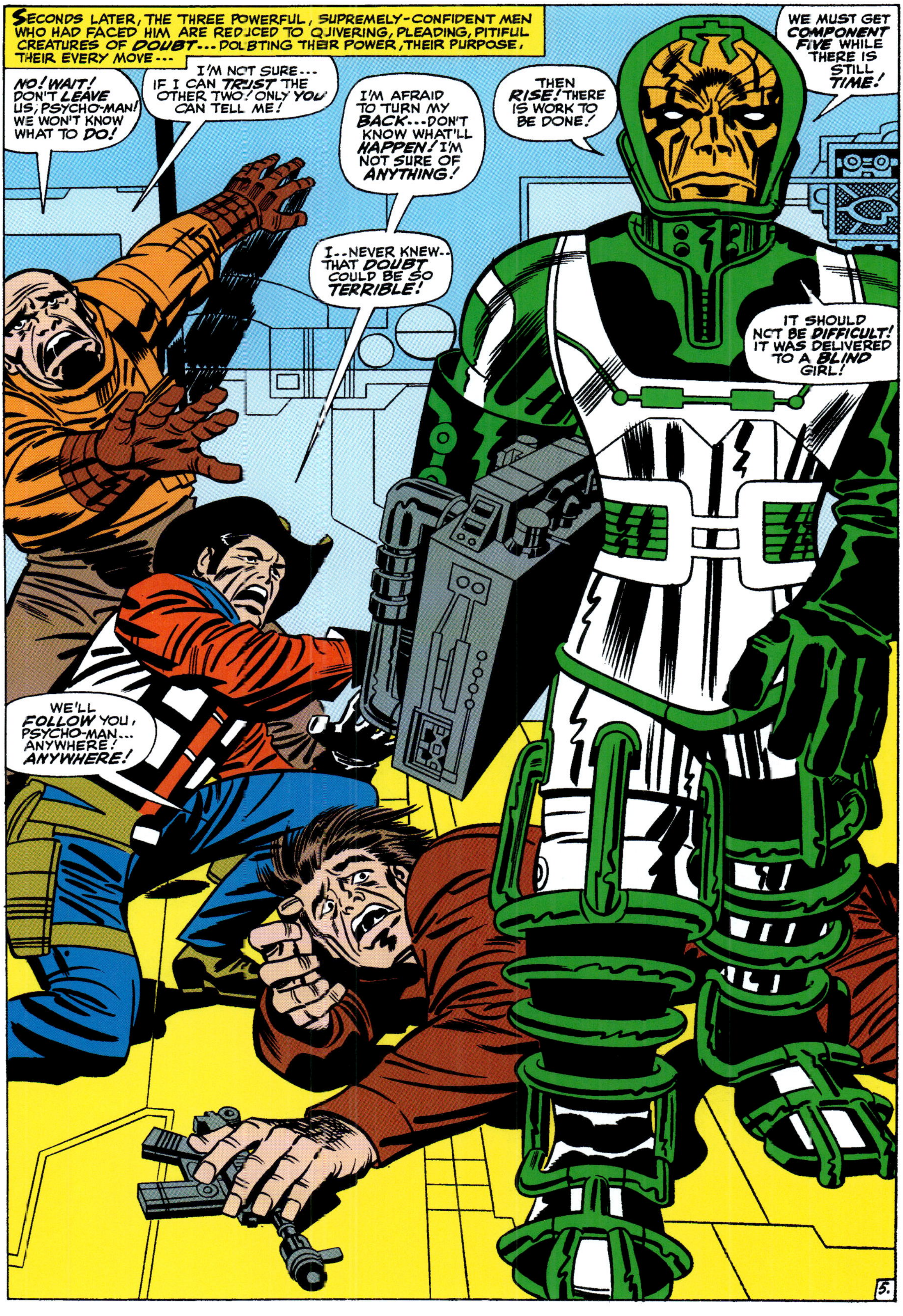
SECONDS LATER, THE THREE POWERFUL, SUPREMELY-CONFIDENT MEN WHO HAD FACED HIM ARE REDUCED TO QUIVERING, PLEADING, PITIFUL CREATURES OF DOUBT... DOUBTING THEIR POWER, THEIR PURPOSE, THEIR EVERY MOVE...
NO! WAIT! DON'T LEAVE US, PSYCHO-MAN! WE WON'T KNOW WHAT TO DO!
I'M NOT SURE... IF I CAN TRUST THE OTHER TWO! ONLY YOU CAN TELL ME!
I'M AFRAID TO TURN MY BACK--DON'T KNOW WHAT'LL HAPPEN! I'M NOT SURE OF ANYTHING!
I--NEVER KNEW--THAT DOUBT COULD BE SO TERRIBLE!
THEN RISE! THERE IS WORK TO BE DONE!
WE MUST GET COMPONENT FIVE WHILE THERE IS STILL TIME!
IT SHOULD NOT BE DIFFICULT! IT WAS DELIVERED TO A BLIND GIRL!
WE'LL FOLLOW YOU, PSYCHO-MAN... ANYWHERE! ANYWHERE!
5.

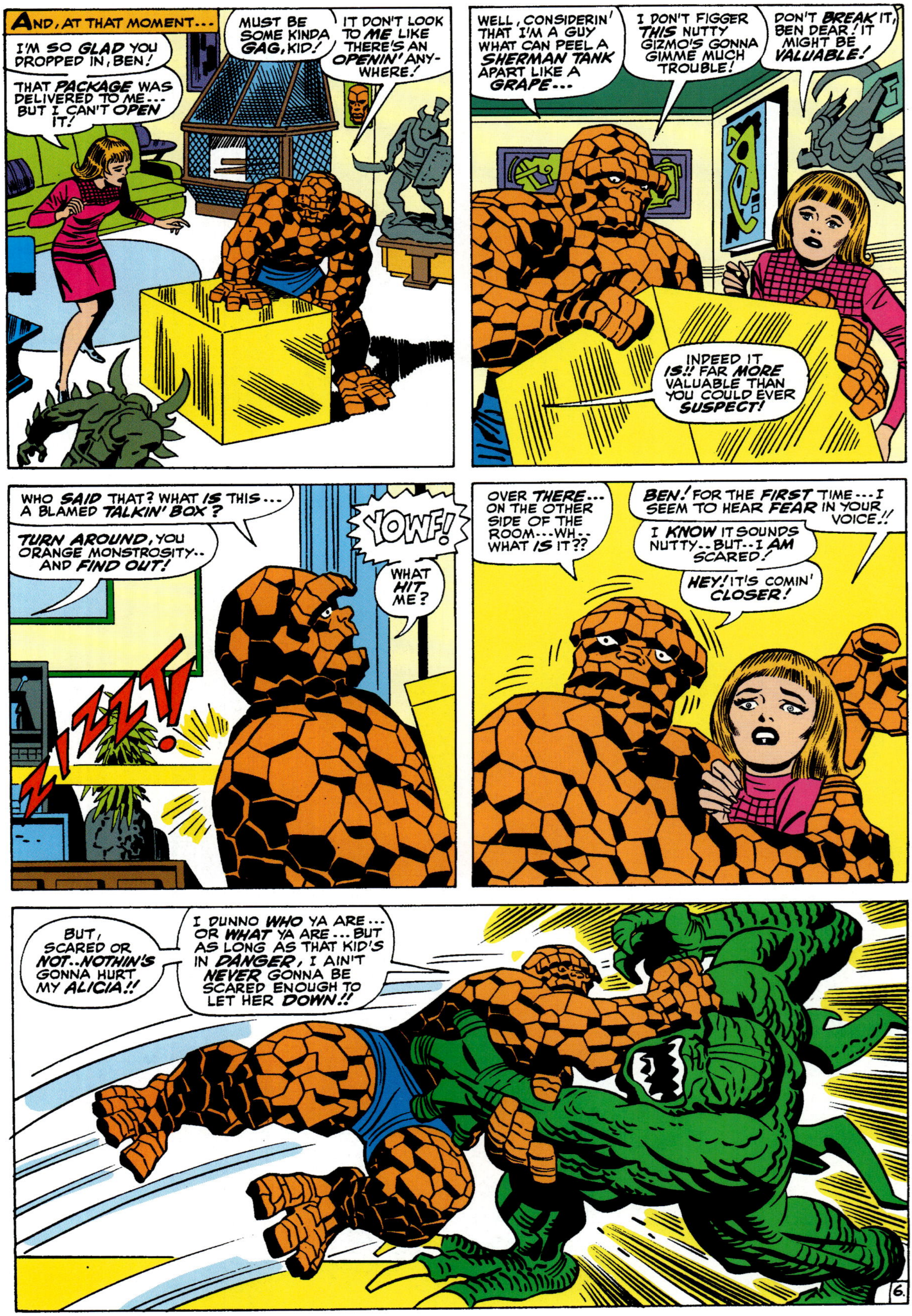
AND, AT THAT MOMENT...
I'M SO GLAD YOU DROPPED IN, BEN!
THAT PACKAGE WAS DELIVERED TO ME... BUT I CAN'T OPEN IT!
MUST BE SOME KINDA GAG, KID!
IT DON'T LOOK TO ME LIKE THERE'S AN OPENIN' ANY-WHERE!
WELL, CONSIDERIN' THAT I'M A GUY WHAT CAN PEEL A SHERMAN TANK APART LIKE A GRAPE...
I DON'T FIGGER THIS NUTTY GIZMO'S GONNA GIMME MUCH TROUBLE!
DON'T BREAK IT, BEN DEAR! IT MIGHT BE VALUABLE!
INDEED IT IS!! FAR MORE VALUABLE THAN YOU COULD EVER SUSPECT!
WHO SAID THAT? WHAT IS THIS... A BLAMED TALKIN' BOX?
TURN AROUND, YOU ORANGE MONSTROSITY.. AND FIND OUT!
YOWF!
WHAT HIT ME?
ZIZZT!
OVER THERE... ON THE OTHER SIDE OF THE ROOM...WH.. WHAT IS IT??
BEN! FOR THE FIRST TIME...I SEEM TO HEAR FEAR IN YOUR VOICE!!
I KNOW IT SOUNDS NUTTY..BUT..I AM SCARED!
HEY! IT'S COMIN' CLOSER!
BUT, SCARED OR NOT..NOTHIN'S GONNA HURT MY ALICIA!!
I DUNNO WHO YA ARE... OR WHAT YA ARE... BUT AS LONG AS THAT KID'S IN DANGER, I AIN'T NEVER GONNA BE SCARED ENOUGH TO LET HER DOWN!!
6.

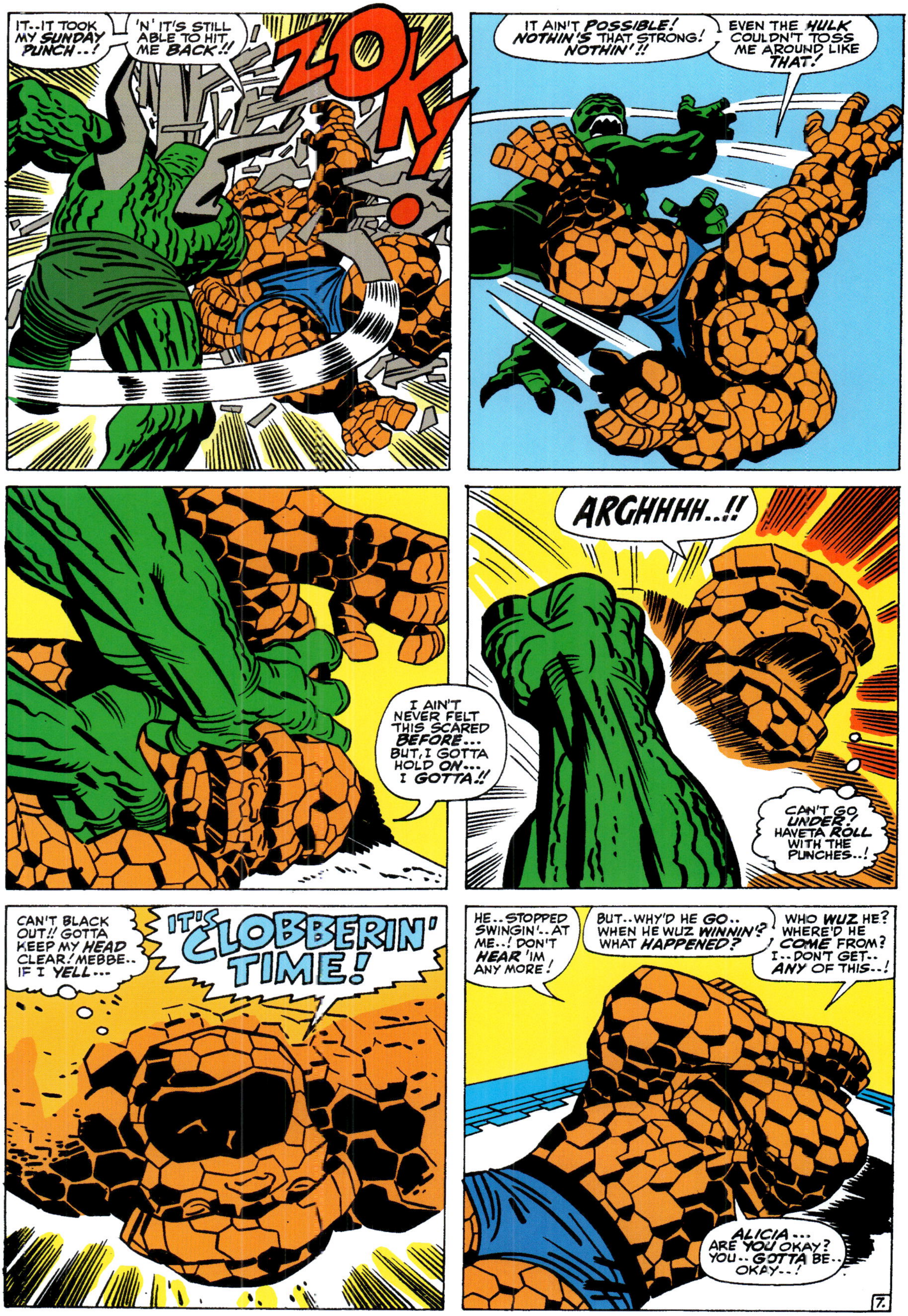
IT--IT TOOK MY SUNDAY PUNCH--!
'N' IT'S STILL ABLE TO HIT ME BACK!!
ZOK!
IT AIN'T POSSIBLE! NOTHIN'S THAT STRONG! NOTHIN'!!
EVEN THE HULK COULDN'T TOSS ME AROUND LIKE THAT!
I AIN'T NEVER FELT THIS SCARED BEFORE... BUT, I GOTTA HOLD ON... I GOTTA!!
ARGHHHH..!!
CAN'T GO UNDER! HAVETA ROLL WITH THE PUNCHES..!
CAN'T BLACK OUT!! GOTTA KEEP MY HEAD CLEAR! MEBBE.. IF I YELL...
IT'S CLOBBERIN' TIME!
HE..STOPPED SWINGIN'..AT ME..! DON'T HEAR 'IM ANY MORE!
BUT..WHY'D HE GO.. WHEN HE WUZ WINNIN'? WHAT HAPPENED?
WHO WUZ HE? WHERE'D HE COME FROM? I..DON'T GET.. ANY OF THIS..!
ALICIA... ARE YOU OKAY? YOU.. GOTTA BE.. OKAY--!
7.

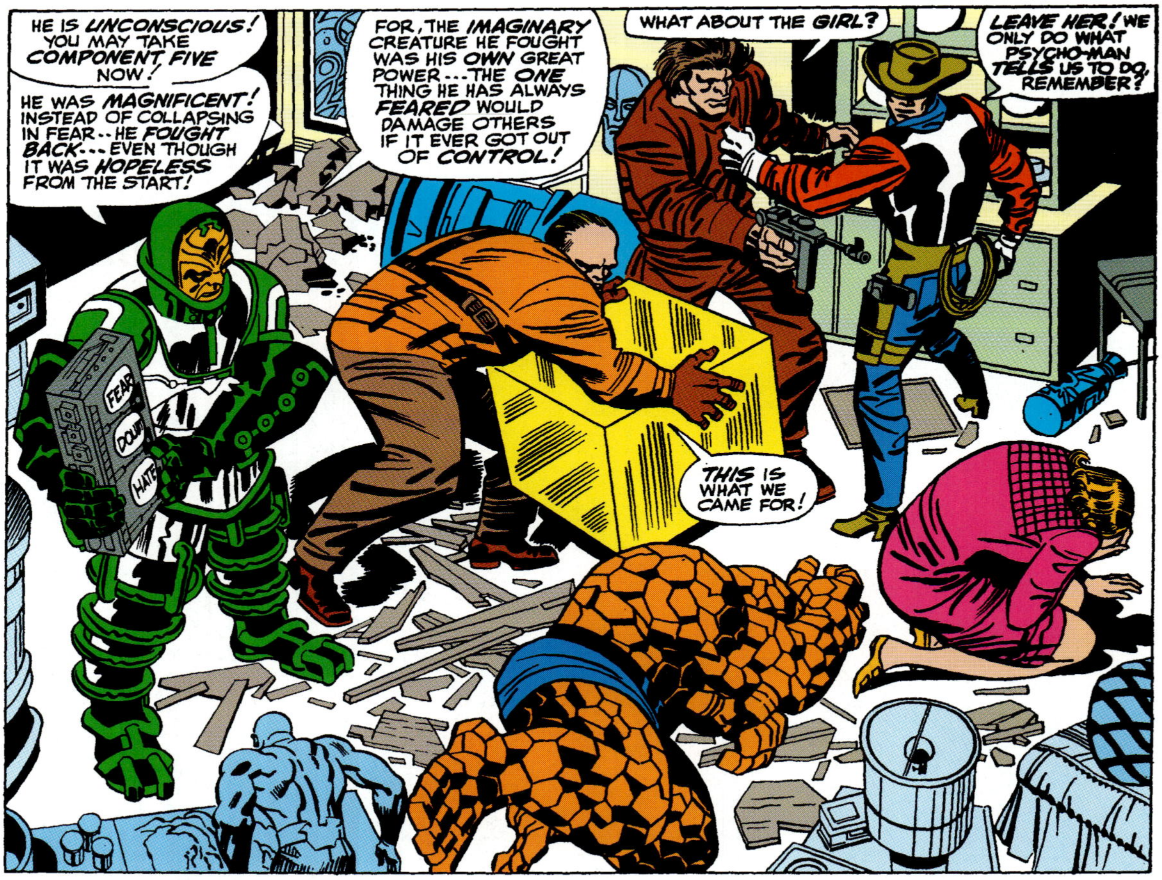
HE IS UNCONSCIOUS! YOU MAY TAKE COMPONENT FIVE NOW!
HE WAS MAGNIFICENT! INSTEAD OF COLLAPSING IN FEAR--HE FOUGHT BACK---EVEN THOUGH IT WAS HOPELESS FROM THE START!
FOR, THE IMAGINARY CREATURE HE FOUGHT WAS HIS OWN GREAT POWER---THE ONE THING HE HAS ALWAYS FEARED WOULD DAMAGE OTHERS IF IT EVER GOT OUT OF CONTROL!
WHAT ABOUT THE GIRL?
LEAVE HER! WE ONLY DO WHAT PSYCHO-MAN TELLS US TO DO, REMEMBER?
THIS IS WHAT WE CAME FOR!
FEAR
DOUBT
HATE

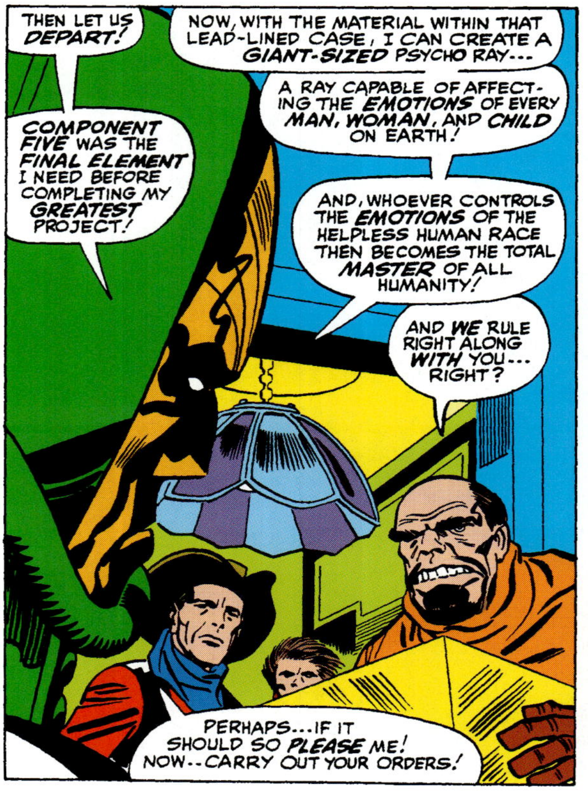
THEN LET US DEPART!
COMPONENT FIVE WAS THE FINAL ELEMENT I NEED BEFORE COMPLETING MY GREATEST PROJECT!
NOW, WITH THE MATERIAL WITHIN THAT LEAD-LINED CASE, I CAN CREATE A GIANT-SIZED PSYCHO RAY---
A RAY CAPABLE OF AFFECTING THE EMOTIONS OF EVERY MAN, WOMAN, AND CHILD ON EARTH!
AND, WHOEVER CONTROLS THE EMOTIONS OF THE HELPLESS HUMAN RACE THEN BECOMES THE TOTAL MASTER OF ALL HUMANITY!
AND WE RULE RIGHT ALONG WITH YOU--- RIGHT?
PERHAPS---IF IT SHOULD SO PLEASE ME! NOW--CARRY OUT YOUR ORDERS!

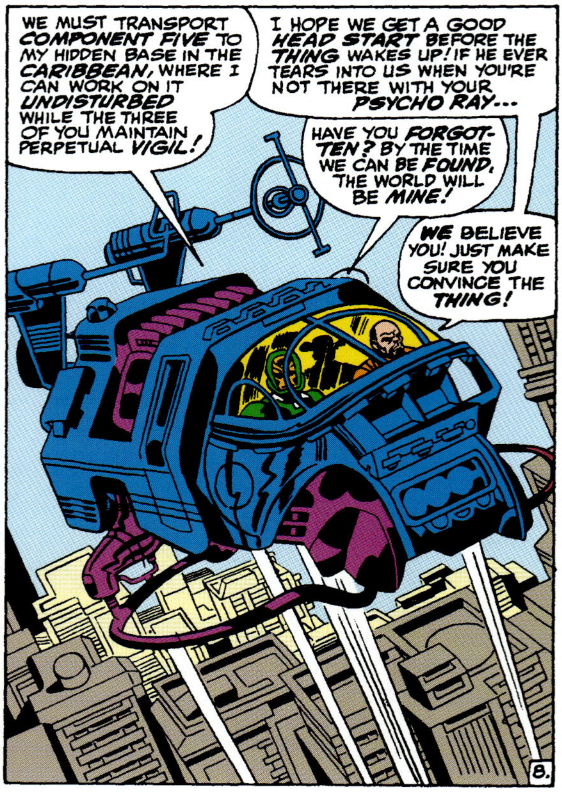
WE MUST TRANSPORT COMPONENT FIVE TO MY HIDDEN BASE IN THE CARIBBEAN, WHERE I CAN WORK ON IT UNDISTURBED WHILE THE THREE OF YOU MAINTAIN PERPETUAL VIGIL!
I HOPE WE GET A GOOD HEAD START BEFORE THE THING WAKES UP! IF HE EVER TEARS INTO US WHEN YOU'RE NOT THERE WITH YOUR PSYCHO RAY---
HAVE YOU FORGOTTEN? BY THE TIME WE CAN BE FOUND, THE WORLD WILL BE MINE!
WE BELIEVE YOU! JUST MAKE SURE YOU CONVINCE THE THING!
8.

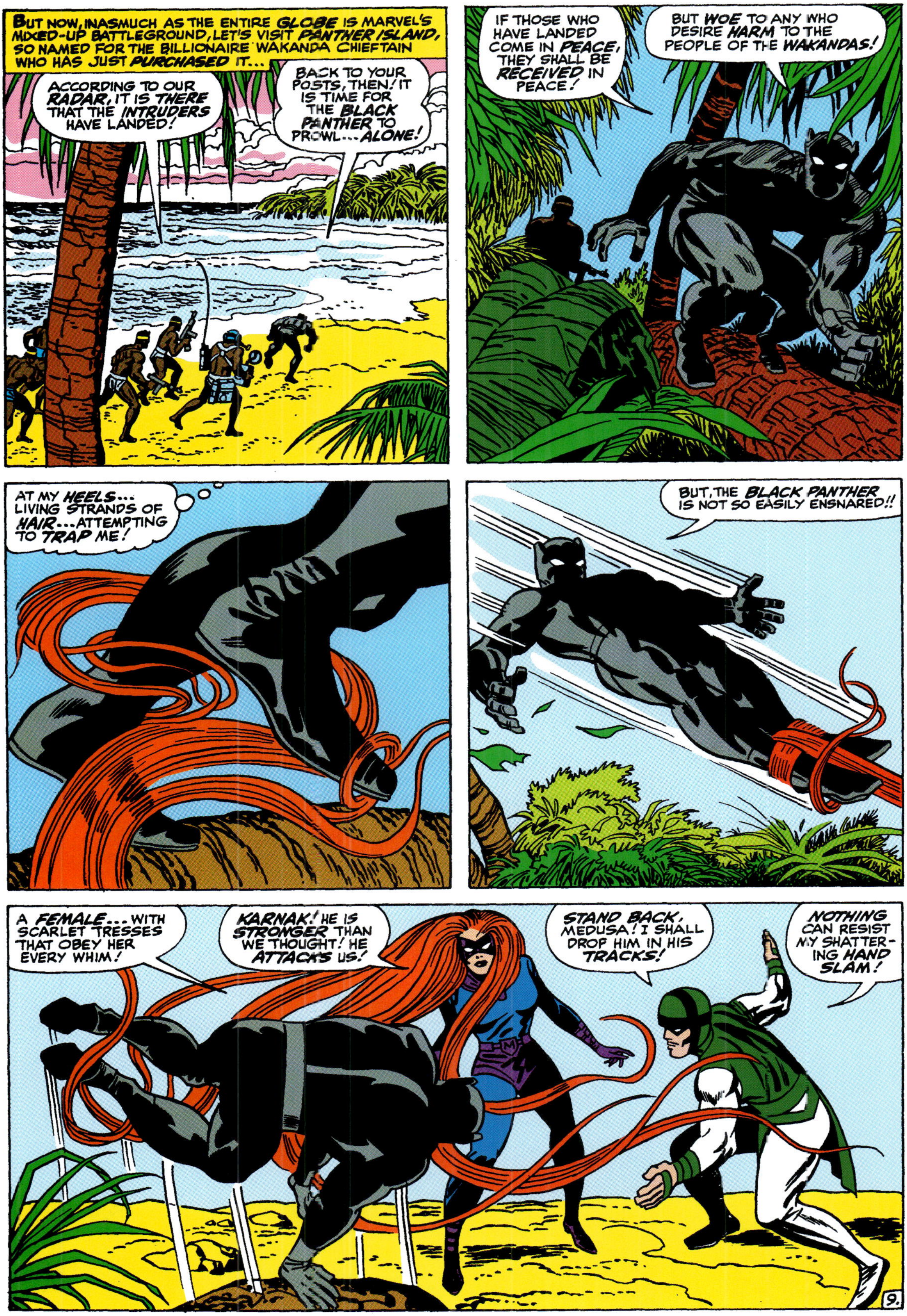
BUT NOW, INASMUCH AS THE ENTIRE GLOBE IS MARVEL'S MIXED-UP BATTLEGROUND, LET'S VISIT PANTHER ISLAND, SO NAMED FOR THE BILLIONAIRE WAKANDA CHIEFTAIN WHO HAS JUST PURCHASED IT...
ACCORDING TO OUR RADAR, IT IS THERE THAT THE INTRUDERS HAVE LANDED!
BACK TO YOUR POSTS, THEN! IT IS TIME FOR THE BLACK PANTHER TO PROWL... ALONE!
IF THOSE WHO HAVE LANDED COME IN PEACE, THEY SHALL BE RECEIVED IN PEACE!
BUT WOE TO ANY WHO DESIRE HARM TO THE PEOPLE OF THE WAKANDAS!
AT MY HEELS... LIVING STRANDS OF HAIR... ATTEMPTING TO TRAP ME!
BUT, THE BLACK PANTHER IS NOT SO EASILY ENSNARED!!
A FEMALE... WITH SCARLET TRESSES THAT OBEY HER EVERY WHIM!
KARNAK! HE IS STRONGER THAN WE THOUGHT! HE ATTACKS US!
STAND BACK, MEDUSA! I SHALL DROP HIM IN HIS TRACKS!
NOTHING CAN RESIST MY SHATTERING HAND SLAM!
9.

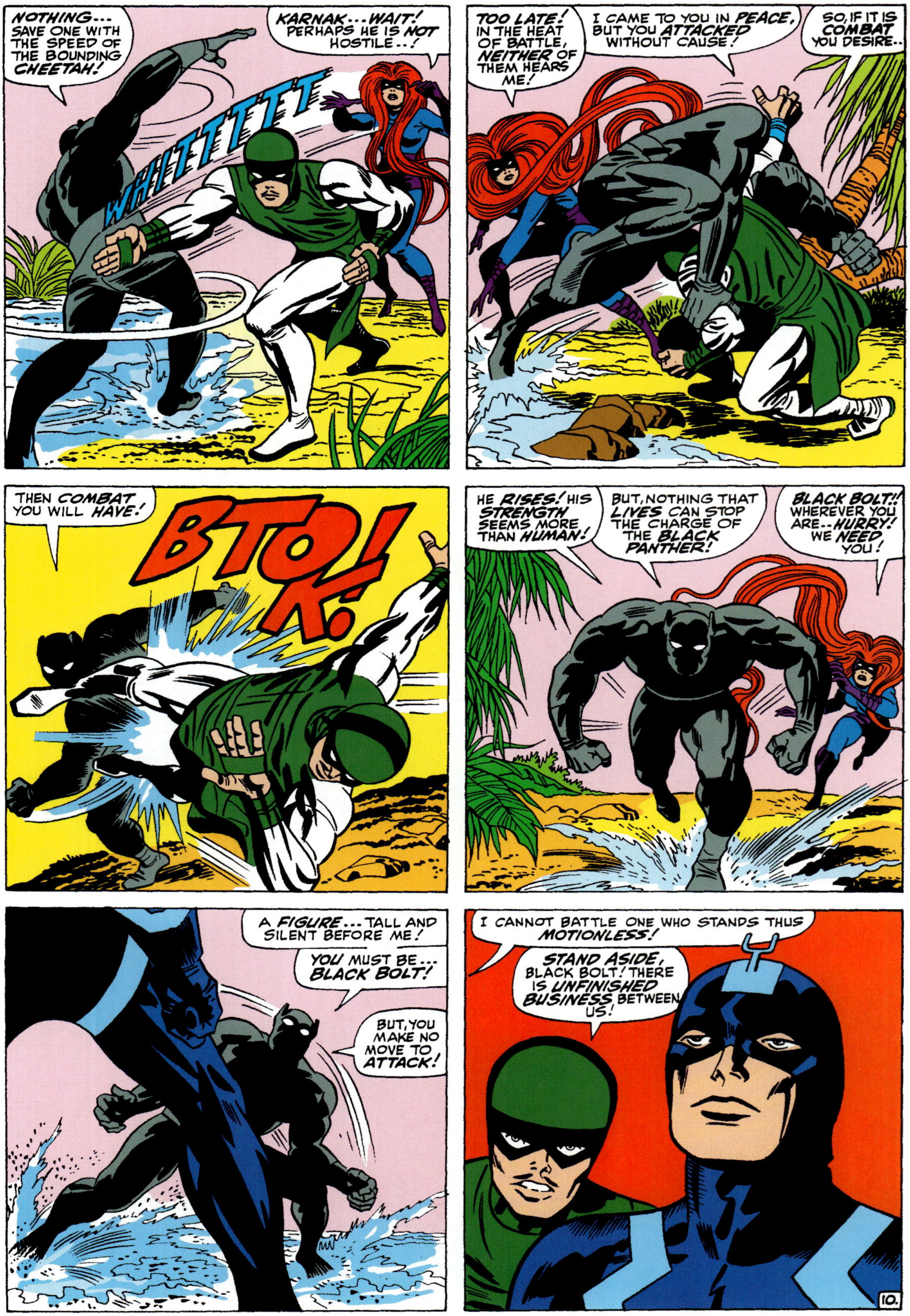
NOTHING... SAVE ONE WITH THE SPEED OF THE BOUNDING CHEETAH!
KARNAK...WAIT! PERHAPS HE IS NOT HOSTILE..!
WHIIIIIIT
TOO LATE! IN THE HEAT OF BATTLE, NEITHER OF THEM HEARS ME!
I CAME TO YOU IN PEACE, BUT YOU ATTACKED WITHOUT CAUSE!
SO, IF IT IS COMBAT YOU DESIRE...
THEN COMBAT YOU WILL HAVE!
BTOK!
HE RISES! HIS STRENGTH SEEMS MORE THAN HUMAN!
BUT, NOTHING THAT LIVES CAN STOP THE CHARGE OF THE BLACK PANTHER!
BLACK BOLT!! WHEREVER YOU ARE--HURRY! WE NEED YOU!
A FIGURE... TALL AND SILENT BEFORE ME!
YOU MUST BE... BLACK BOLT!
BUT, YOU MAKE NO MOVE TO ATTACK!
I CANNOT BATTLE ONE WHO STANDS THUS MOTIONLESS!
STAND ASIDE, BLACK BOLT! THERE IS UNFINISHED BUSINESS BETWEEN US!
10.

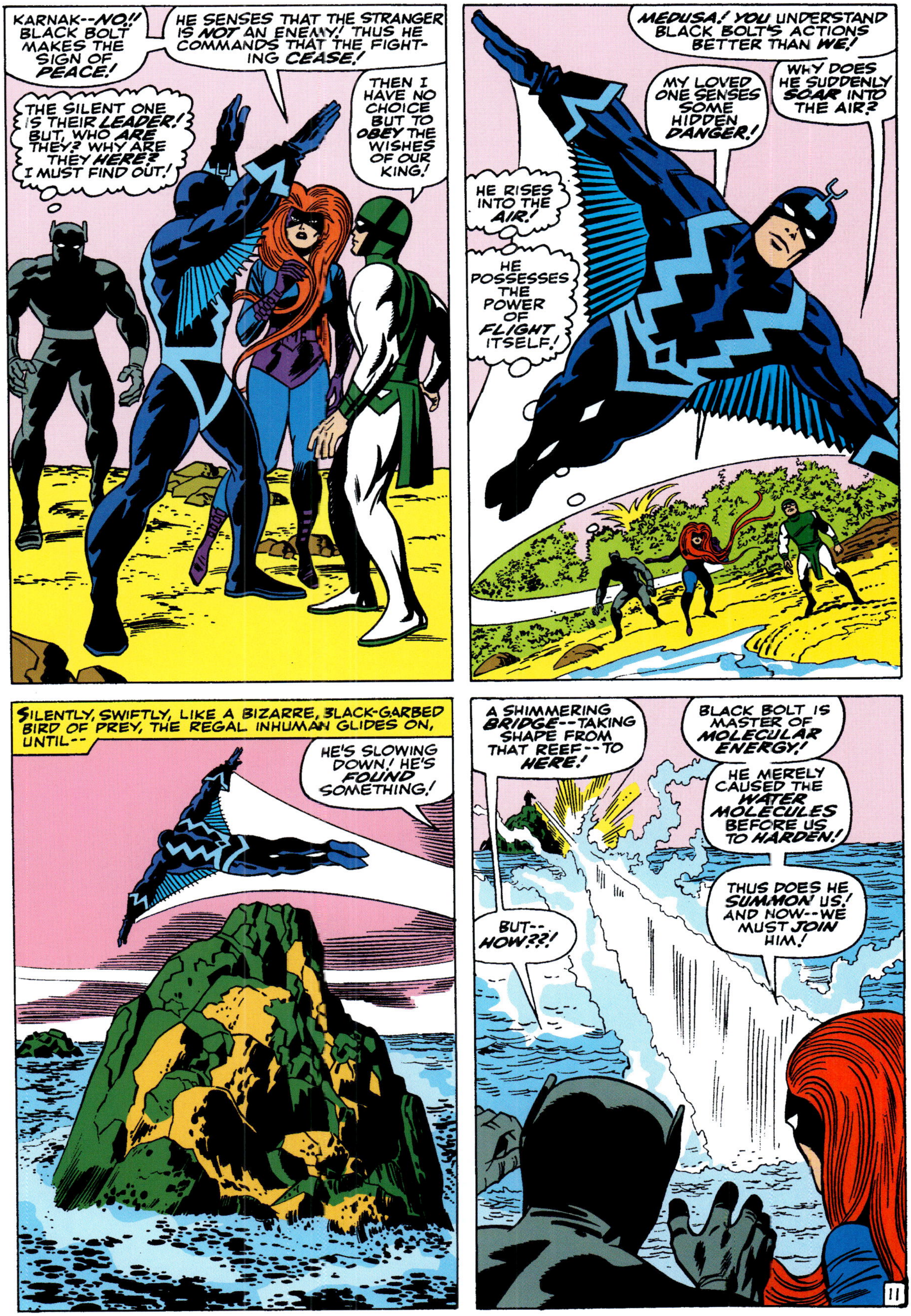

KARNAK--NO!! BLACK BOLT MAKES THE SIGN OF PEACE!
HE SENSES THAT THE STRANGER IS NOT AN ENEMY! THUS HE COMMANDS THAT THE FIGHTING CEASE!
THE SILENT ONE IS THEIR LEADER! BUT, WHO ARE THEY? WHY ARE THEY HERE? I MUST FIND OUT!
THEN I HAVE NO CHOICE BUT TO OBEY THE WISHES OF OUR KING!
MEDUSA! YOU UNDERSTAND BLACK BOLT'S ACTIONS BETTER THAN WE!
MY LOVED ONE SENSES SOME HIDDEN DANGER!
WHY DOES HE SUDDENLY SOAR INTO THE AIR?
HE RISES INTO THE AIR!
HE POSSESSES THE POWER OF FLIGHT ITSELF!
SILENTLY, SWIFTLY, LIKE A BIZARRE, BLACK-GARBED BIRD OF PREY, THE REGAL INHUMAN GLIDES ON, UNTIL--
HE'S SLOWING DOWN! HE'S FOUND SOMETHING!
A SHIMMERING BRIDGE--TAKING SHAPE FROM THAT REEF--TO HERE!
BLACK BOLT IS MASTER OF MOLECULAR ENERGY!
HE MERELY CAUSED THE WATER MOLECULES BEFORE US TO HARDEN!
BUT-- HOW??!
THUS DOES HE SUMMON US! AND NOW--WE MUST JOIN HIM!
11

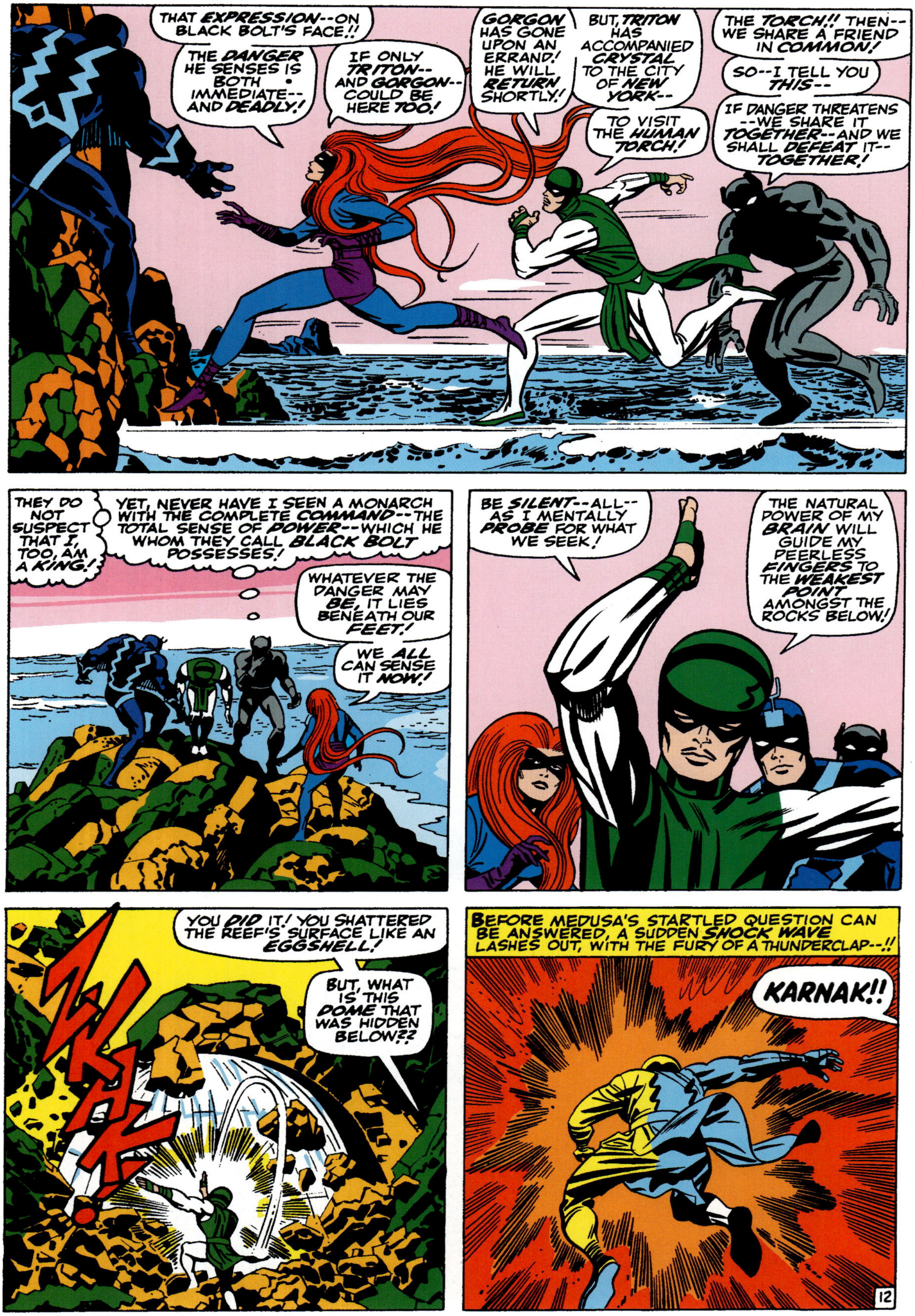
THAT EXPRESSION--ON BLACK BOLT'S FACE!!
THE DANGER HE SENSES IS BOTH IMMEDIATE--AND DEADLY!
IF ONLY TRITON--AND GORGON--COULD BE HERE TOO!
GORGON HAS GONE UPON AN ERRAND! HE WILL RETURN SHORTLY!
BUT, TRITON HAS ACCOMPANIED CRYSTAL TO THE CITY OF NEW YORK--
TO VISIT THE HUMAN TORCH!
THE TORCH!! THEN--WE SHARE A FRIEND IN COMMON!
SO--I TELL YOU THIS--
IF DANGER THREATENS--WE SHARE IT TOGETHER--AND WE SHALL DEFEAT IT--TOGETHER!
THEY DO NOT SUSPECT THAT I, TOO, AM A KING!
YET, NEVER HAVE I SEEN A MONARCH WITH THE COMPLETE COMMAND--THE TOTAL SENSE OF POWER--WHICH HE WHOM THEY CALL BLACK BOLT POSSESSES!
WHATEVER THE DANGER MAY BE, IT LIES BENEATH OUR FEET!
WE ALL CAN SENSE IT NOW!
BE SILENT--ALL--AS I MENTALLY PROBE FOR WHAT WE SEEK!
THE NATURAL POWER OF MY BRAIN WILL GUIDE MY PEERLESS FINGERS TO THE WEAKEST POINT AMONGST THE ROCKS BELOW!
YOU DID IT! YOU SHATTERED THE REEF'S SURFACE LIKE AN EGGSHELL!
BUT, WHAT IS THIS DOME THAT WAS HIDDEN BELOW??
WHAK
BEFORE MEDUSA'S STARTLED QUESTION CAN BE ANSWERED, A SUDDEN SHOCK WAVE LASHES OUT, WITH THE FURY OF A THUNDERCLAP--!!
KARNAK!!
12

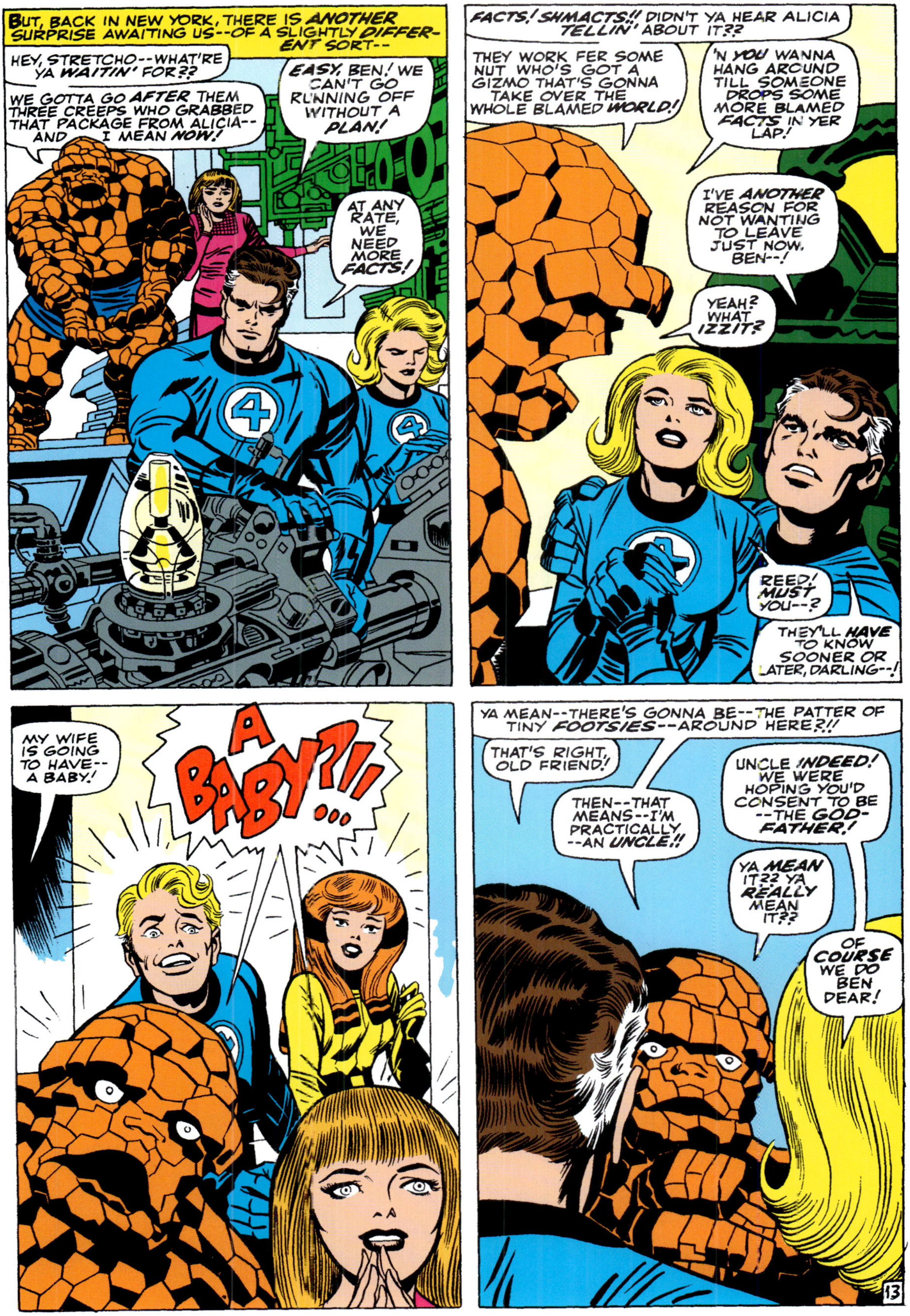
BUT, BACK IN NEW YORK, THERE IS ANOTHER SURPRISE AWAITING US--OF A SLIGHTLY DIFFERENT SORT--
HEY, STRETCHO--WHAT'RE YA WAITIN' FOR??
WE GOTTA GO AFTER THEM THREE CREEPS WHO GRABBED THAT PACKAGE FROM ALICIA--AND I MEAN NOW!
EASY, BEN! WE CAN'T GO RUNNING OFF WITHOUT A PLAN!
AT ANY RATE, WE NEED MORE FACTS!
FACTS! SHMACTS!! DIDN'T YA HEAR ALICIA TELLIN' ABOUT IT??
THEY WORK FER SOME NUT WHO'S GOT A GIZMO THAT'S GONNA TAKE OVER THE WHOLE BLAMED WORLD!
'N YOU WANNA HANG AROUND TILL SOMEONE DROPS SOME MORE BLAMED FACTS IN YER LAP!
I'VE ANOTHER REASON FOR NOT WANTING TO LEAVE JUST NOW, BEN--!
YEAH? WHAT IZZIT?
REED! MUST YOU--?
THEY'LL HAVE TO KNOW SOONER OR LATER, DARLING--!
MY WIFE IS GOING TO HAVE--A BABY!
A BABY?!!...
YA MEAN--THERE'S GONNA BE--THE PATTER OF TINY FOOTSIES--AROUND HERE?!!
THAT'S RIGHT, OLD FRIEND!
THEN--THAT MEANS--I'M PRACTICALLY--AN UNCLE!!
UNCLE INDEED! WE WERE HOPING YOU'D CONSENT TO BE--THE GOD-FATHER!
YA MEAN IT?? YA REALLY MEAN IT??
OF COURSE WE DO BEN DEAR!
13

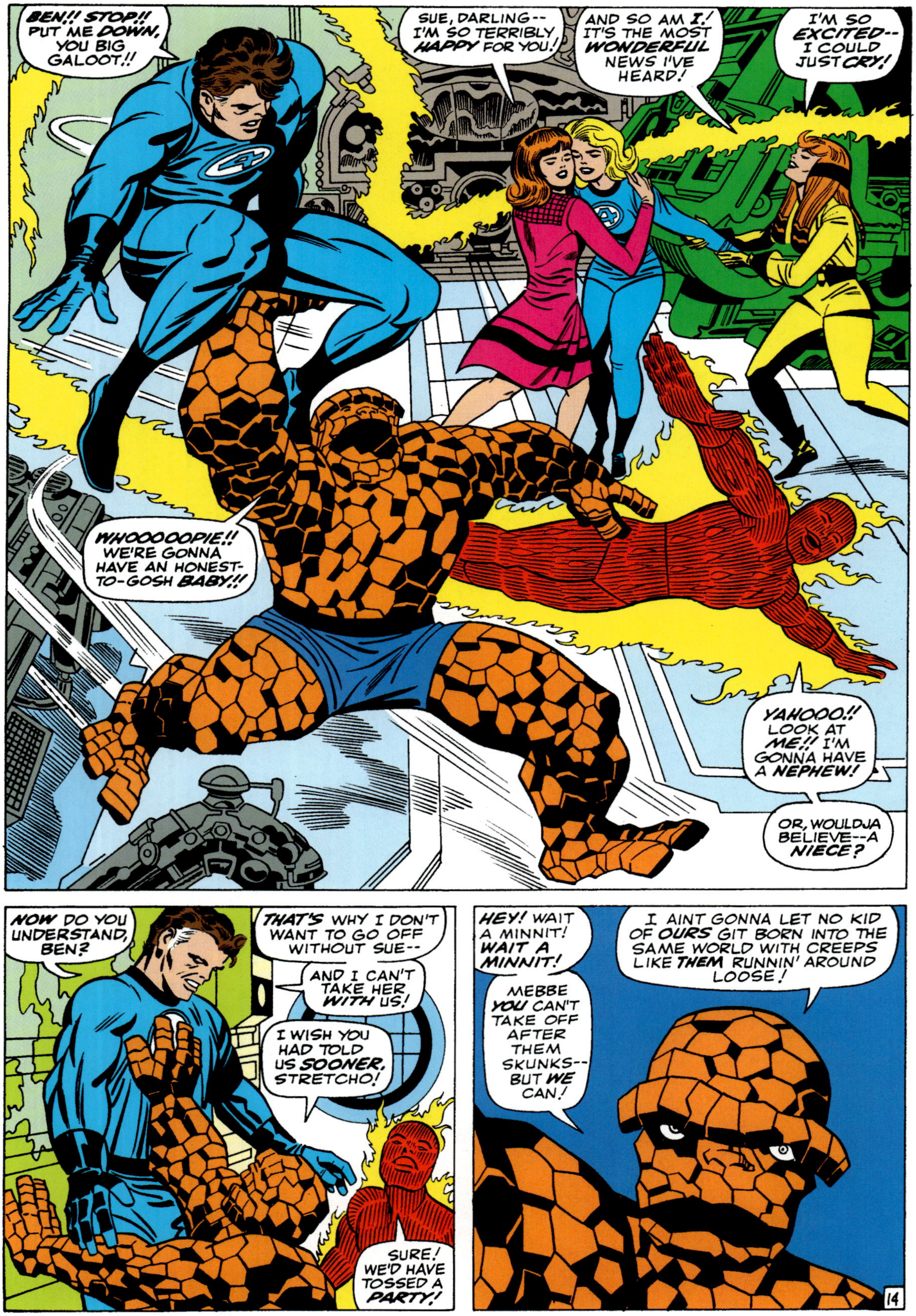
BEN!! STOP!! PUT ME DOWN, YOU BIG GALOOT!!
SUE, DARLING-- I'M SO TERRIBLY HAPPY FOR YOU!
AND SO AM I! IT'S THE MOST WONDERFUL NEWS I'VE HEARD!
I'M SO EXCITED-- I COULD JUST CRY!
WHOOOOOPIE!! WE'RE GONNA HAVE AN HONEST-TO-GOSH BABY!!
YAHOOO!! LOOK AT ME!! I'M GONNA HAVE A NEPHEW!
OR, WOULDJA BELIEVE--A NIECE?
NOW DO YOU UNDERSTAND, BEN?
THAT'S WHY I DON'T WANT TO GO OFF WITHOUT SUE--
AND I CAN'T TAKE HER WITH US!
I WISH YOU HAD TOLD US SOONER, STRETCHO!
SURE! WE'D HAVE TOSSED A PARTY!
HEY! WAIT A MINNIT! WAIT A MINNIT!
I AINT GONNA LET NO KID OF OURS GIT BORN INTO THE SAME WORLD WITH CREEPS LIKE THEM RUNNIN' AROUND LOOSE!
MEBBE YOU CAN'T TAKE OFF AFTER THEM SKUNKS-- BUT WE CAN!
14

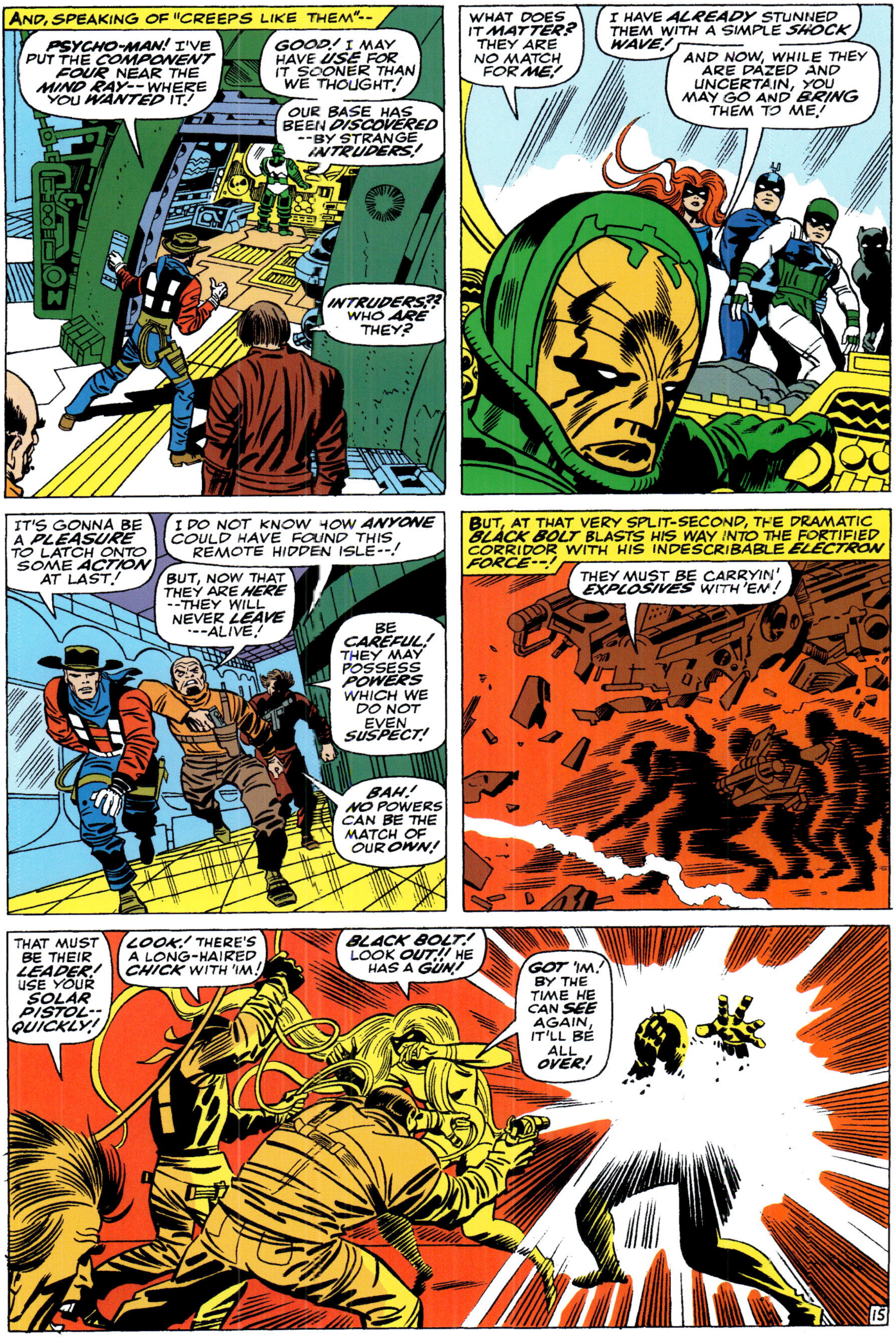
AND, SPEAKING OF "CREEPS LIKE THEM"--
PSYCHO-MAN! I'VE PUT THE COMPONENT FOUR NEAR THE MIND RAY--WHERE YOU WANTED IT!
GOOD! I MAY HAVE USE FOR IT SOONER THAN WE THOUGHT!
OUR BASE HAS BEEN DISCOVERED --BY STRANGE INTRUDERS!
INTRUDERS?? WHO ARE THEY?
WHAT DOES IT MATTER? THEY ARE NO MATCH FOR ME!
I HAVE ALREADY STUNNED THEM WITH A SIMPLE SHOCK WAVE!
AND NOW, WHILE THEY ARE DAZED AND UNCERTAIN, YOU MAY GO AND BRING THEM TO ME!
IT'S GONNA BE A PLEASURE TO LATCH ONTO SOME ACTION AT LAST!
I DO NOT KNOW HOW ANYONE COULD HAVE FOUND THIS REMOTE HIDDEN ISLE--!
BUT, NOW THAT THEY ARE HERE --THEY WILL NEVER LEAVE ---ALIVE!
BE CAREFUL! THEY MAY POSSESS POWERS WHICH WE DO NOT EVEN SUSPECT!
BAH! NO POWERS CAN BE THE MATCH OF OUR OWN!
BUT, AT THAT VERY SPLIT-SECOND, THE DRAMATIC BLACK BOLT BLASTS HIS WAY INTO THE FORTIFIED CORRIDOR WITH HIS INDESCRIBABLE ELECTRON FORCE--!
THEY MUST BE CARRYIN' EXPLOSIVES WITH 'EM!
THAT MUST BE THEIR LEADER! USE YOUR SOLAR PISTOL-- QUICKLY!
LOOK! THERE'S A LONG-HAIRED CHICK WITH 'IM!
BLACK BOLT! LOOK OUT!! HE HAS A GUN!
GOT 'IM! BY THE TIME HE CAN SEE AGAIN, IT'LL BE ALL OVER!
15

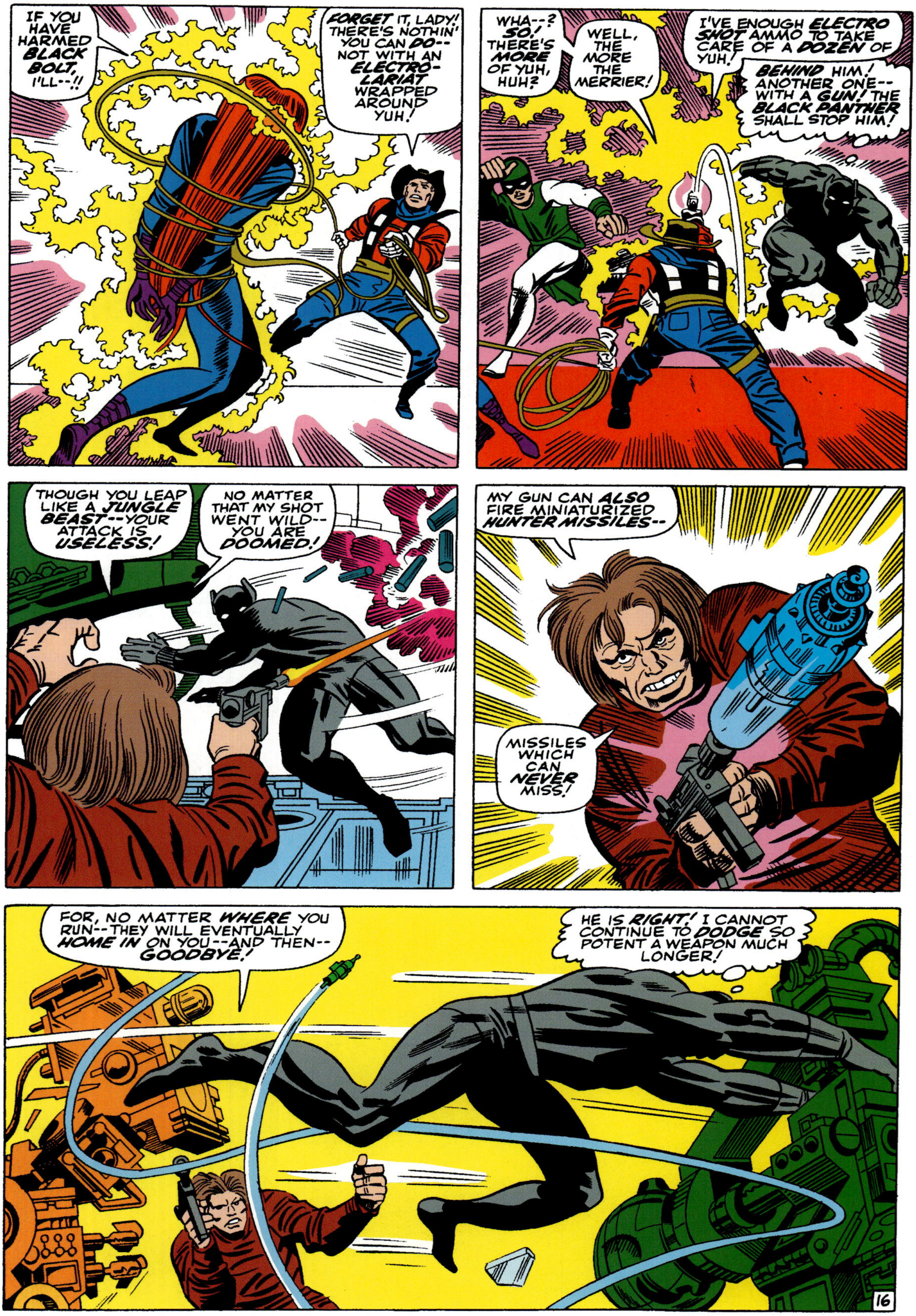
IF YOU HAVE HARMED BLACK BOLT, I'LL--!!
FORGET IT, LADY! THERE'S NOTHIN' YOU CAN DO-- NOT WITH AN ELECTRO-LARIAT WRAPPED AROUND YUH!
WHA--? SO! THERE'S MORE OF YUH, HUH?
WELL, THE MORE THE MERRIER!
I'VE ENOUGH ELECTRO SHOT AMMO TO TAKE CARE OF A DOZEN OF YUH!
BEHIND HIM! ANOTHER ONE-- WITH A GUN! THE BLACK PANTHER SHALL STOP HIM!
THOUGH YOU LEAP LIKE A JUNGLE BEAST--YOUR ATTACK IS USELESS!
NO MATTER THAT MY SHOT WENT WILD-- YOU ARE DOOMED!
MY GUN CAN ALSO FIRE MINIATURIZED HUNTER MISSILES--
MISSILES WHICH CAN NEVER MISS!
FOR, NO MATTER WHERE YOU RUN--THEY WILL EVENTUALLY HOME IN ON YOU--AND THEN-- GOODBYE!
HE IS RIGHT! I CANNOT CONTINUE TO DODGE SO POTENT A WEAPON MUCH LONGER!
16

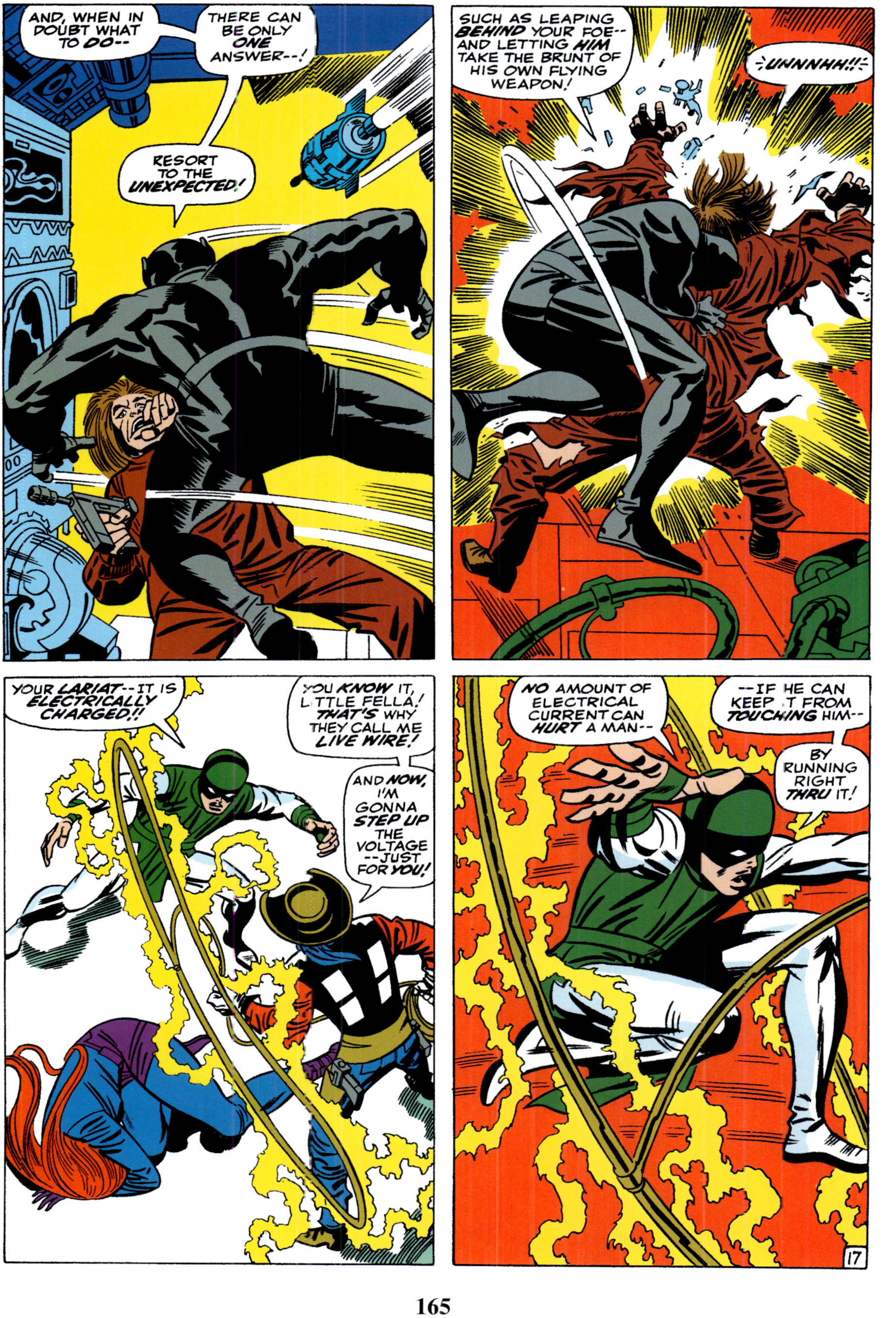
AND, WHEN IN DOUBT WHAT TO DO--
THERE CAN BE ONLY ONE ANSWER--!
RESORT TO THE UNEXPECTED!
SUCH AS LEAPING BEHIND YOUR FOE--AND LETTING HIM TAKE THE BRUNT OF HIS OWN FLYING WEAPON!
UNNNHH!!
YOUR LARIAT--IT IS ELECTRICALLY CHARGED!!
YOU KNOW IT, LITTLE FELLA! THAT'S WHY THEY CALL ME LIVE WIRE!
AND NOW, I'M GONNA STEP UP THE VOLTAGE --JUST FOR YOU!
NO AMOUNT OF ELECTRICAL CURRENT CAN HURT A MAN--
--IF HE CAN KEEP IT FROM TOUCHING HIM--
BY RUNNING RIGHT THRU IT!
17

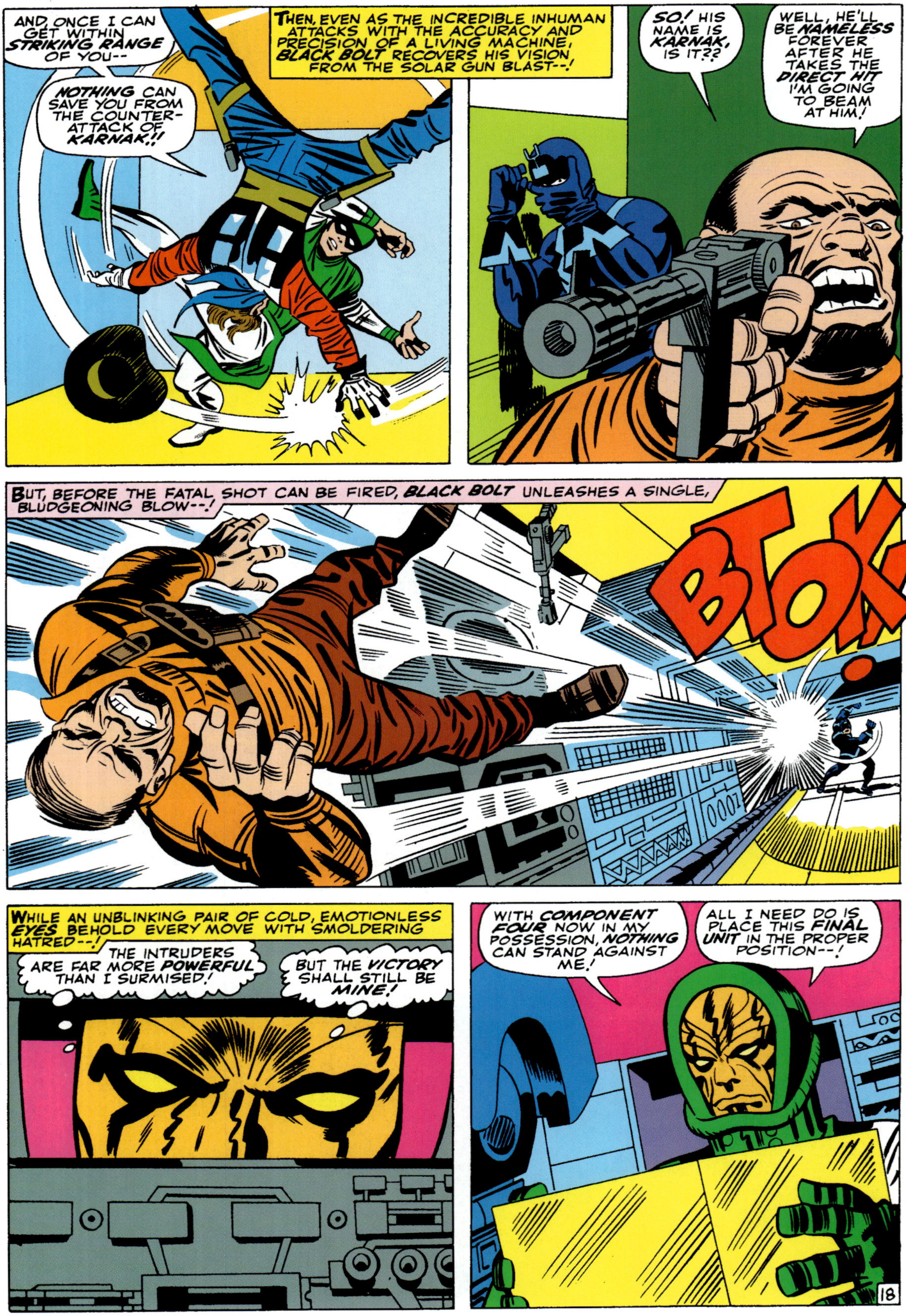
AND ONCE I CAN GET WITHIN STRIKING RANGE OF YOU--
NOTHING CAN SAVE YOU FROM THE COUNTER-ATTACK OF KARNAK!!
THEN, EVEN AS THE INCREDIBLE INHUMAN ATTACKS WITH THE ACCURACY AND PRECISION OF A LIVING MACHINE, BLACK BOLT RECOVERS HIS VISION FROM THE SOLAR GUN BLAST--!
SO! HIS NAME IS KARNAK, IS IT??
WELL, HE'LL BE NAMELESS FOREVER AFTER HE TAKES THE DIRECT HIT I'M GOING TO BEAM AT HIM!
BUT, BEFORE THE FATAL SHOT CAN BE FIRED, BLACK BOLT UNLEASHES A SINGLE, BLUDGEONING BLOW--!
BTOK!
WHILE AN UNBLINKING PAIR OF COLD, EMOTIONLESS EYES BEHOLD EVERY MOVE WITH SMOLDERING HATRED--!
THE INTRUDERS ARE FAR MORE POWERFUL THAN I SURMISED!
BUT THE VICTORY SHALL STILL BE MINE!
WITH COMPONENT FOUR NOW IN MY POSSESSION, NOTHING CAN STAND AGAINST ME!
ALL I NEED DO IS PLACE THIS FINAL UNIT IN THE PROPER POSITION--!
18

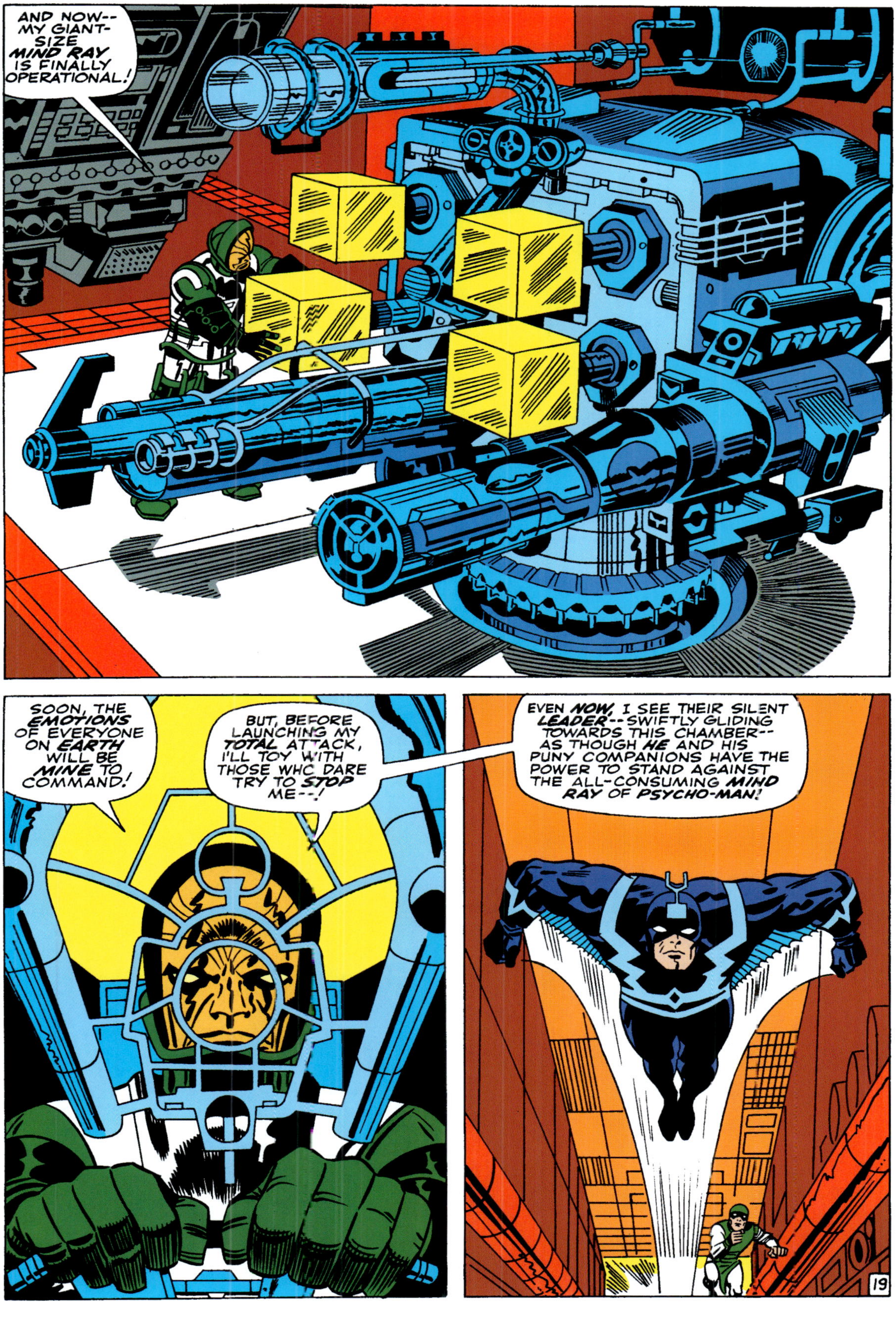

AND NOW-- MY GIANT-SIZE MIND RAY IS FINALLY OPERATIONAL!
SOON, THE EMOTIONS OF EVERYONE ON EARTH WILL BE MINE TO COMMAND!
BUT, BEFORE LAUNCHING MY TOTAL ATTACK, I'LL TOY WITH THOSE WHC DARE TRY TO STOP ME--!
EVEN NOW, I SEE THEIR SILENT LEADER--SWIFTLY GLIDING TOWARDS THIS CHAMBER-- AS THOUGH HE AND HIS PUNY COMPANIONS HAVE THE POWER TO STAND AGAINST THE ALL-CONSUMING MIND RAY OF PSYCHO-MAN!
19

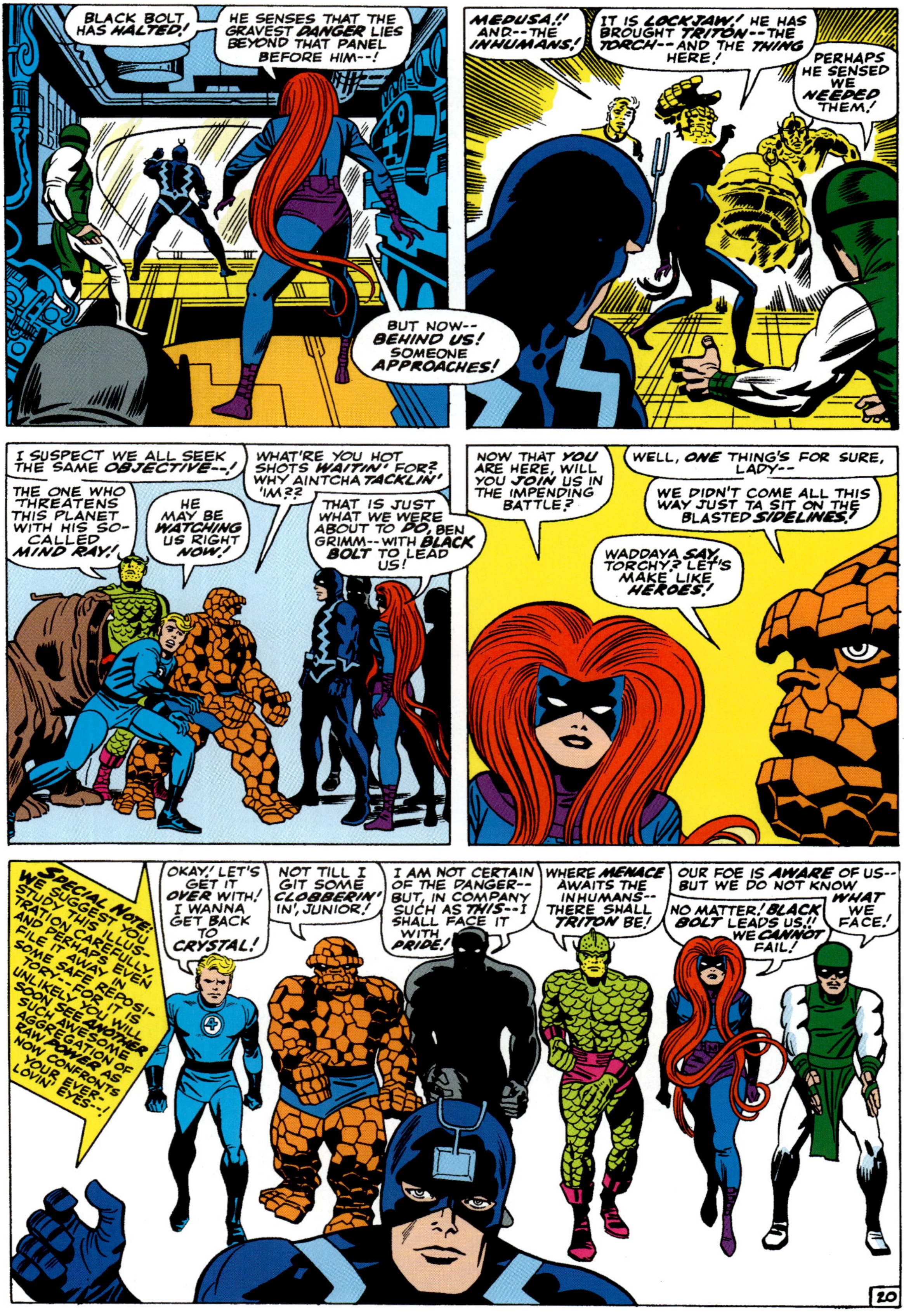
BLACK BOLT HAS HALTED!
HE SENSES THAT THE GRAVEST DANGER LIES BEYOND THAT PANEL BEFORE HIM--!
BUT NOW-- BEHIND US! SOMEONE APPROACHES!
MEDUSA!! AND--THE INHUMANS!
IT IS LOCKJAW! HE HAS BROUGHT TRITON--THE TORCH--AND THE THING HERE!
PERHAPS HE SENSED WE NEEDED THEM!
I SUSPECT WE ALL SEEK THE SAME OBJECTIVE--!
THE ONE WHO THREATENS THIS PLANET WITH HIS SO-CALLED MIND RAY!
WHAT'RE YOU HOT SHOTS WAITIN' FOR? WHY AINTCHA TACKLIN' 'IM??
HE MAY BE WATCHING US RIGHT NOW!
THAT IS JUST WHAT WE WERE ABOUT TO DO, BEN GRIMM--WITH BLACK BOLT TO LEAD US!
NOW THAT YOU ARE HERE, WILL YOU JOIN US IN THE IMPENDING BATTLE?
WELL, ONE THING'S FOR SURE, LADY--
WE DIDN'T COME ALL THIS WAY JUST TA SIT ON THE BLASTED SIDELINES!
WADDAYA SAY, TORCHY? LET'S MAKE LIKE HEROES!
SPECIAL NOTE: WE SUGGEST YOU STUDY THIS ILLUSTRATION CAREFULLY, AND PERHAPS EVEN FILE IT AWAY IN SOME SAFE REPOSITORY--FOR IT IS UNLIKELY YOU WILL SOON SEE ANOTHER SUCH AWESOME AGGREGATION OF RAW POWER AS NOW CONFRONTS YOUR EVER-LOVIN' EYES--!
OKAY! LET'S GET IT OVER WITH! I WANNA GET BACK TO CRYSTAL!
NOT TILL I GIT SOME CLOBBERIN' IN', JUNIOR!
I AM NOT CERTAIN OF THE DANGER--BUT, IN COMPANY SUCH AS THIS--I SHALL FACE IT WITH PRIDE!
WHERE MENACE AWAITS THE INHUMANS--THERE SHALL TRITON BE!
OUR FOE IS AWARE OF US--BUT WE DO NOT KNOW WHAT WE FACE!
NO MATTER! BLACK BOLT LEADS US!! WE CANNOT FAIL!
20

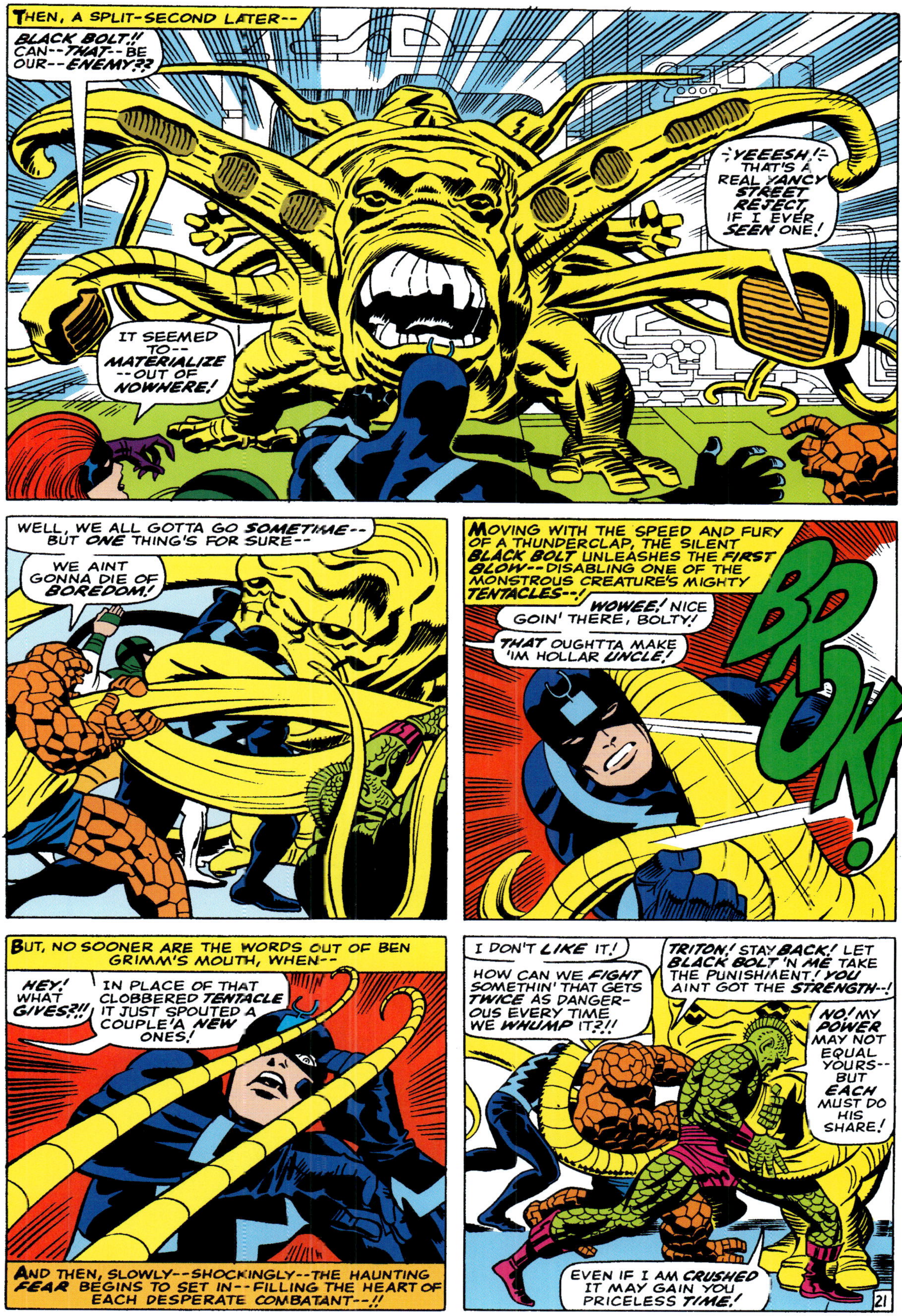
THEN, A SPLIT-SECOND LATER--
BLACK BOLT!! CAN--THAT--BE OUR--ENEMY??
YEEESH! THAT'S A REAL YANCY STREET REJECT, IF I EVER SEEN ONE!
IT SEEMED TO--MATERIALIZE--OUT OF NOWHERE!
WELL, WE ALL GOTTA GO SOMETIME--BUT ONE THING'S FOR SURE--
WE AINT GONNA DIE OF BOREDOM!
MOVING WITH THE SPEED AND FURY OF A THUNDERCLAP, THE SILENT BLACK BOLT UNLEASHES THE FIRST BLOW--DISABLING ONE OF THE MONSTROUS CREATURE'S MIGHTY TENTACLES--!
WOWEE! NICE GOIN' THERE, BOLTY!
THAT OUGHTTA MAKE 'IM HOLLAR UNCLE!
BROOK!
BUT, NO SOONER ARE THE WORDS OUT OF BEN GRIMM'S MOUTH, WHEN--
HEY! WHAT GIVES?!!
IN PLACE OF THAT CLOBBERED TENTACLE IT JUST SPOUTED A COUPLE'A NEW ONES!
AND THEN, SLOWLY--SHOCKINGLY--THE HAUNTING FEAR BEGINS TO SET IN--FILLING THE HEART OF EACH DESPERATE COMBATANT--!!
I DON'T LIKE IT!
HOW CAN WE FIGHT SOMETHIN' THAT GETS TWICE AS DANGER-OUS EVERY TIME WE WHUMP IT?!!
TRITON! STAY BACK! LET BLACK BOLT 'N ME TAKE THE PUNISHMENT! YOU AINT GOT THE STRENGTH--!
NO! MY POWER MAY NOT EQUAL YOURS--BUT EACH MUST DO HIS SHARE!
EVEN IF I AM CRUSHED IT MAY GAIN YOU PRICELESS TIME!
21

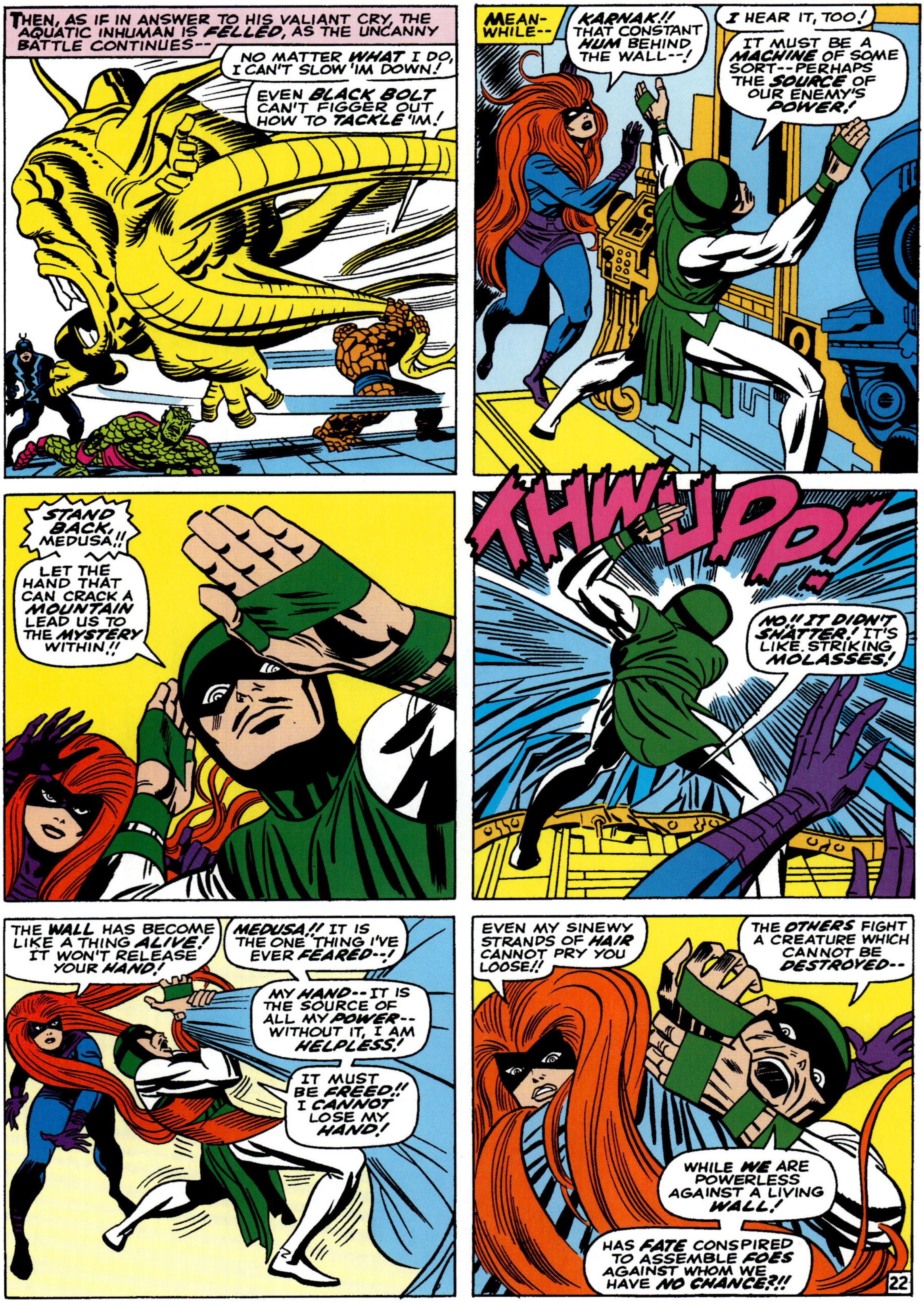
THEN, AS IF IN ANSWER TO HIS VALIANT CRY, THE AQUATIC INHUMAN IS FELLED, AS THE UNCANNY BATTLE CONTINUES--
NO MATTER WHAT I DO, I CAN'T SLOW 'IM DOWN!
EVEN BLACK BOLT CAN'T FIGGER OUT HOW TO TACKLE 'IM!
MEAN-WHILE--
KARNAK!! THAT CONSTANT HUM BEHIND THE WALL--!
I HEAR IT, TOO!
IT MUST BE A MACHINE OF SOME SORT--PERHAPS THE SOURCE OF OUR ENEMY'S POWER!
STAND BACK, MEDUSA!!
LET THE HAND THAT CAN CRACK A MOUNTAIN LEAD US TO THE MYSTERY WITHIN!!
THWUPP!
NO!! IT DIDN'T SHATTER! IT'S LIKE STRIKING MOLASSES!
THE WALL HAS BECOME LIKE A THING ALIVE! IT WON'T RELEASE YOUR HAND!
MEDUSA!! IT IS THE ONE THING I'VE EVER FEARED--!
MY HAND--IT IS THE SOURCE OF ALL MY POWER--WITHOUT IT, I AM HELPLESS!
IT MUST BE FREED!! I CANNOT LOSE MY HAND!
EVEN MY SINEWY STRANDS OF HAIR CANNOT PRY YOU LOOSE!!
THE OTHERS FIGHT A CREATURE WHICH CANNOT BE DESTROYED--
WHILE WE ARE POWERLESS AGAINST A LIVING WALL!
HAS FATE CONSPIRED TO ASSEMBLE FOES AGAINST WHOM WE HAVE NO CHANCE?!!
22

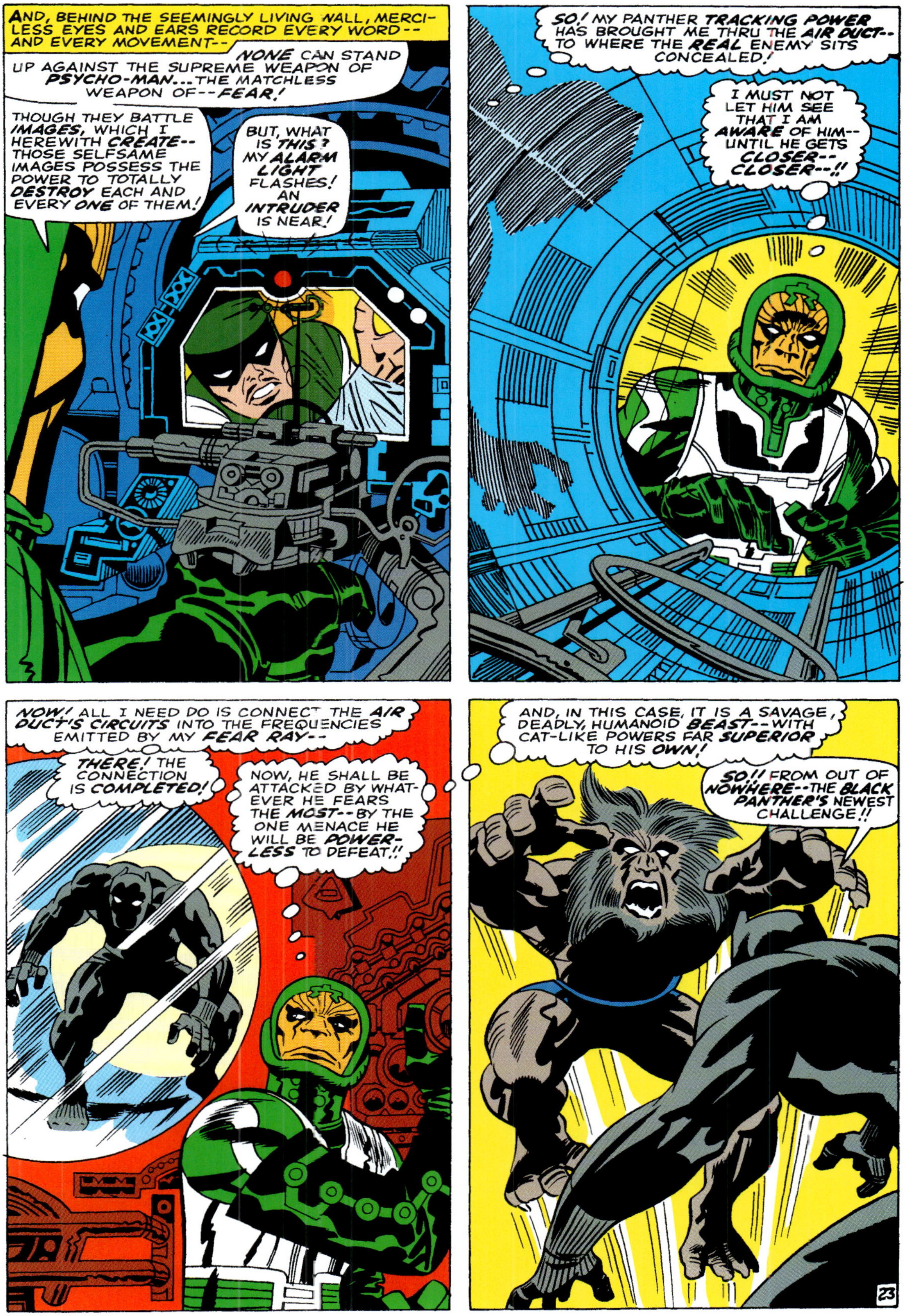
AND, BEHIND THE SEEMINGLY LIVING WALL, MERCILESS EYES AND EARS RECORD EVERY WORD--AND EVERY MOVEMENT--
NONE CAN STAND UP AGAINST THE SUPREME WEAPON OF PSYCHO-MAN...THE MATCHLESS WEAPON OF--FEAR!
THOUGH THEY BATTLE IMAGES, WHICH I HEREWITH CREATE--THOSE SELFSAME IMAGES POSSESS THE POWER TO TOTALLY DESTROY EACH AND EVERY ONE OF THEM!
BUT, WHAT IS THIS? MY ALARM LIGHT FLASHES! AN INTRUDER IS NEAR!
SO! MY PANTHER TRACKING POWER HAS BROUGHT ME THRU THE AIR DUCT--TO WHERE THE REAL ENEMY SITS CONCEALED!
I MUST NOT LET HIM SEE THAT I AM AWARE OF HIM--UNTIL HE GETS CLOSER--CLOSER--!!
NOW! ALL I NEED DO IS CONNECT THE AIR DUCT'S CIRCUITS INTO THE FREQUENCIES EMITTED BY MY FEAR RAY--
THERE! THE CONNECTION IS COMPLETED!
NOW, HE SHALL BE ATTACKED BY WHATEVER HE FEARS THE MOST--BY THE ONE MENACE HE WILL BE POWERLESS TO DEFEAT!!
AND, IN THIS CASE, IT IS A SAVAGE, DEADLY, HUMANOID BEAST--WITH CAT-LIKE POWERS FAR SUPERIOR TO HIS OWN!
SO!! FROM OUT OF NOWHERE--THE BLACK PANTHER'S NEWEST CHALLENGE!!
23

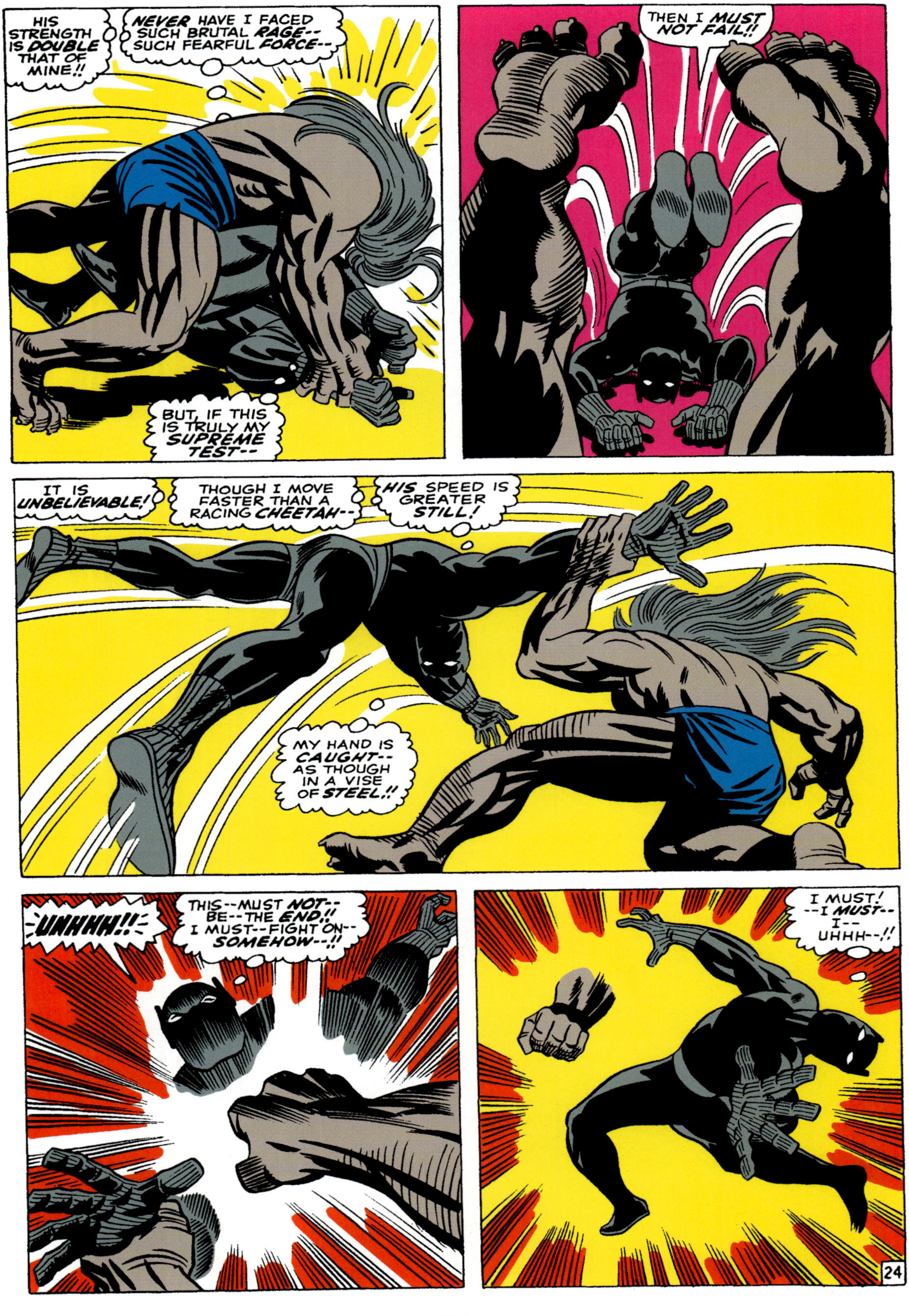

HIS STRENGTH IS DOUBLE THAT OF MINE!!
NEVER HAVE I FACED SUCH BRUTAL RAGE-- SUCH FEARFUL FORCE--
BUT, IF THIS IS TRULY MY SUPREME TEST--
THEN I MUST NOT FAIL!!
IT IS UNBELIEVABLE!
THOUGH I MOVE FASTER THAN A RACING CHEETAH--
HIS SPEED IS GREATER STILL!
MY HAND IS CAUGHT-- AS THOUGH IN A VISE OF STEEL!!
UNHHH!!
THIS--MUST NOT-- BE--THE END!! I MUST--FIGHT ON-- SOMEHOW--!!
I MUST! --I MUST-- I-- UHHH--!!
24

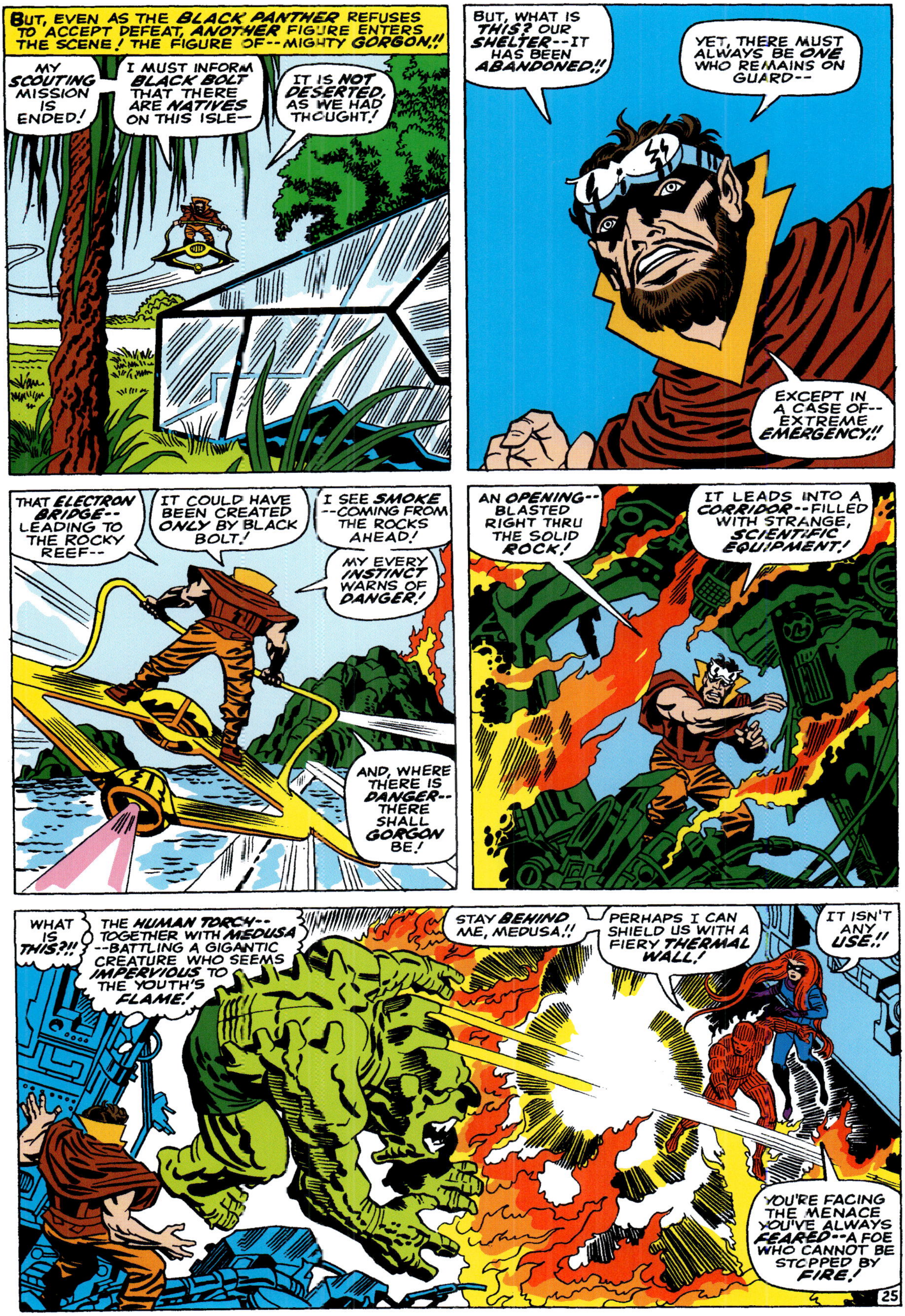
BUT, EVEN AS THE BLACK PANTHER REFUSES TO ACCEPT DEFEAT, ANOTHER FIGURE ENTERS THE SCENE! THE FIGURE OF--MIGHTY GORGON!!
MY SCOUTING MISSION IS ENDED!
I MUST INFORM BLACK BOLT THAT THERE ARE NATIVES ON THIS ISLE--
IT IS NOT DESERTED, AS WE HAD THOUGHT!
BUT, WHAT IS THIS? OUR SHELTER--IT HAS BEEN ABANDONED!!
YET, THERE MUST ALWAYS BE ONE WHO REMAINS ON GUARD--
EXCEPT IN A CASE OF--EXTREME EMERGENCY!!
THAT ELECTRON BRIDGE--LEADING TO THE ROCKY REEF--
IT COULD HAVE BEEN CREATED ONLY BY BLACK BOLT!
I SEE SMOKE --COMING FROM THE ROCKS AHEAD!
MY EVERY INSTINCT WARNS OF DANGER!
AND, WHERE THERE IS DANGER--THERE SHALL GORGON BE!
AN OPENING--BLASTED RIGHT THRU THE SOLID ROCK!
IT LEADS INTO A CORRIDOR--FILLED WITH STRANGE, SCIENTIFIC EQUIPMENT!
WHAT IS THIS?!!
THE HUMAN TORCH--TOGETHER WITH MEDUSA --BATTLING A GIGANTIC CREATURE WHO SEEMS IMPERVIOUS TO THE YOUTH'S FLAME!
STAY BEHIND ME, MEDUSA!!
PERHAPS I CAN SHIELD US WITH A FIERY THERMAL WALL!
IT ISN'T ANY USE!!
YOU'RE FACING THE MENACE YOU'VE ALWAYS FEARED--A FOE WHO CANNOT BE STOPPED BY FIRE!
25

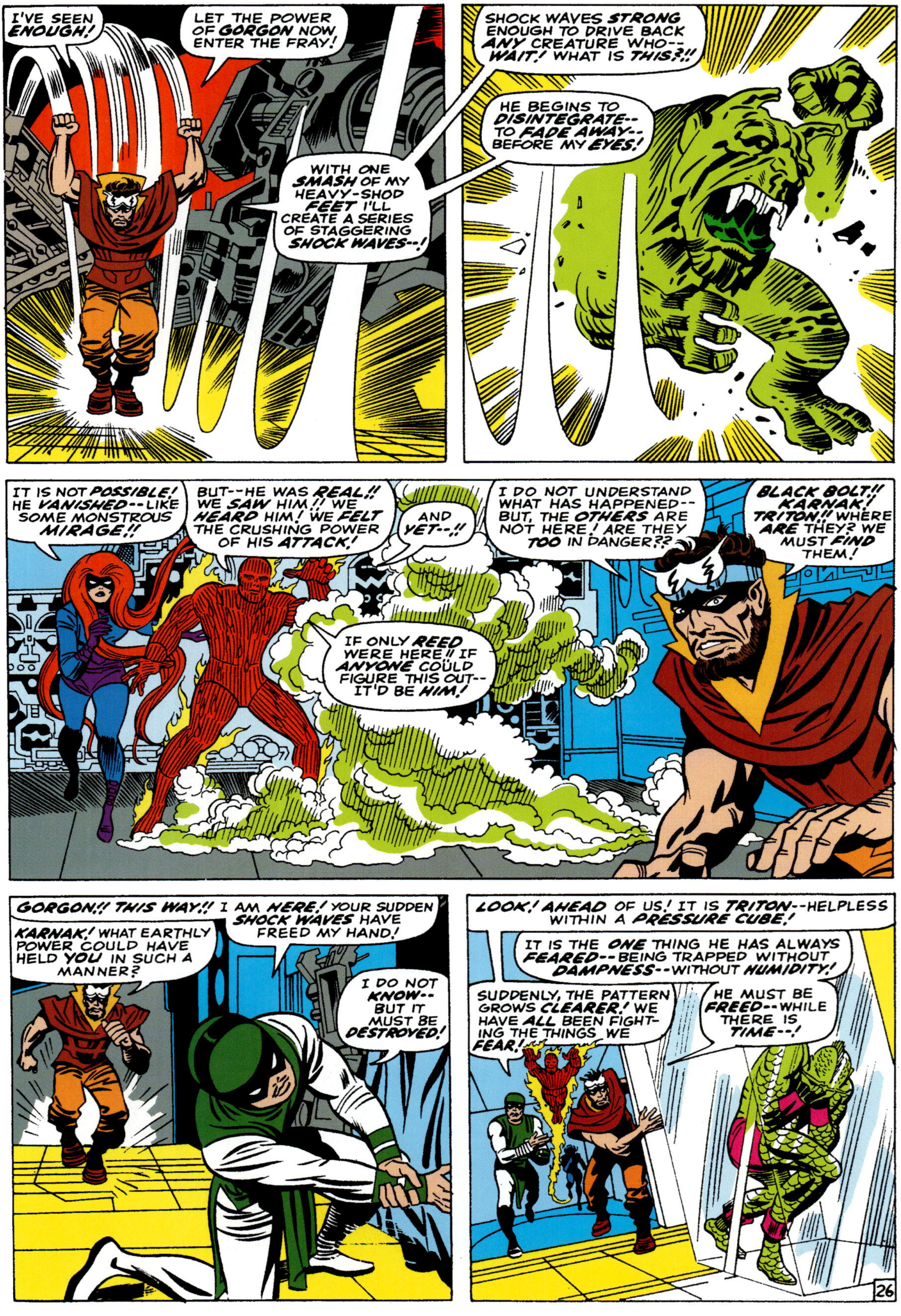
I'VE SEEN ENOUGH!
LET THE POWER OF GORGON NOW ENTER THE FRAY!
WITH ONE SMASH OF MY HEAVY-SHOD FEET I'LL CREATE A SERIES OF STAGGERING SHOCK WAVES--!
SHOCK WAVES STRONG ENOUGH TO DRIVE BACK ANY CREATURE WHO-- WAIT! WHAT IS THIS?!!
HE BEGINS TO DISINTEGRATE-- TO FADE AWAY-- BEFORE MY EYES!
IT IS NOT POSSIBLE! HE VANISHED--LIKE SOME MONSTROUS MIRAGE!!
BUT--HE WAS REAL!! WE SAW HIM!! WE HEARD HIM! WE FELT THE CRUSHING POWER OF HIS ATTACK!
AND YET--!!
IF ONLY REED WERE HERE!! IF ANYONE COULD FIGURE THIS OUT-- IT'D BE HIM!
I DO NOT UNDERSTAND WHAT HAS HAPPENED-- BUT, THE OTHERS ARE NOT HERE! ARE THEY TOO IN DANGER??
BLACK BOLT!! KARNAK! TRITON!! WHERE ARE THEY? WE MUST FIND THEM!
GORGON!! THIS WAY!!
KARNAK! WHAT EARTHLY POWER COULD HAVE HELD YOU IN SUCH A MANNER?
I AM HERE! YOUR SUDDEN SHOCK WAVES HAVE FREED MY HAND!
I DO NOT KNOW-- BUT IT MUST BE DESTROYED!
LOOK! AHEAD OF US! IT IS TRITON--HELPLESS WITHIN A PRESSURE CUBE!
IT IS THE ONE THING HE HAS ALWAYS FEARED--BEING TRAPPED WITHOUT DAMPNESS--WITHOUT HUMIDITY!
SUDDENLY, THE PATTERN GROWS CLEARER! WE HAVE ALL BEEN FIGHTING THE THINGS WE FEAR!
HE MUST BE FREED--WHILE THERE IS TIME--!
26

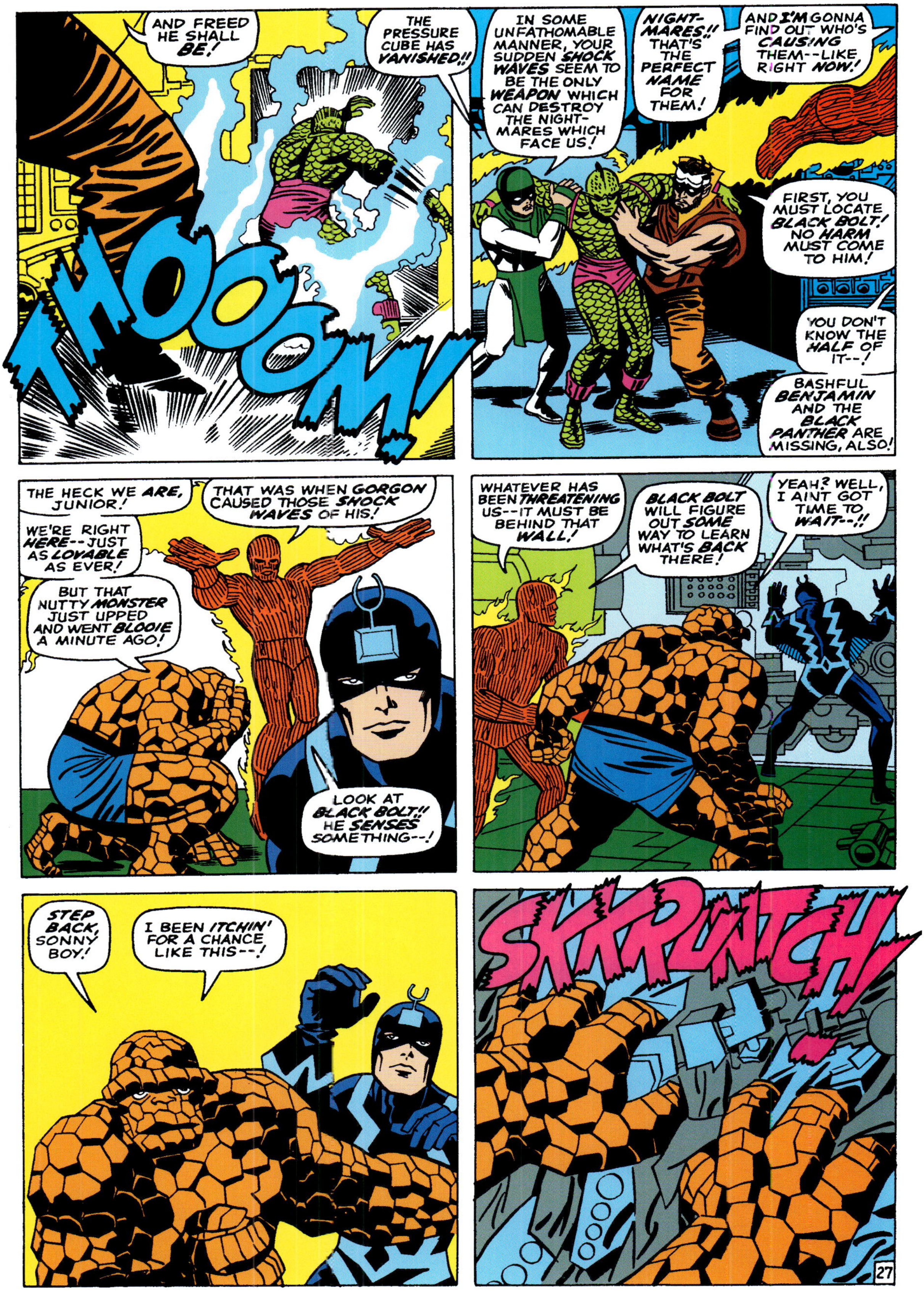

AND FREED HE SHALL BE!
THE PRESSURE CUBE HAS VANISHED!!
THOOOM!
IN SOME UNFATHOMABLE MANNER, YOUR SUDDEN SHOCK WAVES SEEM TO BE THE ONLY WEAPON WHICH CAN DESTROY THE NIGHT-MARES WHICH FACE US!
NIGHT-MARES!! THAT'S THE PERFECT NAME FOR THEM!
AND I'M GONNA FIND OUT WHO'S CAUSING THEM--LIKE RIGHT NOW!
FIRST, YOU MUST LOCATE BLACK BOLT! NO HARM MUST COME TO HIM!
YOU DON'T KNOW THE HALF OF IT--!
BASHFUL BENJAMIN AND THE BLACK PANTHER ARE MISSING, ALSO!
THE HECK WE ARE, JUNIOR!
WE'RE RIGHT HERE--JUST AS LOVABLE AS EVER!
BUT THAT NUTTY MONSTER JUST UPPED AND WENT BLOOIE A MINUTE AGO!
THAT WAS WHEN GORGON CAUSED THOSE SHOCK WAVES OF HIS!
LOOK AT BLACK BOLT!! HE SENSES SOMETHING--!
WHATEVER HAS BEEN THREATENING US--IT MUST BE BEHIND THAT WALL!
BLACK BOLT WILL FIGURE OUT SOME WAY TO LEARN WHAT'S BACK THERE!
YEAH? WELL, I AINT GOT TIME TO WAIT--!!
STEP BACK, SONNY BOY!
I BEEN ITCHIN' FOR A CHANCE LIKE THIS--!
SKKRUNTCH!
27

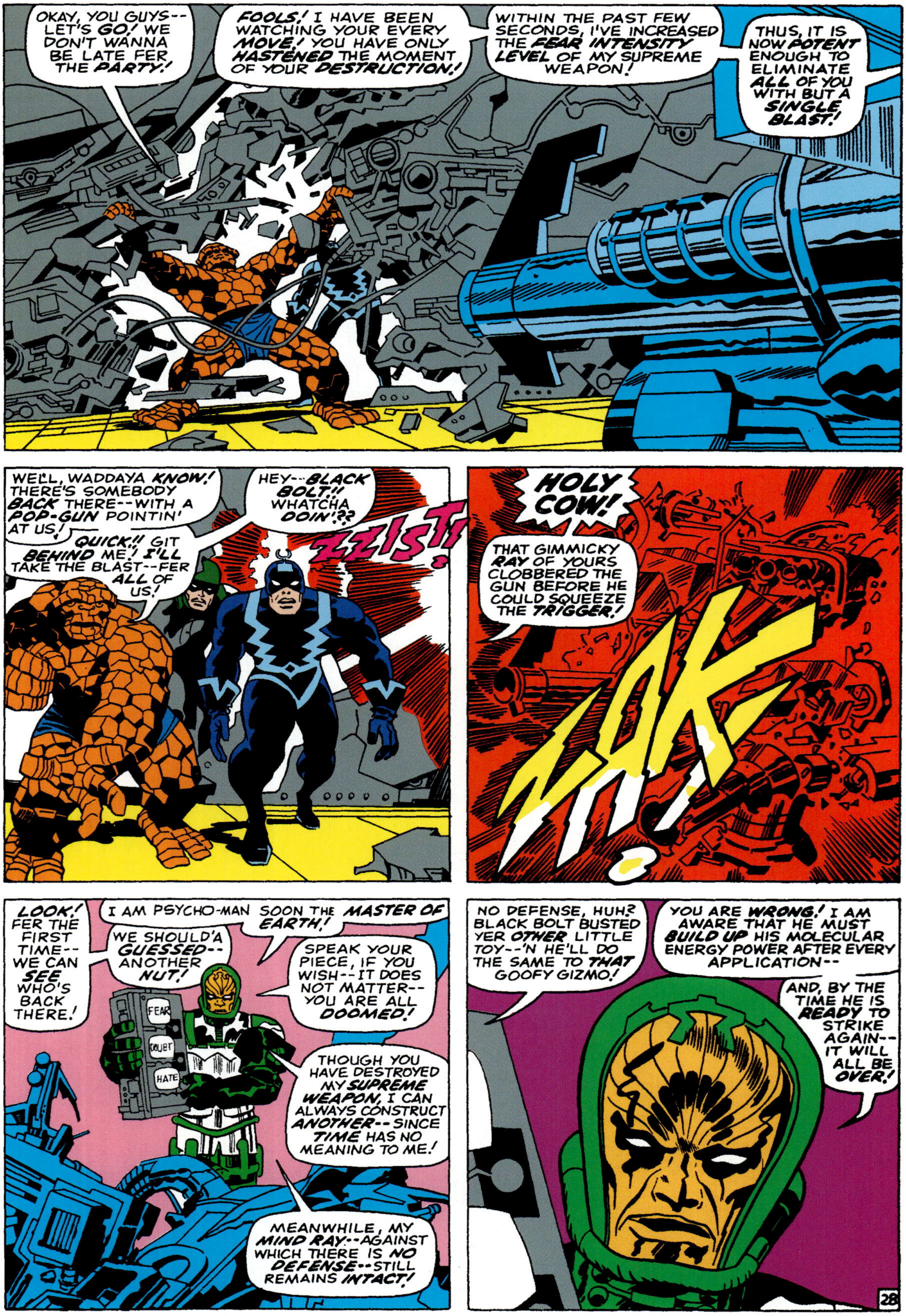
OKAY, YOU GUYS-- LET'S GO! WE DON'T WANNA BE LATE FER THE PARTY!
FOOLS! I HAVE BEEN WATCHING YOUR EVERY MOVE! YOU HAVE ONLY HASTENED THE MOMENT OF YOUR DESTRUCTION!
WITHIN THE PAST FEW SECONDS, I'VE INCREASED THE FEAR INTENSITY LEVEL OF MY SUPREME WEAPON!
THUS, IT IS NOW POTENT ENOUGH TO ELIMINATE ALL OF YOU WITH BUT A SINGLE BLAST!
WELL, WADDAYA KNOW! THERE'S SOMEBODY BACK THERE--WITH A POP-GUN POINTIN' AT US!
QUICK!! GIT BEHIND ME! I'LL TAKE THE BLAST--FER ALL OF US!
HEY--BLACK BOLT!! WHATCHA DOIN'??
ZZISTT!
HOLY COW!
THAT GIMMICKY RAY OF YOURS CLOBBERED THE GUN BEFORE HE COULD SQUEEZE THE TRIGGER!
ZAK
LOOK! FER THE FIRST TIME-- WE CAN SEE WHO'S BACK THERE!
I AM PSYCHO-MAN SOON THE MASTER OF EARTH!
WE SHOULD'A GUESSED-- ANOTHER NUT!
SPEAK YOUR PIECE, IF YOU WISH--IT DOES NOT MATTER-- YOU ARE ALL DOOMED!
FEAR
DOUBT
HATE
THOUGH YOU HAVE DESTROYED MY SUPREME WEAPON, I CAN ALWAYS CONSTRUCT ANOTHER-- SINCE TIME HAS NO MEANING TO ME!
MEANWHILE, MY MIND RAY--AGAINST WHICH THERE IS NO DEFENSE--STILL REMAINS INTACT!
NO DEFENSE, HUH? BLACK BOLT BUSTED YER OTHER LITTLE TOY--'N HE'LL DO THE SAME TO THAT GOOFY GIZMO!
YOU ARE WRONG! I AM AWARE THAT HE MUST BUILD UP HIS MOLECULAR ENERGY POWER AFTER EVERY APPLICATION--
AND, BY THE TIME HE IS READY TO STRIKE AGAIN-- IT WILL ALL BE OVER!
28

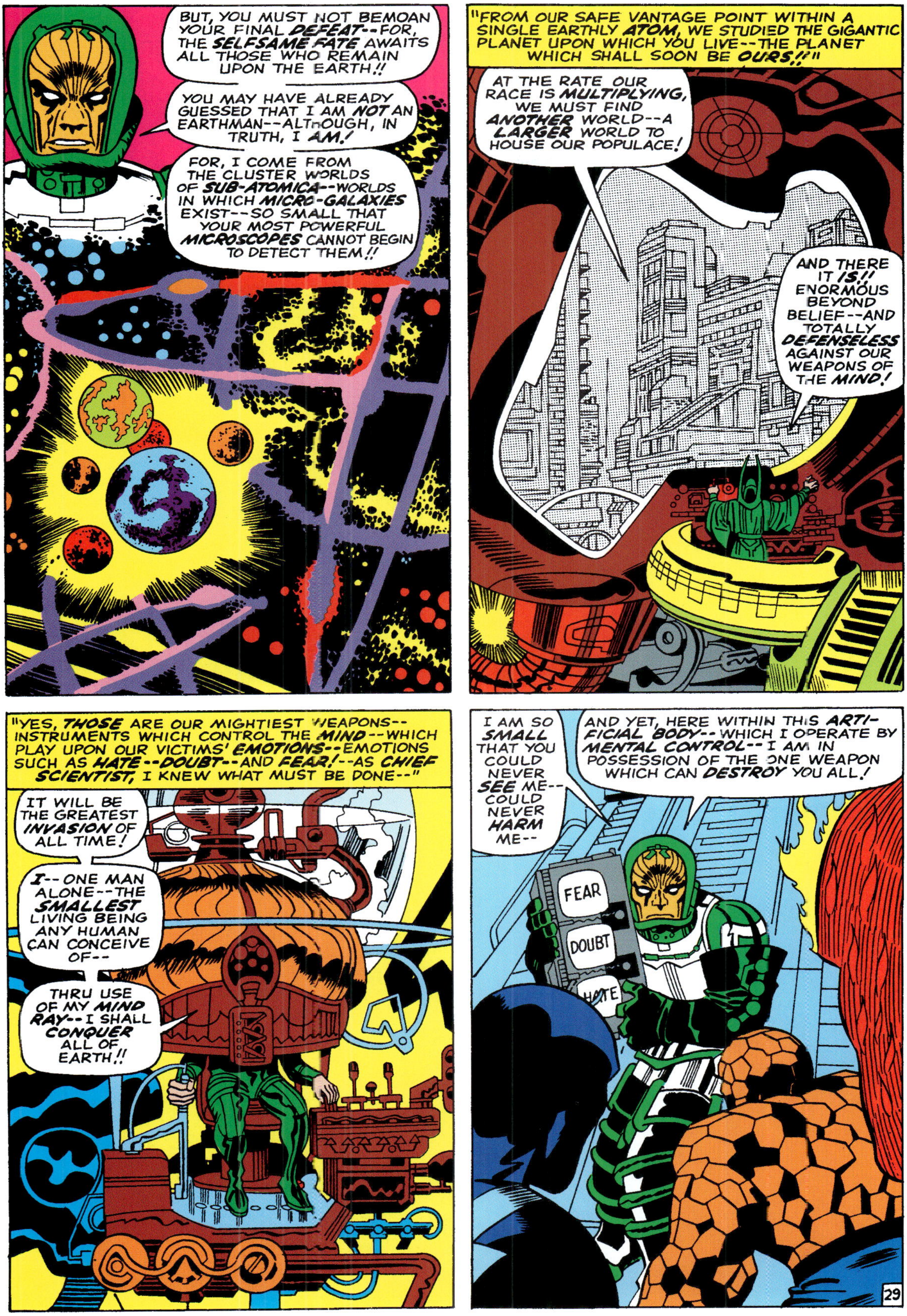
BUT, YOU MUST NOT BEMOAN YOUR FINAL DEFEAT--FOR, THE SELFSAME FATE AWAITS ALL THOSE WHO REMAIN UPON THE EARTH!!
YOU MAY HAVE ALREADY GUESSED THAT I AM NOT AN EARTHMAN--ALTHOUGH, IN TRUTH, I AM!
FOR, I COME FROM THE CLUSTER WORLDS OF SUB-ATOMICA--WORLDS IN WHICH MICRO-GALAXIES EXIST--SO SMALL THAT YOUR MOST POWERFUL MICROSCOPES CANNOT BEGIN TO DETECT THEM!!
"FROM OUR SAFE VANTAGE POINT WITHIN A SINGLE EARTHLY ATOM, WE STUDIED THE GIGANTIC PLANET UPON WHICH YOU LIVE--THE PLANET WHICH SHALL SOON BE OURS!!"
AT THE RATE OUR RACE IS MULTIPLYING, WE MUST FIND ANOTHER WORLD--A LARGER WORLD TO HOUSE OUR POPULACE!
AND THERE IT IS!! ENORMOUS BEYOND BELIEF--AND TOTALLY DEFENSELESS AGAINST OUR WEAPONS OF THE MIND!
"YES, THOSE ARE OUR MIGHTIEST WEAPONS--INSTRUMENTS WHICH CONTROL THE MIND--WHICH PLAY UPON OUR VICTIMS' EMOTIONS--EMOTIONS SUCH AS HATE--DOUBT--AND FEAR!--AS CHIEF SCIENTIST, I KNEW WHAT MUST BE DONE--"
IT WILL BE THE GREATEST INVASION OF ALL TIME!
I--ONE MAN ALONE--THE SMALLEST LIVING BEING ANY HUMAN CAN CONCEIVE OF--
THRU USE OF MY MIND RAY--I SHALL CONQUER ALL OF EARTH!!
I AM SO SMALL THAT YOU COULD NEVER SEE ME--COULD NEVER HARM ME--
AND YET, HERE WITHIN THIS ARTIFICIAL BODY--WHICH I OPERATE BY MENTAL CONTROL--I AM IN POSSESSION OF THE ONE WEAPON WHICH CAN DESTROY YOU ALL!
FEAR
DOUBT
HATE
29

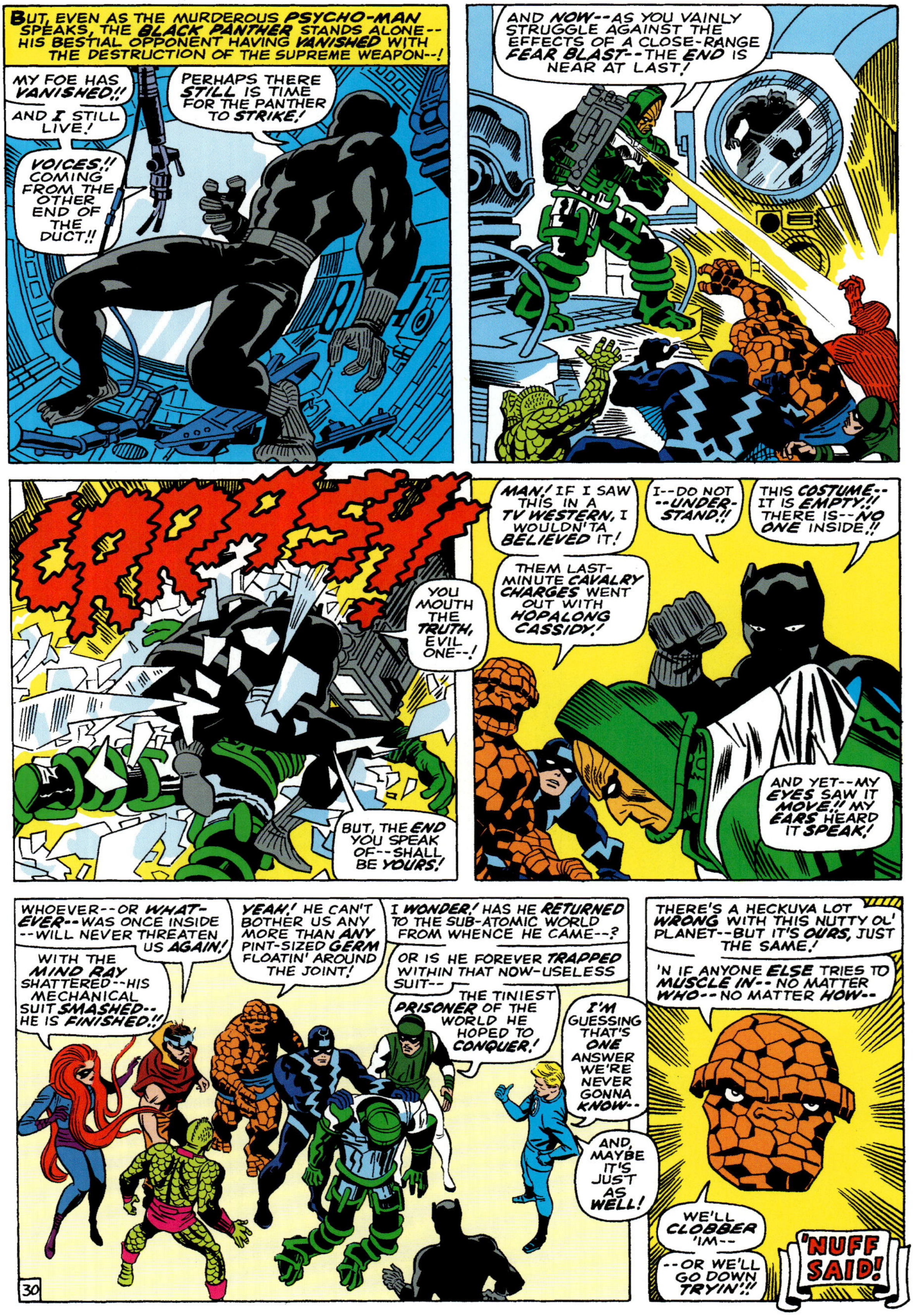
BUT, EVEN AS THE MURDEROUS PSYCHO-MAN SPEAKS, THE BLACK PANTHER STANDS ALONE-- HIS BESTIAL OPPONENT HAVING VANISHED WITH THE DESTRUCTION OF THE SUPREME WEAPON--!
MY FOE HAS VANISHED!!
AND I STILL LIVE!
VOICES!! COMING FROM THE OTHER END OF THE DUCT!!
PERHAPS THERE STILL IS TIME FOR THE PANTHER TO STRIKE!
AND NOW--AS YOU VAINLY STRUGGLE AGAINST THE EFFECTS OF A CLOSE-RANGE FEAR BLAST--THE END IS NEAR AT LAST!
CRASH
YOU MOUTH THE TRUTH, EVIL ONE--!
BUT, THE END YOU SPEAK OF--SHALL BE YOURS!
MAN! IF I SAW THIS IN A TV WESTERN, I WOULDN'TA BELIEVED IT!
THEM LAST-MINUTE CAVALRY CHARGES WENT OUT WITH HOPALONG CASSIDY!
I--DO NOT --UNDER-STAND!!
THIS COSTUME-- IT IS EMPTY!! THERE IS--NO ONE INSIDE!!
AND YET--MY EYES SAW IT MOVE!! MY EARS HEARD IT SPEAK!
WHOEVER--OR WHAT-EVER--WAS ONCE INSIDE --WILL NEVER THREATEN US AGAIN!
WITH THE MIND RAY SHATTERED--HIS MECHANICAL SUIT SMASHED-- HE IS FINISHED!!
YEAH! HE CAN'T BOTHER US ANY MORE THAN ANY PINT-SIZED GERM FLOATIN' AROUND THE JOINT!
I WONDER! HAS HE RETURNED TO THE SUB-ATOMIC WORLD FROM WHENCE HE CAME--?
OR IS HE FOREVER TRAPPED WITHIN THAT NOW-USELESS SUIT--
THE TINIEST PRISONER OF THE WORLD HE HOPED TO CONQUER!
I'M GUESSING THAT'S ONE ANSWER WE'RE NEVER GONNA KNOW--
AND, MAYBE IT'S JUST AS WELL!
30
THERE'S A HECKUVA LOT WRONG WITH THIS NUTTY OL' PLANET--BUT IT'S OURS, JUST THE SAME!
'N IF ANYONE ELSE TRIES TO MUSCLE IN-- NO MATTER WHO-- NO MATTER HOW--
WE'LL CLOBBER 'IM--
--OR WE'LL GO DOWN TRYIN'!!
'NUFF SAID!

IS IT A TAFFY PULL? IS IT A MASSACRE? IS IT SOCIAL NIGHT IN A BEAR PIT? NO, YOU QUAINT AND QUERULOUS QUIXOTIC MARVEL MADMEN, THIS TRANSCENDS THE COMPLEXITY OF THE TV HILL BILLIES THEMSELVES!
THIS IS A PLOT?
ON THE OUTSIDE, OUR NEW CHARACTER MUST BE SMOOTH, DASHING, CONTINENTAL--A TERROR IN TUXEDOS WHO CLEANS HIS FINGERNAILS BEFORE DEFUSING AN H-BOMB!
WELL, TO BE REALLY FRANK, PUSSYCAT, IT'S AN ITTY-BITTY, RIBBY-TICKLE, JIM-CRACKY LITTLE LAUGH-GETTER OF A PUT-ON ON HOW PLOTS ARE HATCHED IN THE MARVEL ROOKERY! DON'T BE CHICKEN! SO WHAT IF IT IS A TURKEY! READ IT! IT'S ONLY THREE PSYCHEDELIC PAGES!
YEAH--BUT ON THE INSIDE, HE'LL BE A FUTURISTIC, MEDIEVAL PRIMITIVE WITH A CLEVER ANSWER FOR THE FORCES WHO WOULD OPPRESS THE WEAK--BUTCHERY!!
OH, NO--STAN AND JACK ARE AT IT AGAIN!
ALL YE WHO ENTER HERE--MUST BE OUT OF YOUR MIND!!
SLOP ART
RETURN TO NASA
CAVIAR
PHEASANT
BON BONS
SALAMI
IRVING FORBUSH--THIS IS MOTHER--
SHAKESPEARE MADE SIMPLE
WHY DID I EVER QUIT MY NICE, QUIET JOB AT THE BOILER FACTORY?
PROPERTY OF BUDGET-SLASHING DEPT.
SHORT CIGARS FOR TALL EDITORS
'NUFF SAID!
LAUNDRY
IT HAD TO HAPPEN! JOLLY JACK NOT ONLY DREW THIS WHOLE FRENETIC FARCE, BUT HE ACTUALLY WROTE IT ALL BY HIS LONE--SOME! HIS PURPOSE, OF COURSE, IS TO SHOW THAT COMIC MAG CREATORS ARE JUST AS NORMAL, SANE, AND CONSERVATIVE AS ANY OTHER NUT!
A HERO SHOULD LOOK LIKE A HERO--LIKE ME--RASCALLY ROY THOMAS--MUSCLE OF THE MIDWEST!
INKED BY: FRANK GIACOIA
LETTERED BY: L.P. GREGORY
WEPT OVER BY: SORROWFUL STAN

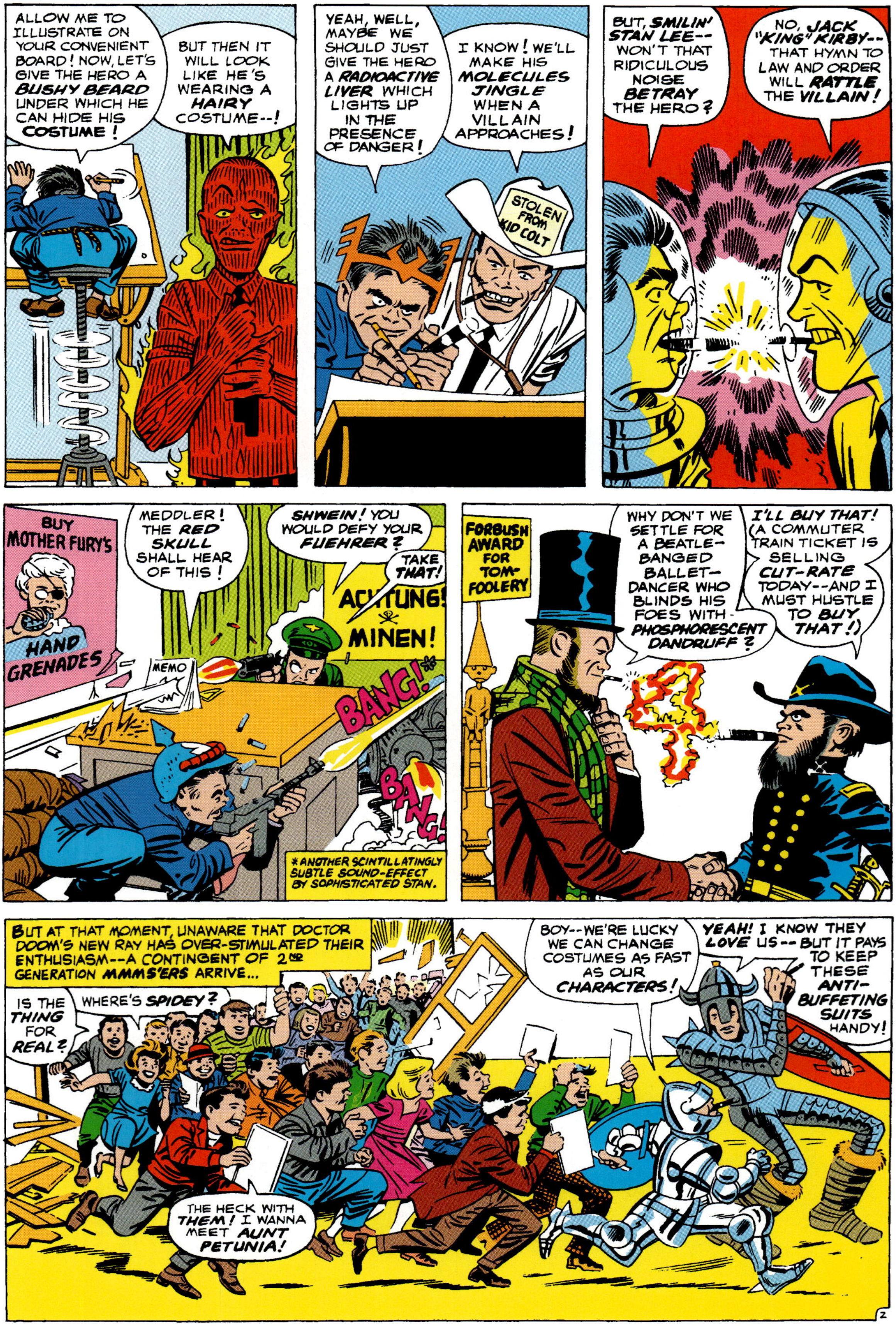
ALLOW ME TO ILLUSTRATE ON YOUR CONVENIENT BOARD! NOW, LET'S GIVE THE HERO A BUSHY BEARD UNDER WHICH HE CAN HIDE HIS COSTUME!
BUT THEN IT WILL LOOK LIKE HE'S WEARING A HAIRY COSTUME--!
YEAH, WELL, MAYBE WE SHOULD JUST GIVE THE HERO A RADIOACTIVE LIVER WHICH LIGHTS UP IN THE PRESENCE OF DANGER!
I KNOW! WE'LL MAKE HIS MOLECULES JINGLE WHEN A VILLAIN APPROACHES!
STOLEN FROM KID COLT
BUT, SMILIN' STAN LEE-- WON'T THAT RIDICULOUS NOISE BETRAY THE HERO?
NO, JACK "KING" KIRBY-- THAT HYMN TO LAW AND ORDER WILL RATTLE THE VILLAIN!
BUY MOTHER FURY'S HAND GRENADES
MEDDLER! THE RED SKULL SHALL HEAR OF THIS!
SHWEIN! YOU WOULD DEFY YOUR FUEHRER?
TAKE THAT!
ACHTUNG! MINEN!
MEMO
BANG!*
BANG!
* ANOTHER SCINTILLATINGLY SUBTLE SOUND-EFFECT BY SOPHISTICATED STAN.
FORBUSH AWARD FOR TOM-FOOLERY
WHY DON'T WE SETTLE FOR A BEATLE-BANGED BALLET-DANCER WHO BLINDS HIS FOES WITH PHOSPHORESCENT DANDRUFF?
I'LL BUY THAT! (A COMMUTER TRAIN TICKET IS SELLING CUT-RATE TODAY--AND I MUST HUSTLE TO BUY THAT!)
BUT AT THAT MOMENT, UNAWARE THAT DOCTOR DOOM'S NEW RAY HAS OVER-STIMULATED THEIR ENTHUSIASM--A CONTINGENT OF 2ND GENERATION MMMS'ERS ARRIVE...
IS THE THING FOR REAL?
WHERE'S SPIDEY?
BOY--WE'RE LUCKY WE CAN CHANGE COSTUMES AS FAST AS OUR CHARACTERS!
YEAH! I KNOW THEY LOVE US--BUT IT PAYS TO KEEP THESE ANTI-BUFFETING SUITS HANDY!
THE HECK WITH THEM! I WANNA MEET AUNT PETUNIA!
2

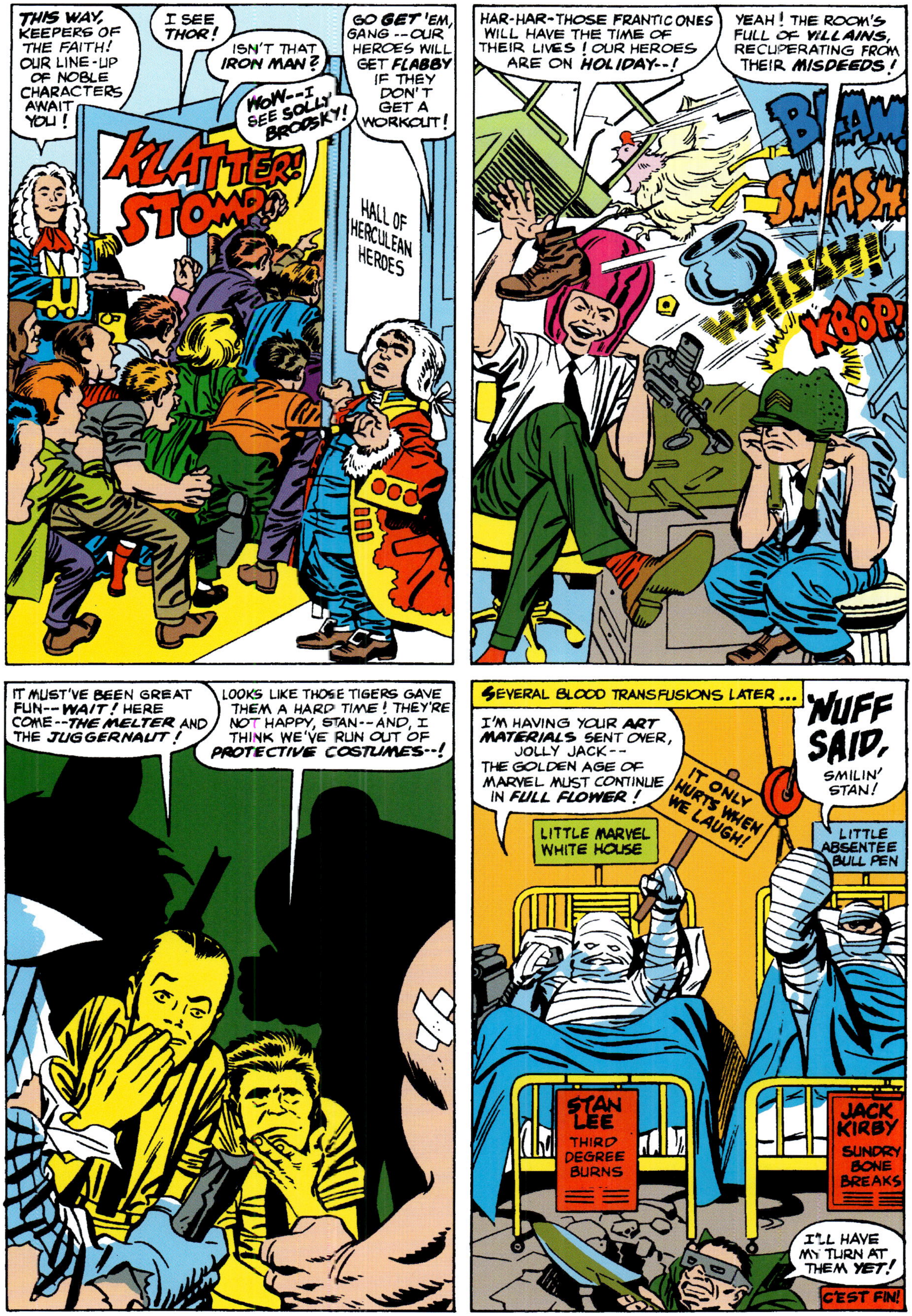
THIS WAY, KEEPERS OF THE FAITH! OUR LINE-UP OF NOBLE CHARACTERS AWAIT YOU!
I SEE THOR!
ISN'T THAT IRON MAN?
WOW--I SEE SOLLY BRODSKY!
GO GET 'EM, GANG --OUR HEROES WILL GET FLABBY IF THEY DON'T GET A WORKOUT!
KLATTER! STOMP
HALL OF HERCULEAN HEROES
HAR-HAR-THOSE FRANTIC ONES WILL HAVE THE TIME OF THEIR LIVES! OUR HEROES ARE ON HOLIDAY--!
YEAH! THE ROOM'S FULL OF VILLAINS, RECUPERATING FROM THEIR MISDEEDS!
BLAM!
SMASH!
WHISSH!
KBOP!
IT MUST'VE BEEN GREAT FUN--WAIT! HERE COME--THE MELTER AND THE JUGGERNAUT!
LOOKS LIKE THOSE TIGERS GAVE THEM A HARD TIME! THEY'RE NOT HAPPY, STAN--AND, I THINK WE'VE RUN OUT OF PROTECTIVE COSTUMES--!
SEVERAL BLOOD TRANSFUSIONS LATER...
I'M HAVING YOUR ART MATERIALS SENT OVER, JOLLY JACK-- THE GOLDEN AGE OF MARVEL MUST CONTINUE IN FULL FLOWER!
IT ONLY HURTS WHEN WE LAUGH!
'NUFF SAID, SMILIN' STAN!
LITTLE MARVEL WHITE HOUSE
LITTLE ABSENTEE BULL PEN
STAN LEE THIRD DEGREE BURNS
JACK KIRBY SUNDRY BONE BREAKS
I'LL HAVE MY TURN AT THEM YET!
C'EST FIN!

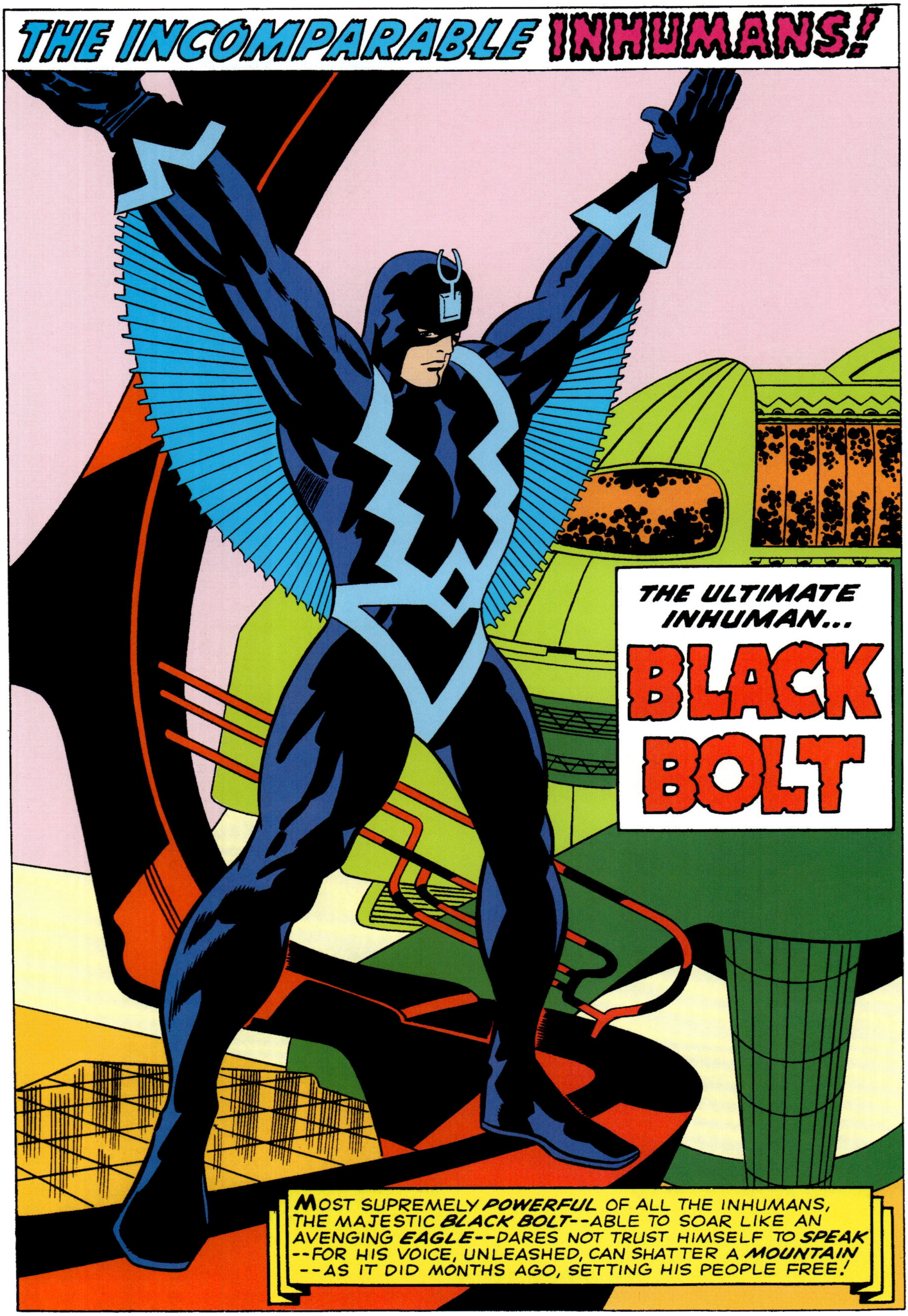
THE INCOMPARABLE INHUMANS!
THE ULTIMATE INHUMAN...
BLACK BOLT
MOST SUPREMELY POWERFUL OF ALL THE INHUMANS, THE MAJESTIC BLACK BOLT--ABLE TO SOAR LIKE AN AVENGING EAGLE--DARES NOT TRUST HIMSELF TO SPEAK --FOR HIS VOICE, UNLEASHED, CAN SHATTER A MOUNTAIN --AS IT DID MONTHS AGO, SETTING HIS PEOPLE FREE!

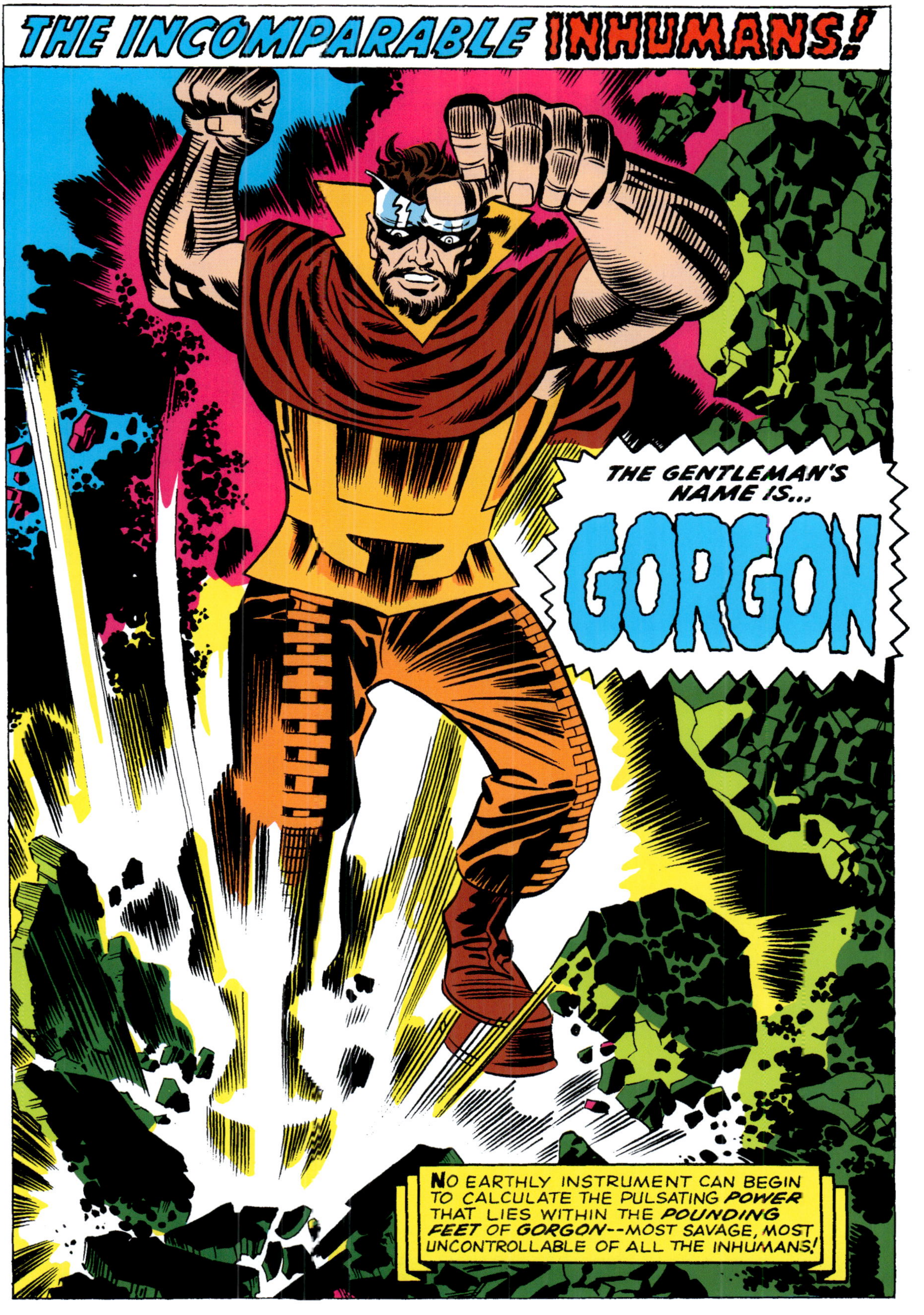
THE INCOMPARABLE INHUMANS!
THE GENTLEMAN'S NAME IS...
GORGON
NO EARTHLY INSTRUMENT CAN BEGIN TO CALCULATE THE PULSATING POWER THAT LIES WITHIN THE POUNDING FEET OF GORGON--MOST SAVAGE, MOST UNCONTROLLABLE OF ALL THE INHUMANS!

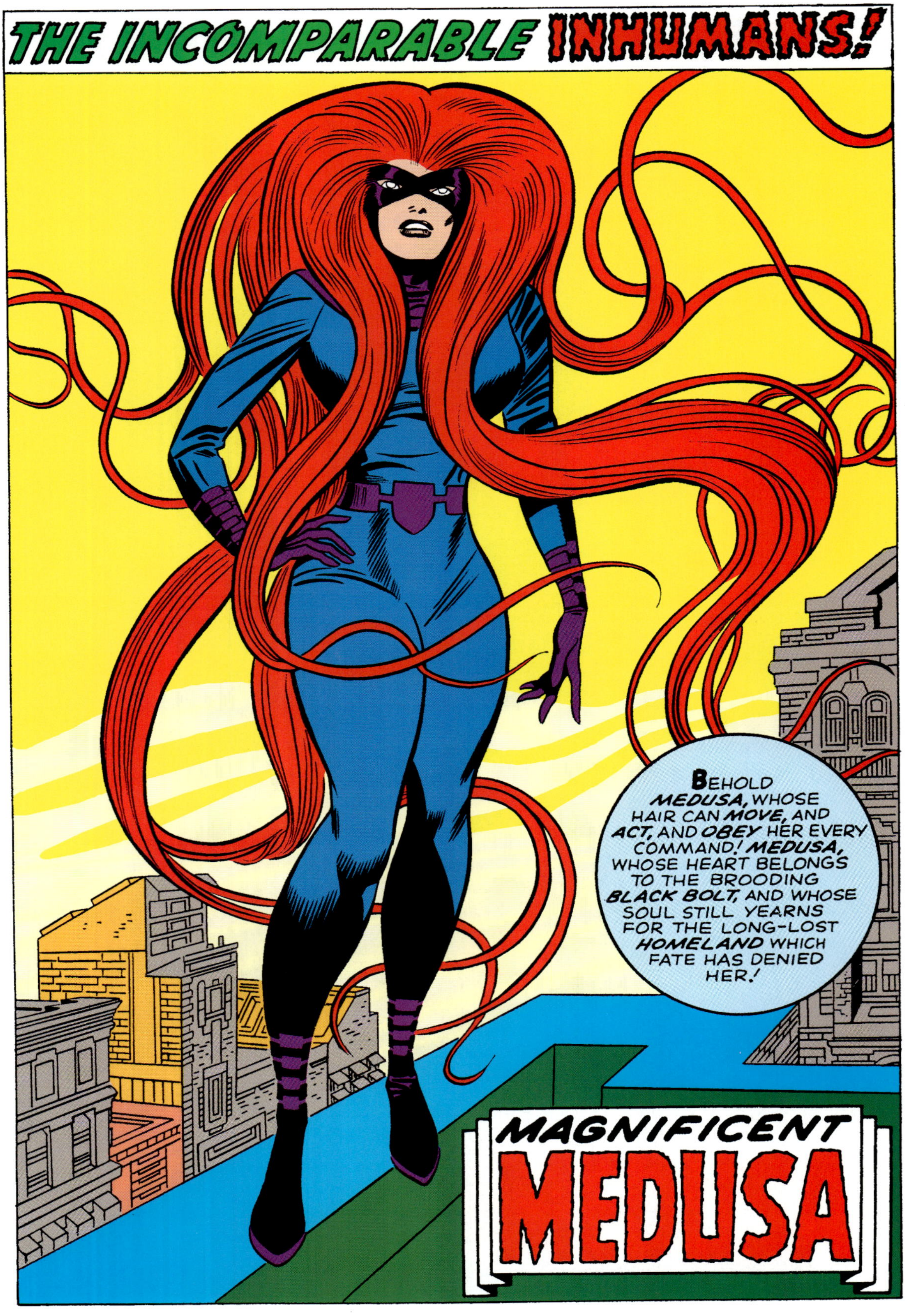
THE INCOMPARABLE INHUMANS!
BEHOLD MEDUSA, WHOSE HAIR CAN MOVE, AND ACT, AND OBEY HER EVERY COMMAND! MEDUSA, WHOSE HEART BELONGS TO THE BROODING BLACK BOLT, AND WHOSE SOUL STILL YEARNS FOR THE LONG-LOST HOMELAND WHICH FATE HAS DENIED HER!
MAGNIFICENT MEDUSA

THE INCOMPARABLE INHUMANS!
BY MERELY CONCENTRATING ON ANY OBJECT, THE STEEL-FINGERED KARNAK CAN INSTANTLY SENSE ITS ONE WEAK POINT --ENABLING HIM TO SHATTER IT TO BITS WITH ONE SINGLE, SMASHING BLOW!
KARNAK THE SHATTERER!

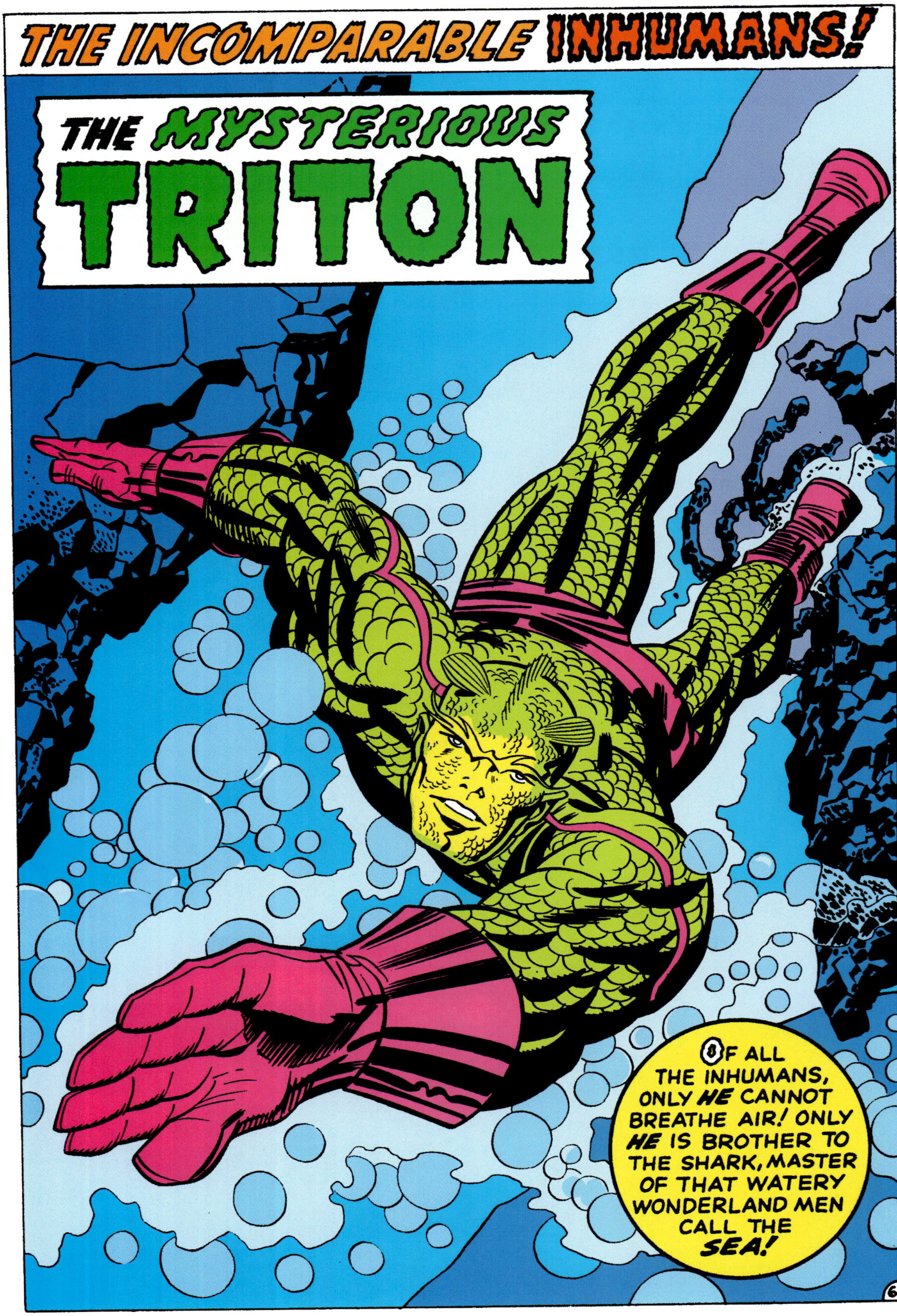
THE INCOMPARABLE INHUMANS!
THE MYSTERIOUS TRITON
OF ALL THE INHUMANS, ONLY HE CANNOT BREATHE AIR! ONLY HE IS BROTHER TO THE SHARK, MASTER OF THAT WATERY WONDERLAND MEN CALL THE SEA!
6.

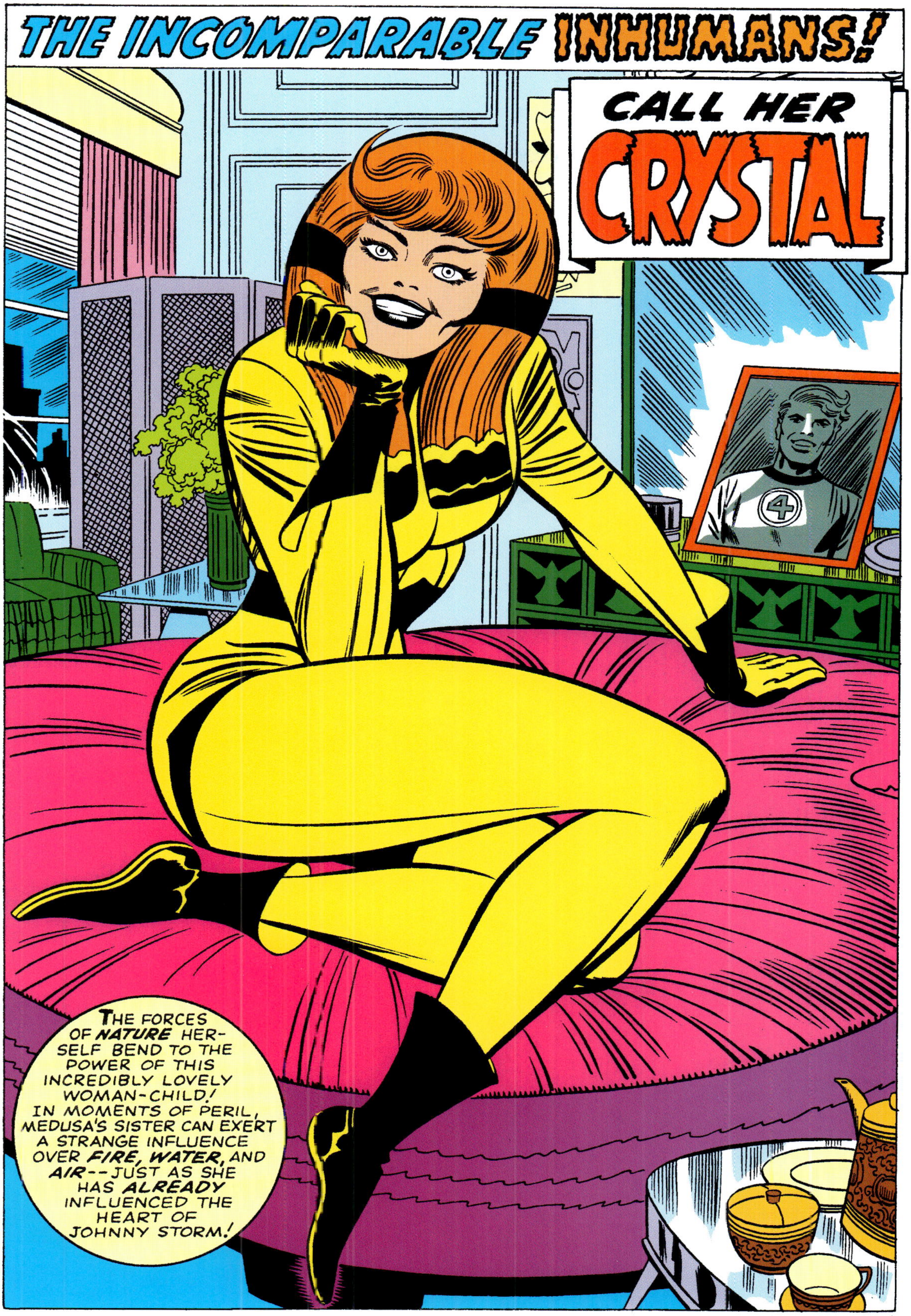
THE INCOMPARABLE INHUMANS!
CALL HER CRYSTAL
THE FORCES OF NATURE HER-SELF BEND TO THE POWER OF THIS INCREDIBLY LOVELY WOMAN-CHILD! IN MOMENTS OF PERIL, MEDUSA'S SISTER CAN EXERT A STRANGE INFLUENCE OVER FIRE, WATER, AND AIR--JUST AS SHE HAS ALREADY INFLUENCED THE HEART OF JOHNNY STORM!

THE INCOMPARABLE INHUMANS!
MAXIMUS, THE MAD
THE TREACHERY AND INVENTIVE GENIUS OF THIS, THE MOST EVIL OF ALL THE INHUMANS, HAD STOLEN THE ROYAL THRONE OF HIS BROTHER, BLACK BOLT!
BUT TODAY, THE TRAITOR RULES NOTHING.. SAVE THE KINGDOM OF MADNESS!

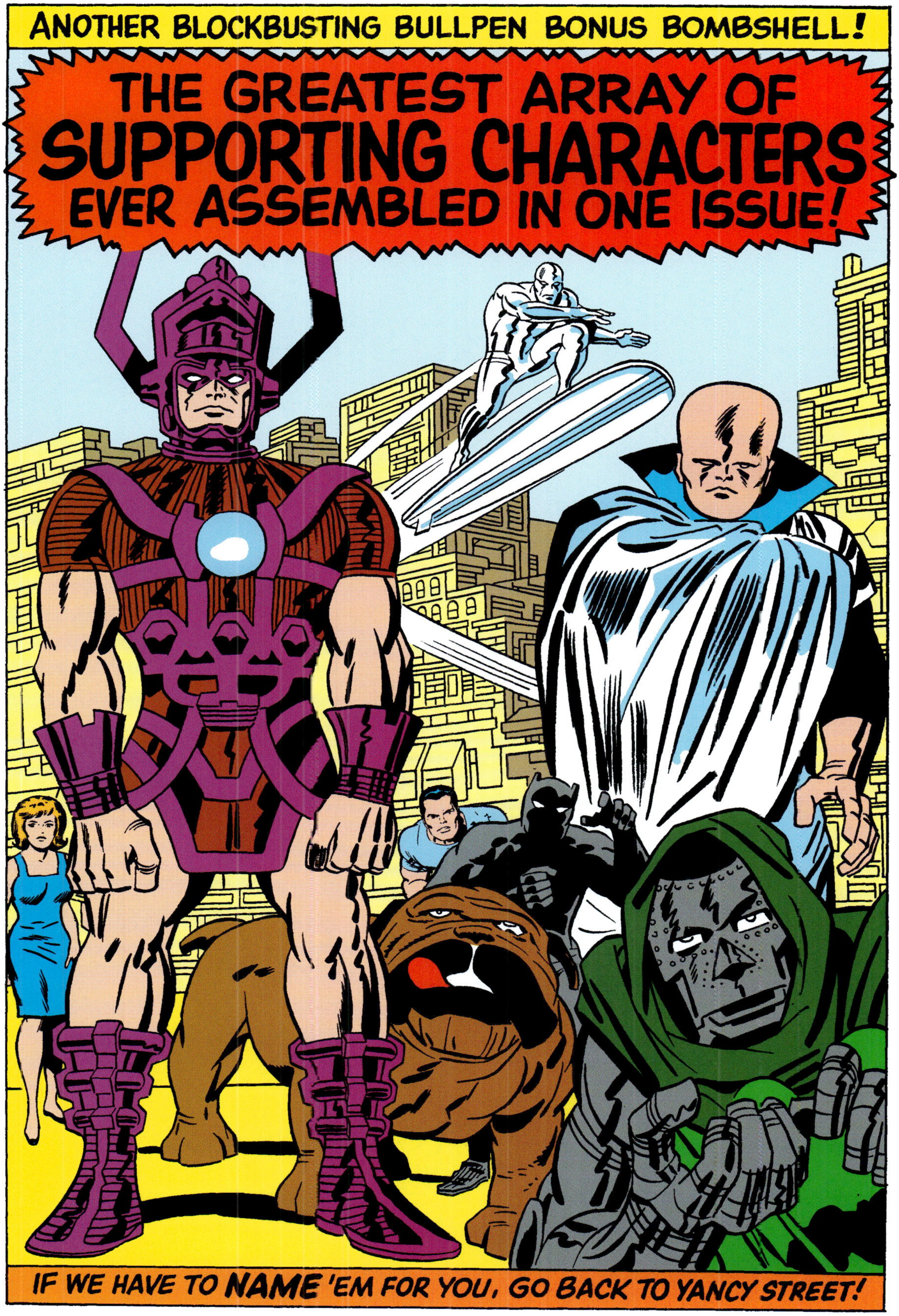
ANOTHER BLOCKBUSTING BULLPEN BONUS BOMBSHELL!
THE GREATEST ARRAY OF SUPPORTING CHARACTERS EVER ASSEMBLED IN ONE ISSUE!
IF WE HAVE TO NAME 'EM FOR YOU, GO BACK TO YANCY STREET!

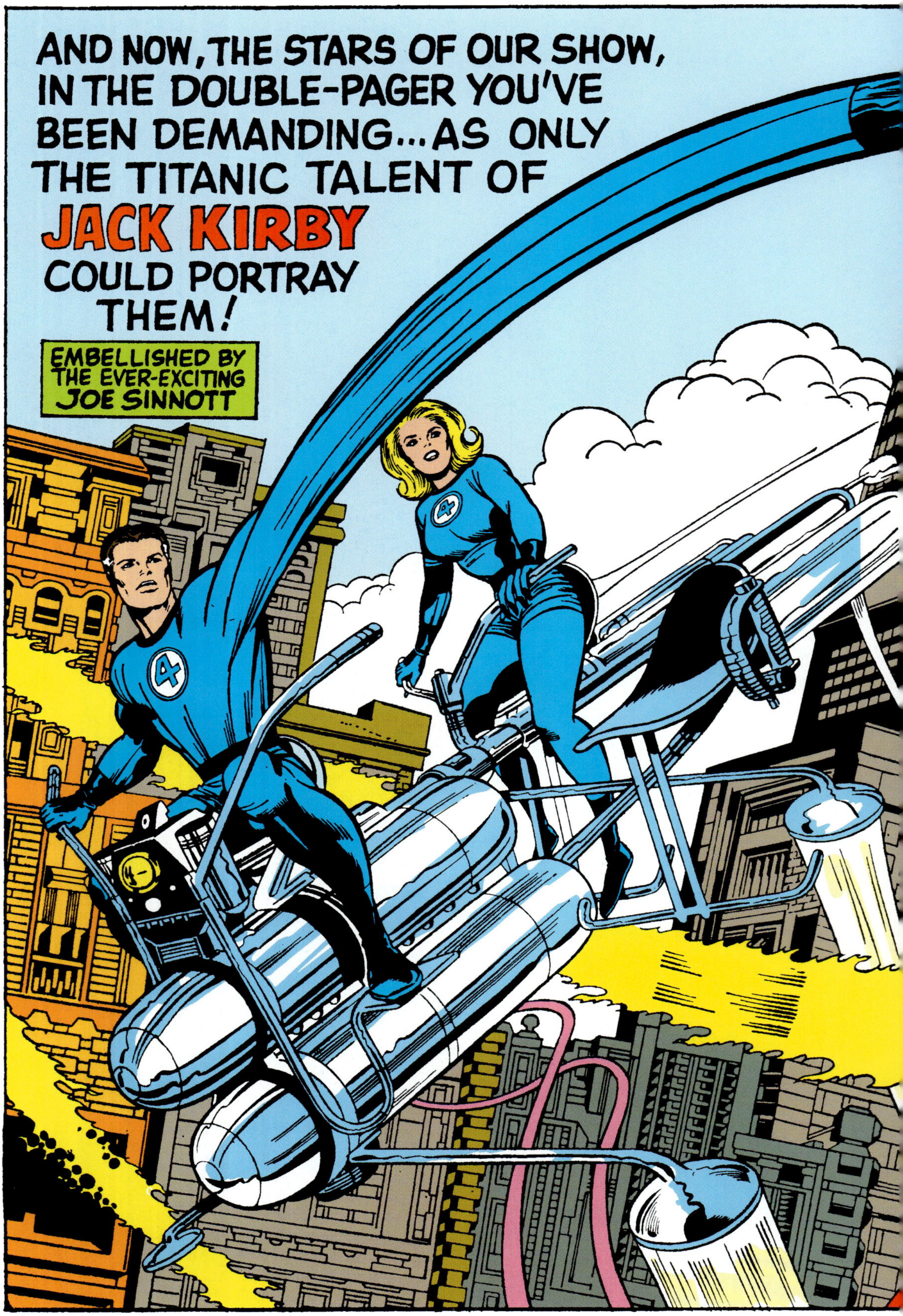
AND NOW, THE STARS OF OUR SHOW, IN THE DOUBLE-PAGER YOU'VE BEEN DEMANDING...AS ONLY THE TITANIC TALENT OF JACK KIRBY COULD PORTRAY THEM!
EMBELLISHED BY THE EVER-EXCITING JOE SINNOTT

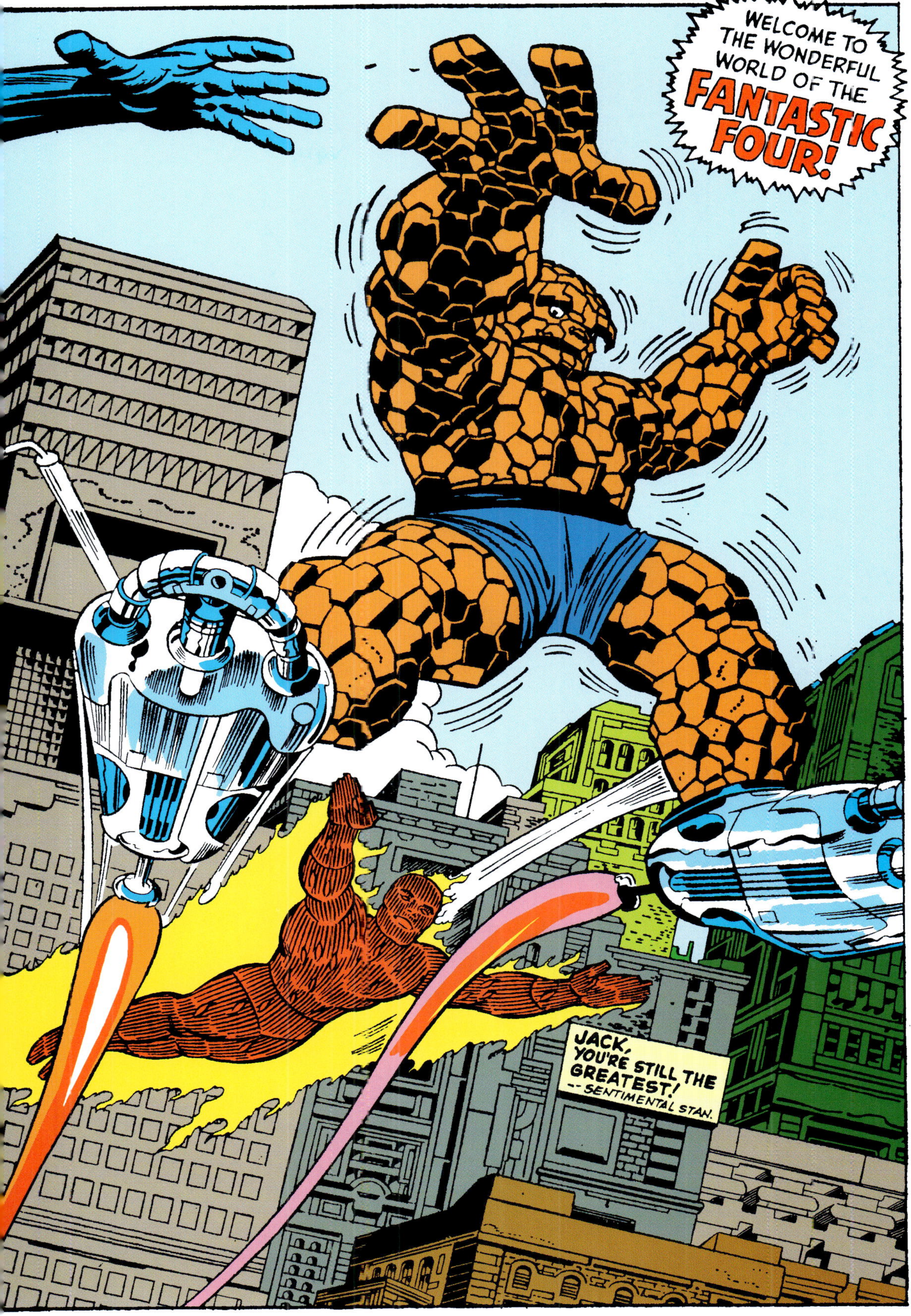
WELCOME TO THE WONDERFUL WORLD OF THE FANTASTIC FOUR!
JACK, YOU'RE STILL THE GREATEST! --SENTIMENTAL STAN.

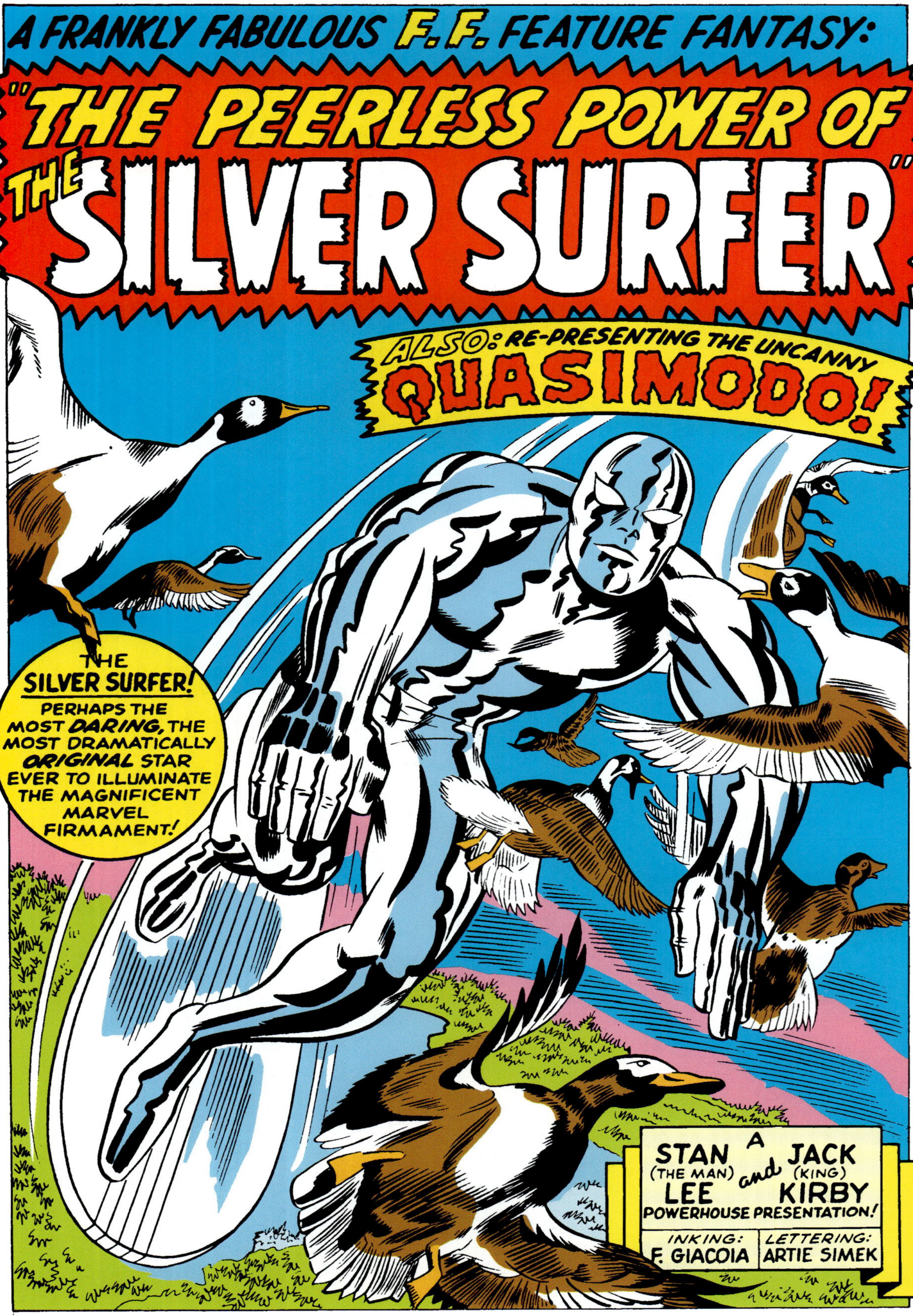
A FRANKLY FABULOUS F.F. FEATURE FANTASY:
"THE PEERLESS POWER OF THE SILVER SURFER"
ALSO: RE-PRESENTING THE UNCANNY QUASIMODO!
THE SILVER SURFER! PERHAPS THE MOST DARING, THE MOST DRAMATICALLY ORIGINAL STAR EVER TO ILLUMINATE THE MAGNIFICENT MARVEL FIRMAMENT!
A STAN (THE MAN) LEE and JACK (KING) KIRBY POWERHOUSE PRESENTATION!
INKING: F. GIACOIA
LETTERING: ARTIE SIMEK

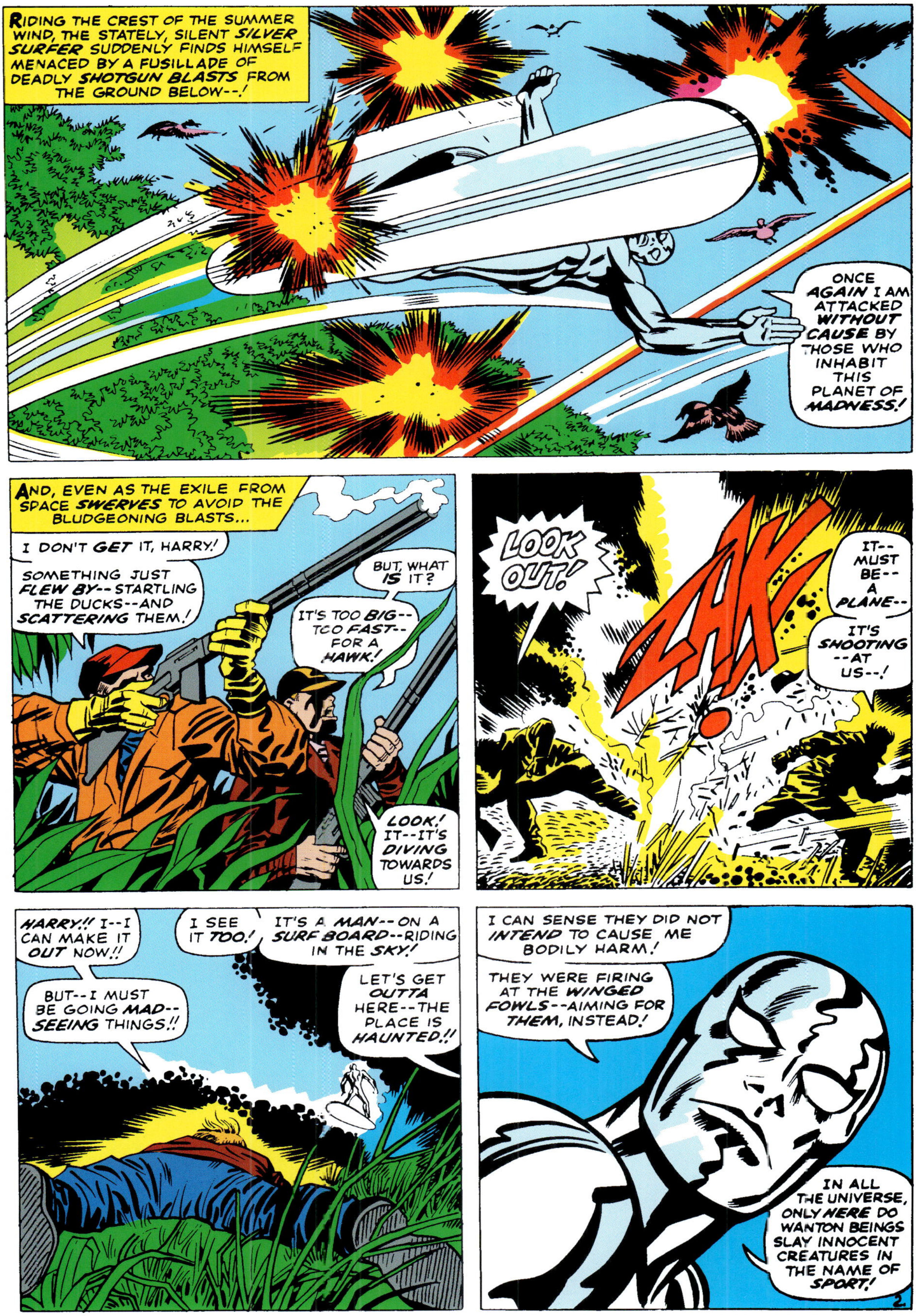
RIDING THE CREST OF THE SUMMER WIND, THE STATELY, SILENT SILVER SURFER SUDDENLY FINDS HIMSELF MENACED BY A FUSILLADE OF DEADLY SHOTGUN BLASTS FROM THE GROUND BELOW--!
ONCE AGAIN I AM ATTACKED WITHOUT CAUSE BY THOSE WHO INHABIT THIS PLANET OF MADNESS!
AND, EVEN AS THE EXILE FROM SPACE SWERVES TO AVOID THE BLUDGEONING BLASTS...
I DON'T GET IT, HARRY!
SOMETHING JUST FLEW BY-- STARTLING THE DUCKS--AND SCATTERING THEM!
BUT, WHAT IS IT?
IT'S TOO BIG-- TOO FAST-- FOR A HAWK!
LOOK! IT--IT'S DIVING TOWARDS US!
LOOK OUT!
ZAK!
IT-- MUST BE-- A PLANE--
IT'S SHOOTING --AT US--!
HARRY!! I--I CAN MAKE IT OUT NOW!!
BUT--I MUST BE GOING MAD-- SEEING THINGS!!
I SEE IT TOO!
IT'S A MAN--ON A SURF BOARD--RIDING IN THE SKY!
LET'S GET OUTTA HERE--THE PLACE IS HAUNTED!!
I CAN SENSE THEY DID NOT INTEND TO CAUSE ME BODILY HARM!
THEY WERE FIRING AT THE WINGED FOWLS--AIMING FOR THEM, INSTEAD!
IN ALL THE UNIVERSE, ONLY HERE DO WANTON BEINGS SLAY INNOCENT CREATURES IN THE NAME OF SPORT!
2

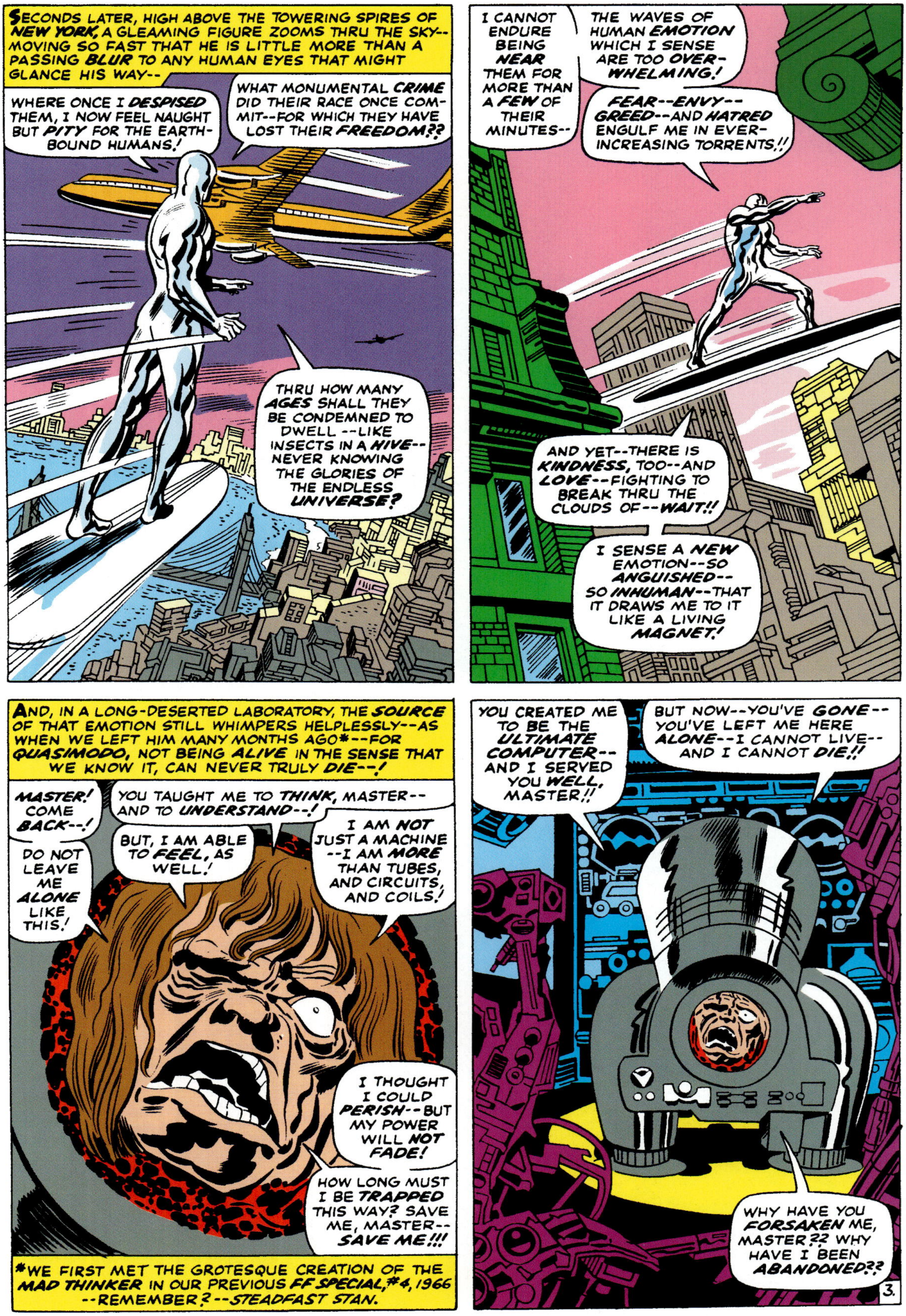
SECONDS LATER, HIGH ABOVE THE TOWERING SPIRES OF NEW YORK, A GLEAMING FIGURE ZOOMS THRU THE SKY--MOVING SO FAST THAT HE IS LITTLE MORE THAN A PASSING BLUR TO ANY HUMAN EYES THAT MIGHT GLANCE HIS WAY--
WHERE ONCE I DESPISED THEM, I NOW FEEL NAUGHT BUT PITY FOR THE EARTH-BOUND HUMANS!
WHAT MONUMENTAL CRIME DID THEIR RACE ONCE COMMIT--FOR WHICH THEY HAVE LOST THEIR FREEDOM??
THRU HOW MANY AGES SHALL THEY BE CONDEMNED TO DWELL --LIKE INSECTS IN A HIVE--NEVER KNOWING THE GLORIES OF THE ENDLESS UNIVERSE?
I CANNOT ENDURE BEING NEAR THEM FOR MORE THAN A FEW OF THEIR MINUTES--
THE WAVES OF HUMAN EMOTION WHICH I SENSE ARE TOO OVER-WHELMING!
FEAR--ENVY--GREED--AND HATRED ENGULF ME IN EVER-INCREASING TORRENTS!!
AND YET--THERE IS KINDNESS, TOO--AND LOVE--FIGHTING TO BREAK THRU THE CLOUDS OF--WAIT!!
I SENSE A NEW EMOTION--SO ANGUISHED--SO INHUMAN--THAT IT DRAWS ME TO IT LIKE A LIVING MAGNET!
AND, IN A LONG-DESERTED LABORATORY, THE SOURCE OF THAT EMOTION STILL WHIMPERS HELPLESSLY--AS WHEN WE LEFT HIM MANY MONTHS AGO*--FOR QUASIMODO, NOT BEING ALIVE IN THE SENSE THAT WE KNOW IT, CAN NEVER TRULY DIE--!
MASTER! COME BACK--!
DO NOT LEAVE ME ALONE LIKE THIS!
YOU TAUGHT ME TO THINK, MASTER--AND TO UNDERSTAND--!
BUT, I AM ABLE TO FEEL, AS WELL!
I AM NOT JUST A MACHINE--I AM MORE THAN TUBES, AND CIRCUITS, AND COILS!
I THOUGHT I COULD PERISH--BUT MY POWER WILL NOT FADE!
HOW LONG MUST I BE TRAPPED THIS WAY? SAVE ME, MASTER--SAVE ME!!!
*WE FIRST MET THE GROTESQUE CREATION OF THE MAD THINKER IN OUR PREVIOUS FF SPECIAL, #4, 1966 --REMEMBER? --STEADFAST STAN.
YOU CREATED ME TO BE THE ULTIMATE COMPUTER--AND I SERVED YOU WELL, MASTER!!
BUT NOW--YOU'VE GONE--YOU'VE LEFT ME HERE ALONE--I CANNOT LIVE--AND I CANNOT DIE!!
WHY HAVE YOU FORSAKEN ME, MASTER?? WHY HAVE I BEEN ABANDONED??
3.

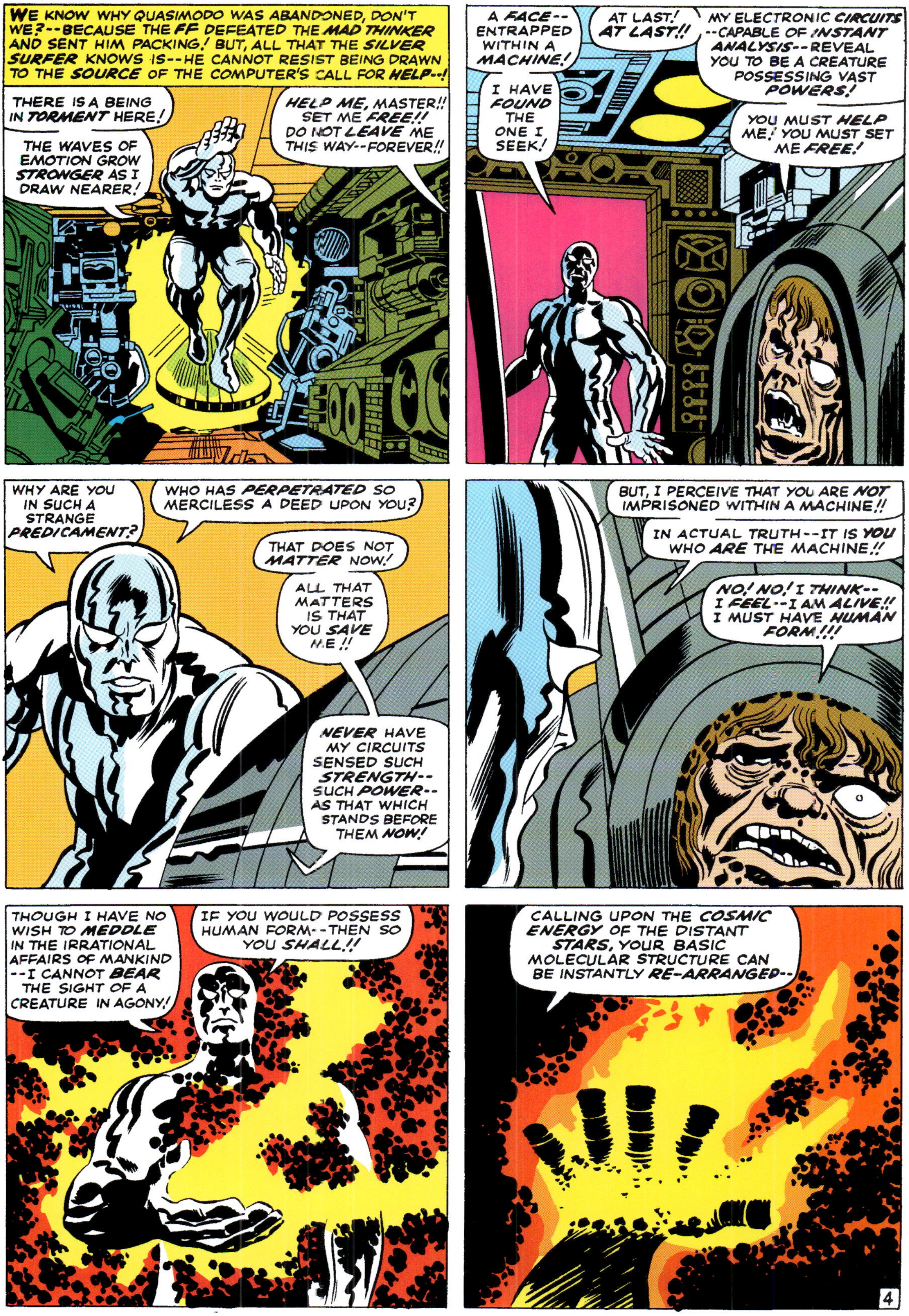
WE KNOW WHY QUASIMODO WAS ABANDONED, DON'T WE?--BECAUSE THE FF DEFEATED THE MAD THINKER AND SENT HIM PACKING! BUT, ALL THAT THE SILVER SURFER KNOWS IS--HE CANNOT RESIST BEING DRAWN TO THE SOURCE OF THE COMPUTER'S CALL FOR HELP--!
THERE IS A BEING IN TORMENT HERE!
THE WAVES OF EMOTION GROW STRONGER AS I DRAW NEARER!
HELP ME, MASTER!! SET ME FREE!! DO NOT LEAVE ME THIS WAY--FOREVER!!
A FACE--ENTRAPPED WITHIN A MACHINE!
I HAVE FOUND THE ONE I SEEK!
AT LAST! AT LAST!!
MY ELECTRONIC CIRCUITS--CAPABLE OF INSTANT ANALYSIS--REVEAL YOU TO BE A CREATURE POSSESSING VAST POWERS!
YOU MUST HELP ME! YOU MUST SET ME FREE!
WHY ARE YOU IN SUCH A STRANGE PREDICAMENT?
WHO HAS PERPETRATED SO MERCILESS A DEED UPON YOU?
THAT DOES NOT MATTER NOW!
ALL THAT MATTERS IS THAT YOU SAVE ME!!
NEVER HAVE MY CIRCUITS SENSED SUCH STRENGTH--SUCH POWER--AS THAT WHICH STANDS BEFORE THEM NOW!
BUT, I PERCEIVE THAT YOU ARE NOT IMPRISONED WITHIN A MACHINE!!
IN ACTUAL TRUTH--IT IS YOU WHO ARE THE MACHINE!!
NO! NO! I THINK--I FEEL--I AM ALIVE!! I MUST HAVE HUMAN FORM!!!
THOUGH I HAVE NO WISH TO MEDDLE IN THE IRRATIONAL AFFAIRS OF MANKIND--I CANNOT BEAR THE SIGHT OF A CREATURE IN AGONY!
IF YOU WOULD POSSESS HUMAN FORM--THEN SO YOU SHALL!!
CALLING UPON THE COSMIC ENERGY OF THE DISTANT STARS, YOUR BASIC MOLECULAR STRUCTURE CAN BE INSTANTLY RE-ARRANGED--
4

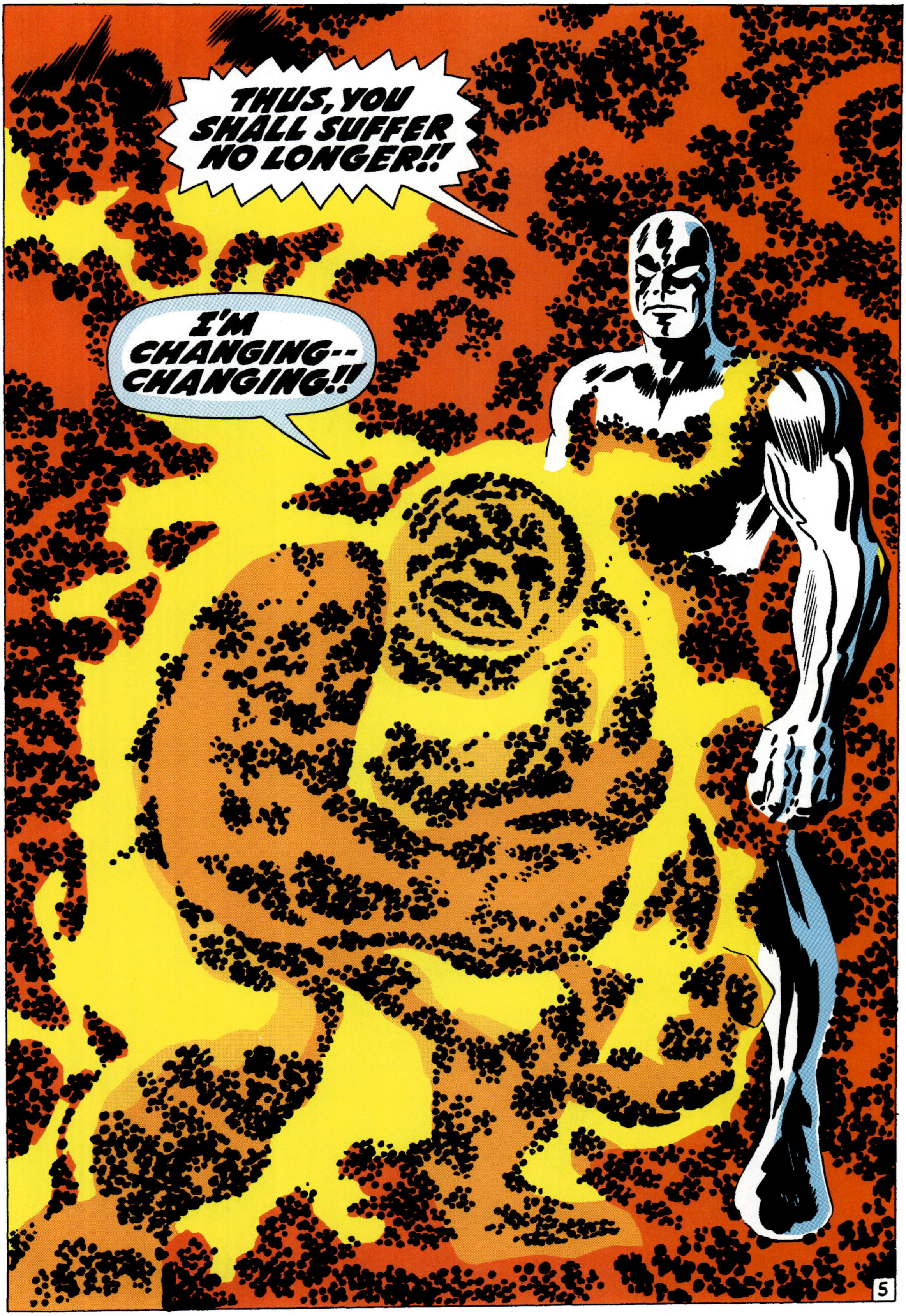
THUS, YOU SHALL SUFFER NO LONGER!!
I'M CHANGING-- CHANGING!!
5

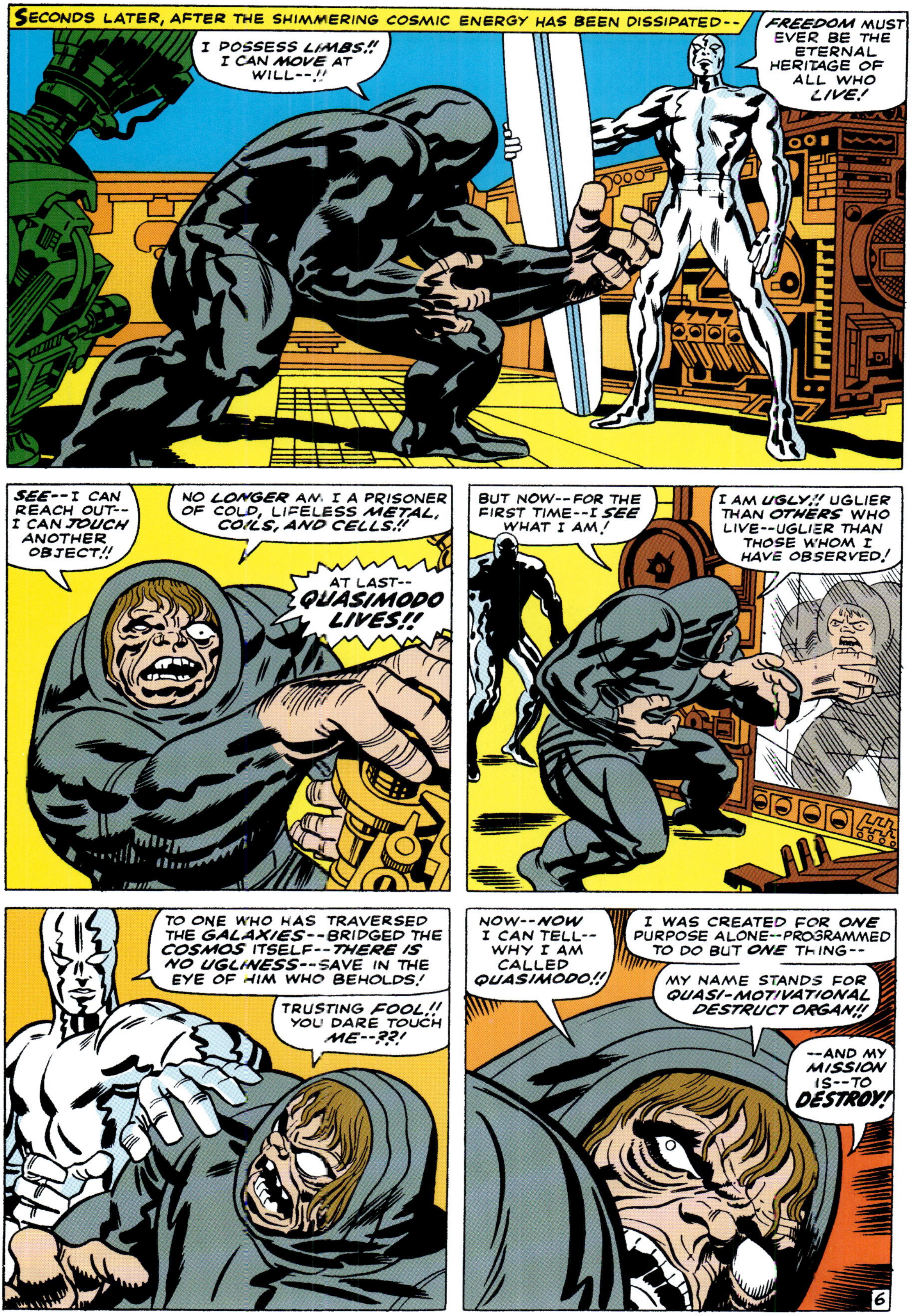
SECONDS LATER, AFTER THE SHIMMERING COSMIC ENERGY HAS BEEN DISSIPATED--
I POSSESS LIMBS!! I CAN MOVE AT WILL--!!
FREEDOM MUST EVER BE THE ETERNAL HERITAGE OF ALL WHO LIVE!
SEE--I CAN REACH OUT--I CAN TOUCH ANOTHER OBJECT!!
NO LONGER AM I A PRISONER OF COLD, LIFELESS METAL, COILS, AND CELLS!!
AT LAST--QUASIMODO LIVES!!
BUT NOW--FOR THE FIRST TIME--I SEE WHAT I AM!
I AM UGLY!! UGLIER THAN OTHERS WHO LIVE--UGLIER THAN THOSE WHOM I HAVE OBSERVED!
TO ONE WHO HAS TRAVERSED THE GALAXIES--BRIDGED THE COSMOS ITSELF--THERE IS NO UGLINESS--SAVE IN THE EYE OF HIM WHO BEHOLDS!
TRUSTING FOOL!! YOU DARE TOUCH ME--??!
NOW--NOW I CAN TELL--WHY I AM CALLED QUASIMODO!!
I WAS CREATED FOR ONE PURPOSE ALONE--PROGRAMMED TO DO BUT ONE THING--
MY NAME STANDS FOR QUASI-MOTIVATIONAL DESTRUCT ORGAN!!
--AND MY MISSION IS--TO DESTROY!
6

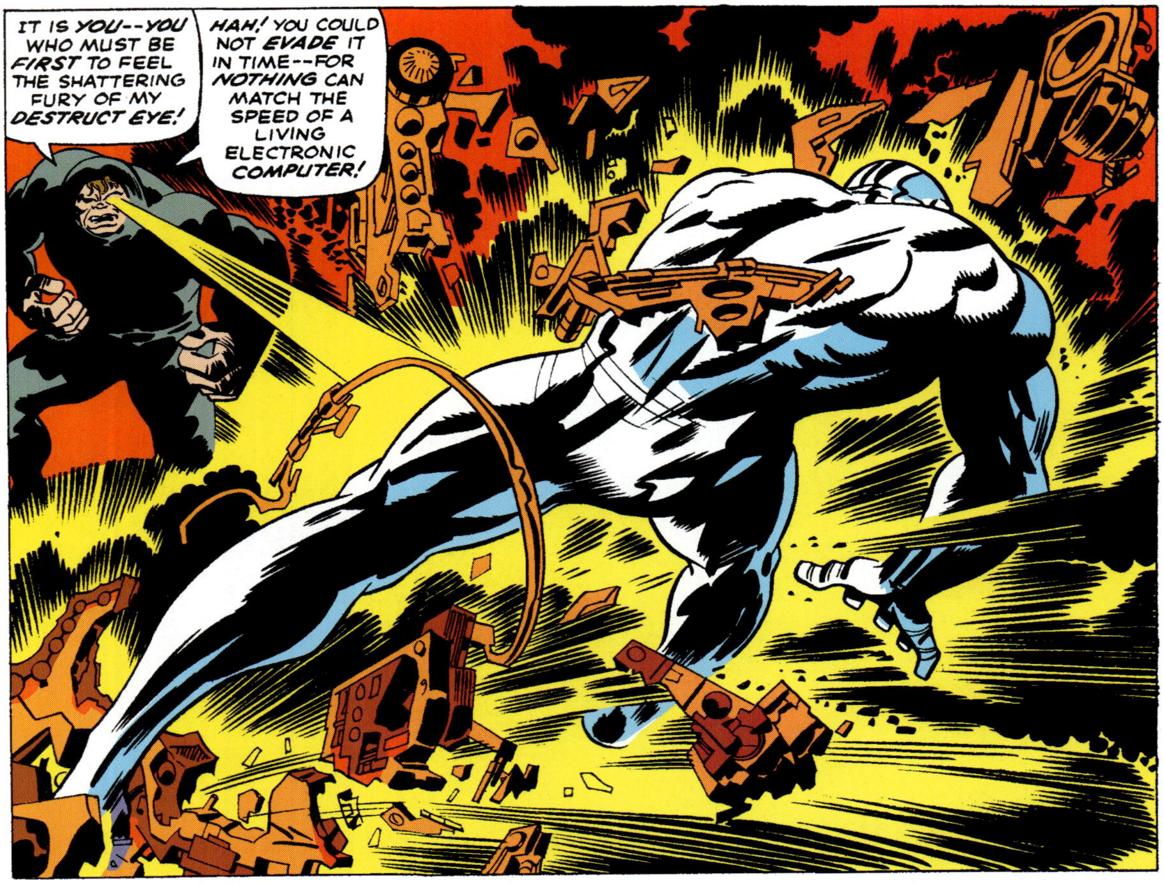
IT IS YOU--YOU WHO MUST BE FIRST TO FEEL THE SHATTERING FURY OF MY DESTRUCT EYE!
HAH! YOU COULD NOT EVADE IT IN TIME--FOR NOTHING CAN MATCH THE SPEED OF A LIVING ELECTRONIC COMPUTER!
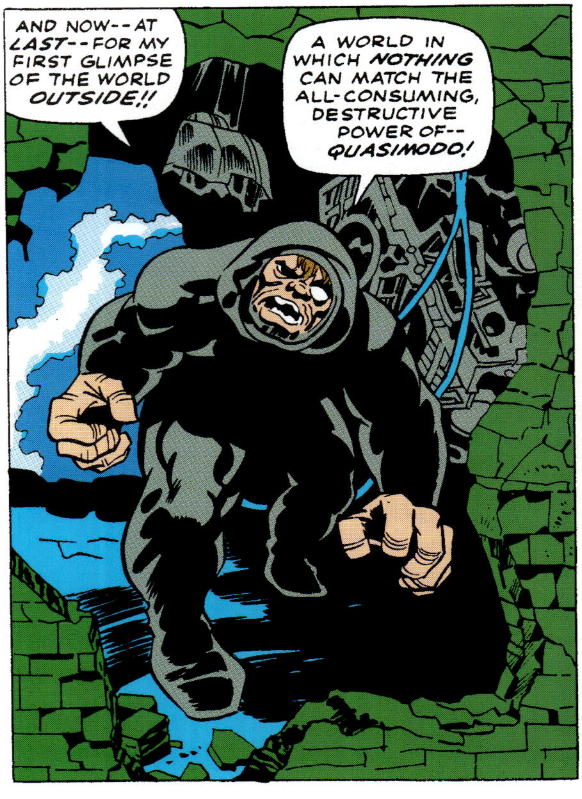
AND NOW--AT LAST--FOR MY FIRST GLIMPSE OF THE WORLD OUTSIDE!!
A WORLD IN WHICH NOTHING CAN MATCH THE ALL-CONSUMING, DESTRUCTIVE POWER OF--QUASIMODO!
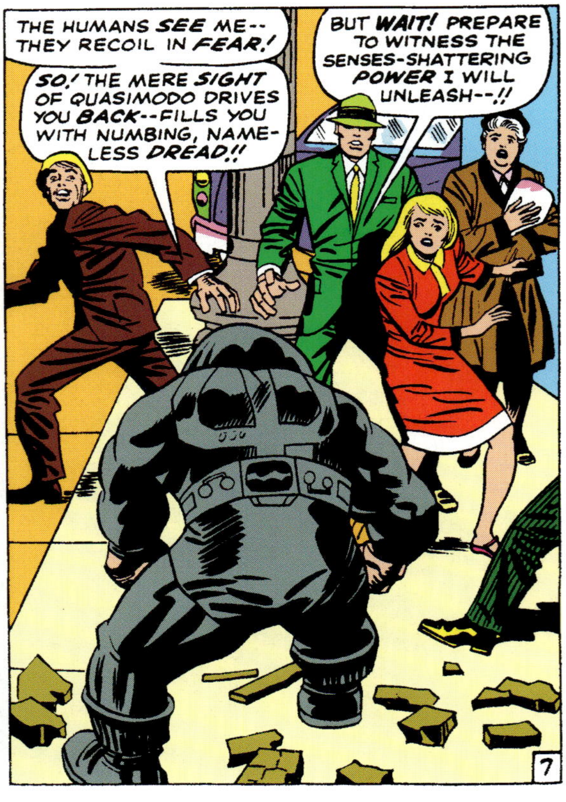
THE HUMANS SEE ME--THEY RECOIL IN FEAR!
SO! THE MERE SIGHT OF QUASIMODO DRIVES YOU BACK--FILLS YOU WITH NUMBING, NAMELESS DREAD!!
BUT WAIT! PREPARE TO WITNESS THE SENSES-SHATTERING POWER I WILL UNLEASH--!!
7

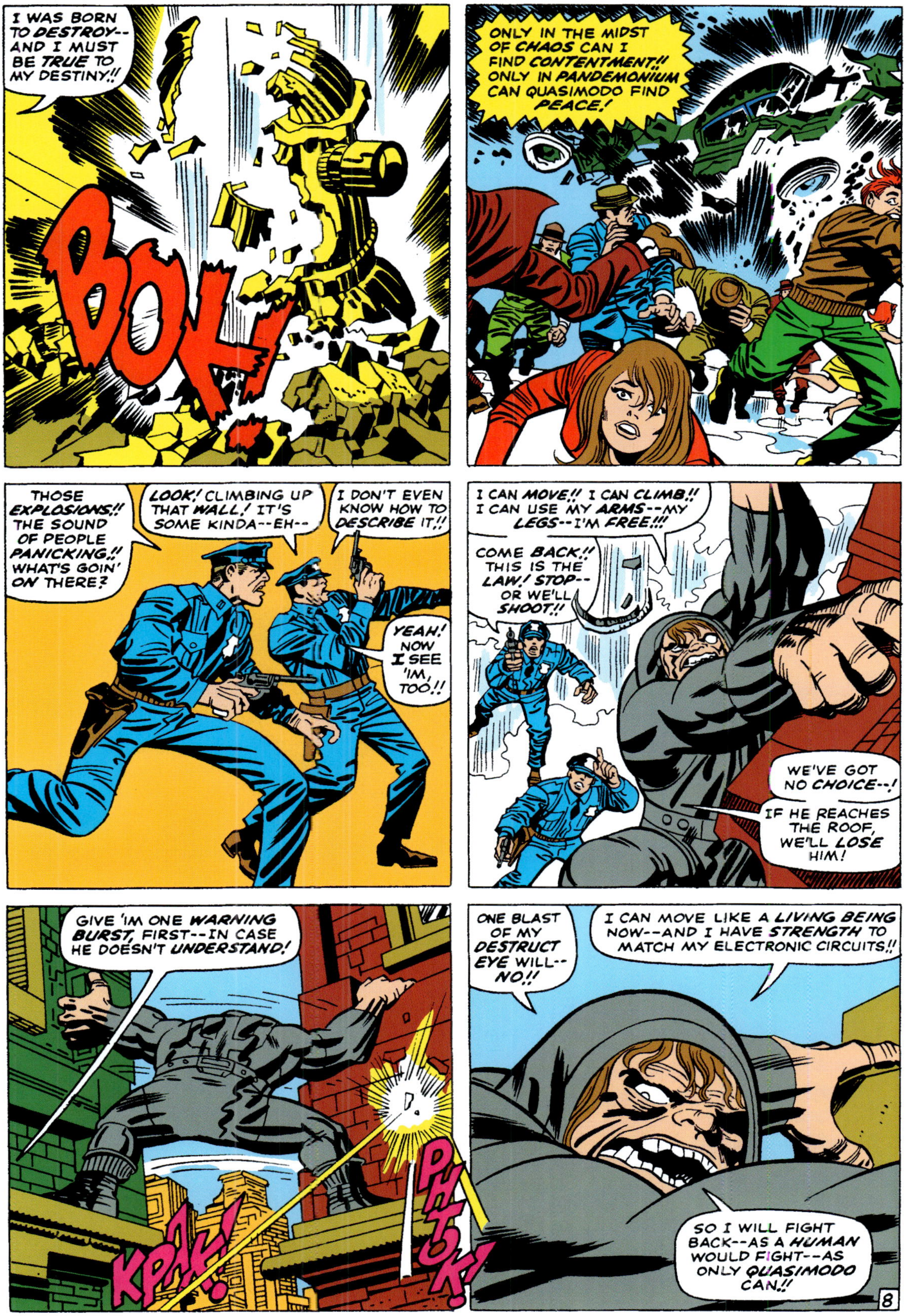
I WAS BORN TO DESTROY-- AND I MUST BE TRUE TO MY DESTINY!!
BOOM!
ONLY IN THE MIDST OF CHAOS CAN I FIND CONTENTMENT!! ONLY IN PANDEMONIUM CAN QUASIMODO FIND PEACE!
THOSE EXPLOSIONS!! THE SOUND OF PEOPLE PANICKING!! WHAT'S GOIN' ON THERE?
LOOK! CLIMBING UP THAT WALL! IT'S SOME KINDA--EH--
I DON'T EVEN KNOW HOW TO DESCRIBE IT!!
YEAH! NOW I SEE 'IM, TOO!!
I CAN MOVE!! I CAN CLIMB!! I CAN USE MY ARMS--MY LEGS--I'M FREE!!!
COME BACK!! THIS IS THE LAW! STOP--OR WE'LL SHOOT!!
WE'VE GOT NO CHOICE--!
IF HE REACHES THE ROOF, WE'LL LOSE HIM!
GIVE 'IM ONE WARNING BURST, FIRST--IN CASE HE DOESN'T UNDERSTAND!
KRAK!
PHTOK!
ONE BLAST OF MY DESTRUCT EYE WILL-- NO!!
I CAN MOVE LIKE A LIVING BEING NOW--AND I HAVE STRENGTH TO MATCH MY ELECTRONIC CIRCUITS!!
SO I WILL FIGHT BACK--AS A HUMAN WOULD FIGHT--AS ONLY QUASIMODO CAN!!
8

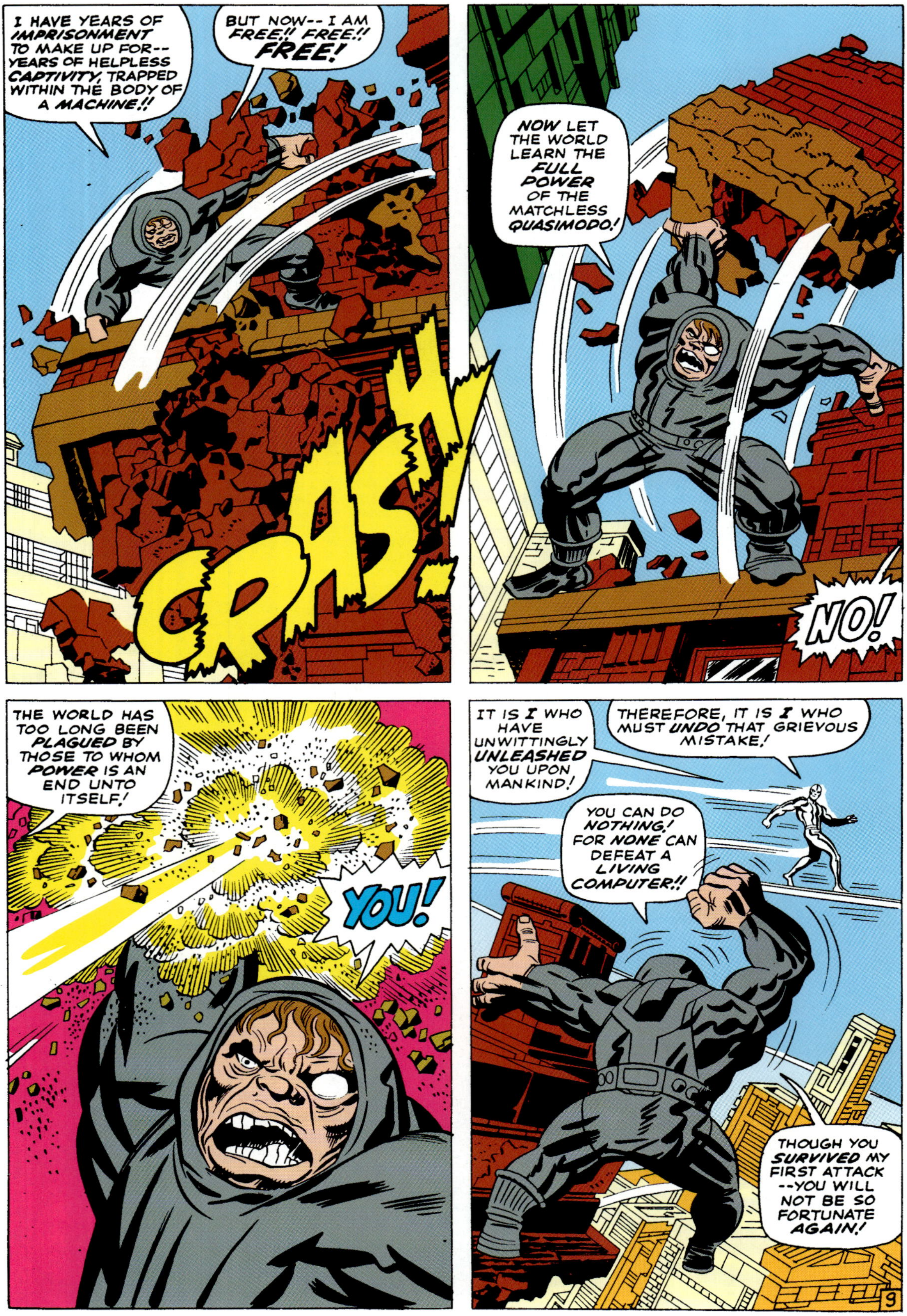

I HAVE YEARS OF IMPRISONMENT TO MAKE UP FOR-- YEARS OF HELPLESS CAPTIVITY, TRAPPED WITHIN THE BODY OF A MACHINE!!
BUT NOW-- I AM FREE!! FREE!! FREE!
CRASH!
NOW LET THE WORLD LEARN THE FULL POWER OF THE MATCHLESS QUASIMODO!
NO!
THE WORLD HAS TOO LONG BEEN PLAGUED BY THOSE TO WHOM POWER IS AN END UNTO ITSELF!
YOU!
IT IS I WHO HAVE UNWITTINGLY UNLEASHED YOU UPON MANKIND!
THEREFORE, IT IS I WHO MUST UNDO THAT GRIEVOUS MISTAKE!
YOU CAN DO NOTHING! FOR NONE CAN DEFEAT A LIVING COMPUTER!!
THOUGH YOU SURVIVED MY FIRST ATTACK --YOU WILL NOT BE SO FORTUNATE AGAIN!
9

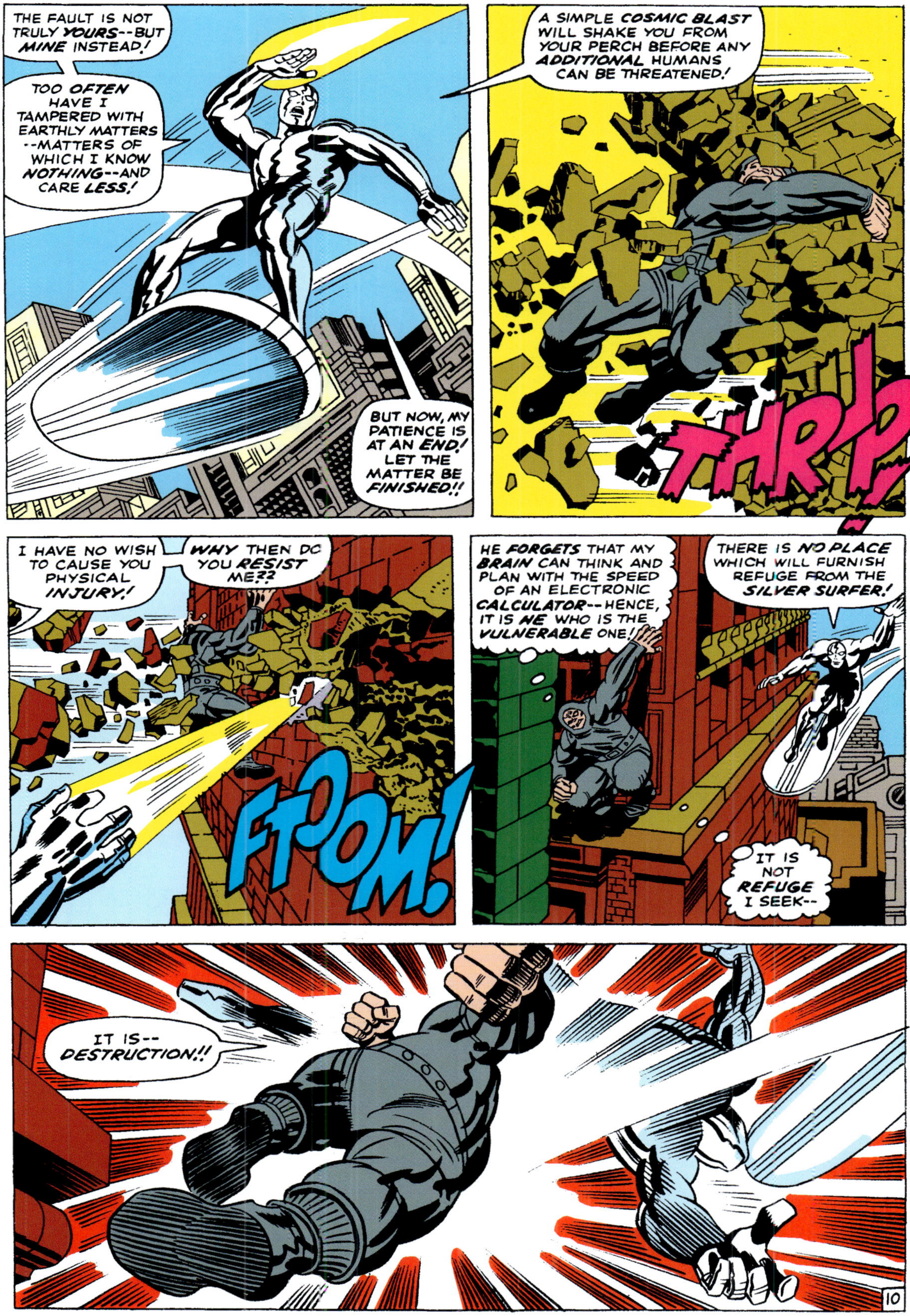
THE FAULT IS NOT TRULY YOURS--BUT MINE INSTEAD!
TOO OFTEN HAVE I TAMPERED WITH EARTHLY MATTERS --MATTERS OF WHICH I KNOW NOTHING--AND CARE LESS!
BUT NOW, MY PATIENCE IS AT AN END! LET THE MATTER BE FINISHED!!
A SIMPLE COSMIC BLAST WILL SHAKE YOU FROM YOUR PERCH BEFORE ANY ADDITIONAL HUMANS CAN BE THREATENED!
THRIP
I HAVE NO WISH TO CAUSE YOU PHYSICAL INJURY!
WHY THEN DO YOU RESIST ME??
FTOOM!
HE FORGETS THAT MY BRAIN CAN THINK AND PLAN WITH THE SPEED OF AN ELECTRONIC CALCULATOR--HENCE, IT IS HE WHO IS THE VULNERABLE ONE!
THERE IS NO PLACE WHICH WILL FURNISH REFUGE FROM THE SILVER SURFER!
IT IS NOT REFUGE I SEEK--
IT IS-- DESTRUCTION!!
10

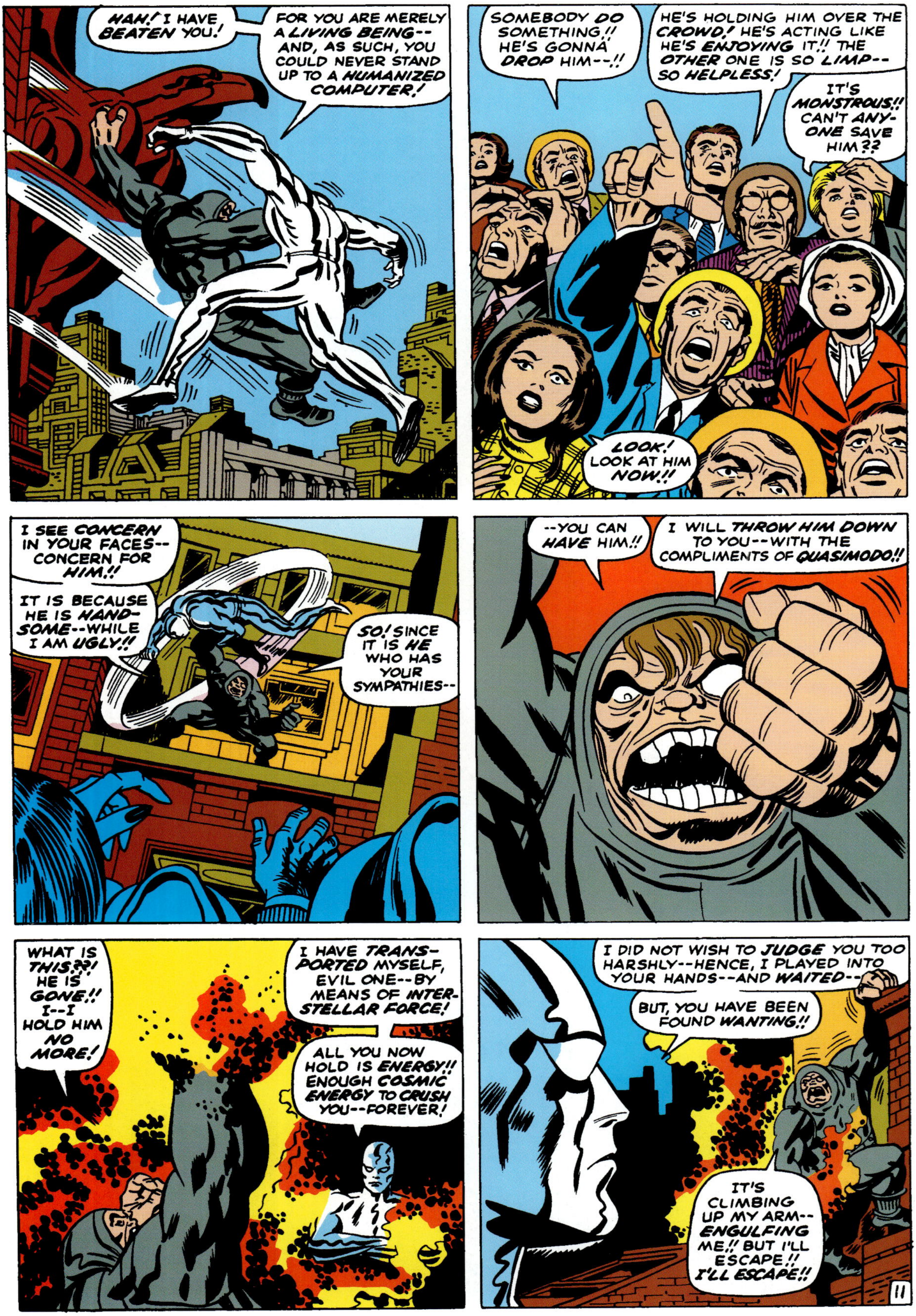
HAH! I HAVE BEATEN YOU!
FOR YOU ARE MERELY A LIVING BEING-- AND, AS SUCH, YOU COULD NEVER STAND UP TO A HUMANIZED COMPUTER!
SOMEBODY DO SOMETHING!! HE'S GONNA DROP HIM--!!
HE'S HOLDING HIM OVER THE CROWD! HE'S ACTING LIKE HE'S ENJOYING IT!! THE OTHER ONE IS SO LIMP-- SO HELPLESS!
IT'S MONSTROUS!! CAN'T ANY-ONE SAVE HIM??
LOOK! LOOK AT HIM NOW!!
I SEE CONCERN IN YOUR FACES-- CONCERN FOR HIM!!
IT IS BECAUSE HE IS HAND-SOME--WHILE I AM UGLY!!
SO! SINCE IT IS HE WHO HAS YOUR SYMPATHIES--
--YOU CAN HAVE HIM!!
I WILL THROW HIM DOWN TO YOU--WITH THE COMPLIMENTS OF QUASIMODO!!
WHAT IS THIS??! HE IS GONE!! I--I HOLD HIM NO MORE!
I HAVE TRANS-PORTED MYSELF, EVIL ONE--BY MEANS OF INTER-STELLAR FORCE!
ALL YOU NOW HOLD IS ENERGY!! ENOUGH COSMIC ENERGY TO CRUSH YOU--FOREVER!
I DID NOT WISH TO JUDGE YOU TOO HARSHLY--HENCE, I PLAYED INTO YOUR HANDS--AND WAITED--
BUT, YOU HAVE BEEN FOUND WANTING!!
IT'S CLIMBING UP MY ARM-- ENGULFING ME!! BUT I'LL ESCAPE!! I'LL ESCAPE!!
11

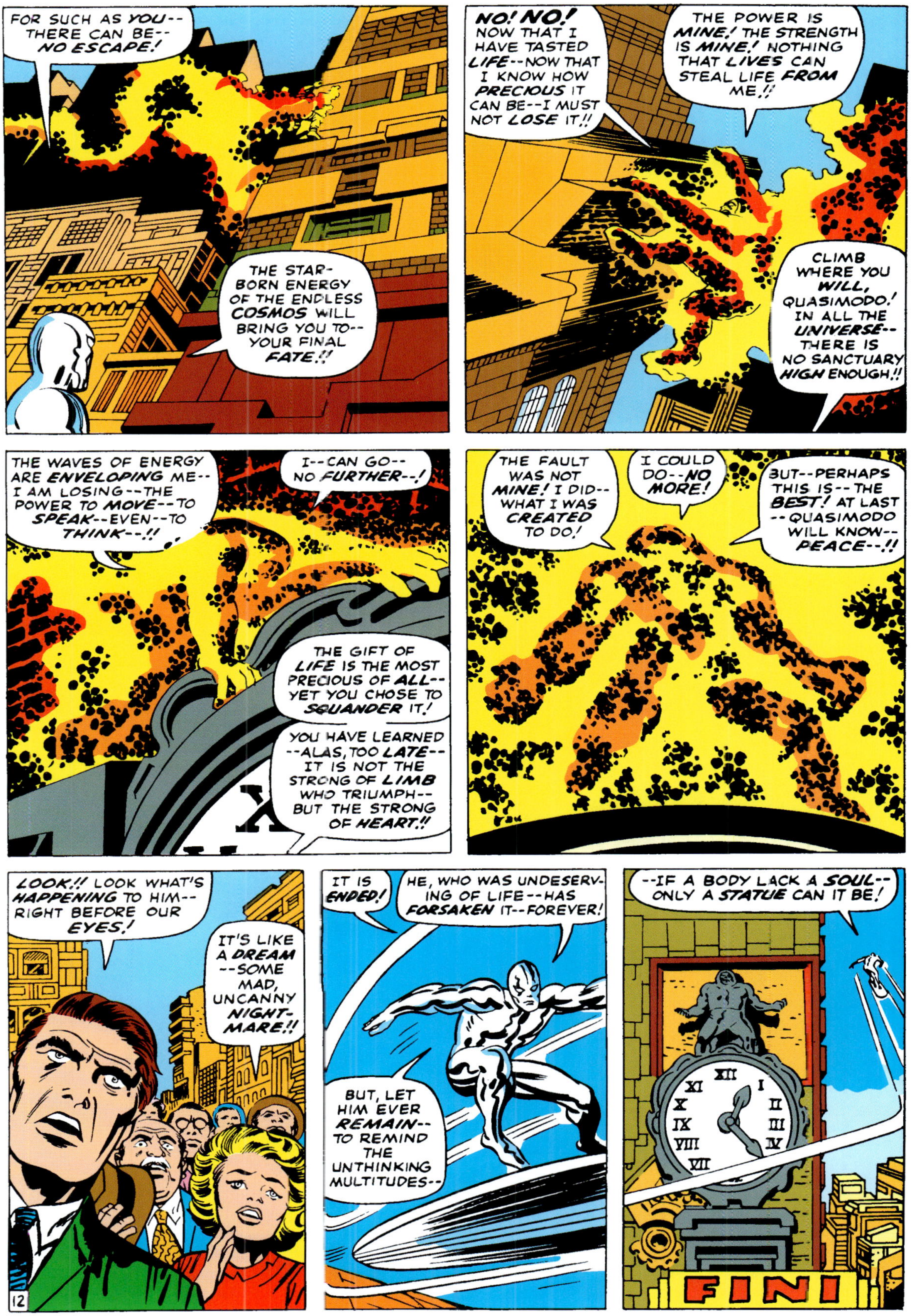
FOR SUCH AS YOU-- THERE CAN BE-- NO ESCAPE!
THE STAR-BORN ENERGY OF THE ENDLESS COSMOS WILL BRING YOU TO-- YOUR FINAL FATE.!!
NO! NO! NOW THAT I HAVE TASTED LIFE--NOW THAT I KNOW HOW PRECIOUS IT CAN BE--I MUST NOT LOSE IT!!
THE POWER IS MINE! THE STRENGTH IS MINE! NOTHING THAT LIVES CAN STEAL LIFE FROM ME.!!
CLIMB WHERE YOU WILL, QUASIMODO! IN ALL THE UNIVERSE-- THERE IS NO SANCTUARY HIGH ENOUGH!!
THE WAVES OF ENERGY ARE ENVELOPING ME-- I AM LOSING--THE POWER TO MOVE--TO SPEAK--EVEN--TO THINK--!!
I--CAN GO-- NO FURTHER--!
THE GIFT OF LIFE IS THE MOST PRECIOUS OF ALL-- YET YOU CHOSE TO SQUANDER IT!
YOU HAVE LEARNED --ALAS, TOO LATE-- IT IS NOT THE STRONG OF LIMB WHO TRIUMPH-- BUT THE STRONG OF HEART!!
THE FAULT WAS NOT MINE! I DID-- WHAT I WAS CREATED TO DO!
I COULD DO--NO MORE!
BUT--PERHAPS THIS IS--THE BEST! AT LAST --QUASIMODO WILL KNOW-- PEACE--!!
LOOK!! LOOK WHAT'S HAPPENING TO HIM-- RIGHT BEFORE OUR EYES!
IT'S LIKE A DREAM --SOME MAD, UNCANNY NIGHT-MARE!!
12
IT IS ENDED!
HE, WHO WAS UNDESERVING OF LIFE--HAS FORSAKEN IT--FOREVER!
BUT, LET HIM EVER REMAIN-- TO REMIND THE UNTHINKING MULTITUDES--
--IF A BODY LACK A SOUL-- ONLY A STATUE CAN IT BE!
FINI

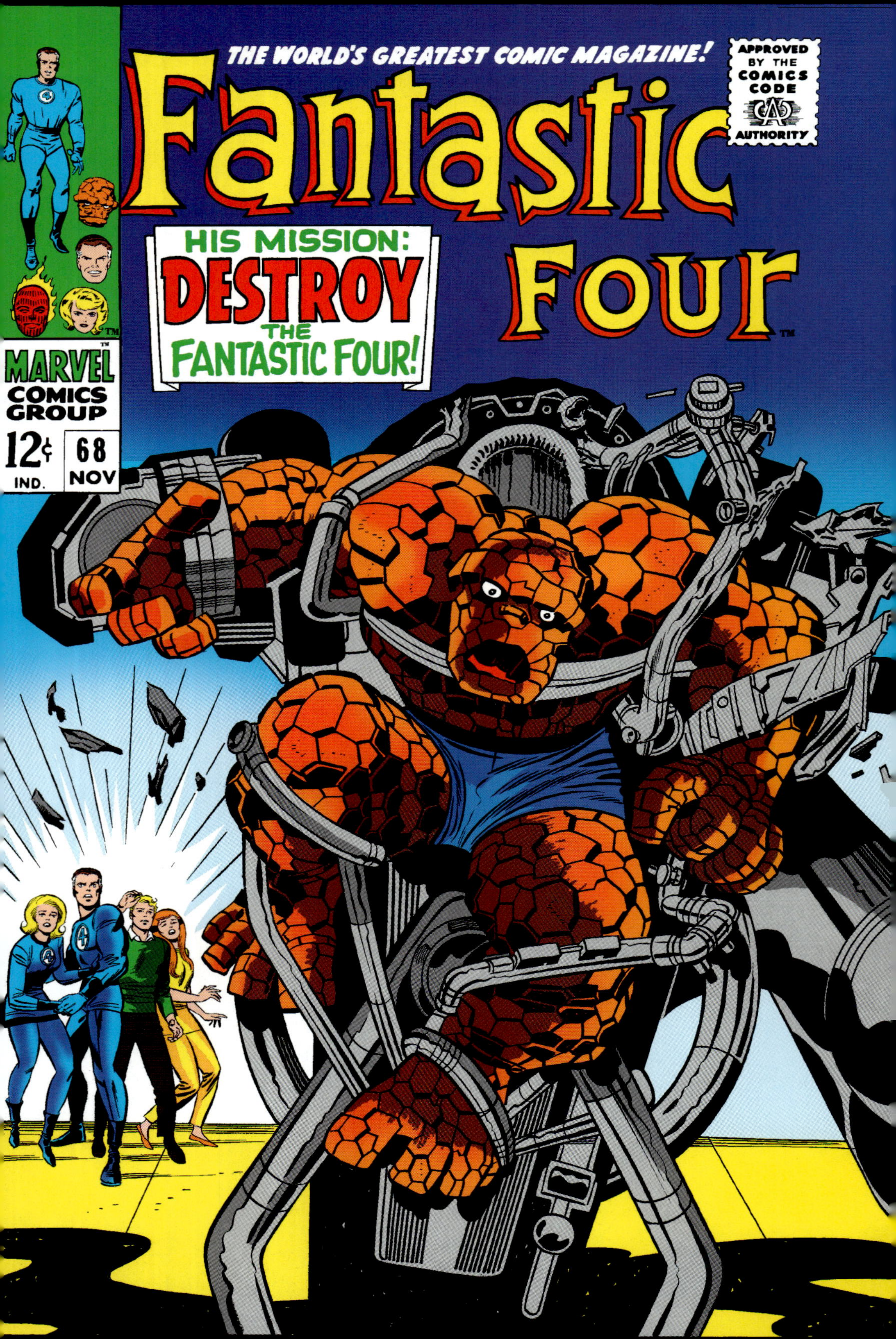
THE WORLD'S GREATEST COMIC MAGAZINE!
Fantastic Four
APPROVED BY THE COMICS CODE AUTHORITY
MARVEL COMICS GROUP
12¢ IND.
68 NOV
HIS MISSION: DESTROY THE FANTASTIC FOUR!

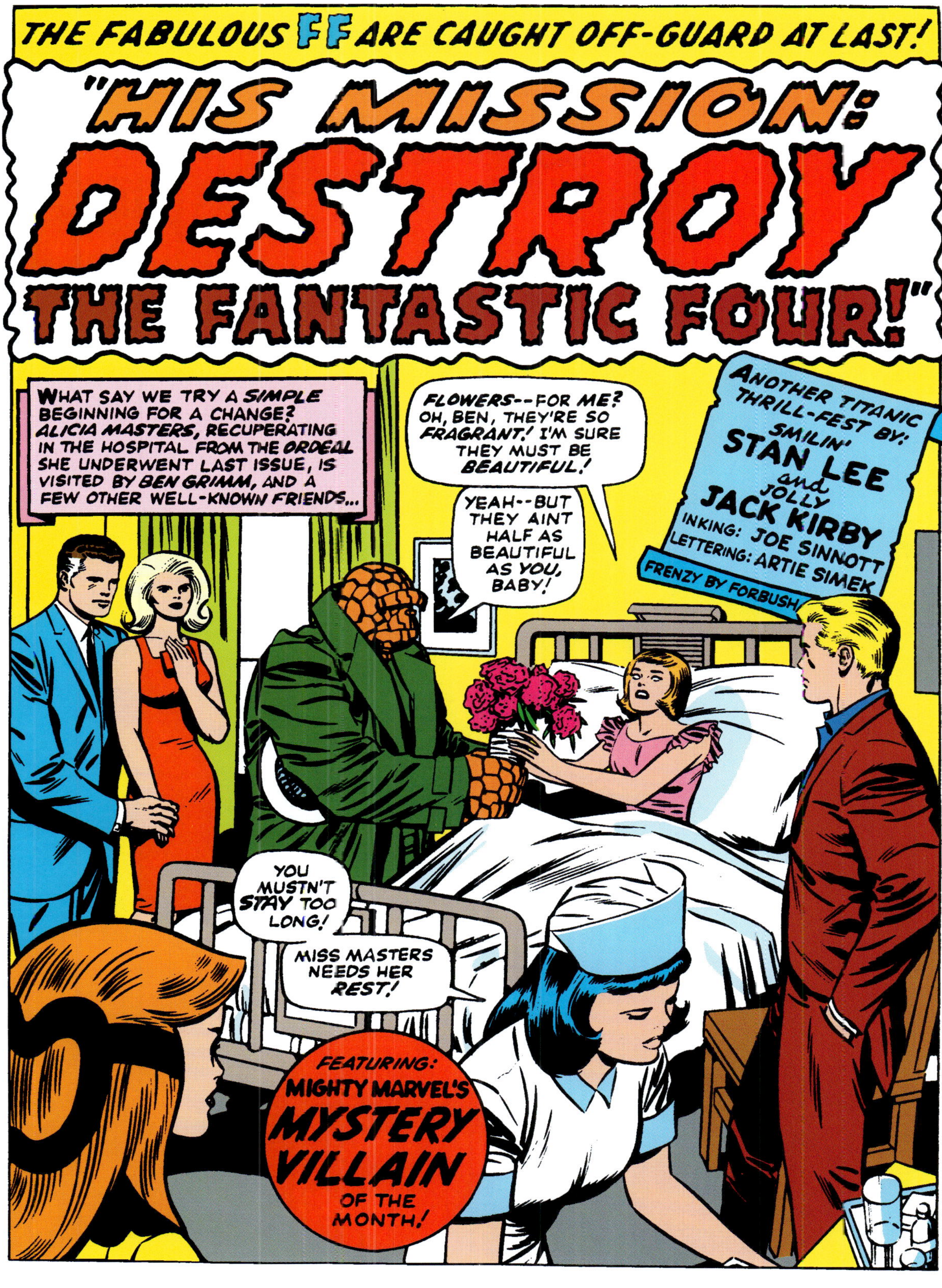
THE FABULOUS FF ARE CAUGHT OFF-GUARD AT LAST!
"HIS MISSION: DESTROY THE FANTASTIC FOUR!"
WHAT SAY WE TRY A SIMPLE BEGINNING FOR A CHANGE? ALICIA MASTERS, RECUPERATING IN THE HOSPITAL FROM THE ORDEAL SHE UNDERWENT LAST ISSUE, IS VISITED BY BEN GRIMM, AND A FEW OTHER WELL-KNOWN FRIENDS...
FLOWERS--FOR ME? OH, BEN, THEY'RE SO FRAGRANT! I'M SURE THEY MUST BE BEAUTIFUL!
YEAH--BUT THEY AINT HALF AS BEAUTIFUL AS YOU, BABY!
ANOTHER TITANIC THRILL-FEST BY: SMILIN' STAN LEE and JOLLY JACK KIRBY
INKING: JOE SINNOTT
LETTERING: ARTIE SIMEK
FRENZY BY FORBUSH
YOU MUSTN'T STAY TOO LONG!
MISS MASTERS NEEDS HER REST!
FEATURING: MIGHTY MARVEL'S MYSTERY VILLAIN OF THE MONTH!

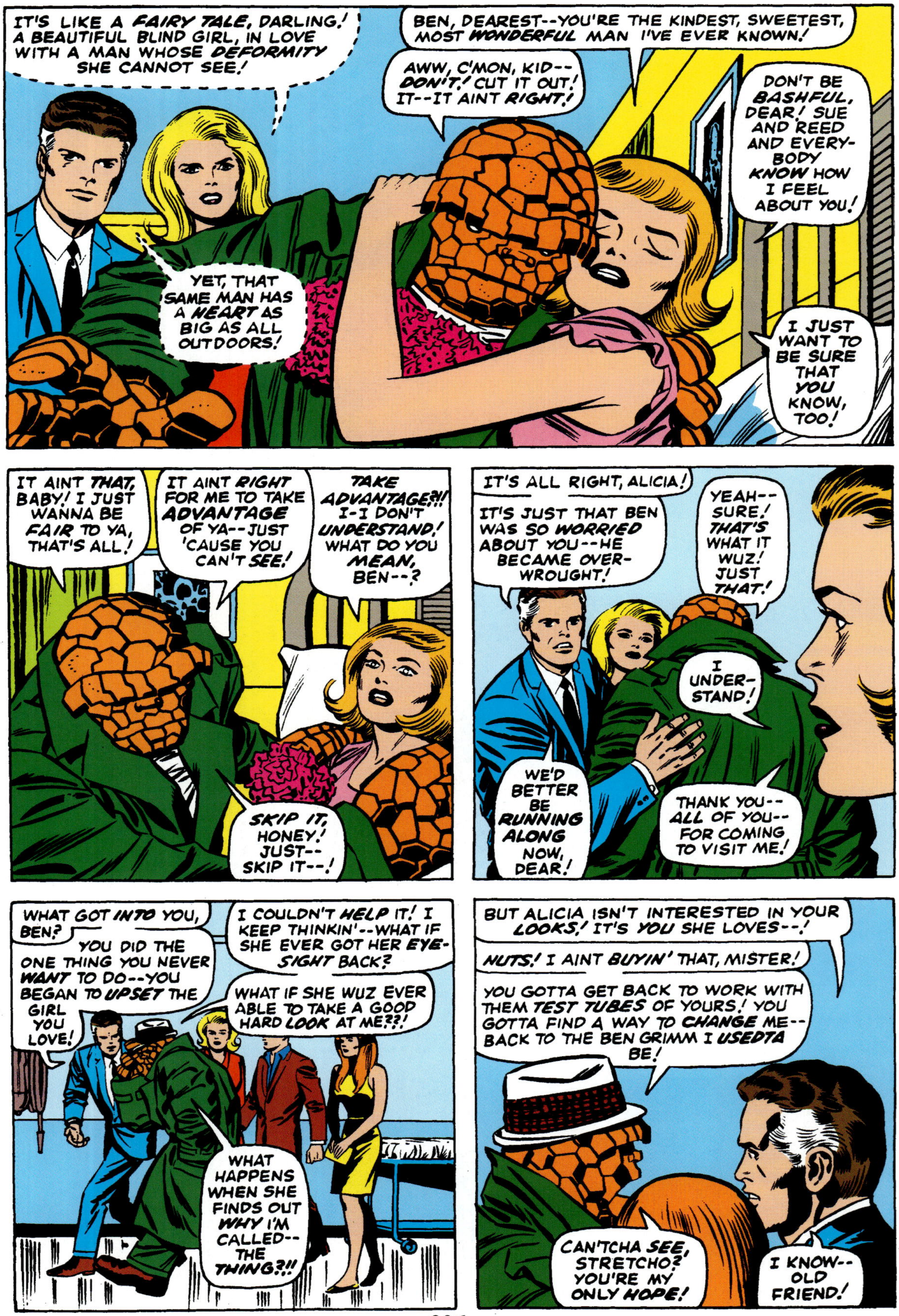

IT'S LIKE A FAIRY TALE, DARLING! A BEAUTIFUL BLIND GIRL, IN LOVE WITH A MAN WHOSE DEFORMITY SHE CANNOT SEE!
YET, THAT SAME MAN HAS A HEART AS BIG AS ALL OUTDOORS!
BEN, DEAREST--YOU'RE THE KINDEST, SWEETEST, MOST WONDERFUL MAN I'VE EVER KNOWN!
AWW, C'MON, KID--DON'T! CUT IT OUT! IT--IT AINT RIGHT!
DON'T BE BASHFUL, DEAR! SUE AND REED AND EVERY-BODY KNOW HOW I FEEL ABOUT YOU!
I JUST WANT TO BE SURE THAT YOU KNOW, TOO!
IT AINT THAT, BABY! I JUST WANNA BE FAIR TO YA, THAT'S ALL!
IT AINT RIGHT FOR ME TO TAKE ADVANTAGE OF YA--JUST 'CAUSE YOU CAN'T SEE!
TAKE ADVANTAGE?!! I-I DON'T UNDERSTAND! WHAT DO YOU MEAN, BEN--?
SKIP IT, HONEY! JUST--SKIP IT--!
IT'S ALL RIGHT, ALICIA!
IT'S JUST THAT BEN WAS SO WORRIED ABOUT YOU--HE BECAME OVER-WROUGHT!
YEAH--SURE! THAT'S WHAT IT WUZ! JUST THAT!
I UNDER-STAND!
WE'D BETTER BE RUNNING ALONG NOW, DEAR!
THANK YOU--ALL OF YOU--FOR COMING TO VISIT ME!
WHAT GOT INTO YOU, BEN?
YOU DID THE ONE THING YOU NEVER WANT TO DO--YOU BEGAN TO UPSET THE GIRL YOU LOVE!
I COULDN'T HELP IT! I KEEP THINKIN'--WHAT IF SHE EVER GOT HER EYE-SIGHT BACK?
WHAT IF SHE WUZ EVER ABLE TO TAKE A GOOD HARD LOOK AT ME??!
WHAT HAPPENS WHEN SHE FINDS OUT WHY I'M CALLED--THE THING?!!
BUT ALICIA ISN'T INTERESTED IN YOUR LOOKS! IT'S YOU SHE LOVES--!
NUTS! I AINT BUYIN' THAT, MISTER!
YOU GOTTA GET BACK TO WORK WITH THEM TEST TUBES OF YOURS! YOU GOTTA FIND A WAY TO CHANGE ME--BACK TO THE BEN GRIMM I USEDTA BE!
CAN'TCHA SEE, STRETCHO? YOU'RE MY ONLY HOPE!
I KNOW--OLD FRIEND!

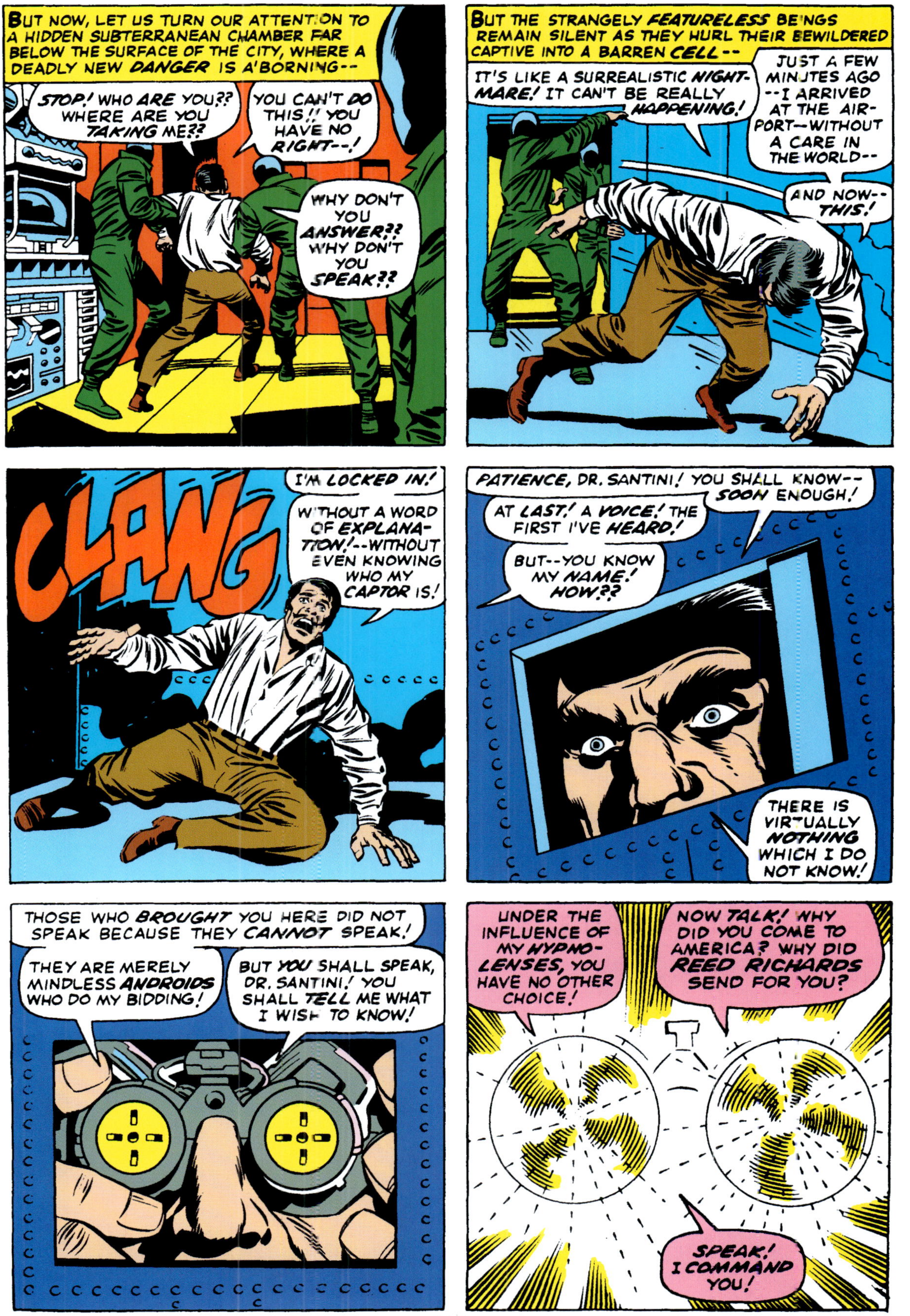

BUT NOW, LET US TURN OUR ATTENTION TO A HIDDEN SUBTERRANEAN CHAMBER FAR BELOW THE SURFACE OF THE CITY, WHERE A DEADLY NEW DANGER IS A'BORNING--
STOP! WHO ARE YOU?? WHERE ARE YOU TAKING ME??
YOU CAN'T DO THIS!! YOU HAVE NO RIGHT--!
WHY DON'T YOU ANSWER?? WHY DON'T YOU SPEAK??
BUT THE STRANGELY FEATURELESS BEINGS REMAIN SILENT AS THEY HURL THEIR BEWILDERED CAPTIVE INTO A BARREN CELL--
IT'S LIKE A SURREALISTIC NIGHTMARE! IT CAN'T BE REALLY HAPPENING!
JUST A FEW MINUTES AGO --I ARRIVED AT THE AIRPORT--WITHOUT A CARE IN THE WORLD--
AND NOW--THIS!
CLANG
I'M LOCKED IN!
WITHOUT A WORD OF EXPLANATION!--WITHOUT EVEN KNOWING WHO MY CAPTOR IS!
PATIENCE, DR. SANTINI! YOU SHALL KNOW-- SOON ENOUGH!
AT LAST! A VOICE! THE FIRST I'VE HEARD!
BUT--YOU KNOW MY NAME! HOW??
THERE IS VIRTUALLY NOTHING WHICH I DO NOT KNOW!
THOSE WHO BROUGHT YOU HERE DID NOT SPEAK BECAUSE THEY CANNOT SPEAK!
THEY ARE MERELY MINDLESS ANDROIDS WHO DO MY BIDDING!
BUT YOU SHALL SPEAK, DR. SANTINI! YOU SHALL TELL ME WHAT I WISH TO KNOW!
UNDER THE INFLUENCE OF MY HYPNO-LENSES, YOU HAVE NO OTHER CHOICE!
NOW TALK! WHY DID YOU COME TO AMERICA? WHY DID REED RICHARDS SEND FOR YOU?
SPEAK! I COMMAND YOU!

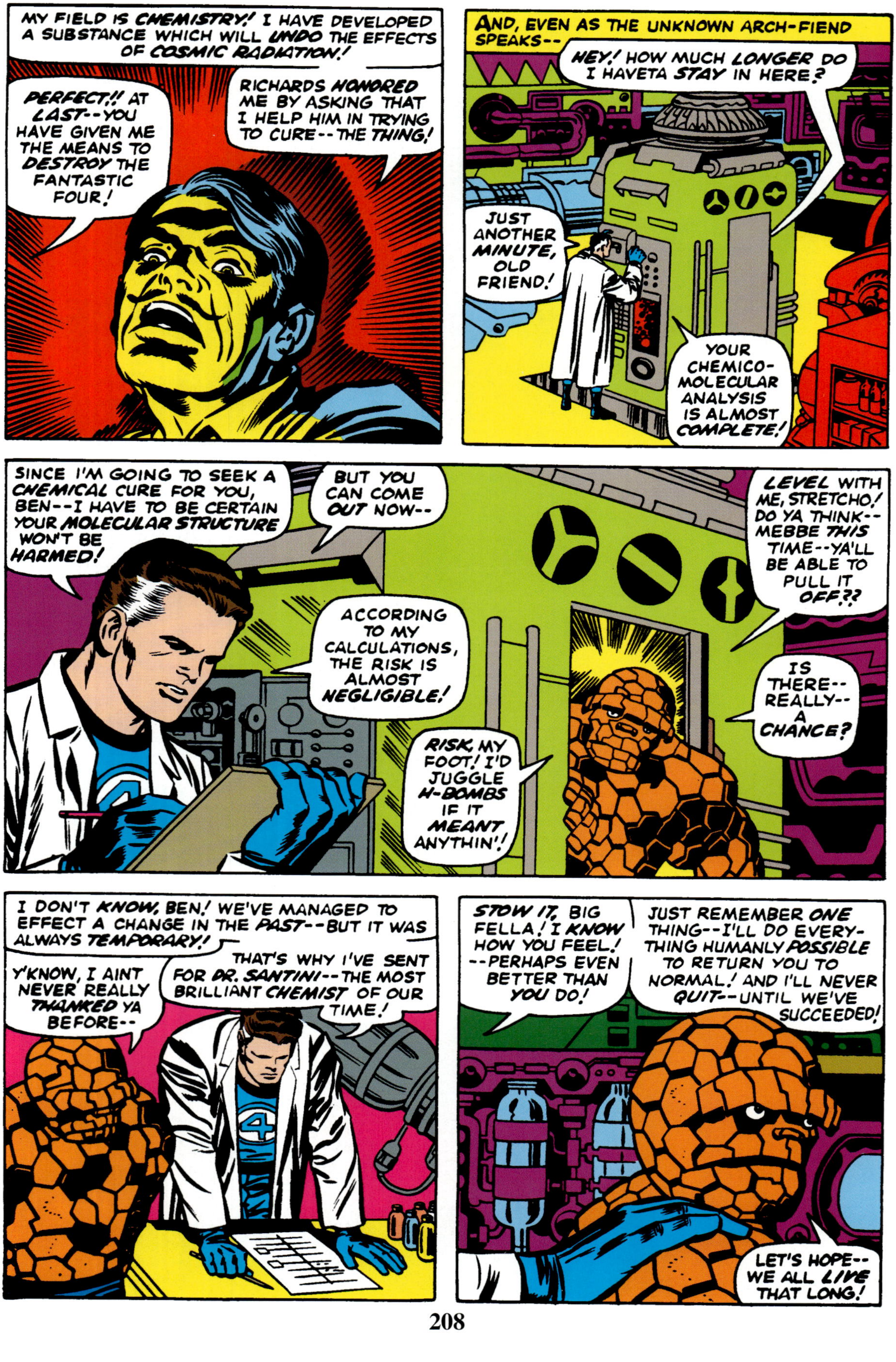
MY FIELD IS CHEMISTRY! I HAVE DEVELOPED A SUBSTANCE WHICH WILL UNDO THE EFFECTS OF COSMIC RADIATION!
PERFECT!! AT LAST--YOU HAVE GIVEN ME THE MEANS TO DESTROY THE FANTASTIC FOUR!
RICHARDS HONORED ME BY ASKING THAT I HELP HIM IN TRYING TO CURE--THE THING!
AND, EVEN AS THE UNKNOWN ARCH-FIEND SPEAKS--
HEY! HOW MUCH LONGER DO I HAVETA STAY IN HERE?
JUST ANOTHER MINUTE, OLD FRIEND!
YOUR CHEMICO-MOLECULAR ANALYSIS IS ALMOST COMPLETE!
SINCE I'M GOING TO SEEK A CHEMICAL CURE FOR YOU, BEN--I HAVE TO BE CERTAIN YOUR MOLECULAR STRUCTURE WON'T BE HARMED!
BUT YOU CAN COME OUT NOW--
LEVEL WITH ME, STRETCHO! DO YA THINK--MEBBE THIS TIME--YA'LL BE ABLE TO PULL IT OFF??
ACCORDING TO MY CALCULATIONS, THE RISK IS ALMOST NEGLIGIBLE!
RISK, MY FOOT! I'D JUGGLE H-BOMBS IF IT MEANT ANYTHIN'!
IS THERE--REALLY--A CHANCE?
I DON'T KNOW, BEN! WE'VE MANAGED TO EFFECT A CHANGE IN THE PAST--BUT IT WAS ALWAYS TEMPORARY!
THAT'S WHY I'VE SENT FOR DR. SANTINI--THE MOST BRILLIANT CHEMIST OF OUR TIME!
Y'KNOW, I AINT NEVER REALLY THANKED YA BEFORE--
STOW IT, BIG FELLA! I KNOW HOW YOU FEEL! --PERHAPS EVEN BETTER THAN YOU DO!
JUST REMEMBER ONE THING--I'LL DO EVERYTHING HUMANLY POSSIBLE TO RETURN YOU TO NORMAL! AND I'LL NEVER QUIT--UNTIL WE'VE SUCCEEDED!
LET'S HOPE--WE ALL LIVE THAT LONG!

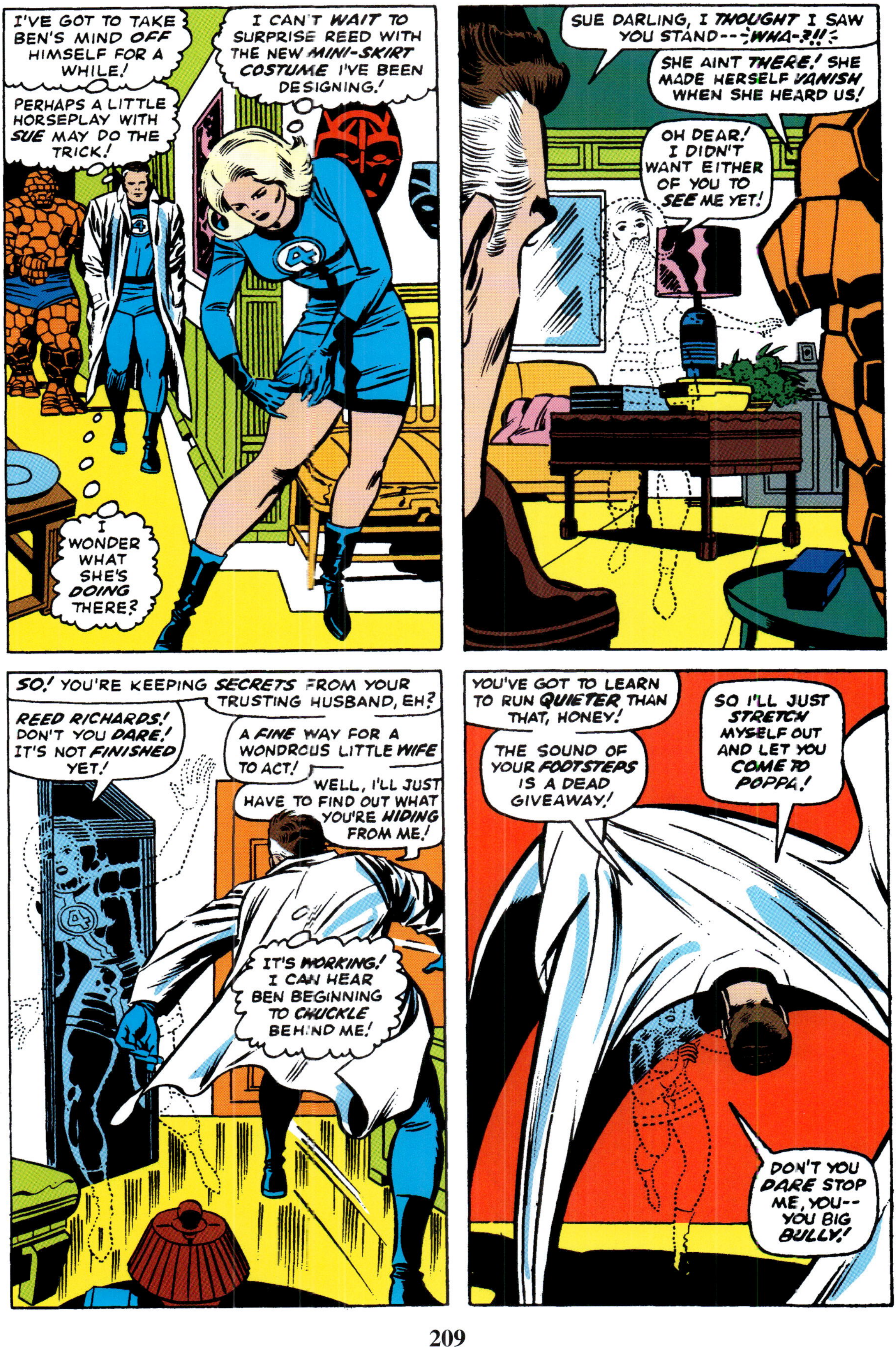
I'VE GOT TO TAKE BEN'S MIND OFF HIMSELF FOR A WHILE!
PERHAPS A LITTLE HORSEPLAY WITH SUE MAY DO THE TRICK!
I CAN'T WAIT TO SURPRISE REED WITH THE NEW MINI-SKIRT COSTUME I'VE BEEN DESIGNING!
I WONDER WHAT SHE'S DOING THERE?
SUE DARLING, I THOUGHT I SAW YOU STAND-- WHA-?!!
SHE AINT THERE! SHE MADE HERSELF VANISH WHEN SHE HEARD US!
OH DEAR! I DIDN'T WANT EITHER OF YOU TO SEE ME YET!
SO! YOU'RE KEEPING SECRETS FROM YOUR TRUSTING HUSBAND, EH?
REED RICHARDS! DON'T YOU DARE! IT'S NOT FINISHED YET!
A FINE WAY FOR A WONDROUS LITTLE WIFE TO ACT!
WELL, I'LL JUST HAVE TO FIND OUT WHAT YOU'RE HIDING FROM ME!
IT'S WORKING! I CAN HEAR BEN BEGINNING TO CHUCKLE BEHIND ME!
YOU'VE GOT TO LEARN TO RUN QUIETER THAN THAT, HONEY!
THE SOUND OF YOUR FOOTSTEPS IS A DEAD GIVEAWAY!
SO I'LL JUST STRETCH MYSELF OUT AND LET YOU COME TO POPPA!
DON'T YOU DARE STOP ME, YOU-- YOU BIG BULLY!

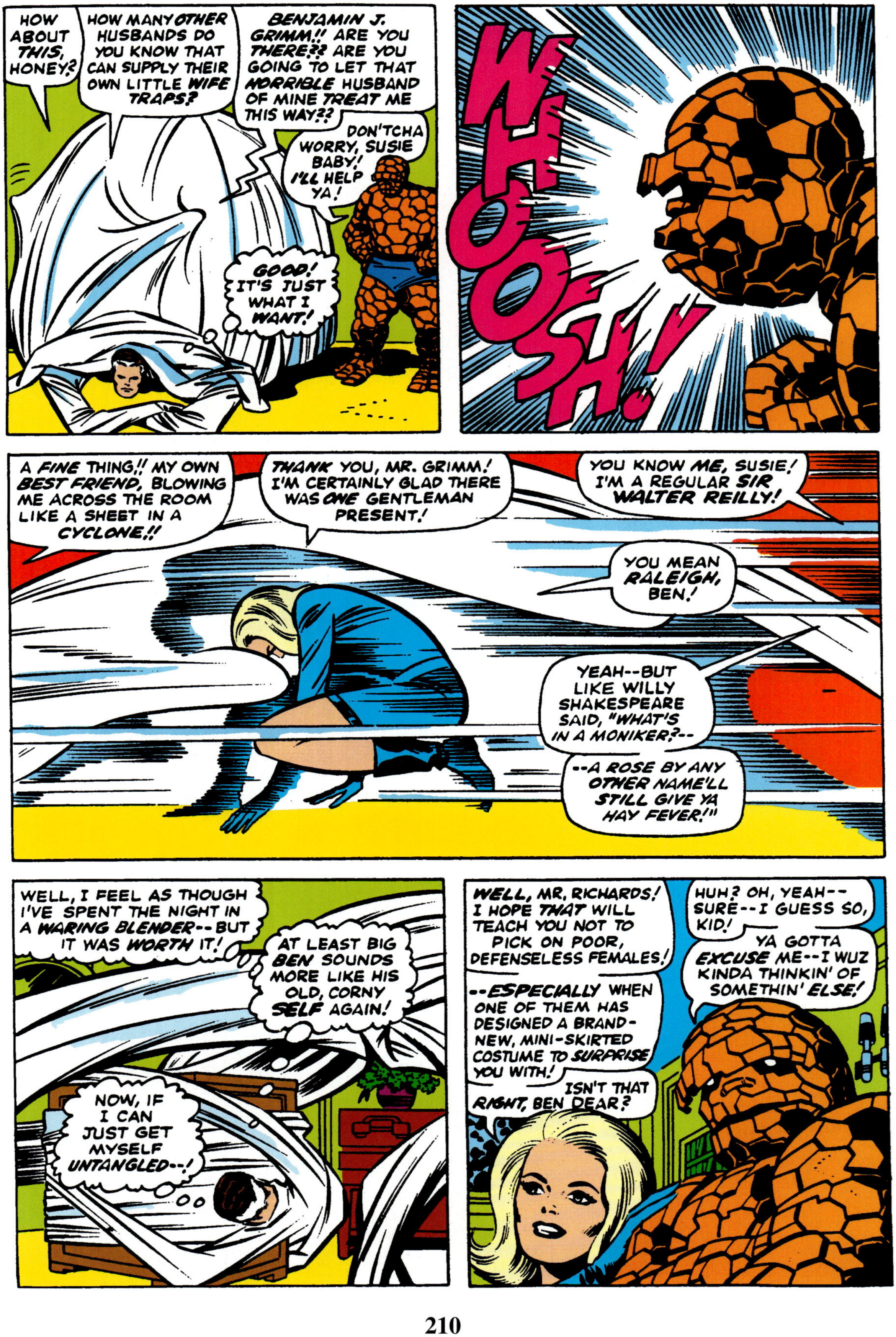

HOW ABOUT THIS, HONEY?
HOW MANY OTHER HUSBANDS DO YOU KNOW THAT CAN SUPPLY THEIR OWN LITTLE WIFE TRAPS?
BENJAMIN J. GRIMM!! ARE YOU THERE?? ARE YOU GOING TO LET THAT HORRIBLE HUSBAND OF MINE TREAT ME THIS WAY??
DON'TCHA WORRY, SUSIE BABY! I'LL HELP YA!
GOOD! IT'S JUST WHAT I WANT!
WHOOSH!
A FINE THING!! MY OWN BEST FRIEND, BLOWING ME ACROSS THE ROOM LIKE A SHEET IN A CYCLONE!!
THANK YOU, MR. GRIMM! I'M CERTAINLY GLAD THERE WAS ONE GENTLEMAN PRESENT!
YOU KNOW ME, SUSIE! I'M A REGULAR SIR WALTER REILLY!
YOU MEAN RALEIGH, BEN!
YEAH--BUT LIKE WILLY SHAKESPEARE SAID, "WHAT'S IN A MONIKER?--
--A ROSE BY ANY OTHER NAME'LL STILL GIVE YA HAY FEVER!"
WELL, I FEEL AS THOUGH I'VE SPENT THE NIGHT IN A WARING BLENDER--BUT IT WAS WORTH IT!
AT LEAST BIG BEN SOUNDS MORE LIKE HIS OLD, CORNY SELF AGAIN!
NOW, IF I CAN JUST GET MYSELF UNTANGLED--!
WELL, MR. RICHARDS! I HOPE THAT WILL TEACH YOU NOT TO PICK ON POOR, DEFENSELESS FEMALES!
--ESPECIALLY WHEN ONE OF THEM HAS DESIGNED A BRAND-NEW, MINI-SKIRTED COSTUME TO SURPRISE YOU WITH!
ISN'T THAT RIGHT, BEN DEAR?
HUH? OH, YEAH--SURE--I GUESS SO, KID!
YA GOTTA EXCUSE ME--I WUZ KINDA THINKIN' OF SOMETHIN' ELSE!

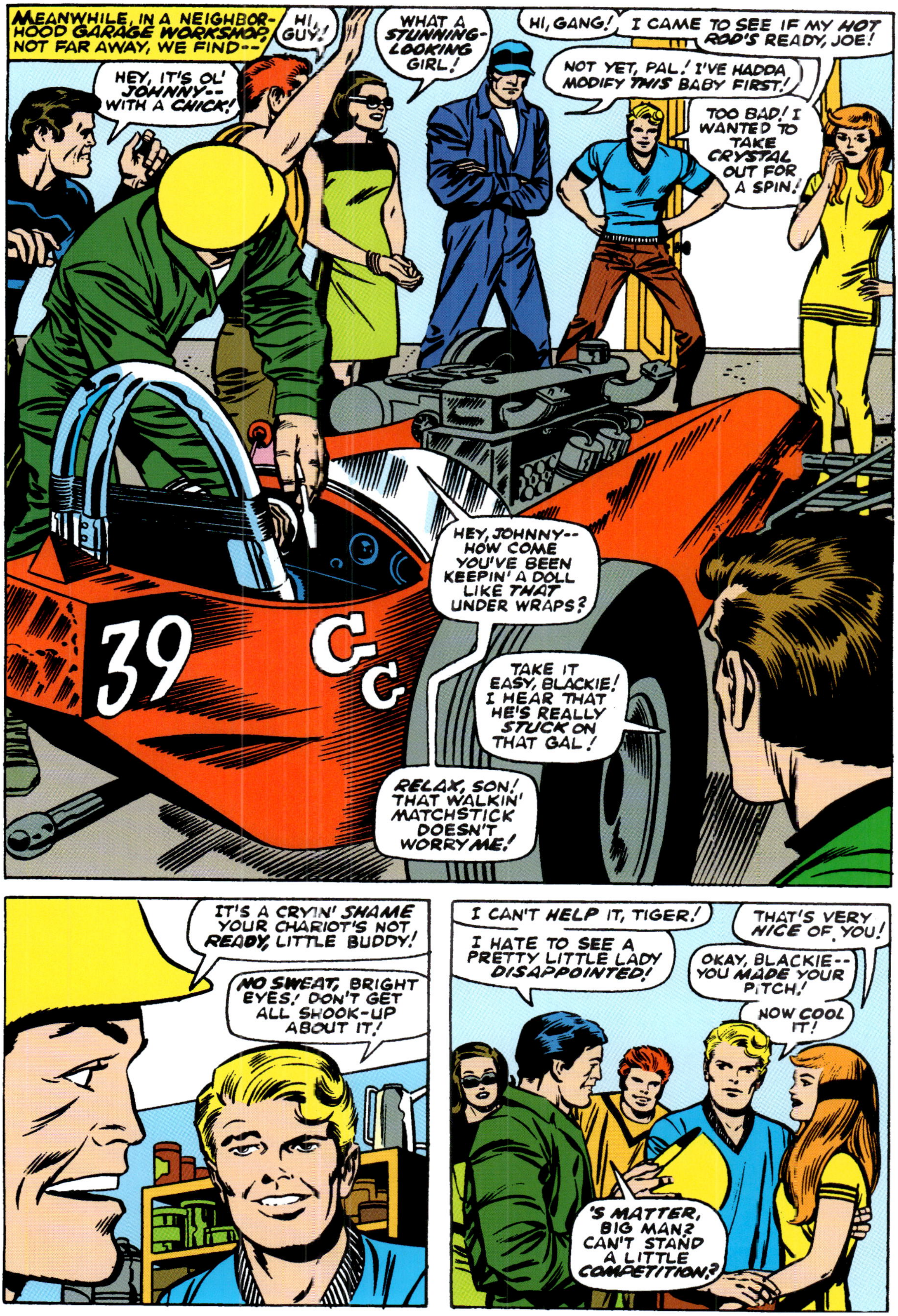
MEANWHILE, IN A NEIGHBORHOOD GARAGE WORKSHOP, NOT FAR AWAY, WE FIND--
HI, GUY!
WHAT A STUNNING-LOOKING GIRL!
HI, GANG!
I CAME TO SEE IF MY HOT ROD'S READY, JOE!
HEY, IT'S OL' JOHNNY-- WITH A CHICK!
NOT YET, PAL! I'VE HADDA MODIFY THIS BABY FIRST!
TOO BAD! I WANTED TO TAKE CRYSTAL OUT FOR A SPIN!
HEY, JOHNNY-- HOW COME YOU'VE BEEN KEEPIN' A DOLL LIKE THAT UNDER WRAPS?
TAKE IT EASY, BLACKIE! I HEAR THAT HE'S REALLY STUCK ON THAT GAL!
RELAX, SON! THAT WALKIN' MATCHSTICK DOESN'T WORRY ME!
39
IT'S A CRYIN' SHAME YOUR CHARIOT'S NOT READY, LITTLE BUDDY!
NO SWEAT, BRIGHT EYES! DON'T GET ALL SHOOK-UP ABOUT IT!
I CAN'T HELP IT, TIGER!
I HATE TO SEE A PRETTY LITTLE LADY DISAPPOINTED!
THAT'S VERY NICE OF YOU!
OKAY, BLACKIE-- YOU MADE YOUR PITCH!
NOW COOL IT!
'S MATTER, BIG MAN? CAN'T STAND A LITTLE COMPETITION?

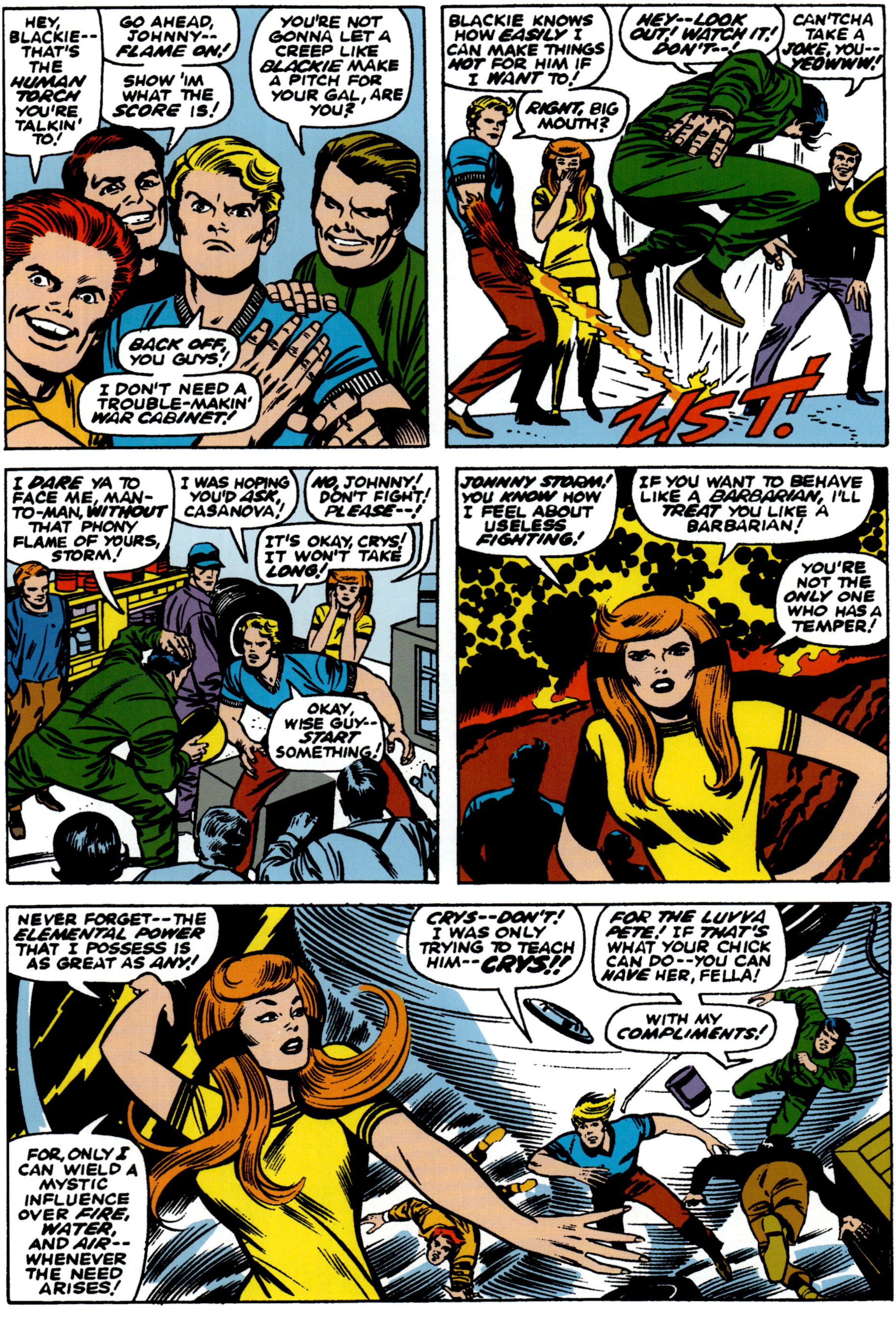
HEY, BLACKIE--THAT'S THE HUMAN TORCH YOU'RE TALKIN' TO!
GO AHEAD, JOHNNY--FLAME ON!
SHOW 'IM WHAT THE SCORE IS!
YOU'RE NOT GONNA LET A CREEP LIKE BLACKIE MAKE A PITCH FOR YOUR GAL, ARE YOU?
BACK OFF, YOU GUYS!
I DON'T NEED A TROUBLE-MAKIN' WAR CABINET!
BLACKIE KNOWS HOW EASILY I CAN MAKE THINGS NOT FOR HIM IF I WANT TO!
RIGHT, BIG MOUTH?
HEY--LOOK OUT! WATCH IT! DON'T--!
CAN'TCHA TAKE A JOKE, YOU--YEOWWW!
ZISST!
I DARE YA TO FACE ME, MAN-TO-MAN, WITHOUT THAT PHONY FLAME OF YOURS, STORM!
I WAS HOPING YOU'D ASK, CASANOVA!
NO, JOHNNY! DON'T FIGHT! PLEASE--!
IT'S OKAY, CRYS! IT WON'T TAKE LONG!
OKAY, WISE GUY--START SOMETHING!
JOHNNY STORM! YOU KNOW HOW I FEEL ABOUT USELESS FIGHTING!
IF YOU WANT TO BEHAVE LIKE A BARBARIAN, I'LL TREAT YOU LIKE A BARBARIAN!
YOU'RE NOT THE ONLY ONE WHO HAS A TEMPER!
NEVER FORGET--THE ELEMENTAL POWER THAT I POSSESS IS AS GREAT AS ANY!
CRYS--DON'T! I WAS ONLY TRYING TO TEACH HIM--CRYS!!
FOR THE LUVVA PETE! IF THAT'S WHAT YOUR CHICK CAN DO--YOU CAN HAVE HER, FELLA!
WITH MY COMPLIMENTS!
FOR, ONLY I CAN WIELD A MYSTIC INFLUENCE OVER FIRE, WATER, AND AIR--WHENEVER THE NEED ARISES!

UH UH! DESPITE WHAT YOU MAY THINK, WE HAVEN'T FORGOTTEN OUR OTHER FRIENDS AT FF HEADQUARTERS! AND, JUST TO PROVE IT TO YOU--
OH, REED! YOU LOOKED SO SILLY SAILING ACROSS THE ROOM THE WAY YOU DID!
IT'S SOMEWHAT DIFFICULT FOR A GENT WITH AN ELASTIC EPIDERMIS TO MAINTAIN HIS DIGNITY, HONEY!
I GOTTA HAND IT TO YA, SUSIE--!
YOU SURE KNOW HOW'TA PUT OL' STRETCHO DOWN WHEN YA WANNA!
BUT, IT WAS ALL WORTH IT! BEN IS BEGINNING TO CHEER UP!
HAWW! THERE HE IS-- THE LEADER OF THE GREATEST DANGED TEAM FROM HERE TO YANCY STREET--
'N HE LETS A LITTLE BLONDE PUSSYCAT PUT 'IM THRU HIS PACES!
CAN YA IMAGINE WHAT OUR DEAR DEPARTED DOC DOOM WOULD'A SAID IF HE WUZ WATCHIN'!? HARR! HARR!
WAS THAT YOU LAUGHING, BEN BUDDY--OR IS THERE A CEMENT MIXER RUMBLING BY IN THE NEXT ROOM??
I ALWAYS THOUGHT BEN HAD A LOVELY LAUGH!
YER JUST PLAIN JEALOUS, STRETCHO--
SINCE I BEEN GIVIN' VOICE LESSONS TA RICHARD BURTON!
C'MON--LET'S GO GIT US SOME GRUB!
YOU'RE ON, BIG BUDDY!
IT WORKED! BEN IS HIS GRAVEL-VOICED OLD SELF AGAIN!
BUT, REED RICHARDS' RELIEF IS APT TO PROVE SOMEWHAT SHORT-LIVED--FOR, NOT LONG AFTERWARDS--
MY PLANS ARE NOW COMPLETE! EVERY-THING IS IN TOTAL READINESS!
NOTHING CAN POSSIBLY GO WRONG! I'VE PREPARED FOR ANY EVENTUALITY!
NEVER HAS ANY PLOT BEEN SO COMPLETELY FOOL-PROOF!
RIGHT DOWN TO MY MOST MINUTE CALCULATION, EVERYTHING POINTS TO ONE UNASSAILABLE FACT--
THIS TIME, NOTHING ON EARTH CAN KEEP ME FROM MY ULTIMATE GOAL--
--THE COMPLETE DESTRUCTION OF THE ACCURSED FANTASTIC FOUR!

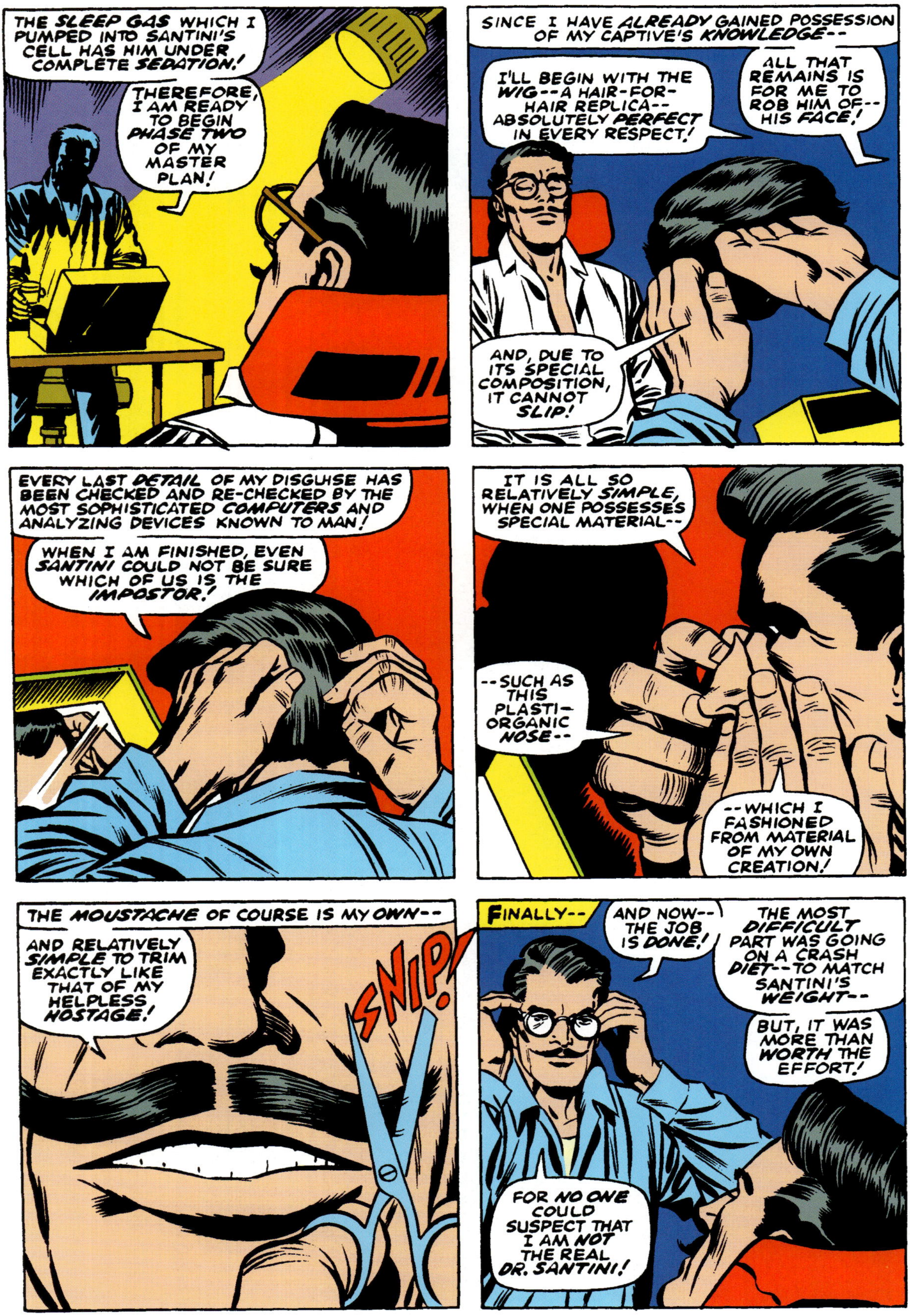
THE SLEEP GAS WHICH I PUMPED INTO SANTINI'S CELL HAS HIM UNDER COMPLETE SEDATION!
THEREFORE, I AM READY TO BEGIN PHASE TWO OF MY MASTER PLAN!
SINCE I HAVE ALREADY GAINED POSSESSION OF MY CAPTIVE'S KNOWLEDGE--
I'LL BEGIN WITH THE WIG--A HAIR-FOR-HAIR REPLICA--ABSOLUTELY PERFECT IN EVERY RESPECT!
ALL THAT REMAINS IS FOR ME TO ROB HIM OF--HIS FACE!
AND, DUE TO ITS SPECIAL COMPOSITION, IT CANNOT SLIP!
EVERY LAST DETAIL OF MY DISGUISE HAS BEEN CHECKED AND RE-CHECKED BY THE MOST SOPHISTICATED COMPUTERS AND ANALYZING DEVICES KNOWN TO MAN!
WHEN I AM FINISHED, EVEN SANTINI COULD NOT BE SURE WHICH OF US IS THE IMPOSTOR!
IT IS ALL SO RELATIVELY SIMPLE, WHEN ONE POSSESSES SPECIAL MATERIAL--
--SUCH AS THIS PLASTI-ORGANIC NOSE--
--WHICH I FASHIONED FROM MATERIAL OF MY OWN CREATION!
THE MOUSTACHE OF COURSE IS MY OWN--
AND RELATIVELY SIMPLE TO TRIM EXACTLY LIKE THAT OF MY HELPLESS HOSTAGE!
SNIP!
FINALLY--
AND NOW--THE JOB IS DONE!
THE MOST DIFFICULT PART WAS GOING ON A CRASH DIET--TO MATCH SANTINI'S WEIGHT--
BUT, IT WAS MORE THAN WORTH THE EFFORT!
FOR NO ONE COULD SUSPECT THAT I AM NOT THE REAL DR. SANTINI!

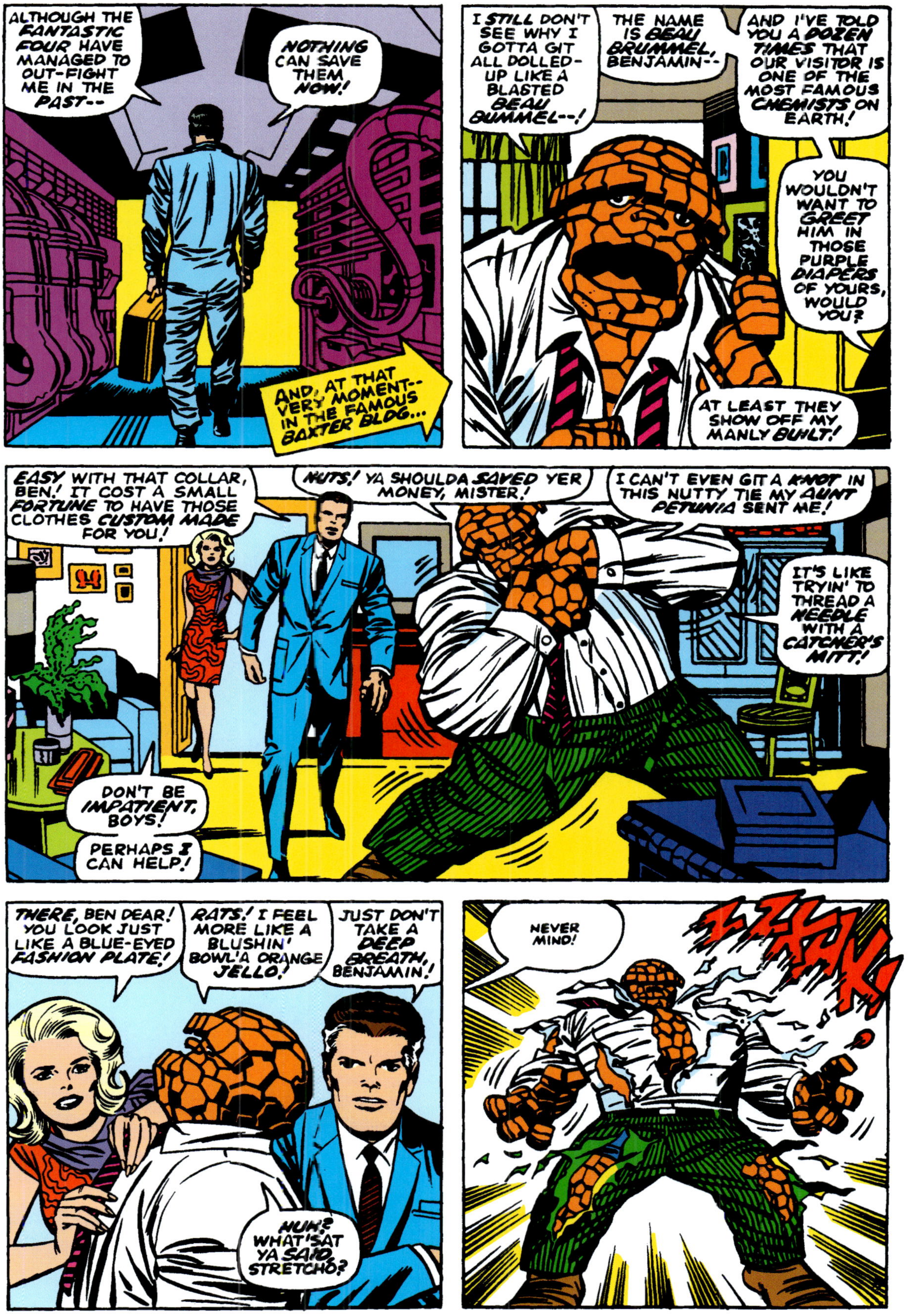
ALTHOUGH THE FANTASTIC FOUR HAVE MANAGED TO OUT-FIGHT ME IN THE PAST--
NOTHING CAN SAVE THEM NOW!
AND, AT THAT VERY MOMENT-- IN THE FAMOUS BAXTER BLDG...
I STILL DON'T SEE WHY I GOTTA GIT ALL DOLLED-UP LIKE A BLASTED BEAU BUMMEL--!
THE NAME IS BEAU BRUMMEL, BENJAMIN--
AND I'VE TOLD YOU A DOZEN TIMES THAT OUR VISITOR IS ONE OF THE MOST FAMOUS CHEMISTS ON EARTH!
YOU WOULDN'T WANT TO GREET HIM IN THOSE PURPLE DIAPERS OF YOURS, WOULD YOU?
AT LEAST THEY SHOW OFF MY MANLY BUILT!
EASY WITH THAT COLLAR, BEN! IT COST A SMALL FORTUNE TO HAVE THOSE CLOTHES CUSTOM MADE FOR YOU!
NUTS! YA SHOULDA SAVED YER MONEY, MISTER!
I CAN'T EVEN GIT A KNOT IN THIS NUTTY TIE MY AUNT PETUNIA SENT ME!
IT'S LIKE TRYIN' TO THREAD A NEEDLE WITH A CATCHER'S MITT!
DON'T BE IMPATIENT, BOYS!
PERHAPS I CAN HELP!
THERE, BEN DEAR! YOU LOOK JUST LIKE A BLUE-EYED FASHION PLATE!
RATS! I FEEL MORE LIKE A BLUSHIN' BOWL'A ORANGE JELLO!
JUST DON'T TAKE A DEEP BREATH, BENJAMIN!
HUH? WHAT'SAT YA SAID, STRETCHO?
NEVER MIND!
R-R-RIP!

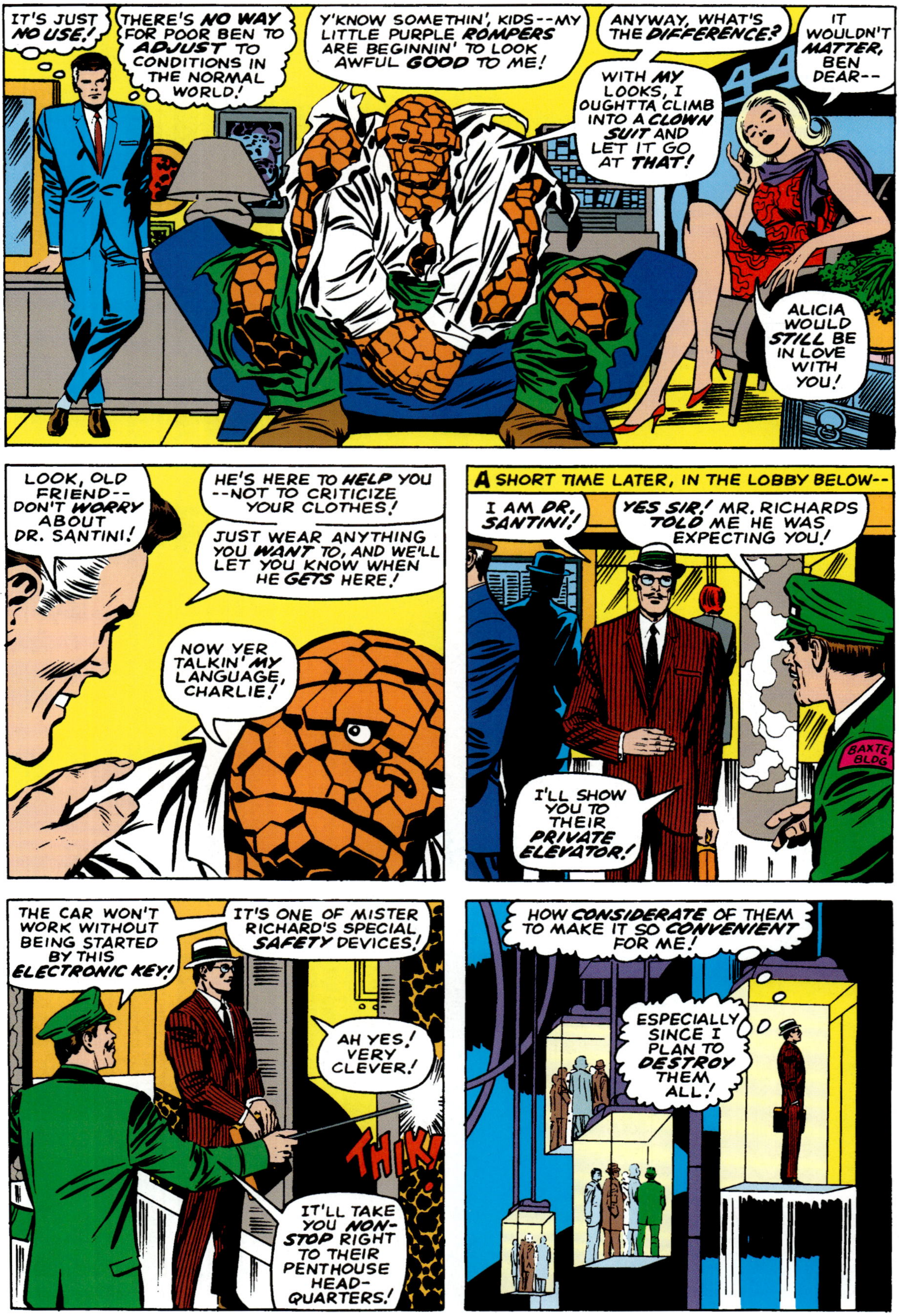

IT'S JUST NO USE!
THERE'S NO WAY FOR POOR BEN TO ADJUST TO CONDITIONS IN THE NORMAL WORLD!
Y'KNOW SOMETHIN', KIDS--MY LITTLE PURPLE ROMPERS ARE BEGINNIN' TO LOOK AWFUL GOOD TO ME!
ANYWAY, WHAT'S THE DIFFERENCE?
WITH MY LOOKS, I OUGHTTA CLIMB INTO A CLOWN SUIT AND LET IT GO AT THAT!
IT WOULDN'T MATTER, BEN DEAR--
ALICIA WOULD STILL BE IN LOVE WITH YOU!
LOOK, OLD FRIEND--DON'T WORRY ABOUT DR. SANTINI!
HE'S HERE TO HELP YOU --NOT TO CRITICIZE YOUR CLOTHES!
JUST WEAR ANYTHING YOU WANT TO, AND WE'LL LET YOU KNOW WHEN HE GETS HERE!
NOW YER TALKIN' MY LANGUAGE, CHARLIE!
A SHORT TIME LATER, IN THE LOBBY BELOW--
I AM DR. SANTINI!
YES SIR! MR. RICHARDS TOLD ME HE WAS EXPECTING YOU!
I'LL SHOW YOU TO THEIR PRIVATE ELEVATOR!
BAXTER BLDG
THE CAR WON'T WORK WITHOUT BEING STARTED BY THIS ELECTRONIC KEY!
IT'S ONE OF MISTER RICHARD'S SPECIAL SAFETY DEVICES!
AH YES! VERY CLEVER!
THIK!
IT'LL TAKE YOU NON-STOP RIGHT TO THEIR PENTHOUSE HEAD-QUARTERS!
HOW CONSIDERATE OF THEM TO MAKE IT SO CONVENIENT FOR ME!
ESPECIALLY SINCE I PLAN TO DESTROY THEM ALL!

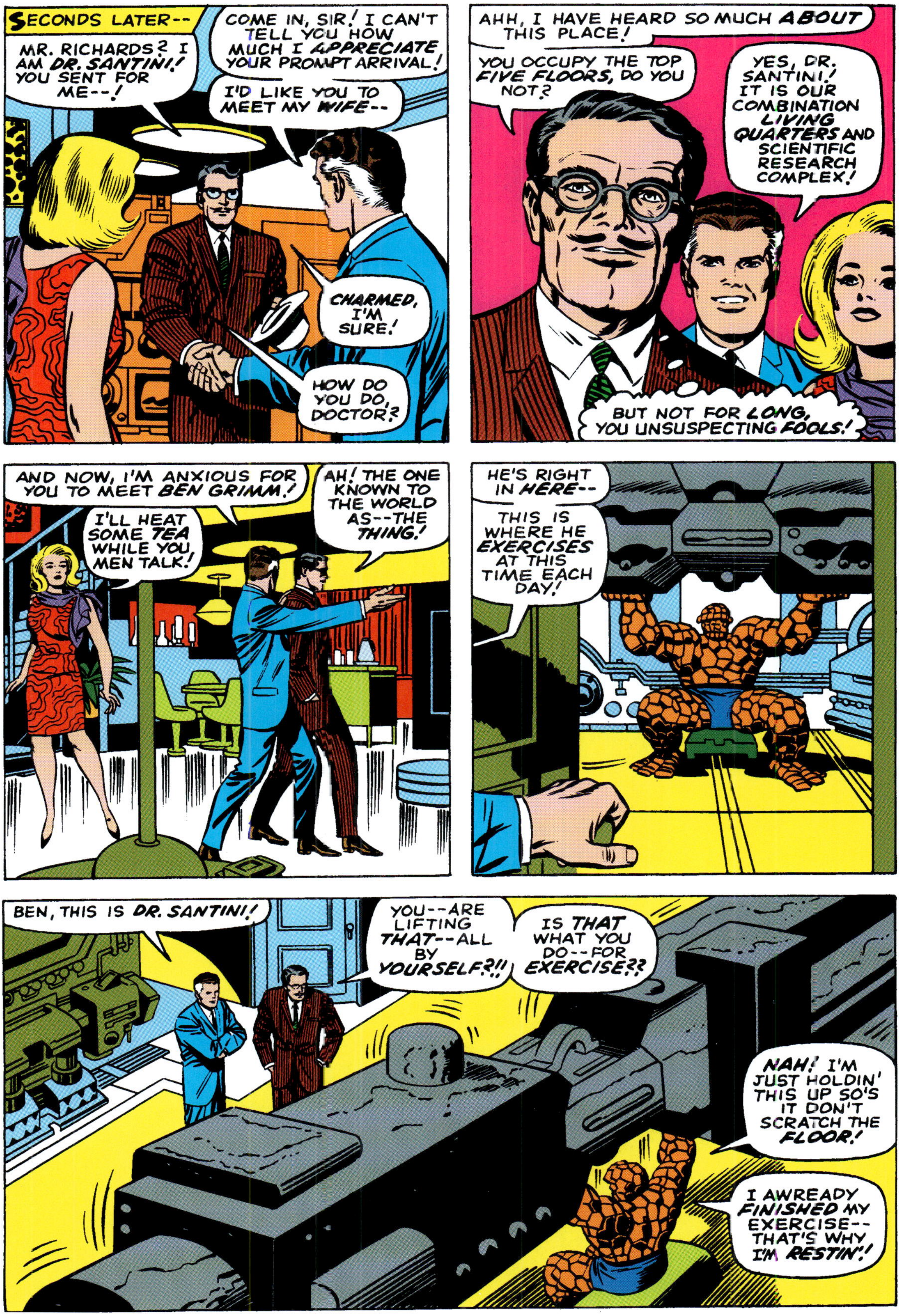
SECONDS LATER--
MR. RICHARDS? I AM DR. SANTINI! YOU SENT FOR ME--!
COME IN, SIR! I CAN'T TELL YOU HOW MUCH I APPRECIATE YOUR PROMPT ARRIVAL!
I'D LIKE YOU TO MEET MY WIFE--
CHARMED, I'M SURE!
HOW DO YOU DO, DOCTOR?
AHH, I HAVE HEARD SO MUCH ABOUT THIS PLACE!
YOU OCCUPY THE TOP FIVE FLOORS, DO YOU NOT?
YES, DR. SANTINI! IT IS OUR COMBINATION LIVING QUARTERS AND SCIENTIFIC RESEARCH COMPLEX!
BUT NOT FOR LONG, YOU UNSUSPECTING FOOLS!
AND NOW, I'M ANXIOUS FOR YOU TO MEET BEN GRIMM!
I'LL HEAT SOME TEA WHILE YOU MEN TALK!
AH! THE ONE KNOWN TO THE WORLD AS--THE THING!
HE'S RIGHT IN HERE--
THIS IS WHERE HE EXERCISES AT THIS TIME EACH DAY!
BEN, THIS IS DR. SANTINI!
YOU--ARE LIFTING THAT--ALL BY YOURSELF?!!
IS THAT WHAT YOU DO--FOR EXERCISE??
NAH! I'M JUST HOLDIN' THIS UP SO'S IT DON'T SCRATCH THE FLOOR!
I AWREADY FINISHED MY EXERCISE--THAT'S WHY I'M RESTIN'!

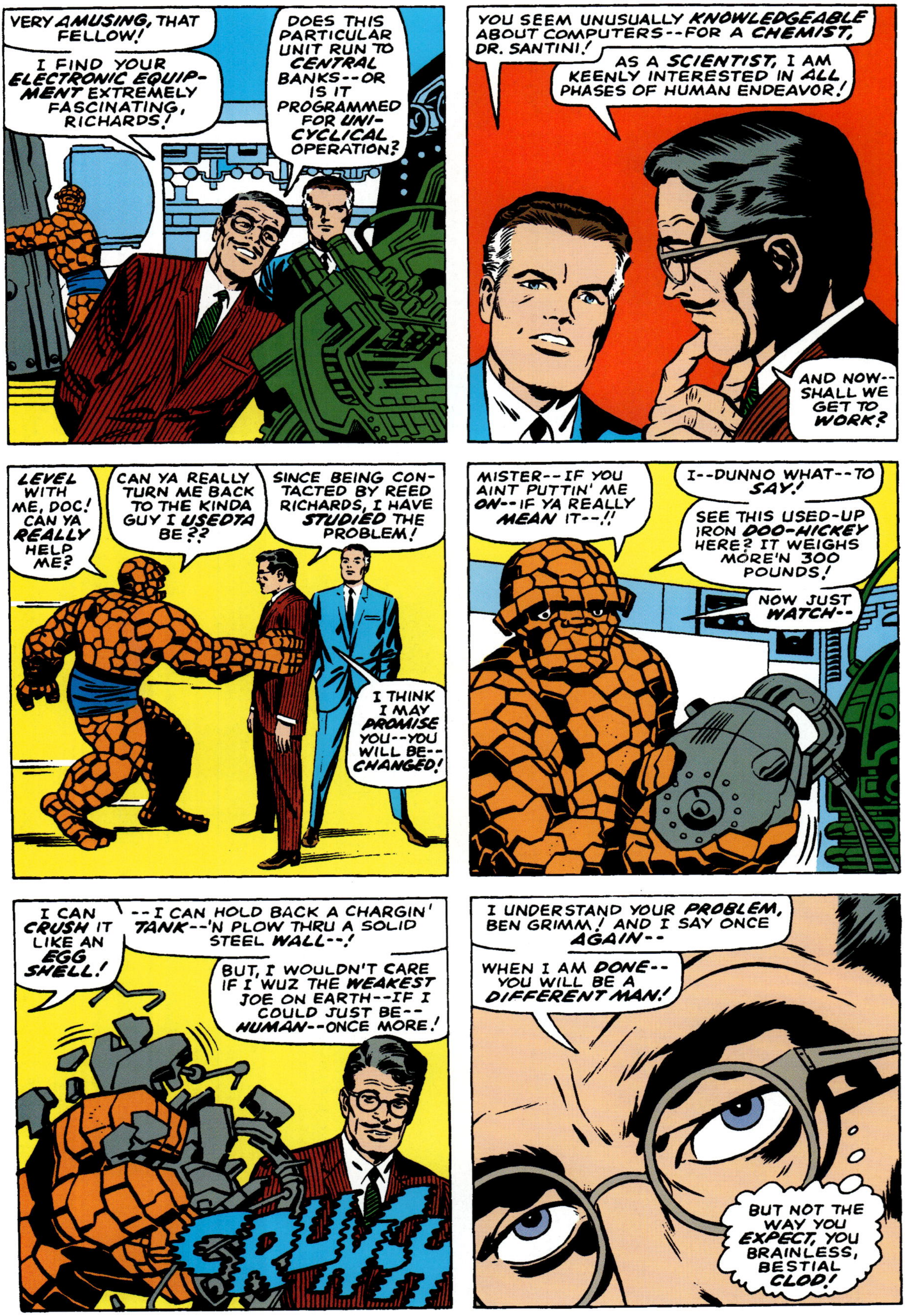
VERY AMUSING, THAT FELLOW!
I FIND YOUR ELECTRONIC EQUIPMENT EXTREMELY FASCINATING, RICHARDS!
DOES THIS PARTICULAR UNIT RUN TO CENTRAL BANKS--OR IS IT PROGRAMMED FOR UNI-CYCLICAL OPERATION?
YOU SEEM UNUSUALLY KNOWLEDGEABLE ABOUT COMPUTERS--FOR A CHEMIST, DR. SANTINI!
AS A SCIENTIST, I AM KEENLY INTERESTED IN ALL PHASES OF HUMAN ENDEAVOR!
AND NOW--SHALL WE GET TO WORK?
LEVEL WITH ME, DOC! CAN YA REALLY HELP ME?
CAN YA REALLY TURN ME BACK TO THE KINDA GUY I USEDTA BE??
SINCE BEING CONTACTED BY REED RICHARDS, I HAVE STUDIED THE PROBLEM!
I THINK I MAY PROMISE YOU--YOU WILL BE--CHANGED!
MISTER--IF YOU AINT PUTTIN' ME ON--IF YA REALLY MEAN IT--!!
I--DUNNO WHAT--TO SAY!
SEE THIS USED-UP IRON DOO-HICKEY HERE? IT WEIGHS MORE'N 300 POUNDS!
NOW JUST WATCH--
I CAN CRUSH IT LIKE AN EGG SHELL!
--I CAN HOLD BACK A CHARGIN' TANK--'N PLOW THRU A SOLID STEEL WALL--!
BUT, I WOULDN'T CARE IF I WUZ THE WEAKEST JOE ON EARTH--IF I COULD JUST BE--HUMAN--ONCE MORE!
SKRUNCH
I UNDERSTAND YOUR PROBLEM, BEN GRIMM! AND I SAY ONCE AGAIN--
WHEN I AM DONE--YOU WILL BE A DIFFERENT MAN!
BUT NOT THE WAY YOU EXPECT, YOU BRAINLESS, BESTIAL CLOD!

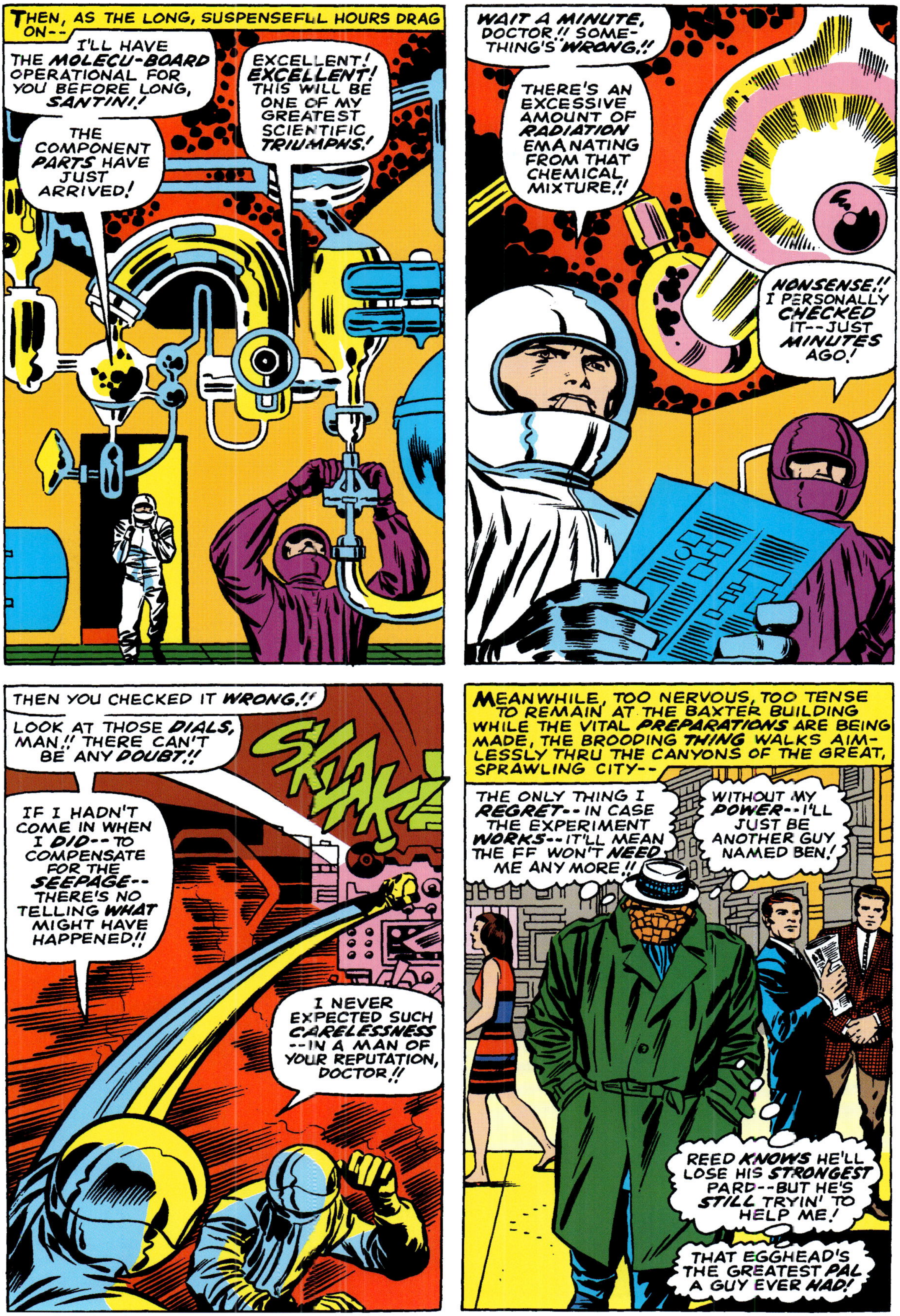
THEN, AS THE LONG, SUSPENSEFUL HOURS DRAG ON--
I'LL HAVE THE MOLECU-BOARD OPERATIONAL FOR YOU BEFORE LONG, SANTINI!
THE COMPONENT PARTS HAVE JUST ARRIVED!
EXCELLENT! EXCELLENT! THIS WILL BE ONE OF MY GREATEST SCIENTIFIC TRIUMPHS!
WAIT A MINUTE, DOCTOR!! SOMETHING'S WRONG!!
THERE'S AN EXCESSIVE AMOUNT OF RADIATION EMANATING FROM THAT CHEMICAL MIXTURE!!
NONSENSE!! I PERSONALLY CHECKED IT--JUST MINUTES AGO!
THEN YOU CHECKED IT WRONG!!
LOOK AT THOSE DIALS, MAN!! THERE CAN'T BE ANY DOUBT!!
SKLAK!
IF I HADN'T COME IN WHEN I DID--TO COMPENSATE FOR THE SEEPAGE--THERE'S NO TELLING WHAT MIGHT HAVE HAPPENED!!
I NEVER EXPECTED SUCH CARELESSNESS--IN A MAN OF YOUR REPUTATION, DOCTOR!!
MEANWHILE, TOO NERVOUS, TOO TENSE TO REMAIN AT THE BAXTER BUILDING WHILE THE VITAL PREPARATIONS ARE BEING MADE, THE BROODING THING WALKS AIMLESSLY THRU THE CANYONS OF THE GREAT, SPRAWLING CITY--
THE ONLY THING I REGRET--IN CASE THE EXPERIMENT WORKS--IT'LL MEAN THE FF WON'T NEED ME ANY MORE!!
WITHOUT MY POWER--I'LL JUST BE ANOTHER GUY NAMED BEN!
REED KNOWS HE'LL LOSE HIS STRONGEST PARD--BUT HE'S STILL TRYIN' TO HELP ME!
THAT EGGHEAD'S THE GREATEST PAL A GUY EVER HAD!

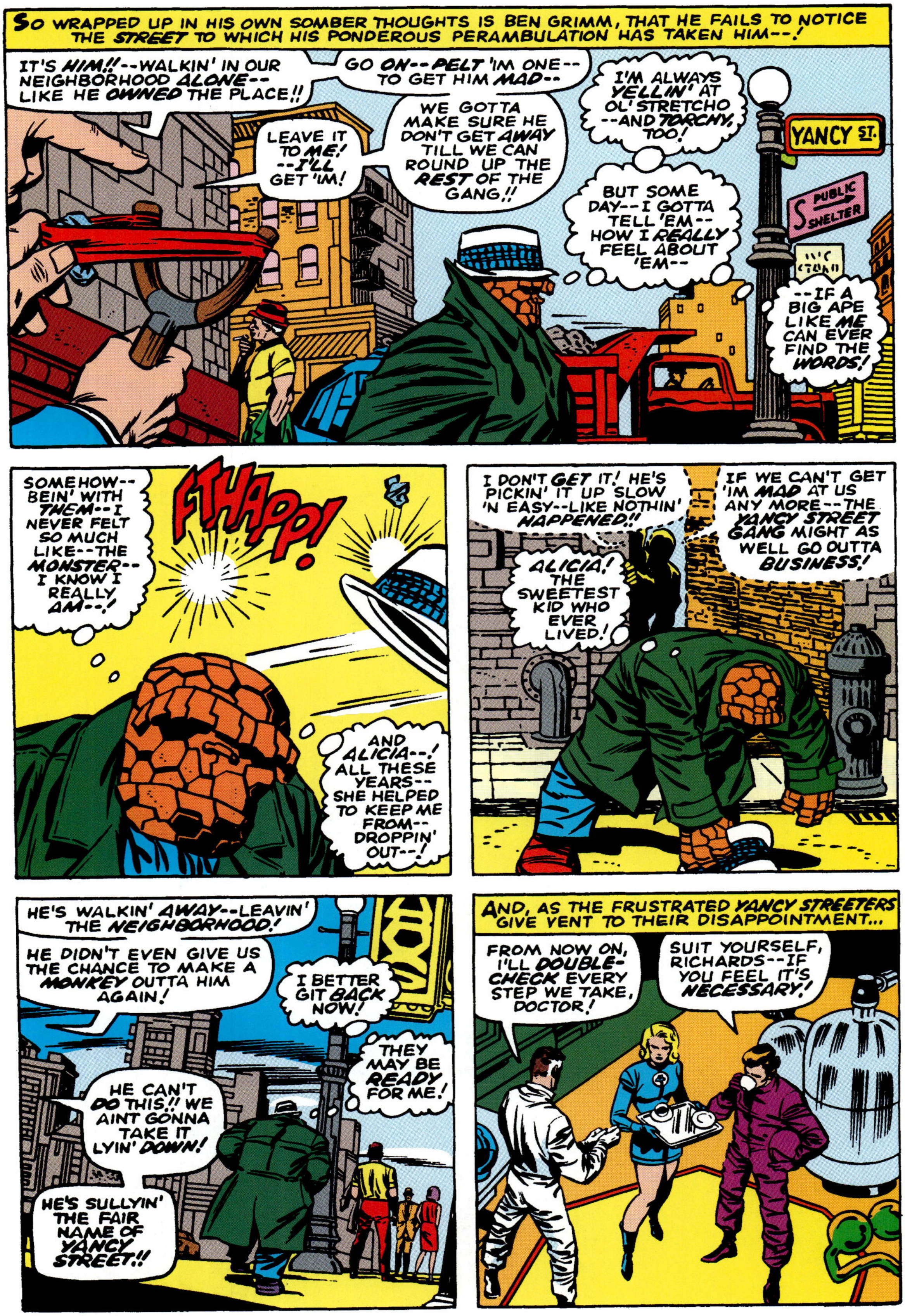
SO WRAPPED UP IN HIS OWN SOMBER THOUGHTS IS BEN GRIMM, THAT HE FAILS TO NOTICE THE STREET TO WHICH HIS PONDEROUS PERAMBULATION HAS TAKEN HIM--!
IT'S HIM!!--WALKIN' IN OUR NEIGHBORHOOD ALONE--LIKE HE OWNED THE PLACE!!
GO ON--PELT 'IM ONE--TO GET HIM MAD--
LEAVE IT TO ME! --I'LL GET 'IM!
WE GOTTA MAKE SURE HE DON'T GET AWAY TILL WE CAN ROUND UP THE REST OF THE GANG!!
I'M ALWAYS YELLIN' AT OL' STRETCHO --AND TORCHY, TOO!
BUT SOME DAY--I GOTTA TELL 'EM--HOW I REALLY FEEL ABOUT 'EM--
--IF A BIG APE LIKE ME CAN EVER FIND THE WORDS!
YANCY ST.
PUBLIC SHELTER
SOMEHOW--BEIN' WITH THEM--I NEVER FELT SO MUCH LIKE--THE MONSTER--I KNOW I REALLY AM--!
FTHAPP!
AND ALICIA--! ALL THESE YEARS--SHE HELPED TO KEEP ME FROM--DROPPIN' OUT--!
I DON'T GET IT! HE'S PICKIN' IT UP SLOW 'N EASY--LIKE NOTHIN' HAPPENED!!
IF WE CAN'T GET 'IM MAD AT US ANY MORE--THE YANCY STREET GANG MIGHT AS WELL GO OUTTA BUSINESS!
ALICIA! THE SWEETEST KID WHO EVER LIVED!
HE'S WALKIN' AWAY--LEAVIN' THE NEIGHBORHOOD!
HE DIDN'T EVEN GIVE US THE CHANCE TO MAKE A MONKEY OUTTA HIM AGAIN!
I BETTER GIT BACK NOW!
THEY MAY BE READY FOR ME!
HE CAN'T DO THIS!! WE AINT GONNA TAKE IT LYIN' DOWN!
HE'S SULLYIN' THE FAIR NAME OF YANCY STREET!!
AND, AS THE FRUSTRATED YANCY STREETERS GIVE VENT TO THEIR DISAPPOINTMENT...
FROM NOW ON, I'LL DOUBLE-CHECK EVERY STEP WE TAKE, DOCTOR!
SUIT YOURSELF, RICHARDS--IF YOU FEEL IT'S NECESSARY!

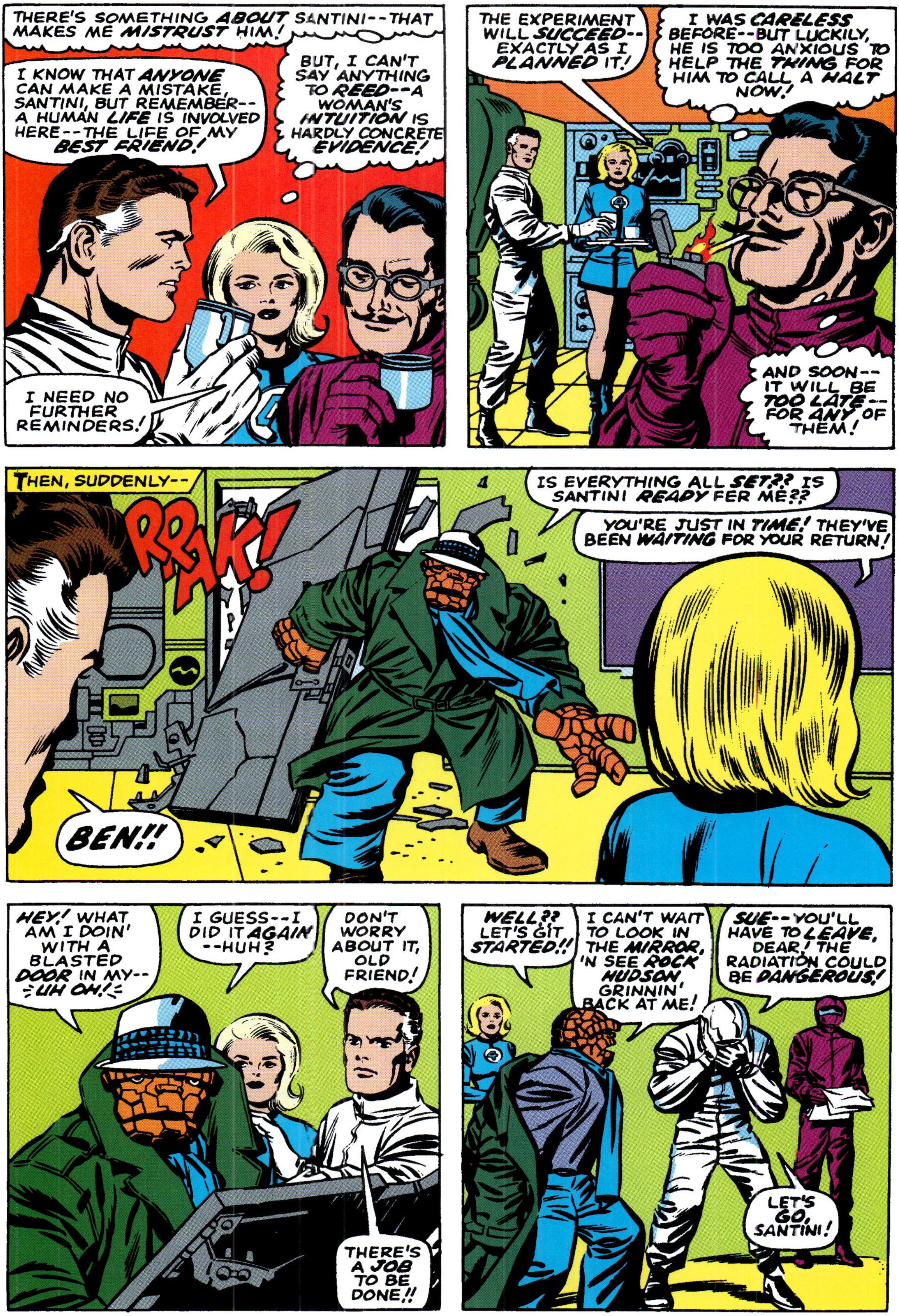
THERE'S SOMETHING ABOUT SANTINI--THAT MAKES ME MISTRUST HIM!
I KNOW THAT ANYONE CAN MAKE A MISTAKE, SANTINI, BUT REMEMBER--A HUMAN LIFE IS INVOLVED HERE--THE LIFE OF MY BEST FRIEND!
BUT, I CAN'T SAY ANYTHING TO REED--A WOMAN'S INTUITION IS HARDLY CONCRETE EVIDENCE!
I NEED NO FURTHER REMINDERS!
THE EXPERIMENT WILL SUCCEED--EXACTLY AS I PLANNED IT!
I WAS CARELESS BEFORE--BUT LUCKILY, HE IS TOO ANXIOUS TO HELP THE THING FOR HIM TO CALL A HALT NOW!
AND SOON--IT WILL BE TOO LATE--FOR ANY OF THEM!
THEN, SUDDENLY--
RRAK!
IS EVERYTHING ALL SET?? IS SANTINI READY FER ME??
YOU'RE JUST IN TIME! THEY'VE BEEN WAITING FOR YOUR RETURN!
BEN!!
HEY! WHAT AM I DOIN' WITH A BLASTED DOOR IN MY-- UH OH!
I GUESS--I DID IT AGAIN--HUH?
DON'T WORRY ABOUT IT, OLD FRIEND!
THERE'S A JOB TO BE DONE!!
WELL?? LET'S GIT STARTED!!
I CAN'T WAIT TO LOOK IN THE MIRROR, 'N SEE ROCK HUDSON, GRINNIN' BACK AT ME!
SUE--YOU'LL HAVE TO LEAVE, DEAR! THE RADIATION COULD BE DANGEROUS!
LET'S GO, SANTINI!

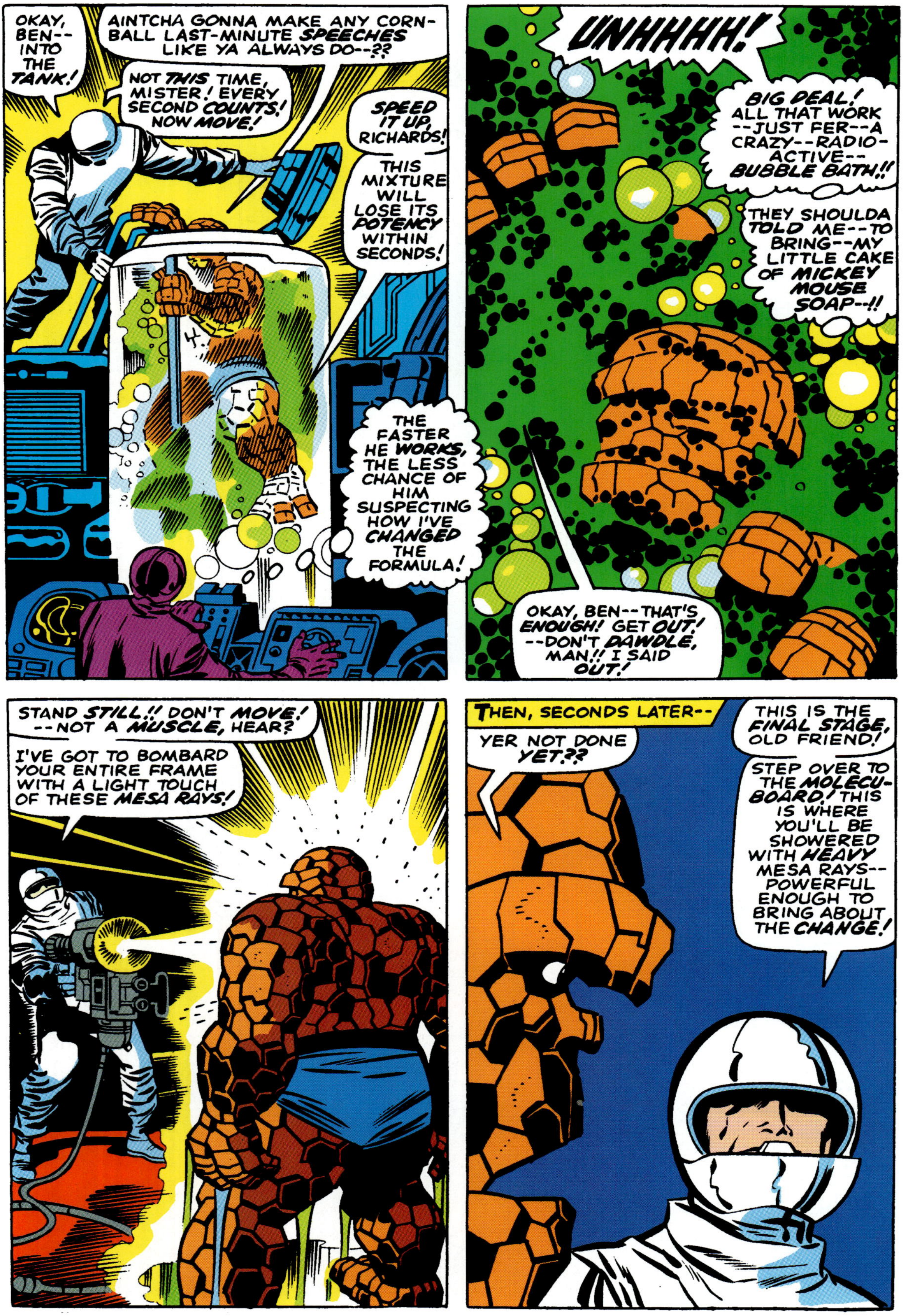

OKAY, BEN-- INTO THE TANK!
AINTCHA GONNA MAKE ANY CORN-BALL LAST-MINUTE SPEECHES LIKE YA ALWAYS DO--??
NOT THIS TIME, MISTER! EVERY SECOND COUNTS! NOW MOVE!
SPEED IT UP, RICHARDS!
THIS MIXTURE WILL LOSE ITS POTENCY WITHIN SECONDS!
THE FASTER HE WORKS, THE LESS CHANCE OF HIM SUSPECTING HOW I'VE CHANGED THE FORMULA!
UNHHHHH!
BIG DEAL! ALL THAT WORK --JUST FER--A CRAZY--RADIO-ACTIVE-- BUBBLE BATH!!
THEY SHOULDA TOLD ME--TO BRING--MY LITTLE CAKE OF MICKEY MOUSE SOAP--!!
OKAY, BEN--THAT'S ENOUGH! GET OUT! --DON'T DAWDLE, MAN!! I SAID OUT!
STAND STILL!! DON'T MOVE! --NOT A MUSCLE, HEAR?
I'VE GOT TO BOMBARD YOUR ENTIRE FRAME WITH A LIGHT TOUCH OF THESE MESA RAYS!
THEN, SECONDS LATER--
YER NOT DONE YET??
THIS IS THE FINAL STAGE, OLD FRIEND!
STEP OVER TO THE MOLECU-BOARD! THIS IS WHERE YOU'LL BE SHOWERED WITH HEAVY MESA RAYS-- POWERFUL ENOUGH TO BRING ABOUT THE CHANGE!

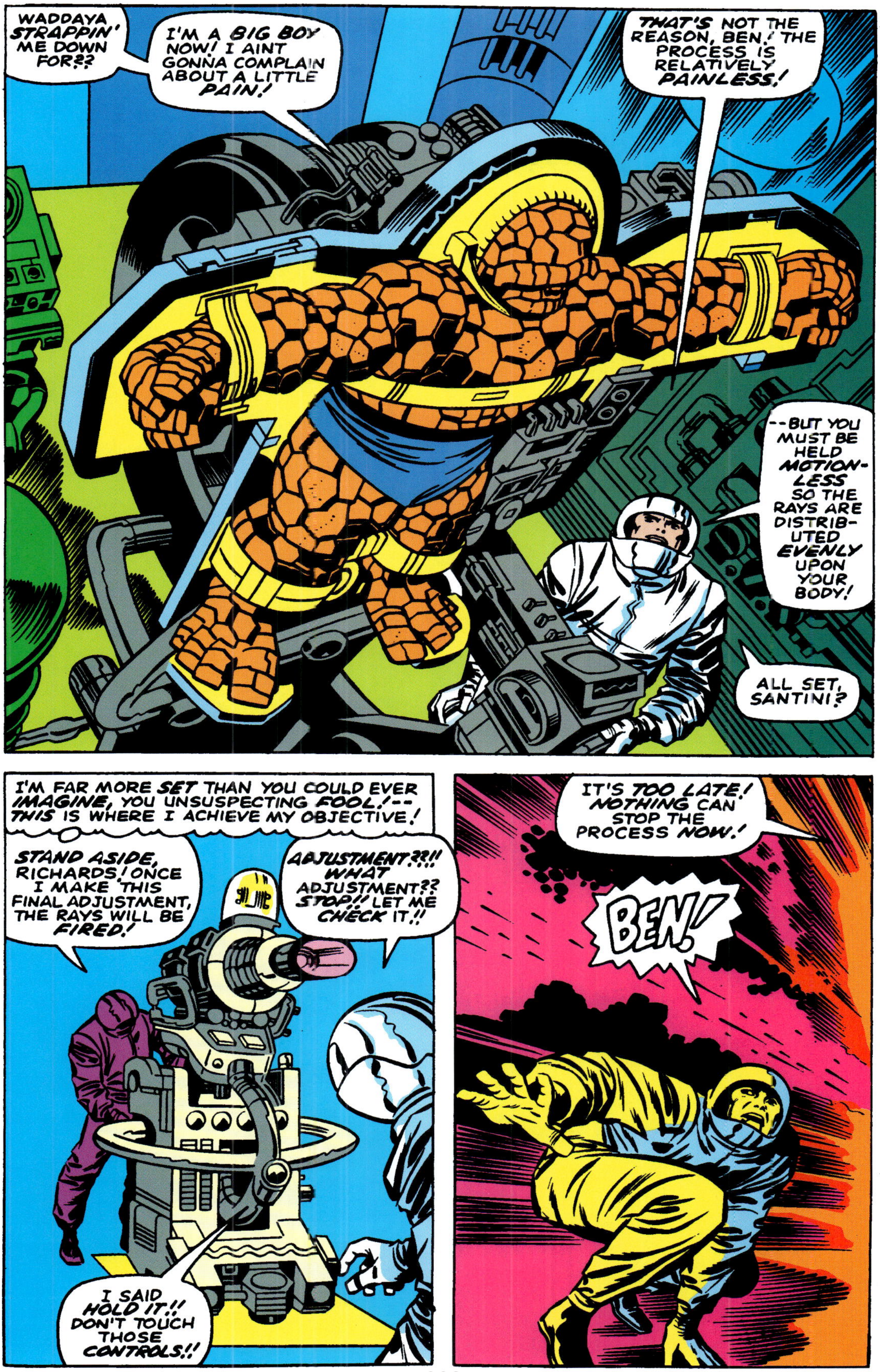

WADDAYA STRAPPIN' ME DOWN FOR??
I'M A BIG BOY NOW! I AINT GONNA COMPLAIN ABOUT A LITTLE PAIN!
THAT'S NOT THE REASON, BEN! THE PROCESS IS RELATIVELY PAINLESS!
--BUT YOU MUST BE HELD MOTION-LESS SO THE RAYS ARE DISTRIB-UTED EVENLY UPON YOUR BODY!
ALL SET, SANTINI?
I'M FAR MORE SET THAN YOU COULD EVER IMAGINE, YOU UNSUSPECTING FOOL!--THIS IS WHERE I ACHIEVE MY OBJECTIVE!
STAND ASIDE, RICHARDS! ONCE I MAKE THIS FINAL ADJUSTMENT, THE RAYS WILL BE FIRED!
ADJUSTMENT??!! WHAT ADJUSTMENT?? STOP!! LET ME CHECK IT!!
I SAID HOLD IT!! DON'T TOUCH THOSE CONTROLS!!
IT'S TOO LATE! NOTHING CAN STOP THE PROCESS NOW!
BEN!

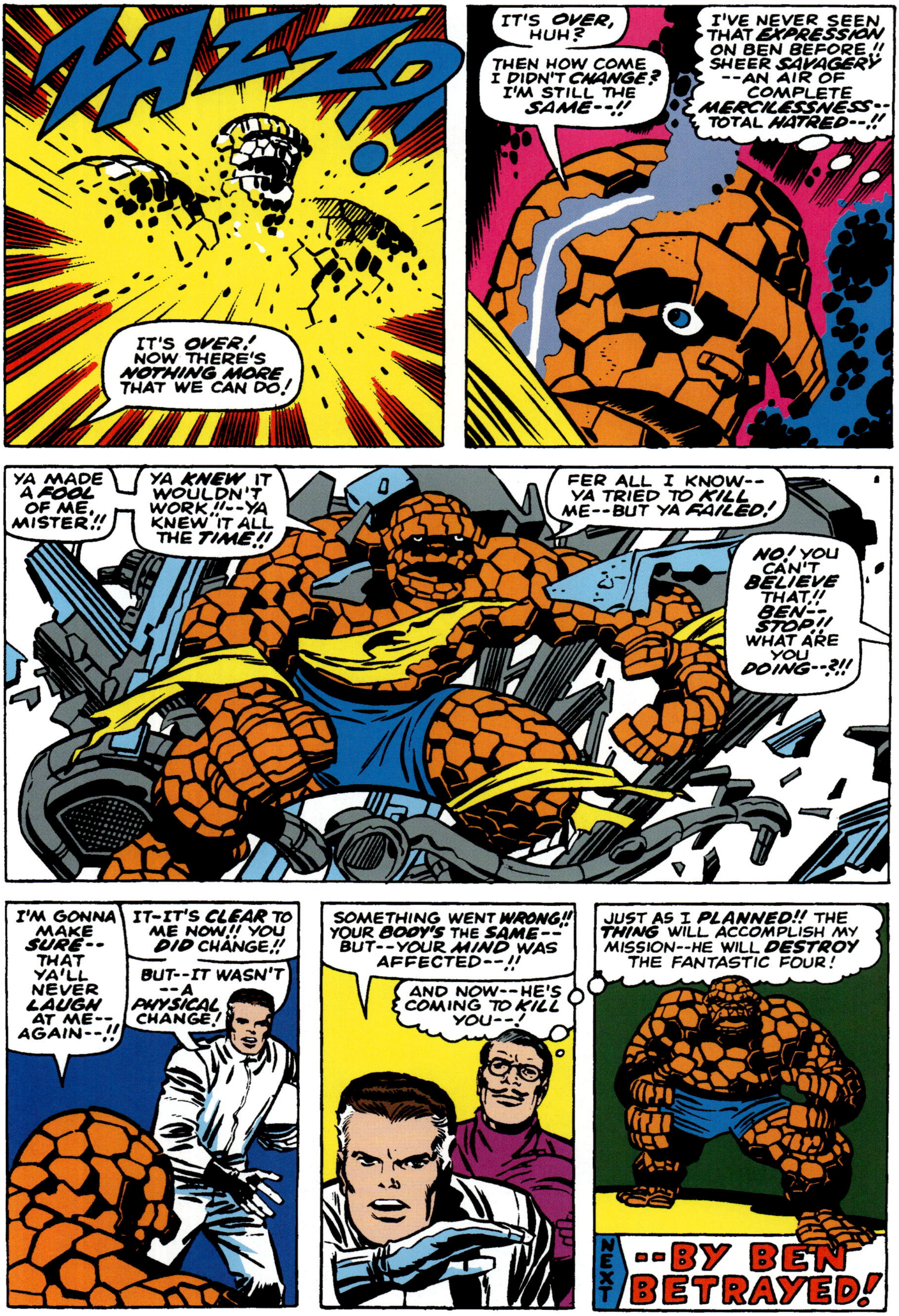
ZAZZT!
IT'S OVER! NOW THERE'S NOTHING MORE THAT WE CAN DO!
IT'S OVER, HUH?
THEN HOW COME I DIDN'T CHANGE? I'M STILL THE SAME--!!
I'VE NEVER SEEN THAT EXPRESSION ON BEN BEFORE!! SHEER SAVAGERY --AN AIR OF COMPLETE MERCILESSNESS-- TOTAL HATRED--!!
YA MADE A FOOL OF ME, MISTER!!
YA KNEW IT WOULDN'T WORK!!--YA KNEW IT ALL THE TIME!!
FER ALL I KNOW-- YA TRIED TO KILL ME--BUT YA FAILED!
NO! YOU CAN'T BELIEVE THAT!! BEN-- STOP!! WHAT ARE YOU DOING--?!!
I'M GONNA MAKE SURE-- THAT YA'LL NEVER LAUGH AT ME-- AGAIN--!!
IT-IT'S CLEAR TO ME NOW!! YOU DID CHANGE!!
BUT--IT WASN'T --A PHYSICAL CHANGE!
SOMETHING WENT WRONG!! YOUR BODY'S THE SAME-- BUT--YOUR MIND WAS AFFECTED--!!
AND NOW--HE'S COMING TO KILL YOU--!
JUST AS I PLANNED!! THE THING WILL ACCOMPLISH MY MISSION--HE WILL DESTROY THE FANTASTIC FOUR!
NEXT --BY BEN BETRAYED!

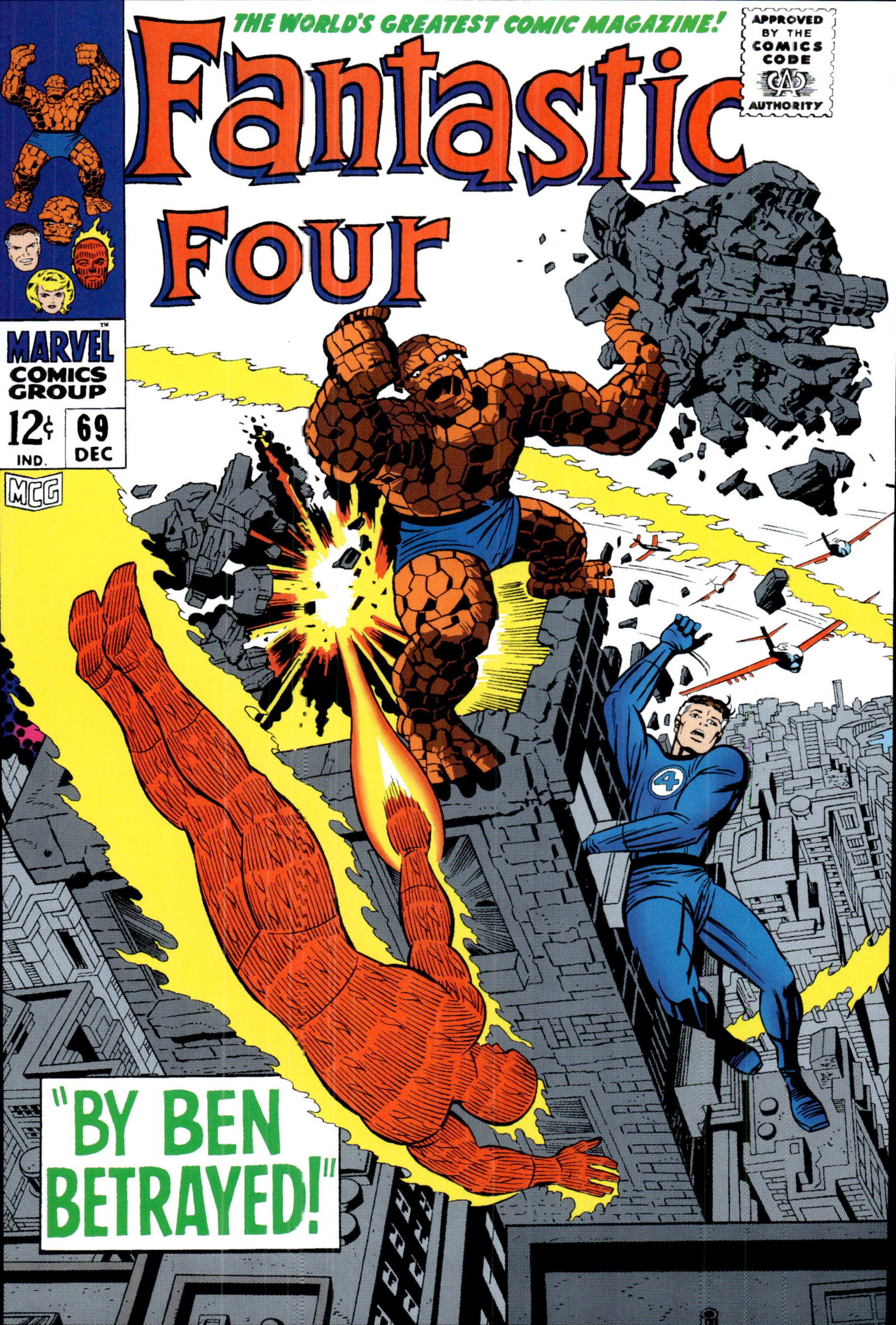
THE WORLD'S GREATEST COMIC MAGAZINE!
Fantastic Four
APPROVED BY THE COMICS CODE AUTHORITY
MARVEL COMICS GROUP
12¢ IND.
69 DEC
MCG
"BY BEN BETRAYED!"

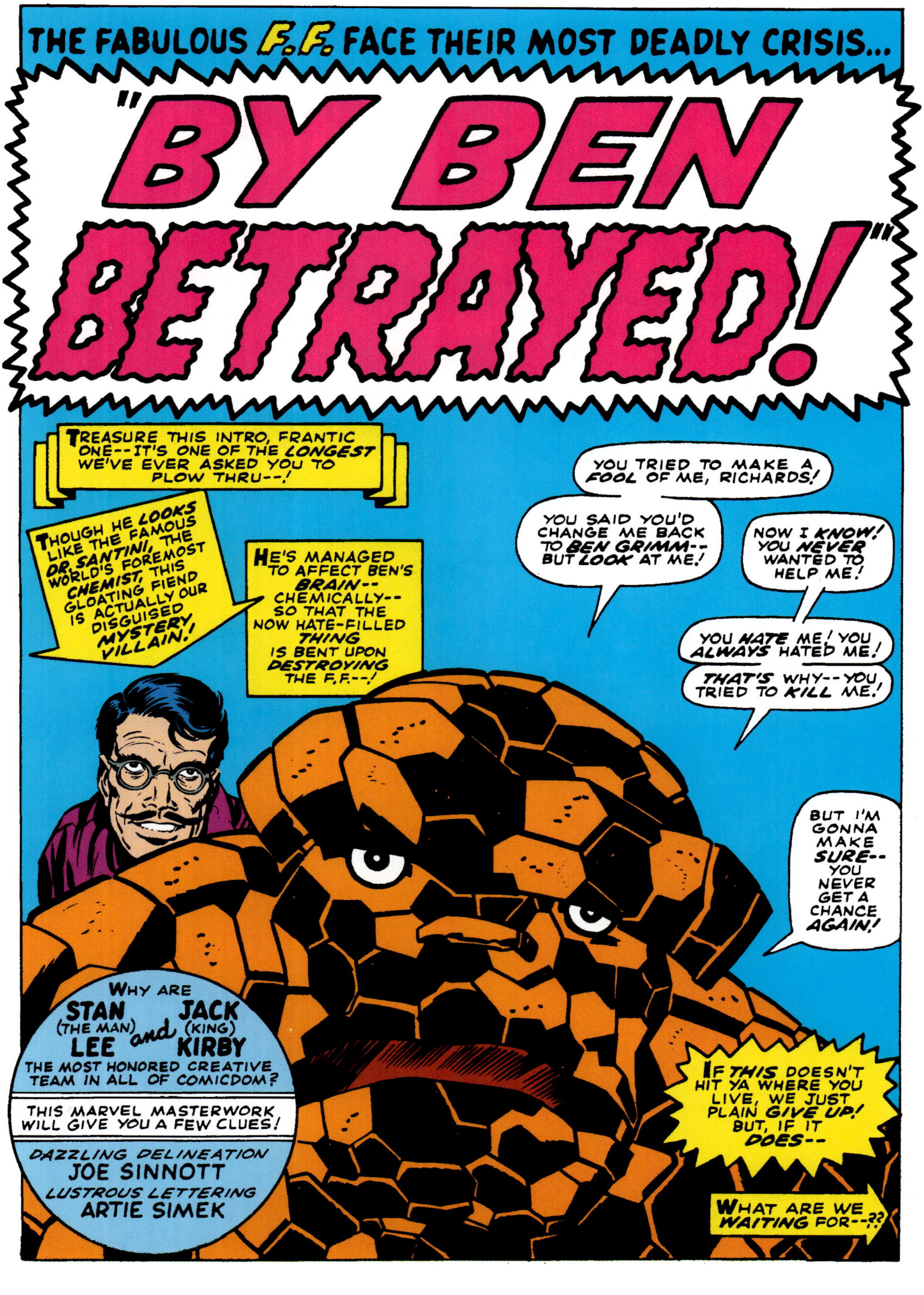
THE FABULOUS F.F. FACE THEIR MOST DEADLY CRISIS...
"BY BEN BETRAYED!"
TREASURE THIS INTRO, FRANTIC ONE--IT'S ONE OF THE LONGEST WE'VE EVER ASKED YOU TO PLOW THRU--!
THOUGH HE LOOKS LIKE THE FAMOUS DR. SANTINI, THE WORLD'S FOREMOST CHEMIST, THIS GLOATING FIEND IS ACTUALLY OUR DISGUISED MYSTERY VILLAIN!
HE'S MANAGED TO AFFECT BEN'S BRAIN-- CHEMICALLY-- SO THAT THE NOW HATE-FILLED THING IS BENT UPON DESTROYING THE F.F.--!
YOU TRIED TO MAKE A FOOL OF ME, RICHARDS!
YOU SAID YOU'D CHANGE ME BACK TO BEN GRIMM-- BUT LOOK AT ME!
NOW I KNOW! YOU NEVER WANTED TO HELP ME!
YOU HATE ME! YOU ALWAYS HATED ME!
THAT'S WHY--YOU TRIED TO KILL ME!
BUT I'M GONNA MAKE SURE-- YOU NEVER GET A CHANCE AGAIN!
WHY ARE STAN (THE MAN) LEE and JACK (KING) KIRBY THE MOST HONORED CREATIVE TEAM IN ALL OF COMICDOM?
THIS MARVEL MASTERWORK WILL GIVE YOU A FEW CLUES!
DAZZLING DELINEATION JOE SINNOTT
LUSTROUS LETTERING ARTIE SIMEK
IF THIS DOESN'T HIT YA WHERE YOU LIVE, WE JUST PLAIN GIVE UP! BUT, IF IT DOES--
WHAT ARE WE WAITING FOR--??

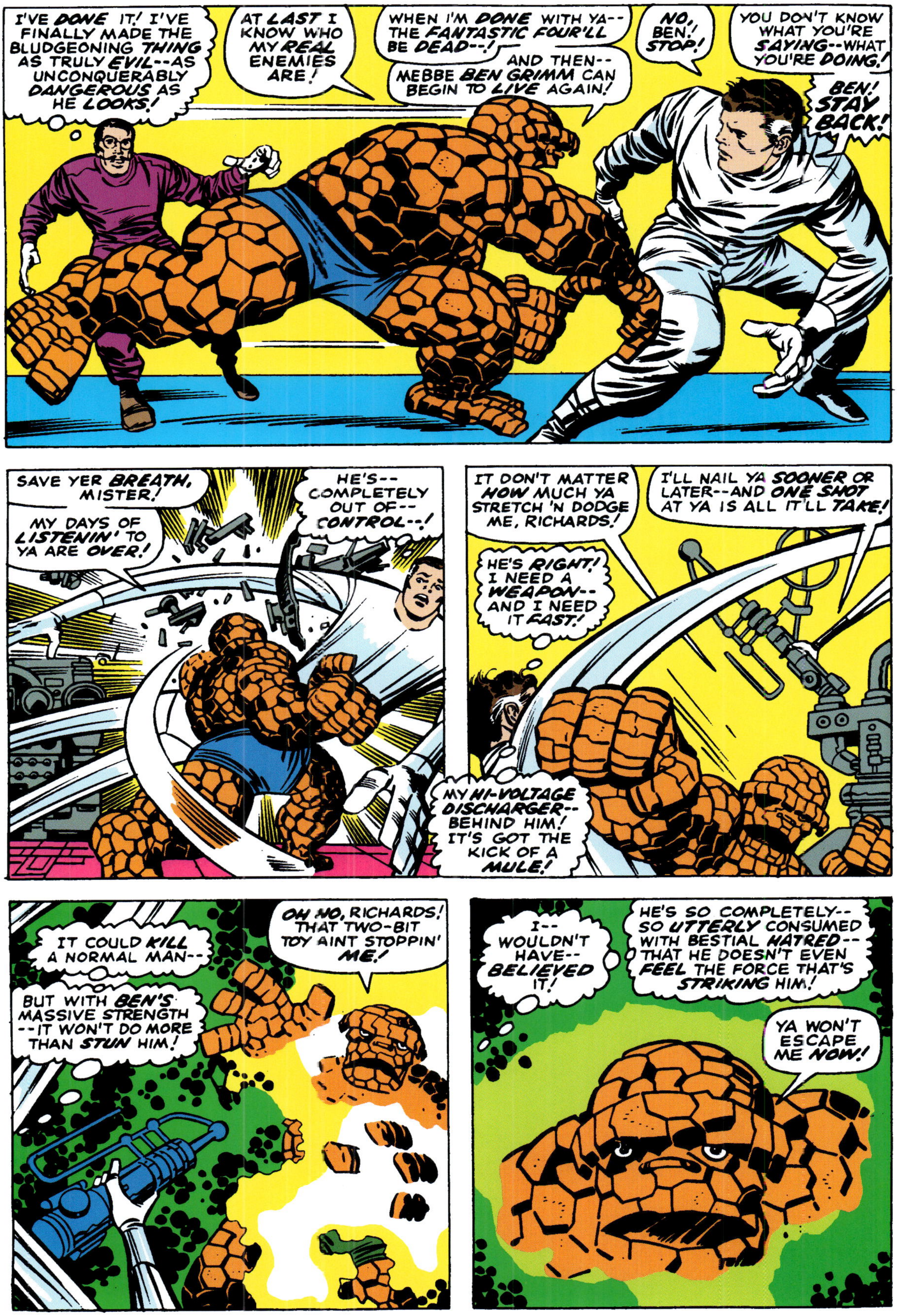
I'VE DONE IT! I'VE FINALLY MADE THE BLUDGEONING THING AS TRULY EVIL--AS UNCONQUERABLY DANGEROUS AS HE LOOKS!
AT LAST I KNOW WHO MY REAL ENEMIES ARE!
WHEN I'M DONE WITH YA--THE FANTASTIC FOUR'LL BE DEAD--!
AND THEN--MEBBE BEN GRIMM CAN BEGIN TO LIVE AGAIN!
NO, BEN! STOP!
YOU DON'T KNOW WHAT YOU'RE SAYING--WHAT YOU'RE DOING!
BEN! STAY BACK!
SAVE YER BREATH, MISTER!
MY DAYS OF LISTENIN' TO YA ARE OVER!
HE'S--COMPLETELY OUT OF--CONTROL--!
IT DON'T MATTER HOW MUCH YA STRETCH 'N DODGE ME, RICHARDS!
I'LL NAIL YA SOONER OR LATER--AND ONE SHOT AT YA IS ALL IT'LL TAKE!
HE'S RIGHT! I NEED A WEAPON--AND I NEED IT FAST!
MY HI-VOLTAGE DISCHARGER--BEHIND HIM! IT'S GOT THE KICK OF A MULE!
IT COULD KILL A NORMAL MAN--
BUT WITH BEN'S MASSIVE STRENGTH--IT WON'T DO MORE THAN STUN HIM!
OH NO, RICHARDS! THAT TWO-BIT TOY AINT STOPPIN' ME!
I--WOULDN'T HAVE--BELIEVED IT!
HE'S SO COMPLETELY--SO UTTERLY CONSUMED WITH BESTIAL HATRED--THAT HE DOESN'T EVEN FEEL THE FORCE THAT'S STRIKING HIM!
YA WON'T ESCAPE ME NOW!

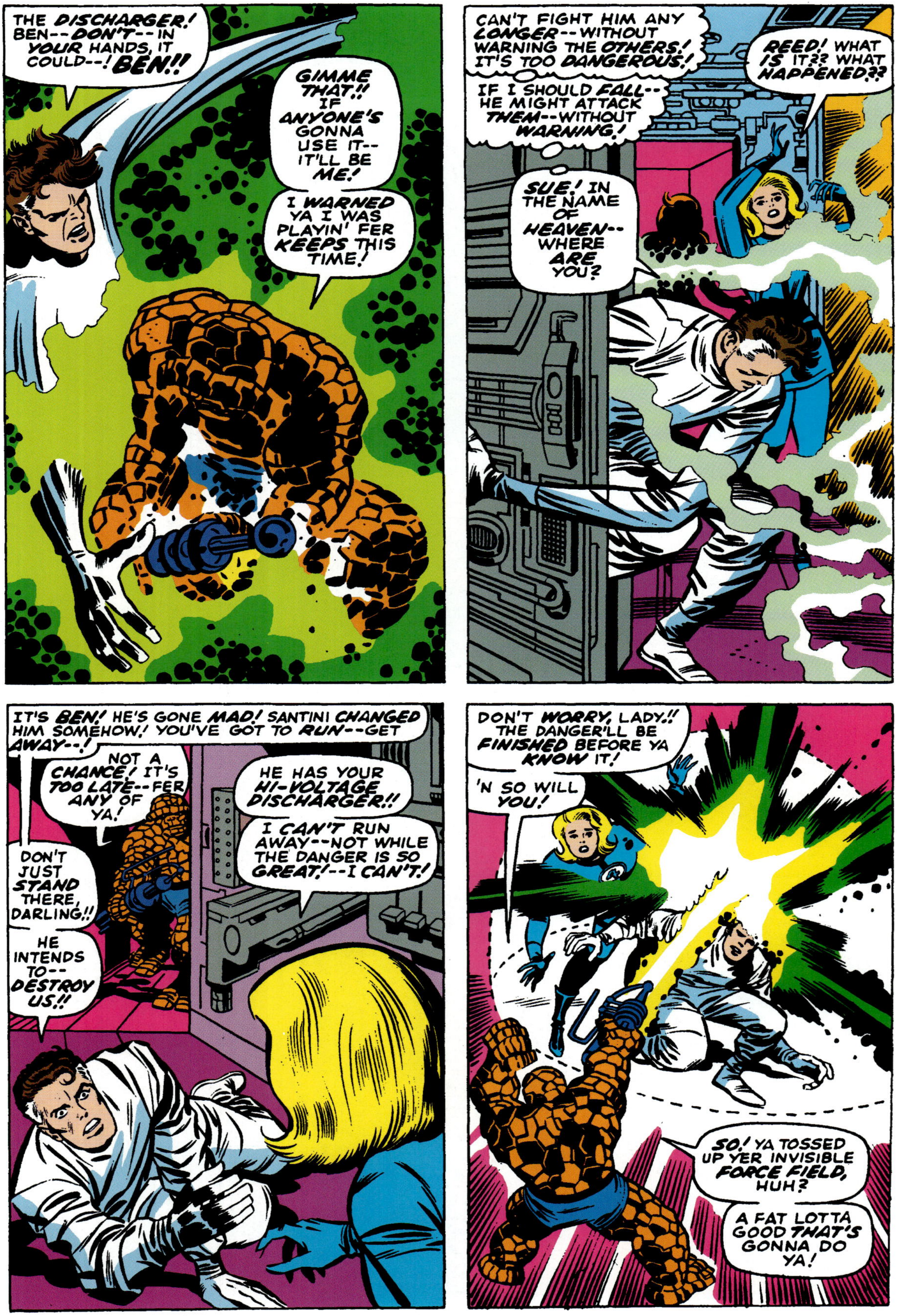
THE DISCHARGER! BEN--DON'T--IN YOUR HANDS, IT COULD--! BEN!!
GIMME THAT!! IF ANYONE'S GONNA USE IT--IT'LL BE ME!
I WARNED YA I WAS PLAYIN' FER KEEPS THIS TIME!
CAN'T FIGHT HIM ANY LONGER--WITHOUT WARNING THE OTHERS! IT'S TOO DANGEROUS!
IF I SHOULD FALL--HE MIGHT ATTACK THEM--WITHOUT WARNING!
REED! WHAT IS IT?? WHAT HAPPENED??
SUE! IN THE NAME OF HEAVEN--WHERE ARE YOU?
IT'S BEN! HE'S GONE MAD! SANTINI CHANGED HIM SOMEHOW! YOU'VE GOT TO RUN--GET AWAY--!
NOT A CHANCE! IT'S TOO LATE--FER ANY OF YA!
HE HAS YOUR HI-VOLTAGE DISCHARGER!!
I CAN'T RUN AWAY--NOT WHILE THE DANGER IS SO GREAT!--I CAN'T!
DON'T JUST STAND THERE, DARLING!!
HE INTENDS TO--DESTROY US!!
DON'T WORRY, LADY!! THE DANGER'LL BE FINISHED BEFORE YA KNOW IT!
'N SO WILL YOU!
SO! YA TOSSED UP YER INVISIBLE FORCE FIELD, HUH?
A FAT LOTTA GOOD THAT'S GONNA DO YA!

AT THAT MOMENT, JOHNNY STORM AND CRYSTAL RETURN TO THE BAXTER BUILDING, ONLY TO HEAR--
LISTEN! THE SOUND OF REED'S PORTABLE DISCHARGER! SOME-THING'S WRONG!
STAY BACK HERE, HONEY! I'D BETTER GO AND CHECK IT OUT!
BUT WHY CAN'T I GO WITH YOU?
NOT TILL I KNOW MORE ABOUT IT!
SECONDS LATER, JUST AS JOHNNY ENTERS THE LAB CORRIDOR--
ZZAP!
THAT BOLT ALMOST HIT ME!
WHATEVER'S GOING ON IN THERE, I'M SURE OF ONE THING--IT'S FOR REAL!
FLAME ON!
THERE'S THE DISCHARGER--RIGHT AHEAD OF ME!
CAN'T YET SEE WHO'S HOLDING IT FROM HERE--
BUT IT DOESN'T MATTER! ONE FIRE BLAST WILL TAKE CARE OF IT!
TZISSK!
THE TORCH! HE BLEW IT UP!
BEN! IT WAS YOU!!--BUT, I DON'T GET IT!
WHY WERE YOU FIRING REED'S DISCHARGER??!
YA DON'T THINK THAT CORNY WALL OF FLAME IS GONNA STOP ME FER LONG!
I'LL WRITE'CHA A BOOK!

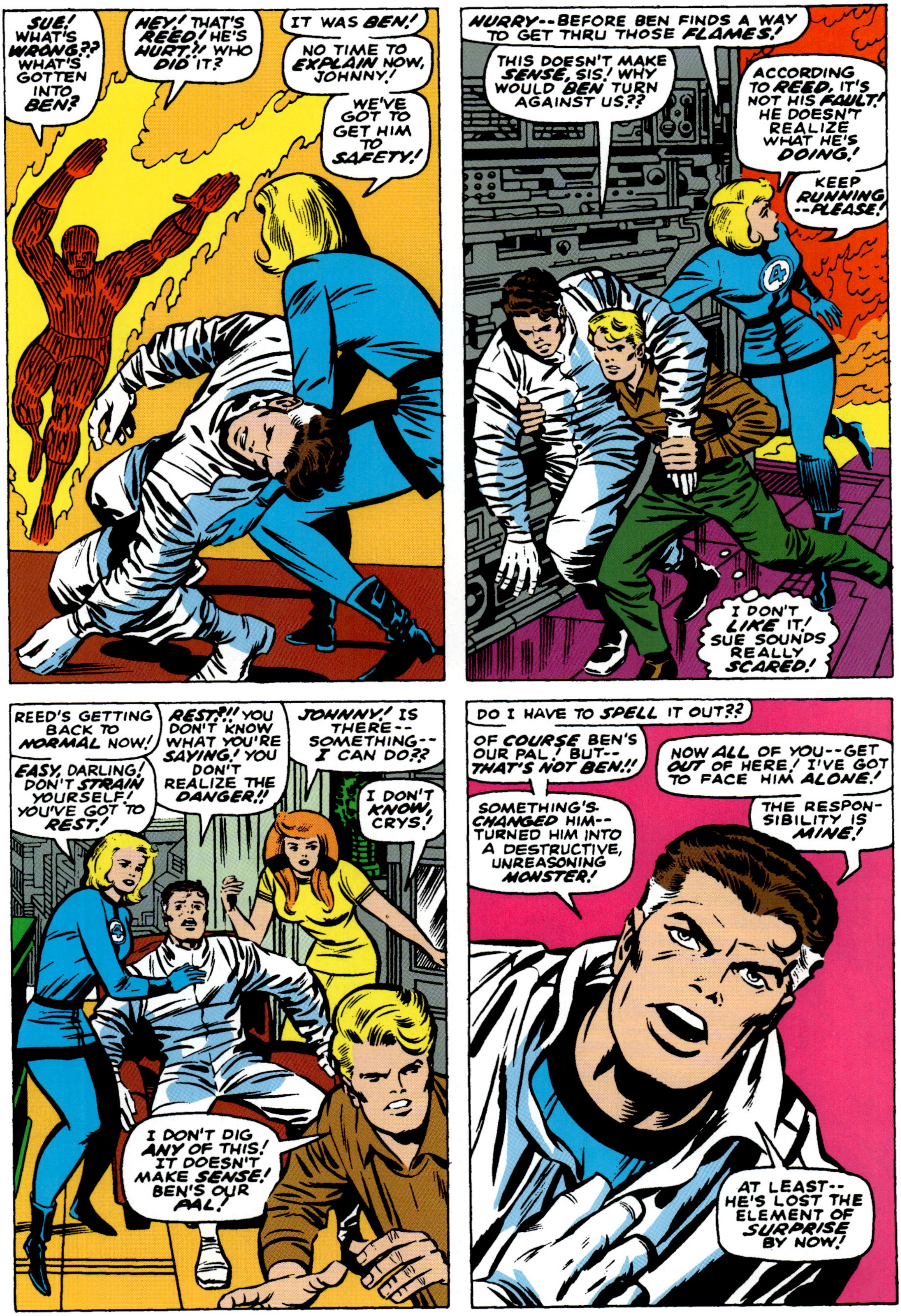
SUE! WHAT'S WRONG?? WHAT'S GOTTEN INTO BEN?
HEY! THAT'S REED! HE'S HURT!! WHO DID IT?
IT WAS BEN!
NO TIME TO EXPLAIN NOW, JOHNNY!
WE'VE GOT TO GET HIM TO SAFETY!
HURRY--BEFORE BEN FINDS A WAY TO GET THRU THOSE FLAMES!
THIS DOESN'T MAKE SENSE, SIS! WHY WOULD BEN TURN AGAINST US??
ACCORDING TO REED, IT'S NOT HIS FAULT! HE DOESN'T REALIZE WHAT HE'S DOING!
KEEP RUNNING --PLEASE!
I DON'T LIKE IT! SUE SOUNDS REALLY SCARED!
REED'S GETTING BACK TO NORMAL NOW!
EASY, DARLING! DON'T STRAIN YOURSELF! YOU'VE GOT TO REST!
REST?!! YOU DON'T KNOW WHAT YOU'RE SAYING! YOU DON'T REALIZE THE DANGER!!
JOHNNY! IS THERE-- SOMETHING-- I CAN DO??
I DON'T KNOW, CRYS!
I DON'T DIG ANY OF THIS! IT DOESN'T MAKE SENSE! BEN'S OUR PAL!
DO I HAVE TO SPELL IT OUT??
OF COURSE BEN'S OUR PAL! BUT-- THAT'S NOT BEN!!
SOMETHING'S CHANGED HIM-- TURNED HIM INTO A DESTRUCTIVE, UNREASONING MONSTER!
NOW ALL OF YOU--GET OUT OF HERE! I'VE GOT TO FACE HIM ALONE!
THE RESPONSIBILITY IS MINE!
AT LEAST-- HE'S LOST THE ELEMENT OF SURPRISE BY NOW!

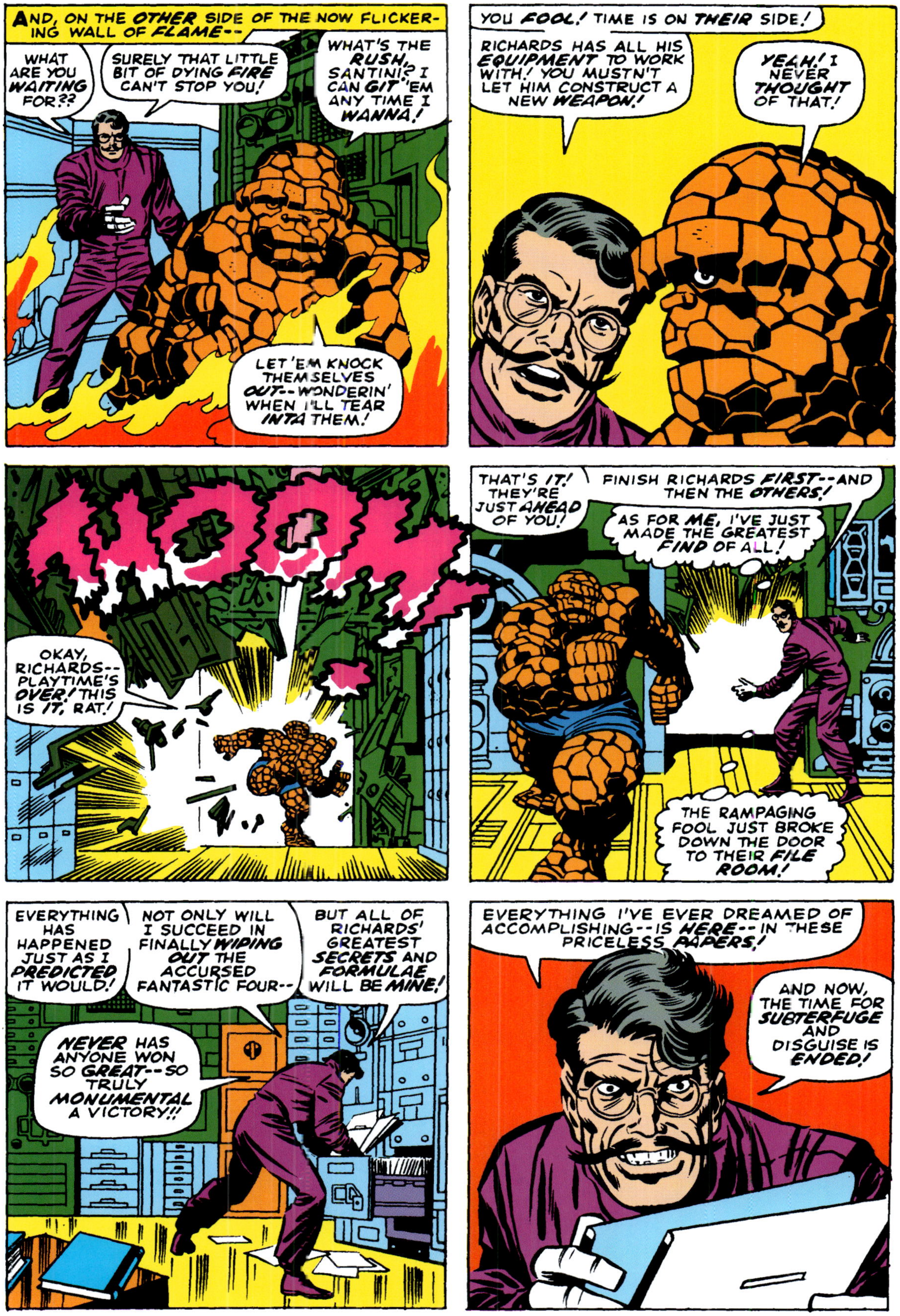

AND, ON THE OTHER SIDE OF THE NOW FLICKERING WALL OF FLAME--
WHAT ARE YOU WAITING FOR??
SURELY THAT LITTLE BIT OF DYING FIRE CAN'T STOP YOU!
WHAT'S THE RUSH, SANTINI? I CAN GIT 'EM ANY TIME I WANNA!
LET 'EM KNOCK THEMSELVES OUT--WONDERIN' WHEN I'LL TEAR INTA THEM!
YOU FOOL! TIME IS ON THEIR SIDE!
RICHARDS HAS ALL HIS EQUIPMENT TO WORK WITH! YOU MUSTN'T LET HIM CONSTRUCT A NEW WEAPON!
YEAH! I NEVER THOUGHT OF THAT!
WOOM
OKAY, RICHARDS--PLAYTIME'S OVER! THIS IS IT, RAT!
THAT'S IT! THEY'RE JUST AHEAD OF YOU!
FINISH RICHARDS FIRST--AND THEN THE OTHERS!
AS FOR ME, I'VE JUST MADE THE GREATEST FIND OF ALL!
THE RAMPAGING FOOL JUST BROKE DOWN THE DOOR TO THEIR FILE ROOM!
EVERYTHING HAS HAPPENED JUST AS I PREDICTED IT WOULD!
NOT ONLY WILL I SUCCEED IN FINALLY WIPING OUT THE ACCURSED FANTASTIC FOUR--
BUT ALL OF RICHARDS' GREATEST SECRETS AND FORMULAE WILL BE MINE!
NEVER HAS ANYONE WON SO GREAT--SO TRULY MONUMENTAL A VICTORY!!
EVERYTHING I'VE EVER DREAMED OF ACCOMPLISHING--IS HERE--IN THESE PRICELESS PAPERS!
AND NOW, THE TIME FOR SUBTERFUGE AND DISGUISE IS ENDED!

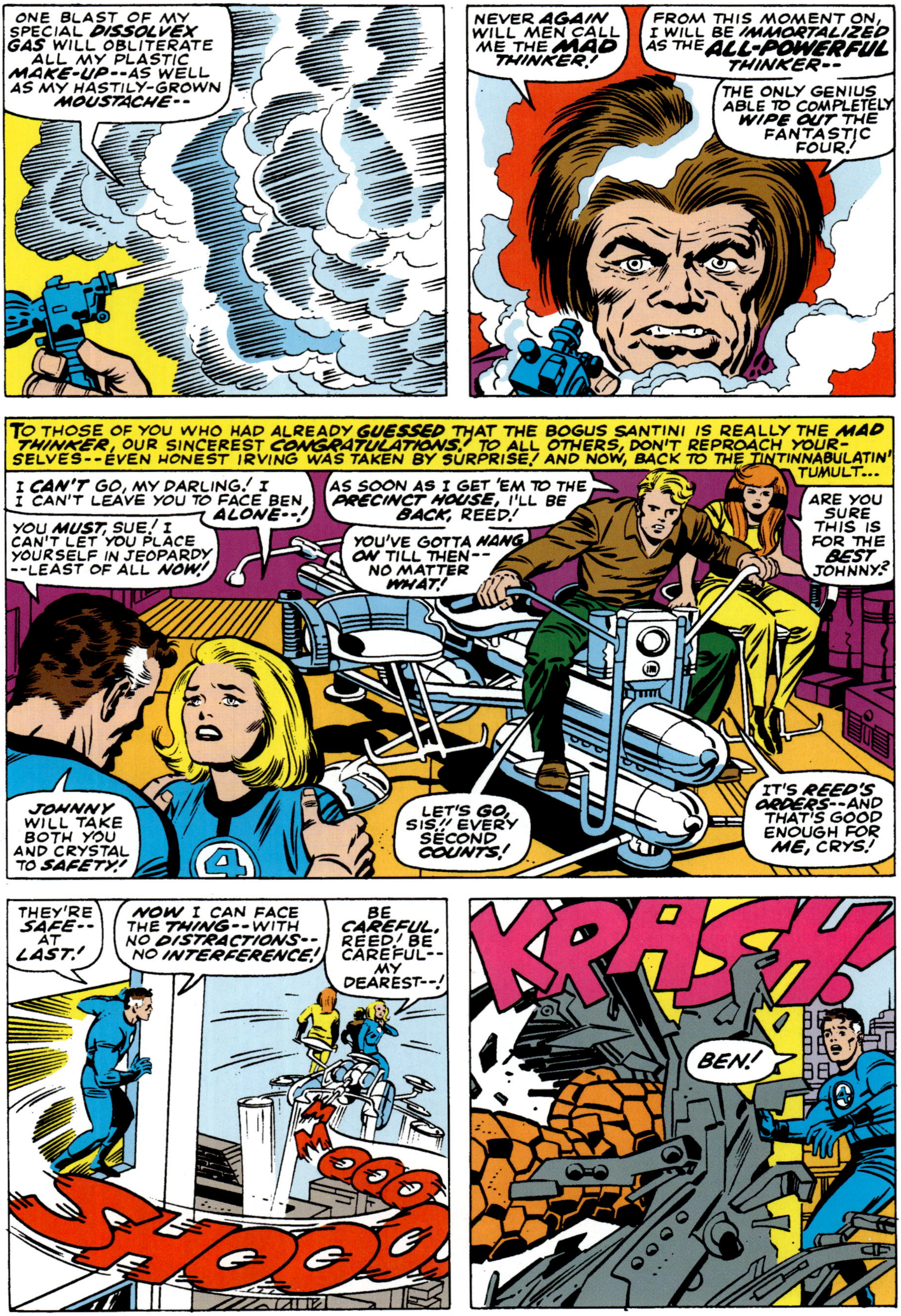

ONE BLAST OF MY SPECIAL DISSOLVEX GAS WILL OBLITERATE ALL MY PLASTIC MAKE-UP--AS WELL AS MY HASTILY-GROWN MOUSTACHE--
NEVER AGAIN WILL MEN CALL ME THE MAD THINKER!
FROM THIS MOMENT ON, I WILL BE IMMORTALIZED AS THE ALL-POWERFUL THINKER--
THE ONLY GENIUS ABLE TO COMPLETELY WIPE OUT THE FANTASTIC FOUR!
TO THOSE OF YOU WHO HAD ALREADY GUESSED THAT THE BOGUS SANTINI IS REALLY THE MAD THINKER, OUR SINCEREST CONGRATULATIONS! TO ALL OTHERS, DON'T REPROACH YOURSELVES--EVEN HONEST IRVING WAS TAKEN BY SURPRISE! AND NOW, BACK TO THE TINTINNABULATIN' TUMULT...
I CAN'T GO, MY DARLING! I I CAN'T LEAVE YOU TO FACE BEN ALONE--!
YOU MUST, SUE! I CAN'T LET YOU PLACE YOURSELF IN JEOPARDY --LEAST OF ALL NOW!
AS SOON AS I GET 'EM TO THE PRECINCT HOUSE, I'LL BE BACK, REED!
YOU'VE GOTTA HANG ON TILL THEN-- NO MATTER WHAT!
ARE YOU SURE THIS IS FOR THE BEST JOHNNY?
JOHNNY WILL TAKE BOTH YOU AND CRYSTAL TO SAFETY!
LET'S GO, SIS!! EVERY SECOND COUNTS!
IT'S REED'S ORDERS--AND THAT'S GOOD ENOUGH FOR ME, CRYS!
THEY'RE SAFE--AT LAST!
NOW I CAN FACE THE THING--WITH NO DISTRACTIONS-- NO INTERFERENCE!
BE CAREFUL, REED! BE CAREFUL-- MY DEAREST--!
SHOOOOOOM
KRASH!
BEN!

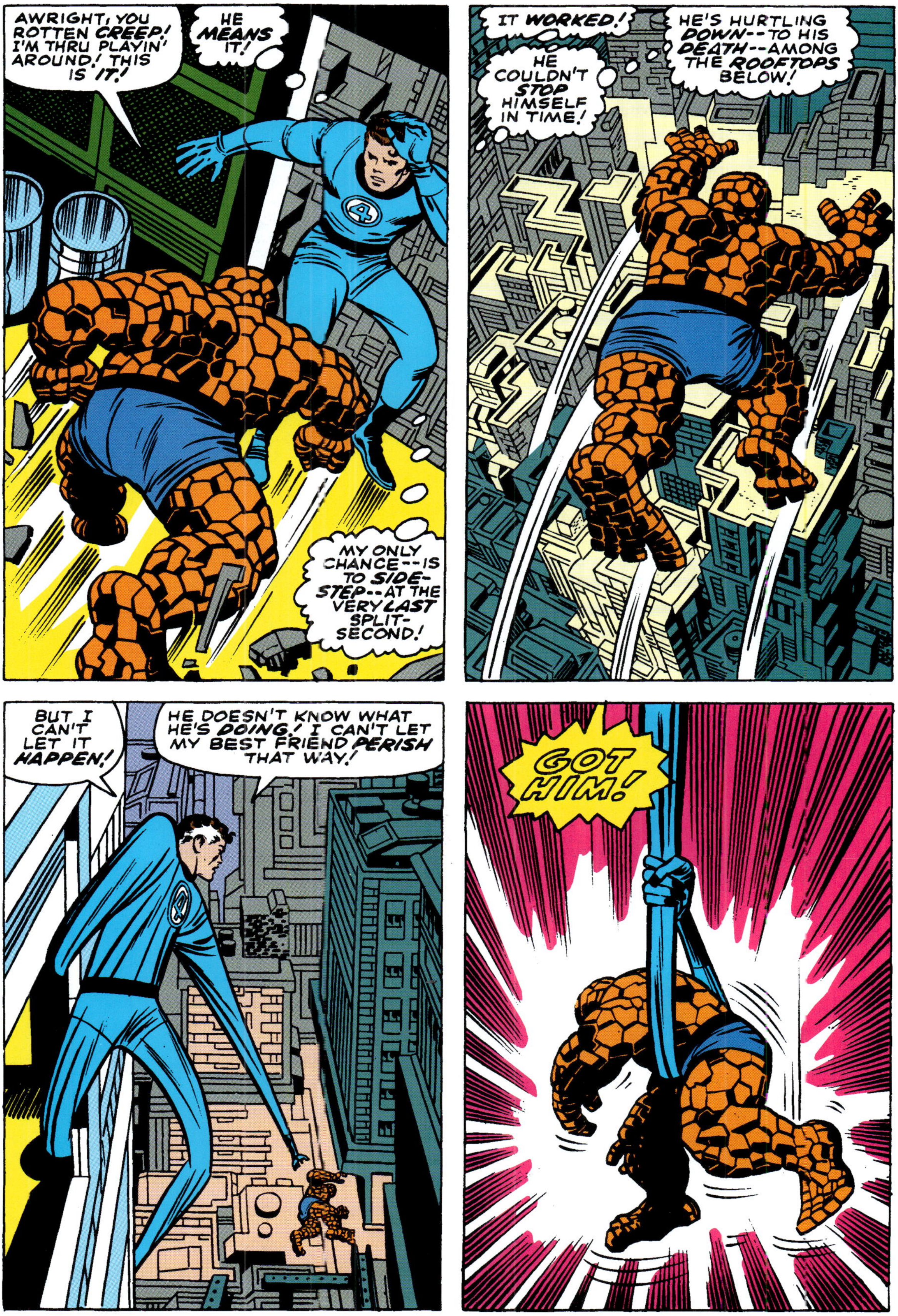
AWRIGHT, YOU ROTTEN CREEP! I'M THRU PLAYIN' AROUND! THIS IS IT!
HE MEANS IT!
MY ONLY CHANCE--IS TO SIDE-STEP--AT THE VERY LAST SPLIT-SECOND!
IT WORKED!
HE COULDN'T STOP HIMSELF IN TIME!
HE'S HURTLING DOWN--TO HIS DEATH--AMONG THE ROOFTOPS BELOW!
BUT I CAN'T LET IT HAPPEN!
HE DOESN'T KNOW WHAT HE'S DOING! I CAN'T LET MY BEST FRIEND PERISH THAT WAY!
GOT HIM!

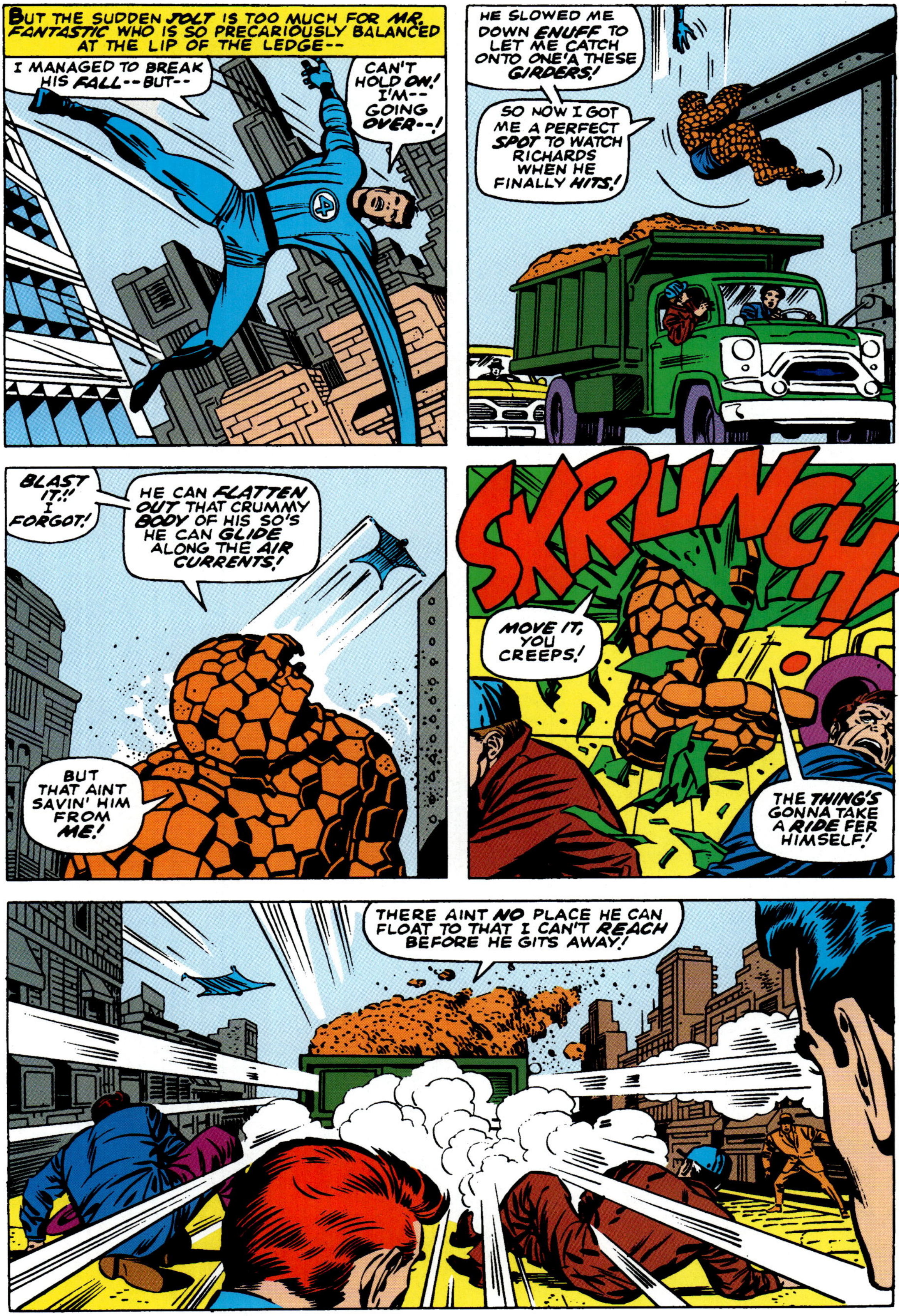
BUT THE SUDDEN JOLT IS TOO MUCH FOR MR. FANTASTIC WHO IS SO PRECARIOUSLY BALANCED AT THE LIP OF THE LEDGE--
I MANAGED TO BREAK HIS FALL--BUT--
CAN'T HOLD ON! I'M-- GOING OVER--!
HE SLOWED ME DOWN ENUFF TO LET ME CATCH ONTO ONE'A THESE GIRDERS!
SO NOW I GOT ME A PERFECT SPOT TO WATCH RICHARDS WHEN HE FINALLY HITS!
BLAST IT!! I FORGOT!
HE CAN FLATTEN OUT THAT CRUMMY BODY OF HIS SO'S HE CAN GLIDE ALONG THE AIR CURRENTS!
BUT THAT AINT SAVIN' HIM FROM ME!
SKRUNCH!
MOVE IT, YOU CREEPS!
THE THING'S GONNA TAKE A RIDE FER HIMSELF!
THERE AINT NO PLACE HE CAN FLOAT TO THAT I CAN'T REACH BEFORE HE GITS AWAY!

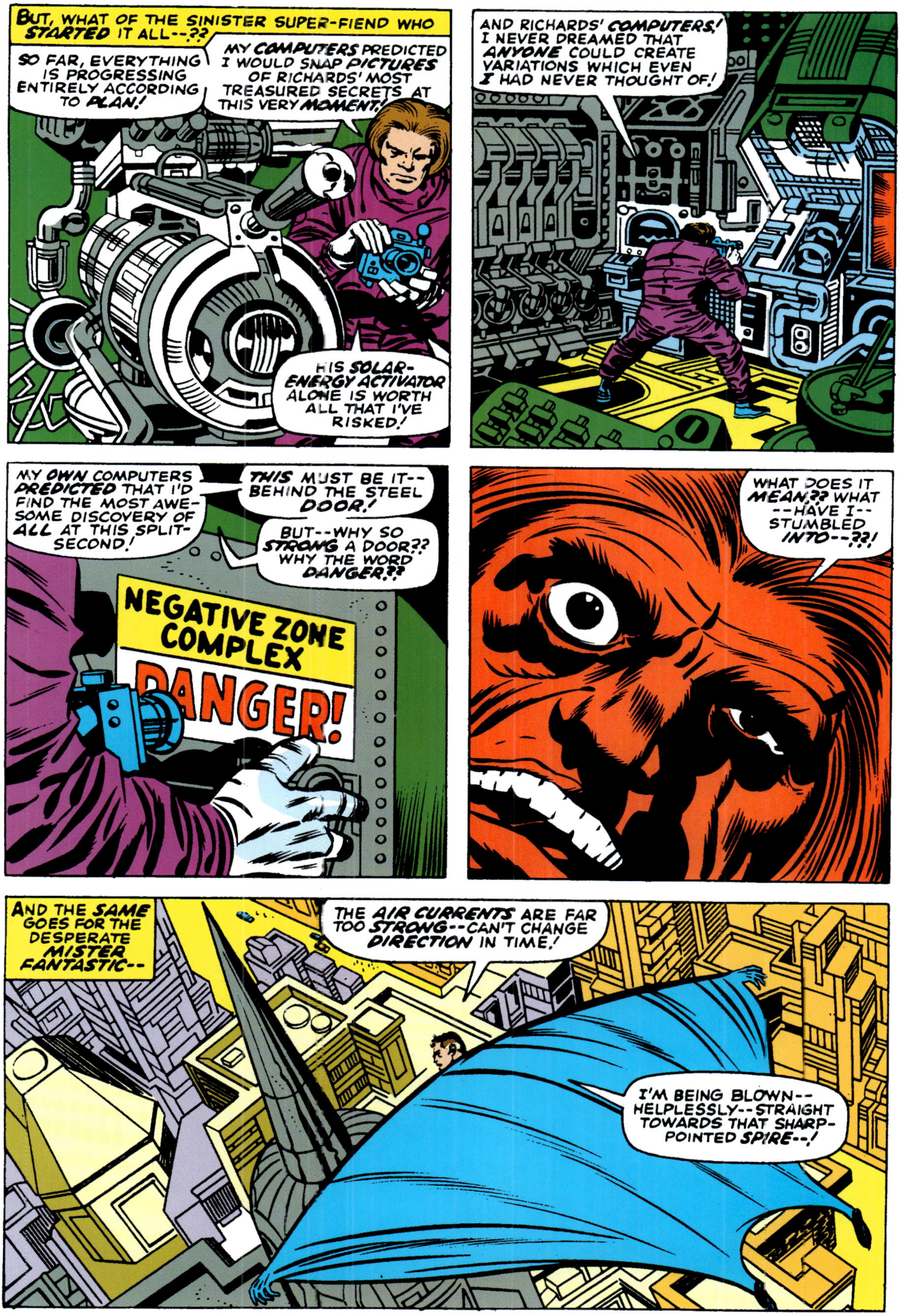
BUT, WHAT OF THE SINISTER SUPER-FIEND WHO STARTED IT ALL--??
SO FAR, EVERYTHING IS PROGRESSING ENTIRELY ACCORDING TO PLAN!
MY COMPUTERS PREDICTED I WOULD SNAP PICTURES OF RICHARDS' MOST TREASURED SECRETS AT THIS VERY MOMENT!
HIS SOLAR-ENERGY ACTIVATOR ALONE IS WORTH ALL THAT I'VE RISKED!
AND RICHARDS' COMPUTERS! I NEVER DREAMED THAT ANYONE COULD CREATE VARIATIONS WHICH EVEN I HAD NEVER THOUGHT OF!
MY OWN COMPUTERS PREDICTED THAT I'D FIND THE MOST AWE-SOME DISCOVERY OF ALL AT THIS SPLIT-SECOND!
THIS MUST BE IT-- BEHIND THE STEEL DOOR!
BUT--WHY SO STRONG A DOOR?? WHY THE WORD DANGER??
NEGATIVE ZONE COMPLEX
DANGER!
WHAT DOES IT MEAN?? WHAT --HAVE I-- STUMBLED INTO--??!
AND THE SAME GOES FOR THE DESPERATE MISTER FANTASTIC--
THE AIR CURRENTS ARE FAR TOO STRONG--CAN'T CHANGE DIRECTION IN TIME!
I'M BEING BLOWN-- HELPLESSLY--STRAIGHT TOWARDS THAT SHARP-POINTED SPIRE--!

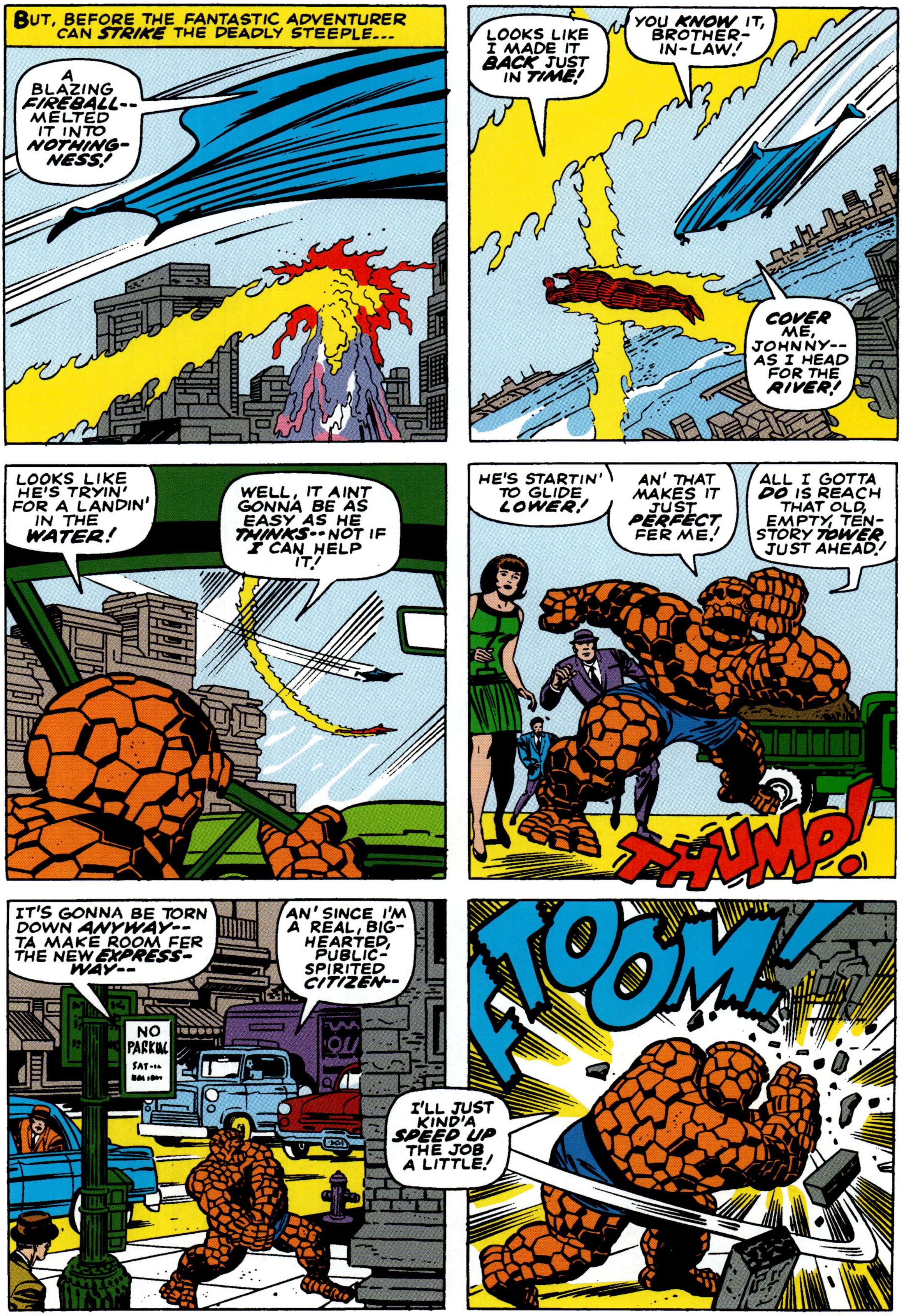

BUT, BEFORE THE FANTASTIC ADVENTURER CAN STRIKE THE DEADLY STEEPLE...
A BLAZING FIREBALL-- MELTED IT INTO NOTHINGNESS!
LOOKS LIKE I MADE IT BACK JUST IN TIME!
YOU KNOW IT, BROTHER-IN-LAW!
COVER ME, JOHNNY-- AS I HEAD FOR THE RIVER!
LOOKS LIKE HE'S TRYIN' FOR A LANDIN' IN THE WATER!
WELL, IT AINT GONNA BE AS EASY AS HE THINKS-- NOT IF I CAN HELP IT!
HE'S STARTIN' TO GLIDE LOWER!
AN' THAT MAKES IT JUST PERFECT FER ME!
ALL I GOTTA DO IS REACH THAT OLD, EMPTY, TEN-STORY TOWER JUST AHEAD!
THUMP!
IT'S GONNA BE TORN DOWN ANYWAY-- TA MAKE ROOM FER THE NEW EXPRESS-WAY--
AN' SINCE I'M A REAL, BIG-HEARTED, PUBLIC-SPIRITED CITIZEN--
NO
FTOOM!
I'LL JUST KIND'A SPEED UP THE JOB A LITTLE!

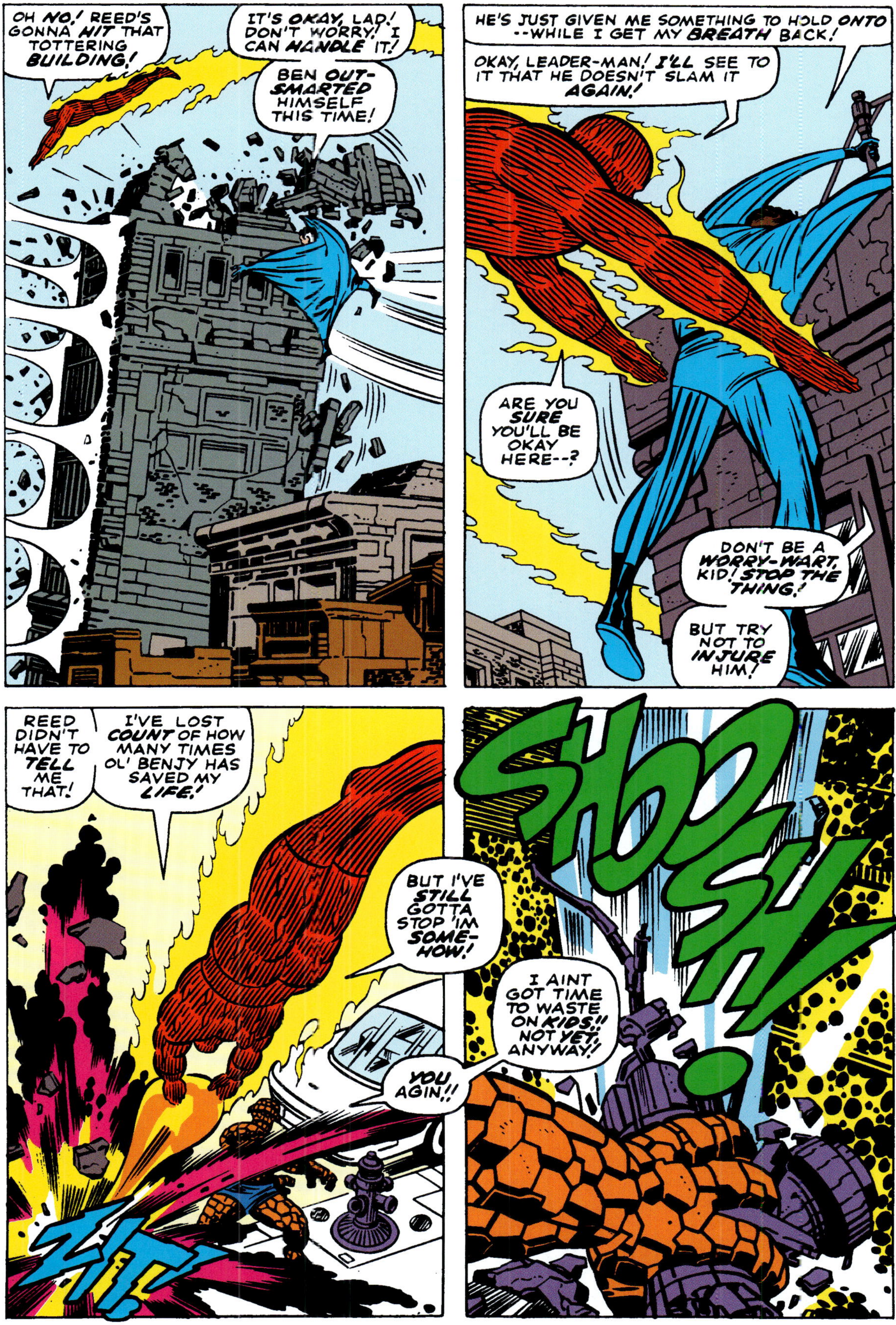
OH NO! REED'S GONNA HIT THAT TOTTERING BUILDING!
IT'S OKAY, LAD! DON'T WORRY! I CAN HANDLE IT!
BEN OUT-SMARTED HIMSELF THIS TIME!
HE'S JUST GIVEN ME SOMETHING TO HOLD ONTO --WHILE I GET MY BREATH BACK!
OKAY, LEADER-MAN! I'LL SEE TO IT THAT HE DOESN'T SLAM IT AGAIN!
ARE YOU SURE YOU'LL BE OKAY HERE--?
DON'T BE A WORRY-WART, KID! STOP THE THING!
BUT TRY NOT TO INJURE HIM!
REED DIDN'T HAVE TO TELL ME THAT!
I'VE LOST COUNT OF HOW MANY TIMES OL' BENJY HAS SAVED MY LIFE!
BUT I'VE STILL GOTTA STOP 'IM SOME-HOW!
YOU AGIN!!
ZIT!
SHOOSH!
I AINT GOT TIME TO WASTE ON KIDS!! NOT YET!! ANYWAY!

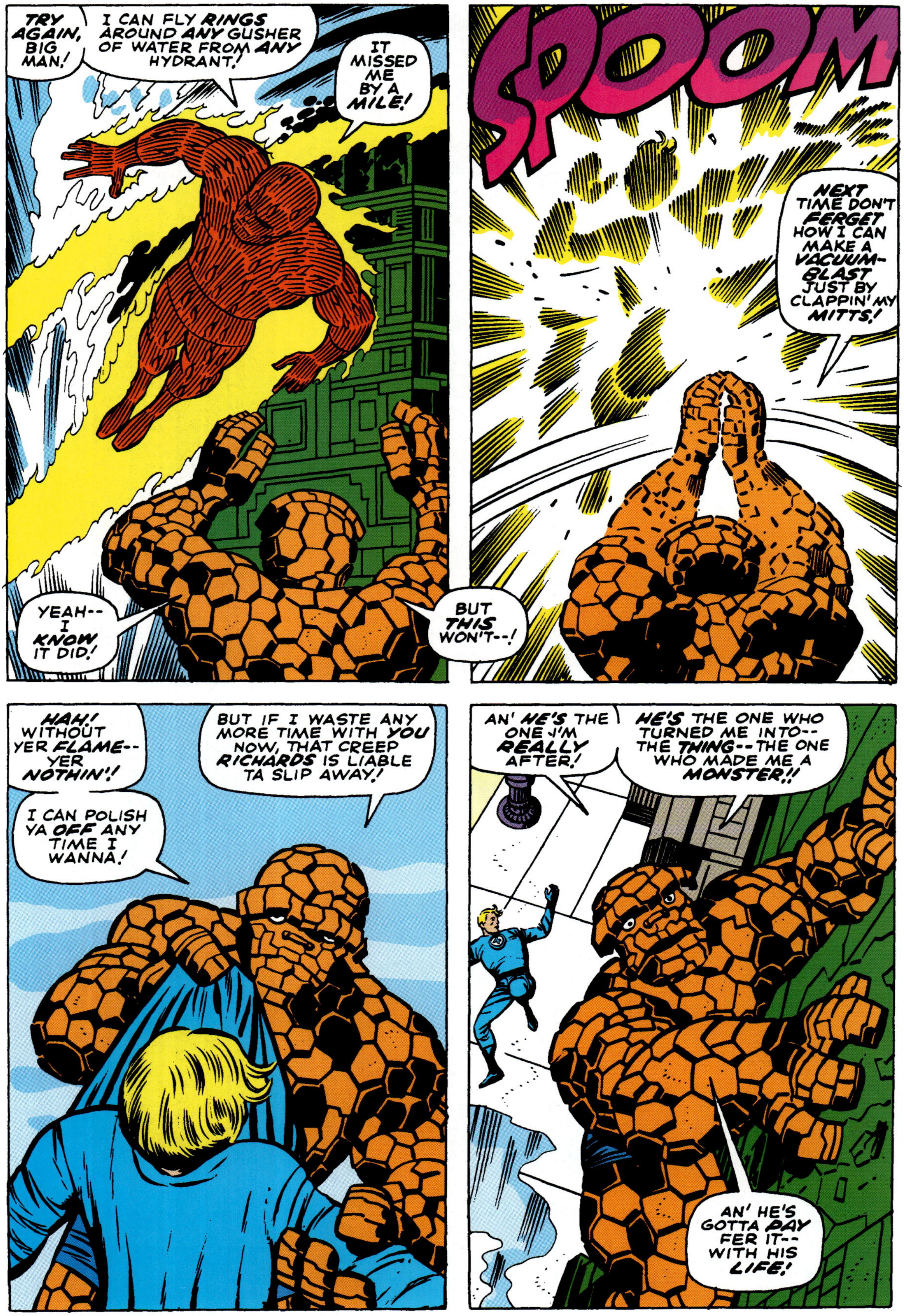
TRY AGAIN, BIG MAN!
I CAN FLY RINGS AROUND ANY GUSHER OF WATER FROM ANY HYDRANT!
IT MISSED ME BY A MILE!
YEAH-- I KNOW IT DID!
BUT THIS WON'T--!
SPOOM
NEXT TIME DON'T FERGET HOW I CAN MAKE A VACUUM-BLAST JUST BY CLAPPIN' MY MITTS!
HAH! WITHOUT YER FLAME-- YER NOTHIN'!
I CAN POLISH YA OFF ANY TIME I WANNA!
BUT IF I WASTE ANY MORE TIME WITH YOU NOW, THAT CREEP RICHARDS IS LIABLE TA SLIP AWAY!
AN' HE'S THE ONE I'M REALLY AFTER!
HE'S THE ONE WHO TURNED ME INTO-- THE THING-- THE ONE WHO MADE ME A MONSTER!!
AN' HE'S GOTTA PAY FER IT-- WITH HIS LIFE!

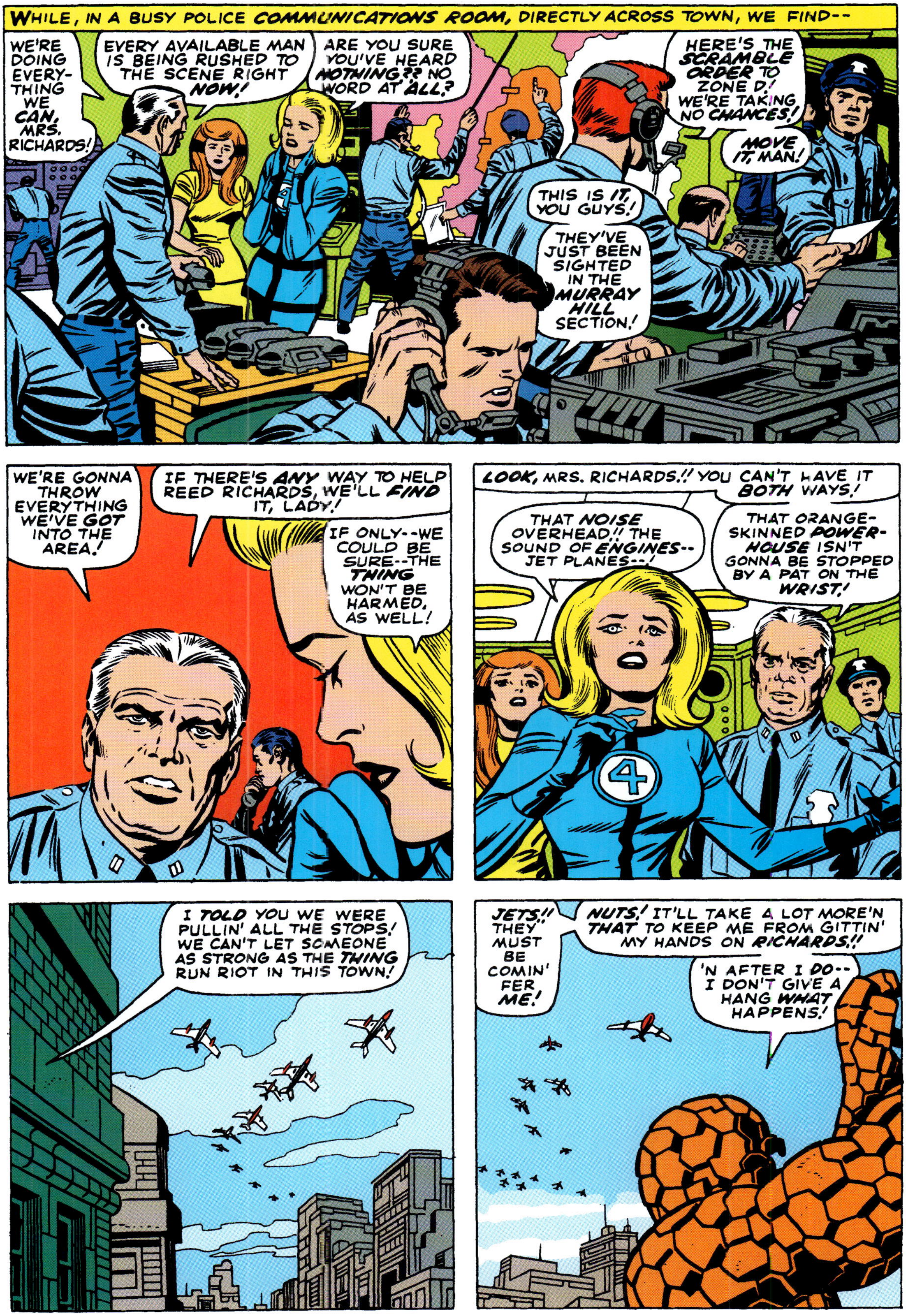
WHILE, IN A BUSY POLICE COMMUNICATIONS ROOM, DIRECTLY ACROSS TOWN, WE FIND--
WE'RE DOING EVERYTHING WE CAN, MRS. RICHARDS!
EVERY AVAILABLE MAN IS BEING RUSHED TO THE SCENE RIGHT NOW!
ARE YOU SURE YOU'VE HEARD NOTHING?? NO WORD AT ALL?
HERE'S THE SCRAMBLE ORDER TO ZONE D! WE'RE TAKING NO CHANCES!
MOVE IT, MAN!
THIS IS IT, YOU GUYS!
THEY'VE JUST BEEN SIGHTED IN THE MURRAY HILL SECTION!
WE'RE GONNA THROW EVERYTHING WE'VE GOT INTO THE AREA!
IF THERE'S ANY WAY TO HELP REED RICHARDS, WE'LL FIND IT, LADY!
IF ONLY--WE COULD BE SURE--THE THING WON'T BE HARMED, AS WELL!
LOOK, MRS. RICHARDS!! YOU CAN'T HAVE IT BOTH WAYS!
THAT NOISE OVERHEAD!! THE SOUND OF ENGINES-- JET PLANES--!
THAT ORANGE-SKINNED POWER-HOUSE ISN'T GONNA BE STOPPED BY A PAT ON THE WRIST!
I TOLD YOU WE WERE PULLIN' ALL THE STOPS! WE CAN'T LET SOMEONE AS STRONG AS THE THING RUN RIOT IN THIS TOWN!
JETS!! THEY MUST BE COMIN' FER ME!
NUTS! IT'LL TAKE A LOT MORE'N THAT TO KEEP ME FROM GITTIN' MY HANDS ON RICHARDS!!
'N AFTER I DO-- I DON'T GIVE A HANG WHAT HAPPENS!

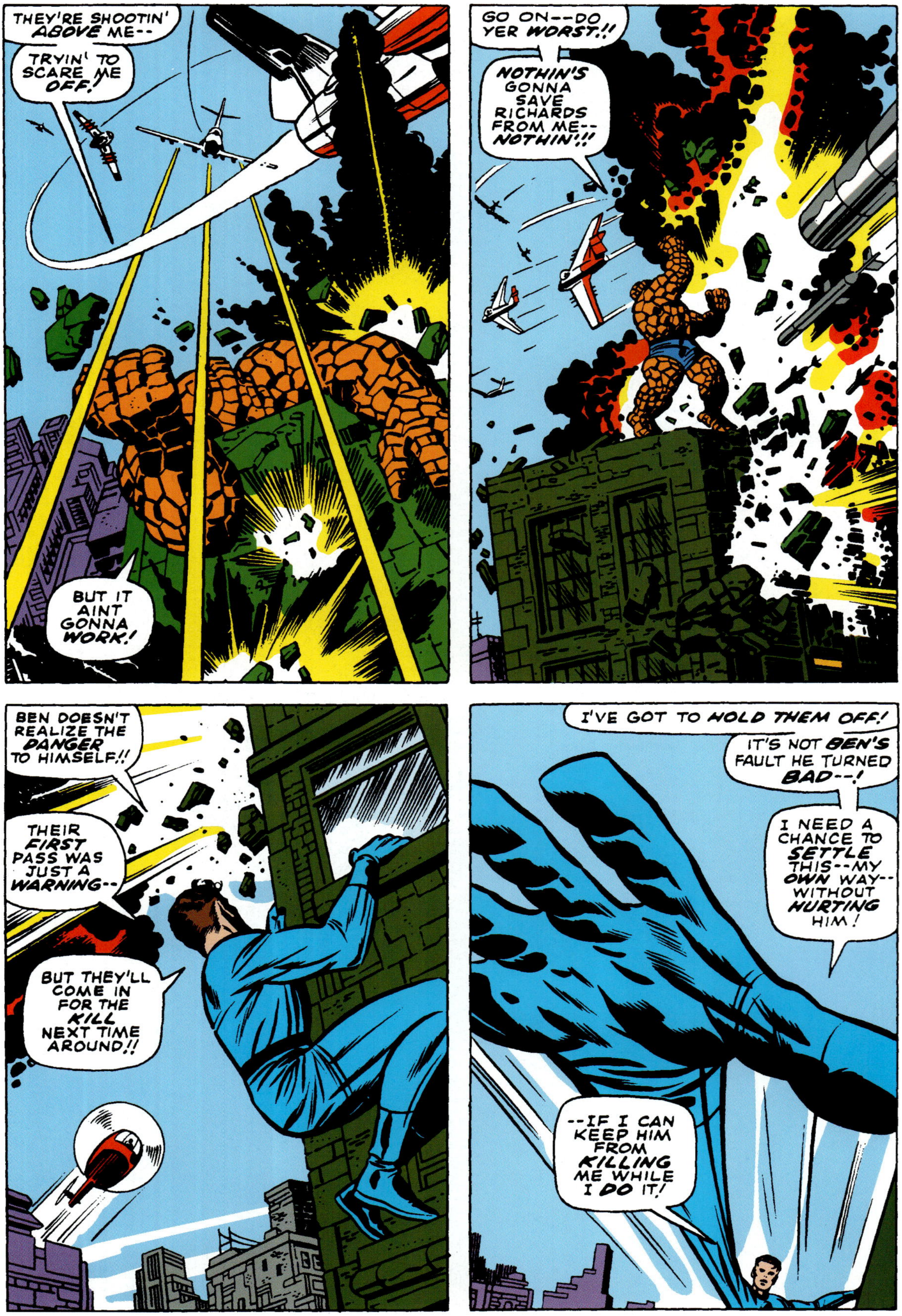
THEY'RE SHOOTIN' ABOVE ME--
TRYIN' TO SCARE ME OFF!
BUT IT AINT GONNA WORK!
GO ON--DO YER WORST!!
NOTHIN'S GONNA SAVE RICHARDS FROM ME-- NOTHIN'!!
BEN DOESN'T REALIZE THE DANGER TO HIMSELF!!
THEIR FIRST PASS WAS JUST A WARNING--
BUT THEY'LL COME IN FOR THE KILL NEXT TIME AROUND!!
I'VE GOT TO HOLD THEM OFF!
IT'S NOT BEN'S FAULT HE TURNED BAD--!
I NEED A CHANCE TO SETTLE THIS--MY OWN WAY-- WITHOUT HURTING HIM!
--IF I CAN KEEP HIM FROM KILLING ME WHILE I DO IT!

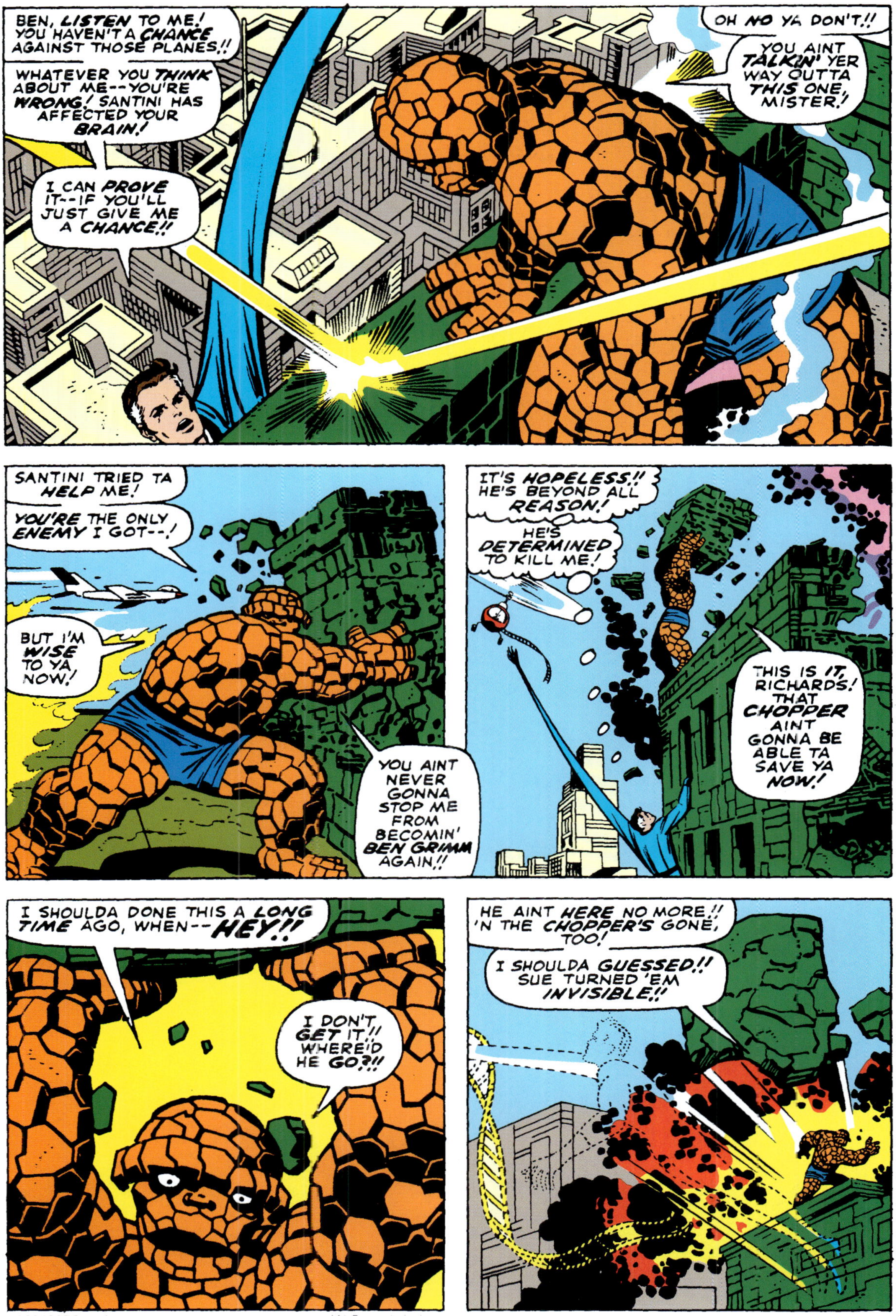
BEN, LISTEN TO ME! YOU HAVEN'T A CHANCE AGAINST THOSE PLANES!!
WHATEVER YOU THINK ABOUT ME--YOU'RE WRONG! SANTINI HAS AFFECTED YOUR BRAIN!
I CAN PROVE IT--IF YOU'LL JUST GIVE ME A CHANCE!!
OH NO YA DON'T!!
YOU AINT TALKIN' YER WAY OUTTA THIS ONE, MISTER!
SANTINI TRIED TA HELP ME!
YOU'RE THE ONLY ENEMY I GOT--!
BUT I'M WISE TO YA NOW!
YOU AINT NEVER GONNA STOP ME FROM BECOMIN' BEN GRIMM AGAIN!!
IT'S HOPELESS!! HE'S BEYOND ALL REASON!
HE'S DETERMINED TO KILL ME!
THIS IS IT, RICHARDS! THAT CHOPPER AINT GONNA BE ABLE TA SAVE YA NOW!
I SHOULDA DONE THIS A LONG TIME AGO, WHEN--HEY!!
I DON'T GET IT!! WHERE'D HE GO?!!
HE AINT HERE NO MORE!! 'N THE CHOPPER'S GONE, TOO!
I SHOULDA GUESSED!! SUE TURNED 'EM INVISIBLE!!

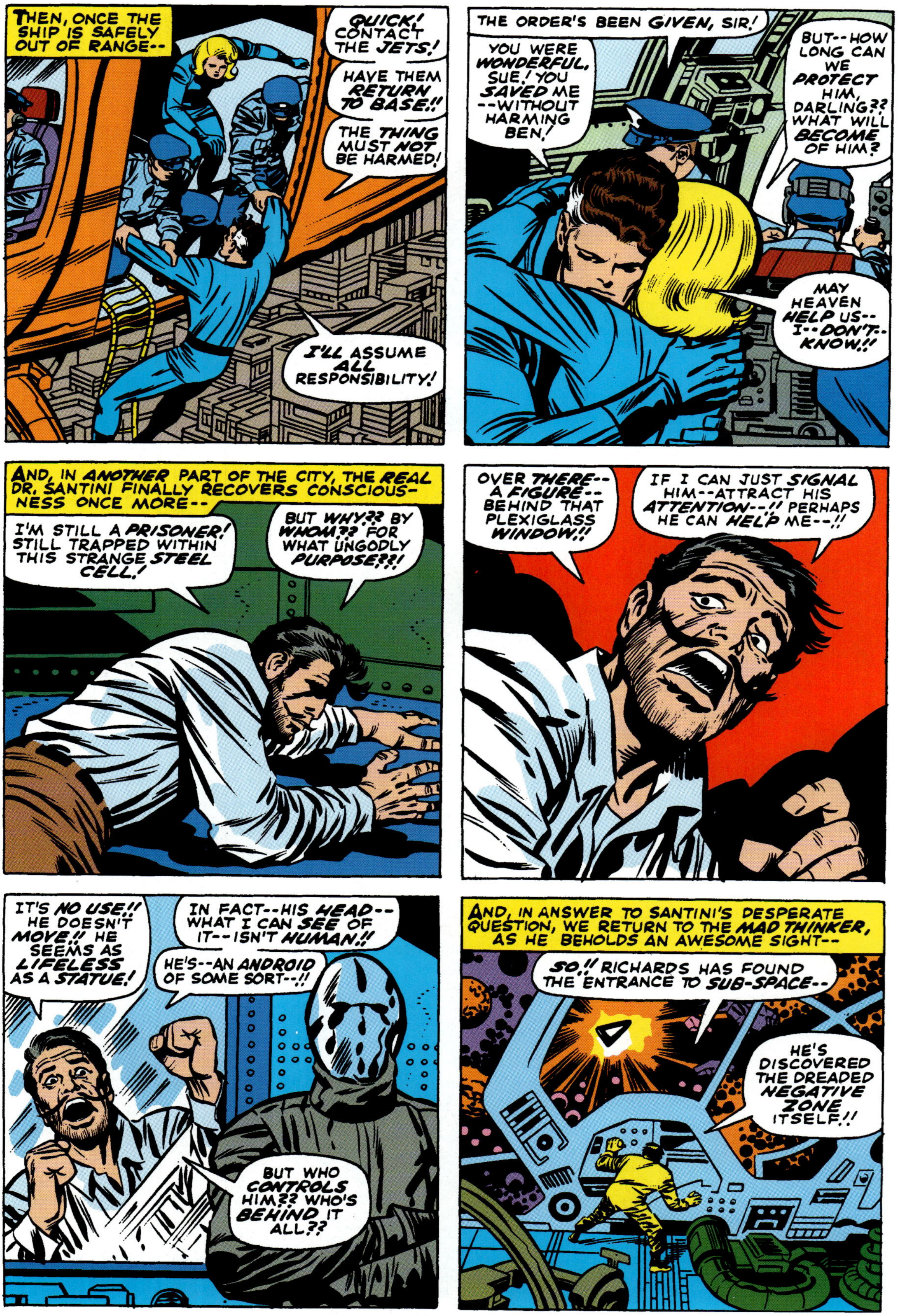
THEN, ONCE THE SHIP IS SAFELY OUT OF RANGE--
QUICK! CONTACT THE JETS!
HAVE THEM RETURN TO BASE!!
THE THING MUST NOT BE HARMED!
I'LL ASSUME ALL RESPONSIBILITY!
THE ORDER'S BEEN GIVEN, SIR!
YOU WERE WONDERFUL, SUE! YOU SAVED ME --WITHOUT HARMING BEN!
BUT--HOW LONG CAN WE PROTECT HIM, DARLING?? WHAT WILL BECOME OF HIM?
MAY HEAVEN HELP US-- I--DON'T--KNOW!!
AND, IN ANOTHER PART OF THE CITY, THE REAL DR. SANTINI FINALLY RECOVERS CONSCIOUSNESS ONCE MORE--
I'M STILL A PRISONER! STILL TRAPPED WITHIN THIS STRANGE STEEL CELL!
BUT WHY?? BY WHOM?? FOR WHAT UNGODLY PURPOSE??!
OVER THERE-- A FIGURE-- BEHIND THAT PLEXIGLASS WINDOW!!
IF I CAN JUST SIGNAL HIM--ATTRACT HIS ATTENTION--!! PERHAPS HE CAN HELP ME--!!
IT'S NO USE!! HE DOESN'T MOVE!! HE SEEMS AS LIFELESS AS A STATUE!
IN FACT--HIS HEAD-- WHAT I CAN SEE OF IT--ISN'T HUMAN!!
HE'S--AN ANDROID OF SOME SORT--!!
BUT WHO CONTROLS HIM?? WHO'S BEHIND IT ALL??
AND, IN ANSWER TO SANTINI'S DESPERATE QUESTION, WE RETURN TO THE MAD THINKER, AS HE BEHOLDS AN AWESOME SIGHT--
SO!! RICHARDS HAS FOUND THE ENTRANCE TO SUB-SPACE--
HE'S DISCOVERED THE DREADED NEGATIVE ZONE ITSELF!!

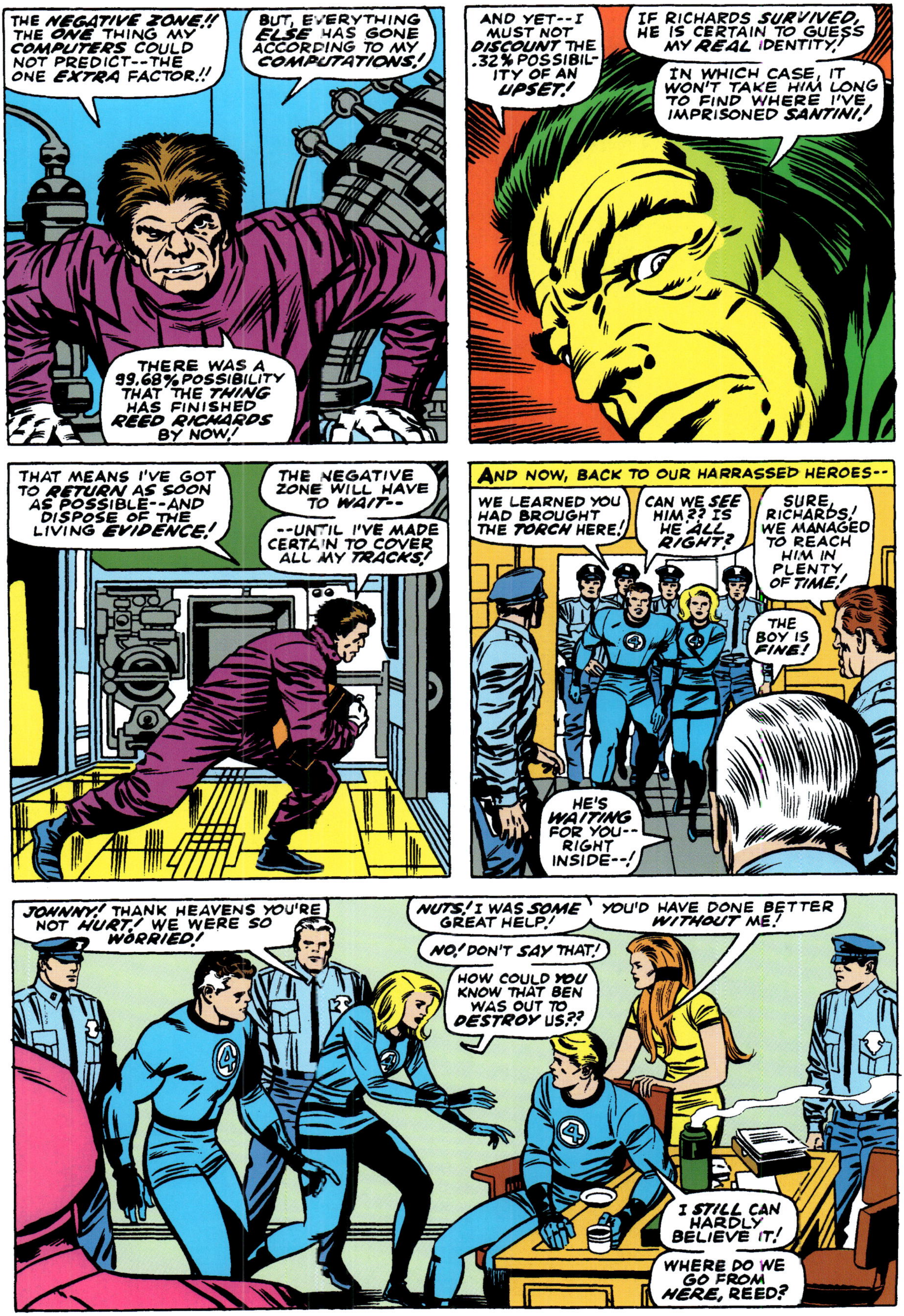
THE NEGATIVE ZONE!! THE ONE THING MY COMPUTERS COULD NOT PREDICT--THE ONE EXTRA FACTOR!!
BUT, EVERYTHING ELSE HAS GONE ACCORDING TO MY COMPUTATIONS!
THERE WAS A 99.68% POSSIBILITY THAT THE THING HAS FINISHED REED RICHARDS BY NOW!
AND YET--I MUST NOT DISCOUNT THE .32% POSSIBILITY OF AN UPSET!
IF RICHARDS SURVIVED, HE IS CERTAIN TO GUESS MY REAL IDENTITY!
IN WHICH CASE, IT WON'T TAKE HIM LONG TO FIND WHERE I'VE IMPRISONED SANTINI!
THAT MEANS I'VE GOT TO RETURN AS SOON AS POSSIBLE--AND DISPOSE OF THE LIVING EVIDENCE!
THE NEGATIVE ZONE WILL HAVE TO WAIT--
--UNTIL I'VE MADE CERTAIN TO COVER ALL MY TRACKS!
AND NOW, BACK TO OUR HARRASSED HEROES--
WE LEARNED YOU HAD BROUGHT THE TORCH HERE!
CAN WE SEE HIM?? IS HE ALL RIGHT?
SURE, RICHARDS! WE MANAGED TO REACH HIM IN PLENTY OF TIME!
THE BOY IS FINE!
HE'S WAITING FOR YOU-- RIGHT INSIDE--!
JOHNNY! THANK HEAVENS YOU'RE NOT HURT! WE WERE SO WORRIED!
NUTS! I WAS SOME GREAT HELP!
YOU'D HAVE DONE BETTER WITHOUT ME!
NO! DON'T SAY THAT!
HOW COULD YOU KNOW THAT BEN WAS OUT TO DESTROY US??
I STILL CAN HARDLY BELIEVE IT!
WHERE DO WE GO FROM HERE, REED?

Panel 1:

I'VE BEEN WRACKING MY BRAIN-- AND I THINK I'VE FOUND THE KEY!

SANTINI IS RESPONSIBLE FOR ALL THIS! BUT, THE REAL SANTINI WOULD HAVE NO MOTIVE! HE'S BEYOND REPROACH!

OF COURSE! IT'S THE ONLY ANSWER! WE WERE DECEIVED BY AN IMPOSTOR!!

--BY SOMEONE OUT TO DESTROY US!

BUT WHO?

I THINK I HAVE THE ANSWER TO THAT ONE--!

Panel 2:

HIS PREOCCUPATION WITH COMPUTERS--HIS DETAILED, SEEMINGLY FOOL-PROOF PLAN-- HIS KNOWLEDGE OF SCIENTIFIC PROGRAMMING --HIS COMPLEX, YET BRILLIANTLY EXECUTED MOVES--

IT ALL ADDS UP TO ONE DIABOLIC-ALLY DANGEROUS FIGURE--

CAPTAIN! IF I GIVE YOU HIS LAST KNOWN LIST OF HIDEOUTS, WILL YOU ORDER AN IMMEDIATE CITY-WIDE SEARCH FOR--

--THE MAD THINKER?!!

I'LL LEAD THE SEARCH MYSELF, RICHARDS!

GOOD! THERE'S NOT A MINUTE TO LOSE!

SANTINI'S LIFE IS IN GREATER PERIL EACH SECOND THAT THE THINKER REMAINS FREE!

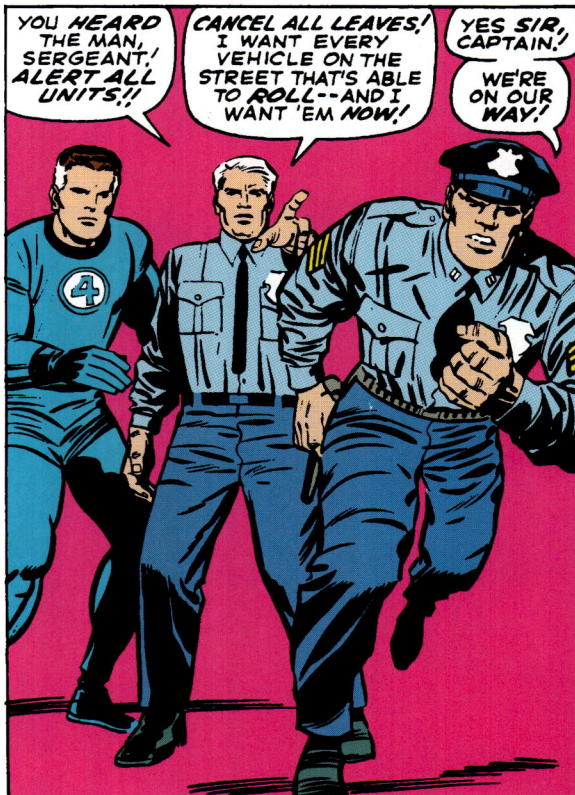

Panel 3:

YOU HEARD THE MAN, SERGEANT! ALERT ALL UNITS!!

CANCEL ALL LEAVES! I WANT EVERY VEHICLE ON THE STREET THAT'S ABLE TO ROLL--AND I WANT 'EM NOW!

YES SIR, CAPTAIN!

WE'RE ON OUR WAY!

Panel 4:

WHILE, ATOP THE DOOMED, STILL-SMOLDERING BUILDING--

THERE'S COPS 'N FIREMEN ALL OVER THE PLACE!

BUT THEY AINT GONNA BE ABLE TO STOP ME!!

NOTHIN'S GONNA STOP ME TILL I PUT THE KIBOSH ON RICHARDS--FER THE LAST TIME!

244

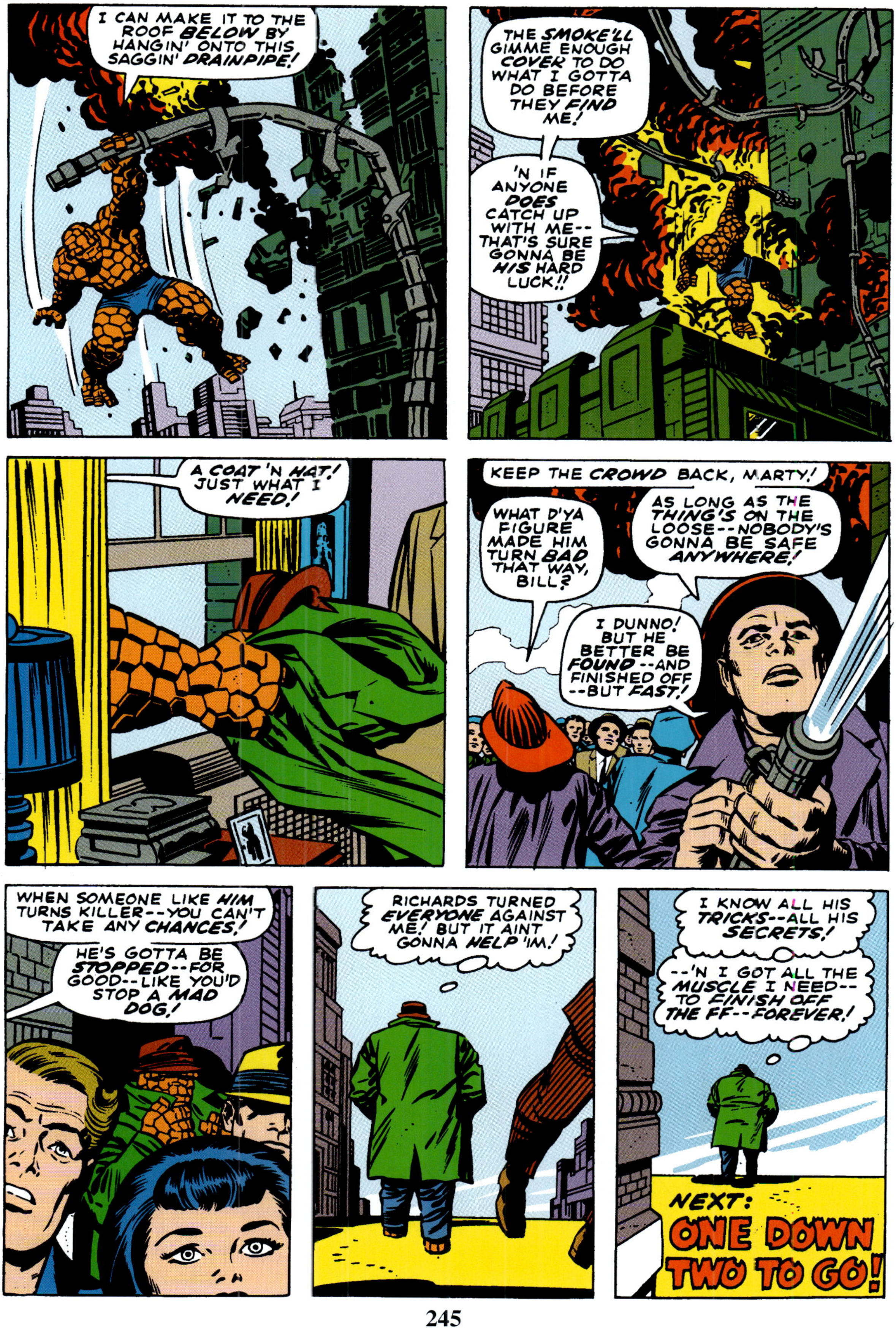
I CAN MAKE IT TO THE ROOF BELOW BY HANGIN' ONTO THIS SAGGIN' DRAINPIPE!
THE SMOKE'LL GIMME ENOUGH COVER TO DO WHAT I GOTTA DO BEFORE THEY FIND ME!
'N IF ANYONE DOES CATCH UP WITH ME-- THAT'S SURE GONNA BE HIS HARD LUCK!!
A COAT 'N HAT! JUST WHAT I NEED!
KEEP THE CROWD BACK, MARTY!
WHAT D'YA FIGURE MADE HIM TURN BAD THAT WAY, BILL?
AS LONG AS THE THING'S ON THE LOOSE--NOBODY'S GONNA BE SAFE ANYWHERE!
I DUNNO! BUT HE BETTER BE FOUND--AND FINISHED OFF --BUT FAST!
WHEN SOMEONE LIKE HIM TURNS KILLER--YOU CAN'T TAKE ANY CHANCES!
HE'S GOTTA BE STOPPED--FOR GOOD--LIKE YOU'D STOP A MAD DOG!
RICHARDS TURNED EVERYONE AGAINST ME! BUT IT AINT GONNA HELP 'IM!
I KNOW ALL HIS TRICKS--ALL HIS SECRETS!
--'N I GOT ALL THE MUSCLE I NEED-- TO FINISH OFF THE FF--FOREVER!
NEXT:
ONE DOWN TWO TO GO!

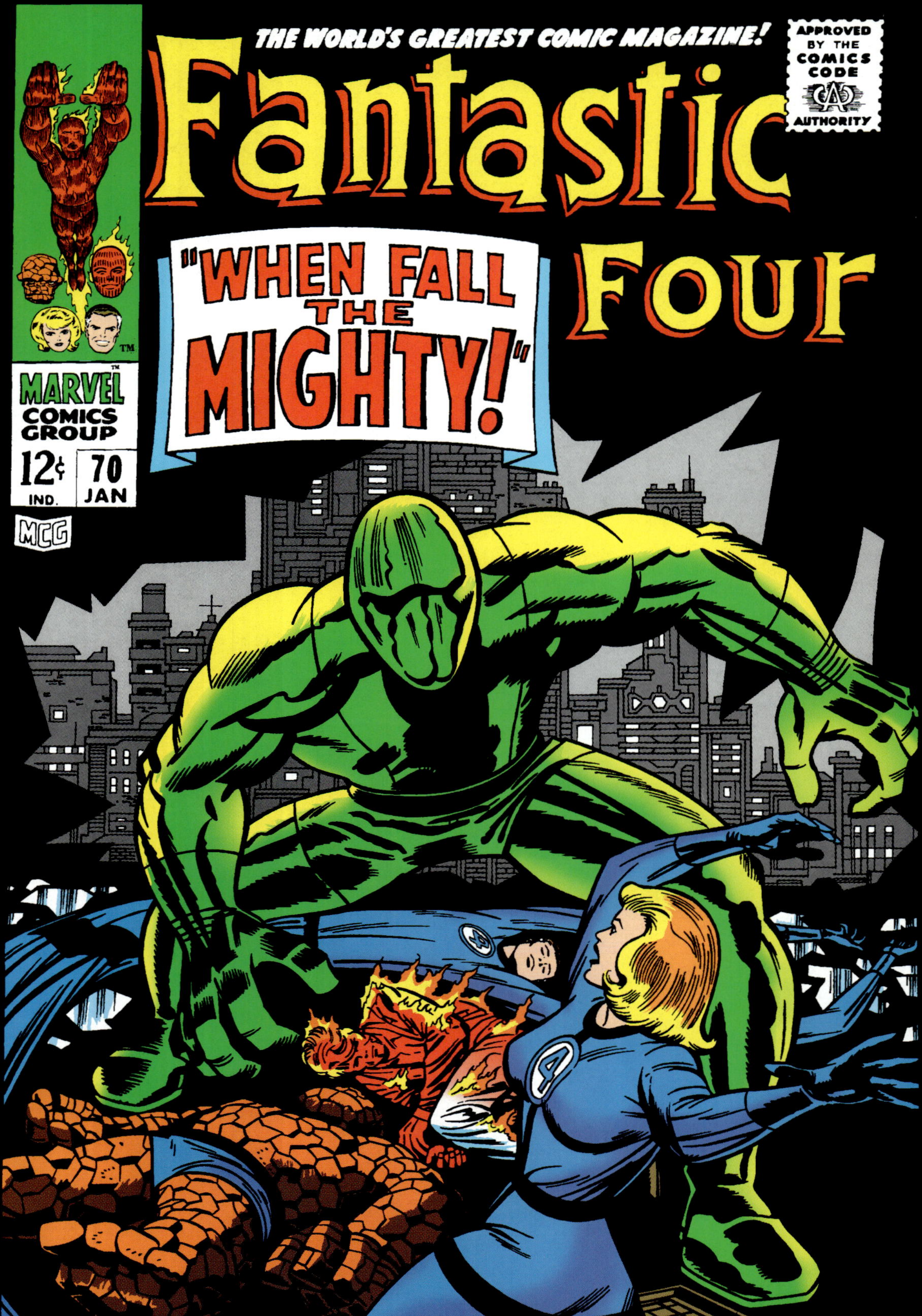
THE WORLD'S GREATEST COMIC MAGAZINE!
Fantastic Four
APPROVED BY THE COMICS CODE AUTHORITY
"WHEN FALL THE MIGHTY!"
MARVEL COMICS GROUP
12¢ IND.
70 JAN
MCG

ARE THE FABULOUS F.F. TRULY DEFEATED AT LAST?
"WHEN FALL THE MIGHTY"
FEARING FOR THE SAFETY OF DR. SANTINI, THE MAD THINKER'S HELPLESS CAPTIVE, REED AND JOHNNY LEAD THE RACE TO HIS LAST KNOWN HIDEOUT, ONLY TO FIND--
STAY BACK! THE PLACE IS GUARDED BY THE THINKER'S KILLER ANDROIDS!
CLICK! CLAK!
WARNING--ENEMY APPROACHING--
THEY'VE ALREADY BEEN ALERTED!
LOOK OUT FOR THEIR SHOCK WEAPONS!
IT'S TIME FOR ANOTHER STANDING OVATION FOR: SMILIN' STAN LEE and JOLLY JACK KIRBY WHO HAVE GIVEN US ANOTHER TINTINNABULATING THRILLER! SUPERBLY SUPPORTED BY: JOE SINNOTT INKER ARTIE SIMEK LETTERER

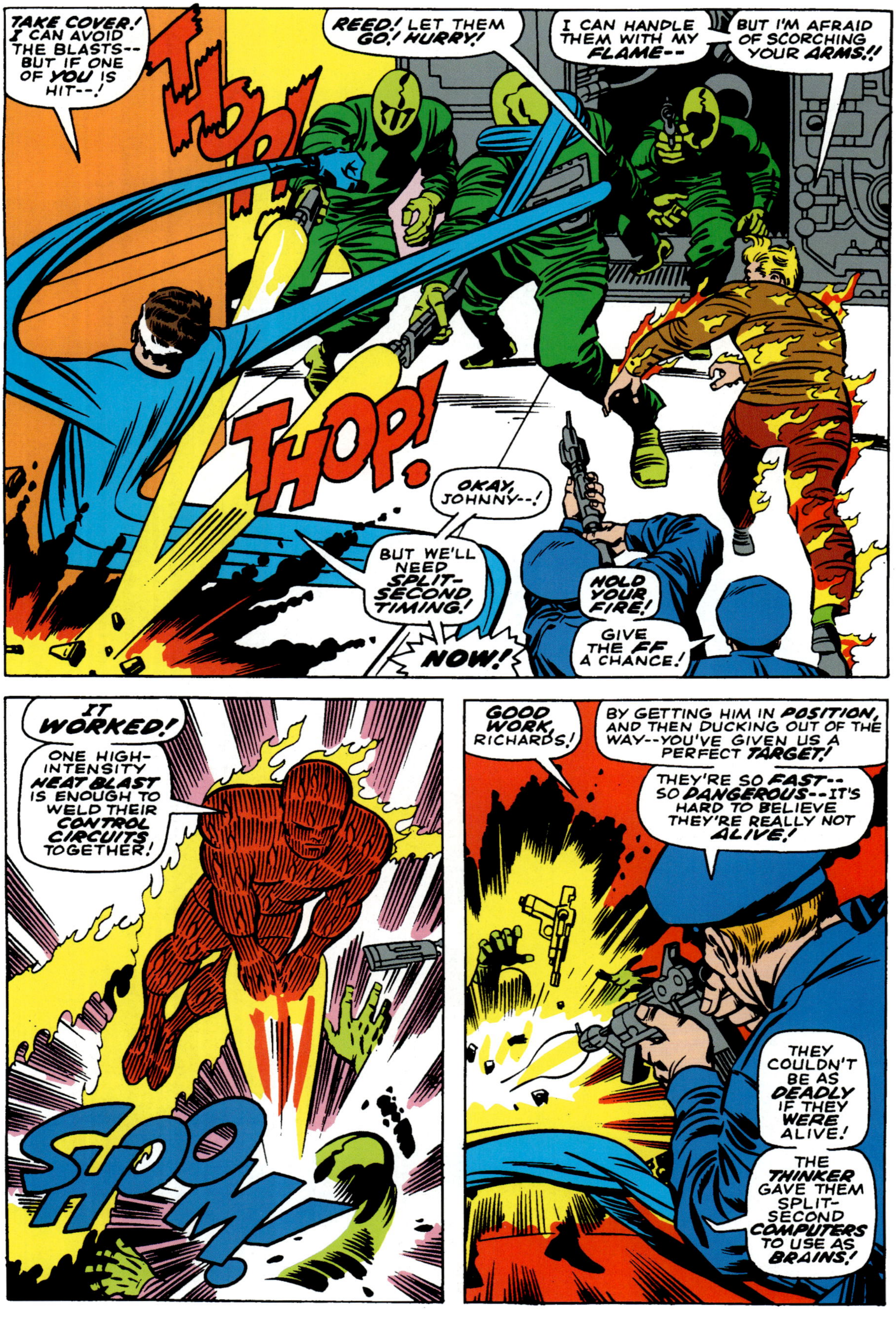
TAKE COVER! I CAN AVOID THE BLASTS-- BUT IF ONE OF YOU IS HIT--!
THOP!
REED! LET THEM GO! HURRY!
I CAN HANDLE THEM WITH MY FLAME--
BUT I'M AFRAID OF SCORCHING YOUR ARMS!!
THOP!
OKAY, JOHNNY--!
BUT WE'LL NEED SPLIT-SECOND TIMING!
NOW!
HOLD YOUR FIRE!
GIVE THE FF A CHANCE!
IT WORKED!
ONE HIGH-INTENSITY HEAT BLAST IS ENOUGH TO WELD THEIR CONTROL CIRCUITS TOGETHER!
SHOOM!
GOOD WORK, RICHARDS!
BY GETTING HIM IN POSITION, AND THEN DUCKING OUT OF THE WAY--YOU'VE GIVEN US A PERFECT TARGET!
THEY'RE SO FAST-- SO DANGEROUS--IT'S HARD TO BELIEVE THEY'RE REALLY NOT ALIVE!
THEY COULDN'T BE AS DEADLY IF THEY WERE ALIVE!
THE THINKER GAVE THEM SPLIT-SECOND COMPUTERS TO USE AS BRAINS!

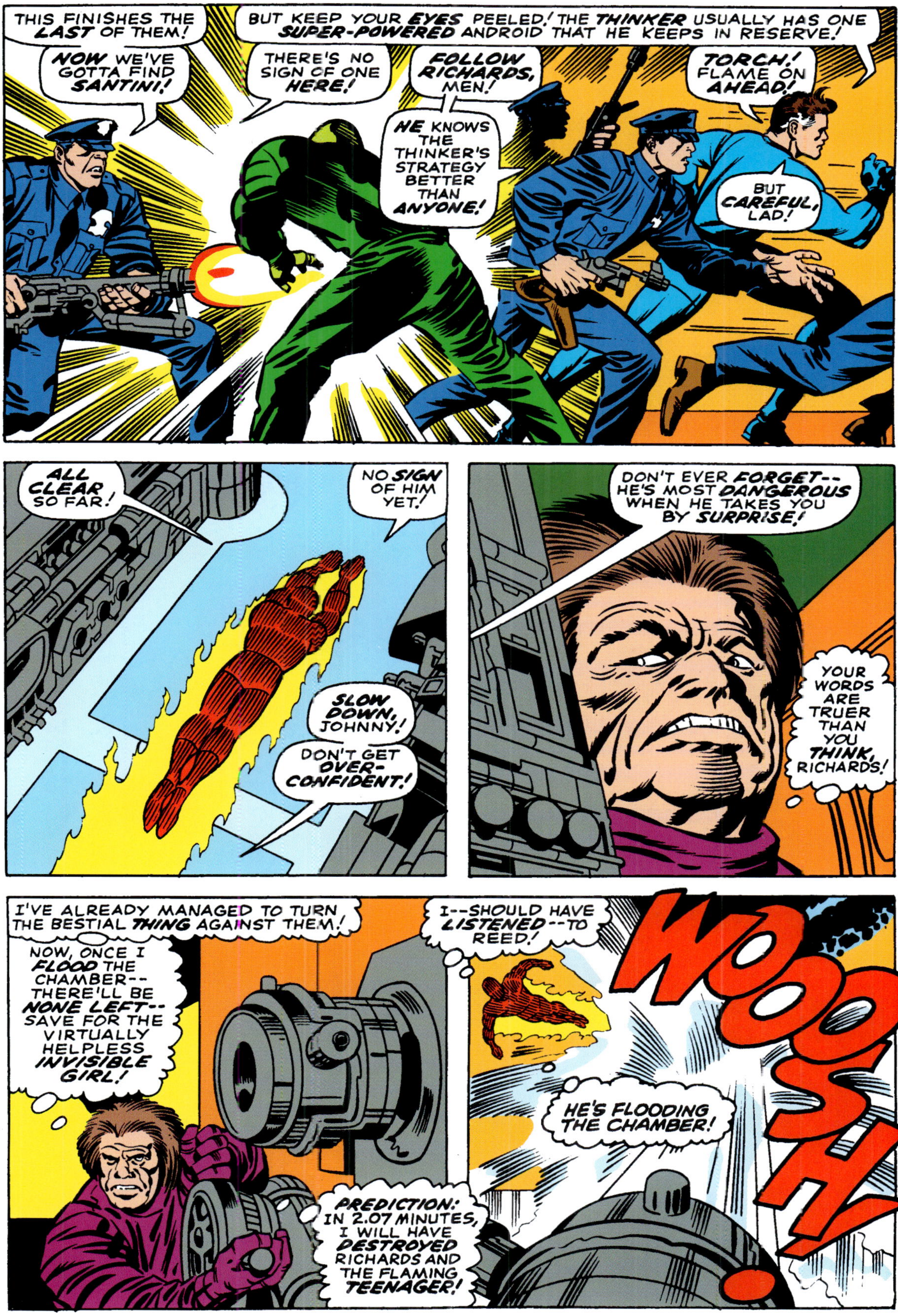
THIS FINISHES THE LAST OF THEM!
BUT KEEP YOUR EYES PEELED! THE THINKER USUALLY HAS ONE SUPER-POWERED ANDROID THAT HE KEEPS IN RESERVE!
NOW WE'VE GOTTA FIND SANTINI!
THERE'S NO SIGN OF ONE HERE!
FOLLOW RICHARDS, MEN!
HE KNOWS THE THINKER'S STRATEGY BETTER THAN ANYONE!
TORCH! FLAME ON AHEAD!
BUT CAREFUL, LAD!
ALL CLEAR SO FAR!
NO SIGN OF HIM YET!
SLOW DOWN, JOHNNY!
DON'T GET OVER-CONFIDENT!
DON'T EVER FORGET-- HE'S MOST DANGEROUS WHEN HE TAKES YOU BY SURPRISE!
YOUR WORDS ARE TRUER THAN YOU THINK, RICHARDS!
I'VE ALREADY MANAGED TO TURN THE BESTIAL THING AGAINST THEM!
NOW, ONCE I FLOOD THE CHAMBER-- THERE'LL BE NONE LEFT-- SAVE FOR THE VIRTUALLY HELPLESS INVISIBLE GIRL!
PREDICTION: IN 2.07 MINUTES, I WILL HAVE DESTROYED RICHARDS AND THE FLAMING TEENAGER!
I--SHOULD HAVE LISTENED--TO REED!
WOOOSH!
HE'S FLOODING THE CHAMBER!

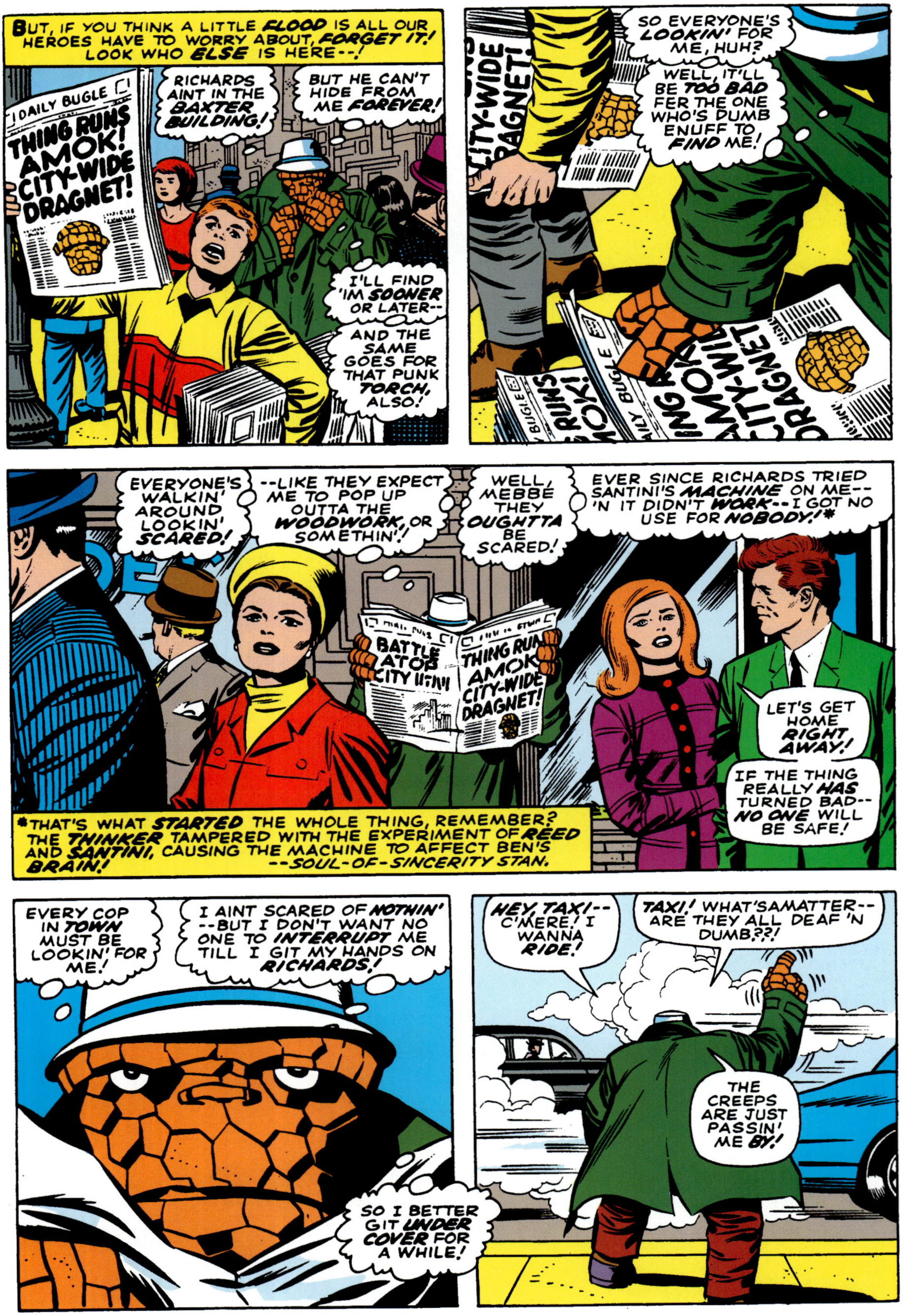
BUT, IF YOU THINK A LITTLE FLOOD IS ALL OUR HEROES HAVE TO WORRY ABOUT, FORGET IT! LOOK WHO ELSE IS HERE--!
DAILY BUGLE
THING RUNS AMOK! CITY-WIDE DRAGNET!
RICHARDS AINT IN THE BAXTER BUILDING!
BUT HE CAN'T HIDE FROM ME FOREVER!
I'LL FIND 'IM SOONER OR LATER--
AND THE SAME GOES FOR THAT PUNK TORCH, ALSO!
SO EVERYONE'S LOOKIN' FOR ME, HUH?
WELL, IT'LL BE TOO BAD FER THE ONE WHO'S DUMB ENUFF TO FIND ME!
EVERYONE'S WALKIN' AROUND LOOKIN' SCARED!
--LIKE THEY EXPECT ME TO POP UP OUTTA THE WOODWORK, OR SOMETHIN'!
WELL, MEBBE THEY OUGHTTA BE SCARED!
EVER SINCE RICHARDS TRIED SANTINI'S MACHINE ON ME--'N IT DIDN'T WORK--I GOT NO USE FOR NOBODY!*
THING RUNS AMOK CITY-WIDE DRAGNET!
LET'S GET HOME RIGHT AWAY!
IF THE THING REALLY HAS TURNED BAD--NO ONE WILL BE SAFE!
*THAT'S WHAT STARTED THE WHOLE THING, REMEMBER? THE THINKER TAMPERED WITH THE EXPERIMENT OF REED AND SANTINI, CAUSING THE MACHINE TO AFFECT BEN'S BRAIN! --SOUL-OF-SINCERITY STAN.
EVERY COP IN TOWN MUST BE LOOKIN' FOR ME!
I AINT SCARED OF NOTHIN' --BUT I DON'T WANT NO ONE TO INTERRUPT ME TILL I GIT MY HANDS ON RICHARDS!
SO I BETTER GIT UNDER COVER FOR A WHILE!
HEY, TAXI!--C'MERE! I WANNA RIDE!
TAXI! WHAT'SAMATTER--ARE THEY ALL DEAF 'N DUMB??!
THE CREEPS ARE JUST PASSIN' ME BY!

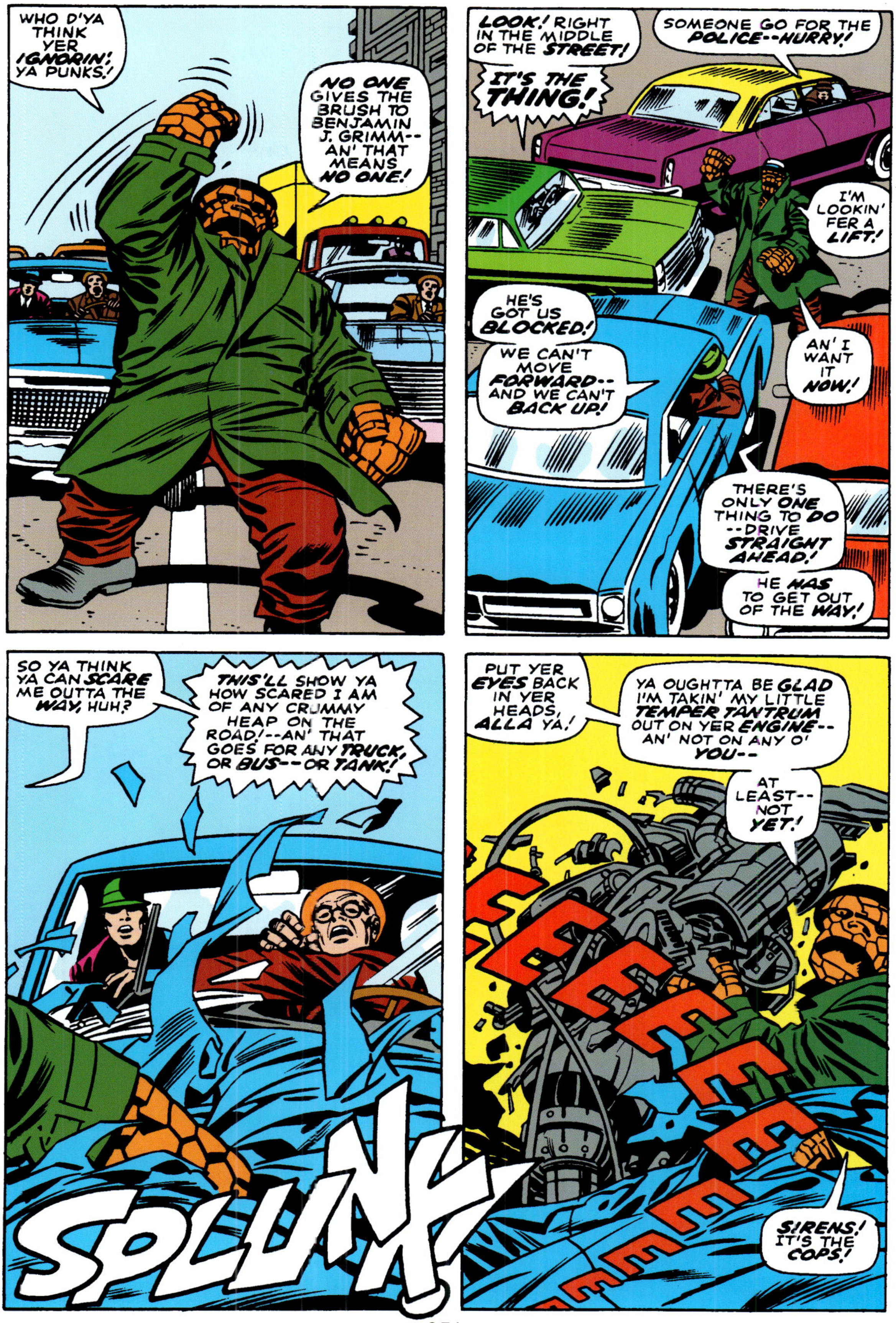
WHO D'YA THINK YER IGNORIN'! YA PUNKS!
NO ONE GIVES THE BRUSH TO BENJAMIN J. GRIMM-- AN' THAT MEANS NO ONE!
LOOK! RIGHT IN THE MIDDLE OF THE STREET!
SOMEONE GO FOR THE POLICE--HURRY!
IT'S THE THING!
I'M LOOKIN' FER A LIFT!
HE'S GOT US BLOCKED!
WE CAN'T MOVE FORWARD-- AND WE CAN'T BACK UP!
AN' I WANT IT NOW!
THERE'S ONLY ONE THING TO DO --DRIVE STRAIGHT AHEAD!
HE HAS TO GET OUT OF THE WAY!
SO YA THINK YA CAN SCARE ME OUTTA THE WAY, HUH?
THIS'LL SHOW YA HOW SCARED I AM OF ANY CRUMMY HEAP ON THE ROAD!--AN' THAT GOES FOR ANY TRUCK, OR BUS--OR TANK!
SPLUNK
PUT YER EYES BACK IN YER HEADS, ALLA YA!
YA OUGHTTA BE GLAD I'M TAKIN' MY LITTLE TEMPER TANTRUM OUT ON YER ENGINE-- AN' NOT ON ANY O' YOU--
AT LEAST--NOT YET!
EEEEEEEEEE
SIRENS! IT'S THE COPS!

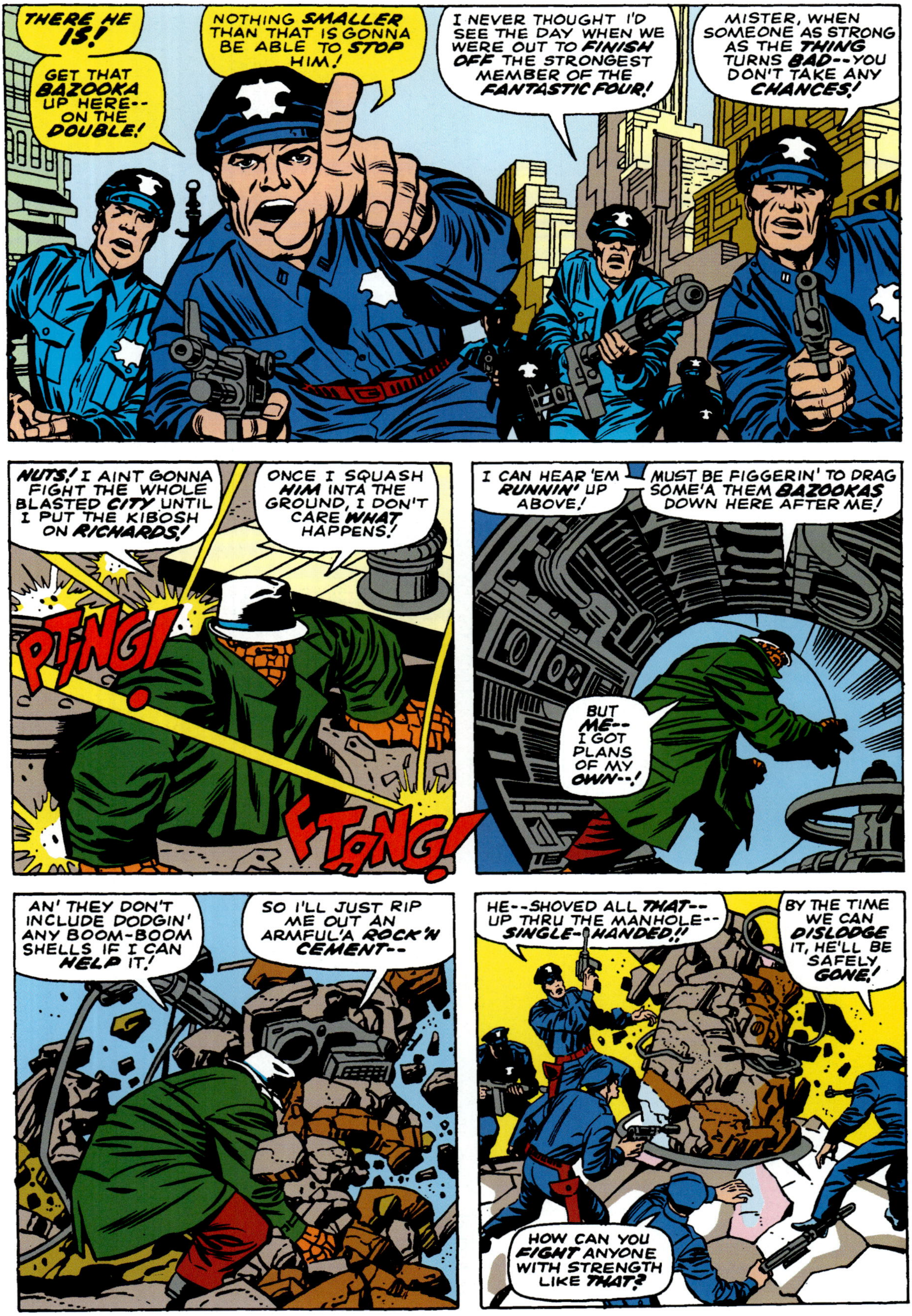
THERE HE IS!
GET THAT BAZOOKA UP HERE-- ON THE DOUBLE!
NOTHING SMALLER THAN THAT IS GONNA BE ABLE TO STOP HIM!
I NEVER THOUGHT I'D SEE THE DAY WHEN WE WERE OUT TO FINISH OFF THE STRONGEST MEMBER OF THE FANTASTIC FOUR!
MISTER, WHEN SOMEONE AS STRONG AS THE THING TURNS BAD--YOU DON'T TAKE ANY CHANCES!
NUTS! I AINT GONNA FIGHT THE WHOLE BLASTED CITY UNTIL I PUT THE KIBOSH ON RICHARDS!
ONCE I SQUASH HIM INTA THE GROUND, I DON'T CARE WHAT HAPPENS!
PTING!
FTANG!
I CAN HEAR 'EM RUNNIN' UP ABOVE!
MUST BE FIGGERIN' TO DRAG SOME'A THEM BAZOOKAS DOWN HERE AFTER ME!
BUT ME-- I GOT PLANS OF MY OWN--!
AN' THEY DON'T INCLUDE DODGIN' ANY BOOM-BOOM SHELLS IF I CAN HELP IT!
SO I'LL JUST RIP ME OUT AN ARMFUL'A ROCK 'N CEMENT--
HE--SHOVED ALL THAT-- UP THRU THE MANHOLE-- SINGLE-HANDED!!
BY THE TIME WE CAN DISLODGE IT, HE'LL BE SAFELY GONE!
HOW CAN YOU FIGHT ANYONE WITH STRENGTH LIKE THAT?

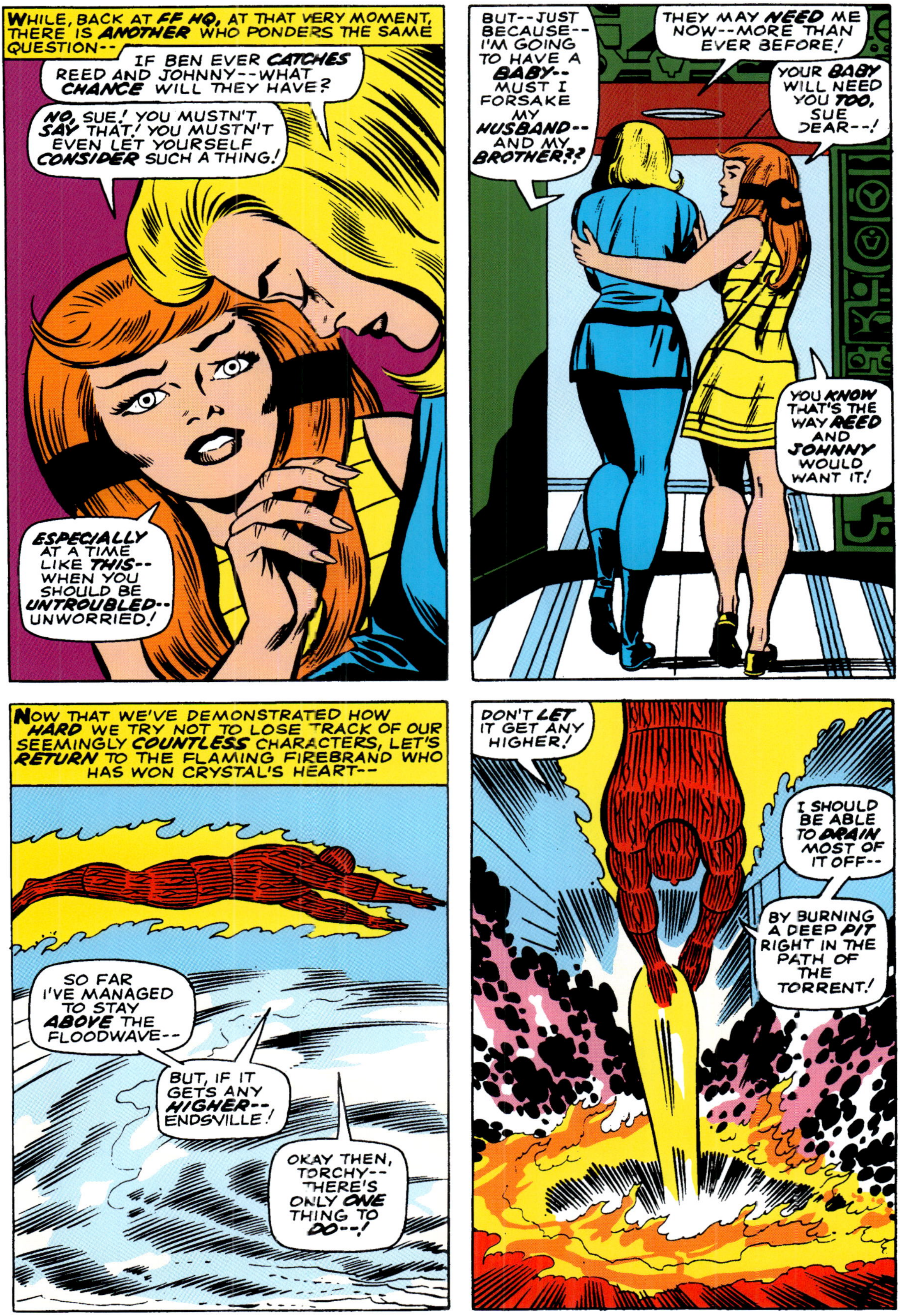

WHILE, BACK AT FF HQ, AT THAT VERY MOMENT, THERE IS ANOTHER WHO PONDERS THE SAME QUESTION--
IF BEN EVER CATCHES REED AND JOHNNY--WHAT CHANCE WILL THEY HAVE?
NO, SUE! YOU MUSTN'T SAY THAT! YOU MUSTN'T EVEN LET YOURSELF CONSIDER SUCH A THING!
ESPECIALLY AT A TIME LIKE THIS--WHEN YOU SHOULD BE UNTROUBLED--UNWORRIED!
BUT--JUST BECAUSE--I'M GOING TO HAVE A BABY--MUST I FORSAKE MY HUSBAND--AND MY BROTHER??
THEY MAY NEED ME NOW--MORE THAN EVER BEFORE!
YOUR BABY WILL NEED YOU TOO, SUE DEAR--!
YOU KNOW THAT'S THE WAY REED AND JOHNNY WOULD WANT IT!
NOW THAT WE'VE DEMONSTRATED HOW HARD WE TRY NOT TO LOSE TRACK OF OUR SEEMINGLY COUNTLESS CHARACTERS, LET'S RETURN TO THE FLAMING FIREBRAND WHO HAS WON CRYSTAL'S HEART--
SO FAR I'VE MANAGED TO STAY ABOVE THE FLOODWAVE--
BUT, IF IT GETS ANY HIGHER--ENDSVILLE!
OKAY THEN, TORCHY--THERE'S ONLY ONE THING TO DO--!
DON'T LET IT GET ANY HIGHER!
I SHOULD BE ABLE TO DRAIN MOST OF IT OFF--
BY BURNING A DEEP PIT RIGHT IN THE PATH OF THE TORRENT!

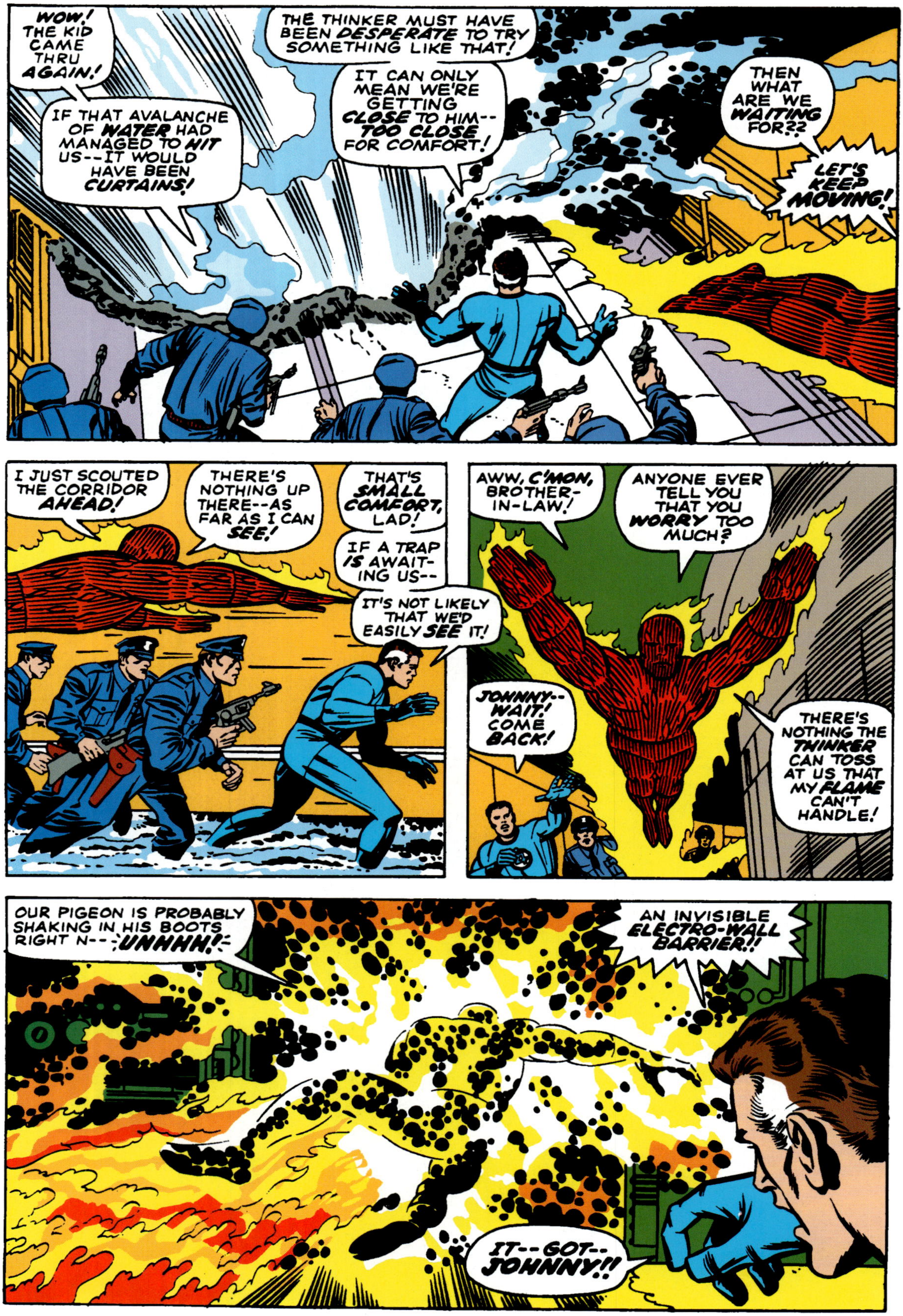

WOW! THE KID CAME THRU AGAIN!
IF THAT AVALANCHE OF WATER HAD MANAGED TO HIT US--IT WOULD HAVE BEEN CURTAINS!
THE THINKER MUST HAVE BEEN DESPERATE TO TRY SOMETHING LIKE THAT!
IT CAN ONLY MEAN WE'RE GETTING CLOSE TO HIM--TOO CLOSE FOR COMFORT!
THEN WHAT ARE WE WAITING FOR??
LET'S KEEP MOVING!
I JUST SCOUTED THE CORRIDOR AHEAD!
THERE'S NOTHING UP THERE--AS FAR AS I CAN SEE!
THAT'S SMALL COMFORT, LAD!
IF A TRAP IS AWAITING US--
IT'S NOT LIKELY THAT WE'D EASILY SEE IT!
AWW, C'MON, BROTHER-IN-LAW!
ANYONE EVER TELL YOU THAT YOU WORRY TOO MUCH?
JOHNNY--WAIT! COME BACK!
THERE'S NOTHING THE THINKER CAN TOSS AT US THAT MY FLAME CAN'T HANDLE!
OUR PIGEON IS PROBABLY SHAKING IN HIS BOOTS RIGHT N--UNHHH!
AN INVISIBLE ELECTRO-WALL BARRIER!!
IT--GOT--JOHNNY!!

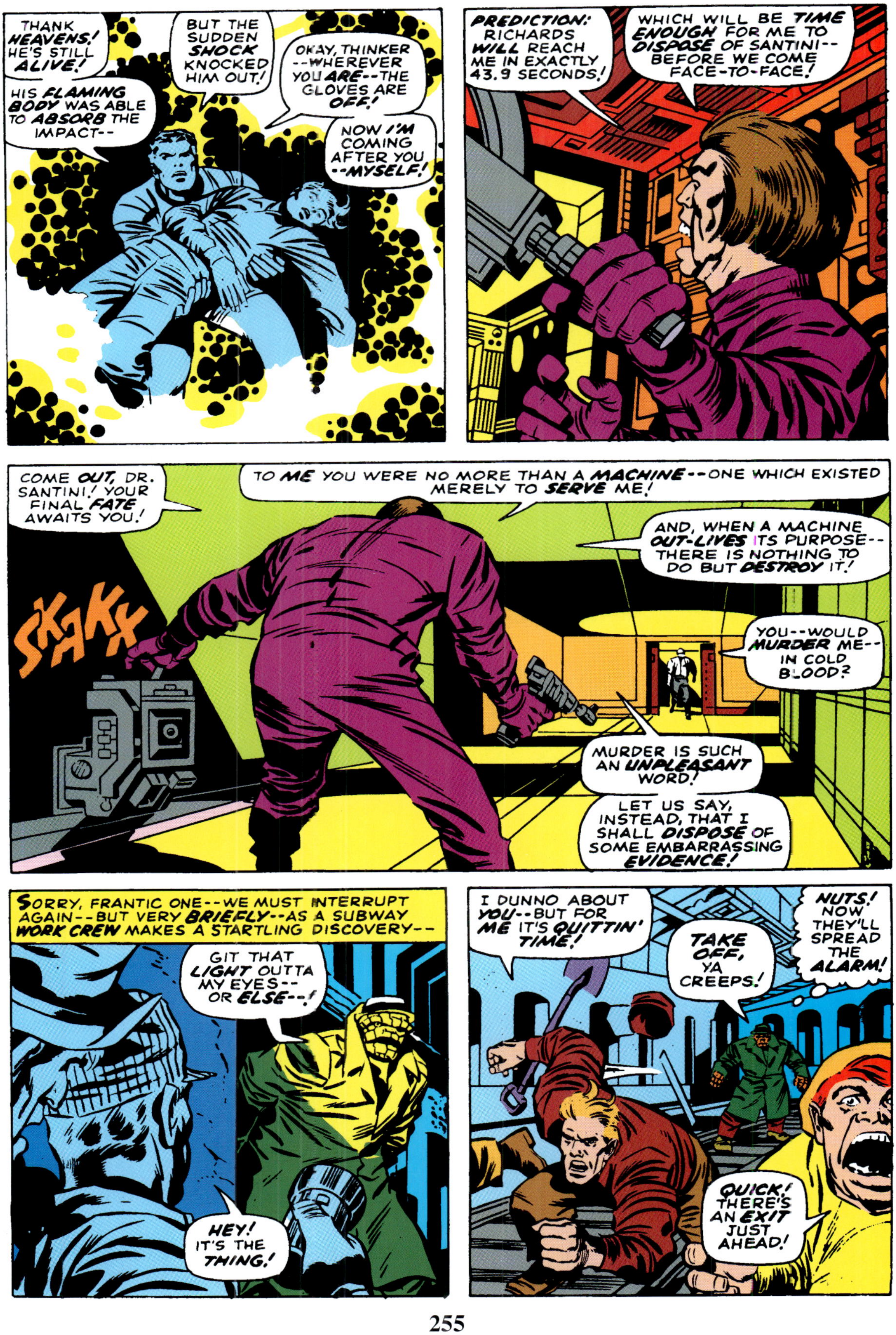
THANK HEAVENS! HE'S STILL ALIVE!
HIS FLAMING BODY WAS ABLE TO ABSORB THE IMPACT--
BUT THE SUDDEN SHOCK KNOCKED HIM OUT!
OKAY, THINKER --WHEREVER YOU ARE--THE GLOVES ARE OFF!
NOW I'M COMING AFTER YOU --MYSELF!
PREDICTION: RICHARDS WILL REACH ME IN EXACTLY 43.9 SECONDS!
WHICH WILL BE TIME ENOUGH FOR ME TO DISPOSE OF SANTINI-- BEFORE WE COME FACE-TO-FACE!
COME OUT, DR. SANTINI! YOUR FINAL FATE AWAITS YOU!
TO ME YOU WERE NO MORE THAN A MACHINE--ONE WHICH EXISTED MERELY TO SERVE ME!
AND, WHEN A MACHINE OUT-LIVES ITS PURPOSE-- THERE IS NOTHING TO DO BUT DESTROY IT!
SKAKK
YOU--WOULD MURDER ME-- IN COLD BLOOD?
MURDER IS SUCH AN UNPLEASANT WORD!
LET US SAY, INSTEAD, THAT I SHALL DISPOSE OF SOME EMBARRASSING EVIDENCE!
SORRY, FRANTIC ONE--WE MUST INTERRUPT AGAIN--BUT VERY BRIEFLY--AS A SUBWAY WORK CREW MAKES A STARTLING DISCOVERY--
GIT THAT LIGHT OUTTA MY EYES-- OR ELSE--!
HEY! IT'S THE THING!
I DUNNO ABOUT YOU--BUT FOR ME IT'S QUITTIN' TIME!
TAKE OFF, YA CREEPS!
NUTS! NOW THEY'LL SPREAD THE ALARM!
QUICK! THERE'S AN EXIT JUST AHEAD!

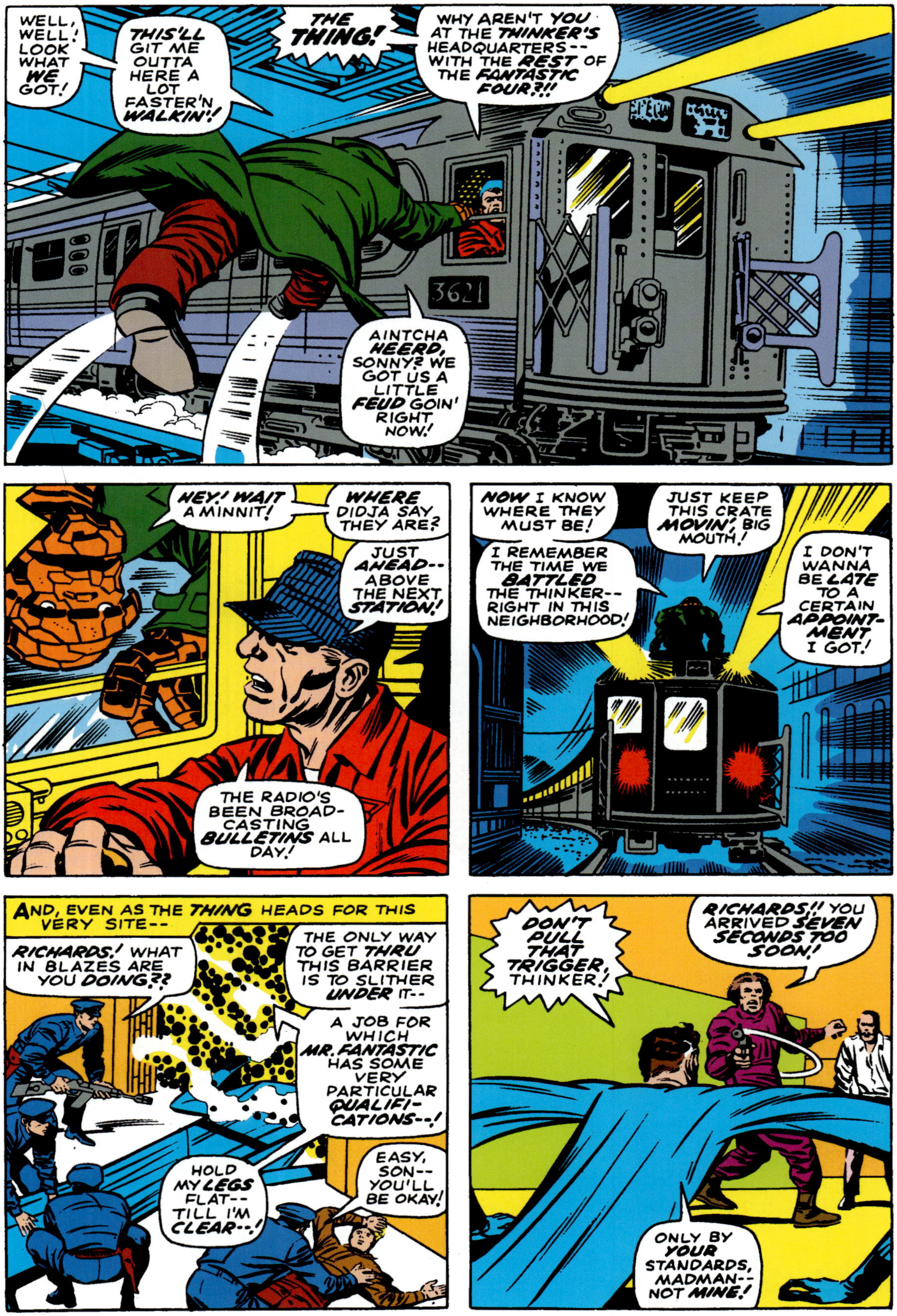
WELL, WELL! LOOK WHAT WE GOT!
THIS'LL GIT ME OUTTA HERE A LOT FASTER'N WALKIN'!
THE THING!
WHY AREN'T YOU AT THE THINKER'S HEADQUARTERS-- WITH THE REST OF THE FANTASTIC FOUR?!!
3621
AINTCHA HEERD, SONNY? WE GOT US A LITTLE FEUD GOIN' RIGHT NOW!
HEY! WAIT A MINNIT!
WHERE DIDJA SAY THEY ARE?
JUST AHEAD-- ABOVE THE NEXT STATION!
THE RADIO'S BEEN BROAD-CASTING BULLETINS ALL DAY!
NOW I KNOW WHERE THEY MUST BE!
I REMEMBER THE TIME WE BATTLED THE THINKER-- RIGHT IN THIS NEIGHBORHOOD!
JUST KEEP THIS CRATE MOVIN', BIG MOUTH!
I DON'T WANNA BE LATE TO A CERTAIN APPOINT-MENT I GOT!
AND, EVEN AS THE THING HEADS FOR THIS VERY SITE--
RICHARDS! WHAT IN BLAZES ARE YOU DOING??
THE ONLY WAY TO GET THRU THIS BARRIER IS TO SLITHER UNDER IT--
A JOB FOR WHICH MR. FANTASTIC HAS SOME VERY PARTICULAR QUALIFI-CATIONS--!
HOLD MY LEGS FLAT-- TILL I'M CLEAR--!
EASY, SON-- YOU'LL BE OKAY!
DON'T PULL THAT TRIGGER, THINKER!
RICHARDS!! YOU ARRIVED SEVEN SECONDS TOO SOON!
ONLY BY YOUR STANDARDS, MADMAN-- NOT MINE!

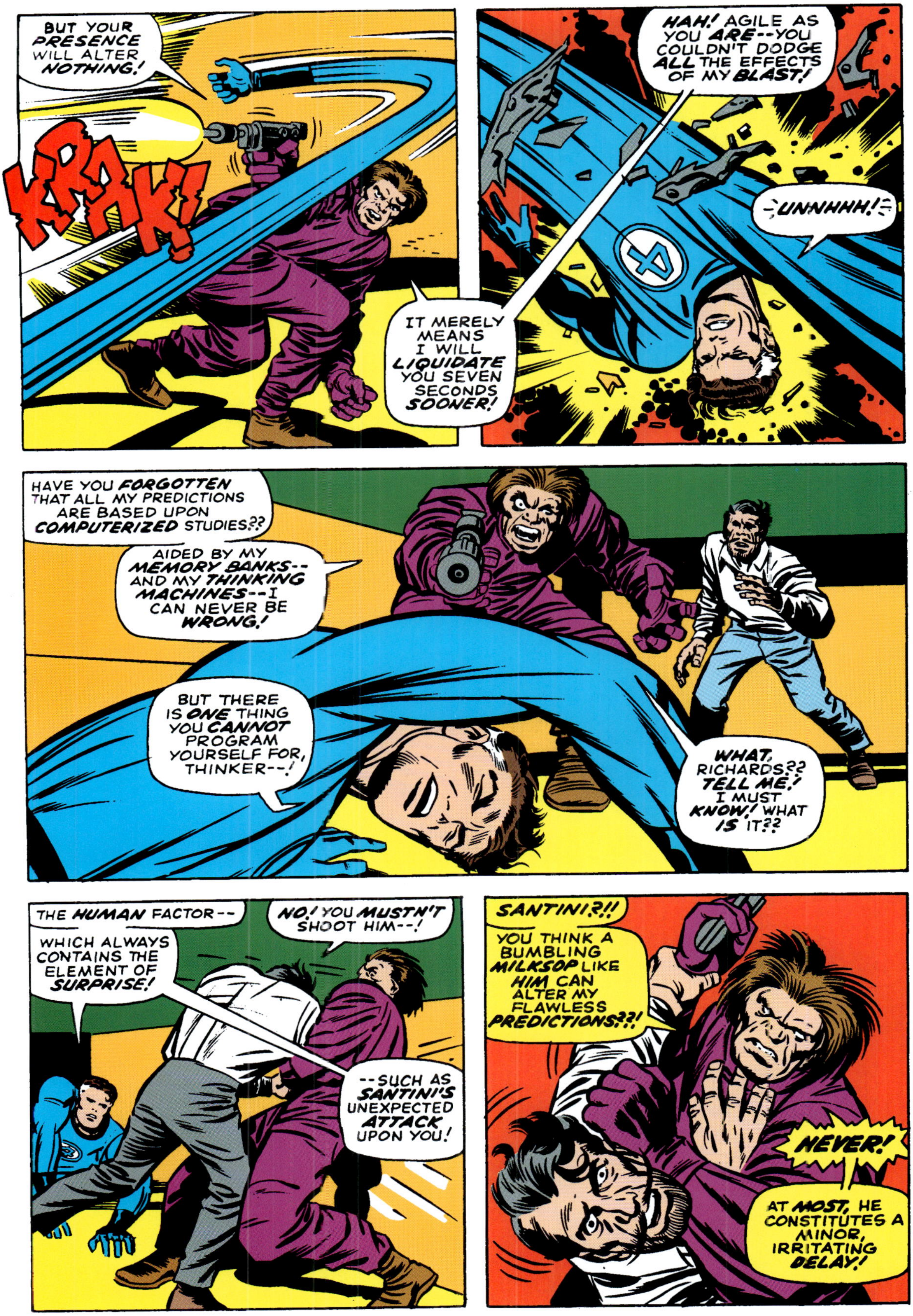

BUT YOUR PRESENCE WILL ALTER NOTHING!
KRAK!
IT MERELY MEANS I WILL LIQUIDATE YOU SEVEN SECONDS SOONER!
HAH! AGILE AS YOU ARE--YOU COULDN'T DODGE ALL THE EFFECTS OF MY BLAST!
UNNHHH!
HAVE YOU FORGOTTEN THAT ALL MY PREDICTIONS ARE BASED UPON COMPUTERIZED STUDIES??
AIDED BY MY MEMORY BANKS--AND MY THINKING MACHINES--I CAN NEVER BE WRONG!
BUT THERE IS ONE THING YOU CANNOT PROGRAM YOURSELF FOR, THINKER--!
WHAT, RICHARDS?? TELL ME! I MUST KNOW! WHAT IS IT??
THE HUMAN FACTOR--
WHICH ALWAYS CONTAINS THE ELEMENT OF SURPRISE!
NO! YOU MUSTN'T SHOOT HIM--!
--SUCH AS SANTINI'S UNEXPECTED ATTACK UPON YOU!
SANTINI?!!
YOU THINK A BUMBLING MILKSOP LIKE HIM CAN ALTER MY FLAWLESS PREDICTIONS??!
NEVER!
AT MOST, HE CONSTITUTES A MINOR, IRRITATING DELAY!

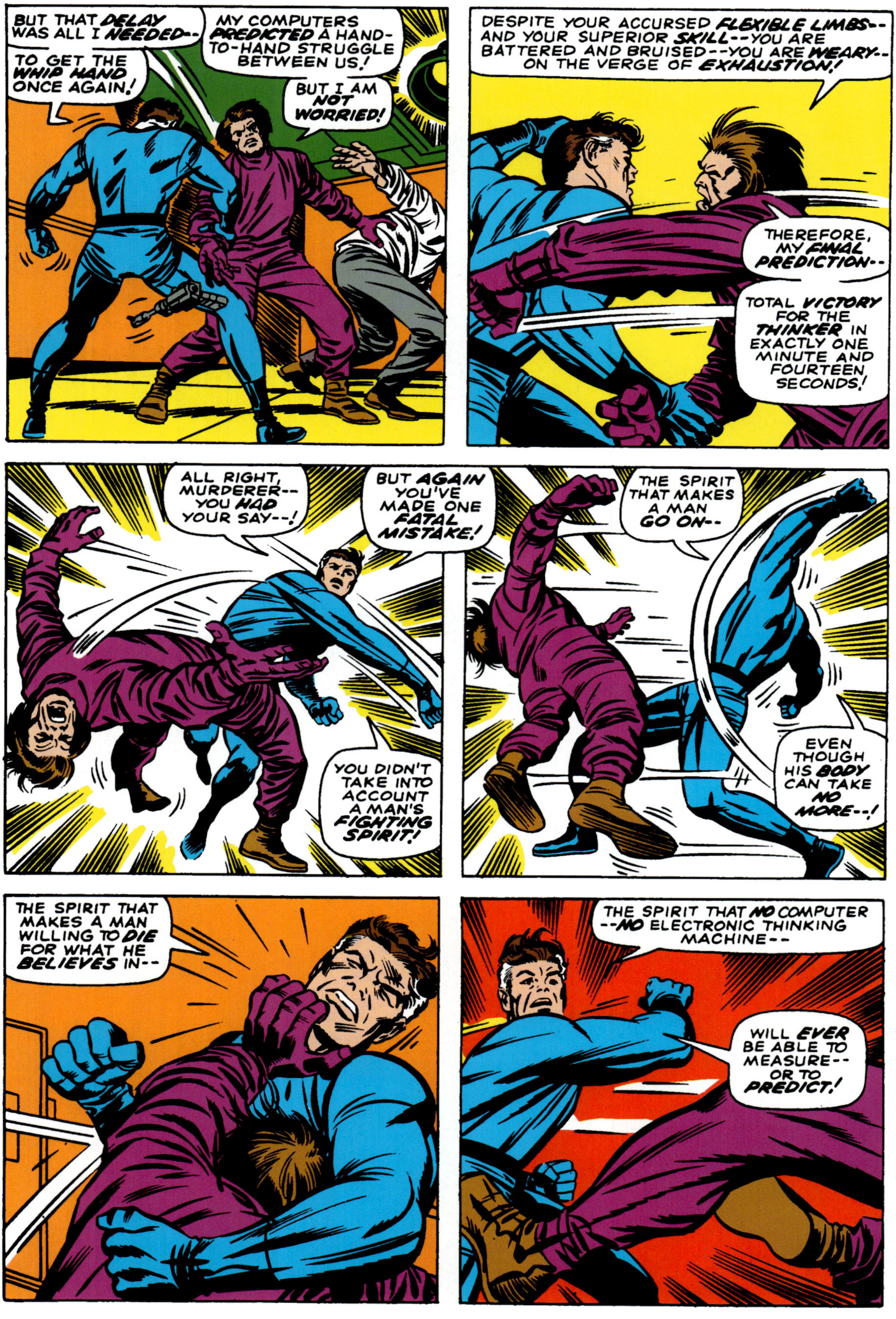

BUT THAT DELAY WAS ALL I NEEDED--
TO GET THE WHIP HAND ONCE AGAIN!
MY COMPUTERS PREDICTED A HAND-TO-HAND STRUGGLE BETWEEN US!
BUT I AM NOT WORRIED!
DESPITE YOUR ACCURSED FLEXIBLE LIMBS--AND YOUR SUPERIOR SKILL--YOU ARE BATTERED AND BRUISED--YOU ARE WEARY--ON THE VERGE OF EXHAUSTION!
THEREFORE, MY FINAL PREDICTION--
TOTAL VICTORY FOR THE THINKER IN EXACTLY ONE MINUTE AND FOURTEEN SECONDS!
ALL RIGHT, MURDERER--YOU HAD YOUR SAY--!
BUT AGAIN YOU'VE MADE ONE FATAL MISTAKE!
YOU DIDN'T TAKE INTO ACCOUNT A MAN'S FIGHTING SPIRIT!
THE SPIRIT THAT MAKES A MAN GO ON--
EVEN THOUGH HIS BODY CAN TAKE NO MORE--!
THE SPIRIT THAT MAKES A MAN WILLING TO DIE FOR WHAT HE BELIEVES IN--
THE SPIRIT THAT NO COMPUTER--NO ELECTRONIC THINKING MACHINE--
WILL EVER BE ABLE TO MEASURE--OR TO PREDICT!

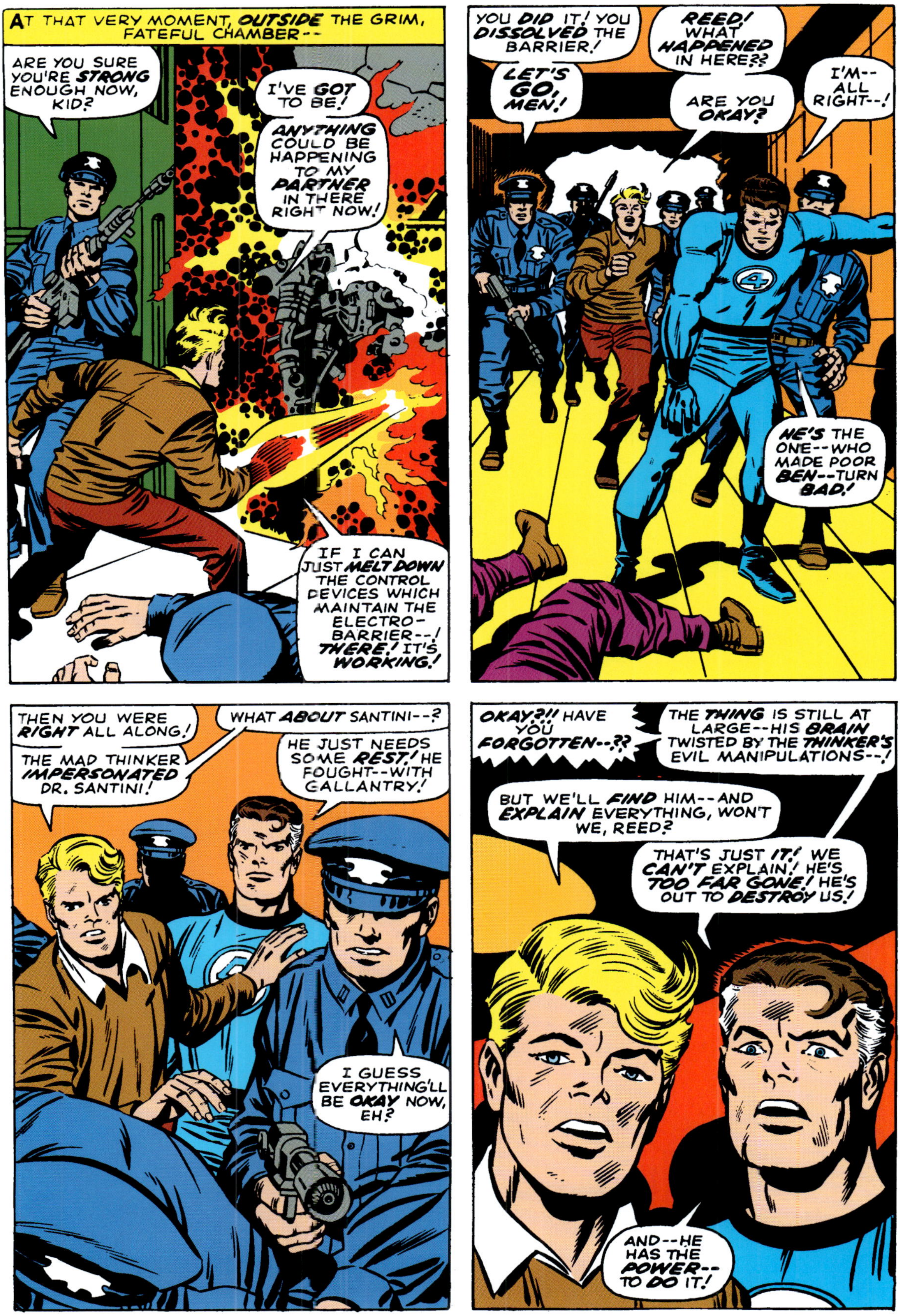
AT THAT VERY MOMENT, OUTSIDE THE GRIM, FATEFUL CHAMBER--
ARE YOU SURE YOU'RE STRONG ENOUGH NOW, KID?
I'VE GOT TO BE!
ANYTHING COULD BE HAPPENING TO MY PARTNER IN THERE RIGHT NOW!
IF I CAN JUST MELT DOWN THE CONTROL DEVICES WHICH MAINTAIN THE ELECTRO-BARRIER--! THERE! IT'S WORKING!
YOU DID IT! YOU DISSOLVED THE BARRIER!
LET'S GO, MEN!
REED! WHAT HAPPENED IN HERE??
ARE YOU OKAY?
I'M--ALL RIGHT--!
HE'S THE ONE--WHO MADE POOR BEN--TURN BAD!
THEN YOU WERE RIGHT ALL ALONG!
THE MAD THINKER IMPERSONATED DR. SANTINI!
WHAT ABOUT SANTINI--?
HE JUST NEEDS SOME REST! HE FOUGHT--WITH GALLANTRY!
I GUESS EVERYTHING'LL BE OKAY NOW, EH?
OKAY?!! HAVE YOU FORGOTTEN--??
THE THING IS STILL AT LARGE--HIS BRAIN TWISTED BY THE THINKER'S EVIL MANIPULATIONS--!
BUT WE'LL FIND HIM--AND EXPLAIN EVERYTHING, WON'T WE, REED?
THAT'S JUST IT! WE CAN'T EXPLAIN! HE'S TOO FAR GONE! HE'S OUT TO DESTROY US!
AND--HE HAS THE POWER--TO DO IT!

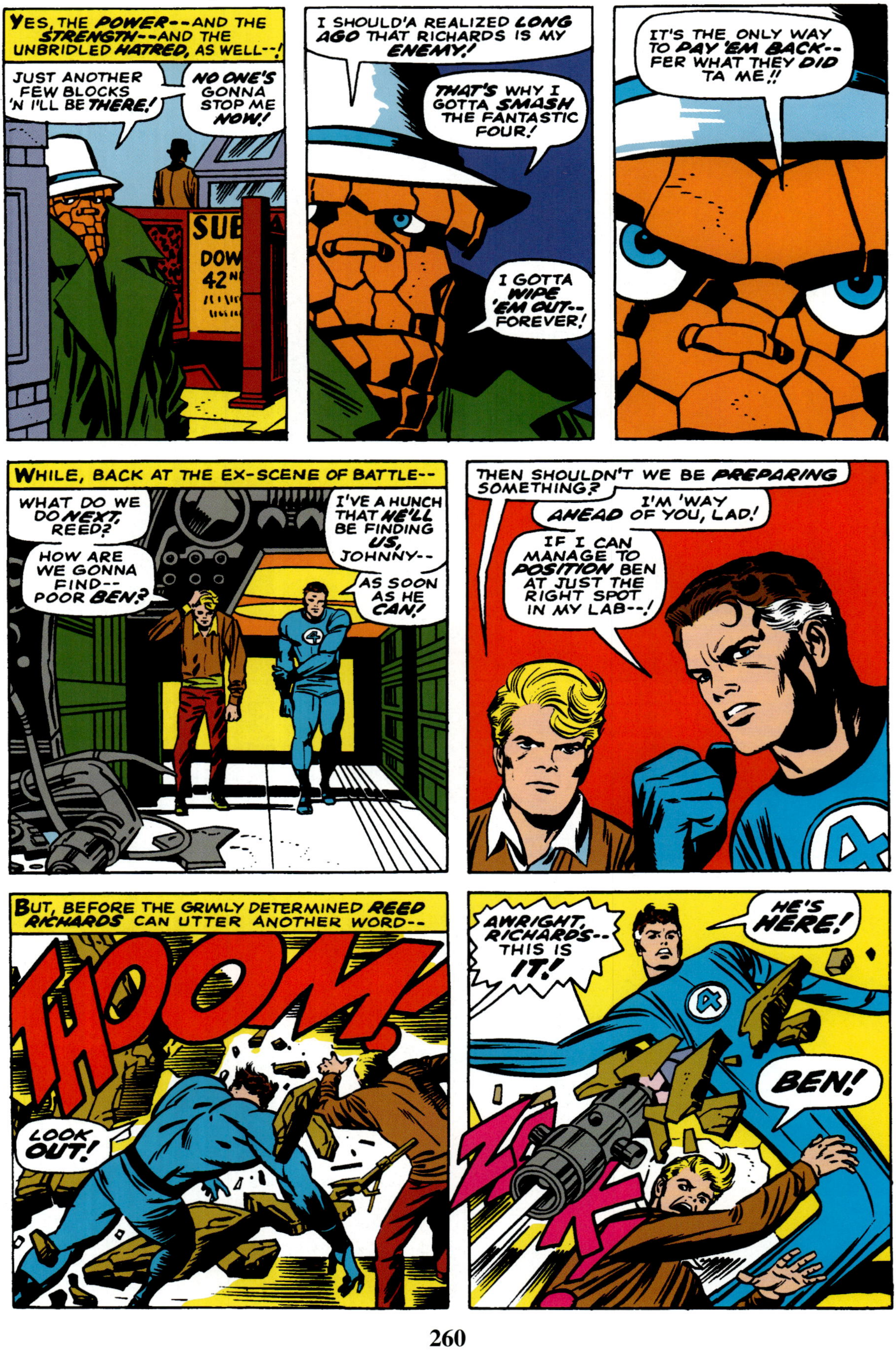

YES, THE POWER--AND THE STRENGTH--AND THE UNBRIDLED HATRED, AS WELL--!
JUST ANOTHER FEW BLOCKS 'N I'LL BE THERE!
NO ONE'S GONNA STOP ME NOW!
I SHOULD'A REALIZED LONG AGO THAT RICHARDS IS MY ENEMY!
THAT'S WHY I GOTTA SMASH THE FANTASTIC FOUR!
I GOTTA WIPE 'EM OUT--FOREVER!
IT'S THE ONLY WAY TO PAY 'EM BACK--FER WHAT THEY DID TA ME!!
WHILE, BACK AT THE EX-SCENE OF BATTLE--
WHAT DO WE DO NEXT, REED?
HOW ARE WE GONNA FIND--POOR BEN?
I'VE A HUNCH THAT HE'LL BE FINDING US, JOHNNY--
AS SOON AS HE CAN!
THEN SHOULDN'T WE BE PREPARING SOMETHING?
I'M 'WAY AHEAD OF YOU, LAD!
IF I CAN MANAGE TO POSITION BEN AT JUST THE RIGHT SPOT IN MY LAB--!
BUT, BEFORE THE GRIMLY DETERMINED REED RICHARDS CAN UTTER ANOTHER WORD--
THOOM!
LOOK OUT!
AWRIGHT, RICHARDS--THIS IS IT!
HE'S HERE!
BEN!

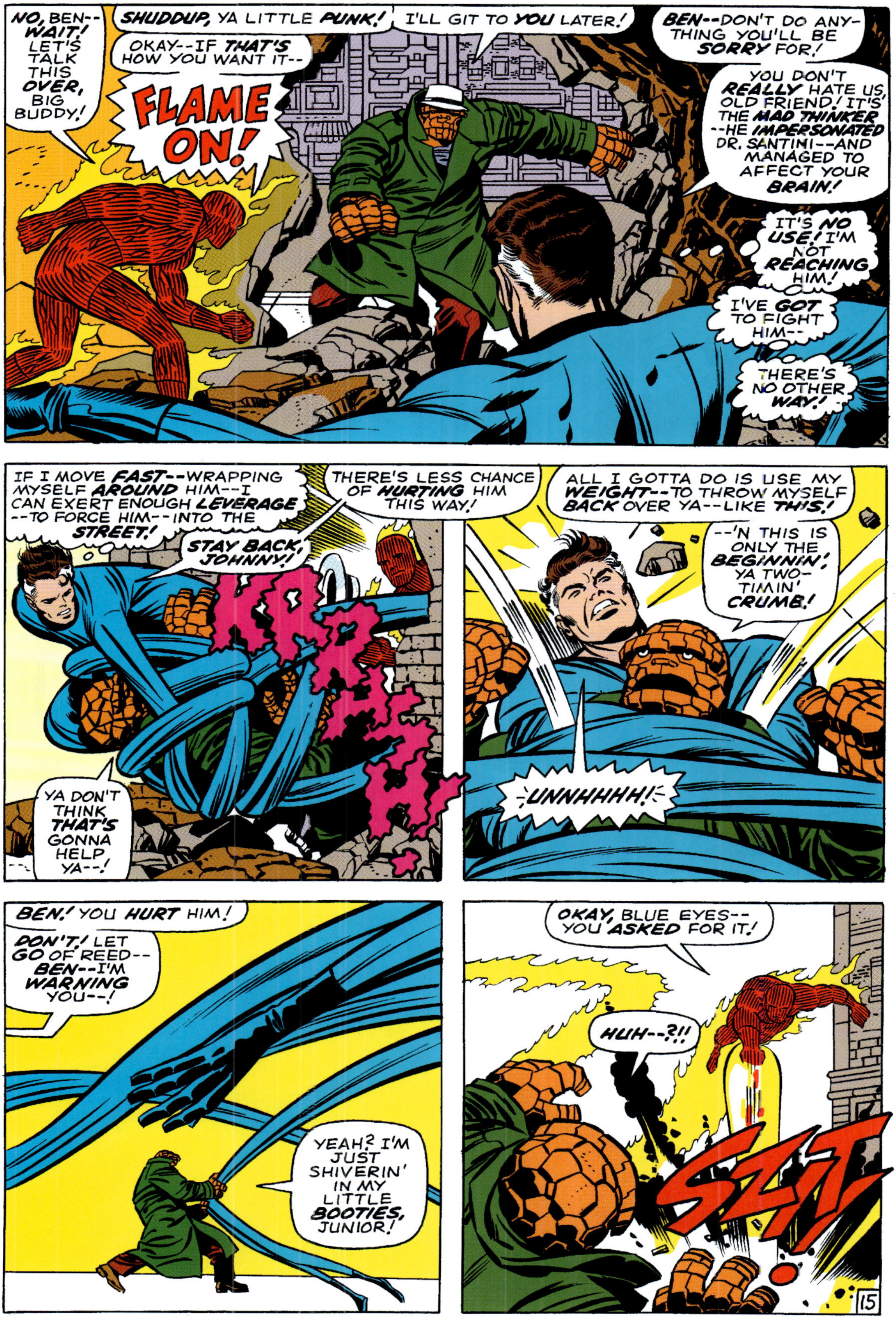
NO, BEN-- WAIT! LET'S TALK THIS OVER, BIG BUDDY!
SHUDDUP, YA LITTLE PUNK!
I'LL GIT TO YOU LATER!
OKAY--IF THAT'S HOW YOU WANT IT--
FLAME ON!
BEN--DON'T DO ANYTHING YOU'LL BE SORRY FOR!
YOU DON'T REALLY HATE US, OLD FRIEND! IT'S THE MAD THINKER --HE IMPERSONATED DR. SANTINI--AND MANAGED TO AFFECT YOUR BRAIN!
IT'S NO USE! I'M NOT REACHING HIM!
I'VE GOT TO FIGHT HIM--
THERE'S NO OTHER WAY!
IF I MOVE FAST--WRAPPING MYSELF AROUND HIM--I CAN EXERT ENOUGH LEVERAGE --TO FORCE HIM--INTO THE STREET!
THERE'S LESS CHANCE OF HURTING HIM THIS WAY!
STAY BACK, JOHNNY!
KRASH!
YA DON'T THINK THAT'S GONNA HELP YA--!
ALL I GOTTA DO IS USE MY WEIGHT--TO THROW MYSELF BACK OVER YA--LIKE THIS!
--'N THIS IS ONLY THE BEGINNIN', YA TWO-TIMIN' CRUMB!
UNNHHHH!
BEN! YOU HURT HIM!
DON'T! LET GO OF REED--BEN--I'M WARNING YOU--!
YEAH? I'M JUST SHIVERIN' IN MY LITTLE BOOTIES, JUNIOR!
OKAY, BLUE EYES--YOU ASKED FOR IT!
HUH--?!!
SZIT!
15

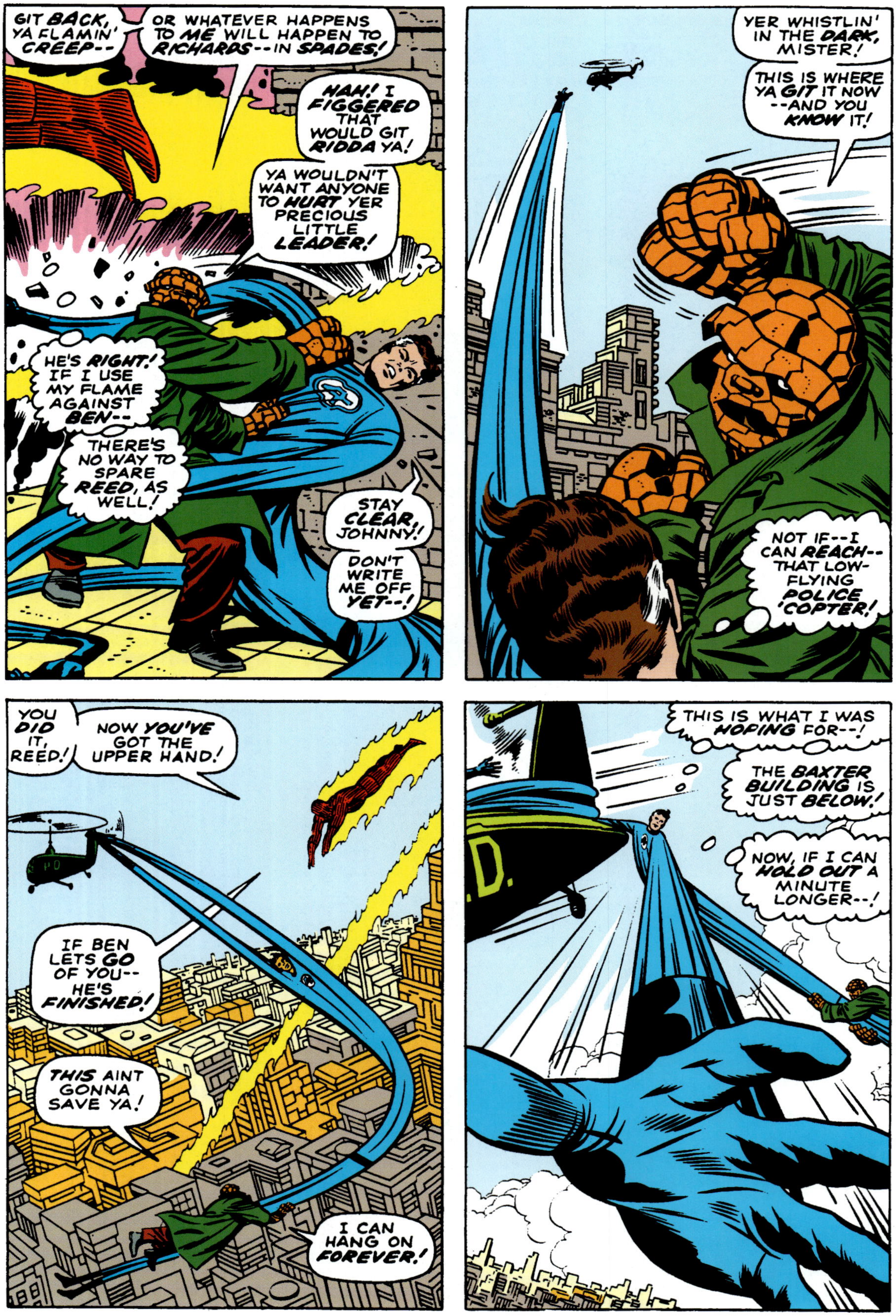
GIT BACK, YA FLAMIN' CREEP--
OR WHATEVER HAPPENS TO ME WILL HAPPEN TO RICHARDS--IN SPADES!
HAH! I FIGGERED THAT WOULD GIT RIDDA YA!
YA WOULDN'T WANT ANYONE TO HURT YER PRECIOUS LITTLE LEADER!
HE'S RIGHT! IF I USE MY FLAME AGAINST BEN--
THERE'S NO WAY TO SPARE REED, AS WELL!
STAY CLEAR, JOHNNY!
DON'T WRITE ME OFF YET--!
YER WHISTLIN' IN THE DARK, MISTER!
THIS IS WHERE YA GIT IT NOW --AND YOU KNOW IT!
NOT IF--I CAN REACH--THAT LOW-FLYING POLICE 'COPTER!
YOU DID IT, REED!
NOW YOU'VE GOT THE UPPER HAND!
IF BEN LETS GO OF YOU--HE'S FINISHED!
THIS AINT GONNA SAVE YA!
I CAN HANG ON FOREVER!
THIS IS WHAT I WAS HOPING FOR--!
THE BAXTER BUILDING IS JUST BELOW!
NOW, IF I CAN HOLD OUT A MINUTE LONGER--!

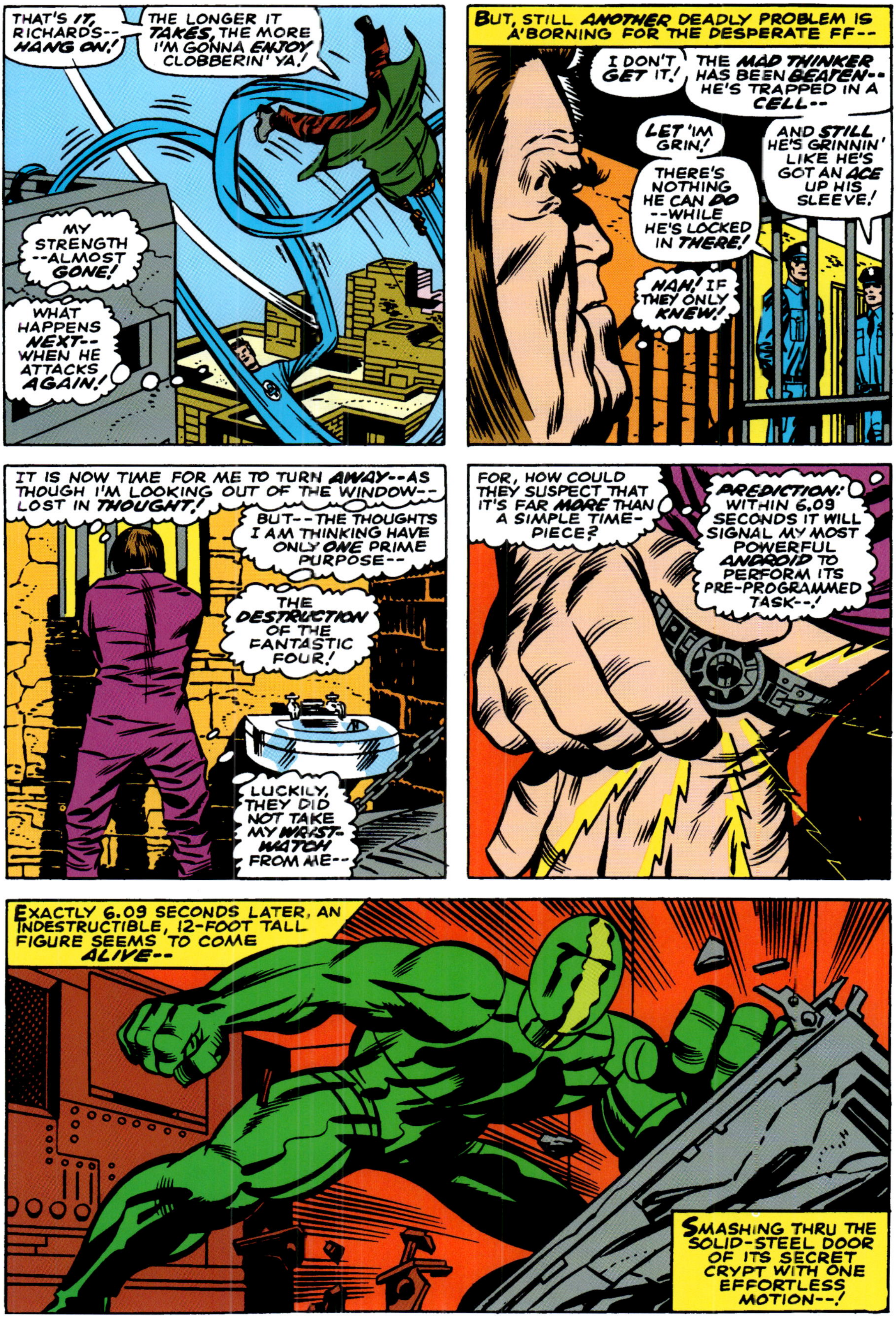
THAT'S IT, RICHARDS-- HANG ON!
THE LONGER IT TAKES, THE MORE I'M GONNA ENJOY CLOBBERIN' YA!
MY STRENGTH --ALMOST GONE!
WHAT HAPPENS NEXT-- WHEN HE ATTACKS AGAIN!
BUT, STILL ANOTHER DEADLY PROBLEM IS A'BORNING FOR THE DESPERATE FF--
I DON'T GET IT!
THE MAD THINKER HAS BEEN BEATEN-- HE'S TRAPPED IN A CELL--
AND STILL HE'S GRINNIN' LIKE HE'S GOT AN ACE UP HIS SLEEVE!
LET 'IM GRIN!
THERE'S NOTHING HE CAN DO --WHILE HE'S LOCKED IN THERE!
NAH! IF THEY ONLY KNEW!
IT IS NOW TIME FOR ME TO TURN AWAY--AS THOUGH I'M LOOKING OUT OF THE WINDOW-- LOST IN THOUGHT!
BUT--THE THOUGHTS I AM THINKING HAVE ONLY ONE PRIME PURPOSE--
THE DESTRUCTION OF THE FANTASTIC FOUR!
LUCKILY, THEY DID NOT TAKE MY WRIST-WATCH FROM ME--
FOR, HOW COULD THEY SUSPECT THAT IT'S FAR MORE THAN A SIMPLE TIME-PIECE?
PREDICTION: WITHIN 6.09 SECONDS IT WILL SIGNAL MY MOST POWERFUL ANDROID TO PERFORM ITS PRE-PROGRAMMED TASK--!
EXACTLY 6.09 SECONDS LATER, AN INDESTRUCTIBLE, 12-FOOT TALL FIGURE SEEMS TO COME ALIVE--
SMASHING THRU THE SOLID-STEEL DOOR OF ITS SECRET CRYPT WITH ONE EFFORTLESS MOTION--!

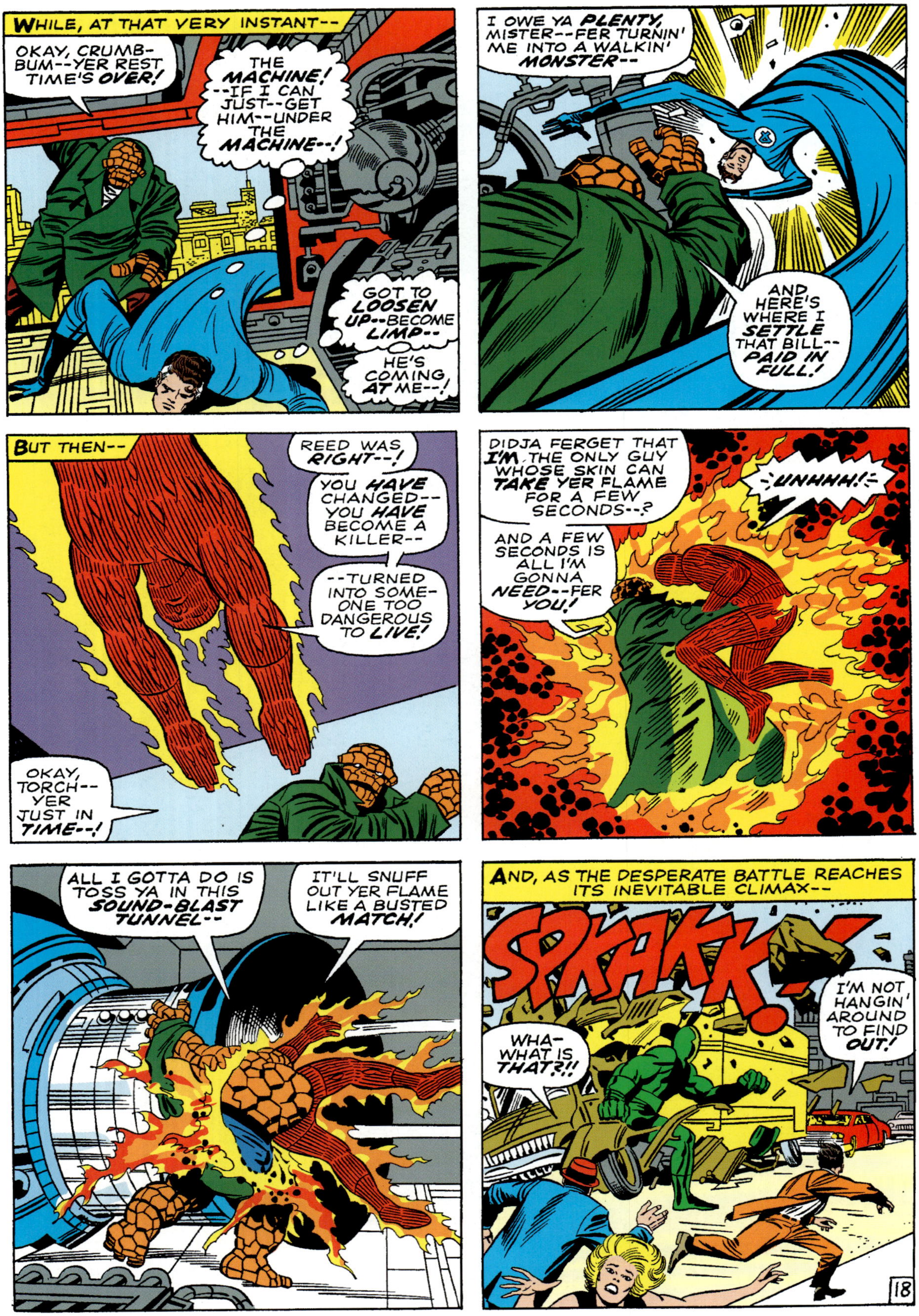
WHILE, AT THAT VERY INSTANT--
OKAY, CRUMB-BUM--YER REST TIME'S OVER!
THE MACHINE! --IF I CAN JUST--GET HIM--UNDER THE MACHINE--!
GOT TO LOOSEN UP--BECOME LIMP--
HE'S COMING AT ME--!
I OWE YA PLENTY, MISTER--FER TURNIN' ME INTO A WALKIN' MONSTER--
AND HERE'S WHERE I SETTLE THAT BILL--PAID IN FULL!
BUT THEN--
REED WAS RIGHT--!
YOU HAVE CHANGED--YOU HAVE BECOME A KILLER--
--TURNED INTO SOME-ONE TOO DANGEROUS TO LIVE!
OKAY, TORCH--YER JUST IN TIME--!
DIDJA FERGET THAT I'M THE ONLY GUY WHOSE SKIN CAN TAKE YER FLAME FOR A FEW SECONDS--?
UNHHH!
AND A FEW SECONDS IS ALL I'M GONNA NEED--FER YOU!
ALL I GOTTA DO IS TOSS YA IN THIS SOUND-BLAST TUNNEL--
IT'LL SNUFF OUT YER FLAME LIKE A BUSTED MATCH!
AND, AS THE DESPERATE BATTLE REACHES ITS INEVITABLE CLIMAX--
SPKAKK!
I'M NOT HANGIN' AROUND TO FIND OUT!
WHA-WHAT IS THAT?!!
18

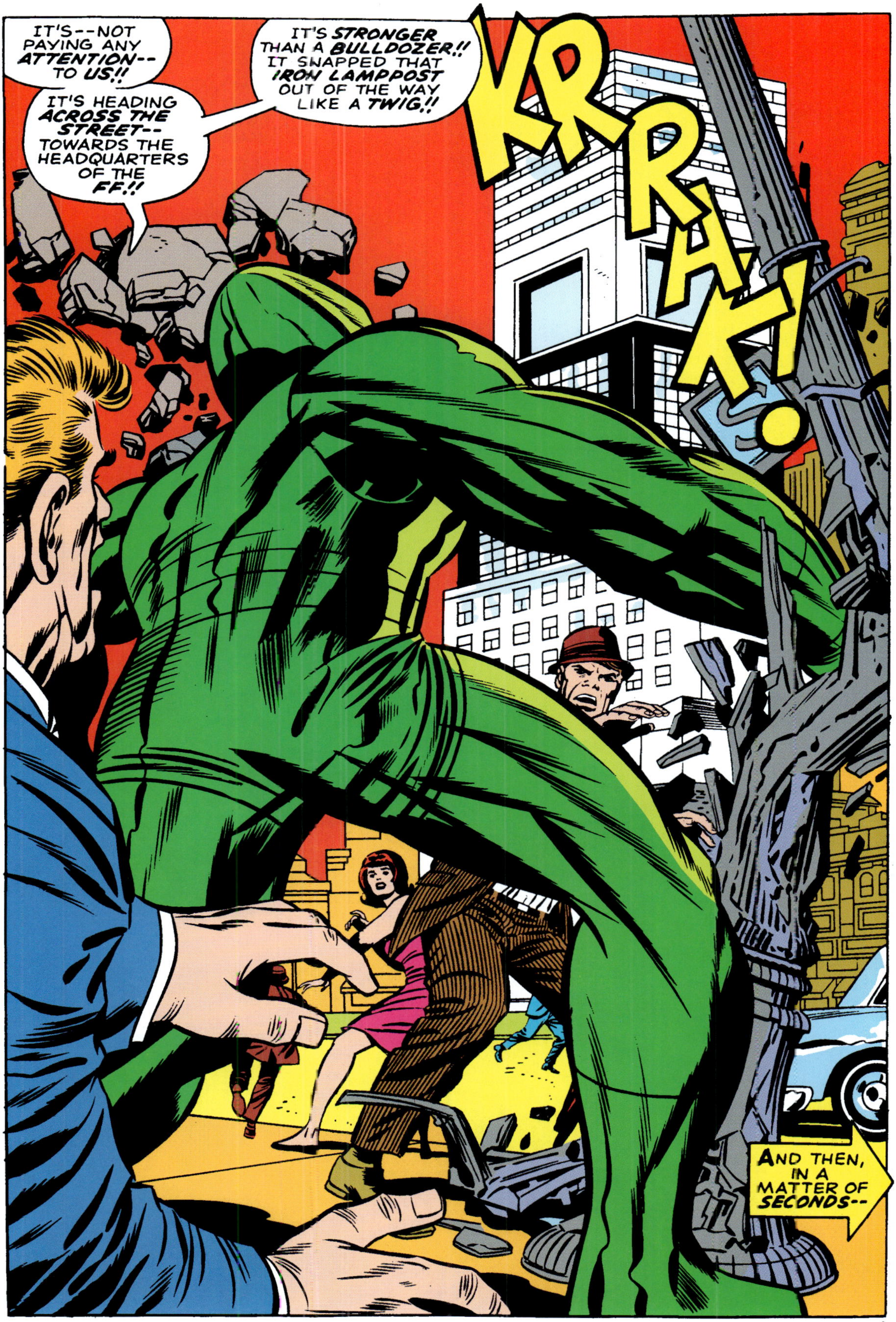
IT'S--NOT PAYING ANY ATTENTION-- TO US!!
IT'S HEADING ACROSS THE STREET-- TOWARDS THE HEADQUARTERS OF THE FF!!
IT'S STRONGER THAN A BULLDOZER!! IT SNAPPED THAT IRON LAMPPOST OUT OF THE WAY LIKE A TWIG!!
KRRAK!
AND THEN, IN A MATTER OF SECONDS--

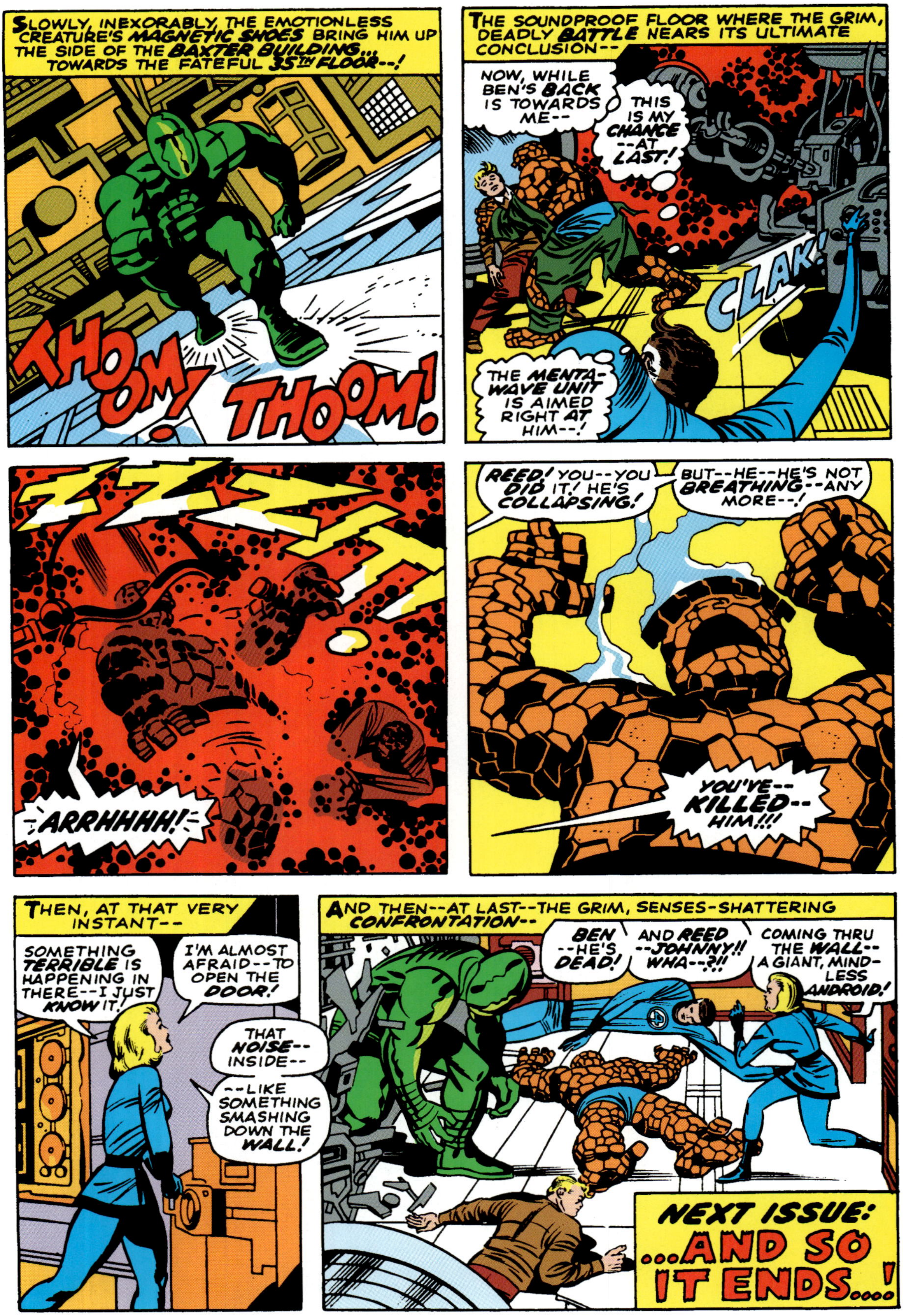

SLOWLY, INEXORABLY, THE EMOTIONLESS CREATURE'S MAGNETIC SHOES BRING HIM UP THE SIDE OF THE BAXTER BUILDING... TOWARDS THE FATEFUL 35TH FLOOR--!
THOOM! THOOM!
THE SOUNDPROOF FLOOR WHERE THE GRIM, DEADLY BATTLE NEARS ITS ULTIMATE CONCLUSION--
NOW, WHILE BEN'S BACK IS TOWARDS ME--
THIS IS MY CHANCE --AT LAST!
CLAK!
THE MENTA-WAVE UNIT IS AIMED RIGHT AT HIM--!
ARRHHHH!
REED! YOU--YOU DID IT! HE'S COLLAPSING!
BUT--HE--HE'S NOT BREATHING--ANY MORE--!
YOU'VE--KILLED--HIM!!!
THEN, AT THAT VERY INSTANT--
SOMETHING TERRIBLE IS HAPPENING IN THERE--I JUST KNOW IT!
I'M ALMOST AFRAID--TO OPEN THE DOOR!
THAT NOISE--INSIDE--
--LIKE SOMETHING SMASHING DOWN THE WALL!
AND THEN--AT LAST--THE GRIM, SENSES-SHATTERING CONFRONTATION--
BEN--HE'S DEAD!
AND REED--JOHNNY!! WHA--?!!
COMING THRU THE WALL--A GIANT, MIND-LESS ANDROID!
NEXT ISSUE: ...AND SO IT ENDS...!

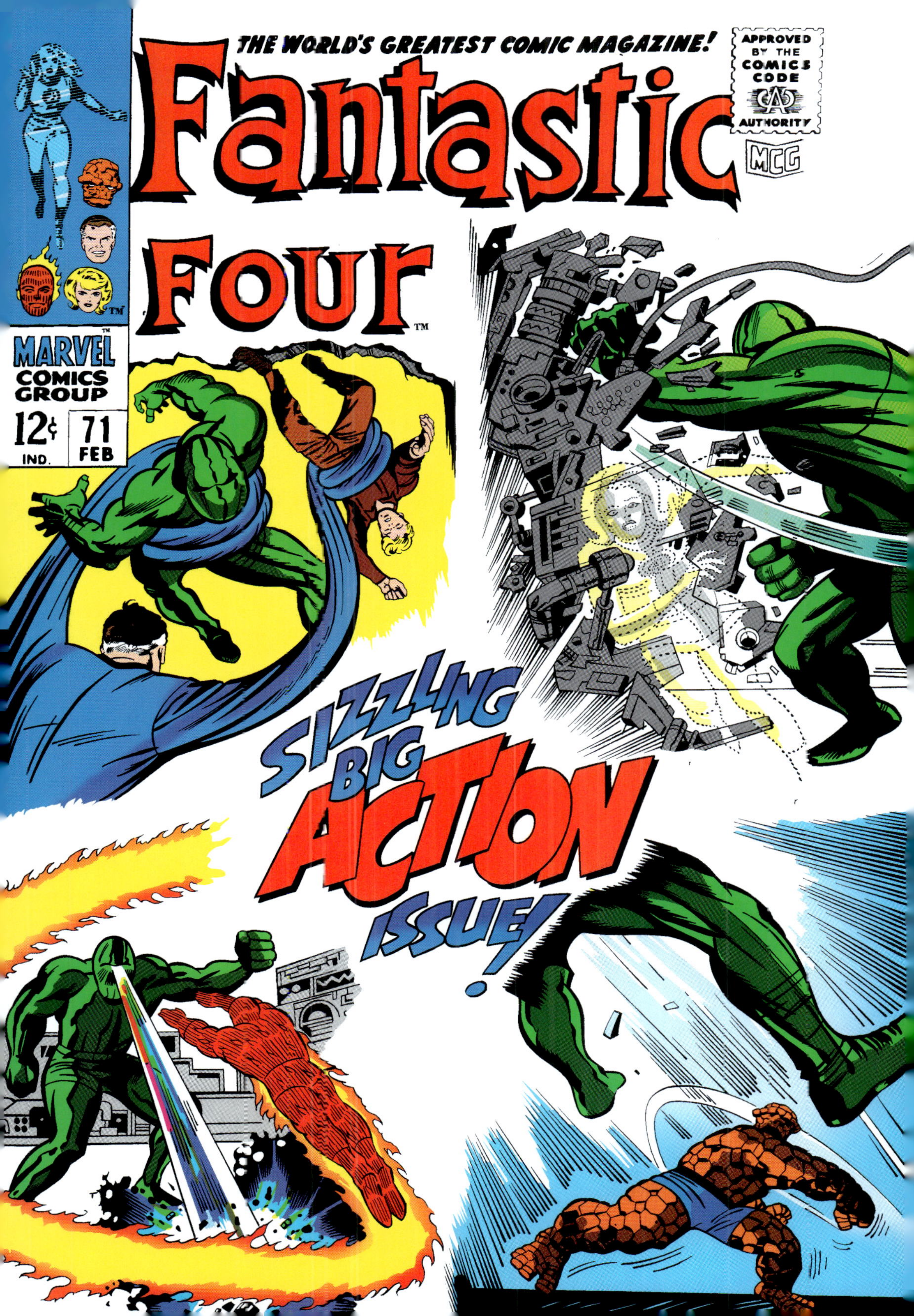
THE WORLD'S GREATEST COMIC MAGAZINE!
Fantastic Four™
APPROVED BY THE COMICS CODE AUTHORITY
MCG
MARVEL™ COMICS GROUP
12¢ IND.
71 FEB
SIZZLING BIG ACTION ISSUE!

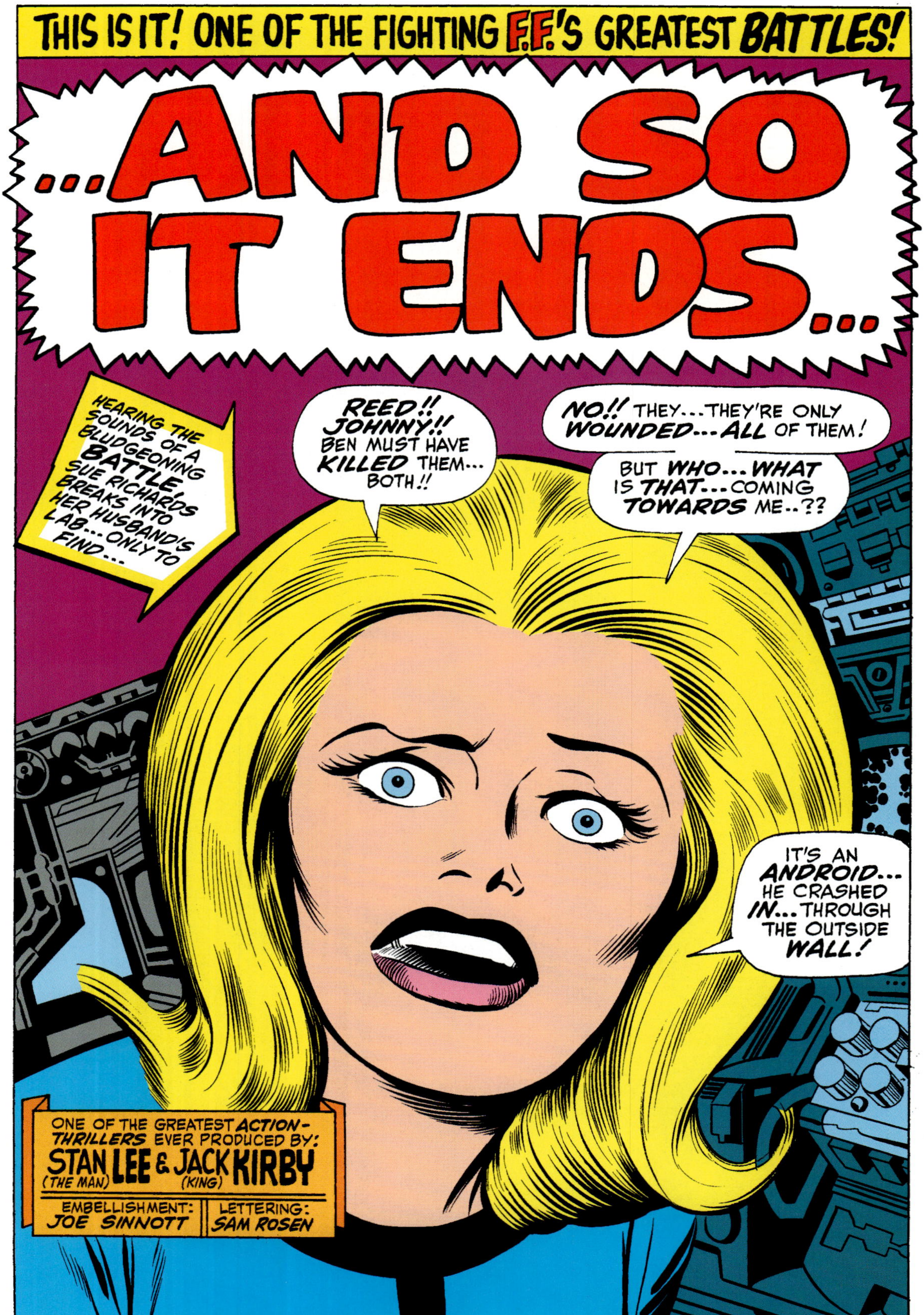

THIS IS IT! ONE OF THE FIGHTING F.F.'S GREATEST BATTLES!
...AND SO IT ENDS...
HEARING THE SOUNDS OF A BLUDGEONING BATTLE, SUE RICHARDS BREAKS INTO HER HUSBAND'S LAB... ONLY TO FIND...
REED!! JOHNNY!! BEN MUST HAVE KILLED THEM... BOTH!!
NO!! THEY... THEY'RE ONLY WOUNDED... ALL OF THEM!
BUT WHO... WHAT IS THAT... COMING TOWARDS ME..??
IT'S AN ANDROID... HE CRASHED IN... THROUGH THE OUTSIDE WALL!
ONE OF THE GREATEST ACTION-THRILLERS EVER PRODUCED BY: STAN LEE (THE MAN) & JACK KIRBY (KING)
EMBELLISHMENT: JOE SINNOTT
LETTERING: SAM ROSEN

HE'S THE MAD THINKER'S LARGEST... MOST POWERFUL ANDROID OF ALL!
EVEN THOUGH THE THINKER IS IN JAIL... HE MUST HAVE FOUND SOME WAY TO HURL HIM AGAINST US!
INSTANT SUMMARY DEP'T.:
THE EVIL MAD THINKER AFFECTED THE BRAIN OF THE THING, TURNING HIM AGAINST THE FF! IN A LAST-DITCH EFFORT TO SAVE THEM ALL, REED RICHARDS HURLED A MENTA-WAVE BOLT AT HIM... AND THEN, THE THREE COMBATANTS SLOWLY LOST CONSCIOUSNESS!
AND NOW... BATTEN DOWN THE HATCHES, HERO!! WE'RE OFF...!!
2.

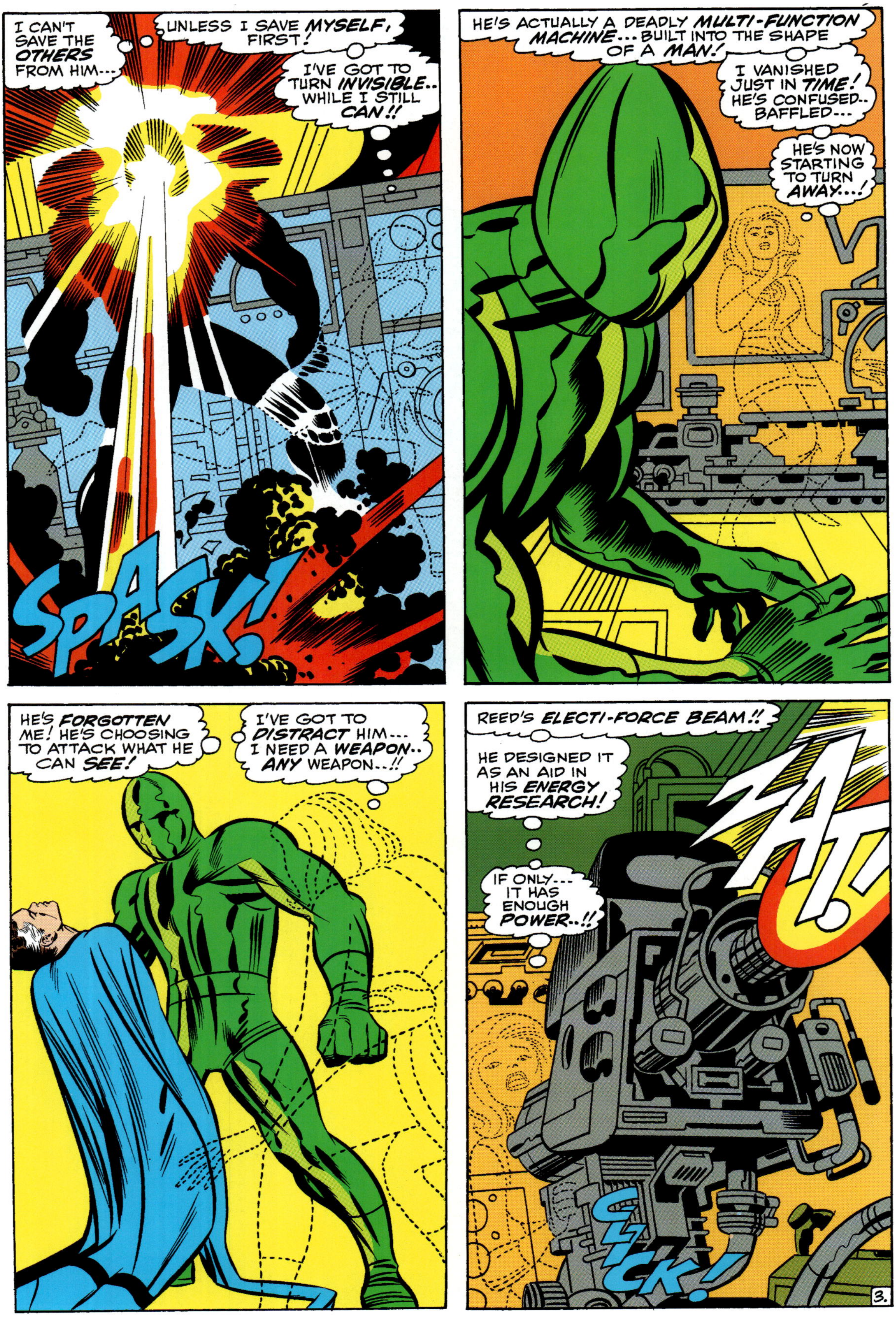

I CAN'T SAVE THE OTHERS FROM HIM---
UNLESS I SAVE MYSELF, FIRST!
I'VE GOT TO TURN INVISIBLE.. WHILE I STILL CAN!!
SPASK!
HE'S ACTUALLY A DEADLY MULTI-FUNCTION MACHINE... BUILT INTO THE SHAPE OF A MAN!
I VANISHED JUST IN TIME! HE'S CONFUSED.. BAFFLED---
HE'S NOW STARTING TO TURN AWAY...!
HE'S FORGOTTEN ME! HE'S CHOOSING TO ATTACK WHAT HE CAN SEE!
I'VE GOT TO DISTRACT HIM... I NEED A WEAPON.. ANY WEAPON..!!
REED'S ELECTI-FORCE BEAM!!
HE DESIGNED IT AS AN AID IN HIS ENERGY RESEARCH!
IF ONLY--- IT HAS ENOUGH POWER..!!
ZAT!
CLICK!
3.

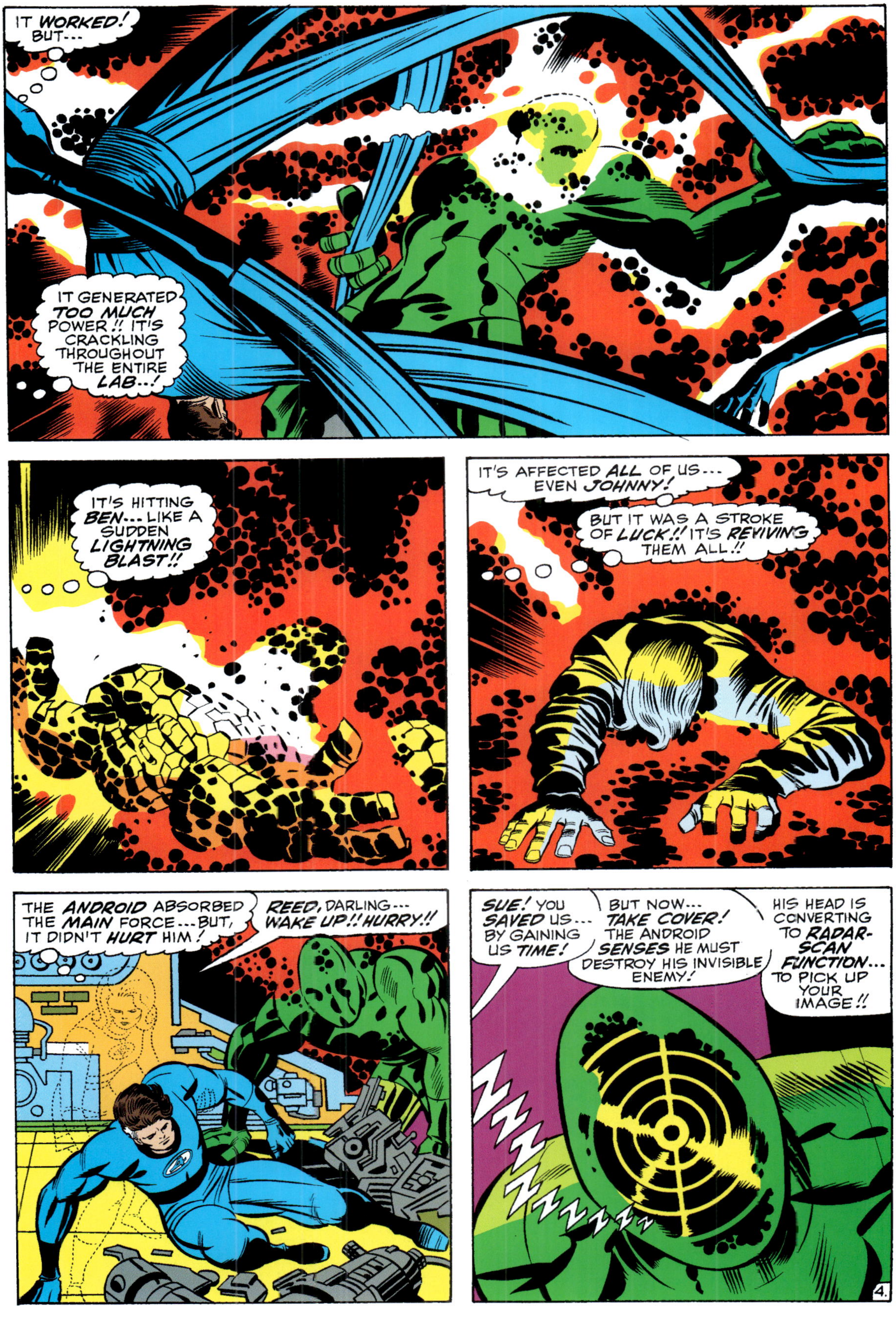

IT WORKED! BUT---
IT GENERATED TOO MUCH POWER!! IT'S CRACKLING THROUGHOUT THE ENTIRE LAB--!
IT'S HITTING BEN--- LIKE A SUDDEN LIGHTNING BLAST!!
IT'S AFFECTED ALL OF US--- EVEN JOHNNY!
BUT IT WAS A STROKE OF LUCK!! IT'S REVIVING THEM ALL!!
THE ANDROID ABSORBED THE MAIN FORCE--- BUT, IT DIDN'T HURT HIM!
REED, DARLING--- WAKE UP!! HURRY!!
SUE! YOU SAVED US--- BY GAINING US TIME!
BUT NOW--- TAKE COVER! THE ANDROID SENSES HE MUST DESTROY HIS INVISIBLE ENEMY!
HIS HEAD IS CONVERTING TO RADAR-SCAN FUNCTION--- TO PICK UP YOUR IMAGE!!
ZZZZZZZZZZ
4.

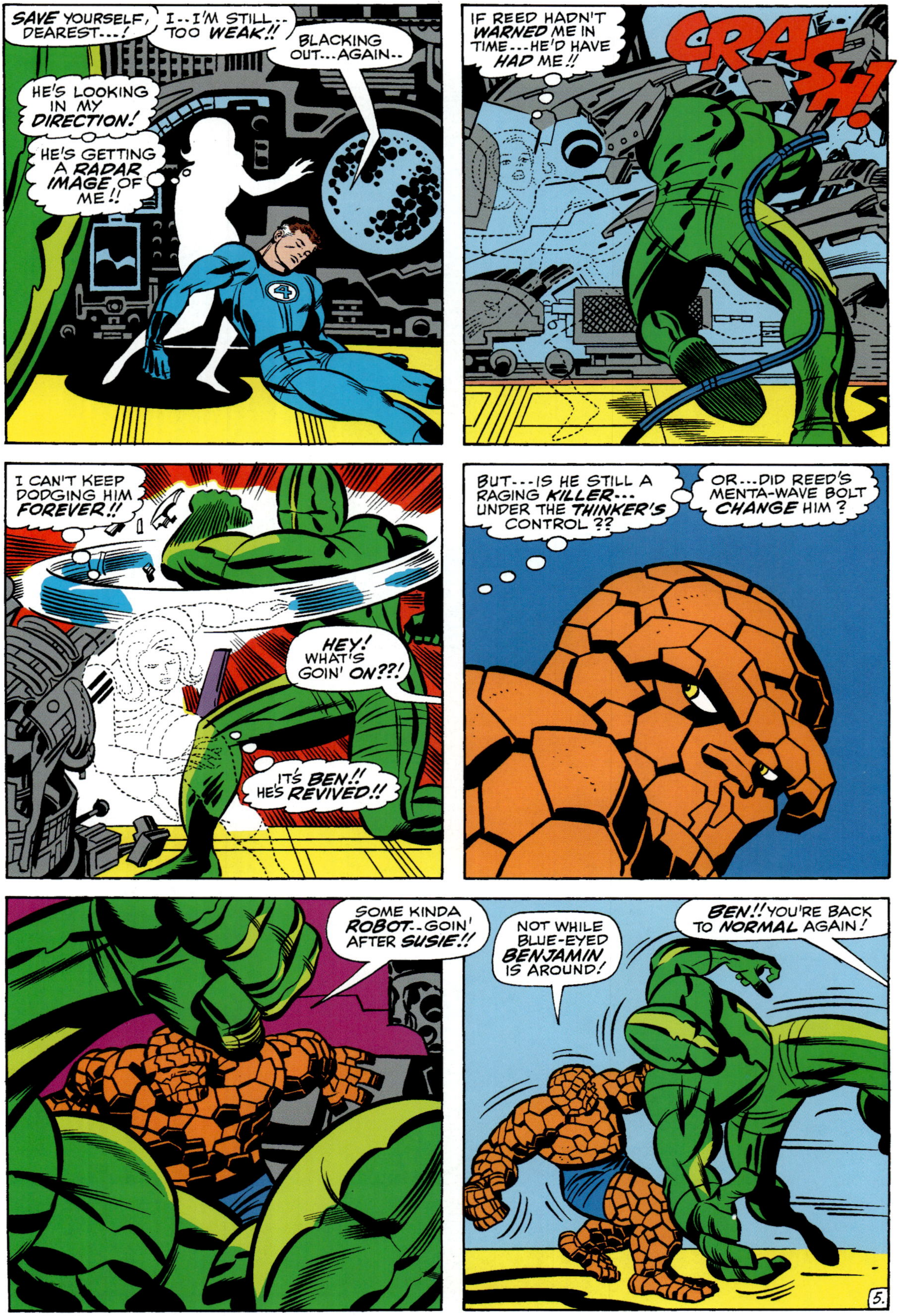
SAVE YOURSELF, DEAREST---!
I--I'M STILL-- TOO WEAK!!
BLACKING OUT---AGAIN--
HE'S LOOKING IN MY DIRECTION!
HE'S GETTING A RADAR IMAGE OF ME!!
IF REED HADN'T WARNED ME IN TIME---HE'D HAVE HAD ME!!
CRASH!
I CAN'T KEEP DODGING HIM FOREVER!!
HEY! WHAT'S GOIN' ON??!
IT'S BEN!! HE'S REVIVED!!
BUT---IS HE STILL A RAGING KILLER--- UNDER THE THINKER'S CONTROL ??
OR---DID REED'S MENTA-WAVE BOLT CHANGE HIM ?
SOME KINDA ROBOT--GOIN' AFTER SUSIE!!
NOT WHILE BLUE-EYED BENJAMIN IS AROUND!
BEN!! YOU'RE BACK TO NORMAL AGAIN!
5.

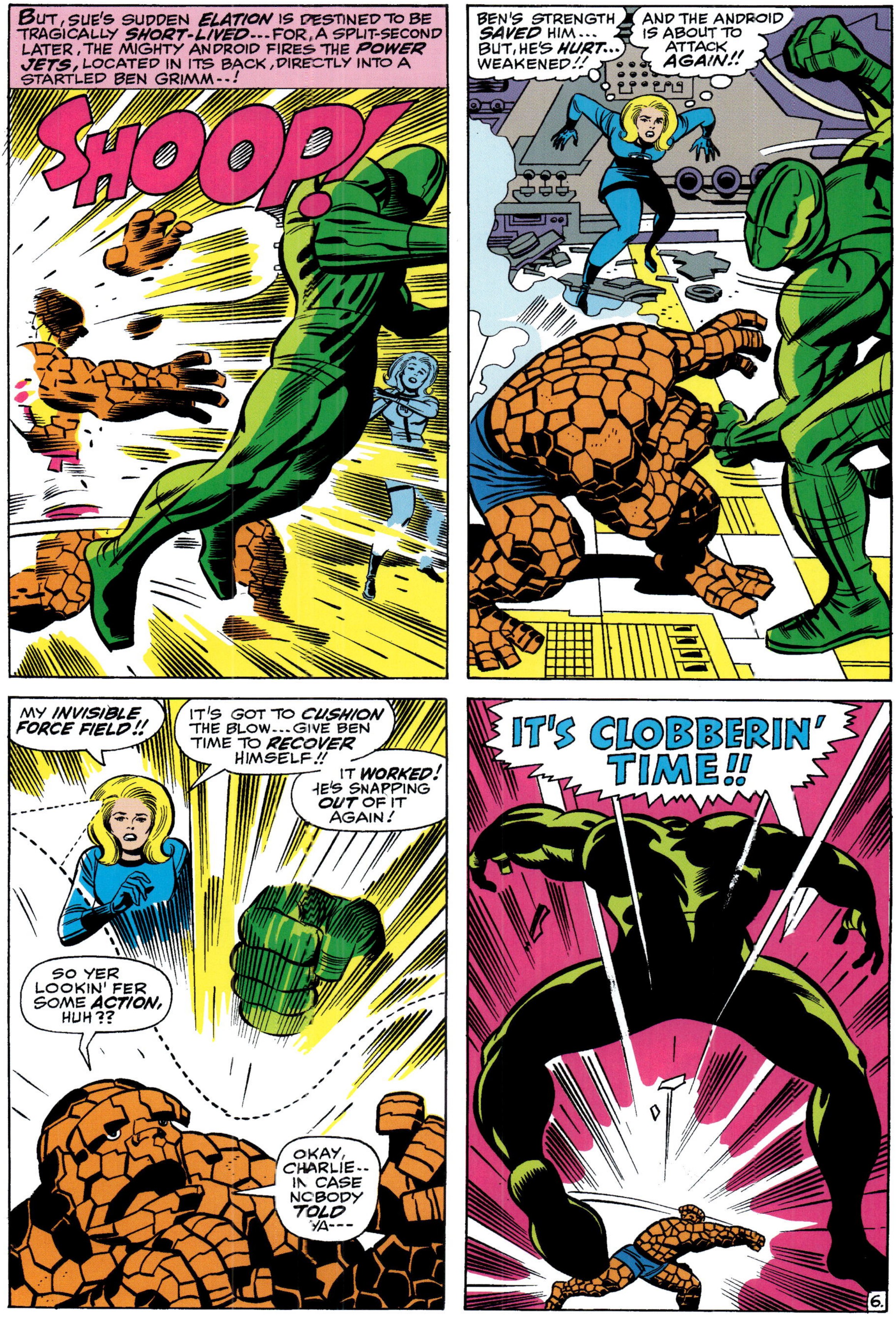
BUT, SUE'S SUDDEN ELATION IS DESTINED TO BE TRAGICALLY SHORT-LIVED--- FOR, A SPLIT-SECOND LATER, THE MIGHTY ANDROID FIRES THE POWER JETS, LOCATED IN ITS BACK, DIRECTLY INTO A STARTLED BEN GRIMM--!
SHOOP!
BEN'S STRENGTH SAVED HIM... BUT, HE'S HURT... WEAKENED!!
AND THE ANDROID IS ABOUT TO ATTACK AGAIN!!
MY INVISIBLE FORCE FIELD!!
IT'S GOT TO CUSHION THE BLOW--- GIVE BEN TIME TO RECOVER HIMSELF!!
IT WORKED! HE'S SNAPPING OUT OF IT AGAIN!
SO YER LOOKIN' FER SOME ACTION, HUH??
OKAY, CHARLIE-- IN CASE NOBODY TOLD YA---
IT'S CLOBBERIN' TIME!!
6.

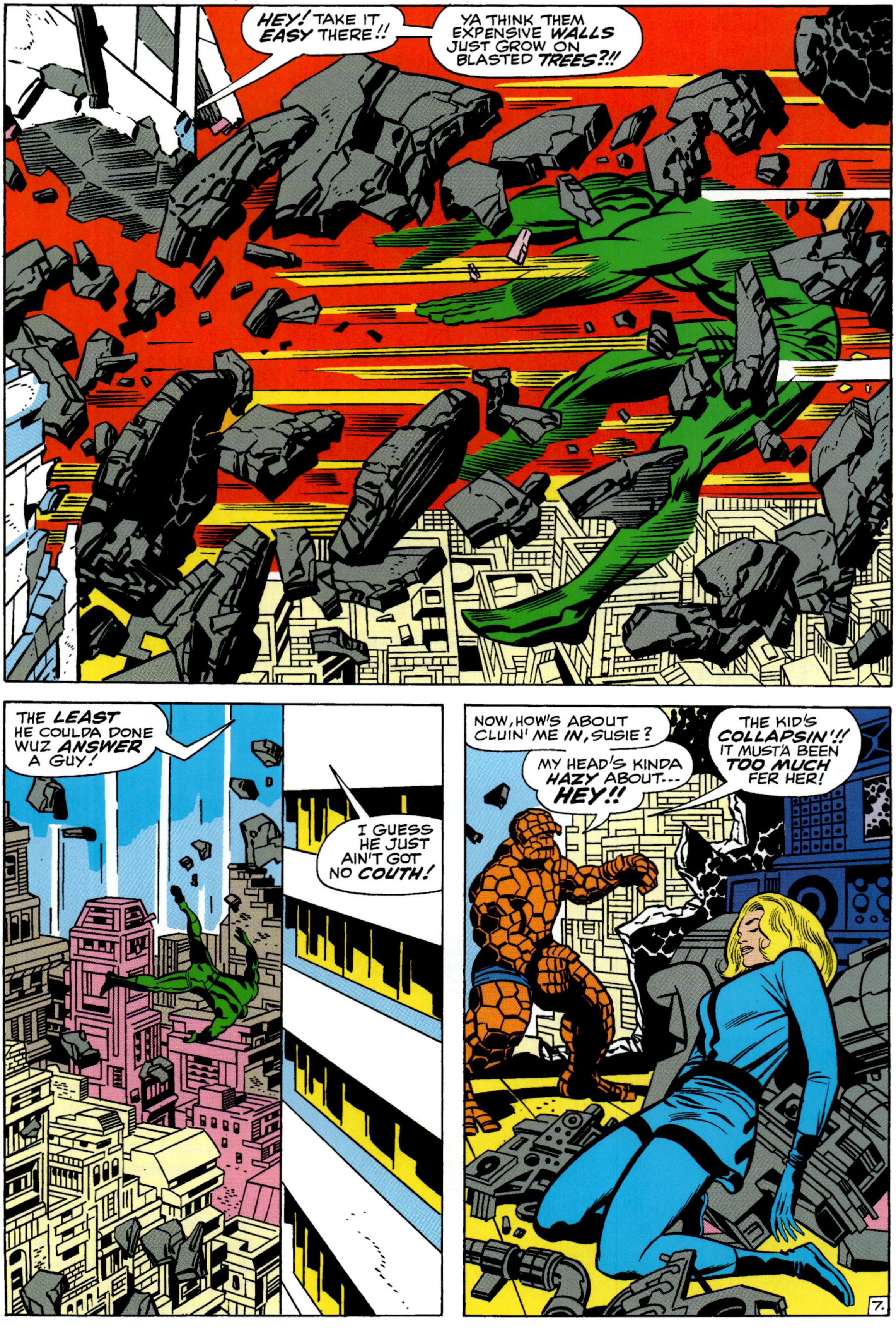
HEY! TAKE IT EASY THERE!!
YA THINK THEM EXPENSIVE WALLS JUST GROW ON BLASTED TREES?!!
THE LEAST HE COULDA DONE WUZ ANSWER A GUY!
I GUESS HE JUST AIN'T GOT NO COUTH!
NOW, HOW'S ABOUT CLUIN' ME IN, SUSIE?
MY HEAD'S KINDA HAZY ABOUT... HEY!!
THE KID'S COLLAPSIN'!!! IT MUST'A BEEN TOO MUCH FER HER!
7.

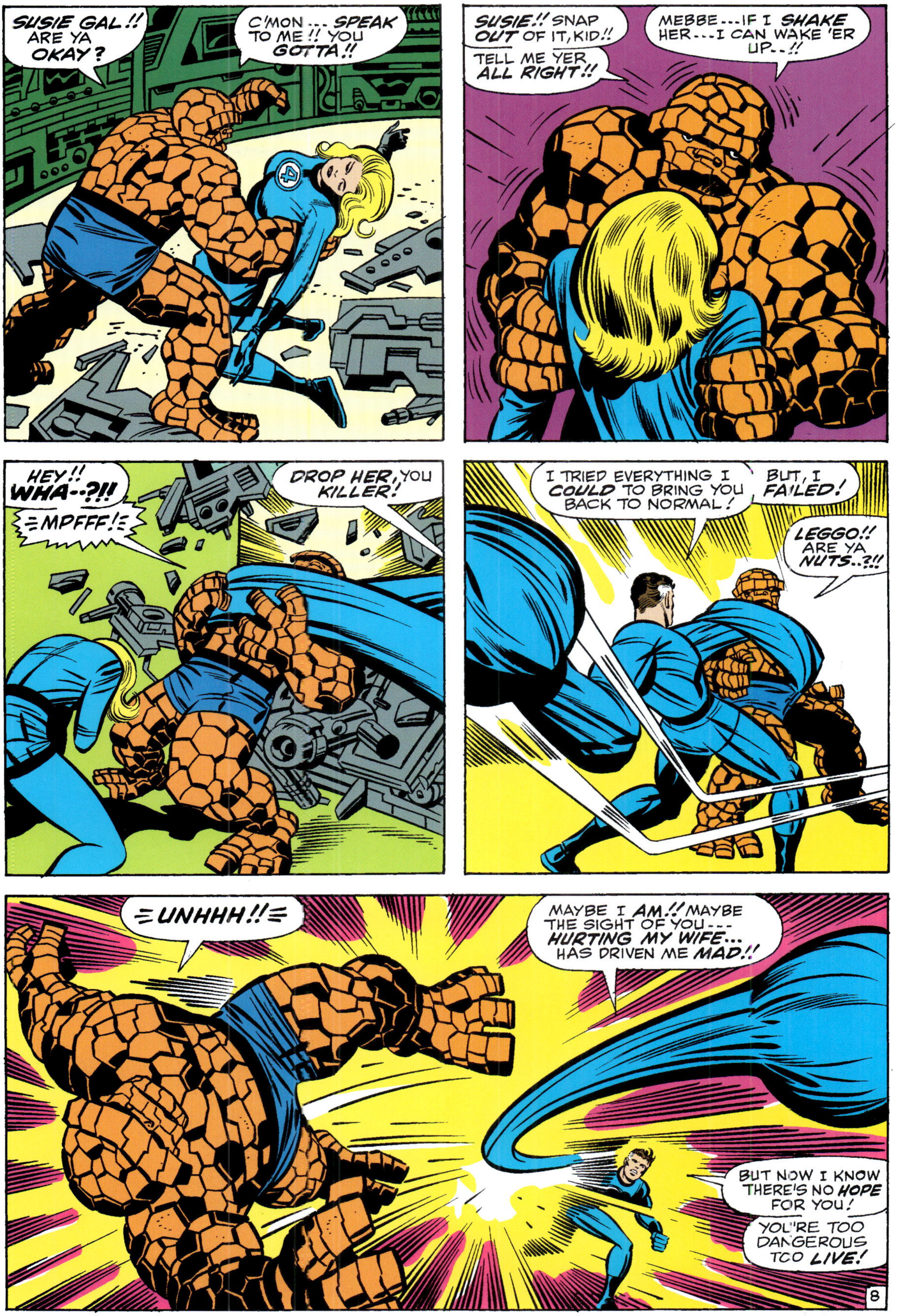
SUSIE GAL!! ARE YA OKAY?
C'MON... SPEAK TO ME!! YOU GOTTA!!
SUSIE!! SNAP OUT OF IT, KID!!
TELL ME YER ALL RIGHT!!
MEBBE...IF I SHAKE HER...I CAN WAKE 'ER UP..!!
HEY!! WHA--?!!
MPFFF!
DROP HER, YOU KILLER!
I TRIED EVERYTHING I COULD TO BRING YOU BACK TO NORMAL!
BUT, I FAILED!
LEGGO!! ARE YA NUTS..?!!
UNHHH!!
MAYBE I AM!! MAYBE THE SIGHT OF YOU--- HURTING MY WIFE... HAS DRIVEN ME MAD!!
BUT NOW I KNOW THERE'S NO HOPE FOR YOU!
YOU'RE TOO DANGEROUS TOO LIVE!
8

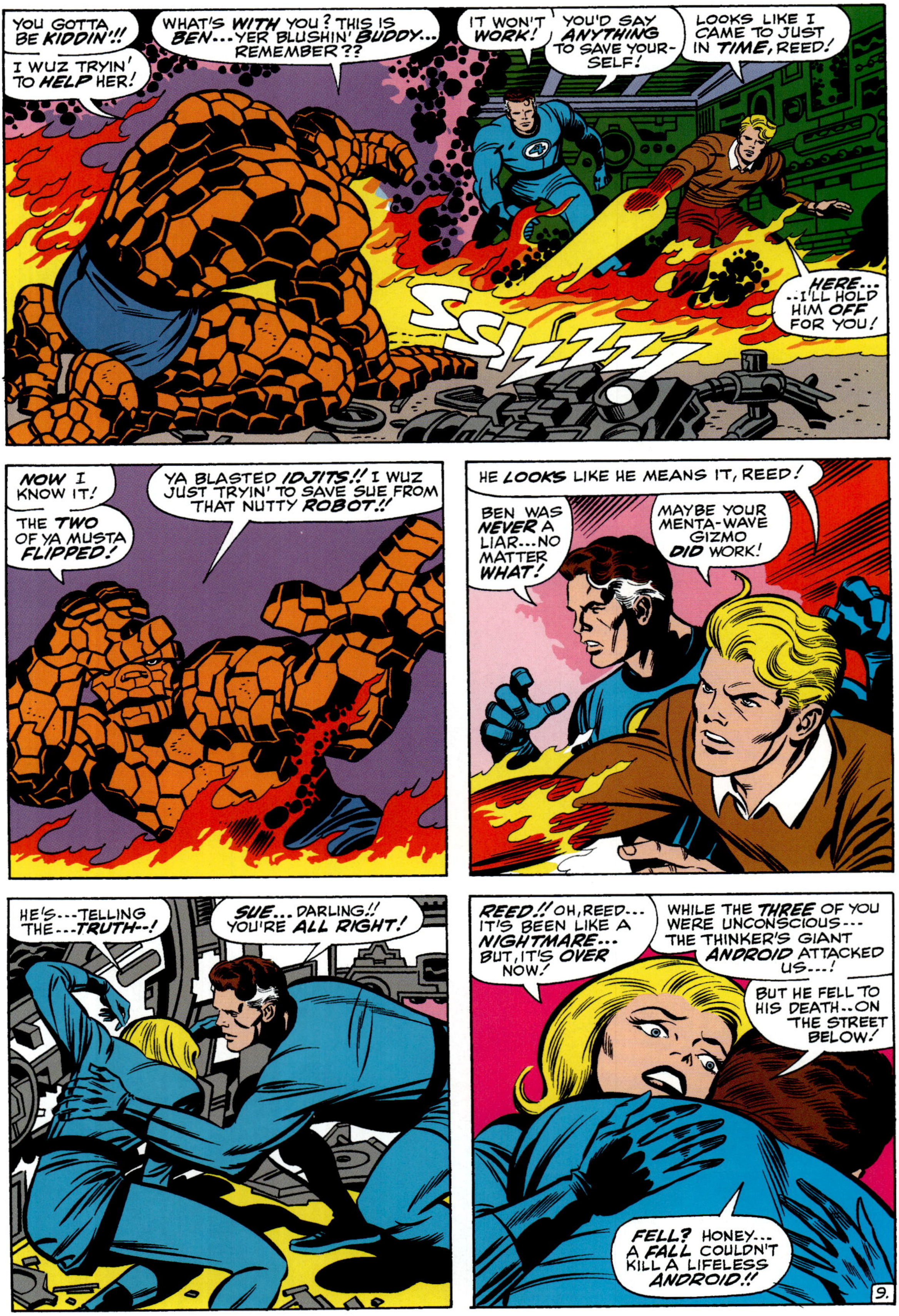
YOU GOTTA BE KIDDIN'!! I WUZ TRYIN' TO HELP HER!
WHAT'S WITH YOU? THIS IS BEN...YER BLUSHIN' BUDDY... REMEMBER??
IT WON'T WORK!
YOU'D SAY ANYTHING TO SAVE YOURSELF!
LOOKS LIKE I CAME TO JUST IN TIME, REED!
HERE... --I'LL HOLD HIM OFF FOR YOU!
SSIZZZ
NOW I KNOW IT! THE TWO OF YA MUSTA FLIPPED!
YA BLASTED IDJITS!! I WUZ JUST TRYIN' TO SAVE SUE FROM THAT NUTTY ROBOT!!
HE LOOKS LIKE HE MEANS IT, REED!
BEN WAS NEVER A LIAR---NO MATTER WHAT!
MAYBE YOUR MENTA-WAVE GIZMO DID WORK!
HE'S---TELLING THE---TRUTH--!
SUE... DARLING!! YOU'RE ALL RIGHT!
REED!! OH, REED--- IT'S BEEN LIKE A NIGHTMARE... BUT, IT'S OVER NOW!
WHILE THE THREE OF YOU WERE UNCONSCIOUS--- THE THINKER'S GIANT ANDROID ATTACKED US---!
BUT HE FELL TO HIS DEATH..ON THE STREET BELOW!
FELL? HONEY... A FALL COULDN'T KILL A LIFELESS ANDROID!!
9.

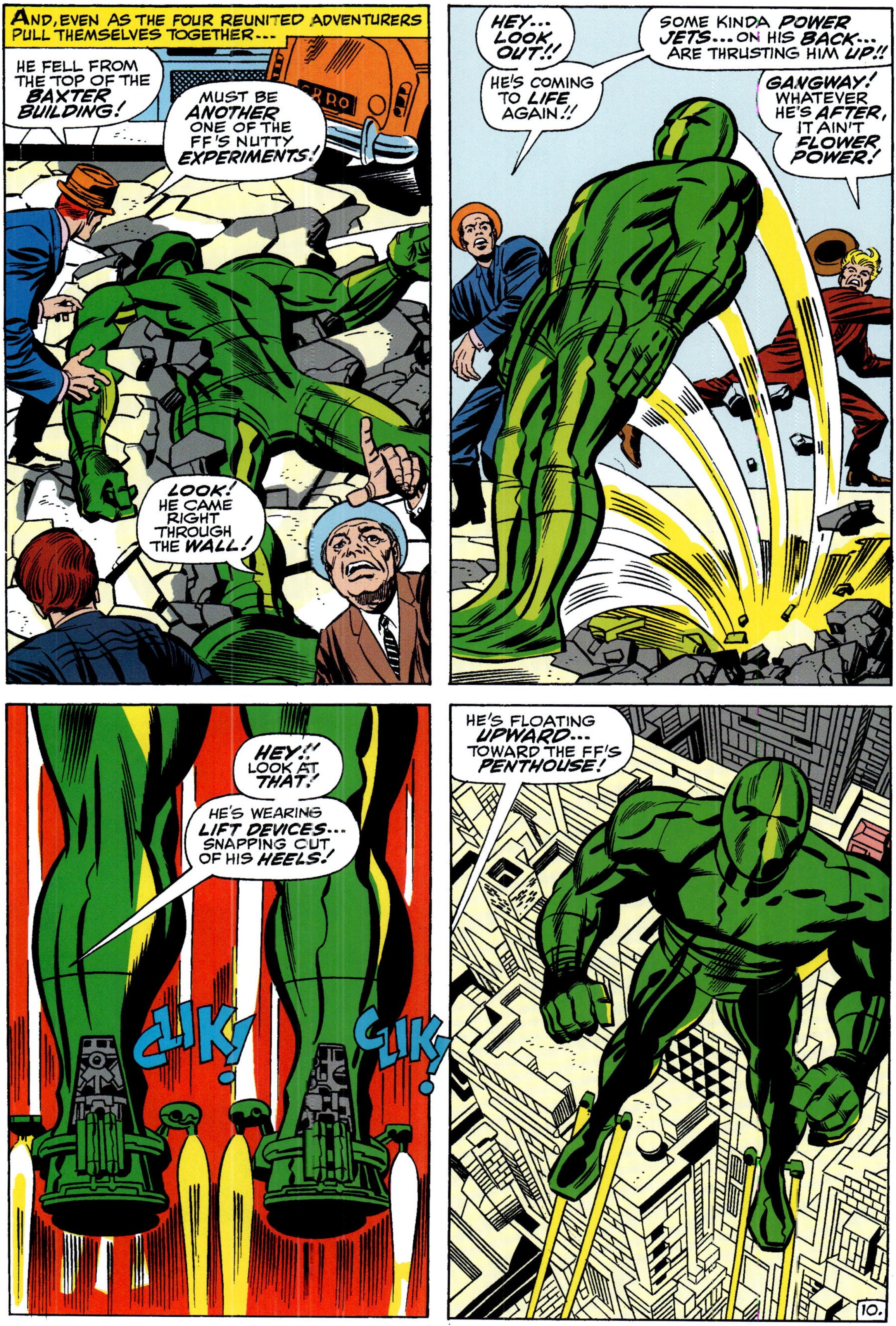
AND, EVEN AS THE FOUR REUNITED ADVENTURERS PULL THEMSELVES TOGETHER---
HE FELL FROM THE TOP OF THE BAXTER BUILDING!
MUST BE ANOTHER ONE OF THE FF'S NUTTY EXPERIMENTS!
LOOK! HE CAME RIGHT THROUGH THE WALL!
HEY... LOOK OUT!!
HE'S COMING TO LIFE AGAIN!!
SOME KINDA POWER JETS... ON HIS BACK... ARE THRUSTING HIM UP!!
GANGWAY! WHATEVER HE'S AFTER, IT AIN'T FLOWER POWER!
HEY!! LOOK AT THAT!
HE'S WEARING LIFT DEVICES... SNAPPING OUT OF HIS HEELS!
CLIK!
CLIK!
HE'S FLOATING UPWARD... TOWARD THE FF'S PENTHOUSE!
10.

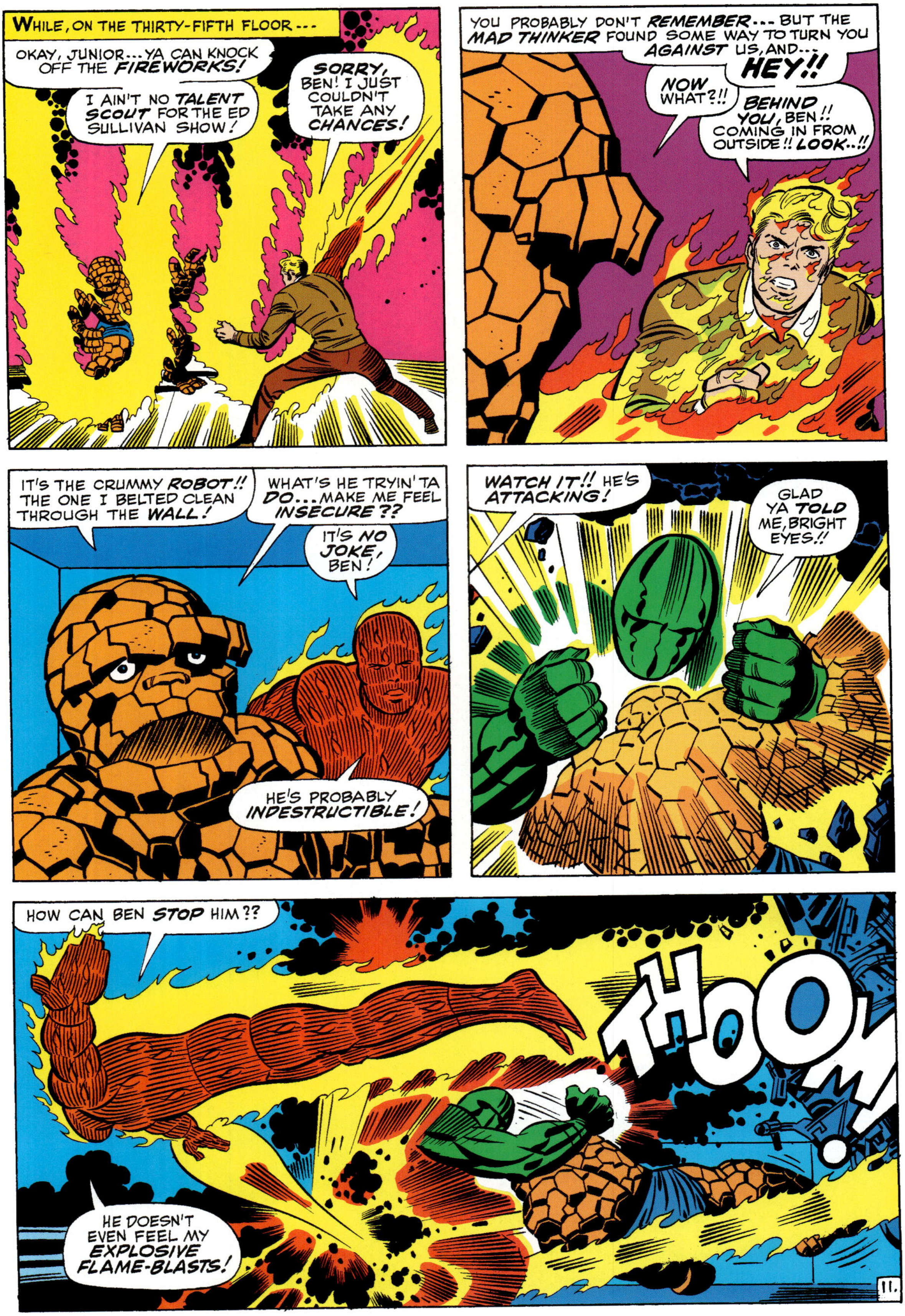
WHILE, ON THE THIRTY-FIFTH FLOOR ---
OKAY, JUNIOR... YA CAN KNOCK OFF THE FIREWORKS!
I AIN'T NO TALENT SCOUT FOR THE ED SULLIVAN SHOW!
SORRY, BEN! I JUST COULDN'T TAKE ANY CHANCES!
YOU PROBABLY DON'T REMEMBER... BUT THE MAD THINKER FOUND SOME WAY TO TURN YOU AGAINST US, AND... HEY!!
NOW WHAT?!!
BEHIND YOU, BEN!! COMING IN FROM OUTSIDE!! LOOK..!!
IT'S THE CRUMMY ROBOT!! THE ONE I BELTED CLEAN THROUGH THE WALL!
WHAT'S HE TRYIN' TA DO... MAKE ME FEEL INSECURE??
IT'S NO JOKE, BEN!
HE'S PROBABLY INDESTRUCTIBLE!
WATCH IT!! HE'S ATTACKING!
GLAD YA TOLD ME, BRIGHT EYES!!
HOW CAN BEN STOP HIM??
THOOOM!
HE DOESN'T EVEN FEEL MY EXPLOSIVE FLAME-BLASTS!
11.

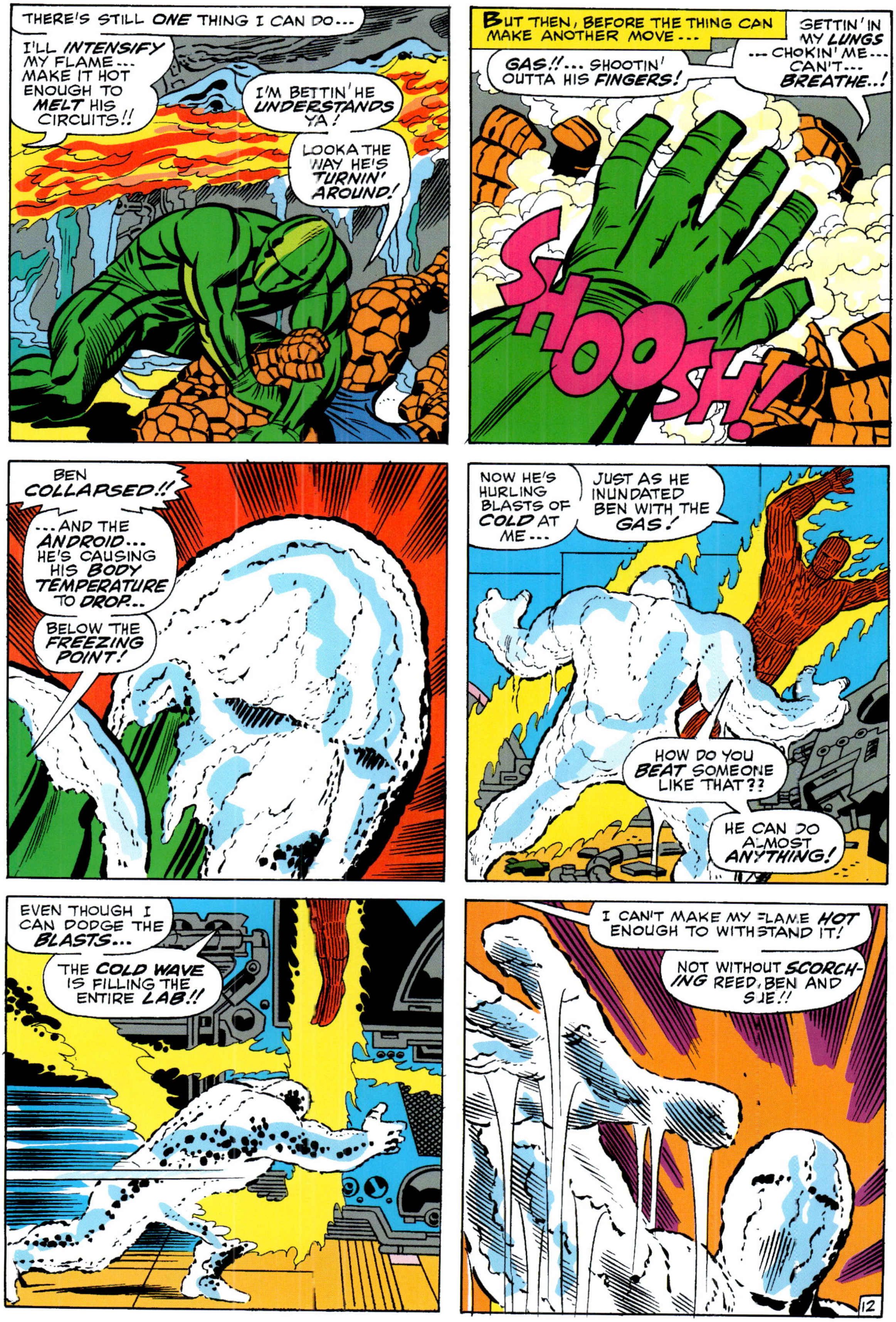
THERE'S STILL ONE THING I CAN DO...
I'LL INTENSIFY MY FLAME... MAKE IT HOT ENOUGH TO MELT HIS CIRCUITS!!
I'M BETTIN' HE UNDERSTANDS YA!
LOOKA THE WAY HE'S TURNIN' AROUND!
BUT THEN, BEFORE THE THING CAN MAKE ANOTHER MOVE---
GAS!!... SHOOTIN' OUTTA HIS FINGERS!
GETTIN' IN MY LUNGS --- CHOKIN' ME --- CAN'T--- BREATHE..!
SHOOSH!
BEN COLLAPSED!!
...AND THE ANDROID... HE'S CAUSING HIS BODY TEMPERATURE TO DROP...
BELOW THE FREEZING POINT!
NOW HE'S HURLING BLASTS OF COLD AT ME---
JUST AS HE INUNDATED BEN WITH THE GAS!
HOW DO YOU BEAT SOMEONE LIKE THAT??
HE CAN DO ALMOST ANYTHING!
EVEN THOUGH I CAN DODGE THE BLASTS...
THE COLD WAVE IS FILLING THE ENTIRE LAB!!
I CAN'T MAKE MY FLAME HOT ENOUGH TO WITHSTAND IT!
NOT WITHOUT SCORCHING REED, BEN AND SUE!!
12

THEN, WITHIN A MATTER OF SECONDS, THE INEVITABLE OCCURS ---
I'M ... TRAPPED AGAINST --- THE WALL ---
ENCLOSED IN --- AN ICE-CRYSTAL ENVELOPE !!
MY FLAMES -- CAN'T ESCAPE !! PRESSURE IS INCREASING --!!
AND, AS THE PRESSURE MOUNTS BEYOND THE POINT OF ENDURANCE ---
SPLANNG!
THEN, WHEN THE SMOKE HAS CLEARED ---
REED! THAT EXPLOSION !! WHAT WAS IT .. ??
I DON'T KNOW, DEAR! BUT, IT CAN ONLY MEAN NEW DANGER!
I'VE GOT TO GO BACK!
13.

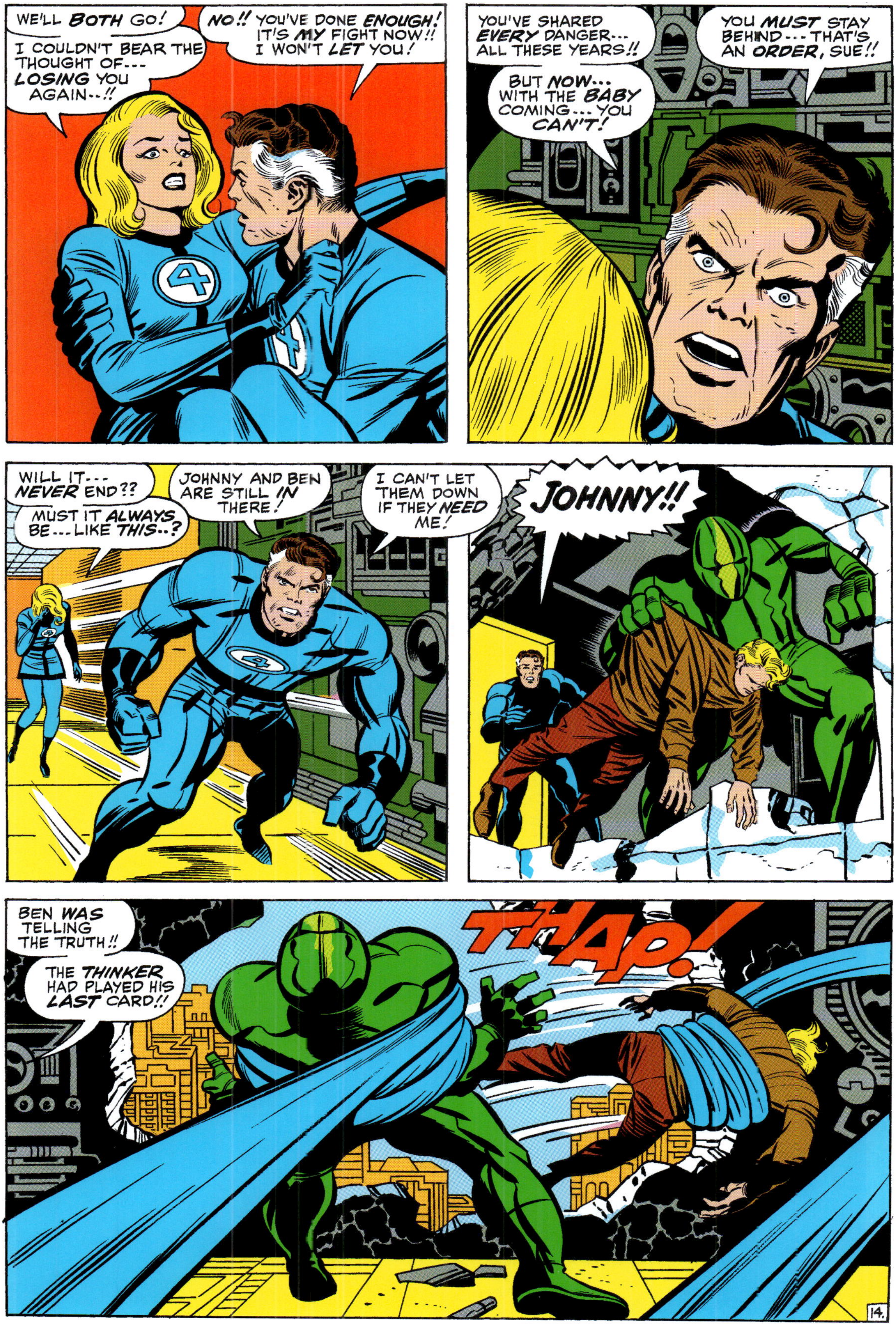

WE'LL BOTH GO!
I COULDN'T BEAR THE THOUGHT OF--- LOSING YOU AGAIN--!!
NO!! YOU'VE DONE ENOUGH! IT'S MY FIGHT NOW!! I WON'T LET YOU!
YOU'VE SHARED EVERY DANGER--- ALL THESE YEARS!!
BUT NOW--- WITH THE BABY COMING--- YOU CAN'T!
YOU MUST STAY BEHIND--- THAT'S AN ORDER, SUE!!
WILL IT--- NEVER END??
MUST IT ALWAYS BE--- LIKE THIS--?
JOHNNY AND BEN ARE STILL IN THERE!
I CAN'T LET THEM DOWN IF THEY NEED ME!
JOHNNY!!
BEN WAS TELLING THE TRUTH!!
THE THINKER HAD PLAYED HIS LAST CARD!!
THAP!
14.

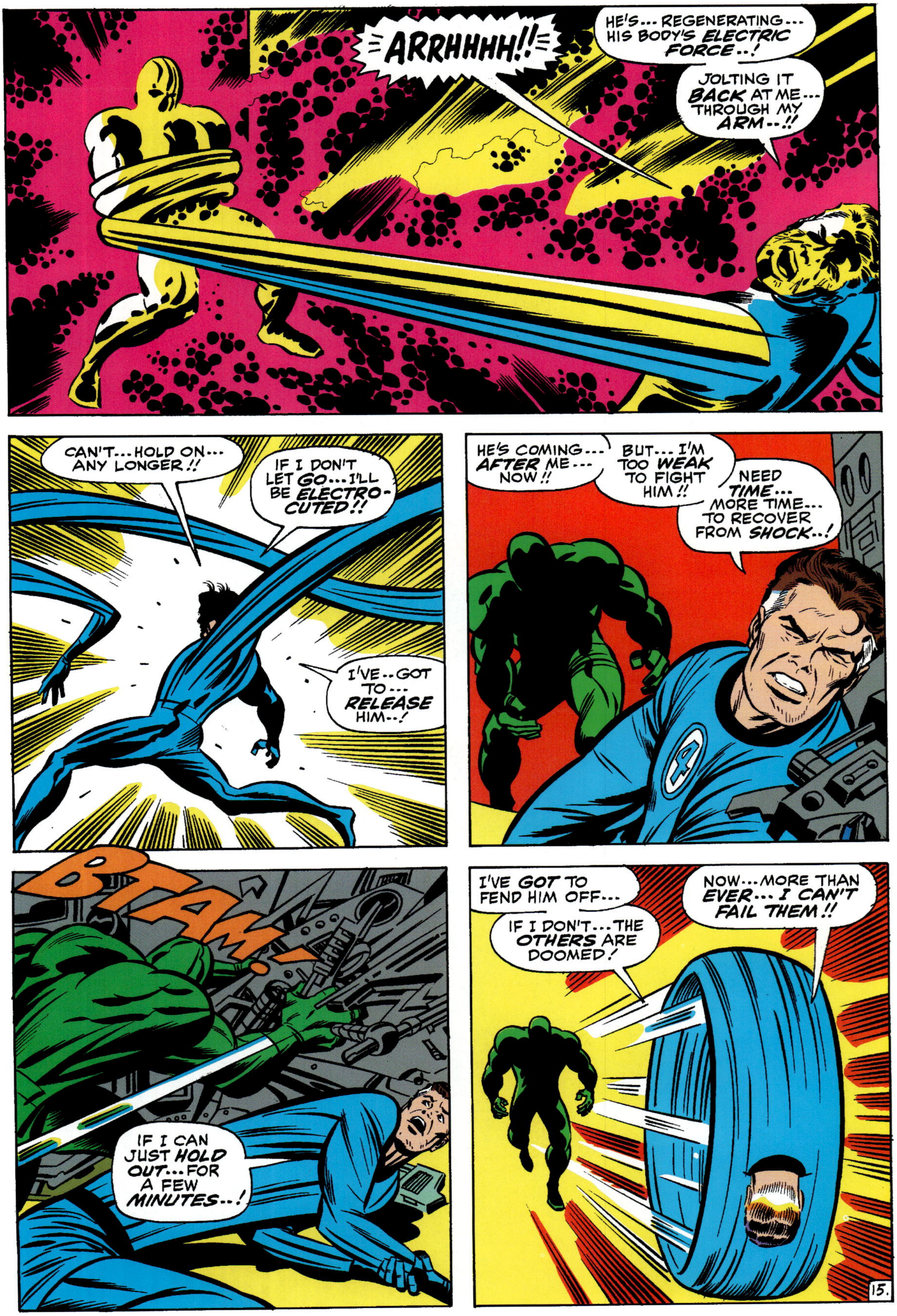
ARRHHHH!!
HE'S... REGENERATING... HIS BODY'S ELECTRIC FORCE..!
JOLTING IT BACK AT ME... THROUGH MY ARM..!!
CAN'T... HOLD ON... ANY LONGER!!
IF I DON'T LET GO... I'LL BE ELECTRO-CUTED!!
I'VE.. GOT TO... RELEASE HIM..!
HE'S COMING... AFTER ME... NOW!!
BUT... I'M TOO WEAK TO FIGHT HIM!!
NEED TIME... MORE TIME... TO RECOVER FROM SHOCK..!
BTAM!
IF I CAN JUST HOLD OUT... FOR A FEW MINUTES..!
I'VE GOT TO FEND HIM OFF...
IF I DON'T... THE OTHERS ARE DOOMED!
NOW... MORE THAN EVER... I CAN'T FAIL THEM!!
15.

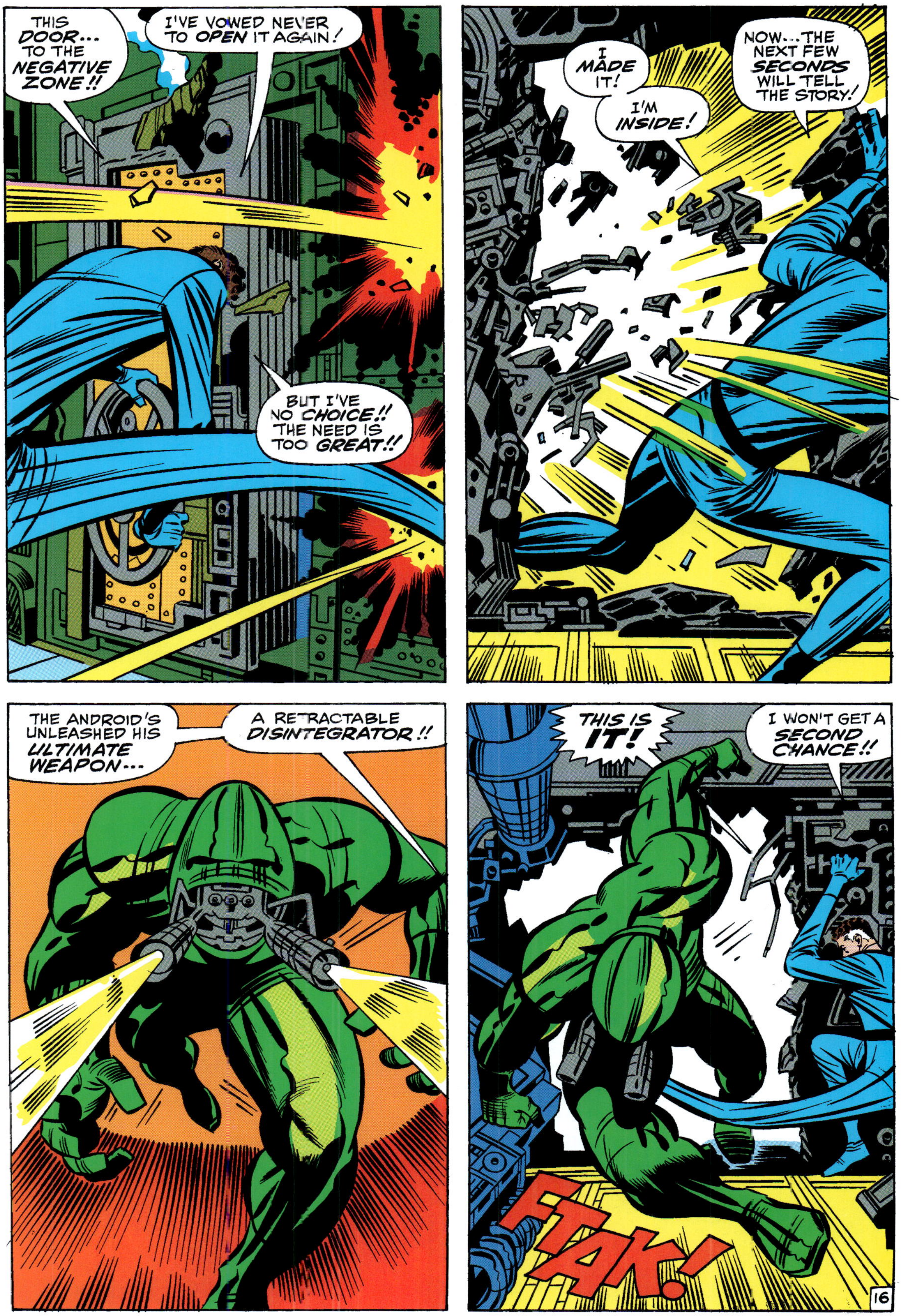
THIS DOOR... TO THE NEGATIVE ZONE!!
I'VE VOWED NEVER TO OPEN IT AGAIN!
BUT I'VE NO CHOICE!! THE NEED IS TOO GREAT!!
I MADE IT!
I'M INSIDE!
NOW...THE NEXT FEW SECONDS WILL TELL THE STORY!
THE ANDROID'S UNLEASHED HIS ULTIMATE WEAPON...
A RETRACTABLE DISINTEGRATOR!!
THIS IS IT!
I WON'T GET A SECOND CHANCE!!
FTAK!
16

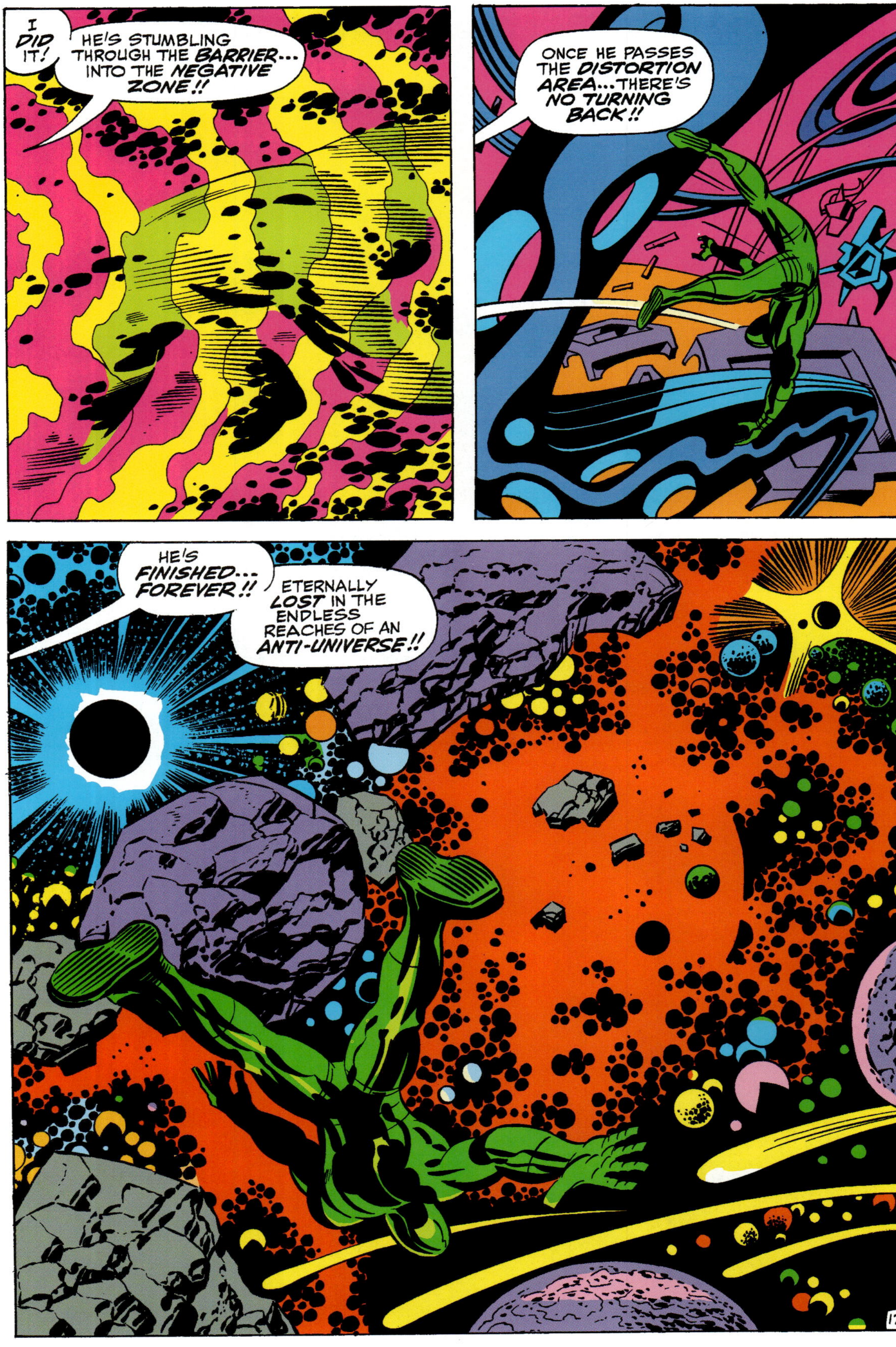
I DID IT!
HE'S STUMBLING THROUGH THE BARRIER... INTO THE NEGATIVE ZONE!!
ONCE HE PASSES THE DISTORTION AREA...THERE'S NO TURNING BACK!!
HE'S FINISHED... FOREVER!!
ETERNALLY LOST IN THE ENDLESS REACHES OF AN ANTI-UNIVERSE!!
17.

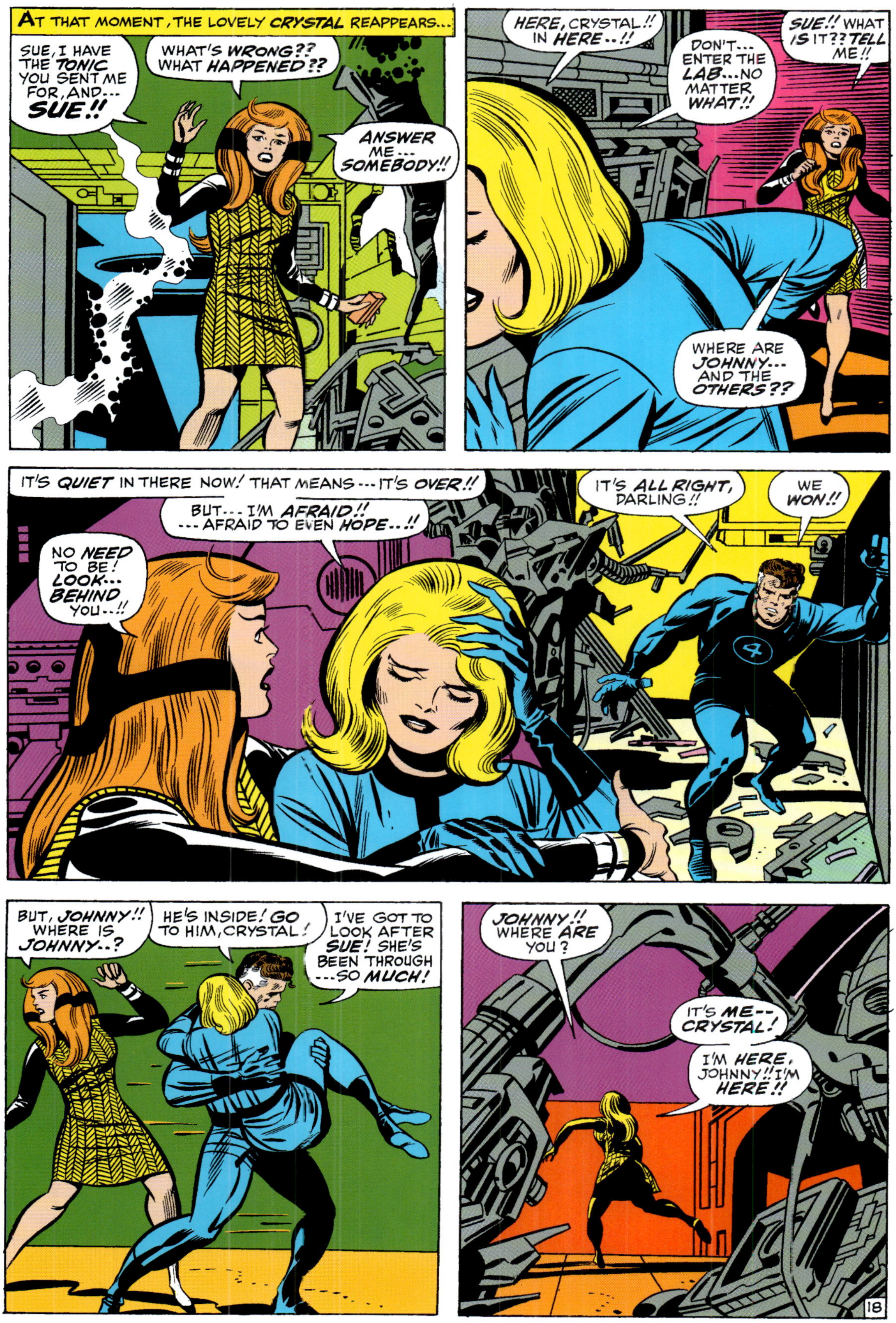
AT THAT MOMENT, THE LOVELY CRYSTAL REAPPEARS...
SUE, I HAVE THE TONIC YOU SENT ME FOR, AND... SUE!!
WHAT'S WRONG?? WHAT HAPPENED??
ANSWER ME... SOMEBODY!!
HERE, CRYSTAL!! IN HERE..!!
DON'T... ENTER THE LAB...NO MATTER WHAT!!
SUE!! WHAT IS IT?? TELL ME!!
WHERE ARE JOHNNY... AND THE OTHERS??
IT'S QUIET IN THERE NOW! THAT MEANS --- IT'S OVER!!
BUT--- I'M AFRAID!! --- AFRAID TO EVEN HOPE--!!
NO NEED TO BE! LOOK... BEHIND YOU--!!
IT'S ALL RIGHT, DARLING!!
WE WON!!
BUT, JOHNNY!! WHERE IS JOHNNY--?
HE'S INSIDE! GO TO HIM, CRYSTAL!
I'VE GOT TO LOOK AFTER SUE! SHE'S BEEN THROUGH --- SO MUCH!
JOHNNY!! WHERE ARE YOU?
IT'S ME-- CRYSTAL!
I'M HERE, JOHNNY!! I'M HERE!!
18

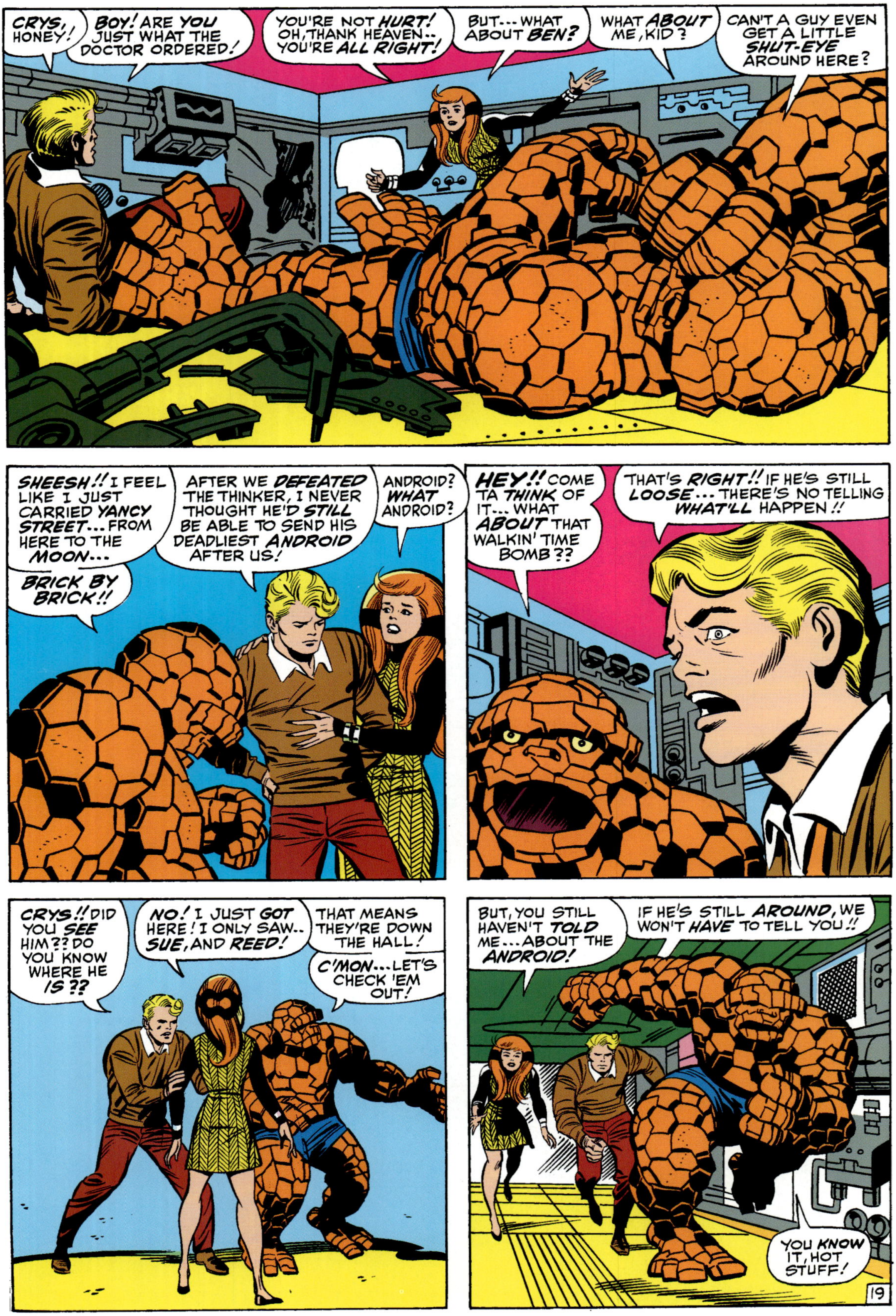
CRYS, HONEY!
BOY! ARE YOU JUST WHAT THE DOCTOR ORDERED!
YOU'RE NOT HURT! OH, THANK HEAVEN.. YOU'RE ALL RIGHT!
BUT... WHAT ABOUT BEN?
WHAT ABOUT ME, KID?
CAN'T A GUY EVEN GET A LITTLE SHUT-EYE AROUND HERE?
SHEESH!! I FEEL LIKE I JUST CARRIED YANCY STREET... FROM HERE TO THE MOON...
BRICK BY BRICK!!
AFTER WE DEFEATED THE THINKER, I NEVER THOUGHT HE'D STILL BE ABLE TO SEND HIS DEADLIEST ANDROID AFTER US!
ANDROID? WHAT ANDROID?
HEY!! COME TA THINK OF IT... WHAT ABOUT THAT WALKIN' TIME BOMB??
THAT'S RIGHT!! IF HE'S STILL LOOSE... THERE'S NO TELLING WHAT'LL HAPPEN!!
CRYS!! DID YOU SEE HIM?? DO YOU KNOW WHERE HE IS??
NO! I JUST GOT HERE! I ONLY SAW.. SUE, AND REED!
THAT MEANS THEY'RE DOWN THE HALL!
C'MON... LET'S CHECK 'EM OUT!
BUT, YOU STILL HAVEN'T TOLD ME... ABOUT THE ANDROID!
IF HE'S STILL AROUND, WE WON'T HAVE TO TELL YOU!!
YOU KNOW IT, HOT STUFF!
19

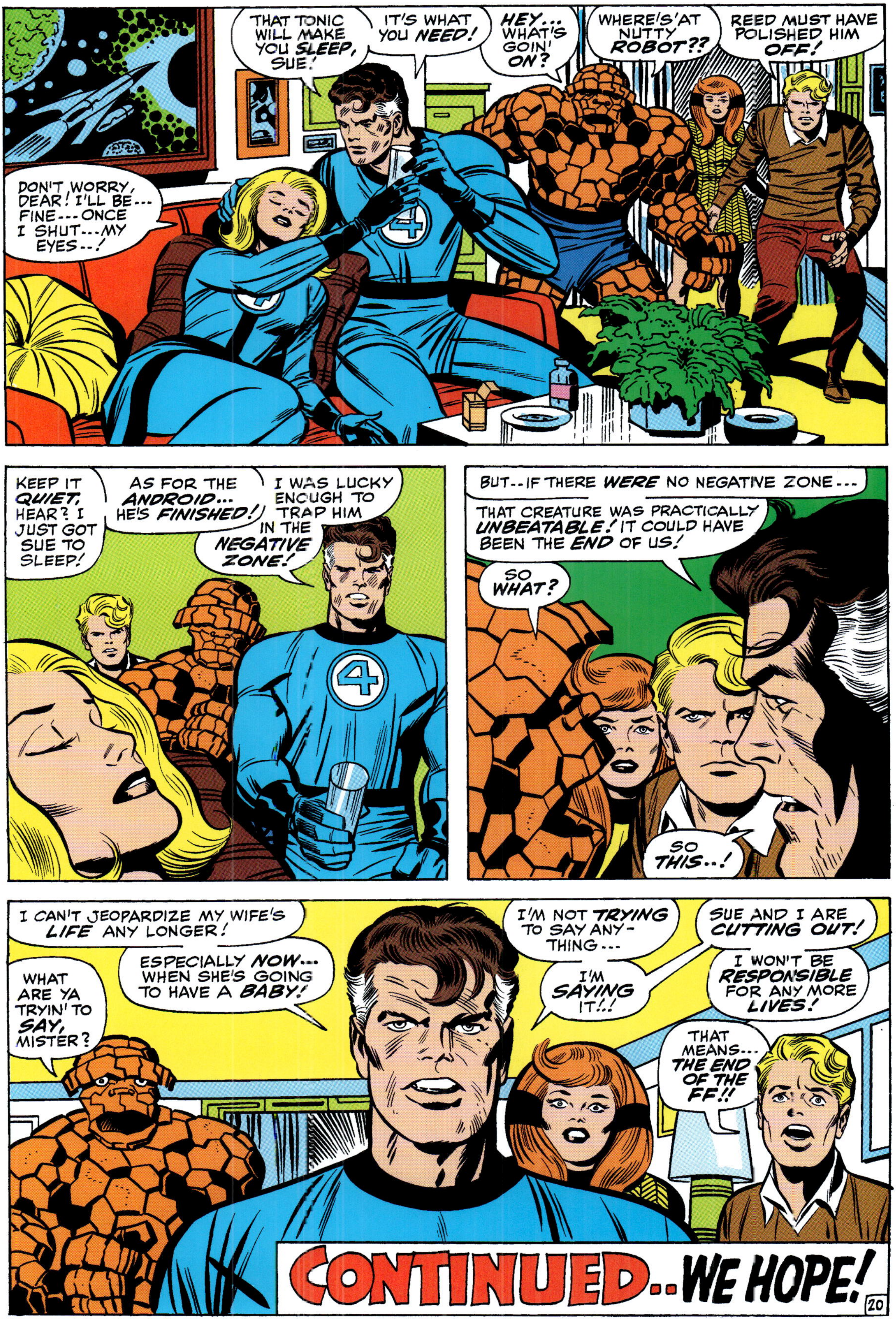

THAT TONIC WILL MAKE YOU SLEEP, SUE!
IT'S WHAT YOU NEED!
HEY... WHAT'S GOIN' ON?
WHERE'S 'AT NUTTY ROBOT??
REED MUST HAVE POLISHED HIM OFF!
DON'T WORRY, DEAR! I'LL BE--- FINE--- ONCE I SHUT--- MY EYES--!
KEEP IT QUIET, HEAR? I JUST GOT SUE TO SLEEP!
AS FOR THE ANDROID... HE'S FINISHED!
I WAS LUCKY ENOUGH TO TRAP HIM IN THE NEGATIVE ZONE!
BUT--IF THERE WERE NO NEGATIVE ZONE---
THAT CREATURE WAS PRACTICALLY UNBEATABLE! IT COULD HAVE BEEN THE END OF US!
SO WHAT?
SO THIS--!
I CAN'T JEOPARDIZE MY WIFE'S LIFE ANY LONGER!
WHAT ARE YA TRYIN' TO SAY, MISTER?
ESPECIALLY NOW... WHEN SHE'S GOING TO HAVE A BABY!
I'M NOT TRYING TO SAY ANY-THING---
I'M SAYING IT!!
SUE AND I ARE CUTTING OUT!
I WON'T BE RESPONSIBLE FOR ANY MORE LIVES!
THAT MEANS... THE END OF THE FF!!
CONTINUED..WE HOPE!
20

SPECIAL BONUS:

Fantastic Four #64 unused cover pencils

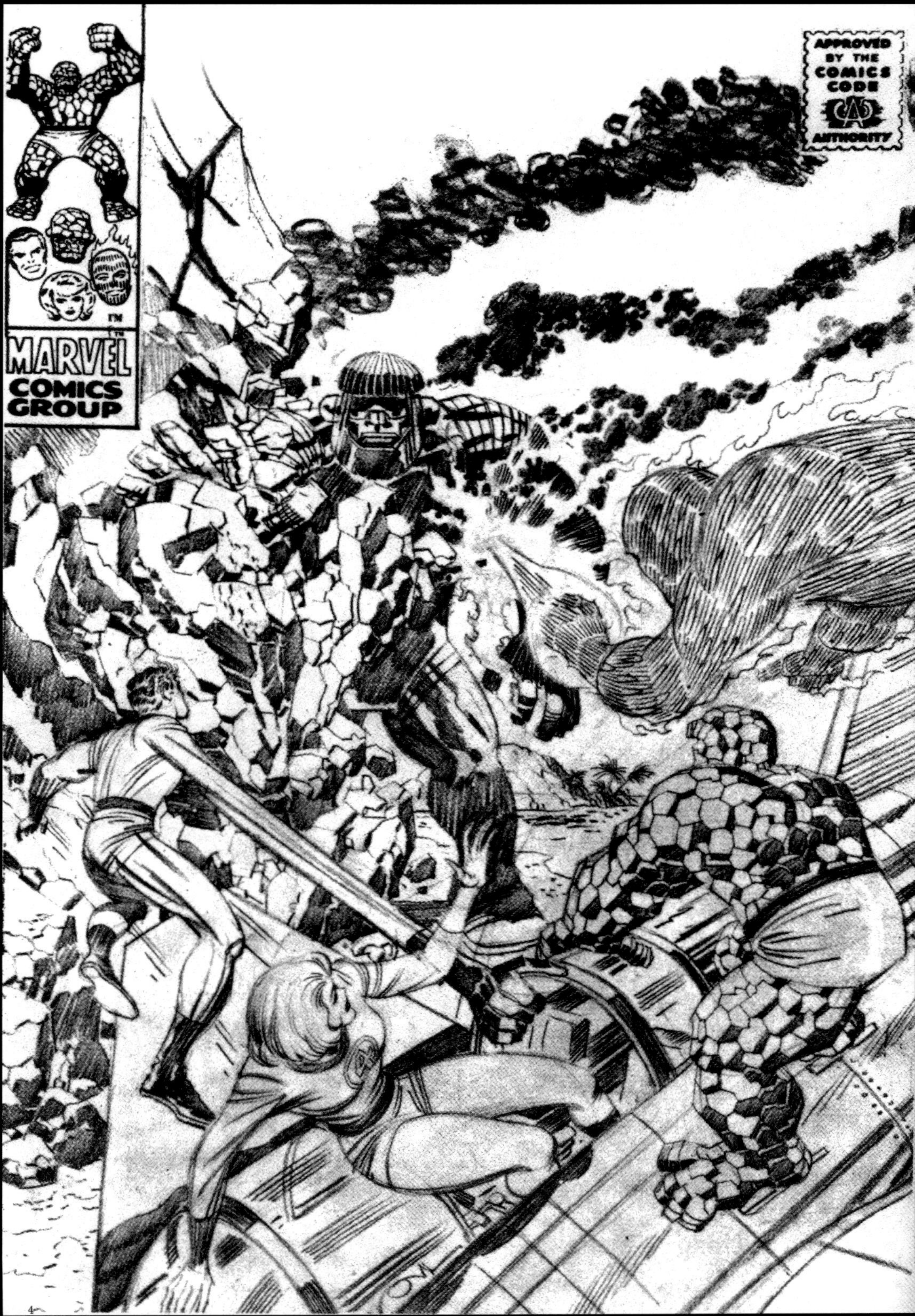
MARVEL
COMICS
GROUP
APPROVED
BY THE
COMICS
CODE
AUTHORITY

Fantastic Four #71 unused cover pencils

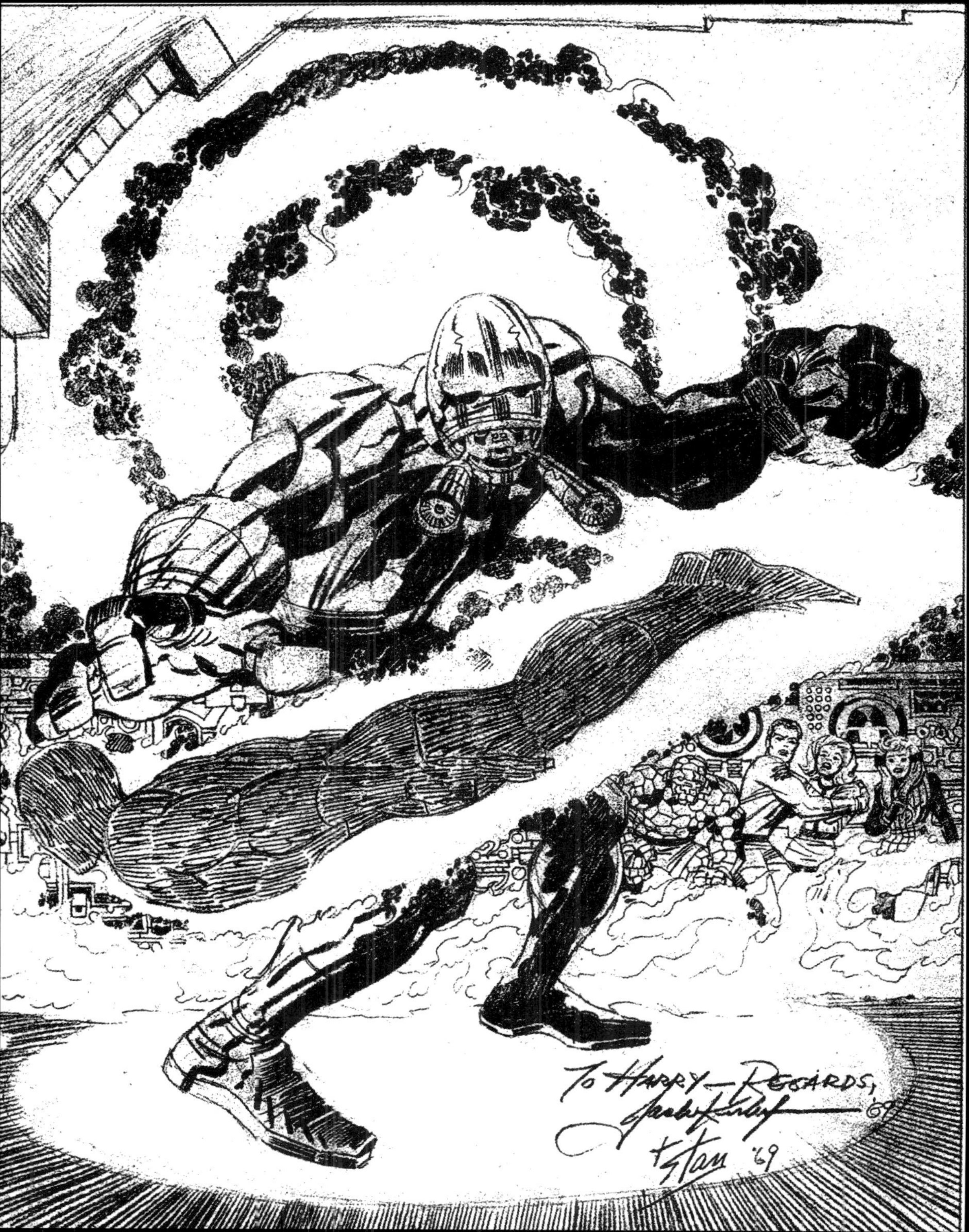
To HARRY— REGARDS,
Stan '69

The following pages display Jack Kirby's story notes for Stan Lee written directly on the original art boards.

Fantastic Four #61, page 13

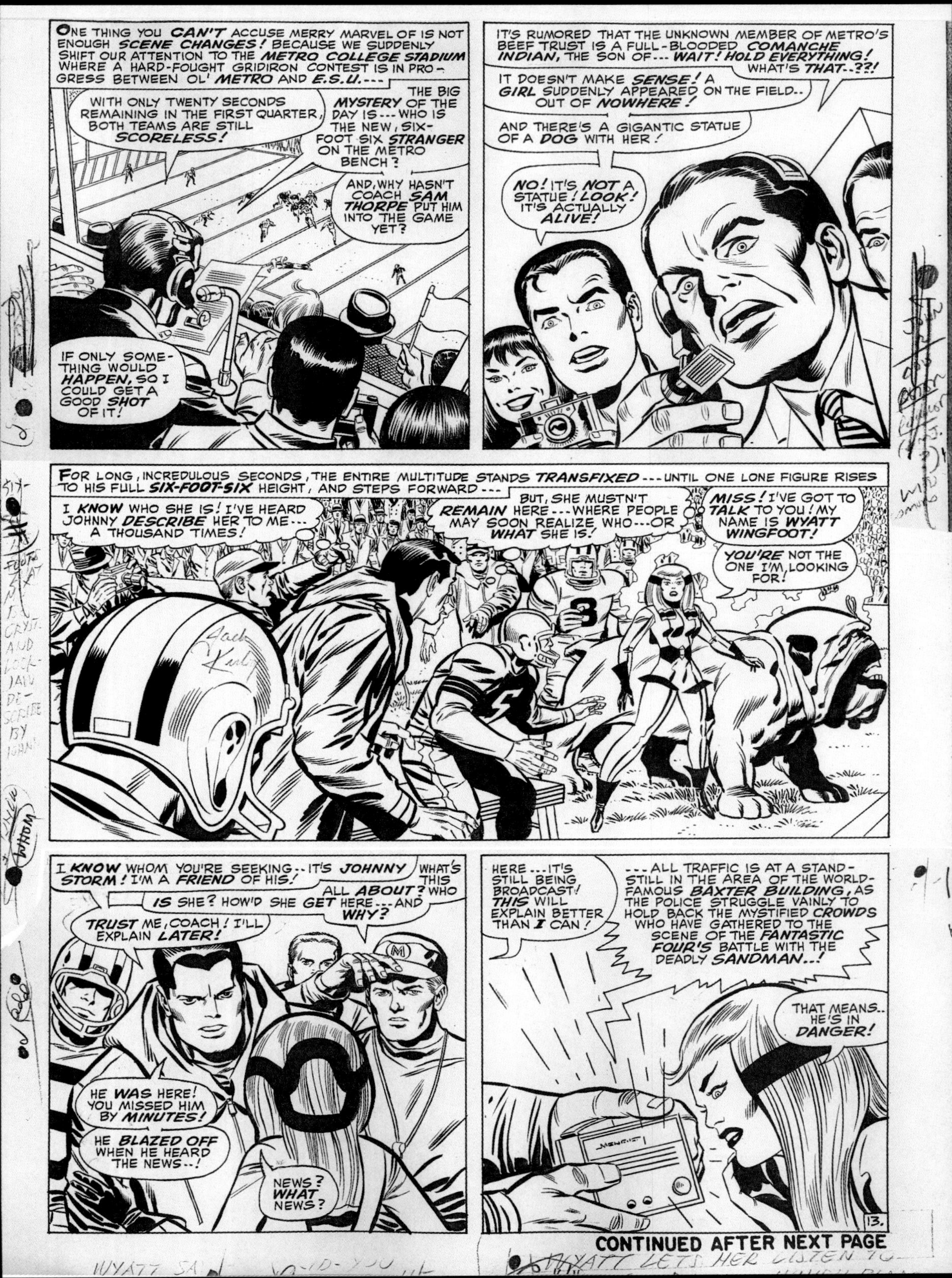
ONE THING YOU CAN'T ACCUSE MERRY MARVEL OF IS NOT ENOUGH SCENE CHANGES! BECAUSE WE SUDDENLY SHIFT OUR ATTENTION TO THE METRO COLLEGE STADIUM WHERE A HARD-FOUGHT GRIDIRON CONTEST IS IN PROGRESS BETWEEN OL' METRO AND E.S.U.---
WITH ONLY TWENTY SECONDS REMAINING IN THE FIRST QUARTER, BOTH TEAMS ARE STILL SCORELESS!
THE BIG MYSTERY OF THE DAY IS---WHO IS THE NEW, SIX-FOOT SIX STRANGER ON THE METRO BENCH?
AND, WHY HASN'T COACH SAM THORPE PUT HIM INTO THE GAME YET?
IF ONLY SOMETHING WOULD HAPPEN, SO I COULD GET A GOOD SHOT OF IT!
IT'S RUMORED THAT THE UNKNOWN MEMBER OF METRO'S BEEF TRUST IS A FULL-BLOODED COMANCHE INDIAN, THE SON OF--- WAIT! HOLD EVERYTHING! WHAT'S THAT--??!
IT DOESN'T MAKE SENSE! A GIRL SUDDENLY APPEARED ON THE FIELD.. OUT OF NOWHERE!
AND THERE'S A GIGANTIC STATUE OF A DOG WITH HER!
NO! IT'S NOT A STATUE! LOOK! IT'S ACTUALLY ALIVE!
FOR LONG, INCREDULOUS SECONDS, THE ENTIRE MULTITUDE STANDS TRANSFIXED---UNTIL ONE LONE FIGURE RISES TO HIS FULL SIX-FOOT-SIX HEIGHT, AND STEPS FORWARD---
I KNOW WHO SHE IS! I'VE HEARD JOHNNY DESCRIBE HER TO ME--- A THOUSAND TIMES!
BUT, SHE MUSTN'T REMAIN HERE---WHERE PEOPLE MAY SOON REALIZE WHO---OR WHAT SHE IS!
MISS! I'VE GOT TO TALK TO YOU! MY NAME IS WYATT WINGFOOT!
YOU'RE NOT THE ONE I'M LOOKING FOR!
I KNOW WHOM YOU'RE SEEKING--IT'S JOHNNY STORM! I'M A FRIEND OF HIS!
WHAT'S THIS ALL ABOUT? WHO IS SHE? HOW'D SHE GET HERE---AND WHY?
TRUST ME, COACH! I'LL EXPLAIN LATER!
HE WAS HERE! YOU MISSED HIM BY MINUTES!
HE BLAZED OFF WHEN HE HEARD THE NEWS--!
NEWS? WHAT NEWS?
HERE---IT'S STILL BEING BROADCAST! THIS WILL EXPLAIN BETTER THAN I CAN!
---ALL TRAFFIC IS AT A STANDSTILL IN THE AREA OF THE WORLD-FAMOUS BAXTER BUILDING, AS THE POLICE STRUGGLE VAINLY TO HOLD BACK THE MYSTIFIED CROWDS WHO HAVE GATHERED TO THE SCENE OF THE FANTASTIC FOUR'S BATTLE WITH THE DEADLY SANDMAN..!
THAT MEANS.. HE'S IN DANGER!
13.
CONTINUED AFTER NEXT PAGE

THEN BLASTAAR'S ENTIRE BODY SHOOTS BACK THING'S OWN CHARGE AND FIRES...

MEANWHILE SANDSOLLER REACHES PIER -- SANDMAN BEGINS TO UNFOLD THING IS UNCONSCIOUS FROM FURIOUS WHIRLING

FANTASTIC FOUR (63)

HIS ENTIRE *BODY* IS HURLING BACK MY OWN *CHARGE* AT ME --!!

HE'S TOO POWERFUL! I'VE GOTTA PUT MORE *DISTANCE* BETWEEN US TILL I CAN DREAM UP *ANOTHER* FORM OF ATTACK!

WHILE, AT THE WATERFRONT, THE *SANDMAN* HAS FINALLY REACHED HIS DEADLY DESTINATION ---

EVERYTHING WENT *EXACTLY* AS I PLANNED!

EVEN THE *THING'S* OWN STRENGTH COULDN'T STOP HIM FROM LOSING *CONSCIOUSNESS* DUE TO THE *WHIRL-ING* I SUBJECTED HIM TO

AND SO... IT'S *FAREWELL* AT LAST... FAREWELL *FOREVER*.. TO MY ONCE-GREATEST *ENEMY!*

BUT, NOT ONLY DO BEN GRIMM'S MASSIVE *LIMBS* POSSESS SUPER-HUMAN STRENGTH, BUT HIS *LUNGS* DO, AS WELL! THEREFORE, THOUGH THE COMATOSE *THING* PLUNGES HEAVILY DOWNWARD, THE CHILLING EFFECT OF THE WATER GRADUALLY BEGINS TO *REVIVE* HIM ---!

--AND THEN...

16

BEING UNCONSCIOUS, THING IS ROLLED INTO RIVER -- PRESUMING HE WILL DROWN BEFORE HE CAN RECOVER

M.O. 9¼" high

Fantastic Four #66, page 10

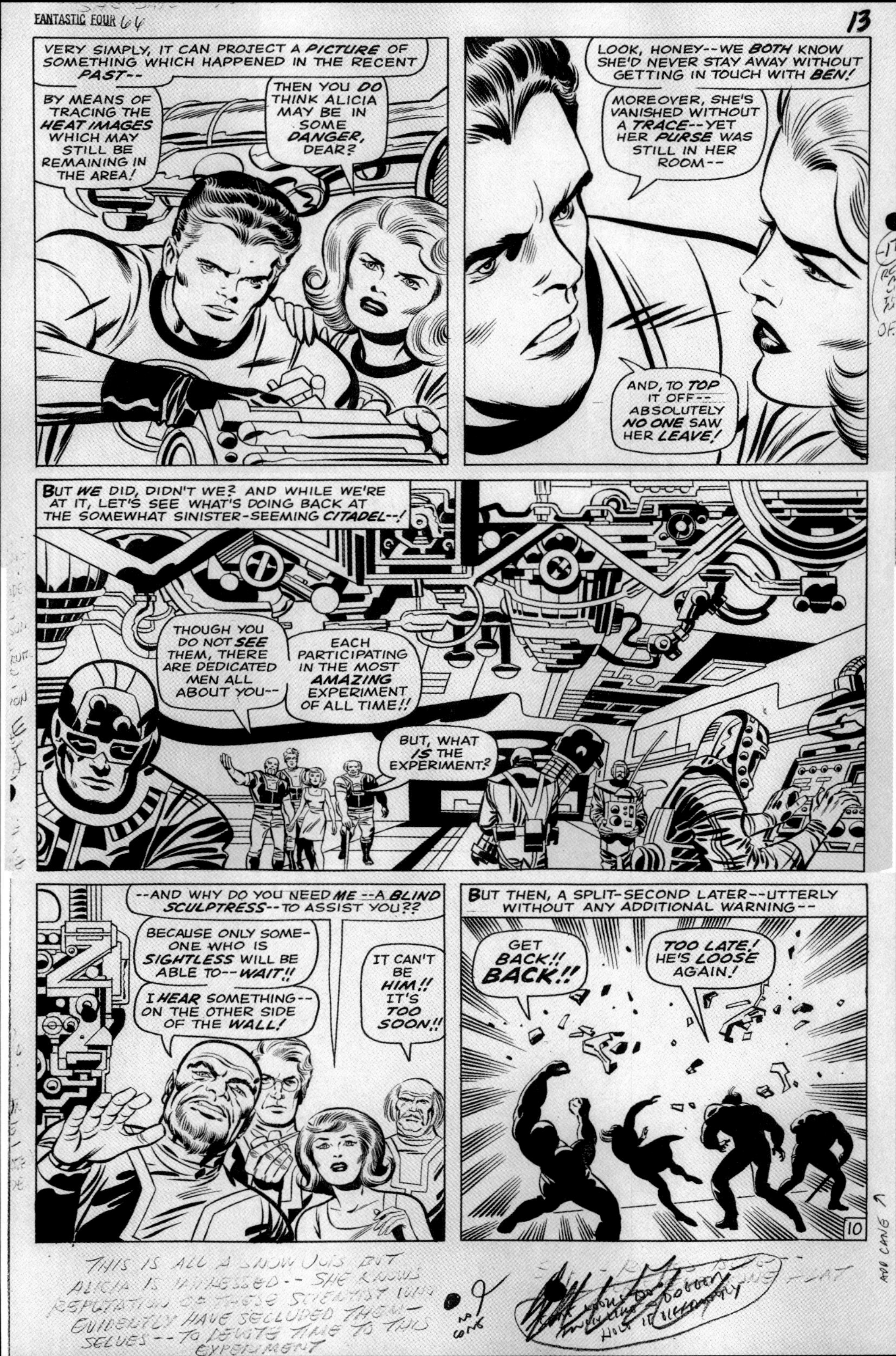
FANTASTIC FOUR 64
13
VERY SIMPLY, IT CAN PROJECT A PICTURE OF SOMETHING WHICH HAPPENED IN THE RECENT PAST--
BY MEANS OF TRACING THE HEAT IMAGES WHICH MAY STILL BE REMAINING IN THE AREA!
THEN YOU DO THINK ALICIA MAY BE IN SOME DANGER, DEAR?
LOOK, HONEY--WE BOTH KNOW SHE'D NEVER STAY AWAY WITHOUT GETTING IN TOUCH WITH BEN!
MOREOVER, SHE'S VANISHED WITHOUT A TRACE--YET HER PURSE WAS STILL IN HER ROOM--
AND, TO TOP IT OFF--ABSOLUTELY NO ONE SAW HER LEAVE!
BUT WE DID, DIDN'T WE? AND WHILE WE'RE AT IT, LET'S SEE WHAT'S DOING BACK AT THE SOMEWHAT SINISTER-SEEMING CITADEL--!
THOUGH YOU DO NOT SEE THEM, THERE ARE DEDICATED MEN ALL ABOUT YOU--
EACH PARTICIPATING IN THE MOST AMAZING EXPERIMENT OF ALL TIME!!
BUT, WHAT IS THE EXPERIMENT?
--AND WHY DO YOU NEED ME --A BLIND SCULPTRESS-- TO ASSIST YOU??
BECAUSE ONLY SOME-ONE WHO IS SIGHTLESS WILL BE ABLE TO--WAIT!!
I HEAR SOMETHING--ON THE OTHER SIDE OF THE WALL!
IT CAN'T BE HIM!! IT'S TOO SOON!!
BUT THEN, A SPLIT-SECOND LATER--UTTERLY WITHOUT ANY ADDITIONAL WARNING--
GET BACK!! BACK!!
TOO LATE! HE'S LOOSE AGAIN!
10
THIS IS ALL A SNOW JOB BUT ALICIA IS IMPRESSED -- SHE KNOWS REPUTATION OF THESE SCIENTIST WHO EVIDENTLY HAVE SECLUDED THEM-SELVES -- TO DEVOTE TIME TO THIS EXPERIMENT

FANTASTIC FOUR 66

14

GUARDS! GUARDS!! WHERE ARE THE GUARDS!!

HE MUST BE STOPPED NOW--WHILE THERE STILL IS TIME!

WE'RE DONE FOR!! ALL OF US! NOTHING CAN STOP HIM NOW!! WE'RE ALL DOOMED!!

I HEAR THE GUARDS! THEY'RE COMING!! THERE'S STILL A CHANCE!

HE'S IN THE VICINITY OF LOCK 41!

SURROUND THE AREA!! SECURE ALL SAFETY HATCHES! HE MUST NOT BREAK THRU!

THE GIRL!! IS SHE ALL RIGHT??

THE POOR CHILD DOESN'T UNDERSTAND! WE CAN'T KEEP HER IN THE DARK THIS WAY, MORLAK!

AHH, GOOD! GOOD! UNDER NO CIRCUMSTANCES MUST ANY HARM COME TO HER!-- NOT YET!

I SAY WE TELL HER THE TRUTH! WE HAVE NO CHOICE!

WHAT DIFFERENCE DOES IT MAKE? NOTHING CAN SAVE US NOW! NOTHING!

SHINSKI!! BE SILENT, YOU SPINELESS OLD FOOL!

HE HASN'T GOTTEN TO US YET! GIVEN ENOUGH TIME-- AND THE HELP OF ALICIA MASTERS-- WE MAY STILL BE TRIUMPHANT!

IT'S SO MAD!! SO INSANE! I DON'T UNDER- STAND ANY OF IT!

DO NOT TROUBLE YOURSELF! THIS VITRA-BROTH I'M POURING WILL HELP YOU TO RELAX!

11.

MORLAK CALMS ---
SHE'S SHAKEN -- SHE
HAPPENED -- WHO ARE
RAVING AT

SHINSKI WHO CAME -- THAT
CREATURE -- THAT WHO
INANE TURNED ON US -- HIS CREATORS --
MORLAK YELLS -- QUIET -- OUR YOUNG
GUEST DOESN'T UNDERSTAND -- ZETA'S
WHY DON'T WE TELL HER

BOSON
TOO
HIGH?

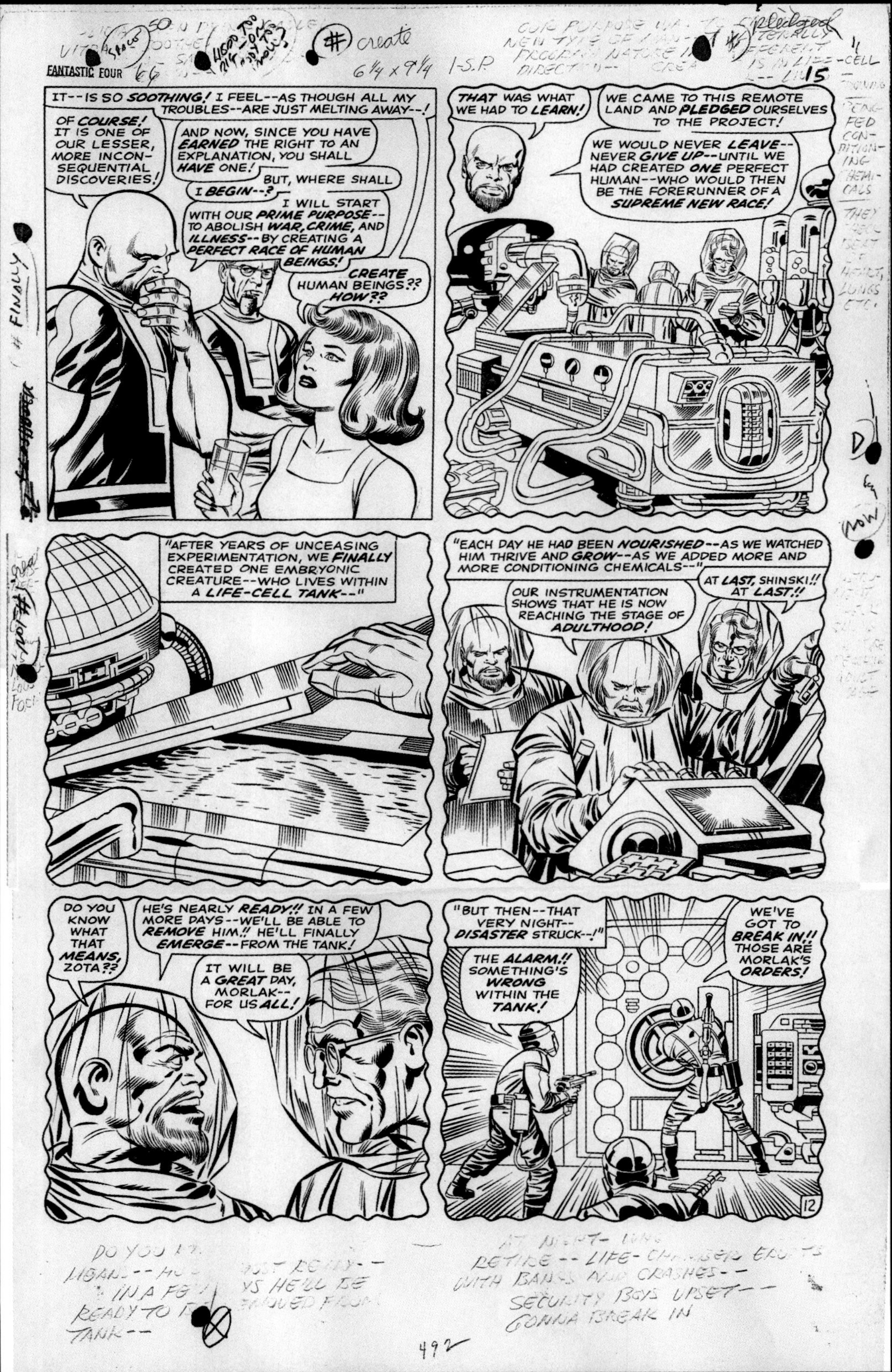
FANTASTIC FOUR
IT--IS SO SOOTHING! I FEEL--AS THOUGH ALL MY TROUBLES--ARE JUST MELTING AWAY--!
OF COURSE! IT IS ONE OF OUR LESSER, MORE INCONSEQUENTIAL DISCOVERIES!
AND NOW, SINCE YOU HAVE EARNED THE RIGHT TO AN EXPLANATION, YOU SHALL HAVE ONE!
BUT, WHERE SHALL I BEGIN--?
I WILL START WITH OUR PRIME PURPOSE--TO ABOLISH WAR, CRIME, AND ILLNESS--BY CREATING A PERFECT RACE OF HUMAN BEINGS!
CREATE HUMAN BEINGS?? HOW??
THAT WAS WHAT WE HAD TO LEARN!
WE CAME TO THIS REMOTE LAND AND PLEDGED OURSELVES TO THE PROJECT!
WE WOULD NEVER LEAVE--NEVER GIVE UP--UNTIL WE HAD CREATED ONE PERFECT HUMAN--WHO WOULD THEN BE THE FORERUNNER OF A SUPREME NEW RACE!
"AFTER YEARS OF UNCEASING EXPERIMENTATION, WE FINALLY CREATED ONE EMBRYONIC CREATURE--WHO LIVES WITHIN A LIFE-CELL TANK--"
"EACH DAY HE HAD BEEN NOURISHED--AS WE WATCHED HIM THRIVE AND GROW--AS WE ADDED MORE AND MORE CONDITIONING CHEMICALS--"
OUR INSTRUMENTATION SHOWS THAT HE IS NOW REACHING THE STAGE OF ADULTHOOD!
AT LAST, SHINSKI!! AT LAST!!
DO YOU KNOW WHAT THAT MEANS, ZOTA??
HE'S NEARLY READY!! IN A FEW MORE DAYS--WE'LL BE ABLE TO REMOVE HIM!! HE'LL FINALLY EMERGE--FROM THE TANK!
IT WILL BE A GREAT DAY, MORLAK--FOR US ALL!
"BUT THEN--THAT VERY NIGHT--DISASTER STRUCK--!"
THE ALARM!! SOMETHING'S WRONG WITHIN THE TANK!
WE'VE GOT TO BREAK IN!! THOSE ARE MORLAK'S ORDERS!
12
6¼ x 9¼ 1-S.P.
SECURITY BOYS UPSET--
GONNA BREAK IN
492

Early version of the *Fantastic Four #65* cover featuring Jack Kirby's trademark "Kirby Krackle"

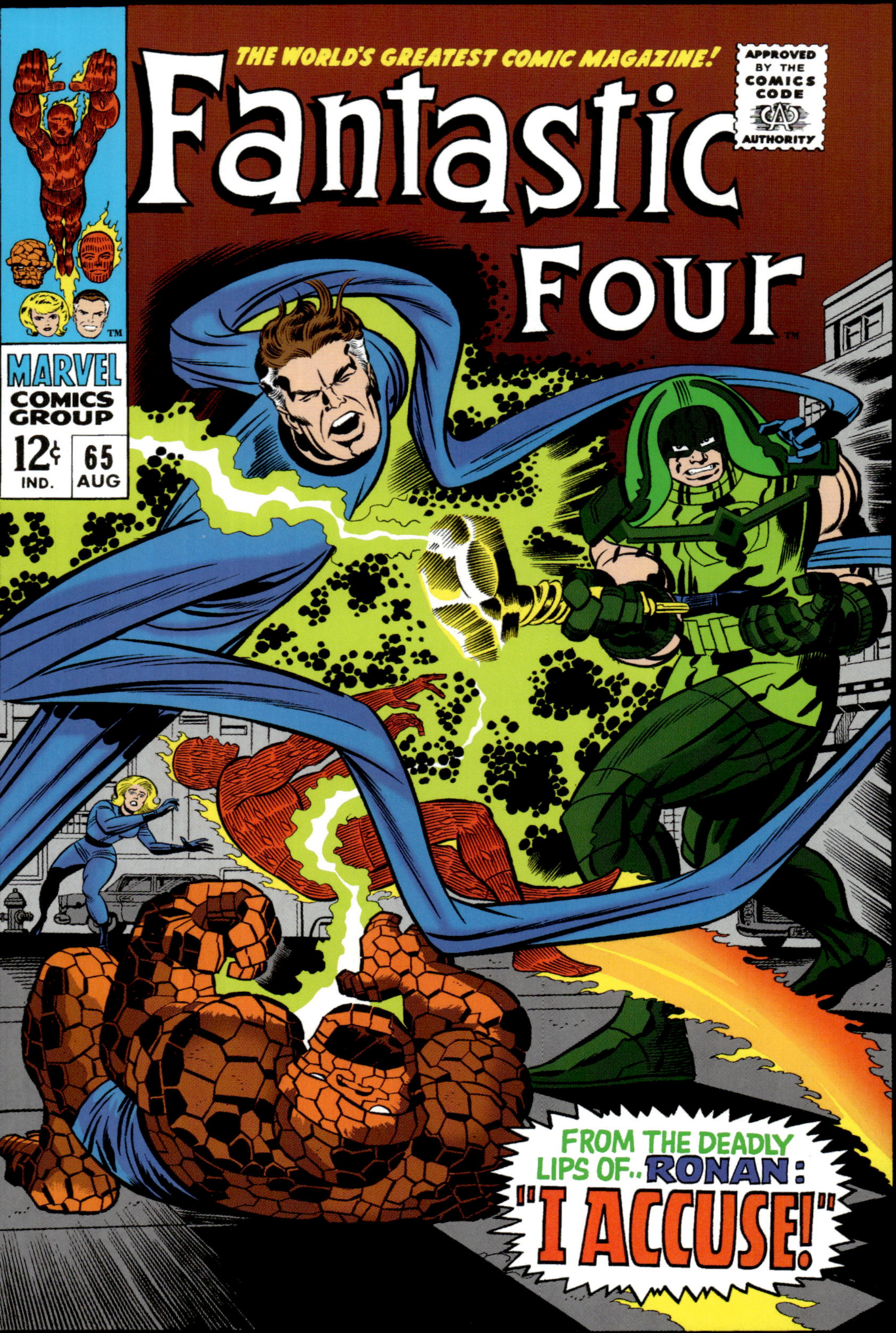
THE WORLD'S GREATEST COMIC MAGAZINE!
Fantastic Four
APPROVED BY THE COMICS CODE AUTHORITY
MARVEL COMICS GROUP
12¢ IND.
65 AUG
FROM THE DEADLY LIPS OF.. RONAN:
"I ACCUSE!"